FIFTH EDITION

Improving Reading Skills

CONTEMPORARY READINGS FOR COLLEGE STUDENTS

Deanne Spears
City College of San Francisco

Boston   Burr Ridge, IL   Dubuque, IA   Madison, WI   New York
San Francisco   St. Louis   Bangkok   Bogotá   Caracas   Kuala Lumpur
Lisbon   London   Madrid   Mexico City   Milan   Montreal   New Delhi
Santiago   Seoul   Singapore   Sydney   Taipei   Toronto

The McGraw-Hill Companies

 Higher Education

IMPROVING READING SKILLS
Published by McGraw-Hill, an imprint of The McGraw-Hill Companies, Inc., 1221 Avenue of the
Americas, New York, NY 10020. Copyright © 2004, 2000, 1996, 1992, 1988 by the McGraw-Hill

This book is printed on acid-free paper.

4 5 6 7 8 9 0 DOC/DOC 0 9 8 7

ISBN: 978-0-07-283070-5
MHID: 0-07-283070-0   (Student Edition)
ISBN: 978-0-07-288049-6
MHID: 0-07-288049-X   (Instructor's Edition)

Publisher: *Steve Debow*
Sponsoring editor: *Alexis Walker*
Development editor: *Jane Carter*
Marketing manager: *David S. Patterson*
Production editor: *Jennifer Chambliss*
Production supervisor: *Tandra Jorgensen*
Design manager: *Cassandra Chu*
Interior design: *Ellen Pettengell*
Cover design: *Cassandra Chu*
Art editor: *Cristin Yancey*
Manager, photo research: *Brian Pecko*
Compositor: *ElectraGraphics, Inc.*
Text and Paper: *Printed in 10/12 Palatino on 45# New era Matte*
Printer: *R. R. Donnelley, Crawfordsville, IN*

On the cover: "Still Life with a Red Rug" by Henri Matisse. Musée des Beaux Arts, Grenoble, France/Peter
Willi/Bridgeman Art Library. © 2003 Succession H. Matisse/Artists Rights Society (ARS), New York.

Library of Congress Cataloging-in-Publication Data

Milan Spears, Deanne.
    Improving reading skills : contemporary readings for college students / Deanne Spears.—
5th ed.
        p. cm.
    Includes bibliographical references (p.) and index.
    ISBN 0-07-283070-0 (student ed.)—ISBN 0-07-288049-X
    1. Reading (Higher education) 2. College readers. 3. Vocabulary. I. Title.

LB2395.3.M56 2003

428.4'071'1—dc21   2003051313

www.mhhe.com

About the Author

Deanne Spears is originally from Portland, Oregon, but she considers herself a Californian, having moved to Los Angeles in the late 1940s when there were still orange groves in the area. She studied comparative literature at the University of Southern California and has taken post-graduate courses at San Francisco State University. Since 1968, she has taught composition and reading courses at City College of San Francisco. Her first passion is reading. Other interests include cooking, hiking, going to the movies, traveling, camping, and exploring the diversity of ethnic food available in the Bay Area. She is married to fellow English teacher and jazz musician, David Spears. She is also the author of *Developing Critical Reading Skills,* the sixth edition of which was published in 2003.

For David

Contents

blacks are often none too sweet—historically at least. And people will see that I'm black only moments after they see that my canoe is green. Maybe even before.

But now we try something new, a real-world test: reading the supermarket advertising inserts from a local newspaper. Each insert is a hodgepodge of food pictures, product names and prices. I point to a word and Ken ponders. "C" he says finally. "And it's got those two e's—so that would be 'coffee'!" I point again. He gets "Pepsi." Silently, he sounds out the letters on a can's label. "So that's 'corn,'" he announces.

Here's another statistical comparison: Eighty-six percent of women look at price tags when they shop. Only 72 percent of men do. For a man, ignoring the price tag is almost a measure of his virility. As a result, men are far more easily upgraded than are women shoppers. They are also far more suggestible than women—men seem so anxious to get out of the store that they'll say yes to almost anything.

My friend Peter claims he cannot open the door to his tiny daughter's bedroom—it is stuffed to the four corners with Barbie dolls and Barbie equipment, with accessories and extras, with vacation houses, gyms, recreational vehicles, costumes, cosmetics. She is six; Barbie, as we all know, is a 40-year-old billionaire.

Americans have always been optimists, and optimists have always liked to speculate. In Texas in the 1880s, the speculative instrument of choice was towns, and there is no tale more American than this. What people would do was buy up enormous tracts of parched and vacant land, lay out a Main Street, nail together some wooden sidewalks, and start slapping up buildings. . . . The developers would erect a flagpole and name a church, and once the workmen had packed up and moved on, the towns would be as empty as the sky.

At Burger King restaurants, frozen hamburger patties are placed on a conveyer belt and emerge from a broiler ninety seconds later fully cooked. The ovens at Pizza Hut and at Domino's also use conveyer belts to ensure standardized cooking times. The ovens at McDonald's look like commercial laundry presses, with big steel hoods that swing down and grill hamburgers on both sides at once. The burgers, chicken, french fries, and buns are all frozen when they arrive at a McDonald's. The shakes and sodas begin as syrup.

two students turned to mass murder because they played nasty computer games associated with the gloomy (but nonviolent) Goths, or had access to Internet bomb-making sites.

Alternate Contents
Arranged by Theme

Preface

Once again, it is gratifying to be able to revise *Improving Reading Skills.* Because I have found that students improve more by reading than just by learning about techniques and strategies, the fifth edition, like the four before it, aims to offer students insightful, engaging, contemporary selections that will both challenge them and make them want to turn the page. To emphasize the nature of the selections as well as the purpose of this text, I have added a subtitle. This book is now called *Improving Reading Skills: Contemporary Readings for College Students.*

Because practice exercises that reinforce good reading skills and help students develop a college-level vocabulary are also important, I continue to include numerous exercises following each reading. This basic principle—including interesting contemporary essays followed by numerous exercises to test comprehension and reinforce basic skills—has accounted for the book's success in the past, and it remains the guiding principle for the fifth edition. A brief discussion of the book's important components—some that remain the same, others that I have changed (and, I hope, improved)—follow.

An Overview of the Text

The fifth edition contains thirty-three reading selections drawn from a variety of sources, representing the kinds of reading students will encounter in their college courses—especially English courses that require students to read expository and persuasive essays—as well as in their lives after their formal education ends. I want students to see that they are members of a larger community and that reading can be instrumental in helping them fill this role. Reading also provides students with a way for them to understand the world around them and to search for meaning in their own lives. The book, however, has no particular underlying philosophy, no "ism" to flog. It seeks only to help students to improve their reading comprehension and to read with better concentration and with enjoyment and confidence.

VOCABULARY DEVELOPMENT

This edition continues to stress vocabulary development in the context of each reading. In my experience, a weak vocabulary—perhaps even more than poor concentration or lack of interest—is a major stumbling block for many students.

Because the interrelationship between comprehension and vocabulary is so strong, intensive vocabulary was an immediate concern when I wrote the first edition. Teaching from the text for several semesters has only strengthened my conviction in this regard. Consequently, vocabulary remains an integral part of both the text and the exercises.

To this end, the organization of the "Vocabulary Previews" preceding each selection remains unchanged. Each preview introduces students to a few words—typically three or four—that they will encounter in the reading. Each contains a short section on word history (etymology), word parts, and word families. These previews have the twin benefits of teaching the students the meanings of a few important words from the reading, but more important, they illustrate a systematic way to acquire new words. Rather than being taught in isolation, the elements of English vocabulary that are useful for developing word recognition skills (roots, prefixes, and suffixes) are taught in context of the readings. Finally, each reading ends with two vocabulary exercises: The first is a simple multiple-choice exercise. The form of the second varies, as a glance through the text will show.

READING SELECTIONS

As with earlier editions, the readings were chosen according to several criteria: They must be well written and relatively easy to understand, especially the first few; they must be of reasonable length so that students can complete the reading and accompanying exercises in one sitting; and they must be of sufficient interest to appeal to the most reluctant of readers. According to the reviewers' preferences and my own tastes and opinions, I have retained the following readings from earlier editions: Dave Barry's humorously entertaining piece, "Tips for Women: How to Have a Relationship with a Guy" (which is now the Practice Essay showing students how to work through a sample reading); Luis J. Rodriguez, "La Vida Loca"; Rose Del Castillo Guilbault, "The Conveyor-Belt Ladies"; Eddy L. Harris, "Mississippi Solo"; Sheldon Campbell, "Games Elephants Play"; Charles Finney, "The Life and Death of a Western Gladiator"; Geoffrey Cowley, "The Language Explosion"; Richard Wolkomir, "Making Up for Lost Time: The Rewards of Reading at Last"; Elliot West, "Wagon Train Children"; Nelson Mandela, "Long Walk to Freedom"; Ellen Alderman and Caroline Kennedy, "*New Jersey v. T.L.O.:* The School Search Cases"; David Ferrell, "Badwater: The Ultra-Marathon"; Arthur Zich, "Japanese Americans: Home at Last"; and Jared Diamond, "Easter's End." This makes a total of fourteen readings retained from the previous edition.

The new readings embrace a wide range of topics. Here are some examples: Josh Sens's piece on weird phenomena in the American West; Lori Hope's *Newsweek* article about racial profiling of airline passengers; Paco Underhill's assessment of men's and women's shopping behavior; Lawrence Shames's essay on optimism and materialism as peculiarly American traits and a by-product of our fascination with the American frontier; an excerpt from Eric Schlosser's highly regarded study of the fast-food industry, *Fast Food Nation;* and a narrative by Val Plumwood about barely surviving a crocodile attack on the northern coast of Australia. As in the fourth edition, Part 4 contains six persuasive pieces on these controversial issues: SUVs and the pollution they cause; excessive competition in American sports and some remedies for the problem; the social repercussions of boys who are raised without fathers; a program to get Los Angeles homeless people off the streets; the prevalence of hero inflation in the wake of the terrorist attacks; and finally, the debate about human cloning. The book ends with an excerpt from Barbara Ehrenreich's instant classic about minimum-wage jobs in America, *Nickel-and-Dimed: On (Not) Getting by in America.*

EXERCISE MATERIAL

The exercises in the fifth edition are more extensive and cover a wider range of skills than those in most other college reading texts. Step by step, each exercise provides students an opportunity to practice these skills at a level appropriate for each reading. By the completion of the course, these exercises will have helped improve students' comprehension and analytical skills. Specifically, the exercises offer practice in the following skills:

- determining the main idea and writer's purpose
- comprehending main ideas
- distinguishing between main ideas and supporting details
- recognizing supporting details
- interpreting meaning
- making inferences and drawing conclusions
- distinguishing between fact and opinion
- analyzing structure
- annotating text and writing paraphrases and summaries.

Changes in the Fifth Edition

For the fifth edition, I have incorporated many of the excellent suggestions made by the reviewers of the previous edition. Here are the most significant ones:

VOCABULARY IMPROVEMENT

The book now opens with a discussion of ways students can improve their reading vocabulary. Specifically covering ways to acquire words, the importance of context clues, and the differences between print and online dictionaries, this section establishes a rationale and a system for students to learn new words as a crucial part of their becoming better readers.

EXPANDED PART INTRODUCTIONS

The five introductory sections offer students both instruction and practice in the skills they will be practicing in the book. Each contains short examples and excerpts to familiarize students with these skills. For example, the introduction to

Part 1 now explains the fundamental concept of main idea as distinguished from supporting ideas, the structure and placement of a thesis statement, the difference between fiction and nonfiction, and so forth. The introduction to Part 2 extensively illustrates the skills of annotating, paraphrasing, and summarizing. Part 3 takes up inference, Part 4 introduces students to some techniques for reading persuasive writing and evaluating evidence, and finally, Part 5 gives an overview of the common patterns of development and transitional devices.

ACCESSIBILITY OF READINGS

Another change is that the table of contents now reflects the problem of under-prepared students in our college reading courses and presents a greater number of easier readings. This has the advantage of promoting students' confidence as they practice with material that they can handle and succeed with at the beginning of the course. And since most of these readings are personal narratives and coming-of-age non-fiction pieces, the interest level is high.

PRACTICE ESSAY

By popular demand, Dave Barry's humorous piece is retained as a practice essay. This section demonstrates the layout and format of the book by means of annotations printed in a different color and font. Each element (headnote, vocabulary preview, and exercise material) is explained and identified.

AN ALTERNATE TABLE OF CONTENTS

For instructors who prefer to teach a thematic course, I have provided an alternate thematic table of contents. Among these themes are Adventure, Race and Ethnicity, Gender Roles and Gender Issues, Coming of Age and Initiation Rites, Our Working Lives, Money and the Consumer, Sports, and Crime and Punishment. A glance at this feature shows that within each thematic section readings are arranged according to level of difficulty.

VARIETY IN EXERCISE MATERIAL

The exercises continue to measure both basic comprehension skills, along with analytical thinking and critical reading. The level of difficulty in the exercises is tailored to each reading, and the type of exercise varies from selection to selection, thereby relieving monotony. Because I believe that students need all the practice they can get in expressing themselves in writing, many exercises require short answers. Thus, the exercises seek to combine multiple-choice questions, which are easy to score, with short-answer questions, which help our students develop their language skills. These exercises are titled "Interpreting Meaning" or "Analyzing Structure," and they appear after the majority of the readings.

For instructors who prefer to have students answer comprehension questions in their own words, I have provided a Critical Reading Worksheet following the practice essays, which can be duplicated for each reading assigned.

INCREASED EMPHASIS ON ANNOTATING, PARAPHRASING, AND SUMMARIZING

Each reading contains an exercise in the interrelated skills of annotating, paraphrasing, and summarizing. In the book's initial selections, these exercises begin with a model. For example, I provide a sentence or two from the reading, along with a sample paraphrase. Then students are instructed to write their paraphrases of other sentences from the selection. The same modeling is provided for annotating and summarizing. Paraphrasing and summarizing are excellent ways to test students' understanding of material, and the emphasis on annotating throughout the text shows students how reading with a pencil in their hand promotes better comprehension. As the readings become more complicated, students are asked to write summaries, typically of sections of the reading, rather than of the reading as a whole.

CONNECTING READING TO THE WORLD WIDE WEB

As in the fourth edition, the section titled "For Further Exploration" includes Web sites for students to explore if they want more information on a subject or if they want to look at photos. Unlike the fourth edition, however, many sites relate to real-world experiences. For example, I have provided job and travel Web sites. However, although I checked the accuracy of Web sites in early summer 2003, I cannot guarantee that Web sites mentioned in this edition will remain current for the life of the book as the Internet is constantly evolving and growing. If students find that a Web site is no longer available, I suggest that they go to one of the popular search engines (like *www.google.com* or *www.yahoo.com*) and perform their own search.

Acknowledgments

I wish to thank the following colleagues at City College of San Francisco for their helpful suggestions: Susanna Bray, Gloria Yee, and Robert Stamps (emeritus). Monilou Carter, of Half Moon Bay, California, gave me some suggestions and recommended interesting articles to read, as did my colleague at City College, Joan Wilson. The reviewers were nearly unanimous in suggesting ways to improve the book, and I wish to extend my most sincere thanks for their help. If this edition is better than previous ones, it is because of these instructors:

Carolyn Conners, Wor-Wic Community College
Fred D'Astoli, College of the Canyons
Marie G. Ekstrom, Rio-Hondo College
James M. Gentile, Manchester Community College
Suzanne Gripenstraw, Butte College
Carole Marquis, Santa Fe Community College
Deborah Naquin, Northern Virginia Community College
Margaret Prothero, Santa Barbara City College
Robin Ramsey, Albuquerque TVI Community College

Washella N. Turner, Lenoir Community College
Patricia Wheeler Andrews, Anoka-Ramsey Community College
Phoebe Wiley, Frostburg State University

I must also thank my previous editor, Sarah Touborg, for her wise counsel and for her continuing support for revisions. Steven Penzinger, formerly of Random House, believed in my original proposal enough to take a chance on publishing the first edition. Jane Carter, development editor, Jennifer Chambliss, production editor, and Jennifer Gordon, copyeditor, ensured the book's accuracy and attractive layout and design. Alexis Walker, sponsoring editor, continued to give me support and encouragement as the revision took shape. To all of them, I am most grateful.

Instructors should feel free to send suggestions, comments, or questions via email to me at *dspears1@mindspring.com* or *dkspears@ccsf.edu*. I can also be reached through the McGraw-Hill Higher Education Web site at *http://www.mhhe.com/ spears*. I will do my best to answer all correspondence within a day or two.

To the Student

The Aims of the Text

This is the fifth edition of *Improving Reading Skills*. Because the book has evolved in many ways in form and content since the first edition, you will benefit from these accumulated changes. If you work through the readings in this text diligently and attentively, with your instructor's help, you will achieve the following goals: better concentration, improved reading comprehension, a more advanced level of vocabulary, a knowledge of important word elements, and most important, a way to connect your reading to the outside world.

Above all, both your instructor and I hope that you will derive the ultimate benefit from the instruction provided in the text: an enjoyment of reading so that it becomes a lifelong pursuit. Reading well allows you to travel from the comfort of your home, to dream, to escape, to learn, to understand the important issues of the day, to question, and, most crucially as a college student, to think.

The thirty-three selections in this edition are drawn from books, magazines, and newspapers. Most are nonfiction, representing both the reading required in your other college courses (especially English courses) and reading material you will encounter the rest of your life after you finish school. The readings have been carefully chosen for their high interest level; they represent a variety of topics and writing styles. Some are entertaining, some are informative, some are persuasive. Most will give you something to think about, and to write about. Since the selections are arranged in order of difficulty, as you work through them you will be able to refine your comprehension, vocabulary, and analytical skills with increasingly harder readings.

The book is divided into five parts. Each part contains instruction in a particular skill that will contribute to your becoming a successful, confident, and accurate reader. Since the material moves from simple to moderate to more difficult, I have attempted to make the introductions conform to that system so that the most important skills are taught first. For example, Part 1 begins with an extensive discussion, explanation, and illustration of main ideas, supporting ideas, and the writer's purpose. Building on these fundamental skills, Part 2 takes up the interrelated skills of annotating, paraphrasing, and summarizing. It is worth taking a few minutes to look over the table of contents to see the overall organization of the contents. Finally, these introductions provide you with an opportunity to study the skills and to practice them with short excerpts before going on to the longer readings that follow.

Post-Reading Exercises

The exercise material following each reading will help you practice a wide variety of important reading skills. Taken together, they will help you read more systematically. They will show you what to look for when you read, and they will provide a structure for your reading. Some of the exercises are multiple-choice, while others require you to formulate answers in your own words. Although the types of exercises vary from selection to selection, the skills are reinforced throughout the text as the material becomes more difficult. Further, these exercises break the process of comprehension and analysis into small, separate steps, so that, little by little, you will understand better what to look for when you read, whether you are reading for a course or for pleasure. Along the way, you should find it easier to concentrate and to focus as you read.

These are the specific skills, apart from vocabulary, that you will work on during the term:

- understanding main ideas
- determining the writer's purpose
- distinguishing between main ideas and supporting details
- making accurate inferences
- distinguishing between fact and opinion
- analyzing structure
- learning how to annotate
- writing paraphrases and summaries.

The exercises for each selection always end with questions for writing or discussion. These ask you to respond to the reading or to consider important questions that the selection raises.

Finally, the sections called "For Further Exploration" make suggestions for examining the subject in more detail. This section includes relevant books to read, movies to watch and Web sites to explore. Concerning Web sites, the Internet is evolving and growing at such a dizzying pace that it is probably presumptuous of me to recommend sites. What I have tried to do is to point you in some directions so that if you are particularly intrigued by a selection and want to read more, you can find a starting place on the Web. Many of the recommended sites will provide you with links to other related sites.

The Importance of Vocabulary

Whether your instructor assigns it or not, be sure to read the introductory material on improving your vocabulary. Good vocabulary is essential for good comprehension skills. Stated another way, if you don't know the meanings of many words a writer uses, it's very difficult to know exactly what he or she is saying. All that you can hope for is to come away with a hazy idea of the main point.

The best way to improve your vocabulary is to commit yourself during the term to looking up many unfamiliar words that you encounter in your reading. At first this task may seem overwhelming, but as you work through the material, you will see that the job is not as daunting as it might at first have appeared. The "Vocabulary Preview" that opens each selection introduces you to a few words that you will encounter in the reading. These previews show you how to break an unfamiliar word down into its component parts—prefix, root, and suffix—as an aid to getting at its meaning.

The section called Improving Your Vocabulary shows you how to use context clues to increase your stock of vocabulary words. You will have ample opportunity to learn definitions of important words from the readings since each selection ends with two vocabulary exercises.

As you work through the vocabulary exercises, remember that it is not cheating to look up unfamiliar words in the dictionary. And since your instructor may test you periodically on these words, another suggestion is to write these new words and their meanings either in a special notebook or on 3" × 5" note cards. This way, you can review them quickly before tests, rather than having to hunt through the book to find them again.

As will be demonstrated throughout the text, good comprehension and good vocabulary skills are interdependent. As the weeks go by, you will be pleasantly surprised to find that words you have come across in earlier selections will turn up again in later ones, and in your other reading as well. One student told me that every morning while riding on a San Francisco city bus, she had seen an advertisement over the window that used a word previously unfamiliar to her: *nostalgia*. Then she encountered the word in a "Vocabulary Preview" section, and suddenly the ad made sense to her.

Calculating Your Comprehension Score

The instructions accompanying each set of exercises ask you to do Exercises A and B without looking back at the selection. Your instructor may ask you to disregard these instructions. Not looking back, however, will force you to read with greater attention and concentration than you would if you know you can look back at the passage to refresh your memory. When you are finished with all the exercises, calculate your comprehension score by counting your correct answers for the first two exercises, according to the formula.

Since the two questions on determining the main idea and writer's purpose are most crucial, each is worth two points, while the main-idea questions in Exercise B are each worth one point. Your final score will be a percentage of 100, the total number of points. Study this example of a hypothetical student who got both questions in section A correct and four questions in section B correct:

A. No. right ____2____ × 2 = ____4____

B. No. right ____4____ × 1 = ____4____

Total points from A and B ____8____ × 10 = ____80____ percent

Since the selections become progressively more difficult, maintaining a score of 70 percent or higher indicates steady improvement. A chart on which you can keep track of your progress is included at the back of the text.

Finally, to be sure that you get the most out of the text and the course, be sure to ask your instructor for help with anything you do not understand. If you have questions, comments, or suggestions for me, you can reach me via email at *dspears1@mindspring.com* or at *dkspears@ccsf.edu,* and also through McGraw-Hill's home page at *http://www.mhhe.com/spears.* I will do my best to respond within a day or two.

Introduction to the Walkthrough

Welcome to the fifth edition of *Improving Reading Skills.* Before you begin the assignments in this text, take a little time to look through this section so that you can become familiar with the book's organization and its many features.

SKILL DEVELOPMENT

Improving Reading Skills contains five instructional sections that will introduce you to some important skills. In addition, the first section of the book shows you ways to improve your vocabulary through the use of context clues, the effective use of your dictionary, and word-of-the-day Web sites.

---

you can see which site might be most appropriate for your level. (Note that by the time you read this text, one or more of these sites may have moved or expired. If you are unable to locate a particular site, use your favorite search engine to get updated addresses.)

WORD-OF-THE-DAY WEB SITES

Dictionary.com Word of the Day
www.dictionary.com/wordoftheday
cataract, torpid, aplomb, insensate, alacrity

Yahoo! Education
education.yahoo.com/college/wotd
exculpate, sublime, corroborate, reprove, dirge

Merriam-Webster's Word of the Day
www.m-w.com
undulate, cerebral, clandestine, vanguard, funicular

A.Word.a.Day
www.wordsmith.org
pangram, decimate, egregious, obsidian, helpmeet

Using Context Clues

We begin this section with an exercise called a *cloze test.* Here is a paragraph from Selection 1 by Josh Sens, "The Truth Is Out Here—Somewhere," with some of the words left out. Your task is to fill in the words that make sense and complete the meaning of the sentence. Be sure to pay attention both to meaning and to grammar and sentence structure. The subject of this paragraph is the mysterious moving stones at a place called Racetrack Playa in California's Death Valley.

What _____ the stones slide remains a _____ . As always, some _____ suspect aliens. If that's _____ case, E.T. is stronger _____ a team of oxen. Some _____ the stones weigh 700 _____ . Other theories _____ emerged. Maybe it's _____ high wind, though _____ alone couldn't budge some _____ these babies. _____ it's the rain, which freezes in _____ weather, forming a thin icy film over which the _____ could slide. _____ it's a combination of the _____ .

Here is the passage again, this time with the missing words restored and bold-faced:

DAVE BARRY

Tips for Women: How to Have a Relationship with a Guy

Dave Barry has written for The Miami Herald since 1983. In 1988 he received a Pulitzer Prize for commentary. His witty observations about American life were the inspiration for the 1990s television show Dave's World. In this excerpt, reprinted from Dave Barry's Complete Guide to Guys, we are introduced to a fictitious couple named Roger and Elaine who have been dating for six months.

Each headnote provides biographical background on the writer, briefly states what the selection is about, and may also list other titles that the writer has published.

Vocabulary Preview

The Vocabulary Preview is divided into three parts; each deals with a word or two that you will find in the reading: the Word History section tells about the etymology or source of an interesting word, the Word Parts section discusses an important prefix or suffix, and the Word Families section explains how knowing one Latin or Greek word root will help you learn other words in the same family.

WORD HISTORY

Petty [paragraph 41] Elaine "explodes with fury" when Roger commits one of his "endless series of *petty* offenses." *Petty* means "of small importance" or "trivial." It derives from the French word *petit* meaning "small." In English, the word suggests something more negative—trivial and unimportant rather than merely small. Barry uses the word humorously or ironically because Roger's "*petty*" offense was to ask Elaine's sister out.

WORD PARTS

-meter [paragraph 7] As they are driving home, instead of paying attention to what Elaine is saying, Roger checks the *odometer* (pronounced ŏ - d ŏm´- ĭ - tər) and wonders if his car needs an oil change. People often confuse a car's odometer with its speedometer. An odometer measures the distance that a vehicle has traveled, while a speedometer measures the speed at which it is moving.

Odometer joins two Greek word parts: *hodos* ("journey") + *metron* ("measure"). Besides the word *meter* itself (as in a water- or gas-meter), this Greek word part is attached to other roots referring to instruments that measure all sorts of things, among them *thermometer* (heat), *chronometer* (time), and *barometer* (atmospheric pressure). What do these two words ending in *-meter* mean? Look them up if you are unsure and write their meanings in the space.

Answers
spectrometer: a device that measures wavelengths
hydrometer: an instrument that uses fluid to measure gravity

spectrometer _____

hydrometer _____

WORD FAMILIES

Transmission [paragraph 9] Roger also worries about his car's *transmission.* This word is formed by two Latin word parts, the prefix *trans* ("across") and the root *mittere*

23

ANNOTATED SAMPLE READING

The first reading in the book, Dave Barry's "How to Have a Relationship with a Guy," is annotated to show you how to use the vocabulary preview that appears before each reading, to explain what you will find in the headnote to each reading, and to prepare you for the exercises you will encounter in the main part of the text.

PART ONE

Before you begin the readings in Part One, you will learn to identify the writer's purpose and to find the main idea in paragraphs, as well as whole articles and essays.

I f your instructor has not assigned the section that begins this book called "To the Student," it would be a good idea to read it before beginning this section. This short introduction previews the book's organization and content and explains what you should accomplish during the term. The introductions to each of the book's five parts discuss a particular skill or set of skills that will make you a better reader, and these skills are organized by order of importance. In Part 1 you will work on the most important areas in the course:

- Recognizing the difference between fiction and nonfiction prose
- Finding the main idea in paragraphs
- Locating thesis statements in articles and essays
- Identifying the writer's purpose

The Difference Between Fiction and Nonfiction

Writing comes in three types: prose, poetry, and drama. This book is concerned with *prose*—ordinary writing that consists of words grouped into sentences and sentences grouped into paragraphs—just like the print that you are reading on this page. *Prose* is further divided into two types: nonfiction and fiction.

Your college textbooks are nonfiction, the daily newspaper is nonfiction, magazine articles are nonfiction, and so are the readings in this book. Nonfiction writing discusses real people with real problems, dealing with real events in their lives, real issues and possible ways to resolve them, real events in the world and their aftermath. The novel you take with you to read at the beach is fiction. Simply put, nonfiction is writing that is real, whereas fiction is writing that is imagined.

> **COMMON TYPES OF NONFICTION**
>
> - Articles, in magazines and newspapers
> - Autobiographies and biographies
> - Books on history, politics, social problems, and so on
> - Editorials or opinion pieces
> - Essays
> - Memoirs and journals
> - Textbooks

ROSE DEL CASTILLO GUILBAULT

5 The Conveyor-Belt Ladies

Rose Guilbault was born in Mexico and later immigrated with her family to the United States, where they settled in the Salinas Valley, an agricultural area in central California. She writes that she discovered books early on in her childhood, but she never had enough of them. The local library allowed kids to check out only two books at a time, and her father could take her to town only twice a month. Guilbault has had a varied career in journalism: She formerly wrote a column for the Sunday San Francisco Chronicle called "Hispanic, USA," which won the Eugene Block Journalism Award for Advancing Social Justice and Human Rights. Currently Guilbault is Vice President of Corporate Communications and Public Affairs for the California State Automobile Association.

In this article, Guilbault describes her summer experiences as a teenager working with Mexican American women from Texas, who migrated each year to Salinas for seasonal work in the packing sheds.

Vocabulary Preview

WORD
HISTORIES

Stigmatize [paragraph 10] Guilbault writes that she feared her Anglo friends would *stigmatize* her for working with the Mexican women in the packing sheds. This verb comes from the Greek word *stigma*, meaning a "tattoo mark." The original meaning, now archaic, referred to a mark burned into a person's skin to identify him or her as a criminal or slave. Today, the word has a more metaphorical meaning, usually referring to a mark of disgrace.

Gregarious [paragraph 12] Guilbault describes her female coworkers as a "*gregarious,* entertaining group." This word, derived from the Latin word *gregarius,* has as its root *grex* meaning "herd" or "flock." *Gregarious* has two meanings: first, "tending to move in a group with others of the same kind," often used to describe animals like sheep; and second, "enjoying the company of others of one's kind," "sociable." It is this second meaning that fits the context as Guilbault uses it.

Melancholic [paragraph 18] As they worked sorting tomatoes, the women described in this article talked about their lives, their husbands and children, their concerns and worries. Guilbault writes that "in unexpected moments, they could turn *melancholic,* recounting the babies who died because their mothers couldn't afford medical care." *Melancholic* is the adjective form of the noun *melancholy.* Medieval

---

HEADNOTES

Each reading begins with a headnote that introduces you to the author. From the headnote, you can learn about the author's background and experience.

PART TWO

The instructional section that precedes Part Two will show you how to annotate, paraphrase, and summarize—all important skills you will use constantly throughout your college career.

Annotating, Paraphrasing, and Summarizing

The skills you will learn in Part 2 follow directly from the work you did in Part 1—finding main ideas and locating supporting details. The three skills you will learn here—annotating, paraphrasing, and summarizing—are not only extraordinarily useful for college students but also for anyone who must understand, absorb, remember, and condense information from the printed page. What are these three skills?

- **Annotating** — A study and comprehension skill, includes: Writing notes in the margin of a text, circling words you don't know, noting questions, and otherwise interacting with the text
- **Paraphrasing** — A comprehension and writing skill, includes: Putting a writer's words into your own words without leaving anything important out, similar to translating
- **Summarizing** — A comprehension and writing skill, includes: Condensing a writer's words by identifying only the main points and omitting unimportant supporting details

What is the relationship among these three skills? Annotating is the first step to writing a successful summary; paraphrasing is also required to produce a good summary. Paraphrasing and summarizing show you and your instructor how well you have understood what you read.

Annotating

More often than not, my students complain about having a bad memory because they claim not to remember a lot of what they read. But I think that one source of this problem lies elsewhere. The culprit is not a bad memory; it's *passive reading*. Rather than being actively involved with the print on the page, a passive reader reads the material once and unwisely thinks that he or she can get the full meaning without doing the hard work that good comprehension requires.

It's almost impossible for a reader—even a very experienced reader—to get the full meaning and to remember what's important when reading a selection for the first time. (I am referring here specifically to your college reading assignments, where good comprehension is required, not to the kind of casual reading you do in popular magazines or the daily paper.) The cure for this kind of bad memory is simple: *annotate the text*, or, in other words, write notes in the margins.

You already have seen this process demonstrated in the introduction to Part 1, where you identified main and supporting ideas. This next section explains and

---

Annotating, Paraphrasing, and Summarizing

demonstrates the process of annotating in more detail. Throughout the text, you will have many opportunities to practice this skill, and your instructor may require you to practice annotation beyond the exercises in this book.

HOW TO ANNOTATE

Annotating is sometimes called reading with a pencil in your hand. (And using a pencil is a good idea, so that you can erase your notes later, if you want to.) Annotating is not the same as highlighting or underlining words with a neon-yellow or -pink marker. Many students rely on such markers as a study aid when they read textbooks; most reading instructors, however, discourage this practice because such marks only delay learning. Marking your text only tells you that the material is important to learn—some day! And my students tell me that they are uncertain what to highlight and so end up highlighting almost everything. Moreover, highlighting is a *passive* activity. Careful annotating, in contrast, allows you both to read *actively* and to pull out the essential ideas at the same time. What makes for good annotating? Here are some suggestions:

TECHNIQUES FOR ANNOTATING	
• Main ideas	Jot down brief phrases in your own words restating the main ideas
• Phrases or sentences you don't understand	Place a question mark in the margin
• Unfamiliar vocabulary words	Circle them in the text
• Questions to ask in class	Write in the margin and mark with a clear symbol
• Ideas you disagree with	Place a star or some other symbol in the margin

To illustrate this process, consider a brief excerpt from a selection that appears in Part 2, Sheldon Campbell's "Games Elephants Play" and the sample annotations. First, read the passage; then study the annotations.

> **Elephants—very intelligent; live in well-organized matriarchies.**
> **Who was Dinesen?**
> **Captive elephants show intelligence by learning complicated, difficult tasks.**
>
> Elephants, female elephants that is, are seen by most zoo visitors as simple, lovable creatures, given to making loud trumpeting noises, tossing dirt onto their backs, addicted to joyous, splashing baths, and cadging peanuts or other goodies by reaching out with their trunks. That picture, as far as it goes, is reasonably accurate. But elephants are not simpletons. Field studies have shown them to be highly intelligent creatures that ordinarily live in well-organized matriarchies, sometimes leisurely browsing, sometimes pacing across a savannah in a deceptively fast and soundless gait as though, in a memorable line from Isak Dinesen, they had "an appointment at the end of the world."
>
> In captivity, elephants best display their great intelligence in shows of various types, rapidly learning complex tasks where it seems the trainer is constantly at risk and never harmed, or in the heavy, often difficult tasks they

---

BOXED INFORMATION

Throughout the introductions to each part, you will find important concepts boxed for easy reference. These boxes will also help reinforce ideas for visual learners.

VOCABULARY PREVIEW

Following each headnote is a Vocabulary Preview to acquaint you with words that will appear in the reading selection that follows. These Vocabulary Previews will help you build your vocabulary as they explain words you will encounter.

---

8 | SHELDON CAMPBELL
Games Elephants Play

Until his death in 1985, Sheldon Campbell had an unusual mix of careers, working as both a teacher and a stockbroker in San Diego, California. But his real interest was animal life. For many years he was president of the San Diego Zoological Society and a trustee of the world-famous San Diego Zoo. In this latter capacity, he pioneered animal exchanges between the San Diego Zoo and the People's Republic of China and was instrumental in arranging with the Chinese for a pair of rare golden monkeys to be brought to the zoo in 1984. This selection comes from his collection of zoo stories, Lifeboats to Ararat.

Vocabulary Preview

WORD HISTORIES

Apocryphal [paragraph 6] Campbell relates an *apocryphal* story, a variant of the fable, "Appointment in Samarra." An *apocryphal* story is one that may or may not be true. It derives from the *Apocrypha*, fourteen books included in the Old Testament. Protestants and Catholics do not consider them authentic because they were not part of the original Hebrew scriptures. The word's origin is from the Greek verb, *apokruptein* ("to hide away").

Alpha [paragraph 7] A male elephant named Tembo, a resident of the Hanover Zoo, obeyed orders only from his *alpha* keeper, so-called because he easily dominated the animals in his care. *Alpha*, the first letter in the Greek alphabet, also means "first" or "beginning." An alpha keeper, then, refers to one who is first in importance. (The *beta* keeper, whom Tembo refused to obey, was second in importance.) You can easily see where the word *alphabet* came from—*alpha* and *beta* are the first two letters of the Greek alphabet.

WORD PARTS

-ly (adverb suffix) Since Campbell uses several adverbs in this selection, perhaps this is a good place to review what adverbs are, how they are formed, and how they are used. Adverbs tell us "in what manner." An adverb's meaning is essentially the same as an adjective's, but the two parts of speech are used differently: Adverbs modify (or describe) verbs, adjectives, other adverbs, and occasionally an entire sentence; adjectives modify nouns. When you read, of course, you do not need to worry about identifying what part of speech an adverb modifies, only the word that it describes. But it's useful to get some practice identifying just what the adverb modifies.

135

Making Inferences

Look carefully at this cartoon:

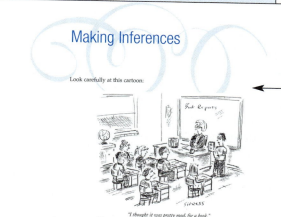

"I thought it was pretty good, for a book."

What can you conclude about the little boy from his remarks? The cartoonist does not tell us the boy's attitude toward books. He suggests or implies it, and from what he implies, we *infer* (draw a conclusion by reading into his remark) that the boy probably prefers to play video games or watch television than read books. You will practice making inferences like this in the readings in the next three parts of the text.

Let's say that on a cloudy winter day you are driving north on a narrow mountain road. Suddenly, you notice that all of the cars coming toward you have their headlights on, and you wonder why. One possibility is that the cars are part of a funeral procession. Another is that they were just driving in an area in which headlights are required during the day (such as on narrow or windy roads) and that all the drivers forgot to turn off their lights at the end. A third is that they have just emerged from dense fog. Which of these conclusions is most likely? (Any one of them could be true, of course, but one is *probably* more likely than the other two.)

223

PART THREE

The discussion of inferences, which precedes Part Three, helps you figure out what the author is implying but not saying outright. This is a crucial skill in college and in the world of work.

READINGS

In each reading, the paragraphs are numbered to help you find information later. Sometimes readings also have illustrations and footnotes to help you understand the ideas and difficult vocabulary.

many young men to run away to work in the mines of Johannesburg, where they often lost their health and their lives. In those days, working in the mines was almost as much of a rite of passage as circumcision school, a myth that helped the mine-owners more than it helped my people.

A custom of circumcision school is that one must perform a daring exploit before the ceremony. In days of old, this might have involved a cattle raid or even a battle, but in our time the deeds were more mischievous than martial. Two nights before we moved to Tyhalarha, we decided to steal a pig. In Mqhekezweni there was a tribesman with an ornery old pig. To avoid making noise and alarming him, we arranged for the pig to do our work for us. We took handfuls of sediment from homemade African beer, which has a strong scent much favored by pigs, and placed it upwind of the pig. The pig was so aroused by the scent that he came out of the kraal,[2] following a trail we had laid, gradually made his way

[2] A South African word denoting either a rural village or an enclosure for livestock. Mandela probably uses the word in the second sense. (Ed.)

Persuasive Writing and Evaluating Evidence

In this introductory section, these are the topics for discussion:

- The principles of persuasive writing
- How to read persuasive writing
- Types of claims
- The structure of an argument
- Kinds of evidence
- The refutation
- Bias

The Principles of Persuasive Writing

As you recall from the introduction to Part 1, to *persuade* is one of the primary purposes in writing. The art of persuasion is a worthwhile skill to develop. Consider its usefulness in practical terms. Let's say that you have been working at your current part-time job for a year; you think you have done a good job, you take on new responsibilities willingly and without complaint, you come on time, and you don't fool around on the job. But you haven't had a raise. How would you approach your boss to ask for a higher salary? What reasons would you give in support of your request? You might point to your fine qualities listed above. You would certainly wait to make sure that he or she was in a good mood and not stressed out about meeting deadlines or dealing with grumpy customers. You would point out your loyalty, your dedication to the job, and other equally stellar traits. And if you were lucky, you might succeed in getting that raise. This real-life example shows that understanding the tactics of persuasion can yield tangible rewards.

Learning to read persuasive prose with understanding and a critical eye also yields rewards. It is the basis on which our democratic society is built. A significant part of being a good citizen is finding out the issues of the day, weighing the arguments for and against proposed policies, and coming to a decision on your own, not one imposed on you by someone else. The right to make informed decisions on one's own is one of many rewards of living in a democratic country with a free press and the unhindered freedom to express oneself without fear of punishment, retaliation, or censorship, as occurs in repressive societies. More broadly, learning to see issues from a variety of perspectives, not merely from one person's (or our own) narrow point of view is an important part of becoming an educated citizen.

339

PART FOUR

Before you begin the readings in Part Four, you will be given instruction in identifying the types of persuasive writing and evidence authors might use to convince you of their positions. You will also learn to look out for bias, prejudice, or preconceived ideas.

---

354   BILL McKIBBEN

2. What is your proposal to help solve this problem? _____
_____
_____

D. USING VOCABULARY

Here are some words from the selection. Write an original sentence using each word that shows both that you know how to use the word and what it means. The number of the paragraph in which the word occurs in the selection is provided for you.

1. *astute* [paragraph 1] _____

2. *penchant* [8] _____

3. *heedless* [10] _____

4. *advocating* [12] _____

5. *subversion* [12] _____

E. LOCATING EVIDENCE

Go through the editorial and locate the evidence that supports this idea:

Consumers who care about solving the problem of global warming should not buy SUVs.

To identify it, put a star in the margin next to the sentence or paragraph, or bracket the words.

F. TOPICS FOR WRITING OR DISCUSSION

1. Imagine that a good friend has decided to buy an SUV. Write a letter in which you try to convince the person to change his or her mind.
2. Write a refutation of your own to McKibben's opinion piece. Can you come up with two or three reasons in favor of buying an SUV?

EXERCISES

Each selection in the text is followed by six or seven different types of exercises that become more difficult and complex as you progress through the text. Both the multiple-choice and fill-in-the blank questions will help you check your understanding and develop better writing skills.

Before you begin the last group of readings in Part Five, the last instructional section will show you how to identify various development patterns authors might use in their essays and articles, and will teach you to recognize transitional elements that make the logical relationships between ideas clear.

Patterns of Development and Transitions

In this final section, we will take up two important skills that are necessary for good comprehension of nonfiction prose: a recognition of various patterns of development. These include a list of facts or details, examples, reasons (cause and effect), process (sequential steps), and contrast (showing differences) as well as transitional elements.

Patterns of Development

Let's say that you are wrestling with a big decision that you must make about your future. You know that you are interested in helping people, and you come up with a list of careers in which such an interest would be required for someone to succeed and be happy. On a sheet of paper you note the following career choices: nurse, doctor, teacher, charity worker, mental health worker, social worker. What you have done is provide *examples*, specific instances of careers in which you could help others.

Now you have another decision facing you: Should you apply to the four-year state university fifty miles away or study for the first two years at your local community college and then transfer? Again, you write down the good and bad aspects of both institutions and analyze their differences. Now you're *contrasting*. And when your counselor asks you why you want to become, say, a social worker, you come up with some *reasons* why the field of social work appeals to you.

These logical processes, which we do all the time in our daily lives, are also present in writing. Called *patterns of development*, they refer to the internal logic of a passage, the way the writer gets his or her ideas across. The choice of the appropriate pattern of development hinges on the subject. But your starting point is to recognize that these patterns of development can pertain to our thought processes as well as to the pattern a writer imposes on his or her material. We will examine each pattern briefly; they are illustrated with some short passages. Studying these patterns will help you keep on track as you read and follow the writer's thinking process.

LISTING FACTS OR DETAILS

The pattern of *listing facts* or *details* is perhaps the simplest one to recognize. Following the main idea, each supporting sentence presents factual evidence to support the main assertion. Consider this passage from a *New Yorker* article on the grueling Tour de France cycling race held every summer. The American cyclist

399

In Country   425

For Further Exploration

BOOKS

- William Langewiesche, *Unbuilding the World Trade Center* (2002). Veteran journalist Langewiesche had unprecedented access to Ground Zero in the weeks following the attacks. In this book, first excerpted in the *Atlantic Monthly*, he tells the behind-the-scenes story of the cleanup efforts.
- Tim O'Brien, *The Things They Carried* (1990). O'Brien's book presents a series of overlapping semi-autobiographical stories relating his experiences in Vietnam as a U.S. marine.

MOVIE

Apocalypse Now (1979), directed by Francis Ford Coppola and starring Marlon Brando and Martin Sheen, adapted Joseph Conrad's novel *Heart of Darkness* to depict the horrors of the Vietnam War.

WEB SITES

Photographs of Ground Zero, both after the attacks and during the cleanup effort, are available at these two sites:

- *http://library.thinkquest.org/CR0212088/grzero.htm*
- *www.digitaljournalist.org/issue0111/aris_intro.htm*

The design that won the international competition to build a memorial at the World Trade Center site was done by Daniel Libeskind, a Berlin architect. A description of his plan can be viewed at:

- *1010wins.com/topstories/winsnews_story_057183025.html*

FOR FURTHER EXPLORATION

After each reading, you will find a section called "For Further Exploration." If a reading interests you and you want to learn more about the topic, you will find a book title or two, a movie, and Web sites on the same theme as the reading listed in this section. (In Part Four, which includes only opinion pieces, only Web sites are offered.)

These tools are designed to help you improve your reading skills by offering you the support you'll need to get the most out of each selection. The readings themselves were chosen because they are interesting and compelling; for the best way to improve as a reader is to *want* to read. My hope is that you will enjoy each assignment and that by the end of your course you will love reading as much as I do.

Deanne Spears

Improving Your Vocabulary

When my students complain in the reading classes I teach that they often have difficulty concentrating and maintaining their focus as they read, we discuss the problem at length. While poor concentration may be the result of many factors—taking too many classes while trying to work, personal problems, lack of sleep, financial worries—the problem may often lie more with lack of vocabulary. Reading is tedious if there are many unfamiliar words on the page, and looking them all up in the dictionary is time-consuming and discouraging. A lack of vocabulary is indeed a significant obstacle to good reading comprehension, and so acquiring a stock of new vocabulary words is crucial if you hope to become a better reader. After all, if you do not know what key words on the page mean, you may not understand very well what a writer is saying.

I hope that this text will be of great use as you embark on this most necessary of skills. Also keep in mind that acquiring a solid reading vocabulary is a lifelong proposition. Your goal for this course should be to acquire as many college-level vocabulary words as you can as you read each selection. Your goal after the course ends should be to continue to acquire words as you read in your everyday life.

For this reason, it is important that you embark on a systematic vocabulary-acquisition program. As you work through the selections, you will practice identifying common prefixes and roots, breaking words down into their meaningful parts, and using context clues. You will turn to your dictionary when context clues aren't enough. This introductory portion of the text explores some techniques to increase the number of words you recognize in your college and everyday reading and to give you measurable, immediate, and long-term results. This introduction discusses these topics:

- Four techniques for acquiring words
- Using context clues
- Using the dictionary effectively
- Comparing print and online dictionaries

As I prepared the selections and the accompanying exercises, I quickly saw that many words from the early selections—actually a surprising number—turned up in subsequent ones. Of course, I did not plan it this way; it just happened. This is the reason I stress that you read the Vocabulary Preview sections that precede each selection, even if your instructor doesn't assign them, and that you work through the two vocabulary exercises after each selection. If you do these steps conscientiously, not only will your stock of vocabulary words improve, but your reading of the later pieces will be easier and more enjoyable. The thrill of recognition does wonders for one's reading morale. ("I saw that word in the Charles Finney selection; even better, I remember what it means!")

The single best way to improve your vocabulary is to read a lot. There is no shortcut or substitute for this method. The idea is simple: The more you read, the more you will be exposed to important vocabulary words. Memorizing long lists of words in isolation or working through vocabulary self-improvement books may fool you into thinking you are learning new words, but their meanings won't stick, and such activities deprive you of encountering words in real writing. What follow are a few suggestions for learning new words.

Four Techniques for Acquiring Words

USE VOCABULARY NOTE CARDS

When I studied German in college, our instructor suggested that we use 3" × 5" index cards to help us learn important vocabulary words. I did this religiously and found the cards' compact size perfect. Index cards can be easily secured with a rubber band and put into your backpack, pocket, or purse. By sorting through the stack, I could quickly review vocabulary words that we were to be tested on, omitting those I already knew and concentrating on those that I wasn't so sure of. When the stack of cards became too unwieldy, I organized them into parts of speech (nouns in one stack, verbs in another, and so on) and continued my study.

I can suggest the same method for improving your reading vocabulary. It takes just a minute to write each card. On one side, write the word (underline it for emphasis), the context in which it occurred (meaning the original sentence), the part of speech, and if necessary, its pronunciation. On the other side, write the definition and etymology. Study this example from Selection 1, "The Truth Is Out Here—Somewhere":

Front side of card—word in original context, part of speech, and pronunciation

... *in the Red Rock Country of Sedona, Ariz., where there are so many <u>pinnacles</u> you nearly expect to see the Marlboro man ...*

noun

pĭn 'ə- kəl

Reverse side of card—major definitions, language word derived from, and its meaning

(1) Architecture: a small turret or spire on a roof
(2) <u>a tall pointed formation, such as a mountain peak</u>
(3) the highest point or culmination
Latin: diminutive of <u>pinna</u> ("feather")

Notice that on the reverse side of the card I included all three dictionary definitions and underlined the appropriate one for the way the word was used in the original sentence. If your time is limited, just write down the definition that fits the way the word was used. Another student might be more interested in learning *variant word forms* (the various forms of the word when other endings are added) as you see on the reverse side of the card below. (The word on the next card comes from Selection 2, "Care in Midair.")

<table>
<tr>
<td>

Front side of card—word in original context, part of speech, and pronunciation

</td>
<td>

. . . if he <u>deteriorated</u>, we'd have to stabilize him

verb

dĭ - tûr′ ē - ə - rāt-əd

</td>
</tr>
<tr>
<td>

Reverse side of card—appropriate definitions, variant word forms, language word derived from, and its meaning

</td>
<td>

(1) to grow worse, degenerate
(2) to weaken or disintegrate
Variant forms: deterioration, deteriorative
Latin: deterior ("worse")

</td>
</tr>
</table>

Which words should you write down? You don't want to overwhelm yourself with hundreds of unfamiliar words, so I would suggest—at least at first—noting those words that you have seen before in your reading but that you can't readily define. Because you have seen these words before, they are not completely unfamiliar, and they are probably common enough in adult prose to make them a worthwhile addition to your vocabulary. As your stock of new vocabulary words grows, you can then turn to learning more unusual words. Keep in mind that even the best reader often encounters a word he or she doesn't know and has to look it up.

An alternate, though less convenient, method is to write new words in a vocabulary notebook. Stenography spiral notebooks are a good choice and, though you can't sort through the words as easily, their compact size makes them convenient to carry around.

USE THE THREE-DOT METHOD

Another technique to help you learn words is the "three-dot method." It works like this: When you look up a word in the dictionary, make a small dot in pencil next to the entry word. The second time you look it up, make another dot. The third time you look it up, add a third dot, and this time, learn the word! Any word that crops up three times within a short amount of time is obviously an important word that belongs in your permanent and active reading vocabulary.

> • • • **eu • tha • na • sia** (yo͞o′ thə -nā′zhə, -zhē-ə) *n.* The act or practice of ending the life of an individual suffering from a terminal illness or an incurable condition. [Gk., a good death : *eu-*, + *thanatos*, death.]

DEVELOP AN INTEREST IN ETYMOLOGY

All of the Vocabulary Preview sections that precede each selection begin with Word Histories, brief discussions of the language or languages that a particular word derived from or an interesting story about a word's origins. *Etymology* refers to the study of word origins, and paying attention to origins can be helpful for remembering new words. You saw on the first note card, for example, that the word *pinnacle* came from the Latin word for "feather." When you think about the shape of a pinnacle—a mountain that is tall and pointed—it does sort of look like a feather.

Something like 60 percent of English words come from Latin and French (as you will see throughout this text); another 15 percent derive from Greek, often through Latin, as well. What of the remaining 25 percent? Many, of course, derive from the original English language, known as Anglo-Saxon. These tend to be the basic building-block words of the language, words like *sun, moon, walk, boy, daughter, house,* and so on. But many words come from more exotic and unusual languages.

Words with Unusual Etymologies	
Arabic	alchemy, algebra, alkali, tariff
Native American languages	canoe, chile, hammock, moccasin, skunk, succotash
Malay	amok (an uncontrolled state)
Tamil	pariah (an outcast)
Alaskan Russian	parka
Hungarian	coach (a type of carriage)
Old Norse	skirt, sky

SUBSCRIBE TO A WORD-OF-THE-DAY WEB SITE

Word-of-the-day Web sites offer a painless and entertaining way to learn new words. Most of them offer the same features: the featured word followed by pronunciation symbols, a definition, a sentence or two using the word, and usually the word's etymology. You can visit a site each day, or more conveniently, you can subscribe (as of May 2003, each service recommended below is free). Each weekday you receive a new word of the day via email. Here are four word-of-the-day sites to check out. I have included some recent sample words from each site so that you can see which site might be most appropriate for your level. (Note that by the time you read this text, one or more of these sites may have moved or expired. If you are unable to locate a particular site, use your favorite search engine to get updated addresses.)

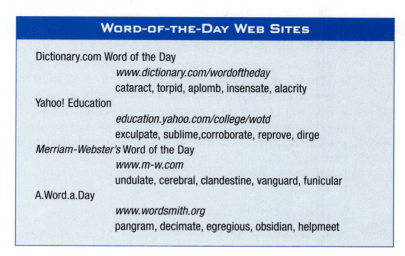

WORD-OF-THE-DAY WEB SITES

Dictionary.com Word of the Day
www.dictionary.com/wordoftheday
cataract, torpid, aplomb, insensate, alacrity
Yahoo! Education
education.yahoo.com/college/wotd
exculpate, sublime, corroborate, reprove, dirge
Merriam-Webster's Word of the Day
www.m-w.com
undulate, cerebral, clandestine, vanguard, funicular
A.Word.a.Day
www.wordsmith.org
pangram, decimate, egregious, obsidian, helpmeet

Using Context Clues

We begin this section with an exercise called a *cloze test*. Here is a paragraph from Selection 1 by Josh Sens, "The Truth Is Out Here—Somewhere," with some of the words left out. Your task is to fill in the words that make sense and complete the meaning of the sentence. Be sure to pay attention both to meaning and to grammar and sentence structure. The subject of this paragraph is the mysterious moving stones at a place called Racetrack Playa in California's Death Valley.

What _____ the stones slide remains a _____. As always, some

_____ suspect aliens. If that's _____ case, E.T. is stronger

_____ a team of oxen. Some _____ the stones weigh 700

_____. Other theories _____ emerged. Maybe it's

_____ high wind, though _____ alone couldn't budge some

_____ these babies. _____ it's the rain, which freezes in

_____ weather, forming a thin icy film over which the _____

could slide. _____ it's a combination of the _____.

Here is the passage again, this time with the missing words restored and bold-faced:

What **makes** the stones slide remains a **question.** As always, some **people** suspect aliens. If that's **the** case, E.T. is stronger **than** a team of oxen. Some **of** the stones weigh 700 **pounds.** Other theories **have** emerged. Maybe it's **the** high wind, though **wind** alone couldn't budge some **of** these babies. **Maybe** it's the rain, which freezes in **cold** weather, forming a thin icy film over which the **rocks** could slide. **Maybe** it's a combination of the **two.**

Give yourself a point for each answer that matches those above. Also give yourself a point if you chose "mystery" (instead of "question"), "icy" (instead of "cold"), or "perhaps" (instead of "maybe").

What process accounts for your ability to fill in at least some of these words? The word *context* refers to the circumstances or setting, more specifically, to the words and phrases that surround a particular word and that *may* help you figure out its meaning. In the Death Valley passage, you used grammatical and context clues to help you find the right word. For example, in the first sentence, the only verb that can really fit into the sentence is "makes." Why not the verb "causes"? If you try to insert "causes" into the sentence, the sentence doesn't work grammatically:

What causes the stones slide remains a question.

"Causes" would work only if the original sentence had been worded like this:

What causes the stones **to** slide remains a question.

Although the method is not perfect or foolproof, context clues can yield a meaning acceptable enough that you don't have to look up every unfamiliar word in the dictionary. Consider all the words you've learned since you were a baby. While growing up, you came across new words all the time, and eventually—even without turning to the dictionary—you figured out their meanings because of the several contexts in which you encountered them. You weren't born with a vocabulary! You learned words by absorption, by osmosis.

This practice of absorbing new words just by reading, however, has one major drawback: It takes years to accomplish. And since time is of the essence in your college courses, you need to develop some shortcuts. When you encounter a new word, first try to break it down into its component parts—prefixes, roots, and suffixes—as you will see in the Vocabulary Preview sections preceding each selection. Next, try to use *context clues* (explained in detail in this section), which are useful when you do not need a precise dictionary definition.

Sometimes using word analysis and context clues together will produce a perfectly acceptable definition. For example, in Selection 9, Charles Finney describes some characteristics of a baby rattlesnake. He writes: "Without moisture, he would die of *dehydration.*" The phrase "without moisture" is a helpful context clue. Further, when we analyze *dehydration,* we break it down into its component parts: *de-* means "removal of" and *hydra* means "water," thus suggesting a dangerous condition: lack of sufficient water.

Of course, if structural analysis or context clues don't produce an adequate definition, and you think an accurate understanding of the word is crucial to your understanding of the passage, you'll have to look it up.

TYPES OF CONTEXT CLUES

To familiarize you with the way these clues work, here are some types of context clues followed by short excerpts from some of the readings in the text that illustrate each clue type. Study them carefully. I have identified the author and selection number in each instance and highlighted the context clues for each italicized word.

Synonyms A *synonym* is a word that is close in meaning to the word in question. This is the easiest of the types of context clues to recognize. For example, in Selection 8, Sheldon Campbell writes:

> While female elephants, even those that play games, are generally friendly and *affable* . . .

Affable means "easy and pleasant to get along with," close enough to "friendly." Also the fact that these adjectives are joined with the conjunction *and* suggests that they are near synonyms. Study this next example from Selection 15 by Eric Schlosser, from the best-seller *Fast Food Nation:*

> Regardless of the billions spent on marketing and promotion, all the ads on radio and TV, all the efforts to create brand loyalty, the major chains must live with the unsettling fact that more than 70 percent of fast food visits are *impulsive.* The decision to stop for fast food is made on the spur of the moment, without much thought.

Impulsive means exactly the same as the two phrases in the next sentence: "on the spur of the moment" and "without much thought"—in other words, on impulse.

Another Synonym Tip Sometimes a writer uses the connecting word *or* to indicate a synonym for an unfamiliar term, especially in scientific material. For example, in Selection 10, Geoffrey Cowley explains how children learn to speak individual words and to distinguish one word from another. He writes:

> Each of the world's approximately 6,000 languages uses a different assortment of *phonemes,* or distinctive sounds, to build words. As adults, we have a hard time even hearing phonemes from foreign languages.

The term *phonemes* comes from linguistics and is not likely to be in the average reader's vocabulary, so Cowley adds a defining phrase separated by "or." (Note that in most contexts the word *or* indicates a choice, as in "We couldn't decide whether to order pizza or a hamburger.")

Antonyms An *antonym* is a word that means the opposite of the one you are unsure of. Consider this example: In Selection 10, Geoffrey Cowley discusses the way small children learn first to produce words, then phrases, and finally sentences. He writes:

Scholars have *bickered* for centuries over how kids accomplish this feat, but most now agree that their brains are wired for the task.

Because *agree* and *bicker* are opposites, we can easily see that *bicker* means "to quarrel." Here is a second example from Selection 17 by Elliott West, "Wagon Train Children":

While they generally enjoyed antelope, bison and other new dishes of the Plains, there was much to *rail at*—like campside baking (bread "plentifully seasoned with mouse pills") and foul water ("drank red mud for coffee").

More than anything, they longed for fresh vegetables and fruit.

Logic tells us that if they *enjoyed* eating the animals they hunted on the Plains, they also *complained about*, or "railed at" the unappetizing bread and coffee.

Examples or Series of Details An *example*—a particular instance of something more general, or a cluster of details in a paragraph—may reveal the meaning of an unfamiliar word. In describing a diamondback rattlesnake in Selection 9, Charles Finney uses the word *formidable*, followed by these examples, which gives you a chance to come up with a suitable meaning on your own:

At two he was *formidable*. He had grown past the stage where a racer [another kind of snake] or a road runner could safely tackle him. He had grown to the size where other desert dwellers—coyotes, foxes, coatis, wildcats—knew it was better to leave him alone.

And a little later, Finney writes:

He had not experienced death for the simple reason that there had never been an opportunity for anything bigger and stronger than himself to kill him. Now at two, because he was so *formidable*, that opportunity became more and more unlikely.

Since both passages describe the rattlesnake as stronger and larger than other creatures around him, you can infer that *formidable* means "impressive" or "arousing fear or dread."

In another example from the article on children's language acquisition, Geoffrey Cowley describes the rapid pace at which toddlers learn new words like this:

Words accrue slowly at first. But around the age of 18 months, children's abilities explode. Most start acquiring new words at the *phenomenal* rate of one every two hours. . . .

It isn't so hard to imagine that an adult might learn one new vocabulary word for every 2 hours he or she reads, but for an 18-month-old to acquire a new word every 2 hours does truly seem *phenomenal.* This word then means "extraordinary" or "remarkable."

Situation   The *situation* or circumstance in which the word is used may give you a hint as to its meaning. Here is Sheldon Campbell in Selection 8 describing elephant behavior around trainers:

Knowing also that the real contest is to determine who is boss, the best elephant keepers establish a *dominance* over their animals that a matador would envy. The test of this dominance can be seen whenever keeper and elephant are walking toward one another on a narrow road or path. The dominant keeper never *deviates.* Without batting an eye he continues forward until the elephant steps aside.

Dominance, required by both elephant trainers and matadors (bullfighters), means "exercising the most influence or control." The situation is clear: The trainer must dominate—completely control—the animal, not the other way around. And the meaning of *deviates* is clearly indicated in the situation described: The keeper must "continue forward," forcing the elephant to step aside, in other words, to deviate.

Emotion   The emotional attitude evident in a passage—its mood—may provide a good enough clue to save you from looking up a word. In "The Environmental Issue from Hell" (Selection 22), Bill McKibben takes up the problem of global warming. He writes,

So maybe we should think of global warming in a different way—as the great moral crisis of our time, the equivalent of the civil rights movement of the 1960s.

Why a moral question? In the first place, no one's ever figured out a more effective way to screw the *marginalized* and poor of this planet than climate change. Having taken their dignity, their resources, and their freedom under a variety of other schemes, we now are taking the very physical ability on which their already difficult lives depend.

CONTEXT CLUES

- Synonym—a word that means the same or nearly the same
- Antonym—a word that means the opposite or nearly the opposite
- Example and detail—a specific instance or series of details that may reveal a word's meaning
- Situation—the specific circumstances in which a word is used, which may help suggest its meaning
- Emotion—the emotional feeling or the mood of the passage

Notice McKibben's strong feelings of anger and disapproval. The passage condemns the powerful and expresses sympathy for the poor. Another clue that points to the meaning of *marginalized* is the slang word *screwed*. Even more clues lie in the last sentence: "Having taken their dignity, their resources, and their freedom." Finally, consider the root of the word *marginalized*: A paper's margins are the edges; similarly, if someone lives on the *margins*, he or she is relegated to the "outer edges" of society. They have low social standing. You can gather all this without opening the dictionary.

WHEN NOT TO LOOK UP WORDS

Some words simply aren't important enough to look up (unless, of course, you have all the time in the world or are simply curious). For example, in Selection 7, Andre Dubus describes his high school years like this:

> That hot June in Lafayette, Louisiana, I was sixteen, I would be seventeen in August. . . . I did not have a girlfriend, so I did not have to buy drinks or food or movie tickets for anyone else. I did not want to work. I wanted to drive around with my friends, or walk with them downtown, to stand in front of the department store, comb our *ducktails*, talk, and look at girls.

Unless you are familiar with 1950s hairstyles, you probably won't have encountered the word *ducktail*. But you can figure out that the word refers to a hairstyle from the word *comb*, making it unnecessary to turn to the dictionary. Also, in the scheme of things, this word is not particularly important. Save the dictionary for words that are essential to your accurate understanding of a passage. Here is another example, from "Sports Centered" (Selection 23), by Jay Weiner:

> Fans applauded the courage of *renegade* Curt Flood, the St. Louis Cardinals outfielder who in 1969 refused to be traded, arguing that baseball players should be free to play where they want to play.

What's a renegade? The "courage" that Curt Flood exhibited, that made fans applaud, suggests that he did something different from what most baseball players of his day did. A *renegade* is a rebel, someone who rejects convention. While not exactly a context clue, the way Flood's behavior is described gives enough of a hint as to the word's meaning that you can safely continue reading without looking it up.

When you are assigned reading for a course, follow these steps for improved comprehension and focus: First, read through the material once without stopping, and circle any unfamiliar vocabulary words. Then read through the material a second time. While reading, try to break unfamiliar words down into their elements or use context clues if any are present and seem reliable. Next, if you are unsure about the meaning of an unfamiliar word and if you need to know its meaning to understand what you are reading, look the word up in the dictionary. Finally, write a brief definition of the word in the margin, and record the word on a vocabulary note card.

PRACTICE EXERCISES

In this discussion I classified context clues into types simply to show you the various possibilities. However, when you read, you should only intuit, or be aware, of these types, for there is no particular advantage in being able to identify them. Here are a few exercises—again, short excerpts from selections in the text—giving you an opportunity to practice using context clues with words that are apt to be unfamiliar. Read the example and study the context carefully. In the first space, write your definition of the word—what you think it means. In the second, verify the word's meaning by consulting your dictionary. See how close you come.

1. Elephants, female elephants that is, are seen by most zoo visitors as simple, lovable creatures, given to making loud trumpeting noises, tossing dirt onto their backs . . . and *cadging* peanuts or other goodies by reaching out with their trunks. (Selection 8: Sheldon Campbell, "Games Elephants Play")

   Your definition _____ Dictionary definition _____

   _____

2. That summer Crotalus [a diamondback rattlesnake] met his first dog. It was a German shepherd which had been reared on a farm in the Midwest and there had gained the reputation of being a snake-killer. Black snakes, garter snakes, pilots, water snakes; it delighted in killing them all. It would seize them by the middle, *heedless* of their tiny teeth, and shake them violently until they died. (Selection 9: Charles Finney, "The Life and Death of a Western Gladiator")

   Your definition _____ Dictionary definition _____

   _____

3. Children surrounded by words almost always become fluent by 3, whatever their general intelligence. And people *deprived of* language as children rarely master it as adults, no matter how smart they are or how intensively they're trained. (Selection 10: Geoffrey Cowley, "The Language Explosion")

   Your definition _____ Dictionary definition _____

   _____

4. A 1993 U.S. Department of Education report on illiteracy said 21–23 percent of U.S. adults—about 40 million—read minimally, enough to *decipher* an uncomplicated meeting announcement. . . . I wanted to meet nonreaders because I could not imagine being unable to *decipher* a street sign, or words printed on supermarket jars, or stories in a book. (Selection 11: Richard Wolkomir, "Making Up for Lost Time: The Rewards of Reading at Last")

   Your definition _____ Dictionary definition _____

   _____

5. When two women shop together, they talk, advise, suggest and consult to their hearts' content, hence the long time in the store; with the kids, she's

partly consumed with herding them along and keeping them entertained; alone, she makes efficient use of her time. But with him [her husband]— well, he makes it plain that he's bored and antsy and likely at any moment to go off and sit in the car and listen to the radio or stand outside and watch girls. So the woman's comfort level *plummets* when he's by her side; she spends the entire trip feeling anxious and rushed. (Selection 12: Paco Underhill, "Shop Like a Man")

Your definition _____ Dictionary definition _____

_____

6. My friend Peter claims he cannot open the door to his tiny daughter's bedroom—it is stuffed to the four corners with Barbie dolls and Barbie equipment, with accessories and extras, with vacation houses, gyms, recreational vehicles, costumes, cosmetics. She is six. . . . What he wants to know is, where will all this lead? Isn't the *surfeit* of things in his daughter's room likely to persuade her that her parents don't really love her, instead of that they do? (Selection 13: Martha Fay, "Sedated by Stuff")

Your definition _____ Dictionary definition _____

_____

7. The speculators, next, would hire people to pass out handbills in the Eastern and Midwestern cities, tracts *limning* the advantages of relocation to "the Athens of the South" or "the new plains Jerusalem." When persuasion failed, the builders might resort to bribery, paying people's moving costs and giving them houses, in exchange for nothing but a pledge to stay until a certain census was taken or a certain inspection made. . . . The speculators' idea, of course, was to *lure* the railroad. (Selection 14: Lawrence Shames, "The Hunger for More")

limning

Your definition _____ Dictionary definition _____

_____

lure

Your definition _____ Dictionary definition _____

_____

8. With discoveries of genetic links to disease and personality announced every week, one could easily misbelieve that identity is written in the language of DNA. It is not. Our physical, cultural and social environments all influence what we become. Even Wilmut, who strongly opposes human cloning, has said he can easily tell his cloned sheep apart by their individual *quirks,* though all are genetic *replicas.* (Selection 27: Rick Weiss, "A Uniquely Human Debate")

quirks

Your definition ———————————— Dictionary definition ——————————

———

replicas

Your definition ———————————— Dictionary definition ——————————

———

9. Despite these and other concerns, Clinton's commission was not convinced that cloning posed unique or *insurmountable* social harms. It did recommend that Congress impose a *moratorium* on human cloning, but not on ethical or moral grounds. Rather, the commission was concerned about safety. And recognizing that research would likely overcome the miscarriages and deformities of early attempts, the commission recommended that any congressional ban automatically expire in five years. (Selection 27: Rick Weiss, "A Uniquely Human Debate")

insurmountable

Your definition ———————————— Dictionary definition ————————

———

moratorium

Your definition ———————————— Dictionary definition ——————————

———

10. Over the past eighteen years, I've been to a dozen-odd war zones around the world. Usually, I went as a journalist, with all the *detachment* and comparative *immunity* that implies. Of course, there were times when both detachment and immunity fell away, when I witnessed things that affected me deeply, or I found myself in harm's way. (Selection 28: Scott Anderson, "In Country")

detachment

Your definition ————————————————————————————————————

Dictionary definition ——————————————————————————————

immunity

Your definition ———————————— Dictionary definition ——————————

———

11. Although many geeks are happy, well-adjusted, popular, and athletic, many are not. They grasp the reality of the *alienated,* the anger of those who inhabit a world that isn't made for them, doesn't work for them or reflect their values, and sometimes systematically excludes and humiliates them—a brutal fact of life in middle school and high school. (Selection 29: Jon Katz, "What Hath Goth Wrought?")

Your definition ———————————————— Dictionary definition ——

——

12. On the morning of my first full day of job searching, I take a red pen to the want ads, which are *auspiciously* numerous. Everyone in Key West's boom-ing "hospitality industry" seems to be looking for someone like me—train-able, flexible, and with suitably humble expectations as to pay. (Selection 32: Barbara Ehrenreich, "On (Not) Getting By in America")

Your definition ——————————————————————————————————

Dictionary definition ————————————————————————————

MASTERING COLLEGE READING

1. Read through the material once without stopping; circle any unfamiliar words.
2. Read through the material again; try to break down any unfamiliar words into their elements, and use context clues to decipher their meaning.
3. Look up unfamiliar words in the dictionary, if they are important to understanding the meaning of what you are reading.
4. Write a brief definition of the words you look up in the margin, and create a vocabulary card for each word.

Using Print and Online Dictionaries

When context clues and your knowledge of word parts aren't enough, you will need to turn to the dictionary. The final section of this part introduces you to spe-cific features of standard college dictionaries; you should study this material closely and refer to it often until you have mastered it. These suggestions show you how best to use this wonderful resource for good results.

First, it is imperative that you have a good, up-to-date dictionary—not some tattered edition you bought at a garage sale or your father's hand-me-down *Web-ster's* from the 1960s. If you can afford to, invest in your academic future and buy two dictionaries: an unabridged and an abridged version. The word *abridged* means "reduced or condensed." Therefore, an *abridged* dictionary, usually pub-lished in an inexpensive paperback format, is shorter than a complete or *unabridged* dictionary because it does not contain as many words. A standard col-lege edition of an *unabridged* dictionary generally contains around 175,000 entries. In contrast, my paperback *American Heritage Dictionary* has about 70,000 entries.

Each kind of dictionary has its own advantages. The light weight of the paper-back dictionary makes it portable. Unabridged versions, besides containing more words, also contain more complete definitions, etymologies, notes on appropriate usage, and explanations of synonyms. But such a dictionary is heavy to lug around and therefore is better kept at home. Ask your instructor to recommend one, or choose one of these three widely used dictionaries. Each comes in both an abridged and an unabridged version. In alphabetical order:

The American Heritage College Dictionary
Merriam-Webster's Collegiate Dictionary
The Random House College Dictionary

THE FEATURES OF A DICTIONARY

No matter which dictionary you choose, all contain the same features. Here is a brief overview of the important ones.

Guide Words *Guide words* are printed in boldface in the top margin of each page; they indicate the first and last words on that page and help you locate words quickly.

Entry The word *entry* is simply a fancy term for the word that you are looking up. It is printed in boldface type in the left margin; dots separate the syllables.

Pronunciation Symbols *Pronunciation symbols* are printed in parentheses and follow each entry. English has a complicated pronunciation system: The language has approximately seventy-five different sounds but only twenty-six letters to represent them. A single vowel like *a,* for example, can be pronounced seven ways, as in these words: *cat* (ă); *lake* (ā); *bar* (är); *bare* (âr); *part* (är); *law* (ô); and *father* (ä). The pronunciation symbols follow a standardized system so that you know how each letter or combination of letters should be pronounced in an unfamiliar word. Ask your instructor for help if you don't know how to pronounce these symbols. In the college edition of the *American Heritage Dictionary,* these symbols are printed in the lower-right corner of each *right-hand* page. Other dictionaries print them across the bottom of both pages.

Stress Marks *Stress,* or *accent,* marks are as important as pronunciation symbols for pronouncing words correctly. Referring to the relative degree of loudness of each syllable, stress marks are printed *after* the syllable to be stressed, as you can see in this word: *solid* (sŏl′ ĭd). In this case, the first syllable, *sol,* receives primary stress or emphasis.

English has three kinds of stress. Primary, or heavy, stress is shown by a heavy boldface mark, like this: ′. Secondary, or weak, stress is shown by the same mark printed in lighter type, like this: ′. And unstressed syllables, such as those containing a neutral vowel sound—symbolized by a pronunciation symbol called a "schwa," which is written like an upside down "e" (ə)—are unmarked. For example, the word *magnification* contains all three types of stress: măg′ nə fĭ kā′ shən. The first syllable takes the secondary stress, the third syllable takes the primary stress, and the second and fourth syllables are unstressed.

Parts of Speech and Inflected Forms Following the dictionary pronunciation symbols is an abbreviation indicating what part of speech the entry word is. For example, *n.* = noun, *v.* = verb, *adj.* = adjective, *adv.* = adverb, and so forth. *Inflected forms*—the forms of the word that take word endings, or *inflections*—are also included. Thus, you can look up the proper way to spell the past tense and present participle of a word like *gratify.* In *gratified* (the past tense form), the *y* changes to *i,* and the ending signifying the past tense (*-ed*) is added. In *gratifying* (the present participle), the ending *-ing* is added; and in *gratifies,* the present tense for the third-person (that is, the form used with "he," "she," or "it") changes to *i* and the ending *-es* is added. Similarly, if you look up the word *ox,* the dictionary indicates the plural form: *n. pl. oxen.*

Order of Definitions The one significant difference in dictionaries is in the order of definitions if a word has more than one meaning. The *American Heritage* and the *Random House* college editions follow this system: If a word has multiple senses (two or more meanings, in other words), the central and often the most commonly sought meaning is listed first. Less common, older forms, and obsolete senses are listed next. *However,* this does not mean that you should grab the first meaning listed. The context is crucial in determining which sense best fits a particular word's meaning. This concept will be illustrated in more detail at the end of this section.

Note that *Merriam-Webster's Collegiate Dictionary* organizes its definitions historically, which means that the earliest sense or senses of a word come first, with more modern senses following. If you are unsure about which method your particular dictionary uses, ask your instructor for help or refer to the early pages of the dictionary, called the *front matter,* where there will be a description of the *Order of Senses* or something similar.

Variant Forms If the word has other grammatical forms, the dictionary will list those after the last definition. If you look up *grateful* (adjective), for example, the dictionary lists as variants *gratefully* (adverb) and *gratefulness* (noun).

Etymology A word's *etymology* refers to its linguistic origin, that is, the language from which it came into English. Etymology also refers to the word's history. It is printed in brackets, [ ], either before or after the definitions, depending on your dictionary. As you will see, each Vocabulary Preview in this text introduces you to the word origins of one or more words in the reading. When you look up a word in the dictionary to see where it came from, the originating language will be abbreviated. For example, *OF* indicates Old French, *ME* indicates Middle English, *L* or *Lat* refers to Latin, and *Gk* means Greek. A complete list of those abbreviations can be found in the front matter of your dictionary.

Other Features Some dictionaries include useful drawings in the margins. The *American Heritage* dictionaries (the college edition and the unabridged edition) are particularly generous in this regard, allowing you to see, for example, the location of El Salvador on a small map of Central America, what a French chateau (castle) looks like, and what Princess Diana looked like, just to cite three random examples from my dictionary. Thus the dictionary goes far beyond being merely a resource for looking up words: It is also a mini-atlas, a biographical index, and a provider of all kinds of useful information from the world around you.

SAMPLE DICTIONARY COLUMN

Now that you are familiar with some of the more important dictionary terminology, reprinted here is one column from *The American Heritage College Dictionary.* Study the arrows to identify the features discussed above.

Entries

Pronunciation symbols

Usage note

Variant forms

Etymology

447

Ellesmere Island

eluvium

Guide words

Parts of speech

Definitions

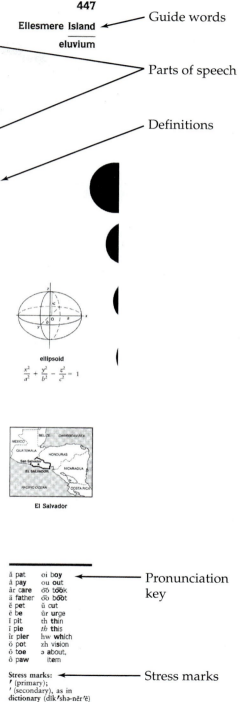

ellipsoid

$$\frac{x^2}{a^2} + \frac{y^2}{b^2} - \frac{z^2}{c^2} = 1$$

El Salvador

chaic. **1.** To remove or carry away to a distance, esp. so as to conceal. **2.** To take (oneself) to a distance. [ME *elongen* < OFr. *esloigner* : *es-*, from (< Lat. *ex-*; see EX-) + *loing*, far (< Lat. *longē*, distant < *longus*, long; see del-¹*).]

e·lon·gate (ĭ-lông′gāt′, ĭ-lŏng′-) *tr. & intr.v.* **-gat·ed, -gat·ing, -gates.** To make or grow longer. — *adj.* or **elongated. 1.** Made longer; extended. **2.** Having more length than width; slender. [LLat. *ēlongāre, ēlongāt-* : Lat. *ē-, ex-*, ex- + Lat. *longē*, distant; see ELOIGN.]

e·lon·ga·tion (ĭ-lông′-gā′shən, ĭ-lŏng′-, ē′lông-, ē′lŏng-) *n.* **1.** The act of elongating or the condition of being elongated. **2.** Something that elongates; an extension. **3.** The angular distance between two celestial bodies as seen from Earth.

e·lope (ĭ-lōp′) *intr.v.* **e·loped, e·lop·ing, e·lopes. 1.** To run away with a lover, esp. with the intention of getting married. **2.** To run away; abscond. [Perh. AN *aloper*, to run away from one's husband with a lover < MDu. *ontlopen*, to run away : *ont-*, away from, along; see ant-* + *lopen*, to run.] — **e·lope′ment** *n.* — **e·lop′er** *n.*

el·o·quence (ĕl′ə-kwəns) *n.* **1.a.** Persuasive powerful discourse. **b.** The skill or power of using such discourse. **2.** The quality of persuasive powerful expression.

el·o·quent (ĕl′ə-kwənt) *adj.* **1.** Characterized by eloquence. **2.** Vividly or movingly expressive. See Syns at **expressive.** [ME < OFr. < Lat. *ēloquēns, ēloquent-*, pr.part. of *ēloquī*, to speak out. See ELOCUTION.] — **el′o·quent·ly** *adv.* — **el′o·quent·ness** *n.*

El Pas·o (păs′ō). A city of extreme W TX on the Rio Grande opposite Ciudad Juárez, Mexico. Pop. 515,342.

El Sal·va·dor (săl′və-dôr′, săl′vä-thôr′). A country of Central America on the Pacific; achieved independence from Spain in 1821. Cap. San Salvador. Pop. 4,949,000. — **El Sal·va·dor′i·an** (săl′və-dôr′ē-ən, -dôr′-) *adj. & n.*

else (ĕls) *adj.* **1.** Other; different: *Ask somebody else.* **2.** Additional; more: *anything else.* — *adv.* **1.** In a different or an additional time, place, or manner: *Where else did he go?* **2.** If not; otherwise: *Be careful, or else you will fall.* — **idiom. or else.** Regardless of any extenuating circumstances: *Be there or else!* [ME *elles* < OE. See al-¹*.]

> **Usage Note:** *Else* is often used redundantly in combination with prepositions such as *but, except,* and *besides*: *No one else but Sam knew* (omit *else*). • When a pronoun is followed by *else*, the possessive form is generally written thus: *someone else's* (not *someone's else*). Both *who else's* and *whose else* are in use but not *whose else's*. See Usage Notes at **who, whose.**

else·where (ĕls′hwâr′, -wâr′) *adv.* In or to a different or another place: *has property at the shore and elsewhere.*

El·si·nore (ĕl′sə-nôr′, -nôr′). See **Helsingør.**

El To·ro (tôr′ō). A community of S CA SE of Santa Ana. Pop. 62,685.

el·u·ant (ĕl′yōō-ənt) *n.* A substance used as a solvent in the process of elution. [< Lat. *ēluēns, ēluent-*, pr.part. of *ēluere*, to wash out. See ELUTE.]

el·u·ate (ĕl′yōō-ĭt, -āt′) *n.* The solution of solvent and dissolved matter resulting from elution. [Lat. *ēluere*, to wash out; see ELUTE + -ATE¹.]

e·lu·ci·date (ĭ-lōō′sĭ-dāt′) *v.* **-dat·ed, -dat·ing, -dates.** — *tr.* To make clear or plain, esp. by explanation. — *intr.* To give an explanation that clarifies. [LLat. *ēlūcidāre, ēlūcidāt-* : Lat. *ē-, ex-*, intensive pref.; see EX- + Lat. *lūcidus*, bright (< *lūcēre*, to shine; see leuk-*).] — **e·lu′ci·da′tion** *n.* — **e·lu′ci·da′tive** *adj.* — **e·lu′ci·da′tor** *n.*

e·lude (ĭ-lōōd′) *tr.v.* **e·lud·ed, e·lud·ing, e·ludes. 1.** To evade or escape from, as by daring, cleverness, or skill. **2.** To escape the understanding or grasp of. [Lat. *ēlūdere* : *ē-, ex-*, ex- + *lūdere*, to play (< *lūdus*, play; see leid-*).]

E·lul (ĕl′ōōl, ē-lōōl′) *n.* The 12th month of the year in the Jewish calendar. [Heb. *'Elûl* < Akkadian *ulūlu, elūlu*, the month Ululu (August/September).]

e·lu·sive (ĭ-lōō′sĭv, -zĭv) *adj.* **1.** Tending to elude capture, perception, comprehension, or memory. **2.** Difficult to define or describe. [< Lat. *ēlūsus*, p.part. of *ēlūdere*, to elude. See ELUDE.] — **e·lu′sive·ly** *adv.* — **e·lu′sive·ness** *n.*

e·lute (ĭ-lōōt′) *tr.v.* **e·lut·ed, e·lut·ing, e·lutes.** To extract (one material) from another, usu. by means of a solvent. [< Lat. *ēluere, ēlūt-*, to wash out : *ē-, ex-*, ex- + *-luere*, to wash; see leu(ə)-*.] — **e·lu′tion** *n.*

e·lu·tri·ate (ĭ-lōō′trē-āt′) *tr.v.* **-at·ed, -at·ing, -ates. 1.** To purify, separate, or remove (ore, for example) by washing, decanting, and settling. **2.** To wash away the lighter or finer particles of (soil, for example). [Lat. *ēlutriāre, ēlutriāt-* (< *ēlutrium*, vat, bath < Gk. *ēlutron*, dim. of *elutron*, tank; see ELYTRON) or *ēlūtriāre* (< *ēlūtor*, one who washes < *ēluere*, to wash out; see ELUTE).] — **e·lu′tri·a′tion** *n.*

e·lu·vi·ate (ĭ-lōō′vē-āt′) *intr.v.* **-at·ed, -at·ing, -ates.** To undergo eluviation.

e·lu·vi·a·tion (ĭ-lōō′vē-ā′shən) *n.* The lateral or downward movement of dissolved or suspended material within soil when rainfall exceeds evaporation. [ELUVI(UM) + -ATION.]

e·lu·vi·um (ĭ-lōō′vē-əm) *n.* Residual deposits of soil, dust, and rock particles produced by the wind. [NLat. *ēluvium* <

Definitions

Pronunciation key

Stress marks

ă pat	oi boy
ā pay	ou out
âr care	ŏŏ took
ä father	ōō boot
ĕ pet	ŭ cut
ē be	ûr urge
ĭ pit	th thin
ī pie	th this
îr pier	hw which
ŏ pot	zh vision
ō toe	ə about,
ô paw	item

Stress marks: ′ (primary); ′ (secondary), as in dictionary (dĭk′shə-nĕr′ē)

CHOOSING THE RIGHT DEFINITION

The tricky part about using the dictionary is determining which sense of the word to choose when you are confronted with several meanings. To illustrate this problem and its resolution, study these two sample paragraphs from two selections you will read. The first is from the concluding paragraph of Selection 1, in which Josh Sens writes about mysterious phenomena in the West. Concerning a place called Castle Lake where flying saucers supposedly once landed, Sens writes:

> No one knows why the aliens traveled here. For a dip in the lake? For a day at leisure with the Lemurians? I stared across the valley at the *looming* elegance of massive, snow-white Shasta. Stunning. Silent. I could well understand the mountain's *allure*.

The American Heritage College Dictionary gives this information about the word *loom:*

> **loom¹** (lōōm) *intr.v.* **loomed. loom·ing, looms. 1.** To come into view as a massive, distorted, or indistinct image. **2.** To appear to the mind in a magnified and threatening form. **3.** To seem imminent; impend: *Revolution loomed.* – *n.* A distorted, threatening appearance of something, as through fog or darkness. [Perh. of Scand. orig.]

> **loom²** (lōōm) *n.* An apparatus for making thread or yarn into cloth by weaving strands together at right angles. [ME *lome* < OE *gelōma*, tool : *ge-*, collective pref.; see YCLEPT + *-lōma*, tool, as in *andlōman*, tools.]

Which definition is appropriate for this context? Let's first look at the way the word is used in the sentence. *Looming* looks like a verb, because of the *-ing* ending. That indicates that you should select the first entry for *loom* (the verb form), not the second one (the noun form). Further evidence of that is suggested by the fact that the second definition makes no sense in the sentence, since Sens isn't talking about a loom used to weave cloth. Of the three definitions in the verb form, which seems correct? "1. To come into view as a massive, distorted, or indistinct image. 2. To appear to the mind in a magnified and threatening form." Or "3. To seem imminent, impend:" as in *"Revolution loomed."* In this case, the first definition seems most appropriate. The second one seems to work at first until you consider the context again. Sens doesn't suggest that Mt. Shasta is threatening in any way.

Now for *allure*. Study this entry from the dictionary:

> **al·lure** (ə-lōōr´) *v.* **-lured, -lur·ing, -lures.** – *tr.* To attract with something desirable; entice: *Promises allure the unwary.* – *intr.* To be highly, often subtly attractive. – *n.* The power to attract; enticement. [ME *aluren* < OFr. *alurer*: *a-*, to (< Lat. *ad-*; see AD–) + *loirre*, bait (of Gmc. orig.).] **– al·lure´- ment** *n.* **–al·lur´er** *n.* **– al·lur´ing·ly** *adv.*

The word is used as a noun: "the mountain's *allure*." So you go to the *n.* definition, and you have only a single choice: "The power to attract, enticement." Further evidence that this is the right choice comes from your being able to substitute these definitions into your phrase: "the mountain's power to attract" or "the mountain's enticement."

Here is a second, more difficult example, from Selection 13, "Sedated by Stuff," by Martha Fay, in which she describes the room of a little girl, the daughter of a friend, whose room is filled floor to ceiling with Barbie dolls and Barbie accessories. (You saw this passage earlier in the context clue section.) Here is the pertinent sentence:

Isn't the *surfeit* of things in his daughter's room likely to persuade her that her parents don't really love her, instead of that they do?

The dictionary lists these meanings for *surfeit*. Which one is appropriate for the context?

sur•feit (sûr′fĭt) *v.* **-feit•ed, -feit•ing, -feits.** – *tr.* To feed or supply to excess, satiety, or disgust. – *intr. Archaic.* To overindulge. – *n.* **1.a.** Overindulgence in food or drink. **b.** The result of such overindulgence; satiety or disgust. **2.** An excessive amount. [ME *surfeten* < *surfait*, excess < OFr. < p.part. of *surfaire*, to overdo : *sur-*, sur- + *faire*, to do (< Lat. *facere;* see **dhē-***).] **– sur′feit•er** *n.*

Again, consider the way the word is used. *Surfeit* is a noun here, which you can tell because it is preceded by the word *the* (called an *article*), so you can safely ignore the verb definitions. Study the three definitions. Which one seems most appropriate to describe a *surfeit* of Barbies? Write your answer here. _____

_____

COMPARING PRINT AND ONLINE DICTIONARIES

Online dictionaries offer a convenient alternative to traditional print dictionaries. Some Web sites even allow you to interact with a text. When you encounter an unfamiliar word, you simply click on it, and you are taken to the *Merriam-Webster* or *American Heritage Dictionary* site, allowing you to locate the word's meaning without leaving your computer. These two dictionaries are probably the most popular; the information from both is derived from the print editions, and since both are respectable sources, you can use either with confidence.

TWO ONLINE DICTIONARY SITES	
Merriam-Webster's Collegiate Dictionary	*www.m-w.com*
The American Heritage Dictionary of the English Language	*www.bartleby.com/61*

To demonstrate the offerings of each, here is the information offered for the word *pinnacle,* which you encountered earlier. The first is from *Merriam-Webster's* (*www.m-w.com*) (See page 2 for the traditional print definitions.)

And here is the same word, this time from the *American Heritage Dictionary* Web site, *www.bartleby.com/61:*

1) pinnacle. The American Heritage® Dictionary of the English Language: Fourth Edition. 2000.
...Architecture A small turret or spire on a roof or buttress. 2. A tall pointed formation, such as a mountain peak. 3. The highest point; the culmination. See synonyms...

American Heritage Dictionary of the English Language: Fourth Edition, 2000.

Comparing these two, you can see that *Merriam-Webster* provides more information, including the possibility of clicking on synonyms and on *pinnacle illustration* for a picture. Study the two samples above, and compare them to the earlier print entries (see p. 18). How do these offerings compare with their print counterparts?

| Dictionary | Thesaurus | Unabridged Dictionary |

2 entries found for **pinnacle**.
To select an entry, click on it.

pinnacle[1,noun]
pinnacle[2,transitive verb]   **Go**

Main Entry: [1]**pin·na·cle** ◀))
Pronunciation: 'pi-ni-k&l
Function: *noun*
Etymology: Middle English *pinacle*, from Middle French, from Late
Latin *pinnaculum* small wing, gable, from Latin *pinna* wing, battlement
Date: 14th century
1 : an upright architectural member generally ending in a small spire and used especially in Gothic construction to give weight especially to a buttress
2 : a structure or formation suggesting a pinnacle; *specifically* : a lofty peak
3 : the highest point of development or achievement : ACME
synonym see SUMMIT
[pinnacle illustration]

What are the advantages of each form? Briefly, here are the advantages and disadvantages of each as I see them:

- *Advantages of Online Dictionaries.* Online dictionaries are undoubtedly more fun to use, and they aren't cluttered with confusing symbols and multiple definitions. Most offer links to word-of-the-day information, word games, sites about linguistic history, and so forth. The general information on both sites mentioned above is free. However, it costs $30 a year or $5 a month to access the unabridged *Merriam-Webster's* dictionary online.[1]
- *Disadvantages of Online Dictionaries.* Unless you have a superfast connection, these dictionary sites may be slow to load. The sites often carry advertisements for their products or for sponsoring Web sites (for example, for online booksellers), or they carry distracting banners or pulsating ads. Except for electronic spellers (like the Franklin models), a computer isn't as portable as a book. Lugging even a compact, notebook-style computer around with you is more trouble than carrying around a paperback book. Your computer won't work in areas that experience frequent electrical storms or blackouts, unless you have a laptop and battery power.
- *Advantages of Print Dictionaries.* Print dictionaries don't depend on fickle battery power; they can be carried around in your backpack or purse; relatively speaking, they cost very little, and they have withstood the test of time. A good paperback college dictionary costs less than $10, and you can buy a good hardback college dictionary for the same price as the yearly fee for the

[1]These figures reflect fall 2002 rates and may have increased by the time you read this.

online version of the *Merriam-Webster's* unabridged dictionary (*www.m-w.com*). Everything that you need is located in the same place, with no need to click on links. Once you become familiar with the layout and the symbols, looking up a word takes less time than typing it in.

- *Disadvantages of Print Dictionaries.* Even the best print dictionary will need to be replaced from time to time, as new editions are published, to reflect changes in the language; this will require a periodic outlay of money. (However, a good hardback dictionary should last you through your college years and beyond.) Print dictionaries require a little more work to learn to use effectively than online versions.

Perhaps both types have their place, depending on your purpose in reading and on your budget.

To conclude this introduction, this course will have been successful if you find yourself unwilling to be content with a haphazard guess as to a new word's meaning and if you find that with each passing year you find fewer and fewer words to look up. Nothing builds confidence as much as a good reading vocabulary.

Practice Selection

What follows is a practice selection in which all the features you'll find throughout this book are explained. Before you begin the readings in Part 1, work through this practice selection and complete the exercises following it. Answers are provided at the end for all of the exercises except for the last one—topics for discussion and writing. Explanations of each element are highlighted in blue. These explanations will show you how to get the most that you can out of the book, will help you focus and concentrate as you read, and will help you learn what to look for when you read.

DAVE BARRY

Tips for Women: How to Have a Relationship with a Guy

Dave Barry has written for The Miami Herald *since 1983. In 1988 he received a Pulitzer Prize for commentary. His witty observations about American life were the inspiration for the 1990s television show* Dave's World. *In this excerpt, reprinted from* Dave Barry's Complete Guide to Guys, *we are introduced to a fictitious couple named Roger and Elaine who have been dating for six months.*

Vocabulary Preview

Each headnote provides biographical background on the writer, briefly states what the selection is about, and may also list other titles that the writer has published.

The Vocabulary Preview is divided into three parts; each deals with a word or two that you will find in the reading: the Word History section tells about the etymology or source of an interesting word, the Word Parts section discusses an important prefix or suffix, and the Word Families section explains how knowing one Latin or Greek word root will help you learn other words in the same family.

WORD HISTORY

Petty [paragraph 41] Elaine "explodes with fury" when Roger commits one of his "endless series of *petty* offenses." *Petty* means "of small importance" or "trivial." It derives from the French word *petit* meaning "small." In English, the word suggests something more negative—trivial and unimportant rather than merely small. Barry uses the word humorously or ironically because Roger's "petty" offense was to ask Elaine's sister out.

WORD PARTS

-meter [paragraph 7] As they are driving home, instead of paying attention to what Elaine is saying, Roger checks the *odometer* (pronounced ō - d ŏm´- ĭ - tər) and wonders if his car needs an oil change. People often confuse a car's odometer with its speedometer. An odometer measures the distance that a vehicle has traveled, while a speedometer measures the speed at which it is moving.

Odometer joins two Greek word parts: *hodos* ("journey") + *metron* ("measure"). Besides the word *meter* itself (as in a water- or gas-meter), this Greek word part is attached to other roots referring to instruments that measure all sorts of things, among them *thermometer* (heat), *chronometer* (time), and *barometer* (atmospheric pressure). What do these two words ending in *-meter* mean? Look them up if you are unsure and write their meanings in the space.

Answers
spectrometer: a device that measures wavelengths
hydrometer: an instrument that uses fluid to measure gravity

spectrometer _____

hydrometer _____

WORD FAMILIES

Transmission [paragraph 9] Roger also worries about his car's *transmission*. This word is formed by two Latin word parts, the prefix *trans* ("across") and the root *mittere* ("to send"). A car's transmission literally transmits or "sends across" power from the engine to the axle. In English, many other words derive from *mittere*, although the idea of "sending" is lost in some of them, for example, *admission, commission, permission,* and *submission* ("sending under").

Now the selection: Follow your instructor's suggestions or requirements for reading. Otherwise, use these directions: Read through the selection once; then answer the questions in Exercises A and B. After finishing these, follow the instructions that appear later to complete the assignment.

DAVE BARRY

Tips for Women: How to Have a Relationship with a Guy

Questions to Ask Yourself: Do you know anything about the writer? What does the selection title suggest to you? What do you already know about the subject?

1   Contrary to what many women believe, it's fairly easy to develop a long-term, stable, intimate, and mutually fulfilling relationship with a guy. Of course this guy has to be a Labrador retriever. With human guys, it's extremely difficult. This is because guys don't really grasp what women mean by the term *relationship.*

2   Let's say a guy named Roger is attracted to a woman named Elaine. He asks her out to a movie; she accepts; they have a pretty good time. A few nights later he asks her out to dinner, and again they enjoy themselves. They continue to see each other regularly, and after a while neither one of them is seeing anybody else.

3   And then, one evening when they're driving home, a thought occurs to Elaine, and, without really thinking, she says it aloud: "Do you realize that, as of tonight, we've been seeing each other for exactly six months?"

4   And then there is silence in the car. To Elaine, it seems like a very loud silence. She thinks to herself: Geez, I wonder if it bothers him that I said that. Maybe he's been feeling confined by our relationship; maybe he thinks I'm trying to push him into some kind of obligation that he doesn't want, or isn't sure of.

5   And Roger is thinking: Gosh. *Six months.*

6   And Elaine is thinking: But, hey, *I'm* not sure I want this kind of relationship, either. Sometimes I wish *I* had a little more space, so I'd have time to think about whether I really want us to keep going the way we are, moving steadily toward . . . I mean, where *are* we going? Are we just going to keep seeing each other at this level of intimacy? Are we heading toward *marriage?* Toward *children?* Toward a *lifetime* together? Am I ready for that level of commitment? Do I really even *know* this person?

7   And Roger is thinking . . . so that means it was . . . let's see . . . *February* when we started going out, which was right after I had the car at the dealer's which means . . . lemme check the odometer . . . *Whoa!* I am *way* overdue for an oil change here.

8   And Elaine is thinking: He's upset. I can see it on his face. Maybe I'm reading this completely wrong. Maybe he wants *more* from our relationship, *more* intimacy, *more* commitment; maybe he has sensed—even before *I* sensed it—that I was feeling some reservations. Yes, I bet that's it. That's why he's so reluctant to say anything about his own feelings: He's afraid of being rejected.

9   And Roger is thinking: And I'm gonna have them look at the transmission again. I don't care *what* those morons say, it's still not shifting right. And they better not try to blame it on the cold weather this time. *What* cold weather? It's eighty-seven degrees out, and this thing is shifting like a goddamn *garbage* truck, and I paid those incompetent thieving cretin bastards *six hundred dollars.*

10   And Elaine is thinking: He's angry. And I don't blame him. I'd be angry, too. God. I feel so *guilty,* putting him through this, but I can't help the way I feel. I'm just not *sure.*

11   And Roger is thinking: They'll probably say it's only a ninety-day warranty. That's exactly what they're gonna say, the scumballs.

12   And Elaine is thinking: Maybe I'm just too idealistic, waiting for a knight to come riding up on his white horse, when I'm sitting right next to a perfectly good person, a person I enjoy being with, a person I truly do care about, a person who seems to truly care about me. A person who is in pain because of my self-centered, schoolgirl romantic fantasy.

13   And Roger is thinking: Warranty? They want a warranty? *I'll* give them a goddamn warranty. I'll take their warranty and stick it right up their . . .

14   "Roger," Elaine says aloud.

15   "What?" says Roger, startled.

16   "Please don't torture yourself like this," she says, her eyes beginning to brim with tears. "Maybe I should never have . . . Oh *God,* I feel so . . ." (*She breaks down, sobbing.*)

17   "What?" says Roger.

18   "I'm such a fool." Elaine sobs. "I mean, I know there's no knight. I really know that. It's silly. There's no knight, and there's no horse."

19   "There's no horse?" says Roger.

20   "You think I'm a fool, don't you?" Elaine says.

21   "No!" says Roger, glad to finally know the correct answer.

22   "It's just that . . . It's that I . . . I need some time," Elaine says.

23   (*There is a fifteen-second pause while Roger, thinking as fast as he can, tries to come up with a safe response. Finally he comes up with one that he thinks might work.*)

24   "Yes," he says.

25   (*Elaine, deeply moved, touches his hand.*)

26   "Oh, Roger, do you really feel that way?" she says.

27   "What way?" says Roger.

28   "That way about time," says Elaine.

29   "Oh," says Roger. "Yes."

30   (*Elaine turns to face him and gazes deeply into his eyes, causing him to become very nervous about what she might say next, especially if it involves a horse. At last she speaks.*)

31   "Thank you, Roger," she says.

32   "Thank *you,*" says Roger.

33   Then he takes her home, and she lies on her bed, a conflicted, tortured soul, and weeps until dawn, whereas when Roger gets back to his place, he opens a bag of Doritos, turns on the TV, and immediately becomes deeply involved in a rerun of a tennis match between two Czechoslovakians he has never heard of. A tiny voice in the far recesses of his mind tells him that something major was going on back there in the car, but he is pretty sure there is no way he would ever understand *what,* and so he figures it's better if he doesn't think about it. (This is also Roger's policy regarding world hunger.)

34   The next day Elaine will call her closest friend, or perhaps two of them, and they will talk about this situation for six straight hours. In painstaking detail, they will analyze everything she said and everything he said, going over it time and time again, exploring every word, expression, and gesture for nuances of meaning, considering every possible ramification. They will continue to discuss this subject, off and on, for weeks, maybe months, never reaching any definite conclusions, but never getting bored with it, either.

35   Meanwhile, Roger, while playing racquetball one day with a mutual friend of his and Elaine's, will pause just before serving, frown, and say: "Norm, did Elaine ever own a horse?"

36   We're not talking about different wavelengths here. We're talking about different *planets,* in completely different *solar systems.* Elaine cannot communicate meaningfully with Roger about their relationship any more than she can meaningfully play chess with a duck. Because the sum total of Roger's thinking on this particular topic is as follows:

37   *Huh?*

38   Women have a lot of trouble accepting this. Despite millions of years of overwhelming evidence to the contrary, women are convinced that guys must spend a certain amount of time thinking about the relationship. How could they not? How could a guy see another human being day after day, night after night, sharing countless hours with this person, becoming physically intimate—how can a guy be doing these things and *not* be thinking about their relationship? This is what women figure.

39   They are wrong. A guy in a relationship is like an ant standing on top of a truck tire. The ant is aware, on a very basic level, that something large is there, but he cannot even dimly comprehend what this thing is, or the nature of his involvement with it. And if the truck starts moving, and the tire starts to roll, the ant will sense that something important is happening, but right up until he rolls around to the bottom and is squashed into a small black blot, the only distinct thought that will form in his tiny brain will be, and I quote.

40   *Huh?*

41   Which is exactly what Roger will think when Elaine explodes with fury at him when he commits one of the endless series of petty offenses, such as asking her sister out, that guys are always committing in relationships because they have virtually no clue that they are in one.

42   "How *could* he?" Elaine will ask her best friends. "What was he thinking?"

43   The answer is, He *wasn't* thinking, in the sense that women mean the word. He can't: He doesn't have the appropriate type of brain. He has a guy brain, which is

basically an analytical, problem-solving type of organ. It likes things to be definite and measurable and specific. It's not comfortable with nebulous and imprecise relationship-type concepts such as *love* and *need* and *trust*. If the guy brain has to form an opinion about another person, it prefers to form that opinion based on something concrete about the person, such as his or her earned-run average.

44 So the guy brain is not well-suited to grasping relationships. But it's good at analyzing and solving mechanical problems. For example, if a couple owns a house, and they want to repaint it so they can sell it, it will probably be the guy who will take charge of this project. He will methodically take the necessary measurements, calculate the total surface area, and determine the per-gallon coverage capacity of the paint; then, using his natural analytical and mathematical skills, he will apply himself to the problem of figuring out a good excuse not to paint the house.

45 "It's too humid," he'll say. Or: "I've read that prospective buyers are actually attracted more to a house with a lot of exterior dirt." Guys simply have a natural flair for this kind of problem-solving. That's why we always have guys in charge of handling the federal budget deficit.

46 But the point I'm trying to make is that, if you're a woman, and you want to have a successful relationship with a guy, the Number One Tip to remember is:

1. Never assume that the guy understands that you and he have a relationship.

47 The guy will not realize this on his own. You have to plant the idea in his brain by constantly making subtle references to it in your everyday conversation, such as:

- "Roger, would you mind passing me a Sweet 'n' Low, inasmuch as we have a relationship?"
- "Wake up, Roger! There's a prowler in the den and we have a relationship. You and I do, I mean."
- "Good news, Roger! The gynecologist says we're going to have our fourth child, which will serve as yet another indication that we have a relationship!"
- "Roger, inasmuch as this plane is crashing and we probably have only about a minute to live, I want you to know that we've had a wonderful fifty-three years of marriage together, which clearly constitutes a relationship."

48 Never let up, women. Pound away relentlessly at this concept, and eventually it will start to penetrate the guy's brain. Some day he might even start thinking about it on his own. He'll be talking with some other guys about women, and, out of the blue, he'll say, "Elaine and I, we have, ummm . . . We have, ahhh . . . We . . . We have this *thing*."

49 And he will sincerely mean it. ✳

From Dave Barry, *Dave Barry's Complete Guide to Guys.* © 1995 by Dave Barry. Reprinted by permission of Random House, Inc.

Exercises

Do not refer to the selection for Exercises A and B unless your instructor directs you to do so.

The first two exercises measure your overall comprehension.

A. DETERMINING THE MAIN IDEA AND PURPOSE

Choose the best answer.

_____ 1. The main idea of the selection is that men and women
   a. are interested in different activities.
   b. think and communicate on completely different wavelengths.
   c. should date for a long time before they begin to think about a long-term commitment.
   d. are not clear about what they want from relationships with the opposite sex.

Exercise A asks you to identify the writer's main idea and purpose. Part 1 will help you with this. For now, see how well you can do on your own.)

_____ 2. With respect to the main idea, the writer's purpose is to
   a. explain why so many relationships fail.
   b. criticize men and women for not understanding the opposite sex.
   c. entertain the reader with an amusing story.
   d. poke fun at men and women's styles of communicating.

Exercise B measures how well you understand the main ideas in the supporting paragraphs. It is not meant to be tricky but meant to determine how well you understand the important ideas in the selection.

B. COMPREHENDING MAIN IDEAS

Choose the correct answer.

_____ 1. According to Barry, guys have trouble understanding what women mean by the term
   a. *commitment.*
   b. *marriage.*
   c. *communication.*
   d. *relationship.*

_____ 2. Roger and Elaine, the couple in this hypothetical story, have been seeing each other for exactly
   a. six weeks.
   b. six months.
   c. a year.
   d. six years.

_____ **3.** After several moments of silence, when Elaine tells Roger "there's no horse," he

    a. knows exactly what she is referring to.
    b. thinks she is crazy.
    c. was also thinking about a horse.
    d. has no idea what she is talking about.

_____ **4.** Barry states that men have trouble communicating about relationships and that women

    a. have trouble accepting this.
    b. have exactly the same problem.
    c. understand men's feelings well.
    d. want to find sensitive men who will share their ideas about relationships.

_____ **5.** Barry describes men's brains as

    a. analytical and problem-solving.
    b. incapable of thinking about two thoughts at the same time.
    c. well-equipped to understand relationship terms like _love_ and _need._
    d. poorly suited to solving mechanical problems, preferring to seek expert advice.

_____ **6.** Barry humorously advises a woman who wants to have a relationship with a guy to

    a. choose a guy who enjoys the same activities as she does.
    b. nag and criticize him for his insensitivity until she finally wears him down.
    c. give up the idea as hopeless and just accept his inability to understand.
    d. plant the idea in his brain by constantly making subtle references to it.

Now check your answers. If you disagree with an answer, ask your instructor for an explanation.

ANSWERS TO EXERCISES A AND B

A. Determining the Main Idea and Purpose

1. b   **2.** d

B. Comprehending Main Ideas

1. d   **2.** b   **3.** d   **4.** a   **5.** a   **6.** d

Next, you can figure out your comprehension score.

COMPREHENSION SCORE

Score your answers for Exercises A and B as follows:

A. No. right _____ × 2 = _____

B. No. right _____ × 1 = _____

Total points from A and B _____ × 10 = _____ percent

You may refer to the selection as you work through the remaining exercises.

Now read the selection again and circle words you don't know and can't figure out from the context. Then look up the words you circled. Now complete the remaining exercises.

C. INTERPRETING MEANING

Write your answers to these questions in your own words.

Exercise C asks you to go beyond the surface ideas. Later you will be asked to study the structure and organization of particular selections.

1. Barry's humor in this piece relies on *overstatement*, sometimes called *hyperbole* (hī-pûr′ bə-lē) or deliberate exaggeration for effect. Here is one example: Barry states in paragraph 36, "We're not talking about different wavelengths here. We're talking about different *planets*, in completely different *solar systems*." Look through the selection and find two other examples of overstatement. _____

_____

_____

2. From Elaine's response in paragraph 18 about there being no knight and no horse, what has occurred in her thinking process? _____

_____

_____

3. Barry writes in paragraphs 36 and 37 that the sum total of Roger's thinking on the subject of his and Elaine's relationship is *"huh?"* What does this response mean? _____

_____

_____

4. At the end of paragraph 48, what is Barry poking fun at when Roger says, "Elaine and I, we have, ummm . . . We have, ahhh . . . We . . . We have this *thing*." _____

_____

_____

Exercise D tests your understanding of some of the most important words in the selection. Since you have looked up the words you didn't know, you should be able to complete this section quickly.

D. UNDERSTANDING VOCABULARY

Choose the best definition according to an analysis of word parts or the context.

_____ **1.** this level of *intimacy* [paragraphs 6 and 8]:
   a. privacy
   b. long-term commitment
   c. closeness, familiarity
   d. friendship

_____ **2.** in *painstaking* detail [34]:
   a. simple
   b. exaggerated
   c. sketchy
   d. extremely careful

_____ **3.** *nuances* of meaning [34]:
   a. slight variations
   b. intentions
   c. direct expressions
   d. examinations

_____ **4.** every possible *ramification* [34]:
   a. interpretation
   b. consequence
   c. use of the imagination
   d. cause or reason

Exercise E varies from selection to selection. This one asks you to consider forms of words that are in the same family but have endings that change their grammatical function. (That is, they are *inflected* forms.) If you aren't sure which form to use, try reading the sentence out loud and inserting each choice to see which one "sounds right," or consult your dictionary for further help.

_____ **5.** pound away *relentlessly* [48]:
   a. harshly
   b. angrily
   c. persistently
   d. politely

E. USING VOCABULARY

In parentheses before each sentence are some inflected forms of words from the selection. Study the context and the sentence. Then write the correct form in the space provided.

1. (*commit, commitment*) Roger and Elaine's imaginary dialogue suggests that

neither of them is ready for a _____ .

2. (*incompetence, incompetent, incompetently*) Roger is convinced that the mechanic who worked on his car was guilty of dishonesty and

_____ .

3. (*pettiness, petty, pettily*) A guy like Roger can never understand why a woman would make a big deal out of something _____ like asking Elaine's sister out.

4. (*subtlety, subtle, subtly*) Barry suggests that a woman can instill the idea of having a relationship by _____ referring to the concept in her everyday conversation.

Now check answers. Any wrong answers? Ask your instructor for an explanation.

ANSWERS FOR EXERCISES C–E

C. Interpreting Meaning

1. Here are two possible answers: Roger commits a "petty offense" by asking Elaine's sister out [paragraph 41]. A guy figures out calculations for painting a house and then devises excuses for not doing the job [paragraphs 44–45].
2. Elaine has mistakenly assumed that Roger, in his silence, is thinking about the same thing she is.
3. "*Huh?*" means that Roger has no idea what Elaine is talking about.
4. Men have difficulty even saying the word *relationship* because it may imply a commitment they are not yet ready to make.

Whether or not your instructor assigns these questions, you should look the questions over in Exercise F. They ask you to respond to what you read and to extend your thinking, perhaps to similar situations in your own life. One of the topics might be the perfect choice for a paper in your composition class.

D. Understanding Vocabulary

1. c   2. d   3. a   4. b   5. c

E. Using Vocabulary

1. commitment   2. incompetence   3. petty
4. subtly

F. TOPICS FOR WRITING OR DISCUSSION

1. Aside from Barry's observation that guys' brains are different from women's, what might be some other reasons that men have difficulty talking about relationships and abstract concepts like *love* and *need* and *commitment?*
2. Is Barry being fair to men? To women?
3. On a separate sheet of paper, write an imaginary dialogue between Roger and Elaine that represents your experience in relationships. The situation is this: Elaine wants to have a relationship with Roger, and she wants him to make a commitment, but Roger isn't so sure that he is ready to make this leap.

For Further Exploration

BOOK

Deborah Tannen, *You Just Don't Understand* (1990). Tannen, a popular linguist, explores the difference between men's and women's communication styles and explains why male–female communication is so often frustrating.

MOVIES

When Harry Met Sally (1989), directed by Rob Reiner and starring Meg Ryan and Billy Crystal, is a romantic comedy that shows the contrast in the way men and women view each other.

A dark look at the breakdown in communication between a husband and wife when tragedy strikes a family can be seen in *Ordinary People* (1980), directed by Robert Redford and starring Donald Sutherland, Mary Tyler Moore, Timothy Hutton, and Judd Hirsch.

WEB SITE

A collection of Dave Barry's recent *Miami Herald* columns can be found at:

- *www.miami.com/mld/miamiherald/living*   Type "Dave Barry" in the search box on the newspaper's home page.

Each selection ends with some recommendations for books to read, movies to rent, and Web sites to explore. The recommended books and movies generally pertain to the same theme that the writer explored in the reading. Some of the Web sites are more practical—for example, sites for finding current movie reviews or for performing job searches.

Critical Reading Worksheet

1. Title of the selection: _____

2. Topic or subject (What or who is it about?): _____

3. Main idea (What does the writer say about the topic?)_____

_____

_____

_____

_____

_____

4. Purpose (Why did the writer write it?): _____

_____

_____

5. Supporting details (How does the author prove his or her main idea?): _____

   a. _____

   _____

   b. _____

   _____

   c. _____

   _____

6. New vocabulary words (include dictionary definitions):

   a. _____

   b. _____

   c. _____

7. Critical evaluation (What do you think about the reading selection? Why?)

_____

_____

_____

8. What other information would you like to have on this subject? _____

_____

_____

_____

Identifying the Main Idea
and the Writer's Purpose

f your instructor has not assigned the section that begins this book called "To the Student," it would be a good idea to read it before beginning this section. This short introduction previews the book's organization and content and explains what you should accomplish during the term. The introductions to each of the book's five parts discuss a particular skill or set of skills that will make you a better reader, and these skills are organized by order of importance. In Part 1 you will work on the most important areas in the course:

- Recognizing the difference between fiction and nonfiction prose
- Finding the main idea in paragraphs
- Locating thesis statements in articles and essays
- Identifying the writer's purpose

The Difference Between Fiction and Nonfiction

Writing comes in three types: prose, poetry, and drama. This book is concerned with *prose*—ordinary writing that consists of words grouped into sentences and sentences grouped into paragraphs—just like the print that you are reading on this page. *Prose* is further divided into two types: nonfiction and fiction.

Your college textbooks are nonfiction, the daily newspaper is nonfiction, magazine articles are nonfiction, and so are the readings in this book. Nonfiction writing discusses real people with real problems, dealing with real events in their lives, real issues and possible ways to resolve them, real events in the world and their aftermath. The novel you take with you to read at the beach is fiction. Simply put, nonfiction is writing that is real, whereas fiction is writing that is imagined.

COMMON TYPES OF NONFICTION
• Articles, in magazines and newspapers
• Autobiographies and biographies
• Books on history, politics, social problems, and so on
• Editorials or opinion pieces
• Essays
• Memoirs and journals
• Textbooks

The Difference Between an Article and an Essay

Two important types of nonfiction are *essays* and *articles*. In this book—as well as in many of your other classes—you will read both. The difference between an article and an essay is a little tricky, and the distinction is not always clear or absolute, especially because magazines may publish both essays and articles.

Probably the easiest way to understand how they differ is to think of an article as being more contemporary; that is, it deals with *immediate* or *current* issues and problems. An essay, on the other hand, tends to be more *universal* in scope, meaning that it offers the writer's perceptions on age-old problems that all human beings have faced since time began. An essay is also more literary, more open in its form, and more enduring.

Journalism has sometimes been defined as "literature in a hurry." News articles should be well written, but their purpose is to inform readers of the day's events and are not intended to last for decades. Essays, however, are more timeless. The story you read in the morning paper about a warehouse fire at the waterfront that did $1 million in damage will most likely be forgotten in a month or a year, except of course by the owners and nearby residents. But the essay "Easter's End," by Jared Diamond in Part 5 of this book is about the destruction of Easter Island's native environment and has significance far beyond the boundaries of that island off the coast of Chile. Diamond's concern is universal: We are ruining the environment.

But these distinctions may not be worth making, and I urge you not to dwell on whether a particular piece of prose is an essay or an article. What *is* important to remember is that essays and articles should be called "essays" and "articles," *not* "stories," which refers only to fiction.

Fiction writers invent the characters, their actions, and the events that happen to them. This is why many books of fiction begin with this warning: "Any similarity to any person, living or dead, is entirely coincidental." Fiction generally comes in two types, or to the use the term English instructors prefer, *genres:* novels and short stories. There are subtypes, or subgenres, of novels and short stories as well, for example, mystery, science fiction, horror, adventure, detective, and romance. In this course, you will read only *nonfiction,* unless, of course, your instructor assigns a book of short stories or a novel to be read in addition to this text.

GENRES OF FICTION		
• Novels	• Novellas (short novels)	• Short stories
SUBGENRES OF FICTION		
• Mysteries	• Romances	• Detective fiction
• Adventure stories	• Science fiction	• Horror fiction

Identifying the Main Idea in Paragraphs

With those important definitions out of the way, we now turn to the comprehension skill that is at the heart of everything in your college career—how to locate the main idea of what you're reading. Let's say that you have just seen *Minority Report,* the 2002 science-fiction thriller made by Steven Spielberg and starring Tom Cruise. The next day your friend asks you what the movie was about. You might say something like this: "The year is 2054. Tom Cruise plays a government agent who works in the Precrime Unit in Washington, DC. Agents in this unit stop people from committing murders before they occur. Three weird creatures, who float in a pool of water, somehow have the power to predict who will commit these crimes, and Cruise and his fellow agents race all over the city arresting them."

What have you just done? In these four sentences you have stated the main point of a 2-hour movie—in other words, what it's about. In short, you have summarized the movie's plot, or conveyed its main idea. In your college reading, finding the main idea, of course, can be a little more difficult. There is no trailer to show you the movie's highlights; there are no annotations in the margins to help you and no way of asking the writer what he or she meant. All you have are print and paper, so it's up to you to wade through the words and sentences to make sense of it all. Step by step, this book—its readings and exercises—will help you make sense of what you're reading and give you the practice to perfect your reading skills.

Your understanding of the main point of the essay as a whole starts with your understanding of the paragraphs that make up the essay because the paragraph is the building block of the essay. Like an essay, a paragraph makes a point, whether that point is stated or not. Further, that point—in essay or paragraph—has to be supported, developed, backed up. If I say that all college students should be required to take a foreign language, you should not just accept the statement because I say so. You should wait to see what reasons I offer to back up my statement. No idea is so good on its own that it can stand undefended. I might support my claim by saying that learning a foreign language advances one's understanding of how languages work, that it allows one to travel to the country where the language is spoken and get around more easily, that one can order from a menu in that language, or that it makes one less isolated, less insulated. These reasons are called the *support* or *supporting details*. Since it's easier to practice finding the main idea in paragraphs, we'll practice that skill first. But we will move on to finding the main idea in longer passages—in essays—before long.

You may have been taught in your writing classes that every paragraph should have a *topic sentence* (or a *main-idea sentence*) and that the topic sentence should be the paragraph's first sentence. Unfortunately, professional writers don't always follow this advice. A writer is under no obligation to make your reading experience easy, and few professional writers structure their paragraphs according to any formula. This advice may get you into trouble when you encounter college and other adult prose because so many paragraphs in the essays you will read don't have topic sentences. A better way to get at the main idea is to ask yourself these questions:

- What's the point of what I'm reading?
- What's the single most important idea that the writer wants me to come away with?

If you can come up with a single sentence—certainly no more than two—that answers these questions, then you will make significant gains in your reading ability.

If there is a main-idea sentence, where should you look for it? It may indeed be the first sentence, but just as often, it might be the sentence *after* the first sentence or two, it might be in the middle of the paragraph, or even at the end. In some instances, there may be no directly stated main-idea sentence at all. We call this last type an *implied main idea,* meaning that the supporting details *suggest* the main point without the main ideas being stated specifically.

Whether it is stated or not, the writer's point must nonetheless be supported with details, examples, stories, anecdotes (little stories), definitions of unfamiliar terms, explanations, analysis—whatever the writer can use to back up his or her point. The trick is to separate the main point from these supporting ideas. Part 5 examines these various types of support; you might want to read it even before your instructor assigns it.

Let's practice first locating the main idea in some individual paragraphs. Three come from two popular magazines, *Harper's* and *Discover,* and another is from Eric Schlosser's book *Fast Food Nation,* an excerpt of which is printed in this text as Selection 15. The first three are annotated for you; that is, I have made notes in the margin showing you the placement of the main idea and the details the writer uses to back up that main idea. Read each example paragraph carefully. If you come across a vocabulary word that you don't know or that you can't figure out from the context clues, circle it in pencil, and look it up the second time you read the passage.

Main idea: The way fish are caught for aquariums needs to be changed.

Reason: Methods of collecting fish are brutal.

Examples: Poisons destroy ecosystems.
- Corals and other fish are killed.
- Only a few stunned fish on the edge are captured.

The worldwide trade in aquarium fish—currently worth $200 million per year and fueled mostly by demand among home aquarists in the United States, Europe, and Japan—is badly in need of transformation. The collection methods are brutal. Using poisons, primarily sodium cyanide, poor people destroy entire ecosystems in order to capture the few stunned fish surviving on the perimeters. The sodium cyanide begins to kill corals and fish within thirty seconds of contact. A handful of fish at the outermost edge of the destruction, disabled but not dead, are then collected by hand.

With each purchase of a lionfish or butterflyfish, the home aquarist, obliviously or uncaringly, funds this devastation.

—Julia Whitty, "Shoals of Time," *Harper's*

Which of these do you think *best* represents Whitty's main idea?

A. Cruel methods are used to collect fish for home aquariums.
B. The way fish are collected for the world's aquariums needs to be changed.
C. People collect fish for aquariums using sodium cyanide.
D. There is great demand for aquarium fish in the United States, Europe, and Japan.

Did you choose *B?* If so, you are correct. Notice that the main idea is indeed represented in the first sentence: "The worldwide trade in aquarium fish . . . is badly in need of transformation." Although answer *A*—"collection methods are brutal"—might look like the main idea, it is actually the main *supporting statement:*

It tells us *why* the way fish are caught needs to be changed. The other two answer choices are minor details; they add extra information and further evidence for the main point.

Here's another way to think about the main idea: Which of these is the best title for the paragraph you just read?

A. "Aquarium Fish"
B. "How Fish Are Captured"
C. "Why Fish Collecting Should Be Prohibited"
D. "Collecting Aquarium Fish: Finding a Better Way"

Did you choose *D?* If so, you chose the right answer. Notice that *A* is too broad and doesn't give the writer's point of view. Similarly, *B* suggests a process but, again, not the author's point of view. And *C* is way off the mark: The writer never says that collecting fish for aquariums should be stopped. By process of elimination, then, and because it includes the essential elements, *D* is the best answer. This outline shows you visually how the writer has constructed her main point:

Aquarium trade in the world needs to be changed. (main idea)

Why? Methods of collection are brutal.

Examples: Poisons are used

Only fish on the boundaries are caught

Other fish and corals are killed

Asbestos has long been used for fire-proofing and insulation.

This is how paragraphs work: A main idea—either stated or suggested—is backed up by supporting information. In the first sample paragraph, the main idea was stated. In the sample paragraph below, the main idea is suggested. Try to figure out the main idea of this paragraph:

Asbestos is a dangerous mineral.

It causes asbestosis, a serious disease.

Asbestos is being removed from buildings.

This process costs a lot and is dangerous.

Because asbestos material is hazardous, it must be disposed of properly.

The ancient Greeks were the first to discover the fireproofing and insulating properties of asbestos, but they knew nothing of the mineral's dangers. When asbestos is inhaled, the fibers can cause asbestosis, a stiffening of lung tissue that contributes to heart disease and lung cancer. Because of this risk, asbestos is being removed from schools, hospitals, and thousands of other buildings around the country. It's a costly, time-consuming, and dangerous process, as workers in protective gear use their hands to scrape out the substance, which must then be disposed of as a hazardous material. To prevent asbestos fibers from escaping in the air, areas being cleaned must be sealed in pressurized tents.

—"Attacking Asbestos," *Discover*

Of the six sets of notes in the margin, which one would you boldface as the one that states the main idea? And within that note, which word seems to be the most important to describe the *subject* of asbestos? Put a circle around that word. Did you boldface the second set? Did you circle "dangerous"? Notice that "dangerous" and "hazardous" used at the end of the paragraph mean the same thing. Because the writer repeats this idea of danger, that's a good indication that it is the writer's point with regard to asbestos.

Which is the best title for this paragraph?

A. "Asbestos Then and Now"
B. "The Hazards of Asbestos"
C. "How to Remove Asbestos"
D. "Asbestos: The Cause of Asbestosis"

Did you mark *B?* If so, you chose the most appropriate title.
Here is what the ideas in this paragraph look like when they are outlined:

Background information: Purpose of asbestos—to fireproof and to insulate.

Asbestos is a dangerous mineral. (main idea)

Why? It causes asbestosis, a very serious illness.

Solutions: Remove asbestos from buildings

Dispose of it properly

Note the pattern of ideas in this paragraph: The opening sentence tells us why asbestos was used in buildings in the first place. Then comes the main idea (suggested rather than stated in one main-idea sentence). Then come the supporting details: the reason it is dangerous, followed by the solutions, or what to do about it. If you visualize the ideas in a paragraph like that below, identifying the main idea should become easier, even when it is not stated directly and you have to come up with your own main-idea sentence. Here is a main-idea sentence for the sample paragraph about asbestos:

Although asbestos was formerly used for insulating and fireproofing, it is a dangerous mineral that causes a serious illness.

And another possibility:

Asbestos is a dangerous mineral that must be removed from buildings.

All of the other sentences in the sample paragraph are **supporting ideas** because they back up the writer's main point. They act like props, holding up the main point and making it more convincing.
Now look at this passage. This time, write your own notes in the space provided.

At Burger King restaurants, frozen hamburger patties are placed on a conveyer belt and emerge from a broiler ninety seconds later fully cooked. The ovens at Pizza Hut and at Domino's also use conveyer belts to ensure standardized cooking times. The ovens at McDonald's look like commercial laundry presses, with big steel hoods

that swing down and grill hamburgers
on both sides at once. The burgers,
chicken, french fries, and buns are all
frozen when they arrive at a McDonald's. The shakes and sodas begin as
syrup. At Taco Bell restaurants the
food is "assembled," not prepared. The
guacamole isn't made by workers in
the kitchen; it's made at a factory in
Michoacán, Mexico, then frozen and
shipped north. The chain's taco meat
arrives frozen and precooked in
vacuum-sealed plastic bags. The beans
are dehydrated and look like brownish
corn flakes. The cooking process is
simple. "Everything's add water," a
Taco Bell employee told me. "Just add
hot water."

—Eric Schlosser, *Fast Food Nation*

What do all of these details add up to? What is Schlosser's main point? Although there is no specific main-idea sentence here—it is *implied*, not stated—
there are plenty of supporting details. Write your answer here: _____

_____

_____

Here is one possibility. Your sentence, of course, may be worded differently, but it
should contain the same elements as this one:

> The food served in fast food restaurants is frozen, and it is assembled and
> cooked with hardly any human intervention.

The main idea of this paragraph, as Schlosser wrote it, is implied because you
have to figure it out for yourself. To do this, ask yourself what all of these details
about fast food being frozen, packaged, precooked, and "prepared" by just adding
hot water add up to. As Schlosser writes later in the selection: "This food is assembled, not prepared or cooked, just as any other factory product is. Bicycles are
assembled, computers are assembled, and Big Macs and Whoppers are assembled,
too."

Here is one final passage to practice with; it is taken from the two opening paragraphs of a magazine article on human transplants. (The word *moniker* in the second sentence is slang for a name or a nickname.) Again, study the notes in the margin.

Pig 23 doesn't have a clever name like Dolly the cloned sheep.

Pig 23 was created at Tufts vet school.

It looks like any other pig.

They hope that Pig 23 will provide organs for human transplants.

He might offer a solution to a vexing medical problem.

Meet Pig 23. Unlike the famous cloned sheep Dolly, this pig has no media-friendly moniker, only a number on a tag stapled to his left ear. "I don't name my animals," says Karl Ebert, chief scientific officer of Midas Biologicals in North Grafton, Massachusetts, and the biologist who created Pig 23 here at the Tufts School of Veterinary Medicine. This particular animal, a male Yorkshire white, has pale pinkish skin covered with light bristles that are softer than they look, an expressive snout, and the stereotypical curly tail—all in all, a very piggy pig, no difference in appearance from his thousands of cousins that end up as pork chops and ham at the butcher counter.

But Pig 23 will serve humans in a different way. He is being grown in the hope that animals like him might one day prove suitable organ donors for humans. In each of his cells, tucked in somewhere among 19 pairs of pig chromosomes, is a bit of humanity: a single human gene. He might not look it, but Pig 23 and a few dozen others like him may harbor the solution to one of the most vexing problems of modern medicine.

—Robert Pool, "Saviors," *Discover*

Which of these sentences best states the writer's main point?

A. Veterinary scientists at Tufts cloned a pig identified only as Pig 23.
B. Pig 23 looks like any other ordinary pig.
C. Pig 23 will serve humans in a way not associated with the butcher counter.
D. Pig 23 and others like him will provide organs for humans.

Notice that the first few sentences in the paragraph provide background information. They lead to the main idea, which comes toward the end of the second paragraph: Pig 23 was cloned because he—and other cloned pigs like him—will be used to provide organs to be transplanted into humans. If you chose *D*, you are correct. Again, if you were asked what the point is of the passage you just read, you would probably say something like this: "Vets are cloning pigs so that they can provide organs for human transplants." That's the writer's point—simple and short.

Which of these would be a good title for this paragraph?

A. "Cloned Pigs: Solving a Medical Problem"
B. "Pig 23: Like Any Ordinary Pig"
C. "Tufts Veterinary School's Cloning Methods"
D. "The Benefits of Cloning"

If you chose *A*, you're on your way to becoming a better reader.

Thesis Statements in Articles and Essays

Now let's consider articles and essays as wholes. Both are composed of individual paragraphs linked together to produce a sustained piece of writing that may be a single page or twenty or more pages. Whatever the length, the writer of an article or essay has in mind a focus or a point, which, like the main idea of a paragraph, may be stated or implied. This main idea is called the *thesis* or *thesis statement*. From your composition classes, you are probably familiar with the concept of a thesis, the statement that conveys the main idea of the essay. After all, the essay that you write has to be about something. A writer may place the thesis near the beginning of the essay, in the middle, or at the end, but usually it comes somewhere near the beginning. In addition, a thesis might be conveyed in two sentences, though rarely more than that.

The passage you just read about Pig 23 illustrates a common placement for a thesis statement. The first few sentences introduce you to an example (Pig 23), give some background, and then point to the direction that the writer will go: ". . . Pig 23 and a few dozens like him may harbor the solution to one of the most vexing problems of modern medicine." We won't know what these vexing problems are unless we keep reading. (In this case, the next couple of paragraphs, which begin the body of the article, discuss the problem of a *shortage* of human organs, not enough for all the people who need them. Pig 23 and other pigs like him are being cloned to provide a ready source of usable organs to save lives.)

To practice locating the thesis within an entire piece, here is a "miniessay," also from *Discover* magazine. The subject is Easter Island, and the unnamed writer gives quite a different view from the one Jared Diamond gives in his examination of the island's doomed culture, which you will read about in Part 5. Read through the essay once, and circle any words you aren't sure of. Then look up the circled words, and read the essay a second time.

1   When Europeans arrived on Easter Island in the eighteenth century, only about 2,000 people lived there. But the legacy of giant *moai* statues[2]—heads carved from hundreds of tons of stone—suggested that a large, complex society once inhabited the island. This populous and isolated group must have fed itself somehow, but researchers had never found extensive signs of agriculture. Now an archeologist has discovered the gardens of Easter hidden under a blanket of stones.

2   Describing an aerial photograph of Easter Island, Chris Stevenson, who works with the Archeological Services Consultants Group in Columbus, Ohio, says, "There's a great huge black blob in the center of these photos, and for months it puzzled me. I thought it might be a natural rock formation." Irregularly shaped patches of rocks, bordered by small clearings, litter the island. Stevenson thought that the islanders might have grown crops in the clearings, but this search had been unsuccessful. "We were looking for nice rectangular field systems," he says. "But they weren't there."

3   Then Joan Wozniak, a graduate student at Oregon State University in Corvallis, suggested looking underneath the rocks. Perhaps, she suggested, the islanders were using rocks as mulch, to keep moisture in the soil. When Stevenson dug a test pit, he found that the soil beneath was thoroughly mixed, as if it had been repeatedly overturned. In other pits he found traces of rotted tubers, and even part of an ancient hoe. The gardens ranged in size

---

[2]For a photograph of the giant *moai* statues on Easter Island, see page 462.

from small household plots 30 feet on a side to giant hilltop plantations covering acres. "Eighty percent of the land was planted at one time or another," says Stevenson. "Easter Island was one big garden."

4   Staple crops were taro, sweet potato, and sugarcane. The islanders surrounded planted stalks with fist-size rocks, forming a pavement over the soil that kept weeds out and moisture in. Near one hilltop plantation, Stevenson found the remains of a chiefly dwelling, suggesting that the island's elite organized labor to work large fields.

5   Small gardens near the coast and in the lowlands were in use from around 1300 to 1800, but the large fields seem to have been abandoned in the 1600s, reflecting the collapse of the island's social structure. Stevenson hopes the newly discovered plots will help answer questions about the island's mysterious fall.

From "The Garden of Easter," *Discover,* June 1998. © *Discover.* Reprinted with permission of *Discover* magazine.

The thesis of this miniessay comes in two adjacent sentences. Which of these pairs of sentences best represents the main idea? Write them here: _____

_____

_____

If you chose the last two sentences of the first paragraph, you are correct. Notice that the thesis does *not* have to include the general subject (Easter Island), because it has already been introduced in the first sentence.

Identifying the Writer's Purpose

Although he or she may not be consciously aware of it when opening a new document on the computer screen, every writer has in mind some *purpose,* the intention or the reason he or she is going to the trouble of writing. The ancient Greeks taught that literature had three aims: to please, to instruct, and to persuade. What exactly did they mean?

THE WRITER'S PURPOSE IN CLASSICAL TERMS	
To please:	To delight, entertain, amuse, give pleasure to, describe, paint a picture in words
To instruct:	To teach, show, inform, examine, expose, analyze, criticize
To persuade:	To convince, change one's mind, influence, argue, recommend, give advice to

Sometimes it is hard to see an exact distinction between "instructing" and "persuading," since the very act of instructing us about something that needs to be changed might also convince us of the need for that change. For example, the writer of "The Garden of Easter" is informing (instructing) us about an intriguing discovery made by archeologists on Easter Island, but there isn't anything particularly controversial here. But in the paragraph you read earlier about changing the ways aquarium fish are caught, the writer is both instructing and persuading.

When you work through Exercise A after the selections in Parts 1, 2, 3, and 5, the second question always refers to the writer's purpose. Once you understand the distinction between the classical purposes, as discussed above, the narrower purposes represented in this question will become clearer. For example, a writer whose topic is global warming may be *persuading* us that it is a serious problem worth our attention. But more specifically, he or she may be *instructing* or *warning* us about the consequences of global warming if the trend is not reversed.

Similarly, Andre Dubus, in his personal narrative essay "Digging" (Selection 7), tells us a story that at first glance might indicate that his purpose is only to please. When we finish reading the piece, though, it's clear that he is doing much more than that. By reflecting on the manual labor he performed as a 15-year-old one summer, he identifies what it taught him about becoming a man. Is his purpose to please, to instruct, or to persuade? Perhaps it is a little of all three.

Here is a final example of a writer's overlapping purposes: Dave Barry's essay "Tips for Women: How to Have a Relationship with a Guy" explores the difficulties men and women have talking to each other. Obviously, his purpose is, at least in part, to entertain. But what other purpose might he have? Because Barry pokes fun at men for their inability to commit to a relationship and at women for exhaustively analyzing every little thing that happens between a man and a woman, his purpose seems more to instruct than to persuade. He is pointing out our differences, not trying to reform us or make us change our ways. Besides, what writer, discussing the age-old battle of the sexes, could ever accomplish that!

PART ONE

Getting Started: Practicing the Basics

JOSH SENS

The Truth Is Out Here— Somewhere

Josh Sens received a B.A. in Brazilian literature from Brown University and an M.A. in journalism from the University of California, Berkeley. After working as a daily reporter for newspapers in Boston, Iowa, and California, he currently writes "quirky vignettes" for the San Francisco Chronicle *and restaurant reviews for* San Francisco Magazine. *He particularly enjoys writing, as he says, "profiles of people who are passionate about unusual pursuits." This article was published in the travel magazine,* Via. *In it, Sens describes visits to seven places in the American West where mysterious natural phenomena have baffled even scientific experts.*

Vocabulary Preview

WORD HISTORIES

Trek [paragraph 9] Sens describes a place called Confusion Hill, where "hikers like to *trek* through coastal forests." Most readers are familiar with the word *trek* because of the popular television and movie series, *Star Trek*. *Trek* is a word of South African origin that originally meant to make a long journey by ox wagon. It derives from Dutch (*trekken*—"to pull" or "to draw"). The White settlers in South Africa speak Afrikaans, a language derived from Dutch, so the connection is easy to see. Today, we use the word *trek* to refer to a slow and difficult journey, often done on foot.

Guru [paragraph 14] *Guru* is another word with an unusual origin. Sens explains that *gurus* "gather to meditate" at the vortices in Sedona, Arizona. In the Buddhist religion, a *guru* is a spiritual teacher or leader; the word is from an ancient Sanskrit word meaning "heavy." But American English has expanded the use of this word beyond the spiritual, so that an outstanding and recognized leader in any field (for example, in science or economics or politics) might be called a "guru."

WORD PARTS

Sub- [paragraph 3] *Submerged* combines the common English prefix *sub-*, originally from Latin, meaning "under," with *mergere* ("to plunge"). This prefix is easy to recognize in words like *submarine* ("under the ocean") or *subplot* ("a secondary plot" or a plot "under" the main plot) but is less easy to detect in other words.

Look up these three words in the dictionary, and write their meanings in the spaces. If "under" is clearly suggested, write "yes" next to the definition. If not, write "no."

subterranean _____

subjugate _____

subject _____

WORD FAMILIES

Incredible [paragraph 5] Visitors often describe the mysterious sites Sens describes as *incredible*. This word derives from the negative Latin prefix *in-*, meaning "not" and *credere*, the Latin verb meaning "to believe." If something is *incredible*, then, it is unbelievable. Here are some other common English words containing the root *cred-*.

creed	A formal statement of religious beliefs
credibility	The power of capability of belief
credit	Belief or confidence in the truth of something; confidence in one's ability to repay money in the future

JOSH SENS

The Truth Is Out Here—Somewhere

1 Memo to agents Scully and Mulder: Here's an assignment. Scour your X-Files for something that explains this.

2 Spring of 1932. A reporter from the *Los Angeles Times* named Edward Lanser shows up in Northern California on the snow-covered slopes of Mount Shasta. He's come to get the scoop on the Lemurians.

3 Yes, Luh-MYUR-ee-ans. Headquarters should have briefed you on them—ancient race of higher humans whose civilization got submerged in some long-ago flood. Now they live in the mountain. In it—not on it. Or so some folks around Shasta say.

4 Stories abound: sightings of strange footprints; lost, lone hikers, getting rescued by beings with huge foreheads. Scoff if you want, Scully. Lanser probably did, until that spring day when he stared up at Shasta and saw bright lights in the wilderness. Flashing, fading. Flashing, fading. He saw them the next night, and the next.

5   "Incredible," Lanser wrote, when he got back to Los Angeles, "that . . . Lemuri-ans . . . have succeeded in secluding themselves in the midst of our teeming state."

6   Interesting, no? But you know our motto: Trust no one.

7   So a few weeks ago, I donned dark glasses, ducked inside a dark sedan, and headed out to investigate the situation for myself. Here's what's top secret: Shasta was only one of my stops. I was on the trail of mysteries, which are plentiful as prairie dogs in the West. Scully and Mulder, you'd love it here. All sorts of stuff goes unexplained.

8   Consider this: In Piercy, Calif., up the northern coast, there's Confusion Hill. Try walking up it and you wobble like a Weeble. Maybe the place was once a landing site for aliens. People have come up with all kinds of ideas.

9   Not far from that spot, hikers, like to trek through the coastal forests. The seldom-seen Sasquatch,[1] some say, likes to hike there, too.

10   But I was working alone; I had to be selective. A man can see only so much. So I started a bit farther south, in the Red Rock Country of Sedona, Ariz., where there are so many buttes and pinnacles you nearly expect to see the Marlboro man. What you see instead are lots of New Age bookstores and crystal shops. And companies offering vortex tours.

11   What's a vortex? No, it's not a cross between velvet and Gore-Tex. It's a spiritual spot where earth's healing energy rises from its core. Skeptics snicker, but believers come in bunches—tens of thousands every year.

12   There are four major vortices in Sedona. (Used to be more, but one got paved over by the post office.) The big ones that remain are Boynton Canyon, Bell Rock, Cathedral Rock, and Airport Mesa. High up on a cliff overlooking the village of Oak Creek there's a vortex known as Apache Leap. Story goes that a small group of fugitive Apache warriors arrived at the cliff's edge and, rather than surrender to the soldiers trailing them, jumped. Not many people go there. It's a heck of a climb.

13   "There is no one singular vortex experience," a local tour operator named Marc Avery told me. "Everyone gets something different out of them."

14   We were standing at the base of the famous Bell Rock vortex, a red rock outcropping that is shaped like—well, let's just say the name rings true. Like all the local vortices, this place was sacred to the American Indians. These days it's a destination for people who hope to cure their hepatitis and for couples who want to heal their marital difficulties. Psychics come here to hold séances. Gurus gather here to meditate. Avery told me that some people stand at a vortex, focus really hard, and swear they can make clouds disappear. Scientists have taken magnetic readings. Some say they found "energy." Others say they didn't.

15   That afternoon I picked up something—a candy bar wrapper on the ground near Cathedral Rock. That piece of litter aside, it's a stunning place, an ornate rock outgrowth standing sentinel near a bend in babbling Oak Creek. I sat on a large stone, listening to the gurgle of the water. There was no special energy that I could sense, except for the intense beauty of the spot. But I didn't give up. As I

[1]Sasquatch is the Native American name for Bigfoot, the legendary huge and hairy humanlike creature who is said to live in the forested areas of Northern California and Oregon. (Ed.)

drove off around sunset, I focused hard and looked out the window. Scout's honor, Scully, I couldn't see a cloud in the whole dang sky.

16　　It was overcast that night when I rolled into Las Vegas, where I bumped into this stumper of a mystery: Why so many Elvises in one place? But Las Vegas wasn't my destination. I was headed up the freeway, 2½ hours northwest through the desert, to Death Valley National Park.

17　　Through the park entrance, down the road dropped, nearly 300 feet below sea level, the lowest point in the Western Hemisphere. I passed Ubehebe Crater, a vast hole in the earth formed by a volcano. The wind whipped at more than 50 miles per hour.

18　　I had swapped the sedan for a big four-wheel drive. I needed it to get where I was going, some 30 miles down a rugged dirt road to Racetrack Playa, home of the mysterious sliding stones.

19　　Racetrack Playa isn't really a racetrack. It's a dried-out lake bed, nearly two miles long. They just call it that because of the stones. I could see them in the distance as I rolled around a bend and rumbled toward the playa. They were like a flock of ducks sitting on a placid pond. I parked the truck and walked half a mile across the cracked-dry lake bed, just barely keeping my balance in the gale-force gusts.

20　　At last, I stood among the sliding stones. There were dozens of them, some barely larger than pebbles, others twice the size of basketballs. I couldn't see them sliding. No one ever has. But I could tell that they'd been on the move. Across the vast expanse of Racetrack Playa, the stones had left snail trails, long snaking furrows in the silt clay. Some of the trails were several hundred feet long.

21　　What makes the stones slide remains a question. As always, some people suspect aliens. If that's the case, E.T. is stronger than a team of oxen. Some of the stones weigh 700 pounds. Other theories have emerged. Maybe it's the high wind, though wind alone couldn't budge some of these babies. Maybe it's the rain, which freezes in cold weather, forming a thin icy film over which the stones could slide. Maybe it's a combination of the two.

22　　Experts have promised to unravel the riddle. They could set up cameras, use fancy measuring devices to watch the stones move over time. Out on the playa, the wind was still howling. I hunched my shoulders and trudged back to the truck. Mulder would take issue, but here's my belief: Some mysteries are better left alone.

23　　That's how I felt when I made my next stop, in the Santa Cruz Mountains, at the fabulously famous Mystery Spot.

24　　Here's your background: During the 1930s, a fellow who'd bought the property was surveying the hillside when he felt a strange force dragging him down. He built a shack with a firm foundation. Soon enough the shack was unaccountably tilting to one side.

25　　It's still tilting today. That much you can see when you pay your $5 and breeze through the half-hour Mystery Spot tour. Lots of odd stuff strikes you as you stroll up the hill. The slope doesn't get steeper, but your legs grow heavy. Each step is harder than the one before.

26　　Stand on a plank—it's perfectly level. Put a cue ball down and it won't roll away. Now walk the plank. Your friends will swear you're shrinking. Walk the other way, and they will insist you've grown. At other spots, try to stand up straight and you'll be leaning backward. You can't help it. Gravity is goofy here.

27   The entire Mystery Spot is just 150 feet in diameter. But, the tour guides say, planes won't fly over it. Rumor has it that it throws their instrumentation off. Some visitors get dizzy and don't know why.

28   But lots of folks have come to their own conclusions. UFO fans insist that some mysterious metal is buried in the earth here. It supposedly helps flying saucers navigate.

29   Then there's the carbon dioxide theory. A scientist once detected high concentrations of the gas here. Said it oozes from the earth and makes you feel lightheaded. Said it refracts the light so it plays tricks on your eyes.

30   No tricks here: When I got back to the office, I read the Mystery Spot brochure. Seems that one scientist visited the Mystery Spot and found "the highest dielectric biocosmic radiation" known in the world. What does that mean? That, my dear agents, is a mystery, too. And here's another one: Do spirits really live in the Winchester Mystery House?

31   Sarah Winchester believed they did. She was the heiress to the Winchester rifle fortune and in 1884, shortly after the deaths of her husband and infant child, she moved to San Jose from Connecticut. She was grief stricken, conscience stricken, and stricken with the sense that spirits trailed her. These were the shades, she thought, of people killed by Winchester guns.

32   Mrs. Winchester consulted a fortune-teller, who gave her advice on keeping ghosts at bay: Start building a house, the seer told her, and never stop building or you'll suffer the same fate as your husband and child. And so she did. Her strange Victorian megamansion stands just a few blocks from the interstate. Guided tours are required. Without them, you might not ever make it out.

33   There are 160 rooms, 2,000 doors, 47 fireplaces, and six kitchens. (Do you know what a bungalow in this neighborhood goes for today?) The place is as endless as a daytime soap opera, with just as many twists and turns. There are stairs that lead to nowhere, doors that open onto nothing, windows that look out at solid walls.

34   Maybe Sarah built it that way to confuse the ghosts. When she died in 1922, construction ceased. But the phantoms, it seems, never skipped town. Folks who work there swear they hear evidence of them: footsteps in the hallway, voices from the kitchen, doors that seem to slam all by themselves.

35   No spirits showed up when I toured the place. But they can't fool me: I know they stay out of sight when there's an agent around. So I left San Jose—I could almost hear the ghosts breathe a sigh of relief—and drove north up the coast to Klamath, Calif., not far from the Oregon border.

36   I rolled through stands of mighty redwoods, then stopped at some of the mightiest trees of all.

37   You know you've arrived at the Trees of Mystery when you see the giant statue of Paul Bunyan standing alongside his giant blue ox, Babe. They guard a patch of forest that the American Indians feared to enter. They believed that spirits lived here. How else could the trees grow so tall?

38   What I wanted to know, as I paid my $15 and lit out down the footpath, is how the trees here could grow so strange. They're twisted and gnarled into

elaborate formations: a tree shaped like an elephant. One that resembles a bolt of lightning. And another that grows upside down, its roots springing forth from some high-hanging branch.

39   I spent an hour wandering amid these ancient monsters. A tree shaped like a candelabra caught my eye. Want to know what I was thinking, Mulder? People may be weird, but Mother Nature is the greatest mystery of all.

40   Or is she? I began to wonder, after driving three more hours from Klamath over the mountains to Gold Hill, Ore., a small town on the state's southern lip. I took a winding road through the forest. Eerie setting. Forget the X-Files—I'm talking *Blair Witch Project II*. A few miles in, I reached the Oregon vortex, home of the "world famous" House of Mystery.

41   Brochure says the place is unique, but it closely resembles the Mystery Spot. Actually, it opened in 1930, a decade before the similar place in Santa Cruz.

42   At any rate, what I saw was a shack and a steep hillside where gravity seems to perform in contrary ways. Hold a broomstick at an angle, handle touching the ground, whisk end up, then let go of it. The broom just stands there. What could explain this? I scratched my head. No shame in that—plenty of scientists have scratched theirs, too.

43   So many questions, so few answers. But lots to ponder on the two-hour drive to Mount Shasta, land of the Lemurians. Arriving downtown, a Mayberry-looking stretch with some shops and stop signs, I moseyed into one of the book-stores. There were crystals in the windows and New Age books on the shelves. I approached the owner.

44   "What about these Lemurians?" I asked. She gave me a grave look.

45   "The problem that I have with the media," she said, "is you're always coming here trying to make us look like a bunch of weirdos." I said I'd be going.

46   And then she said, "But you know, there was this one night when I saw these lights out there . . ."

47   I drove up Lake Street, up the mountain, as far as the snowplows would let me go. Sunlight danced in the bleached-out distance. Or was it the lights of the Lemurians? I drove back down, across the freeway, then seven miles back up the foothills to Castle Lake, which was backed by cliffs, iced over and dusted with a thin layer of snow. Legend has it that in the 1960s, flying saucer landings were common here. Time was, some say, when you could see the burnt patches where the ships touched down.

48   No one knows why the aliens traveled here. For a dip in the lake? For a day at leisure with the Lemurians? I stared across the valley at the looming elegance of massive, snow-white Shasta. Stunning. Silent. I could well understand the mountain's allure. Was there anything out there? Aliens? Lemurians? I don't have the answer. Agents, I leave this one to you. ✳

From Josh Sens, "The Truth Is Out There," *VIA* Magazine, published by the California State Automobile Association.

Exercises

Do not refer to the selection for Exercises A and B unless your instructor directs you to do so.

A. DETERMINING THE MAIN IDEA AND PURPOSE

Choose the best answer.

_____ **1.** The main idea of the selection is that
   a. scientists need to investigate the mysteries of natural phenomena.
   b. travelers have long been fascinated with mysterious spots.
   c. some mysteries are better left unsolved and unexplained.
   d. the American West is home to several unexplained mysterious spots.

_____ **2.** With respect to the main idea, the writer's purpose is to
   a. examine some scientific theories to explain these mysterious phenomena.
   b. encourage the reader to travel to the sites he describes.
   c. provide a first-hand account of his experiences visiting these mysterious places.
   d. encourage scientists to spend more time researching these mysteries.

B. COMPREHENDING MAIN IDEAS

Choose the correct answer.

_____ **1.** The Lemurians, the legendary humans associated with California's Mt. Shasta, are unusual because they supposedly
   a. draw strange pictures on cave walls.
   b. live inside the mountain.
   c. are descended from the inhabitants of the lost continent of Atlantis.
   d. use flashing lights to communicate with each other.

_____ **2.** A vortex, which Sens visited in Sedona, Arizona, is defined as
   a. a spiritual healing spot.
   b. a place without gravity.
   c. a type of water-resistant fabric.
   d. an everlasting cloudless sky.

_____ **3.** Racetrack Playa in California's Death Valley is particularly mysterious because
   a. strange designs have appeared on the lake bed floor.
   b. it is located far below sea level.
   c. aliens have been sighted there pushing heavy animal-shaped rocks.
   d. rocks slide unseen across the lake bed.

    4. The Mystery Spot in the Santa Cruz Mountains deserves its name because

        a. gravity behaves strangely there.
        b. there is no gravity, just like in outer space.
        c. UFOs have been observed landing there.
        d. visitors to the spot develop strange illnesses.

    5. A fortune-teller told Sarah Winchester to start building her mystery house and never to stop building so that she could

        a. ensure enough room for the spirits of her dead husband and child.
        b. prevent her own death and keep ghosts away from her.
        c. make money from tourists who visit the house.
        d. provide a refuge for lost souls.

    6. Concerning all of the mysterious spots Sens visited, he concludes that

        a. all can be explained by modern science.
        b. some mysteries just can't be explained.
        c. tourist bureaus advertise these places to bring in tourist dollars.
        d. all are inhabited by either good or evil spirits.

COMPREHENSION SCORE

Score your answers for Exercises A and B as follows:

A. No. right _____ × 2 = _____

B. No. right _____ × 1 = _____

Total points from A and B _____ × 10 = _____ percent

You may refer to the selection as you work through the remaining exercises.

C. LOCATING SUPPORTING DETAILS

For each main idea stated here, find details that support it.

1. I couldn't see them [the stones] sliding. No one ever has. But I could tell they'd been on the move. [Paragraph 20]

    a. _____

    b. _____

2. The place [the Winchester Mystery House] is as endless as a daytime soap opera. [Paragraph 33]

   a. _____

   b. _____

D. INTERPRETING MEANING

Write your answers to these questions in your own words.

1. Explain the meaning of the article's title. _____

   _____

   _____

2. Look again at paragraphs 43–46. How do you interpret the bookstore

   owner's behavior toward the author? _____

   _____

E. UNDERSTANDING VOCABULARY

Choose the best definition according to an analysis of word parts or the context.

_____ 1. *Scoff* if you want [paragraph 4]:
   a. argue against strongly.
   b. treat with mockery or derision.
   c. consider carefully.
   d. accept as truthful.

_____ 2. in the midst of our *teeming* state [5]:
   a. swarming, abundantly filled.
   b. filled with valuable resources.
   c. rural or agricultural in nature.
   d. popular as a vacation destination.

_____ 3. sitting on a *placid* pond [19]:
   a. dark and murky.
   b. remote, far away.
   c. previously undiscovered.
   d. calm, undisturbed.

_____ 4. it *oozes* from the earth [29]:
   a. slowly leaks out.
   b. strongly gushes.
   c. emerges, appears.
   d. disappears.

_____ **5.** lots to *ponder* on the drive [43]:

    a. investigate, research further.
    b. carefully consider, think about.
    c. look at, regard.
    d. dream, fantasize about.

F. USING VOCABULARY

In parentheses before each sentence are some inflected forms of words from the selection. Study the context and the sentence. Then write the correct form in the space provided.

1. (*submerge, submerged, submersion*). Lemurians were an ancient race of humans

    whose civilization was _____ after a big flood.

2. (*plenty, plentiful, plentifully*) Mysterious sites are _____ in the

    West, as Sens discovered for himself.

3. (*alien, aliens, alienate*) Some people speculate that _____ once
inhabited Confusion Hill and the area surrounding Mt. Shasta.

4. (*skeptic, skeptics, skeptical, skepticism*) Many visitors view the reputed healing

    powers of vortices of Sedona with _____ .

G. TOPICS FOR WRITING OR DISCUSSION

1. Why does Sens mention the old *X-Files* television program and its two lead characters, Scully and Mulder, throughout the article?
2. Write a paragraph or two in which you describe the strangest place you've ever visited or the weirdest natural phenomenon you have ever observed.

For Further Exploration

BOOK

Though not about weird science, Royston M. Roberts's book *Serendipity: Accidental Discoveries in Science* (1989) is an entertaining look at the often unusual or strange origins of everyday items such as: Velcro, graham crackers, cornflakes, and Wite-out.

MOVIE

The Blair Witch Project (1999), directed by Daniel Myrick, is about four teenagers lost in a forest. The movie was so realistic and scary that many thought it was a documentary. The sequel, *The Blair Witch Project II*, is mentioned in paragraph 40.

WEB SITES

Four of the mystery sites described in Sens's article have Web sites:

- *www.mysteryspot.com*
- *www.winchestermysteryhouse.com*
- *www.oregonvortex.com*
- *www.treesofmystery.net*

Photographs and some theories to explain the sliding-rock phenomenon in Death Valley are available at *www.395.com/index.shtml?/deathvalley/.* Click on "Sliding Stones of Racetrack Playa."

2

PAMELA GRIM

Care in Midair

Pamela Grim is an emergency medical physician and research scientist in Cleveland, Ohio. Several of her pieces (such as this one) have appeared in an ongoing series called "Vital Signs" published in Discover *magazine. In addition, she has published a book describing her medical experiences,* Just Here Trying to Save a Few Lives: Tales of Life and Death from the ER *(2000). "Care in Midair" narrates a harrowing helicopter flight she took while trying to save the life of a critically ill patient who was being transported to a larger hospital. In a biographical sketch accompanying this piece, Grim writes, "In the ER, you never know if you've done the right thing. You come home and think, 'Should I have done this? Should I have done that?' In my stories, I am not the hero."*

Vocabulary Preview

WORD HISTORY

Ominous [paragraph 16] During the scary helicopter flight to save the patient, the thunderclouds, as Grim relates, became more *ominous.* Meaning "menacing" or "threatening," this word comes from the Latin noun *omen,* which formerly referred to a prophetic sign, either good or bad. But unlike its Latin root, the English word *ominous* now more often refers to something that promises to bring evil or harm.

WORD PARTS

Micro- [paragraph 3] The helicopter pilot had to speak to the medical crew through his helmet's *microphone* because of the helicopter's noise. The prefix *micro-* came into English from Latin, although it was originally a Greek prefix. Indicating smallness, it is attached to many words to form compounds. In this case *microphone* is derived from *micro-* ("small") + *phonos* ("sound" or "voice"). Other words beginning with *micro-* include *microbiology, microscope,* and *microorganism.*

WORD FAMILIES

Circulatory [paragraph 7] Mr. Prodham, the critically ill subject of this article, suffered from a collapse of his *circulatory* system, referring to the circular movement of blood through the human body. This word comes from the Latin root *circus* ("circle") and the related prefix *circum-* ("around"). In addition to *circus,* a word that derives from the fact that a circus takes place inside a ring, English contains a multitude of words in this family, among them:

circuit	a closed circular line around an object or area
circuitous	taking a roundabout, out-of-the way course
circumference	the boundary line around a circle

| circumnavigate | to go around, as in to circumnavigate the globe |
| circumlocution | using an unnecessary number of words, to "talk around" a subject [circum- + loqui- ("to speak")] |

Other words you will need to know:

| intubation | the process of inserting a breathing tube into a patient's throat |
| extubation | the process of removing this breathing tube |

PAMELA GRIM

Care in Midair

1   We were at 2,000 feet and dropping fast. The flight nurse and I fumbled with our harnesses, preparing to jump out. I was the helicopter physician on duty, and we were rushing to pick up a critically ill patient in a small hospital about 150 miles away. We had to move; the weather was closing in.

2   Skip, the pilot, canted the helicopter toward one of the hospital parking lots. We were to unload hot—that meant we had to jump out with our equipment just as the helicopter touched down and run like crazy through the propeller wash and rotary roar. Already the guards at the hospital entrance were being hit by the wind from the props. Their coats were blown open, and one of them lost his hat.

3   "You have 20 minutes," said Skip as he jockeyed us down. He couldn't just say it, of course; he had to use his helmet's microphone. The rotary blades made too much noise. All our monitor equipment for the patient had to be electronic with visual output only. Our regular stethoscopes were useless.

4   The helicopter struts touched down with a bounce. "Go," Skip shouted through his mike.

5   I opened my door, grabbed two of the monitors and ducked out. Venetra, the flight nurse, was right behind me.

6   The attending physician had already told us about the patient. It was a heart-breaking case. Two weeks earlier Kevin Prodham had had a massive heart attack. Since then he'd had every complication known: blood clots, sepsis, renal failure, liver failure. Most patients would never survive this, but Mr. Prodham was only 42. He'd been a healthy, active businessman until two weeks ago. "He has kids in grade school," one of the nurses told me as we headed for the intensive care unit.

7   I winced when I saw him. He looked like a drowned man, bloated from the collapse of his circulatory system. He was on a ventilator, with leads and monitors and probes going everywhere.

8   Venetra began setting up the monitoring equipment while I flipped through the patient's chart. For the past 24 hours, his oxygen saturation had been less than 70 percent. His blood pressure, despite medication, had gone south early this morning and stayed there. He was comatose; tests of his liver functions were nearly incompatible with life, and he probably should have started dialysis the week before. This man was close to dying.

9   I checked my watch. We had about 15 minutes. First we had to switch all the pumps and monitors from the hospital equipment to our specially designed "helicopter proof" ones. Because the helicopter was not pressurized, the pumps had to operate at varying ambient pressures. And they all had to have visual alarms because we couldn't hear anything. Then we had to move the patient over to the helicopter gurney and disconnect him from the ventilator. The hospital staff had already inserted a breathing tube into his airway; throughout the flight we would have to pump air into his lungs manually, using a device called an Ambu bag.

10   I was worried about the weather, though—within five minutes, I was signaling Venetra. We were taking too much time. She ignored me; a slipup with an IV line or a pump set at the wrong speed could destroy any other attempt to save this man's life.

11   Finally we were ready. We trundled down the hallways. The patient's wife did not let go of his hand until we reached the door.

12   It was colder now, and the sky looked thin and gray. Maybe the wind had picked up, but with the helicopter going, it was hard to tell.

13   We slid the patient into the back of the helicopter. He was a big man, and tall. His feet stuck out over the end of the gurney, nearly tickling Skip's ears. We would have to do everything back here, and if he deteriorated, we'd have to stabilize him. That meant IVs, chest tubes, central lines—all difficult procedures on the ground, much less at a thousand feet and 140 mph. But I had faith in Skip. He had trained as a military pilot in Southeast Asia. In Vietnam, he told us, there were only two kinds of helicopter pilots: good ones and dead ones.

14   We took our places for liftoff. I buckled myself into a seat by the patient's head. Skip contacted base. "This is Air Transport One," he said. "We are lifting off at 4:33. Four souls on board."

15   "Souls." Skip always said that. I patted our patient, hoping his soul was still connected to his body.

16   We lifted off. I could feel the helicopter slip sideways with the gusting wind, recover, then slip again. We kept rising and then leveling off. Rain started pricking at the windows. The thunderclouds looked ominous.

17   The ride seemed to be getting bouncier. I sat pumping the Ambu bag, trying to keep my balance.

18   Skip came on the intercom: "I'm going up another 500 feet. It should be smoother up there. How's the patient?"

19   "Alive," I said.

20   "Barely," Venetra added

21   "You guys buckled in?" Skip asked, and as he did, a gust of wind hit the helicopter. I fell against the window as the entire helicopter swung sideways. I ended up looking straight down at the farm fields 1,500 feet below. It was the last view I saw of the ground. We were enfolded in a cloud of gray mist. Then we ascended and just as quickly dropped back down. Venetra and I were being tossed around like little dolls.

22   We swung sideways again, so far askew that the helicopter blades were almost directly to my right. "We can't stay aloft like this," I thought in the second

we hung that way. With another gust we were righted. I had been in the bumpy helicopter before, but it was never anything like this.

23   It was worse than any roller coaster. The downs weren't like those of going down a hill; they were those of dropping from some great height. As I reached out to hold on to the leather strap above me, I realized my hands were shaking.

24   "Should we go back?" I yelled at Skip through the intercom. There was a long pause. Skip must have contacted base with us out of the circuit. Finally he came back on. "That's a negative. Base states weather worse behind us."

25   I was struggling to pump the Ambu bag to breathe for the patient, but I kept being thrown back into the window. Then the patient showed the only sign of life I saw during the whole trip. He coughed. As he did, the Ambu bag collapsed in my hand. The patient had extubated himself.

26   "We lost the airway," I yelled to Venetra through the microphone. Unless we quickly slipped in a breathing tube, he could suffocate in minutes.

27   This had happened to me once before. We ended up landing in a cornfield long enough for me to get a new endotracheal tube in. I wasn't going to risk an intubation in the air that day, and then the helicopter was a rock compared with how it felt now.

28   "Skip, Skip," I shouted into my microphone. "The patient's extubated himself. Can we land for a few minutes?"

29   There was a long pause. "That's a negative, doctor. Weather conditions do not permit." Skip had never called me "doctor" before.

30   Venetra had unstrapped herself; she wedged her knees under the patient cart and prepared Mr. Prodham for a second intubation.

31   Now I had to get out of my seat belt. As I reached for my buckle I realized I was scared—not just nervous, but deep-in-my-bones frightened. It took an act of conscious will for me to open that metal clasp. Immediately, I was airborne and then slammed down to the left, against a small cabinet. I was too scared to know whether I'd been hurt. I inched my way to the head of the cart and groped for the box containing the intubation equipment. I grabbed a laryngoscope—the tool we use for introducing the breathing tube into the airway. As I did so we made another ascent—gentler this time, but still enough to spill the contents of the box everywhere.

32   "Give me a tube," I said to Venetra. She groped around on the floor, looking for the right size. She found one and handed it to me. I opened up the laryngoscope and slid it into the patient's mouth. I tried to get the tongue up and out of the way. My heart sank along with the next sickening drop of the helicopter—I had forgotten how bloated with water the patient was. His tongue nearly filled his whole mouth. How was I going to see?

33   I looked up at Venetra. She looked green.

34   "I'm airsick," she said. "I'm going to throw up."

35   "Well, don't do it on the patient."

36   She grabbed a bag out of the closet and stuck her head inside.

37   The helicopter took another shaking plunge. As I tried to hold on to the side of the cart, the laryngoscope tumbled out of my hand. I fell after it and caught it as I landed facedown on my seat.

38   This man is going to die now, I thought; no one as sick as he is could survive this. But I would get him reintubated, no matter what. I righted myself and edged back to the front of the cart.

39   Then Venetra was holding the Ambu bag, ready. I snapped open the laryngo-scope and slid the blade into the patient's mouth. Please, I said to myself. Please.

40   I saw for a moment all the landmarks—the epiglottis and beyond to the vocal cords. At least I could see past the tongue.

41   The helicopter lunged again, and the patient's face rolled away. As I tried to pull him back into place, I thought of a helicopter crash I'd seen in Colorado—the doctor in the back with two shattered hips. I knew those injuries. And I could see in the wreckage up front the pilot and the nurse hanging limply in their harnesses. I could hear the wind coming through the shattered glass and see those two figures sway. They had pushed the weather—trying to reach an unstable patient in some far-off clinic.

42   The helicopter bucked again, but this time the movement worked for me. I was flung forward, my hand jerking up, and the tube, as if of its own accord, slipped into place cleanly, right between the vocal cords and down into the air-way.

43   My first thought was, Maybe there is a God.

44   I straightened up. "I'm in," I shouted to Venetra. "I saw it."

45   We dropped again. I struggled to hold the tube in place. We may be about to die, I told myself, but this man will not lose this endotracheal tube.

46   Another ascent and then the rain stopped. For a moment our flight became steady and fairly quiet. Then came a pounding on the roof and walls of the heli-copter. It sounded like someone was beating the helicopter with a baseball bat.

47   "What *is* that?" I shouted at Venetra.

48   "Hail," she said. "That's hail."

49   We sat there, wedged in place, while all around us the metal seemed alive with the force of pounding rocks. I looked back down at my patient. I had no way to listen for breathing sounds, so I had to trust that the tube was in place. As I pumped air, it seemed his color was better. His pulse stayed rock steady at 75.

50   Suddenly the helicopter lit up as if it were on fire. An explosion, I thought. We've exploded. Then I thought, that can't be, I'm still alive. I looked out the window.

51   "Lightning," Venetra said.

52   The intercom buzzed again. "Hang on," Skip shouted to us. "I think we're through the worst of it." And then, as suddenly as it started, the helicopter stopped bouncing around and settled into its customary glide. We broke free from the gray clouds, and the helicopter filled with evening sunlight.

53   The patient's heart rate was 75.

54   When we landed, Skip stepped out of the helicopter, looking shaken and pale. He stood at the edge of the helicopter pad, smoking a cigarette, his head bowed, as if in prayer. When he looked up at me, he was wearing the same expression I had seen on doctors who had just lost patients they didn't expect to lose.

55   "I pushed the weather," he muttered as I patted his shoulder. "I can't believe how I pushed the weather."

56   "Well, we made it," I told him. "It's a happy ending. . . ."

57   And there was another happy ending. Mr. Prodham responded to therapy, the liver failure reversed itself, and his kidneys perked up enough for him not to need dialysis. I stopped by the ICU every day to see how he was doing. His wife

was always sitting there, holding his hand. One day I found her alone in the waiting room, crying because her husband was doing well enough to be taken off the ventilator.

58   "It's a miracle," she said, gripping my hand. "All this has been a miracle."

59   "Yes, yes," I said, squeezing her hand in return. I didn't tell her that during our wild ride I saw no evidence of a miracle. Just fear, hard work, and—well—maybe a little divine nudge to the elbow during the intubation.

60   Or maybe that's not true. Maybe something did hint at the miraculous. It was at the end of the flight, after we had cleared the clouds. First it was sunset, but as we flew east the sunlight disappeared, and it was nearly night when we got back to the city. We were flying at about 1,000 feet, and at that height you could see the grid of streets below, lined with dollhouses and marked by streetlights. The lights were laid out before us, brighter and brighter until they formed a solid mass of light that edged the black ocean. The skyscrapers were to the north and they, too, were marked out only by light. The real buildings, the steel and concrete, were as insubstantial as the night.

61   As I gazed out across the city, I wondered if Vietnam felt like this: you rode like bats out of hell, through the land of death and destruction, suffering everywhere you looked, until at some moment, after you broke free from the ground fire, you'd see as you looked all around you how beautiful the night sky was. ✳

From Pamela Grim, "Care in Midair," *Discover* Magazine, November 1998. Reprinted by permission of the author.

Exercises

Do not refer to the selection for Exercises A and B unless your instructor directs you to do so.

A. DETERMINING THE MAIN IDEA AND PURPOSE

Choose the best answer.

_____ **1.** The main idea of the selection is that

   a. working as a helicopter physician is a difficult job, especially during a storm.

   b. physicians and their crews must sometimes care for their patients under difficult conditions.

   c. physicians risk their lives every day rescuing sick patients.

   d. the writer and her crew faced an enormous challenge trying to save a man's life during a terrifying helicopter ride.

_____ **2.** With respect to the main idea, the writer's purpose is to

   a. defend her actions during the flight.

   b. relate her fears and triumphs by telling a story of a medical crisis.

   c. describe her medical training and experience.

   d. describe the bravery and skill emergency physicians possess.

B. COMPREHENDING MAIN IDEAS

Choose the correct answer.

_____ **1.** Grim and her helicopter crew had only 20 minutes to get the sick patient into the helicopter because the

a. weather was bad and getting worse.
b. emergency room team was ending its shift.
c. patient was near death.
d. helicopter needed routine maintenance.

_____ **2.** Mr. Prodham was suffering primarily from a collapse of his

a. respiratory system.
b. kidneys.
c. circulatory system.
d. liver.

_____ **3.** The writer and Venetra, the flight nurse, had unusual difficulty trying to stabilize the patient during the flight because

a. he was uncooperative.
b. they did not have sufficient training to save such a critically ill patient.
c. the weather was turbulent, making the helicopter bounce around wildly.
d. the equipment wasn't functioning properly.

_____ **4.** Grim says that this particular helicopter ride was worse than

a. any other helicopter ride she had been on.
b. a roller coaster ride.
c. taking a parachute jump.
d. a scary amusement park ride.

_____ **5.** The most terrifying and the most dangerous part of the flight occurred when

a. the crew had to reinsert the patient's breathing tube.
b. the patient's blood pressure dropped quickly.
c. hailstones hit the helicopter.
d. lightning struck the helicopter.

_____ **6.** Throughout the ordeal and despite her obvious fear, Grim exhibited one overriding emotion or feeling:

a. a faith that God or some higher being would intervene and save them with a miracle.
b. a strong determination to save the patient's life.
c. a lack of confidence in her medical skills.
d. a feeling of impending doom.

COMPREHENSION SCORE

Score your answers for Exercises A and B as follows:

A. No. right _____ × 2 = _____

B. No. right _____ × 1 = _____

Total points from A and B _____ × 10 = _____ percent

You may refer to the selection as you work through the remaining exercises.

C. INTERPRETING MEANING

Write your answers to these questions in your own words.

1. See paragraphs 6 and 8. What is the overall effect on the human body when the circulatory system collapses? _____

   _____

2. What did Skip, the pilot, mean when he told the crew that in Vietnam "there were only two kinds of helicopter pilots: good ones and dead ones"? _____

   _____

3. In paragraph 41 Grim describes another medical crew whose helicopter had crashed when the pilot had "pushed the weather." Skip later uses the same phrase in paragraph 55. What does it mean? _____

   _____

D. UNDERSTANDING VOCABULARY

Look through the paragraphs listed below and find a word that matches each definition. Refer to the dictionary if necessary. An example has been done for you.

Ex. cringed in pain [paragraph 7]   _____ winced _____

1. unconscious, lacking alertness [8]   _____

2. surrounding, encircling [9]   _____

3. threatening, menacing [16]   _____

4. at an angle, crookedly [22]   _____

5. voluntary action, done on its own [42—phrase]   _____

6. lacking substance or reality [60]   _____

E. USING VOCABULARY

Write the correct inflected form of the base word (in parentheses) in each of the following sentences. Be sure to add the appropriate ending to fit the grammatical requirements of the sentence. Refer to your dictionary if necessary.

1. (*circulatory*—use a noun) The _____ of blood in the human body affects the functioning of every other organ.

2. (*incompatibility*—use an adjective) The patient's poor liver function was
_____ with life.

3. (*stabilize*—use an adjective) Despite the wild gyrations of the helicopter, Grim and her coworker were able to keep the patient's condition

_____

4. (*ascent*—use a verb) As the helicopter _____, the medical equipment fell out of the box.

F. TOPICS FOR WRITING OR DISCUSSION

1. Write a paragraph or two explaining the many dangerous elements Grim encountered during this helicopter mission.
2. How would you describe Grim's suitability for emergency medicine? What qualities does she embody? Do you agree with her statement quoted in the headnote that she is not a hero?

For Further Exploration

BOOK

Abraham Verghese's *My Own Country* (1995) is an absorbing book describing his experiences treating AIDS patients in Johnson City, located in the Smoky Mountains of eastern Tennessee. Verghese, a young Indian doctor specializing in infectious diseases, confronted his first AIDS patient in 1988; his book chronicles the local townspeople's reactions to what is usually seen as an urban and gay affliction, his own attempts to stop the disease's progression, and the toll that work took on himself and on his family.

MOVIE

A major theme in "Care in Midair" is the determination to save lives, no matter what the personal cost. Such a theme is echoed in the excellent 2001 documentary film, *The Endurance*, which tells of Sir Ernest Shackleton's disastrous 1914 expedition to Antarctica and his heroic attempts to bring his men home alive.

WEB SITES

The following two sites contain reviews of Pamela Grim's book, *Just Here Trying to Save a Few Lives:*

- *www.theonionavclub.com/reviews/words/words_j/justheretryingtosaveafew01.html*
- *www.bookpage.com/0008bp/nonfiction/just_here_trying.html*

3

LORI HOPE

Did I Save Lives or Engage in Racial Profiling?

Lori Hope wrote this article for Newsweek *magazine's weekly column called "My Turn." The incident she describes occurred in December 2001, a few days after the so-called shoe bomber, Richard Reid, was arrested for trying to ignite a shoe containing an explosive device on a flight from Paris to Miami. In the aftermath of the September 11, 2001, World Trade Center terrorist attacks, airlines have struggled with how their employees can ensure their passengers' safety and not violate their civil liberties. In the context of Hope's article, racial profiling refers to singling out male passengers of Middle Eastern descent as being potential terrorists. Hope explores her own dilemma with regard to this civil rights issue.*

Vocabulary Preview

WORD HISTORIES

Paranoid [paragraph 10] At first the author wonders if her fears about the passenger in seat 9-C were simply due to her being *paranoid.* The psychotic disorder known as *paranoia* comes from the Greek word for "madness," *paranoos,* which in turn comes from *para-* ("beyond") + *noos* ("mind"). Physicians use the word *paranoia* to describe a mental disorder whereby the victim experiences delusions of persecution. Hope uses the word more loosely, meaning an irrational or extreme distrust of others.

Jettison [paragraph 17] The word *jettison* literally means "to throw overboard," usually to lighten the weight on board a ship or to get rid of something useless. In this case, a passenger was *jettisoned,* or thrown off the airplane, because of his appearance and suspicious behavior. *Jettison* derives from the Middle English word *jetteson,* with the same literal meaning as today's word; in turn, it comes from the Latin root *iectare,* "to throw."

WORD PARTS

-Ism [paragraph 2] The suffix *-ism* is frequently attached to nouns to indicate a doctrine, practice, theory, or principle. Hope's article concerns racial profiling to prevent acts of *terrorism,* which refers to an individual's or a group's use or threatened use of random violence against others either to intimidate or to coerce them in some way. Although terrorism usually is committed for political or ideological reasons, the recent terrorist attacks against the United States and its allies have been done in the name of religion. English has numerous words ending in *-ism,* among them, *realism, romanticism, barbarism, Catholicism, socialism, sexism,* to cite just a few.

WORD FAMILIES

Potential [paragraph 7] While trying to decide what to do about the suspicious passenger, Hope thought of her son's *potential,* which means an inborn ability that has not yet been realized or the capacity for future development. This word comes from the Latin root *potens,* or "power." Here are two other words in this family:

potent	powerful or capable of commanding attention; convincing
impotent	the opposite of potent—weak and ineffectual; also describing a man who is incapable of sexual intercourse

What is a *potentate?* _____

LORI HOPE

Did I Save Lives or Engage in Racial Profiling?

1   Half a lifetime ago, I read a magazine essay that took deep root within me, and still sprouts whenever I find myself tempted to react to someone based on skin color. The author, an African-American, described what it was like to see people cross the street when he walked toward them on a sidewalk.

2   When racial profiling became an issue in the war against terrorism, I—an avowed liberal—-found myself wondering what I would do if I saw someone who appeared to be of Middle Eastern descent behaving in a way that could be considered "suspicious." A few months ago I stopped wondering.

3   A plane my 16-year-old son and I were scheduled to board was swapped with another because of mechanical problems. Although I was relieved to know we were boarding an aircraft that checked out, I still felt uneasy about flying because of the "shoe bomber" incident three days earlier. I hadn't noticed security checking anyone's shoes.

4   Once settled into the aisle seat, with my son next to the window, I learned there could be another delay because of weather. Before opening my novel I noticed a man in the exit row two seats ahead, looking toward the rear of the plane. He was olive-skinned, black-haired and clean-shaven, with a blanket covering his legs and feet. I thought that was strange, because I felt so warm. No one else was using a blanket.

5   Nine-C, as I called him, sat motionless for 10 minutes, except for glancing nervously down the aisle every few minutes. Then his leg started to shake, and he seemed to be reaching for something under his blanket. He bent over. Adrenaline coursed through my body. I sensed something horrible. The plane was still on the ground, but I felt airsick.

6   "You're being ridiculous," I told myself. "Nine-C just wants to get home. He's cold; he has to use the bathroom. Just relax and keep your water bottle handy, in case he lights a match."

7   But he was very big, and the people sitting near him were not. And I wondered, "What if he goes to the bathroom to light his bomb?" Then I looked at my son—I thought of his potential, his brilliance as a musician and mathematician. How could I tell if 9-C was a terrorist? I couldn't.

8   I forced myself to walk to the rear of the plane. "What should a passenger do if she sees someone behaving in a way she considers odd?" I asked the flight attendant.

9   "Tell me about it."

10   "I'm probably just being paranoid," I started, and described what I'd seen. When I got back to my seat, I tried to forget my suspicions, having turned them over to an expert. A few minutes later, a flight attendant asked the passengers in row nine how they were doing. Another attendant came down the aisle, looking carefully at both sides.

11   "We need to de-ice the wings," announced the captain, apologizing for yet another delay. He emerged from the cockpit, walked back to 9-C's row and looked out to examine the wings. The other pilot did the same.

12   Soon afterward, we learned we were returning to the gate because of "another minor mechanical problem." Absorbed in my book, I hardly paid attention. When I looked up a chapter later, I saw that 9-C was gone. Was he in the bathroom?

13   We took off, and once at cruising altitude, I walked to the rear to see if he'd changed seats. But he was nowhere. I asked the flight attendant where he was. "We don't know what happens once security gets them. After the shoe-bomber, we're glad to get rid of anyone suspicious."

14   I felt awful. I didn't mean for 9-C to be taken away. I had probably ruined an innocent traveler's day, not to mention delaying an already late flight. And I hadn't even noticed he'd gone. I vowed not to scare my son; I'd keep the story to myself.

15   But I couldn't. The head flight attendant asked me to come to the front of the plane. My heart pounded and my cheeks burned; I felt ashamed and afraid. "Thank you for alerting us to that man," he said, smiling. "We all observed him, including our pilots. He seemed depressed, but also very nervous. Security did a background check and decided to question him. If he's OK, we'll compensate him. You did the right thing. Once we're in the air, it's too late."

16   We were moved to first class, and I wrote an incident report. Later, while waiting for our luggage, I reeled with questions: Had other passengers wondered about 9-C? Where was he now? Would I ever know whether he was a danger? Most important, had I become a racial profiler, bulldozing the roots of that powerful essay that had shaped me in my youth?

17   Perhaps I had. But I'm not sure I regret it. I can live with the guilt, grief and anger. Even though I lost a part of myself and may have gotten an innocent man jettisoned from the plane, it's not the same world it was half a lifetime ago. ✳

Exercises

Do not refer to the selection for Exercises A and B unless your instructor directs you to do so.

A. DETERMINING THE MAIN IDEA AND PURPOSE

Choose the best answer.

_____ 1. The main idea of the selection is that the author

    a. experienced mixed feelings after she alerted a flight attendant to a suspicious-looking and -acting passenger.

    b. was convinced that the passenger in seat 9-C was a terrorist.

    c. was tense and nervous about flying in the aftermath of terrorist attacks.

    d. believes that racial profiling is an unfair and dangerous practice.

_____ 2. The writer's purpose in relating the incident she experienced on her flight is to

    a. describe a moral dilemma she confronted.

    b. examine the reasons the number of racial profiling incidents has increased.

    c. present her opinion on a controversial issue.

    d. defend her behavior to those who would criticize her.

B. COMPREHENDING MAIN IDEAS

Choose the correct answer.

_____ 1. Hope recalls a magazine essay written by an African American writer, who described what it was like when other people

    a. denied him a job for which he was qualified.

    b. crossed to the other side of the street when he walked toward them.

    c. looked at him suspiciously wherever he went.

    d. refused to sit next to him on a bus or streetcar.

_____ 2. The man in seat 9-C aroused the author's suspicion

    a. more because of his appearance than his behavior.

    b. more because of his behavior than his appearance.

    c. because of both his appearance and his behavior.

    d. because of a vague, undefined, and unexpressed sense that something was wrong.

_____ 3. The man in 9-C covered his legs with

    a. his coat.

    b. a newspaper.

    c. a large piece of dark plastic.

    d. a blanket.

_____ **4.** What specifically prompted the author to alert the flight attendant to the strange behavior of the man in seat 9-C was

   a. the thought of her son's future.
   b. her fear about flying.
   c. the thought of everything she had to lose in life.
   d. her paranoia.

_____ **5.** The author's suspicions about the passenger were confirmed by

   a. her son.
   b. her fellow passengers.
   c. the flight crew.
   d. a later news account about the man's identity.

_____ **6.** Ultimately, the author concludes that she

   a. made the right decision, given the world we now live in.
   b. made the wrong decision by unfairly targeting an innocent man.
   c. disrupted the lives of her fellow passengers for nothing.
   d. will have to live with the guilt and anger over the situation she was placed in.

COMPREHENSION SCORE

Score your answers for Exercises A and B as follows:

A. No. right _____ × 2 = _____

B. No. right _____ × 1 = _____

Total points from A and B _____ × 10 = _____ percent

You may refer to the selection as you work through the remaining exercises.

C. LOCATING SUPPORTING DETAILS

For the following main idea, which is implied rather than stated, find and write down three supporting details.

The passenger in seat 9-C aroused the writer's suspicions.

1. _____

2. _____

3. _____

D. INTERPRETING MEANING

Write your answers to these questions in your own words.

1. What does Hope suggest about the behavior of the flight attendants, the captain, and the copilot in paragraphs 10–12? Did the plane's wings need de-icing and was there "another minor mechanical problem"? _____

_____

_____

2. What might be one reason that the crew, who had apparently already observed the suspicious passenger, didn't themselves take action? _____

_____

_____

E. UNDERSTANDING VOCABULARY

Choose the best definition according to an analysis of word parts or the context.

_____ 1. an *avowed* liberal [paragraph 2]:
- a. stated boldly and without shame
- b. wishy-washy, indecisive
- c. traditional, conventional
- d. untested, new

_____ 2. I thought of his *potential* [7]:
- a. intellectual achievements
- b. capacity for future development
- c. fear and anxiety
- d. trust and confidence

_____ 3. I *vowed* not to scare my son [14]:
- a. decided
- b. regretted
- c. was indecisive about
- d. promised

_____ 4. we'll *compensate* him [15]:
- a. pay damages to
- b. investigate thoroughly
- c. apologize to
- d. do a background check on

_____ 5. I *reeled* with questions [16] (used figuratively):
- a. drew inward
- b. became dizzy as if whirling around
- c. recited as a list
- d. staggered around

F. USING VOCABULARY

Write the correct inflected form of the base word (in parentheses) in each of the
following sentences. Be sure to add the appropriate ending to fit the grammatical
requirements of the sentence. Refer to your dictionary if necessary.

1. (*suspicion*—use an adverb) The author alerted a flight attendant when she

   observed a fellow passenger behaving _____.

2. (*ridicule*—use an adjective) At first the author decided that she was just

   being _____ and paranoid.

3. (*apology*—use a verb) The pilot came into the cabin and

_____ for yet another delay.

4. (*compensate*—use a noun) If the passenger was judged to be innocent, then

the airline would offer him _____ .

G. TOPICS FOR WRITING OR DISCUSSION

1. If you were in the same situation as Lori Hope, what would you have done? Did she have enough evidence to alert the flight crew?
2. Write a paragraph or two about an incident that caused you great anxiety about the rightness or wrongness of your action.

For Further Exploration

BOOK

Although Lori Hope does not identify the African American writer mentioned in the first paragraph, it sounds very much like Brent Staples, who wrote an essay called "Just Walk on By: A Black Man Ponders His Power to Alter Public Space," first published in *Ms* magazine (September 1986) and later in *Harper's* (December 1987) as "Black Men and Public Space." The same theme is echoed in his 1994 memoir *Parallel Time: Growing Up in Black and White.*

MOVIE

The Terrorists (1975) is a British thriller, directed by Caspar Wrede and starring Sean Connery, about terrorists who hijack an airliner.

WEB SITES

The following three Web sites provide different perspectives about the practice of racial profiling as it affects civil liberties:

- *www.pbs.org/newshour/bb/terrorism/july-dec01/racial_profile.html*
- *www.scu.edu/SCU/Centers/Ethics/publications/ethicalperspectives/profiling.html*
- *http://writ.news.findlaw.com/colb/20011010.html*

4

LUIS J. RODRIGUEZ

La Vida Loca ("The Crazy Life"): Two Generations of Gang Members

The son of Mexican immigrants, Luis Rodriguez grew up in Watts and the East Los Angeles barrio of Las Lomas. This article was originally published in the Los Angeles Times; *it is an early version of the preface and epilogue to* Always Running (La Vida Loca: Gang Days in L.A.), *which was awarded the fifteenth annual Carl Sandburg Literary Arts Award for Nonfiction. In this selection, Rodriguez, a well-regarded poet and fiction writer who now lives in Chicago, tells how he was lured into gang life, the violence and desperation of which eventually dragged him down.*

Vocabulary Preview

WORD HISTORIES

Scapegoat [paragraph 12] Rodriguez questions what society should do with people, like gang members, whom society can't accommodate. Our society, Rodriguez says, uses them as *scapegoats,* or as Rodriguez writes, "We place society's ills on them, then 'stone them.'" A *scapegoat* is a person chosen, often at random, to bear the blame for others. It comes from the Old Testament, Leviticus 16:10, which describes how Aaron, Moses's older brother, arbitrarily chose a goat over whose head he confessed all the sins of the children of Israel. The goat was then sent to wander in the wilderness, where it symbolically carried their sins until the Day of Atonement. This day is celebrated as Yom Kippur, the holiest day in Judaism. (Apparently, the biblical translator was confused about the Hebrew phrase in Leviticus, because it was incorrectly translated into English as "escape goat," which does not really make sense.)

Curfew [paragraph 17] When Rodriguez was young, the police picked up as many 7-year-old boys as they could for various offenses, among them for violating *curfew.* Today, a *curfew* means a time when certain groups of people must be off the streets or out of an area. This word comes from medieval French. Since most houses were made of wood and had thatched roofs, the danger of fire was always great, especially at night. Every evening, therefore, a bell was rung signaling that residents had to put out their candles, or to "cover fire" from the French phrase *couvre-feu.* Its pronunciation has been Anglicized—in other words, made to sound like English.

WORD PARTS

-Cide [paragraph 30] Rodriguez writes, "There is an aspect of *suicide* in gang involvement." Meaning literally "killing oneself," this word is formed from the root *sui* ("self") + the suffix *-cide* ("killing"). Here are three more words using this suffix:

genocide killing an entire race of people
matricide killing one's mother
pesticide an agent that kills insects

What do these three words mean? Consult a dictionary if you are unsure.

patricide _____

infanticide _____

herbicide _____

WORD FAMILIES

Innate [paragraph 35] Rodriguez writes of his hope to make his son Ramiro see that he has _innate_ value. Meaning "inborn," _innate_ comes from this Latin word: _in-_ ("in") + _natus_ ("to be born"). There are a fairly large number of words derived from the root _natus_. Here are some of the most obvious ones: _nation, nationality, natural, nature, prenatal, postnatal,_ and _nativity._ Here are two less obvious ones:

naive lacking worldliness and sophistication
née from the French for "born," meaning the name a married woman was born with, for example, Mrs. Dorothy Koziol, née Dorothy Granter.

LUIS J. RODRIGUEZ

La Vida Loca ("The Crazy Life"): Two Generations of Gang Members

1   Late winter Chicago, 1991: The once-white snow that fell in December has turned into a dark scum, an admixture of salt, car oil and decay; icicles hang from rooftops and window sills like the whiskers of old men. The bone-chilling temperatures force my family to stay inside a one-and-a-half bedroom apartment in a three-flat building in Humboldt Park. My third wife, Trini, our child Ruben and my 15-year-old son Ramiro from a previous marriage huddle around the television set. Tensions build up like a fever.

2   One evening, words of anger bounce back and forth between the walls of our gray-stone flat. Two-year-old Ruben, confused and afraid, crawls up to my leg and hugs it. Trini and I had jumped on Ramiro's case for coming in late following weeks of trouble: Ramiro had joined the Insane Campbell Boys, a group of Puerto Rican and Mexican youth allied with the Spanish Cobras and Dragons.

3   Within moments, Ramiro runs out of the house, entering the freezing Chicago night. I go after him, sprinting down the gangway leading to a debris-strewn alley. I see Ramiro's fleeing figure, his breath rising in quickly dissipating clouds.

4   I follow him toward Division Street, the neighborhood's main drag. People yell out of windows and doorways: "_¿Qué pasa, hombre?_"[1] This is not an unfamiliar sight—father or mother chasing some child down the street.

[1]"What's happening, man?" (Ed.)

5   Watching my son's escape, it is as though he enters the waters of a distant time, back to my youth, back to when I ran, to when I jumped over fences, fleeing *vato locos*,[2] the police or my own shadow, in some drug-induced hysteria.

6   As Ramiro speeds off, I see my body enter the mouth of darkness, my breath cut the frigid flesh of night—my voice crack open the night sky.

7   We are a second-generation gang family. I was involved in gangs in Los Angeles in the late 1960s and early 1970s. When I was 2 years old, in 1956, my family emigrated from Mexico to Watts. I spent my teen years in a barrio called Las Lomas, east of Los Angeles.

8   I was arrested on charges ranging from theft, assaulting an officer to attempted murder. As a teen-ager, I did some time. I began using drugs at age 12—including pills, weed and heroin. I had a near-death experience at 16 from sniffing toxic spray. After being kicked out of three high schools, I dropped out at 15.

9   By the time I turned 18, some 25 friends had been killed by rival gangs, the police, overdoses, car crashes and suicides.

10   Three years ago, I brought Ramiro to Chicago to escape the violence. If I barely survived all this, it appeared unlikely my son would make it. But in Chicago, we found kindred conditions.

11   I had to cut Ramiro's bloodline to the street before it became too late. I had to begin the long intense struggle to save his life from the gathering storm of street violence—some 20 years after I had sneaked out of the hood in the dark of night and removed myself from the death fires of *La Vida Loca*.

12   What to do with those whom society cannot accommodate? Criminalize them. Outlaw their actions and creations. Declare them the enemy, then wage war. Emphasize the differences—the shade of skin, the accent or manner of clothes. Like the scapegoat of the Bible, place society's ills on them, then "stone them" in absolution. It's convenient. It's logical.

13   It doesn't work.

14   Gangs are not alien powers. They begin as unstructured groupings, our children, who desire the same as any young person. Respect. A sense of belonging. Protection. This is no different than the YMCA, Little League or the Boy Scouts. It wasn't any more than what I wanted.

15   When I entered 109th Street School in Watts, I spoke perfect Spanish. But teachers punished me for speaking it on the playground. I peed in my pants a few times because I was unable to say in English that I had to go. One teacher banished me to a corner, to build blocks for a year. I learned to be silent within the walls of my body.

16   The older boys who lived on 103rd Street would take my money or food. They chased me through alleys and side streets. Fear compelled my actions.

17   The police, I learned years later, had a strategy: They picked up as many 7-year-old boys as they could—for loitering, throwing dirt clods, curfew—whatever. By the time a boy turned 13, and had been popped for something like stealing, he had accumulated a detention record, and was bound for "juvey."

---

[2]Crazy dudes. This is what barrio members with intense street reputations were called. (Ed.)

18   One felt besieged, under intense scrutiny. If you spoke out, dared to resist, you were given a "jacket" of troublemaker; I'd tried many times to take it off, but somebody always put it back on.

19   Soon after my family moved to South San Gabriel, a local group, Thee Mystics, rampaged through the school. They carried bats, chains, pipes and homemade zip guns. They terrorized teachers and students alike. I was 12.

20   I froze as the head stomping came dangerously my way. But I was intrigued. I wanted this power. I wanted to be able to bring a whole school to its knees. All my school life until then had been poised against me. I was broken and shy. I wanted what Thee Mystics had. I wanted to hurt somebody.

21   Police sirens broke the spell. Thee Mystics scattered in all directions. But they had done their damage. They had left their mark on the school—and on me.

22   Gangs flourish when there's a lack of social recreation, decent education or employment. Today, many young people will never know what it is to work. They can only satisfy their needs through collective strength—against the police, who hold the power of life and death, against poverty, against idleness, against their impotence in society.

23   Without definitive solutions, it's easy to throw blame. George Bush and Dan Quayle,[3] for example, say the lack of family values is behind our problems.

24   But "family" is a farce among the propertyless and disenfranchised. Too many families are wrenched apart, as even children are forced to supplement meager incomes. At age 9, my mother walked me to the door and, in effect, told me: Now go forth and work.

25   People can't just consume; they have to sell something, including their ability to work. If so-called legitimate work is unavailable, people will do the next best thing—sell sex or dope.

26   You'll find people who don't care about whom they hurt, but nobody I know *wants* to sell death to their children, their neighbors, friends. If there was a viable, productive alternative, they would stop.

27   At 18, I had grown tired. I felt like a war veteran with a kind of posttraumatic syndrome. I had seen too many dead across the pavement; I'd walk the aisles in the church wakes as if in a daze; I'd often watched my mother's weary face in hospital corridors, outside of courtrooms and cells, refusing, finally, to have anything to do with me.

28   In addition, I had fallen through the cracks of two languages; unable to communicate well in any.

29   I wanted the pain to end, the self-consuming hate to wither in the sunlight. With the help of those who saw potential in me, perhaps for some poetry, I got out. No more heroin, spray or pills; no more jails; no more trying to hurt somebody until I stopped hurting—which never seemed to pass.

30   There is an aspect of suicide in gang involvement for those whose options have been cut off. They stand on street corners, flash hand signs and invite the bullets. It's life as stance, as bravado. They say "You can't touch this," but "Come kill me!" is the inner cry. It's either *la torcida*[4] or death, a warrior's path,

[3]George H. W. Bush, president from 1988–1992, and his vice-president, Dan Quayle, made family values an issue during their term in office. (Ed.)
[4]Jail, prison time. (Ed.)

where even self-preservation doesn't make a play. If they murder, the targets are the ones who look like them, walk like them, those closest to who they are—the mirror reflection. They murder and they are killing themselves, over and over.

31 Ramiro stayed away for two weeks the day he ran off. When he returned, we entered him into a psychotherapy hospital. After three months, he was back home. Since then, I've had to pull everyone into the battle for my son. I've spent hours with teachers. I've involved therapists, social workers, the police.

32 We all have some responsibility: Schools, the law, parents. But at the same time, there are factors beyond our control. It's not a simple matter of "good" or "bad" values, or even of choices. If we all had a choice, I'm convinced nobody would choose *la vida loca*, the "insane nation"—to gangbang. But it's going to take collective action and a plan.

33 Recently, Ramiro got up at a Chicago poetry event and read a piece about being physically abused by a stepfather. It stopped everyone cold. He later read the poem at Chicago's Poetry Festival. Its title: "Running Away."

34 The best way to deal with your children is to help construct the conditions for free and healthy development of all, but it's also true you can't be for all children if you can't be for your own.

35 There's a small but intense fire burning in my son. Ramiro has just turned 17; he's made it thus far, but it's day by day. Now I tell him: You have an innate value outside of your job, outside the "jacket" imposed on you since birth. Draw on your expressive powers.

36 Stop running. ✳

Exercises

Do not refer to the selection for Exercises A and B unless your instructor directs you to do so.

A. DETERMINING THE MAIN IDEA AND PURPOSE

Choose the best answer.

_____ 1. The main idea of the article is that

  a. the popularity in gang membership can be traced to many social factors.

  b. the lure of gangs is incredibly strong for young, impressionable boys.

  c. although young boys join gangs for many reasons, the result is a self-destructive, crazy, and suicidal kind of life.

  d. the punishment must be made stiffer for gang members who engage in crime and lawlessness.

_____ 2. With respect to the main idea, the writer's purpose is to

    a. explain why he joined a gang.

    b. relate his experiences as a gang member to warn others.

    c. trace the history of gangs in Los Angeles and Chicago.

    d. examine the effects of poverty on young people.

B. COMPREHENDING MAIN IDEAS

Choose the correct answer.

_____ 1. Rodriguez moved his family to Chicago because he

    a. was afraid that he would be tempted to resume his old gang life if he remained in Los Angeles.

    b. hoped to protect his teenage son from being caught up in the violence he himself had experienced.

    c. wanted to start a new life for himself as a writer.

    d. wanted to keep a promise he had made to his wife.

_____ 2. Rodriguez writes that by the time he turned 18, he had lived through the deaths—from various causes—of

    a. five friends.

    b. ten friends.

    c. fifteen friends.

    d. twenty-five friends.

_____ 3. The author writes that gangs begin as unstructured groups, which children join from the desire to

    a. get back at authority figures, like their teachers and parents.

    b. belong to a group and be protected.

    c. enjoy the status and economic benefits that come with being a gang member.

    d. spend time only with children from their own race or ethnic group.

_____ 4. After the gang called Thee Mystics terrorized his school in South San Gabriel, Rodriguez admits that he was

    a. too terrified to go to school.

    b. intrigued by the gang's power and wanted the same for himself.

    c. forced to join the gang by some older members.

    d. upset and angry about their rampage through the school.

_____ 5. Rodriguez emphasizes that gangs take hold in our urban areas _mainly_ because of

    a. a lack of decent jobs.

    b. insufficient police protection.

    c. boredom.

    d. lack of interest in education.

_____ **6.** According to Rodriguez, being a member of a gang indicates that one

   a. is brave and manly.
   b. is more interested in self-preservation than in self-destruction.
   c. has no concern for his family's or friends' welfare.
   d. has a suicidal impulse.

COMPREHENSION SCORE

Score your answers for Exercises A and B as follows:

A. No. right _____ × 2 = _____
B. No. right _____ × 1 = _____

Total points from A and B _____ × 10 = _____ percent

You may refer to the selection as you work through the remaining exercises.

C. INTERPRETING MEANING

Write your answers to these questions in your own words.

1. Rodriguez describes his feelings as he watches his son escape into the night. How would you describe his emotion? _____

   _____

2. How would you characterize the _tone_ in paragraph 22, that is, Rodriguez's attitude toward the social causes of gang membership?_____

   _____

3. Look through the article again and, from what Rodriguez writes, enumerate two ways to lessen the influence of gangs on urban youth._____

   _____

   _____

D. UNDERSTANDING VOCABULARY

Choose the best definition according to an analysis of word parts or the context.

_____ **1.** _kindred_ conditions [paragraph 10]:

   a. similar
   b. different
   c. troubling
   d. improved

_____ **2.** "stone them" in _absolution_ [12]:

   a. a symbolic action
   b. a fit of anger
   c. pardoning for crimes or sins
   d. a display of mercy

_____ 3. One felt *besieged* [18]:

    a. overwhelmed
    b. threatened
    c. surrounded on all sides
    d. confused, bewildered

_____ 4. their *impotence* in society [22]:

    a. powerlessness
    b. loss of rights
    c. low social status
    d. lack of interest

_____ 5. But "family" is a *farce* [24]:

    a. an illusion
    b. an impossible goal
    c. a ridiculous sham
    d. a lightly humorous theatrical play

_____ 6. an *innate* value [35]:

    a. practical
    b. hidden
    c. traditional
    d. inborn

E. USING VOCABULARY

From the following list of vocabulary words, choose a word that fits in each blank according to both the grammatical structure of the sentence and the context. Use each word in the list only once. Do not change the form of the word. (Note that there are more words than sentences.)

alien	disenfranchise	legitimate
banished	emigrate	meager
bravado	impotence	scapegoats
compelled	intrigued	supplement

1. Rodriguez writes that gangs begin as _____ groupings; however, as he found out, Thee Mystics' power, which at first _____ him, eventually led him into a kind of suicidal life.

2. Making _____ out of gang members is not the answer to the kinds of problems gang members face, especially when people join gangs as a way of fighting back against their feelings of _____ in this society.

3. Another reason that people join gangs, according to Rodriguez, is to

_____ their _____ incomes that they earn

from doing _____ work by turning to crime.

F. TOPICS FOR WRITING OR DISCUSSION

1. In paragraphs 12 and 13 Rodriguez mentions a couple of ways that society has dealt with the problem of gang violence—declaring gang members the enemy, emphasizing their differences, and making them scapegoats. He says that these strategies haven't worked. Write a short paper in which you suggest a more workable solution to the problem of gangs in American cities.
2. What has been your experience with gangs and gang activities? Do you agree with Rodriguez's suggestion that we have been going about dealing with gangs in the wrong way?

For Further Exploration

BOOK

Luis T. Rodriguez, *Always Running (La Vida Loca: Gang Days in L.A.),* published in 1993, is a harsh look at East Los Angeles gangs and the social and economic conditions that give rise to them. Although widely assigned as required reading in high school, many school districts have received complaints from parents about two or three explicit sexual scenes. Rodriguez's most recent book is a collection of short fiction, *The Republic of East L.A.: Stories* (2002).

MOVIES

- *American Me* (1992), directed by and starring Edward James Olmos, offers a tough but inconsistent look at the cycle of gang violence in Southern California's prisons and barrios.
- *My Family, Mi Familia* (1995), directed by Gregory Nava and featuring Jimmy Smits and Edward James Olmos, is an absorbing drama about the hopes, failures, and dreams of three generations of Mexican Americans living in East Los Angeles from the 1930s to the 1960s.

WEB SITES

Find out more about Luis Rodriguez at these two sites. The first is Rodriguez's home page, and the second presents an interview with him.

- *www.luisrodriguez.com*
- *http://poetry.about.com/library/weekly/aa051502a.htm*

5 ROSE DEL CASTILLO GUILBAULT
The Conveyor-Belt Ladies

Rose Guilbault was born in Mexico and later immigrated with her family to the United States, where they settled in the Salinas Valley, an agricultural area in central California. She writes that she discovered books early on in her childhood, but she never had enough of them. The local library allowed kids to check out only two books at a time, and her father could take her to town only twice a month. Guilbault has had a varied career in journalism: She formerly wrote a column for the Sunday San Francisco Chronicle *called "Hispanic, USA," which won the Eugene Block Journalism Award for Advancing Social Justice and Human Rights. Currently Guilbault is Vice President of Corporate Communications and Public Affairs for the California State Automobile Association.*

In this article, Guilbault describes her summer experiences as a teenager working with Mexican American women from Texas, who migrated each year to Salinas for seasonal work in the packing sheds.

Vocabulary Preview

WORD HISTORIES

Stigmatize [paragraph 10] Guilbault writes that she feared her Anglo friends would *stigmatize* her for working with the Mexican women in the packing sheds. This verb comes from the Greek word *stigma,* meaning a "tattoo mark." The original meaning, now archaic, referred to a mark burned into a person's skin to identify him or her as a criminal or slave. Today, the word has a more metaphorical meaning, usually referring to a mark of disgrace.

Gregarious [paragraph 12] Guilbault describes her female coworkers as a *"gregarious,* entertaining group." This word, derived from the Latin word *gregarius,* has as its root *grex* meaning "herd" or "flock." *Gregarious* has two meanings: first, "tending to move in a group with others of the same kind," often used to describe animals like sheep; and second, "enjoying the company of others of one's kind," "sociable." It is this second meaning that fits the context as Guilbault uses it.

Melancholic [paragraph 18] As they worked sorting tomatoes, the women described in this article talked about their lives, their husbands and children, their concerns and worries. Guilbault writes that "in unexpected moments, they could turn *melancholic,* recounting the babies who died because their mothers couldn't afford medical care." *Melancholic* is the adjective form of the noun *melancholy.* Medieval physicians believed that certain human emotions were governed by *humors* or bodily fluids. Meaning "sadness" or "depression of the spirits," *melancholy* (or black bile) was one of the four humors.[1] Therefore, an excess of *melancholy* was thought to cause one to be sullen or sad.

WORD PARTS

Un-, Ir- [paragraphs 2 and 10]   The article contains two words with common negative prefixes: in paragraph 2, *uninspiring* ("not inspiring") and in paragraph 10, *irrevocably*, from the adjective form *irrevocable* ("not able to be revoked or reversed"). *Un-* is probably the most common negative prefix in English, occurring in hundreds of words, among them *unhappy*, *undetermined*, *unimpressive*, and *uninhabited*. *Ir-* is a variant spelling of *-un*, used with words beginning with the consonant *r*. You can see this prefix in such words as *irrational*, *irresponsible*, and *irregular*.

WORD FAMILIES

Monotonous [paragraph 12]   Sorting tomatoes was *monotonous* work for Guilbault and her fellow conveyor-belt workers. The Greek prefix *mono-* ("one" or "single") precedes many common words in English. *Monotonous* ("having one tone," "repetitiously dull") can be broken down like this: *mono-* ("single") + *tonos* ("tone"). Other words with this prefix are *monologue* ("a long speech made by one person") and *monopoly* ("economic control by one group"). What do these three words mean?

monotheism   _____

monochrome   _____

monocle   _____

ROSE DEL CASTILLO GUILBAULT

The Conveyor-Belt Ladies

1   The conveyor-belt ladies were the migrant women, mostly from Texas, I worked with during the summers of my teenage years. I call them conveyor-belt ladies because our entire relationship took place while sorting tomatoes on a conveyor belt.

2   We were like a cast in a play where all the action occurs on one set. We'd return day after day to perform the same roles, only this stage was a vegetable-packing shed, and at the end of the season there was no applause. The players could look forward only to the same uninspiring parts on a string of grim real-life stages.

3   The women and their families arrived in May for the carrot season, spent the summer in the tomato sheds and stayed through October for the bean harvest. After that, they emptied the town, some returning to their homes in Texas (cities

[1]The other three humors were choler (or yellow bile), which was thought to cause anger and bad temper; blood (*sanguin* in Latin), which caused one to have a red face and meant that the person was dominated by passion; and finally, phlegm, which made one sluggish.

Salinas, the Central Valley city near where the author grew up, is the lettuce capital of the United States.

like McAllen, Douglas, Brownsville), while others continued on the migrant trail, picking cotton in the San Joaquin Valley or grapefruits and oranges in the Imperial Valley.

4   Most of these women had started in the fields. The vegetable-packing sheds were a step up, easier than the back-breaking, grueling work the field demanded. The work was more tedious than strenuous, paid better, provided fairly steady hours and clean bathrooms. Best of all, you weren't subjected to the elements.

5   The summer I was 16, my mother got jobs for both of us as tomato sorters. That's how I came to be included in the seasonal sorority of the conveyor belt.

6   The work consisted of standing and picking flawed tomatoes off the conveyor belt before they rolled off into the shipping boxes at the end of the line. These boxes were immediately loaded onto waiting delivery trucks, so it was crucial not to let imperfect tomatoes through.

7   The work could be slow or intense, depending on the quality of the tomatoes and how many there were. Work increased when the company's deliveries got backlogged or after rainy weather had delayed picking.

8   During those times, it was not unusual to work from 7 A.M. to midnight, playing catch-up. I never heard anyone complain about the overtime. Overtime meant desperately needed extra money.

9   I was not happy to be part of the agricultural work force. I would have preferred working in a dress shop or baby-sitting, like my friends. But I had a dream that would cost a lot of money—college. And the fact was, this was the highest-paying work I could do.

10   But it wasn't so much the work that bothered me. I was embarrassed because only Mexicans worked at packing sheds. I had heard my schoolmates joke about the "ugly, fat Mexican women" at the sheds. They ridiculed the way they dressed and laughed at the "funny way" they talked. I feared working with them would irrevocably stigmatize me, setting me further apart from my Anglo classmates.

11   At 16 I was more American than Mexican and, with adolescent arrogance, felt superior to these "uneducated" women. I might be one of them, I reasoned, but I was not like them.

12   But it was difficult not to like the women. They were a gregarious, entertaining group, easing the long, monotonous hours with bawdy humor, spicy gossip and inventive laments. They poked fun at all the male workers and did hysterical impersonations of a dyspeptic Anglo supervisor. Although he didn't speak Spanish (other than *Mujeres, trabajo, trabajo!* Women, work, work!), he seemed to sense he was being laughed at. That would account for the sudden rages when he would stamp his foot and forbid us to talk until break time.

13   "I bet he understands Spanish and just pretends so he can hear what we say," I whispered to Rosa.

14   "*Ay, no, hija,* it's all the buzzing in his ears that alerts him that these *viejas* (old women) are bad-mouthing him!" Rosa giggled.

15   But it would have been easier to tie the women's tongues in a knot than to keep them quiet. Eventually the ladies had their way and their fun, and the men learned to ignore them.

16   We were often shifted around, another strategy to keep us quiet. This gave me ample opportunity to get to know everyone, listen to their life stories and absorb the gossip.

17   Pretty Rosa described her romances and her impending wedding to a handsome field worker. Bertha, a heavy-set, dark-skinned woman, told me that Rosa's marriage would cause nothing but headaches because the man was younger and too handsome. Maria, large, moon-faced and placid, described the births of each of her nine children, warning me about the horrors of childbirth. Pragmatic Minnie, a tiny woman who always wore printed cotton dresses, scoffed at Maria's stupidity, telling me she wouldn't have so many kids if she had ignored that good-for-nothing priest and gotten her tubes tied!

18   In unexpected moments, they could turn melancholic: recounting the babies who died because their mothers couldn't afford medical care; the alcoholic, abusive husbands who were their "cross to bear"; the racism they experienced in

Texas, where they were branded "dirty Mexicans" or "Mexican dogs" and not allowed in certain restaurants.

19   They spoke with the detached fatalism of people with limited choices and alternatives. Their lives were as raw and brutal as ghetto streets—something they accepted with an odd grace and resignation.

20   I was appalled and deeply affected by these confidences. The injustices they endured enraged me; their personal struggles overwhelmed me. I knew I could do little but sympathize.

21   My mother, no stranger to suffering, suggested I was too impressionable when I emotionally told her the women's stories. "That's nothing," she'd say lightly. "If they were in Mexico, life would be even harder. At least there's opportunities here, you can work."

22   My icy arrogance quickly thawed, that first summer, as my respect for the conveyor-belt ladies grew.

23   I worked in the packing sheds for several summers. The last season also turned out to be the last time I lived at home. It was the end of a chapter in my life, but I didn't know it then. I had just finished junior college and was transferring to the university. I was already over-educated for seasonal work, but if you counted the overtime, no other jobs came close to paying so well, so I went back one last time.

24   The ladies treated me with warmth and respect. I was a college student, deserving of special treatment.

25   Aguedita, the crew chief, moved me to softer and better-paying jobs within the plant. I went from conveyor belt to shoving boxes down a chute and finally to weighing boxes of tomatoes on a scale—the highest-paying position for a woman.

26   When the union's dues collector showed up, the women hid me in the bathroom. They had decided it was unfair for me to have to join the union and pay dues, since I worked only during the summer.

27   "Where's the student?" the union rep would ask, opening the door to a barrage of complaints about the union's unfairness.

28   Maria (of the nine children) tried to feed me all summer, bringing extra tortillas, which were delicious. I accepted them guiltily, always wondering if I was taking food away from her children. Others would bring rental contracts or other documents for me to explain and translate.

29   The last day of work was splendidly beautiful, warm and sunny. If this had been a movie, these last scenes would have been shot in soft focus, with a crescendo of music in the background.

30   But real life is anti-climactic. As it was, nothing unusual happened. The conveyor belt's loud humming was turned off, silenced for the season. The women sighed as they removed their aprons. Some of them just walked off, calling *"Hasta la próxima!"* Until next time!

31   But most of the conveyor-belt ladies shook my hand, gave me a blessing or a big hug.

32   "Make us proud!" they said.

33   I hope I have. ✳

From Rose Del Castillo Guilbault, "Hispanic USA: The Conveyor-Belt Ladies," *San Francisco Chronicle,* "This World," April 15, 1990. Reprinted by permission.

Exercises

Do not refer to the selection for Exercises A and B unless your instructor directs you to do so.

A. DETERMINING THE MAIN IDEA AND PURPOSE
Choose the best answer.

_____ 1. The main idea of the selection is that
     a. summer jobs can offer rewarding experiences for students.
     b. working in the vegetable-packing sheds and sorting vegetables was a difficult, tedious job.
     c. the conveyor-belt ladies were accustomed to their daily hardships and injustices.
     d. despite her initial misgivings, the writer learned to respect and admire the conveyor-belt ladies she worked with.

_____ 2. With respect to the main idea, the writer's purpose is to
     a. entertain the reader.
     b. describe her experiences and those of her coworkers.
     c. list facts about migrant workers.
     d. argue for better working conditions in the agricultural industry.

B. COMPREHENDING MAIN IDEAS
Choose the correct answer.

_____ 1. Guilbault's job during her first summers working with the conveyor-belt ladies was
     a. picking beans.
     b. sorting tomatoes.
     c. packing strawberries.
     d. trimming onions.

_____ 2. She writes that the daily lives of the conveyor-belt ladies were
     a. inspiring.
     b. hard but profitable.
     c. grim and tedious.
     d. desperate, nearly hopeless.

_____ 3. At first, Guilbault was afraid that she would
     a. not be physically able to do the work.
     b. be stigmatized by her Anglo friends for working with Mexican women.
     c. not earn enough money to attend college.
     d. be ridiculed by the other workers for her arrogant manner.

_____ 4. The conveyor-belt ladies eased the monotonous hours by

    a. playing jokes on the supervisors.
    b. playing games.
    c. listening to music.
    d. talking and gossiping.

_____ 5. The conveyor-belt ladies accepted their lives, which Guilbault describes as being raw and brutal, with

    a. grace and resignation.
    b. hostility and anger.
    c. detachment and indifference.
    d. good humor.

_____ 6. Because Guilbault was planning to attend college, the conveyor-belt ladies

    a. were envious of her.
    b. treated her with hostility.
    c. treated her with warmth and respect.
    d. complained when she was given easier jobs.

COMPREHENSION SCORE

Score your answers for Exercises A and B as follows:

A. No. right _____ × 2 = _____
B. No. right _____ × 1 = _____
Total points from A and B _____ × 10 = _____ percent

You may refer to the selection as you work through the remaining exercises.

C. IDENTIFYING SUPPORTING DETAILS

Place an X in the space for each detail that *directly* supports this main idea from the selection: [paragraph 18] "In unexpected moments, they could turn melancholic. . . ."

_____ 1. Pretty Rosa described her romances and her impending wedding to a handsome field worker.

_____ 2. They recounted the babies who died because their mothers couldn't afford medical care.

_____ 3. They recounted the alcoholic, abusive husbands who were their "cross to bear."

_____ 4. They recounted the racism they experienced in Texas, where they were branded as "dirty Mexicans" or "Mexican dogs" and not allowed in certain restaurants.

_____ 5. They spoke with the detached fatalism of people with limited choices and alternatives.

_____ 6. Their lives were as raw and brutal as ghetto streets—something they accepted with an odd grace and resignation.

D. INTERPRETING MEANING

Where possible, write your answers to these questions in your own words.

1. Explain this sentence from paragraph 11: "I might be one of them, I reasoned, but I was not like them." _____

_____ 2. Read paragraph 18 again. A good title for this paragraph is
   a. "Problems of Migrant Workers."
   b. "Lack of Opportunities for Migrants."
   c. "The Effects of Poverty and Racism."
   d. "The Melancholy Lives of Mexican Migrant Workers."

2. According to what Guilbault's mother implies, why were the conveyor-belt ladies resigned to their hard lives in America? _____

_____

_____

3. Guilbault eventually came to respect the women she worked with. What specific qualities did she admire? _____

_____

E. UNDERSTANDING VOCABULARY

Look through the paragraphs listed below and find a word that matches each definition. Refer to a dictionary if necessary. An example has been done for you.

Ex. moving from place to place [paragraphs 1–2]   migrant

1. dull, having no excitement [1–2]   _____

2. demanding, exhausting [3–4]   _____

3. tiresome, monotonous, boring [3–4]   _____

4. very important [6–7]   _____

5. describing something that can't be reversed [10–11]   _____

6. sociable, enjoying others' company [11–12]   _____

7. calm, undisturbed [17–18]   _____

8. about to happen [17–18]   _____

9. practical, dealing with facts [18–19]   _____

10. dismayed, filled with consternation [20–21]   _____

F. USING VOCABULARY

In parentheses before each sentence are some inflected forms of words from the selection. Study the context and the sentence. Then write the correct form in the space provided.

1. (*migration, migrants, migrate*) Field workers are often called _____ because they follow the crops and move from place to place.

2. (*arrogance, arrogant, arrogantly*) As the summer went along, the writer's icy _____ finally melted as she got to know the women better.

3. (*monotony, monotonous, monotonously*) The work was characterized by tedium and _____ .

4. (*brutality, brutalize, brutal, brutally*) The lives of the conveyor-belt ladies was characterized by injustice and occasionally _____ , yet they accepted their situation with good grace.

G. TOPICS FOR WRITING OR DISCUSSION

1. Write a paragraph describing Guilbault's experience working with the women on the conveyor belt.
2. Recount an experience in which you learned something you didn't expect to and that taught you something about life or the real world that you didn't know before.
3. Write an essay about a lesson you learned from an unexpected source.

For Further Exploration

BOOKS

- John Steinbeck, *The Grapes of Wrath* (1939). This classic novel centers on the Joad family who, having lost their farm during the 1930s Dust Bowl era, joined thousands of other "Okies" and moved to California, lured by the false promise of high wages picking fruit. This is probably the most important American novel set in California's Central Valley.
- T. Coraghessan Boyle, *The Tortilla Curtain* (1995). This novel, set in the affluent Los Angeles community of Topanga Canyon, describes the intersecting lives of two families—an affluent Anglo couple and a family of illegal Mexican immigrants—and the growing gulf between legal and illegal residents.

MOVIE

An excellent black and white film version of *The Grapes of Wrath* (1940), directed by John Ford and starring Henry Fonda, is well worth renting.

WEB SITES

A compendium of information about Latino/Hispanic culture, including a directory of resources, can be found at this site:

- *directory.google.com/Top/Society/Organizations/Ethnic/Latino*

6 EDDY L. HARRIS
Mississippi Solo

Eddy L. Harris graduated from Stanford University in 1977. He has traveled extensively through Europe, Central America, and Africa as a journalist. "Mississippi Solo" is from his first book of the same title, published in 1988, in which Harris describes a canoe trip he took by himself from Lake Itasca in Minnesota, the headwaters of the Mississippi River, to New Orleans. The incident described here takes place in a little town called La Crescent, Minnesota. Harris's most recent book is Still Life in Harlem *(1999).*

Vocabulary Preview

WORD HISTORY

Fiasco [paragraph 29]   The word *fiasco,* which means "a complete, often ridiculous or shameful failure" in English has little connection with the Italian word from which it comes. In Italian, a *fiasco* is a bottle, and the expression *far fiasco* means "to make a bottle." How "bottle" turned into "a complete failure" is unclear. One theory has it that when a glassblower in Venice discovered a flaw developing in a beautiful piece he was working on, he would turn it into an ordinary bottle to avoid having to destroy the object. The bottle would naturally represent a failure of his art to the glassblower.[1] The *American Heritage Dictionary* offers a different explanation: The French borrowed the Italian word *fiasco* to describe the errors made by Italian actors performing in the eighteenth-century French theater.

WORD PART

Mis- [paragraph 10]   The word *mislaid* begins with the common prefix *mis-.* However, *mis-* has two quite different meanings, and you have to be careful to distinguish between them. *Mislaid* means "to put in the wrong place." This meaning of *mis-,* then, is "wrong" in the sense of "improper." You see the same meaning in words like *misspell, mispronounce,* and *mislead.* The other meaning of *mis-* is "bad," as in *misconduct, misfortune,* and *misbehave.*

   In these two words, does *mis-* mean "wrong" or "bad"?

misunderstand   _____

mismanage   _____

WORD FAMILY

Recognition [paragraph 10]   When Harris enters a Minnesota diner, the other patrons regard him, as Harris says, with looks that were "the recognitions of a stranger." *Recognition* means "knowing something that we have seen before," literally

[1]*Merriam-Webster New Book of Word Histories,* 1991, p. 178.

"knowing it again." The word comes from Latin: *re-* ("again") + *cognoscere* ("to know").

These words share the same Latin root, *cognoscere:*

cognizant   fully informed, conscious
precognition   knowledge of something before it happens
incognito   a person traveling in disguise to avoid being identified

What do these next two words mean? Look them up if you are unsure and write their meanings in the space provided.

cognition   _____

reconnaissance _____

EDDY L. HARRIS

Mississippi Solo

1   The river laps lazily at the sides of my canoe, gently slapping a greeting and rocking me as I drift with the flow of the water and coast for a few moments. The waves are meek and comforting today.

2   I promised myself early on that I would not make race an issue out here. I would try to live my life on the river as I so far have lived my real life; I would not make my being black a part of my success or failure or too great a factor in how I perceive things. After all, I have never considered being black my most significant feature; when I think of myself, black is not the first descriptive term that comes to mind. And yet, how could race not mean a little something extra out here? As my old friend Robert had told me, and he was true so far, here I was traveling from the high north where blacks are pretty scarce and slicing into the deep south where feelings toward blacks are often none too sweet—historically at least. And people will see that I'm black only moments after they see that my canoe is green. Maybe even before.

3   It's not, I hope, what they'll remember later, and long after I'm gone, maybe they'll talk about a black man in a canoe, but perhaps they won't. Perhaps they will pick up on some other aspect of me and will choose to remember what I'm doing out here, what a sweet smile and happy soul I have, and how I let them treat me kindly. People in this country only need a chance and an excuse to be kind, and they respond.

4   Not too long ago a girlfriend tried to enlighten me. She told me I was the dumbest, most naive simpleton she had ever run across, a danger to myself and a step in the wrong direction. I had told her that I had not experienced much bigotry, and she blew a gasket. She violently told me that yes I had and that unless I recognized it I would never be able to do anything about it. And in a way she was right. And I may indeed have been blind to it or too stupid to see, but "if a tree falls in the forest. . . ." If you don't perceive a thing, no matter how real or concrete the occurrence, if it doesn't enter your consciousness or affect your

Harris's solo canoe trip started at Lake Itasca, the headwaters of the Mississippi River, and ended in New Orleans.

awareness, how real could it be? (The converse is true as well.) Or better, what difference does it make?

5   I told her I didn't allow people to deal with me on the basis of my race. I am more than black and my attitude says so. My *attitude!* I think that plays a big and greatly unappreciated role in how we are treated, and in how we face our world and our selves.

6   When as a writer I am rejected, my first reaction questions the stupidity of the editor, my second question concerns the writing itself and the realization that maybe it wasn't what the editor was looking for, or maybe—perish the thought— simply not good enough. Never had the rejection been racially motivated. When I

was accepted to the university, it was because I was qualified, not because I was black.

7   When a man downright doesn't like me, I'm sure he has his reasons; I'm not always so likable. But when he doesn't give me a chance, I find a way to force him to. Certain things, no matter how small, you cannot allow. Idiots screaming bravely from passing cars excepted, people should not get away with stupidity without challenge.

8   Racism—sure it exists, I know that. But its effect and effectiveness depend as much on the reaction as on the action.

9   I stopped for breakfast one morning early in La Crescent, a dinky little town parked at one end of the bridge that reaches over to La Crosse, Wisconsin. The town isn't much for size but it offered a choice of spots to eat, including a place for pizza. I opted for the one that had the most character, a plain looking diner removed from the center of town. A little place, frequented mostly by locals. The lady tripling as waitress and busboy and cashier seemed to know everyone who walked in, and she greeted each one with a different remark, some personal little tidbit that marked the customer like a brand. Early morning laughter to get the body stirring until the coffee comes.

10   The breakfast nook was two rooms worth of booths and a counter up front, and three shallow rows of tables in the rear. Everybody in there looked like a farmer or at least somebody who worked hard for a living, laboring with hands and arms and back, and maybe I didn't look too out of place among them walking in with dirty jeans and smelling like a herring. The looks they tossed my way were the recognitions of a stranger. No one stared for very long and if the waitress took a bit longer to get to me and take my order and return with my breakfast, I understood. She was too busy chatting with the regulars to be bothered with a stranger. And when she came to me she somehow had mislaid her friendly face and became a woman with a job to do.

11   While I waited for my breakfast of chicken livers and scrambled eggs and fried potatoes, a group of three insurance salesmen came in. I don't know if they really sold insurance. They wore ties and jackets and possibly sold farm equipment or maybe held office jobs over in La Crosse, but they reminded me of insurance salesmen. I've yet to see one dressed in a suit that fits well and is not wrinkled, a suit that looks good and is in style and shoes that are more than comfortable. A woman was with them and she wore the female equivalent. They sat in the rear.

12   At the counter an old man was treating his wife to breakfast out but they sat and ate without saying a word to each other, although both spoke happily to the waitress when she came their way. I guess they had lived together so long they had nothing new to say to one another, or else they just knew. The wife passed the salt and ketchup when the husband needed it. He didn't have to ask for it.

13   My food arrived and I asked for a clean fork and for mayonnaise for my potatoes. I said please and the waitress smiled. I noticed after that that no one else used the word. She hurried with the fork, but the mayonnaise took forever. The waitress had stopped to talk to three sturdily built women in the booth nearest the register. They were loud and laughing and wore jackets that said River Rat across the back. I was a river rat by then and I wished for a jacket like that.

14   No one in the place paid any undue attention to my existence or my eating or my being different.

15   I ate quickly and comfortably and paid. A middle aged man with a puffy face came up to pay as well. I hadn't noticed him with them, but he looked like a part of the group of men wearing those badly fitting suits. It turned out that I was right. This man, at least, *was* an insurance broker, and while we waited for the waitress to finish talking to whomever, he brought up the weather and asked me where I was from. I told him and said what I was doing and he laughed, pointing out the women in their jackets, and he said:

16   "You should have a jacket like that. Instead of River Rat it should say River Nigger."

17   He thought it was just the funniest thing and he laughed so loud that everyone looked in our direction. I didn't know if they had heard what he had said and wanted to see my reaction, but they were definitely watching and I felt I could not ignore this man and let him slide by unchallenged, even if he had meant no harm by it. It might, after all, have been a real attempt at friendly though misshapen humor. So why scream and shout?

18   I put on my toothiest grin and my best African accent and I said rapidly, "I'm from Nigeria. You mean river Niger. Aha-aha-aha!"

19   I let him struggle to grasp that one and I paid. His face went blank for a second and then knotted into a frown. By the time I got outside he must have figured out what I was really saying: your little joke upsets me and is not funny. And saying it in a way that does not threaten him, that does not attack him and so he cannot defend with anger and arrogance against it.

20   He hurried out to get me, grabbing me by the arm and saying, "Hey! I didn't mean nothing by it. It was just a joke."

21   I put my lips together and squeezed them tight and nodded once, but he wouldn't let it drop that easily.

22   "You're not from Nigeria, are you?"

23   He wore the most quizzical expression and he was so sincere that I had to laugh.

24   "I told you where I'm from."

25   I could almost hear the gears grinding in his head.

26   "Why'd you say you were from Nigeria? Did what I said bother you that much that you'd rather be from there than here?"

27   I hadn't meant that, but if it works. . . .

28   "I know I shouldn't have said it but you know how it is. You hear things and you repeat them and you get used to it. You don't even stop to think." Then he stopped to think. "Unless," he said and his head hung a little lower, "you're the one who's offended. Then it's a different story, isn't it?"

29   He went on to tell me about the final two games of the World Series which I had missed because of the journey and which had eroded into a fiasco. Grown men throwing tantrums on the ball field and behaving like children, little crybabies because things weren't going their way.

30   "And you could see them, right there on camera, saying F-you this and F-you that and I didn't appreciate it. It was uncalled for and I didn't like it one bit. And I'm not a prude, mind you. I was in the Navy, you know."

31   Twenty years as an insurance broker had done little for him but cause his hair to fall out and make him drink too much. Those little capillaries in his nose and cheeks inflamed his face and gave him the appearance of constant sunburn. Business wasn't too good. Premiums too high. A lot of businesses just can't afford insurance anymore. It's cheaper for them to go out of business, he said, but what can you do, he wanted to know, except close down the law schools for six years. Too many lawyers with nothing to do so they sue sue sue.

32   But twenty years ago, back when he was in the Navy pulling submarine duty and rearranging the Vietnamese coastline, life was leaner and not so cluttered up.

33   "Maybe it was Vietnam," he muses. "Maybe that's what did it to us. We could have won that war, you know, and Korea too."

34   "I guess you miss those Navy days." I'm beginning to feel compassion for this man when only moments before I was feeling contempt. It saddened me that I had made him feel so rotten over a harmless little joke.

35   "Those were the happiest times of my life."

36   And now he's back where he started. He's wound around full circle and he gets to the point of this conversation. He tells me about the stint he served in Puerto Rico. A simple story really about a beautiful heiress from Philadelphia who had come to San Juan to get over her grief. The two had met and spent all of their free time together. They slept together in the same room, in the same bed even, but never once did they make love.

37   "It wasn't that kind of relationship."

38   Instead, they would tell each other secrets, things they would dare tell no one else. And only once in a while if ever in your life does there appear a soul you truly trust with your own soul. And most likely she's a stranger you'll never see again. And since those days in Puerto Rico, he's not seen the woman ever again and had only received one letter from her, the one that said, "We shouldn't see each other again because we would only try to force something to happen that will only warp the memories." He sent her flowers after that, and that was the last they corresponded.

39   But in San Juan on hot days when the slightest breeze from the sea felt like a miracle, they would walk and sip rum drinks and talk forever and she told him of the man she was there to forget. The man she loved but whom she could never have because of her family. The only man with whom she had ever. . . .

40   The story stops while he clears his throat and swallows.

41   "The only man that she ever, you know," he whispers now, "climaxed with." His eyebrows lift. The whisper disappears. "His name was Raoul and he was a black man and she told me she loved him very very much and she cried and cried and I said to her, 'There's no reason why you shouldn't love him' and I meant it."

42   I reckon he did at that. And, I suppose, every man out here who has waved at me so far and wished me luck would get to carving at the core of American racism that lies inside if given the chance. The chance to be helpful. The chance to be friendly. The chance to know that we're not so very different, none of us from the others. I hoped so, anyway. I was traveling south, and because the South still doesn't get very good press, in the back of my mind gnawed a little apprehensive wondering.

43   Working on that core of American racism is certainly an easier task man-to-man, but on a grand scale chipping at it is as laborious as carving granite. Or so it seems, and I struggle with the confusion the same as I struggle with this river.

44   If only the racism could be tamed as easily. I should call in the Corps of Engineers for the task.

45   I waved goodbye to my friend the insurance broker and hoped he would find better days ahead. ✳

From Eddy L. Harris, *Mississippi Solo.* Reprinted by permission of Lyons Press, New York.

Exercises

Do not refer to the selection for Exercises A and B unless your instructor directs you to do so.

A. DETERMINING THE MAIN IDEA AND PURPOSE

Choose the best answer.

_____ 1. The main idea of the passage is
a. that Harris came to understand that race is the single most important issue American society faces today.
b. the way our attitude affects our dealings with others.
c. that racism and our perception of it depend as much on our reactions to racial incidents as to the incidents themselves.
d. that dealing with others on the basis of our race is unfortunate but necessary.

_____ 2. With respect to the main idea, the author's purpose is to
a. examine the origins of racism in American history.
b. explain why he undertook a solo canoe trip as a black man in an essentially white part of the country.
c. illustrate through one incident how racist attitudes can be changed bit by bit.
d. analyze the thinking that results in racist behavior.

B. COMPREHENDING MAIN IDEAS

Choose the correct answer.

_____ 1. Harris promised himself that on his river journey that he would
a. avoid contact with others, thereby avoiding any racial problems.
b. be himself and not make race an issue.
c. try to meet as many inhabitants as possible.
d. act the way whites wanted him to act.

_____ **2.** Harris's girlfriend became upset when he admitted that he had not experienced much bigotry and that he

    a. didn't allow others to deal with him on the basis of race.
    b. wanted to prove that bigotry didn't exist by undertaking the canoe trip.
    c. doubted that it was as common as everyone said.
    d. wanted to find out if Midwesterners were less preoccupied with race than Southerners.

_____ **3.** According to Harris, when an editor rejects his writing, the reason is that

    a. the writing isn't good enough or it isn't what the editor wants.
    b. the subject is uninteresting.
    c. the editor is stupid and racist.
    d. he is an unproven writer and, therefore, editors won't take a chance on his work.

_____ **4.** When the insurance salesman made a supposedly humorous racial joke, Harris pretended he was

    a. deaf.
    b. angry.
    c. amused.
    d. African.

_____ **5.** Harris's intention in responding to the joke as he did was

    a. to make the agent realize how offensive his joke was without threatening him and causing the situation to escalate.
    b. to show the agent how dangerous it is to tell racist jokes.
    c. to allow the agent to save face and to avoid being humiliated in front of his friends.
    d. to make the agent look foolish in front of his friends and the diner's other patrons.

_____ **6.** Harris eventually looks upon the insurance agent with

    a. contempt.
    b. compassion.
    c. indifference.
    d. fear.

COMPREHENSION SCORE

Score your answers for Exercises A and B as follows:

A. No. right _____ × 2 = _____
B. No. right _____ × 1 = _____
Total points from A and B _____ × 10 = _____ percent

You may refer to the selection as you work through the remaining exercises.

C. IDENTIFYING SUPPORTING DETAILS

For each main idea stated here, find a detail in the essay that supports it.

1. "I promised myself that I would not make race an issue out here."
   [paragraph 2] _____

   _____

2. "Racist thinking has its origin in these common practices." [paragraph 28]

   _____

D. INTERPRETING MEANING

Where appropriate, write your answers to these questions in your own words.

1. From what Harris writes in paragraphs 1–5, what *is* his attitude? _____

   _____

   _____

2. In paragraph 2, what is Harris referring to with the phrase "a little something

   extra out here"? _____

3. In paragraph 7, why does Harris say that he makes an exception for idiots

   screaming from passing cars? _____

   _____

4. In paragraph 5, Harris begins to quote an old saying, "If a tree falls in the
   forest. . . . " This quotation usually ends with the question, "Does it make
   a sound"? How does this old question relate to Harris's thinking about

   bigotry? _____

5. In choosing not to get angry over the joke, what, in essence, has Harris ac
   complished? (See paragraph 19.) _____

   _____

   _____

6. Explain what Harris means in the first sentence of paragraph 43. _____

   _____

   _____

7. Why does the insurance agent tell Harris about the Philadelphia woman's

   secret love for Raoul? _____

E. UNDERSTANDING VOCABULARY

Choose the best definition according to an analysis of word parts or the context.

_____ 1. The waves are *meek* [paragraph 1]:
- **a.** small
- **b.** quiet
- **c.** dangerous
- **d.** huge

_____ 2. hadn't experienced *bigotry* [2]:
- **a.** hatred
- **b.** incompetence
- **c.** intolerance
- **d.** a wide range of emotions

_____ 3. The *converse* is true [2]:
- **a.** principle
- **b.** opposite
- **c.** observation
- **d.** remark

_____ 4. any *undue* attention [14]:
- **a.** excessive, improper
- **b.** easily observed
- **c.** unwelcome, unwanted
- **d.** hostile, resentful

_____ 5. a *quizzical* expression [23]:
- **a.** relaxed
- **b.** disturbed
- **c.** puzzling
- **d.** teasing

_____ 6. eroded into a *fiasco* [29]:
- **a.** tragedy
- **b.** complete failure
- **c.** free-for-all, violent altercation
- **d.** humiliating defeat

_____ 7. the *stint* he served [36]:
- **a.** a limited period of time
- **b.** punishment
- **c.** an unhappy period
- **d.** time of confinement

_____ 8. a little *apprehensive* [42]:
- **a.** unconcerned
- **b.** somber
- **c.** sincere
- **d.** uneasy

F. USING VOCABULARY

Write the correct inflected form of the base word in each of the following sentences. Be sure to add the appropriate ending to fit the grammatical requirements of the sentence. Refer to your dictionary if necessary.

1. (*enlightenment*—use a verb) Harris writes that his girlfriend tried to

    _____ him about his odd ideas about race.

2. (*naive*—use an adverb) Harris _____ thought that he had not experienced much bigotry in his life.

3. (*arrogance*—use an adverb) The insurance salesman could not react angrily or

    _____ when Harris responded to his bad joke in a nonthreatening way.

4. (*compassion*—use an adjective) After hearing the salesman's story, Harris

    actually began to feel _____ toward him.

5. (*contempt*—use an adjective) Before he heard the salesman's life story, Harris

    felt _____ about his stereotyped thinking.

G. TOPICS FOR WRITING OR DISCUSSION

1. What are some other ways Harris could have reacted to the insurance agent's joke? What would have been the likely result?
2. Write a short essay examining a situation in which you or someone you know was being treated unjustly. Examine the motivation, the reaction, and the outcome. Compare that situation to the one Harris describes in this essay.

For Further Exploration

BOOKS

- Mark Twain, *Life on the Mississippi* (1883). Twain's classic book details the author's experiences as a Mississippi riverboat captain.
- Eddy L. Harris, *Native Stranger: A Black Man's Journey into the Heart of Africa* (1992). Harris's second book is a nonfiction account of an extensive trip he made through Africa, recording his impressions of the continent through the eyes of an African American.

MOVIE

Deliverance (1972) is a classic film based on James Dickey's novel of the same name. Directed by John Boorman and starring Jon Voight and Burt Reynolds, it tells the story of four men on a weekend canoe trip and the terrible fate that befalls them.

WEB SITES

These sites offer information on sports, particularly river sports, and adventure travel:

- *www.gorp.com*
- *www.canoekayak.about.com*
- *www.amrivers.org*

7 ANDRE DUBUS

Digging

Andre Dubus was an American writer who published nine books of fiction before his death in 1999. His writing received many awards, including the prestigious PEN/Malamud Award and an award from the American Academy of Arts and Letters. "Digging" is a coming-of-age essay in which Dubus recounts a summer job in Lafayette, Louisiana, performing hard manual labor. The essay was included in The Art of the Essay: The Best of 1999, *edited by Phillip Lopate.*

Vocabulary Preview

WORD HISTORIES

Marvel [paragraph 22]   Toward the end of the essay, Dubus recalls finishing the trench he had dug with his fellow workers. He writes, "I was part of the trench, it was part of me," and after it was finished he says that they should have gathered to "marvel at what we had made." The verb *marvel* means "to become filled with wonder." It can also be used as a noun. It comes from the Middle English word *marvail,* in turn from the Latin root *miribilia* or "wonderful things." *Mirus* ("wonderful") is also the source of the English words *mirage* and *miracle.*

Cajun [paragraph 9]   Dubus worked with a Cajun carpenter. The Cajuns, who inhabit the bayous of southern Louisiana, are the descendants of people who emigrated from Acadia, an area in eastern Canada and Maine originally inhabited by people of French descent. Thus, the word *Cajun* is an alteration of "Acadian." When they migrated to Louisiana, many intermarried with whites, blacks, and Indians. Today, the Cajuns of southern Louisiana retain their own distinctive dialect, music (especially zydeco), and food.

WORD PARTS

Trans- [paragraphs 3 and 23]   This essay contains two words with the Latin prefix *trans-: transgressions* and *transferred. Trans-* means "over" or "across" before the root it precedes. A *transgression* is a violation of a law or rule, derived from *trans- + gradi-* ("to step" or "to go"). *Transfer* means "to shift something from one person to another," from *trans- + ferre* ("to bear" or "to carry"). What is the meaning of these words?

transcontinental   _____

transmit   _____

transport   _____

transcribe   _____

**WORD
FAMILIES**

Provoke [paragraph 3]   Dubus writes that many of his friends "quarreled with their fathers, provoked them." *Provoke,* meaning "to cause or incite anger in," comes from the Latin word parts *pro-* ("forth") + *vocare* ("to call") from *vox* ("voice"). English has a large number of words in the family of words derived from these two companion roots. Here are a few:

vocal	outspoken
vocation	one's career or occupation; in other words, one's "calling"
vociferous	making an outcry, speaking loudly and strongly

What is the meaning of these two words?

advocate   _____

revoke   _____

ANDRE DUBUS

Digging

1   That hot June in Lafayette, Louisiana, I was sixteen, I would be seventeen in August, I weighed 105 pounds, and my ruddy, broad-chested father wanted me to have a summer job. I only wanted the dollar allowance he gave me each week, and the dollar and a quarter I earned caddying for him on weekend and Wednesday afternoons. With a quarter I could go to a movie, or buy a bottle of beer, or a pack of cigarettes to smoke secretly. I did not have a girlfriend, so I did not have to buy drinks or food or movie tickets for anyone else. I did not want to work. I wanted to drive around with my friends, or walk with them downtown, to stand in front of the department store, comb our ducktails, talk, look at girls.

2   My father was a civil engineer, and the district manager for the Gulf States Utilities Company. He had been working for them since he left college, beginning as a surveyor, wearing boots and khakis and, in a holster on his belt, a twenty-two caliber pistol for cottonmouths. At home he was quiet; in the evenings he sat in his easy chair, and smoked, and read: *Time, The Saturday Evening Post, Collier's, The Reader's Digest,* detective novels, books about golf, and Book-of-the-Month Club novels. He loved to talk, and he did this at parties I listened to from my bedroom, and with his friends on the golf course, and drinking in the clubhouse after playing eighteen holes. I listened to more of my father's conversations about politics and golf and his life and the world than I ever engaged in, during the nearly twenty-two years I lived with him. I was afraid of angering him, seeing his blue eyes, and reddening face, hearing the words he would use to rebuke me; but what I feared most was his voice, suddenly and harshly rising. He never yelled for long, only a few sentences, but they emptied me, as if his voice had pulled my soul from my body. His voice seemed to empty the house, too, and, when he stopped yelling, the house filled with silence. He did not yell often. That sound was not part of our family life. The fear of it was part of my love for him.

3 I was shy with him. Since my forties I have believed that he was shy with me too, and I hope it was not as painful for him as it was for me. I think my shyness had very little to do with my fear. Other boys had fathers who yelled longer and more often, fathers who spanked them or, when they were in their teens, slapped or punched them. My father spanked me only three times, probably because he did not know of most of my transgressions. My friends with harsher fathers were neither afraid nor shy; they quarreled with their fathers, provoked them. My father sired a sensitive boy, easily hurt or frightened, and he worried about me; I knew he did when I was a boy, and he told me this on his deathbed, when I was a Marine captain.

4 My imagination gave me a dual life: I lived in my body, and at the same time lived a life no one could see. All my life I have told myself stories, and have talked in my mind to friends. Imagine my father sitting at supper with my mother and two older sisters and me: I am ten and small and appear distracted. Every year at school there is a bully, sometimes a new one, sometimes the one from the year before. I draw bullies to me, not because I am small, but because they know I will neither fight nor inform on them. I will take their pushes or pinches or punches, and try not to cry, and I will pretend I am not hurt. My father does not know this. He only sees me at supper, and I am not there. I am riding a horse and shooting bad men. My father eats, glances at me. I know he is trying to see who I am, who I will be.

5 Before my teens, he took me to professional wrestling matches because I wanted to go; he told me they were fake, and I did not believe him. We listened to championship boxing matches on the radio. When I was not old enough to fire a shotgun he took me dove hunting with his friends: we crouched in a ditch facing a field, and I watched the doves fly toward us and my father rising to shoot, then I ran to fetch the warm, dead and delicious birds. In summer he took me fishing with his friends; we walked in woods to creeks and bayous and fished with bamboo poles. When I was ten he learned to play golf and stopped hunting and fishing, and on weekends I was his caddy. I did not want to be, I wanted to play with my friends, but when I became a man and left home, I was grateful that I had spent those afternoons watching him, listening to him. A minor league baseball team made our town its home, and my father took me to games, usually with my mother. When I was twelve or so, he taught me to play golf, and sometimes I played nine holes with him; more often and more comfortably, I played with other boys.

6 If my father and I were not watching or listening to something and responding to it, or were not doing something, but were simply alone together, I could not talk, and he did not, and I felt that I should, and I was ashamed. That June of my seventeenth year, I could not tell him that I did not want a job. He talked to a friend of his, a building contractor, who hired me as a carpenter's helper; my pay was seventy-five cents an hour.

7 On a Monday morning my father drove me to work. I would ride the bus home and, next day, would start riding the bus to work. Probably my father drove me that morning because it was my first day; when I was twelve he had taken me to a store to buy my first pair of long pants; we boys wore shorts and, in fall and winter, knickers and long socks till we were twelve; and he had taken

me to a barber for my first haircut. In the car I sat frightened, sadly resigned, and feeling absolutely incompetent. I had the lunch my mother had put in a brown paper bag, along with a mason jar with sugar and squeezed lemons in it, so I could make lemonade with water from the cooler. We drove to a street with houses and small stores and parked at a corner where, on a flat piece of land, men were busy. They were building a liquor store, and I assumed I would spend my summer handing things to a carpenter. I hoped he would be patient and kind.

8   As a boy in Louisiana's benevolent winters and hot summers I had played out-doors with friends: we built a clubhouse, chased each other on bicycles, shot air rifles at birds, tin cans, bottles, trees; in fall and winter, wearing shoulder pads and helmets, we played football on someone's very large side lawn; and in sum-mer we played baseball in a field that a father mowed for us; he also built us a backstop of wood and chicken wire. None of us played well enough to be on a varsity team; but I wanted that gift, not knowing that it was a gift, and I felt ashamed that I did not have it. Now we drove cars, smoked, drank in nightclubs. This was French Catholic country; we could always buy drinks. Sometimes we went on dates with girls, but more often looked at them and talked about them; or visited them, when several girls were gathered at the home of a girl whose parents were out for the evening. I had never done physical work except caddy-ing, pushing a lawn mower, and raking leaves, and I was walking from the car with my father toward working men. My father wore his straw hat and seer-sucker suit. He introduced me to the foreman and said: "Make a man of him."

9   Then he left. The foreman wore a straw hat and looked old; everyone looked old; the foreman was probably thirty-five. I stood mutely, waiting for him to as-sign me to some good-hearted Cajun carpenter. He assigned me a pickaxe and a shovel and told me to get into the trench and go to work. In all four sides of the trench were files of black men, swinging picks, and shoveling. The trench was about three feet deep and it would be the building's foundation; I went to where the foreman pointed, and laid my tools on the ground; two black men made a space for me, and I jumped between them. They smiled and we greeted each other. I would learn days later that they earned a dollar an hour. They were men with families and I knew this was unjust, as everything else was for black peo-ple. But on that first morning I did not know what they were being paid. I did not know their names, only that one was working behind me and one in front, and they were good to me and stronger than I could ever be. All I really knew in those first hours under the hot sun was raising the pickaxe and swinging it down, raising it and swinging, again and again till the earth was loose; then putting the pick on the ground beside me and taking the shovel and plunging it into dirt that I lifted and tossed beside the trench.

10   I did not have the strength for this: not in my back, my legs, my arms, my shoulders. Certainly not in my soul. I only wanted it to end. The air was very humid, and sweat dripped on my face and arms, soaked my shirts and jeans. My hands gripping the pick or shovel were sore, my palms burned, the muscles in my arms ached, and my breath was quick. Sometimes I saw tiny black spots before my eyes. Weakly I raised the pick, straightening my back, then swung it down, bending my body with it, and it felt heavier than I was, more durable, this thing of wood and steel that was melting me. I laid it on the ground and

picked up the shovel and pushed it into the dirt, lifted it, grunted, and emptied it beside the trench. The sun, always my friend till now, burned me, and my mouth and throat were dry, and often I climbed out of the trench and went to the large tin water cooler with a block of ice in it and water from a hose. At the cooler were paper cups and salt tablets, and I swallowed salt and drank and drank, and poured water onto my head and face; then I went back to the trench, the shovel, the pick.

11   Nausea came in the third or fourth hour. I kept swinging the pick, pushing and lifting the shovel. I became my sick and hot and tired and hurting flesh. Or it became me; so, for an hour or more, I tasted a very small piece of despair. At noon in Lafayette a loud whistle blew, and in the cathedral the bell rang. I could not hear the bell where we worked, but I heard the whistle, and lowered the shovel and looked around. I was dizzy and sick. All the men had stopped working and were walking toward shade. One of the men with me said it was time to eat, and I climbed out of the trench and walked with black men to the shade of the tool shed. The white men went to another shaded place; I do not remember what work they had been doing that morning, but it was not with picks and shovels in the trench. Everyone looked hot but comfortable. The black men sat talking and began to eat and drink. My bag of lunch and jar with lemons and sugar were on the ground in the shade. Still I stood, gripped by nausea. I looked at the black men and at my lunch bag. Then my stomach tightened and everything in it rose, and I went around the corner of the shed where no one could see me and, bending over, I vomited and moaned and heaved until it ended. I went to the water cooler and rinsed my mouth and spat, and then I took another paper cup and drank. I walked back to the shade and lay on my back, tasting vomit. One of the black men said: "You got to eat."

12   "I threw up," I said, and closed my eyes and slept for the rest of the hour that everyone—students and workers—had for the noon meal. At home my nineteen-year-old sister and my mother and father were eating dinner, meat and rice and gravy, vegetables and salad and iced tea with a leaf of mint; and an oscillating fan cooled them. My twenty-two-year-old sister was married. At one o'clock the whistle blew, and I woke up and stood and one of the black men said: "Are you all right?"

13   I nodded. If I had spoken, I may have wept. When I was a boy I could not tell a man what I felt, if I believed what I felt was unmanly. We went back to the trench, down into it, and I picked up the shovel I had left there at noon, and shoveled out all the loose earth between me and the man in front of me, then put the shovel beside the trench, lifted the pick, raised it over my shoulder, and swung it down into the dirt. I was dizzy and weak and hot; I worked for forty minutes or so; then, above me, I heard my father's voice, speaking my name. I looked up at him; he was here to take me home, to forgive my failure, and in my great relief I could not know that I would not be able to forgive it. I was going home. But he said: "Let's go buy you a hat."

14   Every man there wore a hat, most of them straw, the others baseball caps. I said nothing. I climbed out of the trench, and went with my father. In the car, in a voice softened with pride, he said: "The foreman called me. He said the Nigras told him you threw up, and didn't eat, and you didn't tell him."

15   "That's right," I said, and shamefully watched the road, and cars with people who seemed free of all torment, and let my father believe I was brave, because I was afraid to tell him that I was afraid to tell the foreman. Quietly we drove to town and he parked and took me first to a drugstore with air-conditioning and a lunch counter, and bought me a 7-Up for my stomach, and told me to order a sandwich. Sweet-smelling women at the counter were smoking. The men in the trench had smoked while they worked, but my body's only desire had been to stop shoveling and swinging the pick, to be with no transition at all in the shower at home, then to lie on my bed, feeling the soft breath of the fan on my damp skin. I would not have smoked at work anyway, with men. Now I wanted a cigarette. My father smoked, and I ate a bacon and lettuce and tomato sandwich.

16   Then we walked outside, into humidity and the heat and glare of the sun. We crossed the street to the department store where, in the work clothes section, my father chose a pith helmet. I did not want to wear a pith helmet. I would happily wear one in Africa, hunting lions and rhinoceroses. But I did not want to wear such a thing in Lafayette. I said nothing; there was no hat I wanted to wear. I carried the helmet in its bag out of the store and, in the car, laid it beside me. At that place where sweating men worked, I put it on; a thin leather strap looped around the back of my head. I went to my two comrades in the trench. One of them said: "That's a good hat."

17   I jumped in.

18   The man behind me said: "You going to be all right now."

19   I was; and I still do not know why. A sandwich and a soft drink had not given me any more strength than the breakfast I had vomited. An hour's respite in the car and the cool drugstore and buying the helmet that now was keeping my wet head cool certainly helped. But I had the same soft arms and legs, the same back and shoulders I had demanded so little of in my nearly seventeen years of stewardship. Yet all I remember of that afternoon is the absence of nausea.

20   At five o'clock the whistle blew downtown and we climbed out of the trench and washed our tools with the hose, then put them in the shed. Dirt was on my arms and hands, my face and neck and clothes. I could have wrung sweat from my shirt and jeans. I got my lunch from the shade. My two comrades said, See you tomorrow. I said I would see them. I went to the bus stop at the corner and sat on the bench. My wet clothes cooled my skin. I looked down at my dirty tennis shoes; my socks and feet were wet. I watched people in passing cars. In one were teenaged boys, and they laughed and shouted something about my helmet. I watched the car till it was blocks away, then took off the helmet and held it on my lap. I carried it aboard the bus; yet all summer I wore it at work, maybe because my father bought it for me and I did not want to hurt him, maybe because it was a wonderful helmet for hard work outdoors in Louisiana.

21   My father got home before I did and told my mother and sister the story, the only one he knew, or the only one I assumed he knew. The women proudly greeted me when I walked into the house. They were also worried. They wanted to know how I felt. They wore dresses, they smelled of perfume or cologne, they were drinking bourbon and water, and my sister and father were smoking cigarettes. Standing in the living room, holding my lunch and helmet, I said I was

fine. I could not tell the truth to these women who loved me, even if my father were not there. I could not say that I was not strong enough and that I could not bear going back to work tomorrow, and all summer, anymore than I could tell them I did not believe I was as good at being a boy as other boys were: not at sports, or with girls; and now not with a man's work. I was home, where vases held flowers, and things were clean, and our manners were good.

22   Next morning, carrying my helmet and lunch, I rode the bus to work and joined the two black men in the trench. I felt that we were friends. Soon I felt this about all the black men at work. We were digging the foundation; we were the men and the boy with picks and shovels in the trench. One day the foundation was done. I use the passive voice, because this was a square or rectangular trench, men were working at each of its sides. I had been working with my comrades on the same side for weeks, moving not forward but down. Then it was done. Someone told us. Maybe the contractor was there, with the foreman. Who dug out that last bit of dirt? I only knew that I had worked as hard as I could, I was part of the trench, it was part of me, and it was finished; it was there in the earth to receive concrete and probably never to be seen again. Someone should have blown a bugle, we should have climbed exultant from the trench, gathered to wipe sweat from our brows, drink water, shake hands, then walk together to each of the four sides and marvel at what we had made.

23   On that second morning of work I was not sick, and at noon I ate lunch with the blacks in the shade, then we all slept on the grass till one o'clock. We worked till five, said goodbye to each other, and they went to the colored section of town, and I rode the bus home. When I walked into the living room, into cocktail hour, and my family asked me about my day, I said it was fine. I may have learned something if I had told them the truth: the work was too hard, but after the first morning I could bear it. And all summer it would be hard; after we finished the foundation, I would be transferred to another crew. We would build a mess hall at a Boy Scout camp and, with a black man, I would dig a septic tank in clay so hard that the foreman kept hosing water into it as we dug; black men and I would push wheelbarrows of mixed cement; on my shoulder I would carry eighty-five pound bags of dry cement, twenty-five pounds less than my own weight; and at the summer's end my body would be twenty pounds heavier. If I had told these three people who loved me that I did not understand my weak body's stamina, they may have taught me why something terrible had so quickly changed to something arduous.

24   It is time to thank my father for wanting me to work and telling me I had to work and getting the job for me and buying me lunch and a pith helmet instead of taking me home to my mother and sister. He may have wanted to take me home. But he knew he must not, and he came tenderly to me. My mother would have been at home that afternoon; if he had taken me to her she would have given me iced tea and, after my shower, a hot dinner. When my sister came home from work, she would have understood, and told me not to despise myself because I could not work with a pickaxe and a shovel. And I would have spent the summer at home, nestled in the love of the two women, peering at my father's face, and yearning to be someone I respected, a varsity second baseman, a halfback, someone cheerleaders and drum majorettes and pretty scholars

loved; yearning to be a man among men, and that is where my father sent me
with a helmet on my head. ✱

Exercises

Do not refer to the selection for Exercises A and B unless your instructor directs
you to do so.

A. DETERMINING THE MAIN IDEA AND PURPOSE

Choose the best answer.

_____ 1. The main idea of the selection is that

    a. working at a difficult summer job is essential for all teenagers.

    b. the writer's father and mother had different ideas about how to
raise their son.

    c. the writer's coworkers taught him a great deal about race rela-
tions.

    d. working at a difficult summer job taught the writer an important
lesson about adulthood.

_____ 2. The writer's purpose in telling the story of his first summer job
experience is to

    a. show how his first job taught him to become a man.

    b. criticize his father's decision to make him work.

    c. argue the merits of doing manual labor.

    d. explain how he learned to cope with life's difficulties.

B. COMPREHENDING MAIN IDEAS

Choose the correct answer.

_____ 1. Dubus writes that his feelings toward his father were complicated,
a mixture of

    a. love and fear.

    b. respect and terror.

    c. love and hate.

    d. anger and a desire to please.

_____ 2. As an adolescent Dubus writes that he lived a dual life, as himself
in his body and as

    a. the characters in the movies he saw.

    b. the characters in the books he read.

    c. characters in stories from his imagination.

    d. his friends whose lives he envied.

_____ 3. When Dubus's father introduced his son on the first day to the job foreman, he told the foreman,

    a. "Don't work him too hard."
    b. "Teach him everything you know."
    c. "Don't let him get away with anything."
    d. "Make a man of him."

_____ 4. Of the black men with whom Dubus worked, he says that they were strong

    a. and very kind to him.
    b. and glad to have steady work.
    c. yet bitter over their low pay.
    d. yet resigned to their hard lives.

_____ 5. Concerning his first day on the job, which of these did the writer _not_ complain about?

    a. his lack of strength to do the job.
    b. the backbreaking demands of the job.
    c. the sun and high humidity.
    d. his low pay compared to what other workers earned.

_____ 6. At the end of the essay, Dubus looks back at this summer and thanks his father for getting him the job, buying him a helmet, and _not_

    a. taking him home to his mother and sister.
    b. embarrassing him in front of his friends.
    c. criticizing him for his lack of strength.
    d. teaching him to despise himself.

COMPREHENSION SCORE

Score your answers for Exercises A and B as follows:

A. No. right _____ × 2 = _____
B. No. right _____ × 1 = _____
Total points from A and B _____ × 10 = _____ percent

You may refer to the selection as you work through the remaining exercises.

C. LOCATING SUPPORTING DETAILS

For the following main idea, which is implied rather than stated, find and write down two supporting details.

Although he never talked about it, the writer had a difficult time at school.

1. _____

2. _____

D. INTERPRETING MEANING

Write your answers to these questions in your own words.

1. How would you describe Dubus's family life, his relationship with his
   mother, sister, and father? (See in particular paragraphs 2, 3, and 30.) _____

   _____

   _____

   _____

2. In paragraph 8, Dubus writes of his wish to play well enough to be on a varsity team but that he did not know that "it was a gift." What does this mean?

   _____

   _____

3. Besides improving his physical endurance, what are two other lessons that
   Dubus learned from his summer job doing manual labor? _____

   _____

E. UNDERSTANDING VOCABULARY

Choose the best definition according to an analysis of word parts or the context.

_____ 1. my *ruddy*, broad-chested father [paragraph 1]:
   a. red-faced
   b. hot-tempered
   c. kindhearted
   d. athletic

_____ 2. words he would use to *rebuke* me [2]:
   a. offer praise to
   b. give suggestions and advice to
   c. sharply criticize
   d. belittle, put down

_____ 3. most of my *transgressions* [3]:
   a. hopes and dreams
   b. violations of rules
   c. secret desires
   d. criminal acts

_____ 4. in Louisiana's *benevolent* winters [8]:
   a. bitterly cold
   b. undistinguished, ordinary
   c. long, drawn-out
   d. kind, not harsh

_____ **5.** we should have climbed *exultant* [22]:

  a. joyful, triumphant
  b. fatigued, worn out
  c. bitter, resentful
  d. relieved, thankful

_____ **6.** changed to something *arduous* [24]:

  a. valuable, worthwhile
  b. demanding great effort
  c. requiring bravery
  d. demeaning, belittling

F. USING VOCABULARY

In parentheses before each sentence are some inflected forms of words from the selection. Study the context and the sentence. Then write the correct form in the space provided.

1. (*provocation, provoked, provoking, provokingly*) Dubus writes that some of his

friends enjoyed engaging in _____ with their fathers.

2. (*incompetence, incompetent, incompetently*) Before starting his first day of work,

the writer recognized that his _____ would make his work
harder.

3. (*torment, tormented, tormenting, tormentingly*) Rather than admit that the first

day of work was _____ for the writer, he hid his true feelings
from his father.

4. (*exultation, exult, exulted, exultant, exultantly*) On the day when the trench was
finally completed, Dubus writes that he and his coworkers should have

_____ stepped out of the trench and marveled at their
accomplishment.

G. TOPICS FOR WRITING OR DISCUSSION

1. Dubus represents an earlier generation. Do you think his experience—the way his father taught him to "be a man among men"—would be considered unusual in contemporary America? If so, how are boys taught to be men and girls to be women?

2. Read Selection 18 by Nelson Mandela, "Long Walk to Freedom," on pages 276–281. How do the cultures of North America and of the Xhosa in South Africa differ, specifically in the ways boys are initiated into manhood?

3. Write a short essay in which you describe a situation where an older person—a relative, a teacher, a mentor, a friend—taught you something important about what it means to become an adult.

For Further Exploration

BOOK

Studs Terkel, *Working: People Talk About What They Do All Day and How They Feel About What They Do* (1974). Compiled from interviews with hundreds of Americans in the 1970s, Terkel offers profiles of workers at every level of society: why they chose their occupations, the satisfactions they get from their jobs, and the changes they would like to make in their lives.

MOVIE

Roger & Me (1989) is an offbeat, tragicomic, documentary-style movie showing the effect on assembly-line workers when General Motors closed several plants in Flint, Michigan. Directed by and starring Michael Moore, the movie revolves around his attempts to gain access to Roger Smith, then-chairman of GM, to show him how Flint fared after the loss of 40,000 jobs. It is simultaneously funny and tragic.

WEB SITES

Here is a list of top-rated job-search Web sites as recommended by *Yahoo! Internet Life* magazine in May 2002:

- *www.monster.com*
- *www.dice.com*
- *www.vault.com*
- *www.hotjobs.com*
- *www.careers.yahoo.com*
- *www.wantedjobs.com*

Annotating, Paraphrasing, and Summarizing

The skills you will learn in Part 2 follow directly from the work you did in Part 1—finding main ideas and locating supporting details. The three skills you will learn here—annotating, paraphrasing, and summarizing—are not only extraordinarily useful for college students but also for anyone who must understand, absorb, remember, and condense information from the printed page. What are these three skills?

- **Annotating**   A study and comprehension skill, includes:
Writing notes in the margin of a text, circling words you don't know, noting questions, and otherwise interacting with the text
- **Paraphrasing**   A comprehension and writing skill, includes:
Putting a writer's words into your own words without leaving anything important out, similar to translating
- **Summarizing**   A comprehension and writing skill, includes:
Condensing a writer's words by identifying only the main points and omitting unimportant supporting details

What is the relationship among these three skills? Annotating is the first step to writing a successful summary; paraphrasing is also required to produce a good summary. Paraphrasing and summarizing show you and your instructor how well you have understood what you read.

Annotating

More often than not, my students complain about having a bad memory because they claim not to remember a lot of what they read. But I think that one source of this problem lies elsewhere. The culprit is not a bad memory; it's *passive reading.* Rather than being actively involved with the print on the page, a passive reader reads the material once and unwisely thinks that he or she can get the full meaning without doing the hard work that good comprehension requires.

It's almost impossible for a reader—even a very experienced reader—to get the full meaning and to remember what's important when reading a selection for the first time. (I am referring here specifically to your college reading assignments, where good comprehension is required, not to the kind of casual reading you do in popular magazines or the daily paper.) The cure for this kind of bad memory is simple: *annotate the text,* or, in other words, write notes in the margins.

You already have seen this process demonstrated in the introduction to Part 1, where you identified main and supporting ideas. This next section explains and demonstrates the process of annotating in more detail. Throughout the text, you will have many opportunities to practice this skill, and your instructor may require you to practice annotation beyond the exercises in this book.

HOW TO ANNOTATE

Annotating is sometimes called reading with a pencil in your hand. (And using a pencil is a good idea, so that you can erase your notes later, if you want to.) Annotating is not the same as highlighting or underlining words with a neon-yellow or -pink marker. Many students rely on such markers as a study aid when they read textbooks; most reading instructors, however, discourage this practice because such marks only delay learning. Marking your text only tells you that the material is important to learn—some day! And my students tell me that they are uncertain what to highlight and so end up highlighting almost everything. Moreover, highlighting is a *passive* activity. Careful annotating, in contrast, allows you both to read *actively* and to pull out the essential ideas at the same time. What makes for good annotating? Here are some suggestions:

TECHNIQUES FOR ANNOTATING	
• **Main ideas**	Jot down brief phrases in your own words restating the main ideas
• **Phrases or sentences you don't understand**	Place a question mark in the margin
• **Unfamiliar vocabulary words**	Circle them in the text
• **Questions to ask in class**	Write in the margin and mark with a clear symbol
• **Ideas you disagree with**	Place a star or some other symbol in the margin

To illustrate this process, consider a brief excerpt from a selection that appears in Part 2, Sheldon Campbell's "Games Elephants Play" and the sample annotations. First, read the passage; then study the annotations.

Elephants—very intelligent; live in well-organized matriarchies.

Who was Dinesen?

Captive elephants show intelligence by learning complicated, difficult tasks.

Elephants, female elephants that is, are seen by most zoo visitors as simple, lovable creatures, given to making loud trumpeting noises, tossing dirt onto their backs, addicted to joyous, splashing baths, and cadging peanuts or other goodies by reaching out with their trunks. That picture, as far as it goes, is reasonably accurate. But elephants are not simpletons. Field studies have shown them to be highly intelligent creatures that ordinarily live in well-organized matriarchies, sometimes leisurely browsing, sometimes pacing across a savannah in a deceptively fast and soundless gait as though, in a memorable line from Isak Dinesen, they had "an appointment at the end of the world."

In captivity, elephants best display their great intelligence in shows of various types, rapidly learning complex tasks where it seems the trainer is constantly at risk and never harmed, or in the heavy, often difficult tasks they

They're mischievous.

Stories about long memory—probably exaggerated.

May hold a grudge.

Are there any women elephant trainers?

Relationship between elephant and trainer can be affectionate.

Trainers know to be on guard.

Elephants like to test trainers.

Games—like "squash" (doubles or singles) establish animal's dominance.

perform in India, Bangladesh, Sri Lanka, and Thailand. But elephants have a devilish side. One of the oldest bits of conventional wisdom about them is that they have long memories, and while many of the stories about elephants killing men who as small boys put a hot chestnut or peppercorns in their trunks are exaggerated, some elephants do hold grudges against people who have hurt them, or whom for some reason they dislike.

Captive elephants frequently develop great affection for a particular trainer or keeper, but experienced elephant men, who may feel reciprocal affection for their animals, nonetheless know that they must be on their toes around even an affectionate elephant. For elephants play various games to test their keepers. An elephant may use its trunk, that marvelously intricate instrument with one or two fingers at the end, either as a lasso or straight-arm to pull a careless keeper down or punch him to the ground, methods which overwhelmingly demonstrate the elephant's dominance. Another popular game, which might be best described as "squash," though it bears no resemblance to the human sport of that name, can be played by one elephant with a keeper and a wall or in the doubles version by two elephants and a keeper. In the first version the elephant's objective is to sidle around in an innocent and sly way until it traps the keeper between it and the wall. The elephant wins if it can lean against the wall with the keeper in between. In the more difficult doubles version two elephants maneuver until they can trap a keeper between them. Then they lean together and voilà, the keeper becomes meat in a sandwich. . . .

Here is a short excerpt from the same selection for you to practice with. Use the marking suggestions above (see the box on page 124), or try out your own system.

Elephants may also, if they get the opportunity, play little games with unwary visitors. One kindhearted lady who was trying to feed an elephant at the San Diego Zoo made the mistake of holding her purse and the peanut in the hand she stretched out across the moat, while she clung to a no feeding sign with the other. Instead of taking the peanut the elephant grabbed the purse, which in the process fell open. The elephant then turned the purse upside down and emptied its contents on the ground. For the next several moments, while the formerly kindhearted lady watched helplessly, the elephant picked up all the objects one by one—lipstick, car keys, comb, compact, hair curlers, coin holder, wallet, and ballpoint pen—that were in the purse. Eventually the purse and its contents were rescued, but not quite in the shape they had been before the elephant got them.

While female elephants, even those that play games, are generally friendly and affable and in the Asian species fairly easy to handle and train, male elephants are a different story. Among both circus and zoo people legend holds that for every captive bull elephant a keeper has been killed. The truth is that several keepers have been gored or trampled to death by bulls during the animals' "musth,"[1] when for periods of up to five months the males

[1]Sometimes spelled "must," this refers to a period that male elephants go through every year when they become highly aggressive and, therefore, more likely to attack.

become unpredictable, unmanageable, and possessed of superelephant strength. A human male in this condition would be called mad. Little understood, but probably related to sex drive, musth may give a bull elephant the determination, ability, and don't-give-a-damn attitude to drive off rival males and break through the largely female herds in order to mate. The condition is more pronounced in Asian elephants, but in either species it spells trouble for keepers. . . .

One final word: Keep your annotations neat and brief. You don't want to clutter up the margins with too many notes or with words that you can't read in a few weeks. Annotate only the main idea and important supporting details, not unimportant or reinforcing details.

Paraphrasing

Next, we turn to a skill that I use in all of my classes, both reading and composition courses. Paraphrasing can help students focus and read as accurately as possible. As you will recall from the introduction to this section, *paraphrasing* means restating the writer's words in your own words. Paraphrasing can be done both to test comprehension and to clarify meaning. The process requires you to go through *one sentence at a time,* rewriting and changing the words into your own words as much as possible, *without changing the meaning of the original.* That's the hard part. Also it is perfectly all right if your paraphrase turns out to be longer than the original.

HOW TO PARAPHRASE

For a successful paraphrase, consider the suggestions below:

TECHNIQUES FOR PARAPHRASING
• Substitute a synonym for key words in the original.
• An exception to the above: Don't strain to find a synonym for major words. Call an *elephant* an *elephant*, not a *pachyderm* with wrinkly gray skin.
• Omit unimportant ideas if your instructor allows.
• Reorder ideas for logical flow.
• Combine ideas when possible.
• Maintain the flavor and level of formality of the original passage.

First read this passage, which comes from Selection 9, Charles Finney's "The Life and Death of a Western Gladiator." (Crotalus is a diamondback rattlesnake.) Then study the paraphrase and compare it with the original. See if you can identify each of the four techniques from the box above.

Original Passage

During his first two years Crotalus grew
rapidly. He attained the length of two feet; his
tail had five rattles on it and its button. He
rarely bothered with lizards any more, preferring baby rabbits, chipmunks, and round-
tailed ground squirrels. Because of his slow locomotion he could not run down these agile
little things. He had to contrive instead to be
where they were when they would pass. Then
he struck swiftly, injected his poison, and ate
them after they died.

At two he was formidable. He had grown
past the stage where a racer or a road runner
could safely tackle him. He had grown to the
size where other desert dwellers—coyotes,
foxes, coatis, wildcats—knew it was better to
leave him alone. (125 words)

Paraphrase

Crotalus grew quickly for the first two years of his life, eventually
growing to 2 feet long with five rattles and a button on his tail. He
hardly ever hunted lizards any more because he was now able to
catch baby rodents like rabbits and squirrels. But he had to be in
their vicinity when they passed by if he was going to hunt them
successfully, because he moved more slowly than they did. When
he located his prey, he quickly injected his venom, and after the animal died he ate it.

By the time he was 2 years old, he was such a tough opponent
that no other animal would take him on, and he no longer had to
watch out for predators like racers or road runners. Larger desert animals like coyotes and wildcats knew not to bother him. (141 words)

_____

_____

_____

_____

_____

Now you try it. Here is an excerpt from the same selection for you to practice
with.

Original Passage

At twelve he was a magnificent reptile. Not a
single scar defaced his rippling symmetry. He
was diabolically beautiful and deadly poison.

His venom was his only weapon, for he had
no power of constriction. Yellowish in color,
his poison was colorless and tasteless. It was a
highly complex mixture of proteins, each in itself direly toxic. His venom worked on the
blood. The more poison he injected with a bite,

Paraphrase

_____

_____

_____

_____

_____

_____

_____

_____

_____

the more dangerous the wound. The pain ren-   _____

dered by his bite was instantaneous, and the   _____

shock accompanying it was profound.   _____

Swelling began immediately, to be followed by   _____

a ghastly oozing. Injected directly into a large   _____

vein, his poison brought death quickly, for the   _____

victim died when it reached his heart. (122   _____

words)   _____

Summarizing

Summarizing—the last skill—is the culmination of the other two skills. Before you can write a summary, you must first annotate the text, and you must know how to paraphrase important points. Summarizing also requires you to eliminate unimportant supporting details. The point of writing a summary is to *convey only the most important information,* so you have to develop a feel for what to save and what to drop. This process sounds harder than it really is. When one paints a room, one has to spend more time preparing the surface than actually painting it. Writing a summary is the same; it just takes good preparation and practice.

First, study the chart below that lists the techniques for summarizing. You may use them all, or you may decide that some work better than others. Before you begin, I suggest making a photocopy of the selection you are summarizing so that you can mark it up easily.

TECHNIQUES FOR SUMMARIZING

- Read the selection and circle unfamiliar words.
- Read the selection again; annotate it and look up circled words.
- Underline important phrases and sentences, and cross out unimportant material.
- Copy the notes from your margins onto a piece of paper, or type them up on a computer.
- Review your notes: Add or delete information as needed.
- Rewrite the selection, condensing where you can. Substitute your own words for the author's, and add transitions to show the relationship between ideas.
- Read through your summary for accuracy and to make sure you don't introduce your own ideas or opinions.

Study this short example first, which comes from Selection 10, "The Language Explosion" by Geoffrey Cowley. Pay particular attention to the crossed out words and phrases.

Original Passage

~~The journey toward~~ language starts ~~not in the nursery but~~ in the womb, where the fetus is ~~continually~~ bathed in the sounds of its mother's voice. Babies just 4 days old can distinguish one language from another. ~~French newborns suck more vigorously when they hear French spoken than when they hear Russian—and Russian babies show the opposite preference.~~ At first, ~~they notice only~~ general rhythms and melodies. But newborns ~~are also~~ sensitive to speech sounds, ~~and they~~ home in quickly on the ones that matter. (86 words)

Summary

A baby listens to its mother's language in the womb. Even at 4 days, babies can distinguish their mother's language from another. Initially, they hear only general rhythms, but soon they focus on the sounds of their native language. (39 words)

A rule of thumb is that a summary should be about 25 percent of the original length. The sample summary above is longer than 25 percent, but that is because we are working with only a single paragraph with very few ideas to omit. In longer passages, as you will see in the next section, there will be more information to cut.

Forcing yourself to limit a summary to an arbitrary number of words is an intellectually rigorous and challenging exercise. It requires you to think about what to save and what to omit, how to keep the meaning of the original, using the fewest possible words, and how not to distort the meaning. The trick to writing a good summary is to see the difference between main ideas and supporting details. Crossing out unnecessary words and phrases, as demonstrated above, allows you more easily to see what is essential to save and what can be safely eliminated.

For further practice in summarizing, here is a miniessay from *Discover* magazine. Its subject is a strange one—monkeys that eat charcoal. The original passage is around 325 words long, so try to keep your summary between 80 and 100 words.[2]

---

[2]You can count your words manually or, in Microsoft Word, you can select "Word Count" from the "Tools" menu.

Original Passage

Summary

Monkeys in Zanzibar eat charcoal to neutralize toxins in their diet. ("A Briquette a Day," *Discover*)

The human population of Zanzibar, a Tanzanian island off the East African coast, doubles every 15 years or so. The island's red colobus monkeys, however, are dwindling as their habitats are destroyed for firewood and timber. But some monkeys have found a way to coexist with humans: they snack on charcoal.

Thomas Struhsaker, a zoologist at Duke University, has been studying the effects of selective logging on rain forest wildlife in eastern Africa. A Tanzanian biologist told him about the monkeys' charcoal habit in 1981. Over the years, as the human population grew, Struhsaker noticed that the monkeys ate more and more charcoal. "Each animal," he says, "eats about five grams a day."

The monkeys live in an area with almond, mango, and other exotic fruit trees. The leaves of these trees are rich in protein but also contain toxic compounds like tannic acids. Most animals avoid the leaves. But charcoal has a well-known ability to absorb toxins—it is used as a poison control agent, and in Europe people use it in liquid form as a digestive aid. When a monkey eats charcoal after chomping on leaves, its meal goes down a little easier. The charcoal selectively holds on to large tannic acid molecules, allowing them to pass through the body while smaller nutritious proteins are absorbed by the gut.

The monkeys snatch charcoal from kilns and also nibble on charred wood and tree stumps. Struhsaker isn't sure how they acquired the habit. "There must be a quick effect so they can learn by association," he says. Baby monkeys, at least, learn from imitating their mothers, and the mothers themselves may have learned from eating soil containing charcoal particles.

"These are pretty clever animals," says Struhsaker. "They've picked up a habit that allows them to exploit a resource to an extent that was not possible before." Despite this adaptation, red colobus populations are still shrinking in Zanzibar, even in nature reserves, where speeding cars take a large toll. "If they put the potholes back in the road, or built speed bumps, I think the reserve animals would be fine."

"A Briquette a Day," *Discover* Magazine, July 1998. Reprinted by permission.

PART TWO

Refining the Basics

8

Games Elephants Play

Until his death in 1985, Sheldon Campbell had an unusual mix of careers, working as both a teacher and a stockbroker in San Diego, California. But his real interest was animal life. For many years he was president of the San Diego Zoological Society and a trustee of the world-famous San Diego Zoo. In this latter capacity, he pioneered animal exchanges between the San Diego Zoo and the People's Republic of China and was instrumental in arranging with the Chinese for a pair of rare golden monkeys to be brought to the zoo in 1984. This selection comes from his collection of zoo stories, Lifeboats to Ararat.

Vocabulary Preview

WORD HISTORIES

Apocryphal [paragraph 6]   Campbell relates an *apocryphal* story, a variant of the fable, "Appointment in Samarra." An *apocryphal* story is one that may or may not be true. It derives from the *Apocrypha,* fourteen books included in the Old Testament. Protestants and Catholics do not consider them authentic because they were not part of the original Hebrew scriptures. The word's origin is from the Greek verb, *apokruptein* ("to hide away").

Alpha [paragraph 7]   A male elephant named Tembo, a resident of the Hanover Zoo, obeyed orders only from his *alpha* keeper, so-called because he easily dominated the animals in his care. *Alpha,* the first letter in the Greek alphabet, also means "first" or "beginning." An alpha keeper, then, refers to one who is first in importance. (The *beta* keeper, whom Tembo refused to obey, was second in importance.) You can easily see where the word *alphabet* came from—*alpha* and *beta* are the first two letters of the Greek alphabet.

WORD PARTS

-ly (adverb suffix)   Since Campbell uses several adverbs in this selection, perhaps this is a good place to review what adverbs are, how they are formed, and how they are used. Adverbs tell us "in what manner." An adverb's meaning is essentially the same as an adjective's, but the two parts of speech are used differently: Adverbs modify (or describe) verbs, adjectives, other adverbs, and occasionally an entire sentence; adjectives modify nouns. When you read, of course, you do not need to worry about identifying what part of speech an adverb modifies, only the word that it describes. But it's useful to get some practice identifying just what the adverb modifies.

Probably 90 percent of English adverbs are formed by adding the suffix *-ly* to an adjective root. Here are some examples of adverbs from "Games Elephants Play." In the first few examples, an arrow has been drawn indicating the word that the italicized adverb modifies.

- "In captivity elephants best display their great intelligence in shows of various types, *rapidly* learning complex acts where it seems the trainer is *constantly* at risk and never harmed." [paragraph 2]
- "Captive elephants *frequently* develop great affection for a particular trainer or keeper." [paragraph 3]
- "*Clearly,* he was laying down a statement of his *newly* assumed authority." [paragraph 10]

(Note that in this last sentence, the adverb *clearly* modifies the entire sentence rather than a single word.)

Following the examples above, draw an arrow to the word each italicized adverb modifies.

- "An elephant may use its trunk, that *marvelously* intricate instrument with one or two fingers at the end . . . , methods which *overwhelmingly* demonstrate the elephant's dominance." [paragraph 3]
- "For the next several moments, while the *formerly* kindhearted lady watched *helplessly*. . . ." [paragraph 4]
- "*Consequently* . . . the elephants were always chained in the barn at night to prevent them from falling into the moat." [paragraph 9]

WORD FAMILIES   **Matriarchies [paragraph 1]**   According to Campbell, elephants live in well-organized *matriarchies*. This word combines the Latin root *matri-* ("female" or "motherhood") and the Greek root *-archy* ("rule" or "government"). So a *matriarchy* means "rule by the female members of the group." Here are some related words: *matrimony, maternal,* and *matricide* ("killing of a mother"). What is a *matrilineal* society?_____

SHELDON CAMPBELL

Games Elephants Play

1   Elephants, female elephants that is, are seen by most zoo visitors as simple, lovable creatures, given to making loud trumpeting noises, tossing dirt onto their backs, addicted to joyous, splashing baths, and cadging peanuts or other goodies by reaching out with their trunks. That picture, as far as it goes, is reasonably accurate. But elephants are not simpletons. Field studies have shown them to be highly intelligent creatures that ordinarily live in well-organized matriarchies,

sometimes leisurely browsing, sometimes pacing across a savannah[1] in a deceptively fast and soundless gait as though, in a memorable line from Isak Dinesen, they had "an appointment at the end of the world."

2   In captivity elephants best display their great intelligence in shows of various types, rapidly learning complex acts where it seems the trainer is constantly at risk and never harmed, or in the heavy, often difficult tasks they perform in India, Bangladesh, Sri Lanka, and Thailand. But elephants have a devilish side. One of the oldest bits of conventional wisdom about them is that they have long memories, and while many of the stories about elephants killing men who as small boys put a hot chestnut or peppercorns in their trunks are exaggerated, some elephants do hold grudges against people who have hurt them or whom for some reason they dislike.

3   Captive elephants frequently develop great affection for a particular trainer or keeper, but experienced elephant men, who may feel reciprocal affection for their animals, nonetheless know that they must be on their toes around even an affectionate elephant. For elephants play various games to test their keepers. An elephant may use its trunk, that marvelously intricate instrument with one or two fingers at the end, either as a lasso or straight-arm to pull a careless keeper down or punch him to the ground, methods which overwhelmingly demonstrate the elephant's dominance. Another popular game, which might be best described as "squash," though it bears no resemblance to the human sport of that name, can be played by one elephant with a keeper and a wall or in the

[1]Flat grasslands associated with tropical or subtropical regions. (Ed.)

doubles version by two elephants and a keeper. In the first version the elephant's objective is to sidle around in an innocent and sly way until it traps the keeper between it and the wall. The elephant wins if it can lean against the wall with the keeper in between. In the more difficult doubles version two elephants maneuver until they can trap a keeper between them. Then they lean together and *voilà*,[2] the keeper becomes meat in a sandwich. Smart elephant keepers who know that these games will be played carry a shortened elephant hook, marlin spike, or hunting knife whenever they are around the elephants. If the game starts and the keeper is outmaneuvered he can still win by poking his opponent sharply in the side. Knowing also that the real contest is to determine who is boss, the best elephant keepers establish a dominance over their animals that a matador would envy. The test of this dominance can be seen whenever keeper and elephant are walking toward one another on a narrow road or path. The dominant keeper never deviates. Without batting an eye he continues forward until the elephant steps aside.

4   Elephants may also, if they get the opportunity, play little games with unwary visitors. One kindhearted lady who was trying to feed an elephant at the San Diego Zoo made the mistake of holding her purse and the peanut in the hand she stretched out across the moat while she clung to a no feeding sign with the other. Instead of taking the peanut the elephant grabbed the purse, which in the process fell open. The elephant then turned the purse upside down and emptied its contents on the ground. For the next several moments, while the formerly kindhearted lady watched helplessly, the elephant picked up all the objects one by one—lipstick, car keys, comb, compact, hair curlers, coin holder, wallet, and ballpoint pen—that were in the purse. Eventually the purse and its contents were rescued, but not quite in the shape they had been before the elephant got them.

5   While female elephants, even those that play games, are generally friendly and affable and in the Asian species fairly easy to handle and train,[3] male elephants are a different story. Among both circus and zoo people legend holds that for every captive bull elephant a keeper has been killed. The truth is that several keepers have been gored or trampled to death by bulls during the animals' "musth,"[4] when for periods of up to five months the males become unpredictable, unmanageable, and possessed of superelephant strength. A human male in this condition would be called mad. Little understood, but probably related to sex drive, musth may give a bull elephant the determination, ability, and don't-give-a-damn attitude to drive off rival males and break through the largely female herds in order to mate. The condition is more pronounced in Asian elephants, but in either species it spells trouble for keepers.

6   One elephant keeper, an apocryphal story goes, had been made so nervous by the tales of male elephants killing their keepers that he played the leading part

[2]French for "There!" it is pronounced vwä–lä´. (Ed.)

[3]Although the African elephant can be trained, Hannibal probably used a North African subspecies on his famous march across the Alps. Some have been trained in Zaire, and the legendary Jumbo was African.

[4]Sometimes spelled "must," this word refers to a period that male elephants go through every year when they become highly aggressive and sexually active and prone to attack. Elephants in this state are highly dangerous. (Ed.)

in a modern version of the legend about the appointment in Samarra. That legend told of a man who heard that Death was coming to fetch him. Living at the time in Damascus, he sought to avoid his fate by moving to Samarra. On his first day there he encountered Death, who smiled and said, "Ah, my friend, I see you have come to keep your appointment with me in Samarra." The apocryphal keeper, when he heard that the zoo where he worked was acquiring a bull elephant, quit his job and took one like it at another zoo which had only female elephants. One of the females became agitated, pushed him to the ground and trampled him to death.

7   Some of the stories about keepers and bull elephants are more amusing than tragic. Lothar Dittrich, director of the zoo in Hanover, Germany, tells a story about his elephant keeper and a large African bull elephant named Tembo. As is often the case with bull elephants, Tembo had developed an affection bordering on love for his keeper, a type Dittrich calls an "alpha keeper" because he easily dominated the animals in his care. He became one with them, but at the same time their seldom-challenged leader.

8   It was the closeness of the relationship between this keeper and Tembo that created a serious problem for the zoo. The keeper, who tended other animals besides the elephants, was working one day in a pen of Masai cattle, large, tough, half-wild creatures that are the principal basis of wealth among the fierce Masai tribesmen of Kenya and Tanzania. Intent on his work the keeper failed to notice a challenger, a cow who got into position to butt him hard against the wall. The keeper managed to escape, but with a cracked, dislocated vertebra that necessitated his being placed in traction on a hospital bed.

9   On the first night the alpha keeper was in the hospital, a substitute keeper was assigned the task of putting Tembo and his two female companions into the elephant barn that abuts the rear side of Hanover's small African elephant exhibit. This exhibit, adjacent to one holding Asian elephants, is bounded on three sides by a narrow, shallow moat, which had given the zoo a good deal of trouble. Several times the elephants had either fallen or been pushed into the moat, and some had been injured. Consequently, whether the weather required it or not, the elephants were always chained in the barn at night to prevent them from falling into the moat.

10   When the substitute keeper attempted to order Tembo into the barn the big bull would have none of it. For him, it appeared, the substitute was a beta keeper, practically a nonperson, unfit to command his respect and obedience. He flatly refused to enter the barn, trumpeting his displeasure and waving his huge head, ears laid back, massive tusks raised ominously. Moreover, he wouldn't allow the females to enter the barn either. Clearly, he was laying down a statement of his newly assumed authority. "If I stay out, everybody stays out. And I'm staying out!"

11   The keeper was a reasonably brave but not foolish man. Instead of pressing the matter further he reported the rebellion to his superior. That first night the African elephants did not go in the barn.

12   On the following day Tembo found he was up against a stubborn and resourceful man in Director Dittrich. The heart of the problem, Dittrich well knew, was the close relationship between Tembo and the alpha keeper. It appeared that

no one else could command the big elephant's respect. Very well, Dittrich thought, we'll let Tembo hear the alpha keeper—on a tape recorder. So he drove the twelve miles to the hospital, explained the situation to the alpha keeper, who was lying flat on a hard bed with weights attached to his feet, and had the man record a message to Tembo ordering him to enter the barn.

13   That evening Dittrich, the substitute keeper, and several other zoo officials stood by the rail of the elephant enclosure while Dittrich played the tape, turning the volume up so loud the alpha keeper's words cracked out loud and clear, like a German noncom's. But Tembo was not to be fooled. The voice was not the man. He listened, showed signs of interest and recognition, but he would not go in the barn.

14   Now Dittrich saw the full extent of the challenge and determined that no elephant in his zoo was going to defy him. A handsome man in his forties, Dittrich is a dedicated zoo man who fled with his family from East Germany just a few days before the Berlin Wall was built. In the manner of most German zoo directors he made rounds of the zoo each day, getting to know his animals by name and personality. Now he realized that Tembo was not going to be satisfied with anything less than the real thing—the alpha keeper in person.

15   And the real thing was what Tembo got. Dittrich made arrangements with the keeper, his doctor, and the hospital to have the keeper taken out of traction, strapped to a stretcher, and brought by ambulance to the zoo. Attendants then carried the keeper over to the guardrail around the elephant enclosure and held him up so that Tembo could see him. Otherwise immobile, the keeper was allowed the use of one arm and was able to raise his head a few inches above the bed of his stretcher.

16   What followed no doubt seemed strange to the few visitors left in the Hanover Zoo that evening. A man lying flat on a stretcher between two ambulance attendants raised his head a few inches and fixed stern eyes on a large elephant that was looking fondly down at him. Pointing with one arm toward the barn at the rear of the elephant exhibit, the man commanded in a firm voice, "Tembo, go in! Tembo! Go in!" For an instant the tableau held. The man continued to point while he looked the elephant in the eye; the elephant looked down on him. Then obediently, the elephant turned. He had gotten the word from the highest authority he cared to acknowledge. The rebellion was over, the old order reestablished. Placid now, Tembo allowed the substitute keeper to shepherd him into the barn, the two females falling in behind. From that moment until the alpha keeper returned Tembo seemed to understand that the command was permanent. Each night he let the substitute keeper drive him and the females into the barn. ✳

From Sheldon Campbell, *Lifeboats to Ararat*. © 1978 by Sheldon H. Campbell. Reprinted by permission of Times Books, a division of Random House, Inc.

Exercises

Do not refer to the selection for Exercises A and B unless your instructor directs you to do so.

A. DETERMINING THE MAIN IDEA AND PURPOSE

Choose the best answer.

_____ **1.** Which of the following sentences from the selection *best* represents the main idea or thesis?

    a. "But elephants are not simpletons."

    b. "Elephants play various games to test their keepers."

    c. "It was the closeness between this keeper and Tembo that created a serious problem for the zoo."

    d. "The rebellion was over, the old order reestablished."

_____ **2.** With respect to the main idea, the writer's purpose is to

    a. present an argument on a controversial subject.

    b. explain an interesting phenomenon by relating a story.

    c. describe a scene so that the reader can visualize it.

    d. summarize scientific information.

B. COMPREHENDING MAIN IDEAS

Choose the correct answer.

_____ **1.** The writer characterizes elephants as essentially

    a. nasty and unpredictable.

    b. loyal but easily angered.

    c. simpleminded but stubborn.

    d. highly intelligent but mischievous.

_____ **2.** Stories illustrating that an elephant never forgets, for example, by killing a man who as a child was cruel to the animal, are probably

    a. true.

    b. impossible to verify.

    c. improbable.

    d. exaggerated.

_____ **3.** Elephants play games with their keepers to

    a. prove that they are dominant.

    b. test people's intelligence.

    c. show their affection.

    d. get revenge on their captors.

_____ **4.** The main objective of a good elephant keeper is to

    a. win the animal's trust.

    b. establish total dominance over the animal.

    c. let the elephant think that it is smarter than the keeper.

    d. avoid risk and the possibility of injury.

_____ 5. Tembo refused to obey the beta, or substitute, keeper, because
  a. he had been cruel to him in the past.
  b. he wanted to test the new keeper's wits.
  c. only his regular keeper was fit to command his obedience and respect.
  d. he was new and inexperienced, and Tembo sensed this.

_____ 6. Tembo was not fooled by
  a. a picture of his real keeper.
  b. a tape recording of his real keeper's voice.
  c. bribes of favorite foods to eat.
  d. his keeper lying on a stretcher.

COMPREHENSION SCORE

Score your answers for Exercises A and B as follows:

A. No. right _____ × 2 = _____
B. No. right _____ × 1 = _____
Total points from A and B _____ × 10 = _____ percent

You may refer to the selection as you work through the remaining exercises.

C. DISTINGUISHING BETWEEN MAIN IDEAS AND SUPPORTING DETAILS

Label the following statements from the selection as follows: MI if it represents a *main idea* and SD if it represents a *supporting detail.*

_____ 1. While female elephants, even those that play games, are generally friendly and affable and in the Asian species fairly easy to handle and train, male elephants are a different story.

_____ 2. Among both circus and zoo people legend holds that for every captive bull elephant a keeper has been killed.

_____ 3. The truth is that several keepers have been gored or trampled to death by bulls during the animals' "musth," when for periods of up to five months the males become unpredictable, unmanageable, and possessed of superelephant strength.

_____ 4. A human male in this condition would be called mad.

_____ 5. Little understood, but probably related to sex drive, musth may give a bull elephant the determination, ability, and don't-give-a-damn attitude to drive off rival males and break through the largely female herds in order to mate.

_____ 6. The condition is more pronounced in Asian elephants, but in either species it spells trouble for keepers.

D. INTERPRETING MEANING

Write your answers to these questions in your own words.

1. Look again at the quotation by Isak Dinesen at the end of paragraph 1, in which she describes the way elephants walk. What does she mean? _____

   _____

2. What information in the selection supports the idea that elephants are highly intelligent?_____

   _____

3. Why would an elephant keeper and a matador have to establish such a strong dominance over the animals they are associated with? _____

   _____

4. *Irony* is the contrast between what one expects and what actually happens. Look again in paragraph 6 at the legend about the appointment in Samarra and the story about the keeper who wanted to work only with female elephants. Then explain the irony in both stories. _____

   _____

5. *Anthropomorphism* is a device whereby a nonhuman thing—an animal or an object like a tree, for example—is described as if it had human emotions. Look through paragraph 16 and find an example of a word (an adverb) that fits this definition. _____

E. ANALYZING STRUCTURE

Where appropriate, write your answers for these questions in your own words.

1. In relation to the rest of the selection, what is the purpose of paragraph 1? What information does it provide the reader? _____

   _____

2. Look again at paragraph 3 and write the sentence that expresses the main idea. _____

3. *Narrative* writing tells a story, and *expository* writing explains and discusses. What kind of writing is represented in paragraphs 1–3? _____
   In paragraphs 4–16? _____

4. What idea does the story of Tembo and his keeper illustrate about elephants?

   _____

F. UNDERSTANDING VOCABULARY

Choose the best definition according to an analysis of word parts or context.

_____ 1. bits of *conventional* wisdom [paragraph 2]:

    a. simplified
    b. traditional
    c. generally accepted
    d. ordinary

_____ 2. *reciprocal* affection [3]:

    a. fond
    b. shown in return
    c. unearned
    d. deep, profound

_____ 3. the keeper never *deviates* [3]:

    a. changes expression
    b. allows himself to be tricked
    c. turns aside
    d. wanders around with no purpose

_____ 4. an *apocryphal* story [6]:

    a. definitely true
    b. definitely untrue
    c. of questionable authenticity
    d. passed along from generation to generation

_____ 5. tusks raised *ominously* [10]; suggesting:

    a. fear, cowardice
    b. danger, harm
    c. a good sign
    d. anger

_____ 6. *placid* now [16]:

    a. outwardly calm
    b. outsmarted
    c. motionless
    d. suffering from injured pride

G. USING VOCABULARY

Here are some words from the selection. Write an original sentence using each word that shows both that you know how to use the word and what it means.

1. *deceptive* _____

_____

2. *captive* _____

_____

3. *exaggerate* _____

_____

4. *reciprocal* _____

_____

5. *immobile* _____

_____

H. PARAPHRASING EXERCISE

In the left column below is paragraph 13 from the selection, with a paraphrase of it on the right.

Original Passage	**Paraphrase**
That evening Dittrich, the substitute keeper, and several other zoo officials stood by the rail of the elephant enclosure while Dittrich played the tape, turning the volume up so loud the alpha keeper's words cracked out loud and clear, like a German noncom's. But Tembo was not to be fooled. The voice was not the man. He listened, showed signs of interest and recognition, but he would not go in the barn.	Dittrich, the beta keeper, and other zoo officials watched while he played a tape of the alpha keeper's voice at top volume. But the trick didn't fool Tembo, who was smart enough to know that the voice coming from the recorder wasn't the real thing. Although he listened and showed that he recognized the voice, he still refused to go into the barn.

First study the paraphrase above and then write a paraphrase of the sentences below from paragraph 16.

Original Passage	**Paraphrase**
What followed no doubt seemed strange to the few visitors left in the Hanover Zoo that evening. A man lying flat on a stretcher between two ambulance attendants raised his head a few inches and fixed stern eyes on a large elephant that was looking fondly down at him. Pointing with one arm toward the barn at the rear of the elephant exhibit, the man	_____ _____ _____ _____ _____ _____ _____ _____

commanded in a firm voice, "Tembo, go in! Tembo! Go in!" For an instant, the tableau held. The man continued to point while he looked the elephant in the eye; the elephant looked down on him. Then obediently, the elephant turned. He had gotten the word from the highest authority he cared to acknowledge. The rebellion was over, the old order reestablished.

_____

_____

_____

_____

_____

_____

_____

I.   TOPICS FOR WRITING OR DISCUSSION

1. Describe an incident where an animal you have observed demonstrated an unusual or unexpected behavior or quality.
2. Critics of zoos charge that they are cruel institutions that serve no scientific purpose except to provide a place where humans can go to stare at penned-up creatures. Proponents argue that zoos are important for animal research and for preserving threatened species. Write a short essay of two to three paragraphs in which you take a stand on this question. Make sure to give two or three good reasons to back up your opinion.

For Further Exploration

BOOKS

- Jeffrey Masson and Susan McCarthy, *When Elephants Weep* (1995). The authors present the theory that animals not only are intelligent but also have emotions. Though controversial because they are not trained scientists, the authors do suggest through vivid examples that a bear sitting on a log staring at a sunset just might be enjoying its beauty.
- Gerald Durrell, *The Overloaded Ark* (1953). In this classic work, Durrell, who was a prominent British naturalist, describes his private zoo on an island off the English coast and shows how one naturalist helped save endangered species.

MOVIE

Dumbo (1941) remains one of Walt Disney's most charming and poignant animated movies. It tells the story of a little circus elephant born with ears so gigantic that all the other circus animals tease him mercilessly. There are many sad and touching moments before his plight is resolved. It is well worth a trip to the video store.

WEB SITES

- The home page of the San Diego Zoo and the Zoological Society of San Diego is *www.sandiego.zoo.org*.
- Everything you wanted to know about elephants can be found at "Elephanteria," *www.elephanteria.com*.

9

CHARLES FINNEY

The Life and Death of a Western Gladiator

In this fictional account, Charles Finney describes the life cycle of Crotalus, a diamond-back rattlesnake, one of the most feared yet splendid creatures that inhabit the western United States. This article first appeared in Harper's *magazine.*

Vocabulary Preview

WORD HISTORIES

Nemesis [paragraph 12]   Most diamondback rattlers do not survive after birth. The roadrunner is one *nemesis* of baby rattlesnakes. The Greek word *nemesis* ("just fate") comes from *nemein*, "to measure what is due." In Greek mythology, ideas were often associated with gods and goddesses, and *Nemesis* was also the goddess of vengeance. Charles Funk describes her role like this:

> She measured out happiness and unhappiness, and saw to it that any who were too greatly or too frequently blessed by fortune were visited in equal measure by loss or suffering. From this last she became looked upon as the goddess of retribution, as a goddess of vengeance and punishment.[1]

In this context, the word *nemesis* means "an unbeatable rival" or "one who causes a downfall."

Diabolically [paragraph 32]   Finney describes Crotalus in his mature state as being *"diabolically* beautiful and deadly poison." The adverb *diabolically* refers to the devil, from the Latin word *diabolos.* When Finney describes Crotalus as *"diabolically* beautiful" then, he is referring to a kind of beauty that is extraordinarily dangerous.

WORD PARTS

De- [paragraph 3]   The prefix *de-* refers to removal of something. Therefore, *dehydration* means "the process of removing water." Here is how the word is broken down: *de-* ("removal of") + *hydr* ("water") + *-ation.* Incidentally, new words ending with the common noun suffix *-tion* will be easy to pronounce if you remember that the primary accent or stress mark always occurs on the syllable just *before* the suffix: dē hī drā´ shən. Some other words with the prefix *de-*:

defoliate	to remove vegetation
deoxygenate	to remove oxygen from a substance, like water
depilatory	to remove hair from [*de-* + *pilus* ("hair")]

[1]Charles Funk, *Thereby Hangs a Tale* (New York: Harper & Row, 1950), p. 202.

What do these two words mean?

desegregate _____

deflate _____

Somnolent [paragraph 13]   As he lies in his cave, Crotalus becomes sleepy, or *somnolent* (from the Latin word *somnus*). English has a few words in this family that refer to sleep:

somnolence	sleepy
insomnia	the inability to sleep
insomniac	one who suffers from insomnia

If a woman is a *somnambulist,* what does she do? _____

CHARLES FINNEY

Life and Death of a Western Gladiator

1   He was born on a summer morning in the shady mouth of a cave. Three others were born with him, another male and two females. Each was about five inches long and slimmer than a lead pencil.

2   Their mother left them a few hours after they were born. A day after that his brother and sisters left him also. He was all alone. Nobody cared whether he lived or died. His tiny brain was very dull. He had no arms or legs. His skin was delicate. Nearly everything that walked on the ground or burrowed in it, that flew in the air or swam in the water or climbed trees was his enemy. But he didn't know that. He knew nothing at all. He was aware of his own existence, and that was the sum of his knowledge.

3   The direct rays of the sun could, in a short time, kill him. If the temperature dropped too low he would freeze. Without food he would starve. Without moisture he would die of dehydration. If a man or a horse stepped on him he would be crushed. If anything chased him he could run neither very far nor very fast.

4   Thus it was at the hour of his birth. Thus it would be, with modifications, all his life.

5   But against these drawbacks he had certain qualifications that fitted him to be a competitive creature of this world and equipped him for its warfare. He could exist a long time without food or water. His very smallness at birth protected him when he most needed protection. Instinct provided him with what he lacked in experience. In order to eat he first had to kill; and he was eminently adapted for killing. In sacs in his jaws he secreted a virulent poison. To inject that poison he had two fangs, hollow and pointed. Without that poison and those fangs he would have been among the most helpless creatures on earth. With them he was among the deadliest.

6   He was, of course, a baby rattlesnake, a desert diamondback, named Crotalus atrox by the herpetologists Baird and Girard and so listed in the *Catalogue of*

North American Reptiles in its issue of 1853. He was grayish brown in color with a series of large dark diamond-shaped blotches on his back. His tail was white with five black cross-bands. It had a button on the end of it.

7   Little Crotalus lay in the dust in the mouth of his cave. Some of his kinfolk lay there too. It was their home. That particular tribe of rattlers had lived there for scores of years.

8   The cave had never been seen by a white man.

9   Sometimes as many as two hundred rattlers occupied the den. Sometimes the numbers shrunk to as few as forty or fifty.

10   The tribe members did nothing at all for each other except breed. They hunted singly; they never shared their food. They derived some automatic degree of safety from their numbers, but their actions were never concerted toward using their numbers to any end. If an enemy attacked one of them, the others did nothing about it.

11   Young Crotalus's brother was the first of the litter to go out into the world and the first to die. He achieved a distance of fifty feet from the den when a Sonoran racer, four feet long and hungry, came upon him. The little rattler, despite his poison fangs, was a tidbit. The racer, long skilled in such arts, snatched him up by the head and swallowed him down. Powerful digestive juices in the racer's stomach did the rest. Then the racer, appetite whetted, prowled around until it found one of Crotalus's little sisters. She went the way of the brother.

12   Nemesis of the second sister was a chaparral cock. This cuckoo, or road runner as it is called, found the baby amid some rocks, uttered a cry of delight, scissored it by the neck, shook it until it was almost lifeless, banged and pounded it upon a rock until life had indeed left it, and then gulped it down.

13   Crotalus, somnolent in a cranny of the cave's mouth, neither knew nor cared. Even if he had, there was nothing he could have done about it.

14   On the fourth day of his life he decided to go out into the world himself. He rippled forth uncertainly, the transverse plates on his belly serving him as legs.

15   He could see things well enough within his limited range, but a five-inch-long snake can command no great field of vision. He had an excellent sense of smell. But, having no ears, he was stone deaf. On the other hand, he had a pit, a deep pock mark between eye and nostril. Unique, this organ was sensitive to animal heat. In pitch blackness, Crotalus, by means of the heat messages recorded in his pit, could tell whether another animal was near and could also judge its size. That was better than an ear.

16   The single button on his tail could not, of course, yet rattle. Crotalus wouldn't be able to rattle until that button had grown into three segments. Then he would be able to buzz.

17   He had a wonderful tongue. It looked like an exposed nerve and was probably exactly that. It was forked, and Crotalus thrust it in and out as he traveled. It told him things that neither his eyes nor his nose nor his pit told him.

18   Snake fashion, Crotalus went forth, not knowing where he was going, for he had never been anywhere before. Hunger was probably his prime mover. In order to satisfy that hunger he had to find something smaller than himself and kill it.

19   He came upon a baby lizard sitting in the sand. Eyes, nose, pit, and tongue told Crotalus it was there. Instinct told him what it was and what to do. Crotalus

gave a tiny one-inch strike and bit the lizard. His poison killed it. He took it by the head and swallowed it. Thus was his first meal.

20   During his first two years, Crotalus grew rapidly. He attained a length of two feet; his tail had five rattles on it and its button. He rarely bothered with lizards any more, preferring baby rabbits, chipmunks, and round-tailed ground squirrels. Because of his slow locomotion he could not run down these agile little things. He had to contrive instead to be where they were when they would pass. Then he struck swiftly, injected his poison, and ate them after they died.

21   At two he was formidable. He had grown past the stage where a racer or a road runner could safely tackle him. He had grown to the size where other desert dwellers—coyotes, foxes, coatis, wildcats—knew it was better to leave him alone.

22   And, at two, Crotalus became a father, his life being regulated by cycles. His cycles were plantlike. The peach tree does not "know" when it is time to flower, but flower it does because its cycle orders it to do so.

23   In the same way, Crotalus did not "know" when it was time for young desert diamondback rattlers to pair off and breed. But his cycle knew.

24   He found "her" on a rainy morning. Crotalus's courtship at first was sinuous and subtle, slow and stealthy. Then suddenly it became dynamic. A period of exhaustion followed. Two metabolic machines had united to produce new metabolic machines.

25   Of that physical union six new rattlesnakes were born. Thus Crotalus, at two, had carried out his major primary function: he had reproduced his kind. In two years he had experienced everything that was reasonably possible for desert diamondback rattlesnakes to experience except death.

26   He had not experienced death for the simple reason that there had never been an opportunity for anything bigger and stronger than himself to kill him. Now, at two, because he was so formidable, that opportunity became more and more unlikely.

27   He grew more slowly in the years following his initial spurt. At the age of twelve he was five feet long. Few of the other rattlers in his den were older or larger than he.

28   He had a castanet of fourteen segments. It had been broken off occasionally in the past, but with each new molting a new segment appeared.

29   His first skin-shedding back in his babyhood had been a bewildering experience. He did not know what was happening. His eyes clouded over until he could not see. His skin thickened and dried until it cracked in places. His pit and his nostrils ceased to function. There was only one thing to do and that was to get out of that skin.

30   Crotalus managed it by nosing against the bark of a shrub until he forced the old skin down over his head, bunching it like the rolled top of a stocking around his neck. Then he pushed around among rocks and sticks and branches, literally crawling out of his skin by slow degrees. Wriggling free at last, he looked like a brand new snake. His skin was bright and satiny, his eyes and nostrils were clear, his pit sang with sensation.

31   For the rest of his life he was to molt three or four times a year. Each time he did it he felt as if he had been born again.

32   At twelve he was a magnificent reptile. Not a single scar defaced his rippling symmetry. He was diabolically beautiful and deadly poison.

33   His venom was his only weapon, for he had no power of constriction. Yellowish in color, his poison was odorless and tasteless. It was a highly complex mixture of proteids, each in itself direly toxic. His venom worked on the blood. The more poison he injected with a bite, the more dangerous the wound. The pain rendered by his bite was instantaneous, and the shock accompanying it was profound. Swelling began immediately, to be followed by a ghastly oozing. Injected directly into a large vein, his poison brought death quickly, for the victim died when it reached his heart.

34   At the age of twenty Crotalus was the oldest and largest rattler in his den. He was six feet long and weighed thirteen pounds. His whole world was only about a mile in radius. He had fixed places where he avoided the sun when it was hot and he was away from his cave. He knew his hunting grounds thoroughly, every game trail, every animal burrow.

35   He was a fine old machine, perfectly adapted to his surroundings, accustomed to a life of leisure and comfort. He dominated his little world.

36   The mighty seasonal rhythms of the desert were as vast pulsations, and the lives of the rattlesnakes were attuned to them. Spring sun beat down, spring rains fell, and, as the plants of the desert ended their winter hibernations, so did the vipers in their lair. The plants opened forth and budded; the den "opened" too, and the snakes crawled forth. The plants fertilized each other, and new plants were born. The snakes bred, and new snakes were produced. The desert was repopulated.

37   In the autumn the plants began to close; in the same fashion the snake den began to close, the reptiles returned to it, lay like lingering blossoms about its entrance for a while, then disappeared within it when winter came. There they slept until summoned forth by a new spring.

38   Crotalus was twenty years old. He was in the golden age of his viperhood.

39   But men were approaching. Spilling out of their cities, men were settling in that part of the desert where Crotalus lived. They built roads and houses, set up fences, dug for water, planted crops.

40   They homesteaded the land. They brought new animals with them—cows, horses, dogs, cats, barnyard fowl.

41   The roads they built were death traps for the desert dwellers. Every morning new dead bodies lay on the roads, the bodies of the things the men had run over and crushed in their vehicles.

42   That summer Crotalus met his first dog. It was a German shepherd which had been reared on a farm in the Midwest and there had gained the reputation of being a snake-killer. Black snakes, garter snakes, pilots, water snakes; it delighted in killing them all. It would seize them by the middle, heedless of their tiny teeth, and shake them violently until they died.

43   This dog met Crotalus face to face in the desert at dusk. Crotalus had seen coyotes aplenty and feared them not. Neither did the dog fear Crotalus, although Crotalus then was six feet long, as thick in the middle as a motorcycle tire, and had a head the size of a man's clenched fist. Also this snake buzzed and buzzed and buzzed.

44   The dog was brave, and a snake was a snake. The German shepherd snarled and attacked. Crotalus struck him in the underjaw; his fangs sank in almost half an inch and squirted big blobs of hematoxic poison into the tissues of the dog's flesh.

45   The shepherd bellowed with pain, backed off, groveled with his jaws in the desert sand, and attacked again. He seized Crotalus somewhere by the middle of his body and tried to flip him in the air and shake him as, in the past, he had shaken slender black snakes to their death. In return, he received another poison-blurting stab in his flank and a third in the belly and a fourth in the eye as the terrible, writhing snake bit wherever it could sink its fangs.

46   The German shepherd had enough. He dropped the big snake and in sick, agonizing bewilderment crawled somehow back to his master's homestead and died.

47   The homesteader looked at his dead dog and became alarmed. If there was a snake around big enough to kill a dog that size, it could also kill a child and probably a man. It was something that had to be eliminated.

48   The homesteader told his fellow farmers, and they agreed to initiate a war of extermination against the snakes.

49   The campaign during the summer was sporadic. The snakes were scattered over the desert, and it was only by chance that the men came upon them. Even so, at summer's end, twenty-six of the vipers had been killed.

50   When autumn came the men decided to look for the rattlers' den and execute mass slaughter. The homesteaders had become desert-wise and knew what to look for.

51   They found Crotalus's lair, without too much trouble—a rock outcropping on a slope that faced the south. Cast-off skins were in evidence in the bushes. Bees flew idly in and out of the den's mouth. Convenient benches and shelves of rock were at hand where the snakes might lie for a final sunning in the autumn air.

52   They killed the three rattlers they found at the den when they first discovered it. They made plans to return in a few more days when more of the snakes had congregated. They decided to bring along dynamite with them and blow up the mouth of the den so that the snakes within would be sealed there forever and the snakes without would have no place to find refuge.

53   On the day the men chose to return nearly fifty desert diamondbacks were gathered at the portals of the cave. The men shot them, clubbed them, smashed them with rocks, Some of the rattlers escaped the attack and crawled into the den.

54   Crotalus had not yet arrived for the autumn rendezvous. He came that night. The den's mouth was a shattered mass of rock, for the men had done their dynamiting well. Dead members of his tribe lay everywhere. Crotalus nosed among them, tongue flicking as he slid slowly along.

55   There was no access to the cave any more. He spent the night outside among the dead. The morning sun warmed him and awakened him. He lay there at full length. He had no place to go.

56   The sun grew hotter upon him and instinctively he began to slide toward some dark shade. Then his senses warned him of some animal presence near by; he stopped, half coiled, raised his head and began to rattle. He saw two upright figures. He did not know what they were because he had never seen men before.

57   "That's the granddaddy of them all," said one of the homesteaders. "It's a good thing we came back." He raised his shotgun. ✳

From Charles Finney, "The Life and Death of a Western Gladiator." Reprinted by permission of Barthold Fles, Literary Agent.

Exercises

Do not refer to the selection for Exercises A and B unless your instructor directs you to do so.

A. DETERMINING THE MAIN IDEA AND PURPOSE

Choose the best answer.

_____ 1. The main idea of the selection is that
   a. the life of a diamondback rattlesnake is harsh.
   b. Crotalus was well suited to survive in his environment until civilization intruded.
   c. diamondback rattlesnakes are a threat to human settlements.
   d. diamondback rattlesnakes can adapt to even the most hostile environment because of their strong instinct to survive.

_____ 2. The writer's purpose in telling the story of Crotalus is to
   a. encourage the reader to learn more about rattlesnakes.
   b. persuade the reader that rattlesnakes are important to the environment.
   c. describe those physical characteristics of the rattlesnake that enable it to survive so well.
   d. inform and make the reader sympathetic to the rattlesnake's life cycle and behavior.

B. COMPREHENDING MAIN IDEAS

Choose the correct answer.

_____ 1. In describing the baby stage in a rattlesnake's life, Finney emphasizes its
   a. dependence on its mother.
   b. well-developed killing instinct.
   c. deadly effect on its victims.
   d. helplessness and susceptibility to danger.

_____ 2. According to the selection, rattlesnakes
   a. hunt in groups.
   b. have a well-organized and complex society.
   c. must be taught to hunt by adults.
   d. live solitary lives except for breeding.

_____ **3.** The particular group of rattlesnakes described in this selection lived in
  a. an abandoned farmhouse.
  b. a den or cave.
  c. a large underground cavern.
  d. a quarry.

_____ **4.** The rattlesnake "senses" the presence of other animals by using its
  a. pit.
  b. mouth.
  c. eyes.
  d. ears.

_____ **5.** Rattlesnakes molt or shed their skin
  a. once a year.
  b. twice a year.
  c. three or four times a year.
  d. three or four times in a normal life span.

_____ **6.** After the homesteaders found the rattlesnakes, they decided to
  a. alert the authorities.
  b. begin a campaign to decrease their numbers.
  c. exterminate them.
  d. move them to a more isolated location.

COMPREHENSION SCORE

Score your answers for Exercises A and B as follows:

A. No. right _____ × 2 = _____
B. No. right _____ × 1 = _____
Total points from A and B _____ × 10 = _____ percent

You may refer to the selection as you work through the remaining exercises.

C. IDENTIFYING SUPPORTING DETAILS

Place an X beside each statement that _directly_ supports this main idea from the selection: "He had certain qualifications that fitted him to be a competitive creature of this world and equipped him for its warfare."

1. _____ The direct rays of the sun could, in a short time, kill him.

2. _____ Without moisture he would die of dehydration.

3. _____ He could exist a long time without food or water.

4. _____ He was eminently adapted for killing by means of the virulent poison contained in sacs in his jaws.

5. _____ To inject that poison he had two fangs, hollow and pointed.

6. _____ Without that poison and those fangs he would have been the most helpless creature on earth.

D. INTERPRETING MEANING

Write your answers to these questions in your own words.

1. Read paragraph 2 and explain why the survival rate of baby rattlesnakes is so low. _____

2. What single characteristic mentioned in paragraph 5 makes a rattlesnake more deadly than all other creatures on earth? _____

3. In paragraphs 22–25, what does Finney say is the main impetus for Crotalus to reproduce? _____

4. Aside from the danger the snakes presented to children and livestock, what are *two* reasons that the homesteaders were so determined to destroy the rattlesnake population?_____

    _____

5. Did Crotalus survive the homesteaders' assault? How do you know? _____

    _____

    _____

E. ANALYZING STRUCTURE

Write your answers to these questions in your own words.

1. Why does Finney delay identifying Crotalus as a rattlesnake until paragraph 6?

    _____

    _____

2. Look up the meaning of *chronological* in the dictionary. Then explain the connection between this word and the way Finney organizes his ideas._____

    _____

    _____

3. Look again at paragraphs 1–8. Most of the sentences are short and simple. What do sentences like this lend to the story? _____

F. UNDERSTANDING VOCABULARY

Look through the paragraphs listed below and find a word that matches each definition. Refer to the dictionary if necessary. An example has been done for you.

Ex. changes, alterations [paragraphs 3–4]   _____modifications_____

1. actively poisonous, toxic [5]   _____

2. an unbeatable rival or opponent [12–13]   _____

3. sleepy [12–13]   _____

4. to plan cleverly, devise, scheme [20]   _____

5. active, forceful, energetic [24]   _____

6. awesome in strength, intimidating [26]   _____

7. dreadful, horrible [33]   _____

8. thorough, deep, pervasive [33–34]   _____

9. confusion, complete puzzlement [45–46]   _____

10. shelter or protection from danger [51–52]   _____

G. USING VOCABULARY

In parentheses before each sentence are some inflected forms of words from the selection. Study the context and the sentence. Then write the correct form in the space provided.

1. (*formidableness, formidability, formidable, formidably*) Because of Crotalus's

   _____ size and strength, it became less likely that another
   animal could kill him.

2. (*bewilderment, bewilder, bewildered*) Crotalus felt _____ the
   first time he shed his skin.

3. (*symmetry, symmetrical, symmetrically*) As an adult rattlesnake, Crotalus's

   body was an example of perfect _____ .

4. (*domination, dominated, dominant, dominantly*) Crotalus was _____
   over that particular tribe of snakes.

5. (*sporadic, sporadically*) At first the homesteaders carried out their

   extermination campaign _____ .

H. PARAPHRASING EXERCISE

In the left column below is paragraph 32 from the selection, with a paraphrase of it on the right.

Original Passage

At twelve he was a magnificent reptile. Not a single scar defaced his rippling symmetry. He was diabolically beautiful and deadly poison.

Paraphrase

When Crotalus was 12 he was a magnificent specimen with no scars marring his skin, and he was both as beautiful and deadly as the devil.

First, study the paraphrase above and then write a paraphrase for paragraph 26.

Original Passage

He had not experienced death for the simple reason that there had never been an opportu-

Paraphrase

_____

_____

nity for anything bigger and stronger than
himself to kill him. Now, at two, because he
was so formidable, that opportunity became
more and more unlikely.

_____

_____

_____

_____

I. TOPICS FOR WRITING OR DISCUSSION

1. On a separate sheet of paper, write a short summary of the physical changes Crotalus underwent throughout his life, from birth to adulthood.
2. Describe the life cycle of an animal or organism that you have observed or studied.
3. An imbalance among native organisms in an environment is a common problem today. Sometimes these imbalances are a result of human interference with the population; sometimes they have natural causes. For example, in the West, the native deer population has grown to a point where the environment can often no longer support it, mainly because the deer's natural predators—mountain lions and bobcats—no longer exist. Investigate and report on an ecological imbalance in your area.

For Further Exploration

BOOK

Barry Lopez, _Of Wolves and Men_ (1978). This book is an example of nature writing at its best. Lopez examines the wolf through history and man's ongoing attempts to eradicate the species. Lopez's presentation is careful and balanced, yet he creates sympathy in the reader, as Finney does in this selection.

MOVIE

Never Cry Wolf (1983), directed by Carroll Ballard, is a fine adaptation of Farley Mowat's book of the same title. A semidocumentary, it explores the experience of a young biologist who ventures to the Yukon to study white wolves. Ballard captures the essence of the natural world on film.

WEB SITES

Further information about diamondback rattlers of the American Southwest, including photographs, can be found at these sites. The first one is sponsored by the San Diego Natural History Museum:

- _www.sdnhm.org/fieldguide/herps/crot-atr.html_
- _www.biopark.org/Catrox.html_
- _www.photovault.com/Link/Animals/Reptiles/Snakes/Species/ WesternDiamondRattlesnake.html_

This site features photographs of other types of American rattlesnakes:

- _www.coastalreptiles.com/crotalus.htm_

10

GEOFFREY COWLEY

The Language Explosion

Geoffrey Cowley received his undergraduate degree in English from Lewis and Clark College in Portland, Oregon, and a master's degree in English from the University of Washington. His formal interest in language dates back to graduate school when he studied linguistics. Now Newsweek's *senior editor for health and medicine, Cowley covers medical research, fitness trends, and health policy issues. "The Language Explosion" examines the step-by-step process by which very young children acquire language.*

Vocabulary Preview

WORD HISTORIES

Zenith [paragraph 12]   Cowley writes that the *zenith* of a child's language acquisition occurs when he or she becomes aware that the way words are put together determines their meaning. *Zenith* is one of the few words in English derived from Arabic. In English, it means "the highest point." (From this explanation, you can easily see how the Zenith Electronics Corporation got its name.) Literally this word means "the highest point attained by the sun over the observer's horizon." In Arabic *zenith* means a "path over the head" because when the sun is at its *zenith*, it is at its highest point.

WORD PARTS

-fy [paragraph 9]   According to Cowley, children possess certain skills that *simplify* the process of learning language. The verb to *simplify*, meaning "to make simple," ends with the suffix *-fy* ("to cause to become" or "to make"). This suffix comes at the end of many common verbs, among them *codify, pacify, modify,* and *satisfy*. What do these verbs mean? Check a dictionary if you need help with their roots.

deify _____

liquefy _____

stupefy _____

WORD FAMILIES

Linguist [paragraph 3]   The words *linguist* and *psycholinguist* appear throughout this selection. A linguist is one who studies language. Both *linguist* and *language* come from the French *langue*, originally from the Latin root *lingua-* ("tongue"). And in fact, some people use the word *language* and *tongue* interchangeably. Here are four other words in this family:

linguistics	the study of languages
linguaphile	one who loves language [*lingua-* + *philos* ("love")]
linguine	a type of Italian pasta, so called because the broad, flat strands are thought to resemble little tongues
lingo	an unfamiliar or specialized vocabulary of a particular field

GEOFFREY COWLEY

The Language Explosion

1   Barry is a pixie-faced 3-year-old who can't yet draw a circle or stack his blocks in a simple pattern. There is little chance he will ever live independently. He may never learn to tie his own shoes. Yet Barry is as chatty and engaging a person as you could ever hope to meet. He knows his preschool classmates—and their parents—by name. When he wakes his mom in the morning, he strokes her cheek and tells her how beautiful she is. Then he asks her how she slept. Barry has Williams syndrome, a rare congenital disorder caused by abnormalities on chromosome 7. Children with the condition share an array of distinctive traits, including weak hearts, elfin faces and extremely low IQs. But they're unusually sociable, and often display an extraordinary feeling for language. Ask a Williams child to name an animal, says Dr. Ursula Bellugi of the Salk Institute's Laboratory for Cognitive Neuroscience, and you may get a fanciful discourse on yaks, koalas or unicorns.

2   If we learned language in the same way that we learn to add, subtract or play cards, children like Barry would not get much beyond hello and goodbye. Nor, for that matter, would normal toddlers. As anyone who has struggled through college French can attest, picking up a new language as an adult is as simple as picking up a truck. Yet virtually every kid in the world succeeds at it—and without conscious effort. Children attach meanings to sounds long before they shed their diapers. They launch into grammatical analysis before they can tie their shoes. And by the age of 3, most produce sentences as readily as laughter or tears.

3   Scholars have bickered for centuries over how kids accomplish this feat, but most now agree that their brains are wired for the task. Like finches or sparrows, which learn to sing as hatchlings or not at all, we're designed to acquire certain kinds of knowledge at particular stages of development. Children surrounded by words almost always become fluent by 3, whatever their general intelligence. And people deprived of language as children rarely master it as adults, no matter how smart they are or how intensively they're trained. As MIT linguist Steven Pinker observes in his acclaimed 1994 book *The Language Instinct,* "Language is not a cultural artifact that we learn the way we learn to tell time or how the federal government works. It is a distinct piece of [our] biological makeup." Whether they emerge speaking Spanish, Czech or Hindi, kids all acquire lan-

guage on the same general schedule. And as a growing body of research makes clear, they all travel the same remarkable path.

SOUND

4   The journey toward language starts not in the nursery but in the womb, where the fetus is continually bathed in the sounds of its mother's voice. Babies just 4 days old can distinguish one language from another. French newborns suck more vigorously when they hear French spoken than when they hear Russian—and Russian babies show the opposite preference. At first, they notice only general rhythms and melodies. But newborns are also sensitive to speech sounds, and they home in quickly on the ones that matter.

5   Each of the world's approximately 6,000 languages uses a different assortment of phonemes, or distinctive sounds, to build words. As adults, we have a hard time even hearing phonemes from foreign languages. The French don't notice any real difference between the *th* sounds in *thick* and *then*—and to most English speakers, the vowel in the French word *tu* (*ee* through rounded lips) is just another *oo*. Researchers have found that month-old infants register both of those distinctions and countless others from the world's languages. But at 6 and 10 months, they start to narrow their range. They grow oblivious to foreign phonemes while staying attuned to whatever sounds the speakers around them are using.

6   Acquiring a set of phonemes is a first step toward language, but just a baby step. To start decoding speech, you have to recognize words. And as anyone listening to a foreign conversation quickly discovers, people don't talk one . . . word . . . at . . . a . . . time. Real-life language—even the melodious "parentese" that parents use with infants—consists mainly of nonstopstreamofsound. So how do babies suss out the boundaries? Long before they recognize words, says Peter Jusczyk, a cognitive scientist at Johns Hopkins University, they get a feel for how their language uses phonemes to launch syllables. By the time they're 7 months old, American babies are well accustomed to hearing *t* joined with *r* (as in *tram*) and *c* with *l* (as in *clam*), but they've been spared combinations like *db, gd, kt, ts* and *ng,* all of which occur in other languages. And once they have an ear for syllables, word boundaries become less mysterious. *Ten / groaning / deadbeats / are / cleaning / a / train on / blacktop* makes acoustic sense in English even if you don't know the words. *Te / ngroanin / gdea / dbea / tsare / cleani / nga / traino / nbla / cktop* isn't an option.

7   As children start to recognize and play with syllables, they also pick up on the metrical patterns among them. French words tend to end with a stressed syllable. The majority of English words—and virtually all of the *mommy-daddy-doggie* diminutives that parents heap on children—have the accented syllable up front. Until they're 6 months old, American babies are no more responsive to words like *big*ger than they are to words like gui*tar*. But Jusczyk has found that 6- to 10-month-olds develop a clear bias for words with first-syllable accents. They suck more vigorously when they hear such words, regardless of whether they're read from lists or tucked into streams of normal speech. The implication is that children less than a year old hear speech not as a blur of sound but as a series of distinct but meaningless words.

MEANING

8   By their first birthday, most kids start linking words to meanings. Amid their streams of sweet, melodic gibberish, they start to name things—ball, cup, bottle, doggie. And even those who don't speak for a while often gesture to show off their mastery of the nose, eyes, ears, and toes. These may seem small steps; after all, most 1-year-olds are surrounded by people who insist on pointing and naming every object in sight. But as Pinker observes, making the right connections is a complicated business. How complicated? Imagine yourself surrounded by people speaking a strange language. A rabbit runs by, and someone shouts, *"Gavagai!"* What does the word mean? "Rabbit" may seem the obvious inference, but it's just one of countless logical alternatives. *Gavagai* could refer to that particular creature, or it could have a range of broader meanings, from "four-legged plant eater" to "furry thing in motion." How do kids get to the right level of generalization? Why don't they spend their lives trying to figure out what words like "rabbit" mean?

9   Because, says Stanford psychologist Ellen Markman, they come to the game with innate mental biases. Markman has shown that instead of testing endless hypotheses about each word's meaning, kids start from three basic assumptions. First, they figure that labels refer to whole objects, not parts or qualities. Second, they expect labels to denote classes of things (cups, balls, rabbits) rather than in-dividual items. Third, they assume that anything with a name can have only one. These assumptions don't always lead directly to the right inference ("I'm not a noying," Dennis the Menace once told Mr. Wilson, "I'm a cowboy"). But they vastly simplify word learning. In keeping with the "whole object" assump-tion, a child won't consider a label for "handle" until she has one for "cup." And thanks to the "one label per object" assumption, a child who has mastered the word *cup* never assumes that *handle* is just another way of saying the same thing. "In that situation," says Markman, "the child accepts the possibility that the new word applies to some feature of the object."

10   Words accrue slowly at first. But around the age of 18 months, children's abil-ities explode. Most start acquiring new words at the phenomenal rate of one every two hours—and for the first time, they start combining them. Children don't all reach these milestones on exactly the same schedule; their development rates can vary by a year or more, and there's no evidence that late talkers end up less fluent than early talkers. But by their second birthdays, most kids have socked away 1,000 to 2,000 words and started tossing around two-word strings such as "no nap," "all wet," or "bottle juice."

GRAMMAR

11   Once kids can paste two words together, it's not long before they're generating sentences. Between 24 and 30 months, "no nap" may become "I don't want nap," and "bottle juice" may blossom into "I want juice." When kids hit that stage, their repertoires start expanding exponentially. Between 30 and 36 months, most acquire rules for expressing tense (*walk* versus *walked*) and number (*house* versus *houses*), often overextending them to produce statements like "I bringed home three mouses." They also start using "function words"—the *somes,*

woulds, whos, hows and *afters* that enable us to ask either "Do you like milk?" or "Would you like some milk?"

12   More fundamentally, they discover that words can have radically different meanings depending on how they're strung together. Even before children start combining words on their own, most know the difference between "Big Bird is tickling Cookie Monster" and "Cookie Monster is tickling Big Bird." That awareness marks the zenith of language development. A chimp can learn to label things, and a high-powered computer can process more information in a minute than any person could handle in a lifetime. But neither a chimp nor a mainframe is any match for a runny-nosed 3-year-old when it comes to reporting who did what to whom. When a chimp with a signboard signals "Me banana you banana you," chances are he wants you to give him one, but the utterance could mean almost anything. Three-year-olds don't talk that way. The reason, most linguists agree, is that natural selection has outfitted the human brain with software for grammatical analysis. As MIT linguist Noam Chomsky realized more than 30 years ago, the world's languages all build sentences from noun phrases ("The big dog") and verb phrases ("ate my homework"). And toddlers who have never heard of grammar identify them effortlessly.

13   To confirm that point, psycholinguists Stephen Crain and Mineharu Nakayama once invited 3-, 4- and 5-year-olds to interview a talking "Star Wars" doll (Jabba the Hutt). With a child at his side, one researcher would pull out a picture and suggest asking Jabba about it. For example: "Ask Jabba if the boy who is unhappy is watching Mickey Mouse." You can't compose the right sentence—"Is the boy who is unhappy watching Mickey Mouse?"—unless you recognize *the-boy-who-is-unhappy* as a single noun phrase. As Chomsky would have predicted, the kids got it right every time.

14   If children's minds were open to all the possible relationships among words, they would never get very far. No one could memorize 140 million sentences, but a kid who masters 25 common recipes for a noun phrase can produce more than that number from scratch. Too much mental flexibility would confine children. Pinker observes: "innate constraints set them free." Not everyone is blessed with those constraints. Kids with a hereditary condition known as Specific Language Impairment, or SLI, never develop certain aspects of grammar, despite their normal IQs. But those are rare exceptions. Most kids are so primed for grammatical rules that they'll invent them if necessary.

15   Consider hearing adults who take up American Sign Language so they can share it with their deaf children. They tend to fracture phrases and leave verbs unconjugated. Yet their kids still become fluent, grammatical signers. "Children don't need good teachers to master language," says Elissa Newport, a cognitive scientist at the University of Rochester. "They pick up whatever rules they can find, and sharpen and extend them." That, according to University of Hawaii linguist Derek Bickerton, is why the crude pidgins that crop up in mixed-language communities quickly evolve into fully grammatical creoles. When language lacks a coherent grammar, children create one.

16   That's not to say language requires no nurture. Children raised in complete silence grow deaf to grammar. "Chelsea," whose correctable hearing problem went

untreated until she was 31, eventually learned enough words to hold a job in a vet's office. Yet her expressive powers have never surpassed those of a chimp with a signboard. She says things like "The woman is bus the going" or "I Wanda be drive come." Fortunately, Chelsea is a rare exception. Given even a few words to play with, most kids quickly take flight. "You don't need to have left the Stone Age," Pinker says. "You don't need to be middle class." All you need to be is young. ✳

Exercises

Do not refer to the selection for Exercises A and B unless your instructor directs you to do so.

A. DETERMINING THE MAIN IDEA AND PURPOSE

Choose the best answer.

_____ 1. The main idea of the selection is that
   a. no matter what language they speak, children all acquire language following the same remarkable path.
   b. children who are not exposed to language as infants rarely master it well.
   c. linguists disagree about the way children acquire language.
   d. further research must be done before linguists can know exactly how children acquire language.

_____ 2. With respect to the main idea, the writer's purpose is to
   a. summarize recent research on child language acquisition.
   b. show parents how to help their children learn to speak earlier.
   c. convince parents to spend more time talking to their newborn babies.
   d. explain the stages a child goes through on his or her way to acquiring language.

B. COMPREHENDING MAIN IDEAS

Choose the best answer.

_____ 1. Small children who have been deprived of language
   a. never learn to speak.
   b. rarely master it as adults.
   c. must attend special schools and be taught by specially trained teachers.
   d. show signs of mental and physical retardation.

_____ **2.** According to the article, children are designed to acquire certain kinds of knowledge at particular stages of development. This language acquisition usually occurs

    a. before birth to age 3.
    b. between ages 1 and 2.
    c. between ages 4 and 6.
    d. between ages 7 and 9.

_____ **3.** An important step in a baby's language development is the ability to

    a. reproduce sounds she hears.
    b. distinguish phonemes that make up syllables and identify word boundaries.
    c. recognize that sounds are merely symbols for things in the real world.
    d. accept sounds from their own language and reject sounds that are from foreign languages.

_____ **4.** According to Stanford psychologist Ellen Markman, a child learns to attach meaning to words by

    a. testing a whole set of theories about the meaning of each word he hears.
    b. figuring out for himself by process of deduction what each word means.
    c. learning to speak each word independently and then later connecting it to its meaning.
    d. following the assumption that a label refers to a whole object and not to its parts or qualities.

_____ **5.** The sentence "I bringed home three mouses" shows that the child

    a. has not learned correct grammar.
    b. is connecting phonemes that make sense.
    c. is employing common rules to express time and number in her sentences.
    d. has no flexibility in the way she expresses herself.

_____ **6.** When a child recognizes the differences in the sentences "Big Bird is tickling Cookie Monster" and "Cookie Monster is tickling Big Bird," it is a sign that he

    a. is showing a capacity for grammatical analysis.
    b. has learned that sentences are different from two-word phrases.
    c. can perform a remarkable feat that a chimpanzee can't.
    d. recognizes that all the things in the world around him have names.

COMPREHENSION SCORE

Score your answers for Exercises A and B as follows:

A. No. right _____ × 2 = _____

B. No. right _____ × 1 = _____

Total points from A and B _____ × 10 = _____ percent

You may refer to the selection as you work through the remaining exercises.

C. DISTINGUISHING BETWEEN MAIN IDEAS AND SUPPORTING DETAILS

Label the following statements from the selection as follows: MI if it represents a *main idea* and SD if it represents a *supporting detail*.

1. _____ The journey toward language starts not in the nursery but in the womb, where the fetus is continually bathed in the sounds of its mother's voice.

2. _____ Babies just 4 days old can distinguish one language from another.

3. _____ French newborns suck more vigorously when they hear French spoken than when they hear Russian.

4. _____ Russian babies show the opposite preference.

5. _____ At first, they notice only general rhythms and melodies.

6. _____ But newborns are also sensitive to speech sounds, and they home in quickly on the ones that matter.

D. INTERPRETING MEANING

Write your answers to these questions in your own words.

1. From the selection as a whole, state *two* important points Cowley makes

   about the way a child acquires language. _____

   _____

   _____

2. From paragraphs 2 and 3, what does Cowley mean when he says that

   "picking up a new language as an adult is as simple as picking up a truck"?

   _____

   _____

3. In paragraph 3, what does the writer mean in the first sentence when he says

   that children's brains are "wired" for the task of learning language? _____

   _____

4. What point is Cowley trying to make in paragraph 9 when he quotes Dennis the Menace telling Mr. Wilson, "I'm not a noying. I'm a cowboy"? _____

_____

_____

5. Read paragraph 10 again. If the 18-month-old child of a friend or relative were not acquiring words at the phenomenal rate Cowley cites—one word every two hours—what advice would you give the parents? _____

_____

_____

_____

E. ANALYZING STRUCTURE

Where appropriate, write your answers to these questions in your own words.

1. The *body*, or middle portion, of this essay has three distinct parts. Identify them and write the three main divisions in these spaces. (Hint: Look at the capitalized subheads.)

   a. _____   _____

   b. _____   _____

   c. _____   _____

2. The opening paragraph describes the language abilities of Barry, a little boy with Williams syndrome, and the concluding paragraph describes the language abilities of Chelsea, whose correctable hearing problem went untreated until adulthood. What is the point of using these two people to open and close the essay, and how do their experiences relate to the content of the article? _____

   _____

   _____

3. In paragraph 6, why does Cowley use this spacing? "one . . . word . . . at . . . a . . . time" _____

   _____ And this? "nonstopstreamofsound"? _____

   _____ What is the connection between these two examples and a baby's acquisition of language?_____

   _____

4. In paragraph 12, Cowley gives an example of a chimpanzee sentence, "Me banana you banana you." What point does this example support? _____

_____

F. UNDERSTANDING VOCABULARY

Look through the paragraph[s] listed below and find a word that matches each definition. An example has been done for you.

Ex. irregularities, conditions that are not normal [paragraph 1] abnormalities

1. assert, confirm, substantiate [2]   _____

2. quarreled, argued about, disagreed [3]   _____

3. completely unmindful of, lacking conscious awareness of [5] _____

4. choice, alternative [6]   _____

5. nonsense talk, babble [8]   _____

6. inborn, natural, present at birth [9 and 14]   _____

7. complete lists of skills and talents, entire vocabulary [11] _____

8. the highest point, apex, pinnacle [12]   _____

G. USING VOCABULARY

In parentheses before each sentence are some inflected forms of words from the selection. Study the context and the sentence. Then write the correct form in the space provided.

1. (abnormality, abnormal, abnormally) Williams syndrome is caused by an

   _____ chromosome 7, which results in a weak heart and low IQ.

2. (fluency, fluent, fluently) Most children develop complete

   _____ in their native language by the age of 3.

3. (deprivation, deprived, depriving, deprivable) Babies who are routinely

   _____ of hearing language rarely master it well later in life.

4. (vigor, vigorous, vigorously) Researchers have noted that even very small

   babies suck more _____ when they hear their own language than when they hear a foreign language.

5. (simplification, simplify, simple, simply) The innate biases that children bring

   to language learning allow them to _____ the process.

H. ANNOTATING EXERCISE

Annotate paragraphs 8 and 9 in the margin.

I. TOPICS FOR WRITING OR DISCUSSION

1. If you are acquainted with a child younger than 3—a brother or sister, nephew or niece, a neighbor's child or your own child—observe the child for an hour as he or she goes about playing, listen to the child's speech, and take notes. When you're finished with your observations, write a short report in which you evaluate the child's speech in relation to the stages of development Cowley describes in the article.
2. Judging from what you read in this article, what advice would you give to the parents of a newborn?
3. What makes a child's acquisition of language so phenomenal?

For Further Exploration

BOOK

Peter Farb, *Word Play: What Happens When People Talk* (1974). Although now out of print, this book is available in libraries. It remains a readable and comprehensive introduction to linguistics, including a chapter on how children learn to speak.

MOVIE

Helen Keller was blind, deaf, and mute from the age of 19 months, before she had fully developed language skills. She was miserable and out of control. An excellent film, *The Miracle Worker* (1962), was made of her life, and it is far superior to more recent versions. Directed by Arthur Penn, it stars Patty Duke as Helen and Anne Bancroft as Annie Sullivan, the teacher from the Perkins Institute who finally broke through Helen's silence and taught her to communicate.

WEB SITES

These two sites provide general information about language acquisition in children. The second one, sponsored by the Linguistic Society of America, provides links with FAQs (frequently asked questions).

- *www.facstaff.bucknell.edu/rbeard/acquisition.html,* "Mama Teached Me Talk!"
- *www.lsadc.org/web2/faq/lgacquisition.htm*

For parents who want to foster a love of learning in their children, this site offers message boards, academic skill builders, and Backyard Science:

- *www.familyeducation.com*

11

RICHARD WOLKOMIR

Making Up for Lost Time: The Rewards of Reading at Last

Richard Wolkomir graduated in 1964 from Syracuse University where he received a bachelor's degree in American studies with a minor in journalism. After working as a writer-editor for the McGraw-Hill Publishing Company in New York City, he moved to Vermont where he currently lives. A winner of many awards for his writing, Wolkomir has written extensively for Reader's Digest *and* National Geographic, *although now he writes mainly for the* Smithsonian *magazine, where this selection was first published. In it he recounts his experience helping Ken Adams, a 64-year-old Vermont farmer and a most unusual man: He was an illiterate who wanted to learn to read.*

Vocabulary Preview

WORD HISTORIES

Mesmerized (eponymous words) [paragraph 57]   In the course of his tutoring, Wolkomir finds himself just as *mesmerized* by the children's animal stories Adams reads as Adams does himself. The verb *mesmerize* describes a near-hypnotic state, in this case, a state of intense enjoyment. *Mesmerism* is named for Friedrich Anton Mesmer (1734–1815), an Austrian doctor who claimed that he could cure diseases by a process he called "animal magnetism." Apparently, Mesmer demonstrated his theory with patients by fixing his eyes on theirs, and they often later claimed to have been cured. Later, a government commission investigated this practice, and Mesmer was declared a fraud. It wasn't until later that *mesmerism* was understood to be the phenomenon that we know today as hypnotism.

Occasionally, a word for an idea enters the language from the name of a person associated with it. Such words are called *eponymous words* or *eponyms; mesmerize* is one such word. Here are three more eponymous words for you to look up in the dictionary.

gerrymander   _____

_____

_____

sadist   _____

_____

silhouette _____

_____

WORD PARTS

-Ine (animal adjectives) [paragraph 9]   Wolkomir recounts a book he loved as a child about a mouse, Peter Churchmouse, who has a *feline* friend, the rectory cat. The English adjective suffix *-ine* is added to a countless number of Latin roots referring to animals. They can either describe an animal or behavior associated with a particular animal. *Feline* (Latin root *felis*, "cat"), then, refers either to the animal itself or to behavior that is "catlike." Some other words with this suffix are *canine* (referring to a dog, from the Latin word for dog, *canis*); *lupine* (describing a wolf, from Latin, *lupus*); *equine* (referring to a horse, from Latin, *equus*); and *serpentine* (serpentlike, obviously from *serpent*, a word that comes to us, ultimately, from Sanskrit, an ancient language). What animal do these adjectives refer to? Check a dictionary if you are unsure.

leonine   _____

bovine   _____

porcine   _____

piscine   _____

WORD FAMILIES

Illiteracy [paragraph 43]   When Richard Wolkomir decided to help Ken Adams, a 64-year-old illiterate Vermont farmer, learn how to read, he was overwhelmed with the magnitude of the task. Adams's experience illustrates the sad situation of many students who "fall through the cracks." Branded as a "slow learner" by the teachers in his one-room schoolhouse, Adams was passed along year after year and received little help from either his family or his teachers. Yet as Wolkomir finds out, Adams is anything but slow: He is a whiz at fixing mechanical things, and, despite his obvious handicap, he tackles learning to read with diligence and good humor.

Illiteracy is a serious problem, even in a country as affluent as the United States; indeed, Wolkomir cites statistics that 40 percent of American adults read at a very low level of proficiency. The prefix *il-* means "not," and *literacy* refers to the ability to read and write, from the Latin root *littera* ("letter"). English has many words in this family, among them: *literal, literature,* and *obliterate* ("to destroy completely so as not to leave a trace"), from *ob-* ("off" or "away from") + *littera.*

RICHARD WOLKOMIR

Making Up for Lost Time: The Rewards of Reading at Last

1   I decide simply to blurt it out. "Ken?" I ask. "Why didn't you learn to read?" Through the Marshfield community center's window, I see snowy fields and the Vermont village's clapboard houses. Beyond, mountains bulge. "I was a slow

Richard Wolkomir (right) helps Ken Adams with a reading lesson.
Source: © 1999 Sue Owrutsky

learner," Ken says. "In school they just passed me along, and my folks told me I wasn't worth anything and wouldn't amount to anything."

2   Ken Adams is 64, his hair white. He speaks Vermontese, turning "I" into "Oy," and "ice" into "oyce." His green Buckeye Feeds cap is blackened with engine grease from fixing his truck's transmission, and pitch from chain-sawing pine logs. It is 2 degrees below zero outside on this December afternoon; he wears a green flannel shirt over a purple flannel shirt. He is unshaven, weather reddened. He is not a tall man, but a lifetime of hoisting hay bales has thickened his shoulders.

3   Through bifocals, Ken frowns at a children's picture book, *Pole Dog.* He is studying a drawing: an old dog waits patiently by a telephone pole, where its owners abandoned it. He glares at the next pictures. Cars whizzing by. Cruel people tormenting the dog. "Looks like they're shootin' at him, to me!" he announces. "Nobody wants an old dog," he says.

4   Ken turns the page. "He's still by the pole," he says. "But there's that red car that went by with those kids, ain't it?" He turns the page again. The red car has stopped to take the old dog in, to take him home. "*Somebody* wants an old dog!" Ken says. "Look at that!"

5   This is my first meeting with Ken. It is also my first meeting with an adult who cannot read.

6   I decided to volunteer as a tutor after a librarian told me that every day, on the sidewalks of our prim little Vermont town, I walk by illiterate men and women. We are unaware of them because they can be clever at hiding their inability to read. At a post office counter, for instance, when given forms to fill out, they say, "Could you help me with this? I left my glasses home."

7   Ken Adams is not alone in his plight. A 1993 U.S. Department of Education report on illiteracy said 21–23 percent of U.S. adults—about 40 million—read minimally, enough to decipher an uncomplicated meeting announcement. Another 25–28 percent read and write only slightly better. For instance, they can fill out a simple form. That means about *half* of all U.S. adults read haltingly. Millions, like Ken Adams, hardly read at all.

8   I wanted to meet nonreaders because I could not imagine being unable to decipher a street sign, or words printed on supermarket jars, or stories in a book. In fact, my own earliest memory is about reading. In this memory, in our little Hudson River town, my father is home for the evening from the wartime lifeboat factory where he is a foreman. And he has opened a book.

9   "Do you want to hear about Peter Churchmouse?" my father asks. Of course! It is my favorite, from the little library down the street. My father reads me stories about children lost in forests. Cabbage-stealing hares. A fisherman who catches a talking perch. But my favorite is Peter Churchmouse, a small but plucky cheese addict who befriends the rectory cat. Peter is also a poet, given to reciting original verse to his feline friend during their escapades. I cannot hear it enough.

10   My father begins to read. I settle back. I am taking a first step toward becoming literate—I am being read to. And although I am only 2, I know that words can be woven into tales.

11   Now, helping Ken Adams learn to read, I am re-entering that child's land of chatty dogs and spats-wearing frogs. Children's books—simply worded, the sentences short—are perfect primers, even for 60-year-olds who turn the pages with labor-thickened fingers and who never had such books read to them when they were children.

12   "Do you remember what happened from last time?" asks Sherry Olson, of Central Vermont Adult Basic Education, who tutors Ken an hour and a half each week.

13   I have volunteered as Sherry's aide. My work requires too much travel for me to be a full-fledged tutor. But I am actually relieved, not having sole responsibility for teaching an adult to read. That is because—when I think about it—I don't know how I read myself. I scan a printed page; the letters magically reveal meaning. It is effortless. I don't know how I do it. As for teaching a man to read from scratch, how would I even begin?

14   Sherry, a former third-grade teacher, gives me hints, like helping Ken to learn words by sight so that he doesn't have to sound out each letter. Also, we read stories so Ken can pick out words in context. Ken reads Dr. Seuss rhyming books and tales about young hippopotamuses helping on the family farm. At the moment, we are reading a picture book about Central American farmers who experience disaster when a volcano erupts.

15   "The people had to move out, and put handkerchiefs over their noses!" Ken says, staring at the pages. He starts to read: "They . . . prayed? . . . for the . . . fire? . . ." "Yes, that's right, fire," Sherry says. "They prayed for the fire to . . . go out?" "That word is 'stop,'" Sherry says.

16   I listen carefully. A few sessions ahead, it will be my turn to try teaching. "They prayed for the fire to *stop*," Ken says, placing a thick forefinger under each word. "They watched from the s . . ." "Remember we talked about those?" Sherry says. "When a word ends in a silent *e*, what does that silent *e* do to the vowel?" "It makes it say itself," Ken says. "So what's the vowel in *s-i-d-e*?" she asks. "It's *i*, and it would say its own name,'" Ken says, pronouncing it "oy." "So that would be 'side.'" "Good," Sherry says.

17   Ken reads the sentence: "They watched from the side of the hill!" He sounds quietly triumphant. "They-uh," he says, in backcountry Vermontese. "That's done it."

18   After the session, I stand a few minutes with Ken in the frozen driveway. He has one foot on the running board of his ancient truck, which he somehow keeps going. He tells me he was born in 1931 into a family eking out an existence on a hardscrabble farm. His trouble in school with reading is puzzling, because Ken is intelligent.

19   For instance, he says he was late today because he had to fix his truck. And now he launches into a detailed analysis of the transmission mechanisms of various species of trucks. Also, during the tutoring session, we played a game that required strewing word cards upside down on a table and remembering their locations. Ken easily outscored both Sherry and me in this exercise.

20   Ken described himself as a "slow learner," but clearly he is not slow. Sherry has told me he probably suffers from a learning disability. People with these perceptual disorders experience difficulties such as seeing letters reversed. Although their intelligence may actually be above average, learning to read is difficult for them. They need individual tutoring.

21   "It was a one-room school, with eight grades, so I didn't get much attention there," Ken tells me. "It was just the same as the folks at home were doing when they kicked me along through the grades, and when you got to be 16, that's when they kicked you out."

22   After he left school, he left home. "Then you knock around, one farm to another," he says. "I'd get $15 a week, and room and board." Besides farming, he worked in bobbin mills and sawmills and granite quarries. "Then I was at a veneer mill in Bradford," he says. "After that I was caretaker at a farm for six years until I had to give it up because I had heart attacks."

23   Now he subsists on a $400-a-month Social Security disability pension plus $90 a month in food stamps. He lives alone in a farmhouse he built himself more than 25 years ago, five miles up a mountain dirt road. He earns money for his medicines by cutting firewood, haying, digging postholes with his tractor, snowplowing and cutting brush. "I'm doing odds-and-ends jobs where you can take your time, because the doctor told me I have to stop whenever I feel I need to rest," he says.

24   He cannot afford electricity from the power company, but he gets what current he needs, mostly for lights, by—ingeniously—drawing it from car batteries. To recharge the batteries, he hooks them up in his truck for a day. He also can charge them with a diesel generator. He waits until prices dip to buy fuel for his generator and tractor. "I've got a few maples around my house," he tells me. "I'll find a rusted-out evaporator, fix it up and make syrup—there's always a few things I can do, I guess."

25   I ask how he's managed all these years, not reading. He says his bosses did the reading for him. And now a Marshfield couple, lifelong friends, help him read his mail and bills and notices. But they are entering their 80s. "Now I've got to learn to read myself, as a backup," Ken says.

26   To find out more about what illiteracy does to people like Ken, I telephoned the U.S. Department of Education and spoke with the Deputy Secretary, Madeleine Kunin. She told me that only 3–5 percent of adult Americans cannot read at all. "But literacy is a moving target," she said. "We figure the 40 million who do read, but at the lowest proficiency levels, have difficulty handling some

of the tasks they need to hold a job today." Kunin, a former Vermont governor, cited that state's snowplow drivers: "Now they have computers attached, and they need a high school degree just to drive a snowplow."

27 Ken arrives for his next session in a dark mood. It turns out his tape recorder, used for vocabulary practice, is broken. "I can't fix it because the money's all gone for this month," he says. "I had to go to the doctor, and that's $30, and it was $80 for the pills, and they keep going up." He says one of his prescriptions jumped from $6.99 to $13 in two months. "I don't know if I'll keep taking them," he says. Illiteracy has condemned Ken to a lifetime of minimum-wage poverty.

28 He brightens reading a story. It is about a dog, John Brown, who deeply resents his mistress's new cat. Ken stumbles over a word. "Milk?" Sherry and I nod. "Go and give her some milk," Ken reads, then pauses to give us a dispatch from the literacy front: "I was trying to figure that out, and then I see it has an *i*," he says.

29 My own first attempt at solo tutoring finally comes, and I am edgy. Sherry has wryly admonished Ken, "You help Richard out." I show him file cards, each imprinted with a word for Ken to learn by sight. He is supposed to decipher each word, then incorporate it in a sentence. I write his sentence on the card to help him when he reviews at home. Ken peers at the first word. "All," he says, getting it easily. He makes up a sentence: "We all went away."

30 "That's right," I say. Maybe this won't be so hard after all. I write Ken's sentence on the card for him. Then I flip another card. Ken peers at it, his face working as he struggles with the sounds. "As," he says.

31 During our last session, he confused "as" and "at." Now he has it right. So he has been doing his homework.

32 "As we went down the road, we saw a moose," Ken says, composing a sentence. That reminds him that the state recently allowed moose hunting, game officials arguing that moose have become so plentiful they cause highway accidents. "Yesterday, I come around a turn and there was *ten* moose, a big male and females and young ones," Ken says. "They shouldn't be shooting those moose—they ain't hurting anyone, and it ain't the moose's fault if people don't use their brakes."

33 I flip another card. "At!" Ken says, triumphing over another of our last session's troublemakers. "We are at the school." But the next word stumps him. It is "be." I put my finger under the first letter. "What's that sound?" I ask. When he stares in consternation, I make the sound "buh." But Ken is blocked. He can't sound out the next letter, even though he has often done it before. "Eeeee," I say, trying to help. "Now put the two sounds together."

34 Ken stares helplessly at the word. I am beginning to understand the deep patience needed to tutor a man like Ken, who began these sessions a year before, knowing the alphabet but able to sound out only a few words. "Buh . . . eeee," I say, enunciating as carefully as I can. "Buh . . . eeee," Ken repeats. Abruptly, his forehead unfurrows. "Oh, that's 'be,' " he says. "Be—We should be splitting wood!"

35 "Was that what you were doing before the tutoring session?" I ask, to give us both a break. "Nope, plowing snow with my tractor for my friend who broke off his ankle," Ken says.

36 That is arresting information. When I ask what happened, Ken says his octogenarian friend was chain-sawing cherry trees when a bent-back branch lashed

out, smashing his lower leg. Ken, haying a field, saw his friend ease his tractor down from the mountainside woodlot, grimacing in agony, working the tractor's pedals with his one good foot.

37   Ken himself once lost his grip on a hay bale he was hoisting. A twig poking from the bale blinded his right eye. Now learning to read is doubly difficult because his remaining eye often tires and blurs. These grim country stories of Ken's make my worries—delayed flights, missed appointments—seem trivial. I flip another card: "But." "Bat," Ken says cautiously. "Buh . . . uh . . . tuh," I prompt. "But," he finally says. "I would do it, but I have to go somewhere else."

38   I write Ken's sentence on the card and he reads it back. But he stumbles over his own words, unable to sound out "would." I push down rising impatience by remembering the old man in the woods, crawling toward his tractor, dragging that smashed leg.

39   Finally, I put away the cards, glad to be done with them. Tutoring can be frustrating. Why are even easy words sometimes so hard to get? Now we look at a puzzle. On one side it has pictures of various automobile parts. On the other side are printed the parts' names. The idea is to match the pictures and the names. Before I can start asking Ken to try sounding out big terms like "connecting rod," he points to one of the drawings. It looks to me like deer antlers. "Carburetor?" I guess. "Exhaust manifold," Ken says.

40   "What's this one?" I inquire. For all I know, it might be something Han Solo is piloting through hyperspace. "Starter," Ken says. It seems to me he is gloating a little. He points again. "Camshaft?" I ask. Ken corrects me. "Crankshaft," he says, dryly.

41   It is a standoff. I know the printed words. Ken knows the actual objects to which the words refer. "When I was a kid," he tells me, "I bought an old '35 truck. Sometimes it had brakes and sometimes it didn't. I was probably 17. It made lots of smoke, so mosquitoes never bothered me. But one day I got sick of it. I put it under a pine tree and I hoisted the engine up into the tree to look at it. The pressure plate weren't no good. And the fellow showed me how to fix it."

42   That reminds Ken of a later episode. "One time we had to get the hay in, but the baler was jammed. We had the guys from the tractor place, but they could not fix it. Finally I asked the old guy for some wrenches and I adjusted it, and I kept on adjusting, and after that it worked perfectly. I just kept adjusting it a hair until I had it. And then we were baling hay!" No wonder Ken's bosses were happy to do his reading for him. Even so, in our late 20th-century wordscape, illiteracy stymies people like him. And working with Ken has me puzzled: Why do so many people fail to learn to read?

43   I telephoned an expert, Bob Caswell, head of Laubach Literacy International, a nonprofit organization that trains tutors worldwide. He told me many nonreaders, like Ken Adams, suffer from perceptual reading disorders. But there are other reasons for illiteracy, and it is by no means confined to any one part of the population.

44   "People think adult nonreaders are mainly poor, urban minorities, but 41 percent are English-speaking whites," Caswell said, adding that 22 percent are English-speaking blacks, 22 percent are Spanish-speaking, and 15 percent are other non-English speakers. More than half of nonreading adults live in small

towns and suburbs. Caswell cited U.S. Department of Labor figures that put illiteracy's annual national cost at $225 billion in workplace accidents, lost produc-
tivity, unrealized tax revenues, welfare and crime. One big reason for this whop-
ping problem is *parents* who read poorly.

45   Well over a third of all kids now entering public schools have parents who read
inadequately, he said. "Everywhere we find parents who *want* to read to their
kids, but can't," he added. "And a child with functionally illiterate parents is
twice as likely to grow up to be functionally illiterate."

46   But as I met some of Ken Adams' fellow students, I discovered all sorts of
causes for being unable to decipher an English sentence. For instance, I met a
woman who had escaped from Laos to Connecticut knowing only Laotian. She
learned enough English watching *Sesame Street* ("Big Bird and all that," she told
me), and later from being tutored, to become a citizen.

47   I also met a man in his 30s who worked on a newspaper's printing press. He
could not spell the simplest words. He said it was because, at age 10, he had begun bringing alcohol to school in peanut-butter jars. After his son was born, he
turned to Alcoholics Anonymous and mustered the courage to seek tutoring.

48   I met another man who had dropped out of school in frustration. Not until he
tried to enlist in the military did he discover he was nearly deaf. The operator of
a creamery's cheese-cutting machine told me he never learned to read because
his family had been in a perpetual uproar, his mother leaving his father seven
times in one year. And I met a farm wife, 59, who rarely left her mountaintop.
But now, with tutoring she was finally learning to read, devouring novels—"enjoyment books," she called them.

49   In central Vermont, these struggling readers receive free tutoring from nonprofit
Adult Basic Education offices, each employing a few professionals, like Sherry Olson, but relying heavily on armies of volunteers, like me. Other states have their
own systems. Usually, the funding is a combination of federal and state money,
sometimes augmented with donations. Mostly, budgets are bare bones.

50   Many states also rely on nonprofit national organizations, like Laubach Literacy Action (Laubach International's U.S. division) and Literacy Volunteers of
America, both headquartered in Syracuse, New York, to train volunteers.
Laubach's Bob Caswell told me that, nationwide, literacy services reach only 10
percent of adult nonreaders. "Any effort is a help," he said.

51   Help has come late for Ken Adams. Reviewing his portfolio, I found the goals he
set for himself when he began: "To read and write better. And to get out and
meet people and develop more trust." Asked by Sherry to cite things that he
does well, he had mentioned "fixing equipment, going to school and learning to
read, trying new things, telling stories, farming." He remembered being in a
Christmas play in second grade and feeling good about that. And he remembered playing football in school: "They would pass it to me and I'd run across
the goal to make a score." He mentioned no fond family memories. But he had
some good moments. "I remember the first time I learned to drive a tractor," he
had said. "We were working in the cornfields. I was proud of that." And a later
notation, after he had several months of tutoring, made me think of Ken living

alone in his hand-built farmhouse on ten acres atop the mountain. "I like to use recipes," he said. "I use them more as I learn to read and write better. I made Jell-O with fruit, and I make bean salad. I feel good I can do that."

52   In our tutoring sessions, between bouts with the vocabulary cards, Ken tells me he was the oldest of four children. When he was small, his father forced him to come along to roadside bars, and then made Ken sit alone in the car for hours. Ken remembers shivering on subzero nights. "He always said I'd never amount to nothing," Ken says.

53   I ask Ken, one day, if his inability to read has made life difficult. He tells me, "My father said I'd never get a driver's license, and he said nobody would ever help me." Ken had to walk five miles down his mountain and then miles along highways to get to work. "And," he recalls, "I was five years in the quarries in Graniteville—that was a long way." Sometimes he paid neighbors to drive him down the mountain. "They said the same as my father, that I'd never get a license," he says. "They wanted the money."

54   It was not until he was 40 years old that he applied for a license. He had memorized sign shapes and driving rules, and he passed easily. "After I got my license I'd give people a ride down myself," he says. "And they'd ask, 'How much? And I'd always say, 'Nothing, not a danged thing!' "

55   To review the words he has learned, Ken maintains a notebook. On each page, in large block letters, he writes the new word, along with a sentence using the word. He also tapes to each page a picture illustrating the sentence, as a memory aid. To keep him supplied with pictures to snip, I bring him my old magazines. He is partial to animals. He points to one photograph, a black bear cub standing upright and looking back winsomely over its shoulder. "That one there's my favorite," Ken says. And then he tells me, glowering, that he has seen drivers swerve to intentionally hit animals crossing the road. "That rabbit or raccoon ain't hurting anyone," he says.

56   We start a new book, *The Strawberry Dog*. Ken picks out the word "dog" in the title. "That dog must eat strawberries," he says. "I used to have a dog like that. I was picking blackberries. Hey, where were those berries going? Into my dog!"

57   We read these books to help Ken learn words by sight and context. But it seems odd, a white-haired man mesmerized by stories about talkative beavers and foppish toads. Yet, I find myself mesmerized, too. The sessions are reteaching me the exhilaration I found in a narrative as a child, listening to my father read about Peter Churchmouse. Our classes glide by, a succession of vocabulary words—"house," "would," "see"—interwoven with stories about agrarian hippopotamuses and lost dogs befriended.

58   One afternoon it is my last session with Ken. We have wrestled with words through a Christmas and a March sugaring, a midsummer haying, an October when Ken's flannel shirts were specked with sawdust from chain-sawing stove logs. Now the fields outside are snowy; it is Christmas again.

59   My wife and I give Ken a present that she picked out. It is bottles of jam and honey and watermelon pickles, nicely wrapped. Ken quickly slides the package into his canvas tote bag with his homework. "Aren't you going to open it?"

Sherry asks. "I'll open it Christmas day," Ken says. "It's the only present I'll get." "No, it isn't," she says, and she hands him a present she has brought.

60   And so we begin our last session with Ken looking pleased. I start with a vocabulary review. "Ignition coil," Ken says, getting the first card right off. He gets "oil filter," too. He peers at the next card. "Have," he says. And he reads the review sentence: "Have you gone away?"

61   He is cruising today. When I flip the next card, he says "There's that 'for.'" It is a word that used to stump him. I turn another card. He gets it instantly. "But." He gets "at," then another old nemesis, "are." I ask him to read the card's review sentence. "Are we going down . . . street?" he says. He catches himself. "Nope. That's down*town*!"

62   I am amazed at Ken's proficiency. A while ago, I had complained to my wife that Ken's progress seemed slow. She did some math: one and half hours of tutoring a week, with time off for vacations and snowstorms and truck breakdowns, comes to about 70 hours a year. "That's like sending a first grader to school for only 12 days a year," she said. And so I am doubly amazed at how well Ken is reading today. Besides, Sherry Olson has told me that he now sounds out—or just knows—words that he never could have deciphered when he began. And this reticent man has recently read his own poems to a group of fellow tutees—his new friends—and their neighbors at a library get-together.

63   But now we try something new, a real-world test: reading the supermarket advertising inserts from a local newspaper. Each insert is a hodgepodge of food pictures, product names and prices. I point to a word and Ken ponders. "C" he says finally. "And it's got those two *e's*—so that would be 'coffee'!" I point again. He gets "Pepsi." Silently, he sounds out the letters on a can's label. "So that's 'corn,'" he announces. He picks out "brownies." This is great. And then, even better, he successfully sounds out the modifier: "Fudge," he says. "They-uh!"

64   We're on a roll. But now I point to the page's most tortuous word. Ken starts in the middle again, "ta?" I point my finger at the first letters. "Po," he says, unsure. As always when he reads, Ken seems like a beginning swimmer. He goes a few strokes. Flounders.

65   "Po-ta . . . ," Ken says. He's swum another stroke. "To," he says, sounding out the last syllable. "Po-ta-to, po-ta-to—Hey, that's potato!" He's crossed the pond. "Ken!" I say. "Terrific!" He sticks out his chin. He almost smiles. "Well, I done better this time," he says. "Yup, I did good." ✳

From Richard Wolkomir, "Making Up for Lost Time: The Rewards of Reading at Last," *Smithsonian*, August 1996. © 1996 Richard Wolkomir. Reprinted by permission of the author.

Exercises

Do not refer to the selection for Exercises A and B unless your instructor directs you to do so.

A. DETERMINING THE MAIN IDEA AND PURPOSE

Choose the best answer.

_____ **1.** The main idea of the selection is that
  a. illiteracy is the most difficult problem American educators face today.
  b. learning to read as an adult is a tedious but rewarding activity.
  c. teaching an illiterate adult is a frustrating process that requires time, profound patience, and understanding.
  d. adult illiterates can never master reading skills they should have learned as children.

_____ **2.** With respect to the main idea, the writer's purpose is to
  a. urge teachers to do a better job of teaching children to read.
  b. criticize the nation's teachers for passing students along, thereby dooming them to illiteracy and underemployment.
  c. explain the difficulties and triumphs one illiterate adult experienced as he learned to read.
  d. promote adult literacy programs and encourage the reader to volunteer in these programs.

B. COMPREHENDING MAIN IDEAS

Choose the correct answer.

_____ **1.** According to a U.S. Department of Education report on illiteracy and another report cited in the selection, only 3 to 5 percent of adult Americans are completely illiterate; however, the number of adult Americans who read haltingly or minimally is around
  a. 10 percent.
  b. 25 percent.
  c. 40 percent.
  d. 50 percent.

_____ **2.** Wolkomir finds that the most appropriate materials for teaching an adult learner like Ken Adams are
  a. the daily newspaper and supermarket ads.
  b. children's books.
  c. books on subjects that the student is interested in.
  d. comic books.

_____ **3.** Ken Adams displays a special talent for
  a. fixing household appliances.
  b. fixing trucks and other mechanical things.
  c. cooking.
  d. building houses and barns.

_____ **4.** According to Sherry Olson, the primary reading tutor, Ken Adams's difficulty with learning to read as a child was probably the result of
  a. brain damage at birth.
  b. his own unwillingness to do his schoolwork.
  c. his elementary teachers' incompetence.
  d. a perceptual reading disorder.

_____ **5.** Bob Caswell, of Laubach Literacy International, reports that adult nonreaders are

    a. not confined to any one segment of the population.
    b. generally urban minorities.
    c. unwilling to take the necessary steps to learn to read.
    d. living on farms where reading is not a necessary skill.

_____ **6.** One particular problem for more than a third of children now entering public schools is that they may fall behind because

    a. their school districts have cut budgets drastically.
    b. their parents are themselves functionally illiterate and can't help them much.
    c. their classrooms are understaffed.
    d. their instructors can't agree on the best method to teach reading.

COMPREHENSION SCORE

Score your answers for Exercises A and B as follows:

A. No. right _____ × 2 = _____   **B.** No. right _____ × 1 = _____

Total points from A and B _____ × 10 = _____ percent

You may refer to the selection as you work through the remaining exercises.

C. LOCATING SUPPORTING DETAILS

For each main idea stated here, find and write down two supporting details.

1. Sherry, Ken Adams' primary tutor, gives the writer tips on how to go about helping Ken learn to read. [paragraph 14]

    a. _____

    b. _____

2. Ken Adams describes himself as a "slow learner," but clearly he is not slow. [paragraph 19]

    a. _____

    b. _____

D. INTERPRETING MEANING

Write your answers to these questions in your own words.

1. In paragraphs 8–10, Wolkomir describes his own fond memories of reading.

How does he account for his love of reading? _____

2. From the selection as a whole and specifically from paragraph 21, what might be one reason that Ken Adams's teachers didn't recognize his

difficulty and help him? _____

_____

_____

_____

3. From paragraph 26, what is Madeleine Kunin's main point about literacy and
   the work force? _____

   _____

4. For the writer, what does helping Ken Adams learn to read teach him about
   reading? _____

5. Briefly list three benefits that Ken Adams derived from learning to read.

   _____

   _____

   _____

E. ANALYZING STRUCTURE

Where appropriate, write your answers to these questions in your own words.

1. From paragraph 13, what are the two important points Wolkomir makes
   about learning to read, at least for most people. The process is both

   _____ and _____ .

2. What is the purpose of the statistics cited in paragraphs 7 and 26? _____

   _____

3. _____   Read paragraph 26 again. A good title for this paragraph would be
   a. "Literacy: A Moving Target."   c. "A High School Education Isn't Enough."
   b. "Adult Literacy Statistics."   d. "How Illiteracy Affects Its Victims."

4. Look again at paragraphs 36 and 37 in which the writer cites "grim country
   stories." What is the significance for the writer of the chainsaw accident

   mentioned in paragraph 38? _____

   _____

5. Look again at paragraphs 46–48, and write the sentence that states the main

   idea for this section. _____

   _____

F. UNDERSTANDING VOCABULARY

Choose the best definition according to an analysis of word parts or the context.

_____ 1. not alone in his *plight* [paragraph 7]:
   a. bad state
   b. alienation
   c. lack of education
   d. unhappiness

_____ **2.** I *scan* a printed page [13]:

    a. read carefully
    b. open
    c. glance over
    d. study intensely

_____ **3.** by *ingeniously* drawing it [24]:

    a. tightly
    b. with inventive skill
    c. slowly and carefully
    d. intelligently

_____ **4.** Sherry has *wryly admonished* Ken [29]:

    a. harshly criticized
    b. cautiously suggested
    c. humorously warned
    d. subtly reminded

_____ **5.** he stares in *consternation* [33]: Showing

    a. fear and anxiety
    b. uncertainty and bewilderment
    c. amazement and delight
    d. confidence and self-assurance

_____ **6.** this *reticent* man [61]:

    a. restrained, reserved
    b. outspoken, blunt
    c. honest, open
    d. shy, timid

G. USING VOCABULARY

From the following list of vocabulary words, choose a word that fits in each blank according to both the grammatical structure of the sentence and the context. Use each word in the list only once. Do not change the form of the word. (Note that there are more words than sentences.)

augmented	enunciated	nemesis	sole
context	exhilaration	primers	triumph
eking	mesmerized	reticent	trivial

1. The writer _____ each word carefully when working with Ken Adams, and the difficulties his student faces make him realize how

_____ some of his own concerns are.

2. It is clear from the selection that Adams feels both a sense of _____

and of _____ from making such good progress. (   )

3. Adams's life has been difficult: _____ out an existence on

Social Security Disability _____ by food stamps.

4. Despite the fact that Adams is reading children's stories, he appears to be

_____ by the stories; also, the stories allow him to figure out words

from the _____ .

H. LOCATING EVIDENCE

Go through the article and locate any piece of information that supports this idea: Illiteracy presents serious obstacles for adults.

Identify evidence by putting a star in the margin next to the sentence or by putting the words in brackets.

I.   TOPICS FOR WRITING OR DISCUSSION

1. Using Ken Adams as the central example, write a paragraph in which you summarize the plight of adult illiterates.
2. How would you characterize Ken Adams from what you have read? In a paragraph or two, analyze his character, being sure to include pertinent information about his background, his goals, and the difference learning to read made in his life.
3. Do you remember learning to read? Write a short paper describing your first experiences learning to read. Who taught you? Was it pleasurable or frustrating? To what extent have your childhood experiences affected your attitude toward reading as an adult?

For Further Exploration

BOOK

National Academy of Education, *Becoming a Nation of Readers* (1985). This study examines ways teachers and parents can promote literacy among American students.

MOVIE

Stanley and Iris (1990), directed by Martin Ritt and starring Robert De Niro and Jane Fonda, follows the relationship between Fonda, a lonely widow who works as a waitress, and De Niro, a shy loner who finally admits a terrible secret—he can't read. Fonda takes him in hand and changes his life—and hers.

WEB SITES

An updated report with many links on the state of literacy in the United States is available at this site sponsored by the National Institute for Literacy:

• *www.nifl.gov*

These sites list various literacy programs in the United States:

• *www.laubach.org/* (Laubach Literacy Action, mentioned in paragraph 50)
• *literacy.kent.edu/LVA/index.html* (Literacy Volunteers of America, also mentioned in paragraph 50)

12

PACO UNDERHILL

Shop Like a Man

Paco Underhill and his New York company Envirosell are credited with establishing the science of shopping. For over twenty years, Underhill, who has been described as a retail anthropologist, has advised corporate clients—among them Starbucks, McDonald's, and Blockbuster—on how to improve their customer base. He gathers research by following customers around stores and public spaces and videotaping their behavior. In the book that this selection comes from, Why We Buy: The Science of Shopping, *Underhill explains modern-day consumer behavior. This particular excerpt examines the differences in the way male and female shoppers typically behave in stores.*

Vocabulary Preview

WORD HISTORIES

Emporium [paragraph 19] The word *emporium* is a rather old-fashioned word that means simply a "store." Although the word entered English from Latin, it actually derives from two Greek words: *emporion* ("market") and *emporos* ("merchant" or "traveler"). An *emporium* was originally a marketplace where merchants or traveling salesmen could come together and exchange goods.

Accoutrements [paragraph 24] Underhill writes that men are "interested in all the *accoutrements*, all the tools of the bartender trade." This word, also spelled *accouterments*, in this context means "accessory items of equipment." The word most likely derives from the Latin verb *consuere*, "to sew together." In modern English, however, the word's meaning has been enlarged to include all sorts of accessories beyond those associated with clothing. In other contexts, *accoutrements* can also refer to what are called "trappings" or "outward forms of recognition"—that is, possessions that indicate social status, like a certain brand of automobile or entertainment equipment.

WORD PARTS

Proto- [paragraph 14] Underhill's firm conducted a study for "a wireless phone provider that was developing a *prototype* retail store." The Greek prefix *proto-* means "first in time" or "earliest." A *prototype*, then, is the "first type" of something built—in other words, a model—whether it is a store, a computer, or a new automobile. Other words beginning with this prefix are *protohumans* (the first human species), *protohistory*, *proton*, and *protoplasm* (the living matter of plant and animal cells providing essential life functions).

WORD FAMILIES

Unchaperoned   Underhill humorously writes that "any wife who's watching the family budget knows better than to send her husband to the supermarket *unchaperoned*." A *chaperone* usually refers to an older or wiser person who accompanies a young woman in public or who supervises an activity where young people might congregate (for example, school dances). Here, Underhill uses the word facetiously to mean "unaccompanied." The word derives from the French word *chape,* the hood worn by the Knights of the Garter who attended the queen, and it is related to *caput,* the Latin word for "head." Here are a few other words in this family:

cap	a casual head covering
capital	a capital letter, which stands at the head of a word; a capital city, which houses the head of the government; or capital punishment
capitulate	to surrender or come to terms, from the Latin phrase "to draw up under heads or chapters"
decapitate	to cut off a person's head
chapter	the main divisions or heads of a book

PACO UNDERHILL

Shop Like a Man

1   When they were a client I used to tell Woolworth's, if you would just hold Dad's Day at your stores once a week, you'd bring in a lot more money.

2   They didn't listen. You may have heard.

3   Men and women differ in just about every other way, so why shouldn't they shop differently, too? The conventional wisdom on male shoppers is that they don't especially like to do it, which is why they don't do much of it. It's a struggle just to get them to be patient company for a woman while she shops. As a result, the entire shopping experience—from packaging design to advertising to merchandising to store design and fixturing—is generally geared toward the female shopper.

4   Women do have a greater affinity for what we think of as shopping—walking at a relaxed pace through stores, examining merchandise, comparing products and values, interacting with sales staff, asking questions, trying things on and ultimately making purchases. Most purchasing traditionally falls to women, and they usually do it willingly—even when shopping for the mundane necessities, even when the experience brings no particular pleasure, women tend to do it in dependable, agreeable fashion. Women take pride in their ability to shop prudently and well. In a study we ran of baby products, women interviewed insisted that they knew the price of products by heart, without even having to look. (Upon further inquiry, we discovered that they were mostly wrong.) As women's roles change, so does their shopping behavior—they're becoming a lot more like men in that regard—but they're still the primary buyer in the American marketplace.

5   In general, men, in comparison, seem like loose cannons. We've timed enough shoppers to know that men always move faster than women through a store's

aisles. Men spend less time looking, too. In many settings it's hard to get them to look at anything they hadn't intended to buy. They usually don't like asking where things are, or any other questions, for that matter. (They shop the way they drive.) If a man can't find the section he's looking for, he'll wheel about once or twice, then give up and leave the store without ever asking for help. You can watch men just shut down.

6   You'll see a man impatiently move through a store to the section he wants, pick something up, and then, almost abruptly, he's ready to buy, having taken no apparent joy in the process of finding. You've practically got to get out of his way. When a man takes clothing into a dressing room, the only thing that stops him from buying it is if it doesn't fit. Women, on the other hand, try things on as only part of the consideration process, and garments that fit just fine may still be rejected on other grounds. In one study, we found that 65 percent of male shoppers who tried something on bought it, as opposed to 25 percent of female shoppers. This is a good argument for positioning fitting rooms nearer the men's department than the women's, if they are shared accommodations. If they are not, men's dressing rooms should be very clearly marked, because if he has to search for it, he may just decide it's not worth the trouble.

7   Here's another statistical comparison: Eighty-six percent of women look at price tags when they shop. Only 72 percent of men do. For a man, ignoring the price tag is almost a measure of his virility. As a result, men are far more easily upgraded than are women shoppers. They are also far more suggestible than women—men seem so anxious to get out of the store that they'll say yes to almost anything.

8   Now, a shopper such as that could be seen as more trouble than he's worth. But he could also be seen as a potential source of profits, especially given his lack of discipline. Either way, men now do more purchasing than ever before. And that will continue to grow. As they stay single longer than ever, they learn to shop for things their fathers never had to buy. And because they marry women who work long and hard too, they will be forced to shoulder more of the burden of shopping. The manufacturers, retailers and display designers who pay attention to male ways, and are willing to adapt the shopping experience to them, will have an edge in the twenty-first century.

9   The great traditional arena for male shopping behavior has always been the supermarket. It's here, with thousands of products all within easy reach, that you can witness the carefree abandon and restless lack of discipline for which the gender is known. In one supermarket study, we counted how many shoppers came armed with lists. Almost all of the women had them. Less than a quarter of the men did. Any wife who's watching the family budget knows better than to send her husband to the supermarket unchaperoned. Giving him a vehicle to commandeer, even if it is just a shopping cart, only emphasizes the potential for guyness in the experience. Throw a couple of kids in with Dad and you've got a lethal combination; he's notoriously bad at saying no when there's grocery acquisitioning to be done. Part of being Daddy is being the provider, after all. It goes to the heart of a man's self-image.

10   I've spent hundreds of hours of my life watching men moving through supermarkets. One of my favorite video moments starred a dad carrying his little

daughter on his shoulders. In the snacks aisle, the girl gestures toward the animal crackers display. Dad grabs a box off the shelf, opens it and hands it up—without even a thought to the fact that his head and shoulders are about to be dusted with cookie crumbs. It's hard to imagine Mom in such a wanton scenario. Another great lesson in male shopping came about watching a man and his two small sons pass through the cereal aisle. When the boys plead for their favorite brand, he pulls down a box and instead of carefully opening it along the reclosable tab, he just rips the top, knowing full well that once the boys start in, there won't be any need to reclose it.

11   Supermarkets are places of high impulse buying for both sexes—fully 60 to 70 percent of purchases there were unplanned, grocery industry studies have shown us. But men are particularly suggestible to the entreaties of children as well as eye-catching displays.

12   There's another profligate male behavior that invariably shows itself at supermarkets, something we see over and over on the video we shoot at the registers: The man almost always pays. Especially when a man and woman are shopping together, he insists on whipping out his wad and forking it over, lest the cashier mistakenly think it's the woman of the house who's bringing home the bacon. No wonder retailers commonly call men wallet carriers. Or why the conventional wisdom is, sell to the woman, close to the man. Because while the man may not love the experience of shopping, he gets a definite thrill from the experience of paying. It allows him to feel in charge even when he isn't. Stores that sell prom gowns depend on this. Generally, when Dad's along, the girl will get a pricier frock than if just Mom was there with her.

13   In some categories, men shoppers put women to shame. We ran a study for a store where 17 percent of the male customers we interviewed said they visited the place more than once a week! Almost one-quarter of the men there said they had left the house that day with no intention of visiting the store—they just found themselves wandering in out of curiosity. The fact that it was a computer store may have had something to do with it, of course. Computer hardware and software have taken the place of cars and stereo equipment as the focus of male love of technology and gadgetry. Clearly, most of the visits to the store were information-gathering forays. On the videotape, we watched the men reading intently the software packaging and any other literature or signage available. The store was where men bought software, but it was also where they did most of their learning about it. This underscores another male shopping trait—just as they hate to ask directions, they like to get their information firsthand, preferably from written materials, instructional videos or computer screens.

14   A few years back we ran a study for a wireless phone provider that was developing a prototype retail store. And we found that men and women used the place in very different ways. Women would invariably walk right up to the sales desk and ask staffers questions about the phones and the various deals being offered. Men, however, went directly to the phone displays and the signs that explained the agreements. They then took brochures and application forms and left the store—all without ever speaking to an employee. When these men returned to the store, it was to sign up. The women, though, on average required a third visit to the store, and more consultation, before they were ready to close.

15   For the most part, men are still the ones who take the lead when shopping for cars (though women have a big say in most new-car purchases), and men and women perform the division of labor you'd expect when buying for the home: She buys anything that goes inside, and he buys everything that goes outside— mower and other gardening and lawn-care equipment, barbecue grill, water hose and so on. This is changing as the percentage of female-headed households rises, but it still holds.

16   Even when men aren't shopping, they figure prominently in the experience. We know that across the board, how much customers buy is a direct result of how much time they spend in a store. And our research has shown over and over that when a woman is in a store with a man, she'll spend less time there than when she's alone, with another woman or even with children. Here's the actual breakdown of average shopping time from a study we performed at one branch of a national housewares chain:

woman shopping with a female companion: 8 minutes, 15 seconds
woman with children: 7 minutes, 19 seconds
woman alone: 5 minutes, 2 seconds
woman with man: 4 minutes, 41 seconds

17   In each case, what's happening seems clear: When two women shop together, they talk, advise, suggest and consult to their hearts' content, hence the long time in the store; with the kids, she's partly consumed with herding them along and keeping them entertained; alone, she makes efficient use of her time. But with him—well, he makes it plain that he's bored and antsy and likely at any moment to go off and sit in the car and listen to the radio or stand outside and watch girls. So the woman's comfort level plummets when he's by her side; she spends the entire trip feeling anxious and rushed. If he can somehow be occupied, though, she'll be a happier, more relaxed shopper. And she'll spend more time and money. There are two main strategies for coping with the presence of men in places where serious shopping is being done.

18   The first one is passive restraint, which is not to say handcuffs. Stores that sell mainly to women should all be figuring out some way to engage the interest of men. If I owned The Limited or Victoria's Secret, I'd have a place where a woman could check her husband—like a coat. There already exists a traditional space where men have always felt comfortable waiting around. It's called the barbershop. Instead of some ratty old chairs and back issues of *Playboy* and *Boxing Illustrated,* maybe there could be comfortable seats facing a big-screen TV tuned to ESPN or the cable channel that runs the bass-fishing program. Even something that simple would go a long way toward relieving wifely anxiety, but it's possible to imagine more: *Sports Illustrated* in-store programming, for instance—a documentary on the making of the swimsuit issue, perhaps, or highlights of last weekend's NFL action.

19   If I were opening a brand-new store where women could shop comfortably, I'd find a location right next to an emporium devoted to male desire—a computer store, for instance, somewhere he could happily kill half an hour. Likewise, if I were opening a computer software store, I'd put it next to a women's clothing shop and guarantee myself hordes of grateful male browsers.

20   But you could also try to sell to your captive audience. A women's clothing store could prepare a video catalog designed especially for men buying gifts—items like scarves or robes rather than shoes or trousers. Gift certificates would sell easily there; he already knows that she likes the store. Victoria's Secret could really go to town with a video catalog for men. They could even stage a little fashion show.

21   (The only precaution you'd need to take is in where to place such a section. You want customers to be able to find it easily, but you don't want it so near the entrance that the gaze of window shoppers falls on six lumpy guys in windbreakers slumped in BarcaLoungers watching TV.)

22   The second, and ultimately more satisfying, strategy would be to find a way to get the man involved in shopping. Not the easiest thing to do in certain categories, but not impossible either.

23   We were doing a study for Pfaltzgraff, the big stoneware dish manufacturer and retailer. Their typical customer will fall in love with one particular pattern and collect the entire set—many, many pieces, everything from dinner plate and coffee cup to mustard pot, serving platter and napkin ring. It is very time-consuming to shop the store, especially when you figure in how long it takes to ring the items up and wrap them so that they don't break. Just the kind of situation designed to drive most men nuts. A typical sale at Pfaltzgraff outlet stores can run into the hundreds of dollars—all the more reason to find a way to get men involved.

24   As we watched the videotape, we noticed that for some unknown reason men were tending to wander over toward the glassware section of the store. They were steering clear of the gravy boats and the spoon rests and drifting among the tumblers and wineglasses. At one point we saw two guys meander over to the beer glasses, where one of them picked one up and with the other hand grabbed an imaginary beer tap, pulled it and tilted the glass as if to fill it. And I thought, well, of course—when company's over for dinner and the woman's cooking in the kitchen, what does the man do? He makes drinks. That's his socially acceptable role. And so he's interested in all the accoutrements, all the tools of the bartender trade—every different type of glass and what it's for, and the corkscrew and ice tongs and knives and shakers. They're being guys about it.

25   My first thought was that the stores should put in fake beer taps, like props, for men to play with. We ended up advising them to pull together all the glassware into a barware section—to put up on the wall some big graphic, like a photo of a man pulling a beer, or making some martinis in a nice chrome shaker. Something so that men would walk in and see that there was a section meant for them, somewhere they could shop. All the bottle openers in the different patterns, say, would be stocked there, too. And because men prefer to get their information from reading, the store could put up a chart showing what type of glass is used for what—the big balloons and the long stems and the flutes and the rocks glass and steins.

26   And by doing all that you could take the man—who had been seen as a drag on business and an inconvenience to the primary shopper—and turn him into a customer himself. Or at least an interested bystander.

27   We did a study for Thomasville, the furniture maker, and thought that there, too, getting the man more involved would make it easier to sell such big-ticket items. The solution was simple: Create graphic devices, like displays and posters,

showing the steps that go into making the furniture, and use visuals, like cross sections and exploded views, to prove that in addition to looking good, the pieces were well made. Emphasizing construction would do a lot toward overcoming male resistance to the cost of new furniture, but the graphics would also give men something to study while their wives examined upholstery and styling.

28   One product where men consistently outshop women is beer. And that's in every type of setting—supermarket or convenience store, men buy the beer. (They also buy the junk food, the chips and pretzels and nuts and other entertainment food.) So we advised a supermarket client to hold a beer-tasting every Saturday at 3 P.M., right there in the beer aisle. They could feature some microbrew or a new beer from one of the major brewers, it didn't matter. The tastings would probably help sell beer, but even that wasn't the point. It would be worth it just because it would bring more men into the store. And it would help transform the supermarket into a more male-oriented place.

29   That should be the goal of every retailer today. All aspects of business are going to have to anticipate how men's social roles change, and the future is going to belong to whoever gets there first. A good general rule: Take any category where women now predominate, and figure out how to make it appealing to men. ✱

From Paco Underhill, *Why We Buy.* © 1999 by Obat, Inc. Reprinted with permission of Simon & Schuster Adult Publishing Group.

Exercises

Do not refer to the selection for Exercises A and B unless your instructor directs you to do so.

A. DETERMINING THE MAIN IDEA AND PURPOSE

Choose the best answer.

_____ 1. The main idea of the selection is that
   a. men are more suggestible to graphics and physical displays in a retail environment than women are.
   b. men and women behave so differently while shopping that retailers are confused about strategies to increase their sales.
   c. retailers and designers should adapt the shopping experience to involve male shoppers.
   d. men are better shoppers than women, especially when buying cars or technological equipment.

_____ 2. With respect to the main idea, the writer's purpose is to
   a. illustrate how men and women's shopping behavior differs.
   b. persuade retailers and display artists to completely redesign their stores.
   c. warn consumers about deceptive strategies stores use to entice them to buy.
   d. poke fun at men for their peculiar shopping behavior.

B. COMPREHENDING MAIN IDEAS

Choose the correct answer.

_____ 1. One primary difference between the way men and women shop concerns

    a. the amount of time they spend and how quickly or slowly they move through a retail space.
    b. the type of merchandise that they shop for.
    c. the different amounts of money they spend for similar items.
    d. their willingness to comparison shop and the influence of advertising slogans on their buying habits.

_____ 2. When shopping in a supermarket,

    a. men use a list more than women do.
    b. women use a list more than men do.
    c. both men and women use lists about equally.
    d. no reliable statistics exist about which gender uses a list more often.

_____ 3. In a computer store, men prefer to get their information about hardware and software by

    a. doing preliminary research at home before going shopping.
    b. talking to sales clerks.
    c. watching television advertisements.
    d. reading the packaging and other available literature in the store.

_____ 4. The person who spends the _least_ amount of time shopping in a store is a

    a. woman shopping with a female companion.
    b. woman shopping with children.
    c. woman shopping alone.
    d. woman shopping with a man.

_____ 5. Underhill recommends that retailers solve the problem of male boredom while their wives or girlfriends shop by

    a. locating their stores near a male-oriented business like a computer store.
    b. having pretty girls model clothing throughout the store.
    c. opening up a barbershop within the store.
    d. installing large-screen televisions advertising the store's merchandise.

_____ **6.** When Underhill's firm did a study for the furniture maker Thomasville, the researchers found that men would become more involved if

    a. their wives asked their advice about what styles to buy.

    b. the store provided displays and posters showing how the furniture was made.

    c. the male shoppers were allowed to use a computer drawing program to see how the furniture would look in their homes.

    d. the sales staff encouraged male shoppers to try out the furniture themselves.

COMPREHENSION SCORE

Score your answers for Exercises A and B as follows:

A. No. right _____ × 2 = _____

B. No. right _____ × 1 = _____

Total points from A and B _____ × 10 = _____ percent

You may refer to the selection as you work through the remaining exercises.

C. IDENTIFYING SUPPORTING DETAILS

For each main idea stated here, find and write down two supporting details.

1. The great traditional arena for male shopping behavior has always been the supermarket. [paragraph 9]

    a. _____

    b. _____

2. A few years back we ran a study for a wireless phone provider that was developing a prototype retail store. And we found that men and women used the place in very different ways. [paragraph 14]

    a. _____

    b. _____

D. ANALYZING STRUCTURE AND INTERPRETING MEANING

Where appropriate, write your answers to these questions in your own words.

1. _____ Read paragraph 4 again. A good title for this paragraph would be

    a. "The Science of Shopping."

    b. "Why Women Shop."

    c. "Traditional Gender Roles."

    d. "Characteristics of Women Shoppers."

2. What does Underhill mean in paragraph 5 when he writes that in comparison to women shoppers, men seem like "loose cannons." _____

    _____

3. Explain what Underhill means in paragraph 7 when he writes that a man is more likely to ignore price tags "as a measure of his virility."_____

    _____

4. In paragraph 12 Underhill states that retailers follow this "conventional wis-dom": "sell to the woman, close to the man." What does he mean by the word *close?* _____

5. On balance and from a retailer's point of view, whom would you say Underhill favors as shoppers—men or women?_____

    _____ What evidence from

    the selection points to your choice? _____

    _____

E. UNDERSTANDING VOCABULARY

Choose the best definition according to an analysis of word parts or the context.

_____ 1. women do have a greater *affinity* for [paragraph 4]:

   a. practiced habit
   b. economic influence
   c. natural attraction
   d. long-standing domination

_____ 2. shopping for *mundane* necessities [4]:

   a. common, ordinary
   b. expensive, pricey
   c. inexpensive, cheap
   d. worldly, sophisticated

_____ 3. ability to shop *prudently* [4]:

   a. enthusiastically
   b. for hours on end
   c. carefully
   d. extravagantly

_____ **4.** a measure of his *virility* [7]:

    a. courage
    b. generosity
    c. social status
    d. manliness

_____ **5.** a *lethal* combination [here, used humorously—9]:

    a. troublesome
    b. deadly
    c. unusual
    d. poisonous

_____ **6.** such a *wanton* scenario [10]:

    a. unrestrained, excessive
    b. unselfish, bighearted
    c. lacking in good taste
    d. irresponsible, reckless

_____ **7.** suggestible to the *entreaties* of children [11]:

    a. bad-tempered complaints
    b. whining requests
    c. earnest pleas
    d. spoiled behaviors

_____ **8.** *profligate* male behavior [12]:

    a. carefully planned
    b. thrifty, penny-pinching
    c. chauvinistic, prejudiced toward males
    d. extravagant, wasteful

_____ **9.** a *prototype* retail store [14]:

    a. unique, one of a kind
    b. the first model
    c. masculine-oriented
    d. chain, franchise

_____ **10.** the woman's comfort level *plummets* [17]:

    a. drops slowly but steadily
    b. unpredictably goes up and down
    c. increases sharply
    d. drops straight down

F. USING VOCABULARY

Here are some words from the selection. Write an original sentence using each word that shows both that you know how to use the word and what it means.

1. *conventional* _____

2. *prudently* _____

3. *virility* _____

4. *passively* _____

G. TOPICS FOR WRITING OR DISCUSSION

1. Look over Dave Barry's selection, "Tips for Women: How to Have a Relation-ship with a Guy" (pages 25–28). Now that you have read Underhill's selec-tion, what similarities in male–female behavior are evident in both pieces? Based on your experience as a shopper, or as a companion to a shopper of the opposite sex, is Underhill fair and accurate in his characterizations of our behavior?

2. Go to a store that you have frequented in the past and spend half an hour or so observing the customers' behavior. Do men and women behave differently from one another? Do your observations match Underhill's? Write a short es-say in which you summarize your observations and conclusions.

For Further Exploration

BOOK

Underhill's book, *Why We Buy: The Science of Shopping*, from which this selection comes, is an eye-opening, instructive, and often entertaining overview of Ameri-can shopping habits and the techniques stores use to separate our money from our wallets. The book can be read on two levels: (1) Retailers can get advice on ways to improve their service (and, of course, their profits) in the face of in-creased competition and a changed marketplace. (2) Consumers can educate themselves about the tricks and manipulative devices retailers use to get them to spend more.

MOVIE

Frederick Wiseman's excellent documentary *The Store* (1983) offers a behind-the-scenes look at Neiman-Marcus's flagship store in Dallas, Texas, and its corporate headquarters. The film reveals the store's sales, marketing, and advertising strategies, especially for designer clothing, perfume, jewelry, shoes, and other high-end merchandise. Wiseman's documentaries are shown often on American PBS stations. A complete filmography of Wiseman's work is available at *www.subcin.com/wiseman.html*

WEB SITES

Malcolm Gladwell, the renowned *New Yorker* staff writer, published a comprehensive and balanced article in the November 4, 1996, issue about Paco Underhill titled "A Reporter at Large: The Science of Shopping." You can read it online at:

- *www.gladwell.com/1996/1996_11_04_a_shopping.htm*

An archive of all Gladwell's articles is available at:

- *www.gladwell.com*

13

MARTHA FAY

Sedated by Stuff

In the preceding selection Paco Underhill preaches that stores should do more to entice consumers, especially male shoppers, to spend. This article looks at consumerism from a different perspective. Here, Martha Fay argues that an excess of material goods is warping our children's values. She presents the case that, by lavishing everything from Barbie dolls to video games on our children, American parents are relinquishing the chance to shape their offspring's view of the world. This article was originally published in Civilization, *the publication of the Smithsonian Institute.*

Vocabulary Preview

WORD HISTORY

Psychiatrist [paragraph 16] A *psychiatrist* is a medical doctor who specializes in mental and emotional disorders. The root of this word is *psyche,* after Psyche, the Greek goddess who fell in love with Cupid and who personified the soul. In Greek the word *psyche* means "soul," "spirit," or "mind," from the verb *psychein,* meaning, fittingly, "to breathe."

WORD PARTS

Pre- [paragraphs 1 and 6] The Latin prefix *pre-,* meaning "before," is attached to dozens of English roots, for example, *prerequisite, prelude,* and *pretext. A prerequisite* is a requirement that must be completed as a condition of something undertaken later; for example, in most colleges Economics 1A would be a prerequisite to Economics 1B. A *prelude* is an "introductory performance or action that precedes the main event." It comes from the Latin: *pre- + ludere* ("to play"). And finally, a *pretext* is an "ostensible or professed purpose used as an excuse." In this word, the meaning of the prefix is somewhat obscured. What do these words beginning with *pre-* mean? Of the six, which two have little or no connection with "before"?

prearrange _____

precede _____

precarious _____

precursor _____

premonition _____

pretense _____

Seduction [paragraph 17] The Latin verb *ducere* ("to lead") is the basis of a large number of English words. Fay concludes the article by saying that parents must give their children "some perspective on life and how it should be lived that is resistant to commercial *seduction.*" The noun *seduction* and the related verb *seduce* are derived from the Latin verb *seducere,* "to lead astray." Both words also can be used in a sexual sense. Here are some other words in this family:

induct	to lead into, as in the army
abduct	to carry away by force [*ab-* ("away") + *ducere*]
aqueduct	a passage carrying water [*aqua* ("water") + *ducere*]
educate	to provide with knowledge or training, literally "to lead out of" (one's ignorance or the dark) [*e-* ("out of") + *ducere*]

MARTHA FAY

Sedated by Stuff

1   There are few subjects on which I feel as entitled to take a high moral tone as material greed. I was raised in perennial want of stuff, trained from infancy to pretend I didn't care—and to disdain those who did. Being Catholic helped; so did being the fifth of eight children—though I long ago learned that such circumstances are not a prerequisite to the less-is-more disposition. All this is prelude to the subject at hand: the glut of stuff that parents foist on children year after year, all the while protesting, "We can't help it. Who is making us do this? Stop us before we buy again."

2   It's unclear exactly when parents went from knowing what was good for kids to not knowing, but pretty much everybody agrees that things have taken a sharp turn for the worse in the greed department. Therapists tell horror stories about children drowning in plush and plastic tokens of affection. Parents tell tales on themselves.

3   My friend Peter claims he cannot open the door to his tiny daughter's bedroom—it is stuffed to the four corners with Barbie dolls and Barbie equipment, with accessories and extras, with vacation houses, gyms, recreational vehicles, costumes, cosmetics. She is six; Barbie, as we all know, is a 40-year-old billionaire.

4   Peter has been analyzed; he has raised a few children; he was once a child himself, in a family that could afford a new Mercedes every two years and trips to France in summer but did not believe in spoiling children. What he wants to know is, where will all this lead? Isn't the surfeit of things in his daughter's room likely to persuade her that her parents don't really love her, instead of that they do? Why else would they be bringing her daily proofs, if not to mask the truth? And what of ceremony, he asks, what of occasion? When he was a boy, presents arrived on major holidays, on one's birthday, to mark a significant life passage. Presents were *presented.* They were Big Deals.

5   All this I, too, remember (minus the Mercedes and the trips to France), and most of my friends claim to as well: a new sled or a pair of ice skates at Christmas, new clothes at Easter, bar mitzvah pens, a watch when you graduated from

high school, crayons and coloring books for rainy days. I remember the impulse purchase of a yo-yo as a rare event. I remember waiting with my sister for things we might or might not get in the end: new packs of jacks, bikes, roller skates. "We'll see," my mother said when we asked for things we did not strictly need. It was understood that she meant "no." It was not an answer that left me worrying whether she loved me or not.

6   So why do modern parents persist in giving at the slightest pretext, or even none at all—why do we not know when enough is enough?

7   Television is part of it, the agent of contagion certainly, if not the primary source—but you knew that. Children are bombarded from infancy with commercial images of how life is supposed to be lived, with products that scream, "Buy me or die lonely!" They take the messages aimed at them as seriously as their parents do promises of sexual fulfillment by Lexus. So they ask for what they see—the brightly colored things held high by smiling children in front of beaming parents. They think they are supposed to. They are doing their best to get the hang of love. They learn early on that stuff equals acceptance.

8   When my friend Jane's son was seven and had just started a new school, she asked him why he hadn't invited any classmates over to play.

9   "No one will come to my house," he said, "because I have no publicity."

10   "What do you mean, you have no publicity?"

11   "I don't have Nintendo. No one will want to play with me," he said with finality.

12   But why do parents buy into this equation, as well—and buy, and buy, and buy?

13   Because it's easier to say yes than no (and always has been); because it's *fun* to buy stuff; because parents are as addicted as their children to the quick fix of a new toy; because they worry about cutting their kids off from the culture of their peers; because the best is easily confused with the most; and because many parents spend far less time with their children than they think they should and are paying just enough attention to feel guilty about it. Because life doesn't always work out as expected, and things that come in boxes offer the illusion that everything has, in fact, turned out perfectly.

14   Of course, it is not always about giving kids what they or we mistakenly believe they need. In my case—and in many others, I'm sure—going overboard almost always has to do with trying to make up to my child for things that cannot be made right: a dead father, an imperfect mother, a world far scarier than we like to think children notice. We both know such gifts are just another form of whistling in the dark—compensatory paroxysms of longing and desire.

15   And all too often it is about being seen as the kind of parents who can afford to pay for things in a culture with no other agreed-upon value but money. For years, this was not an issue in our house. When my daughter was in public school, no matter how strapped I felt in a given stretch, she was obviously considerably better off than most of her classmates. It was easy to take a we-don't-need-it-and-don't-value-it attitude, and to feel rather virtuous as a result. Then she switched to a private school so rich that it could afford to have *us;* a scholarship bridged the gap between what we could realistically pay and what an education designed for the ruling class actually costs. Our relative worth

plummeted overnight. Suddenly, it became necessary to talk about what it is nice to have (or dream about having), what is more or less necessary, what people like us can afford, and what all this did and didn't say about who we were. I'd like to say it took half an hour to resolve my feelings about this; it took years.

16   "In some ways, it's a no-brainer," psychiatrist Annie Boland said to me. "We're a consumer society. People buy things for a lot of reasons, and just because they become parents doesn't change their behavior."

17   "Just because they become parents": But what does parenting mean if not the obligation to interpret the world, to point out dangers, to draw distinctions? More interesting, why are parents so ready to surrender the best part of the job—where you get to influence, to shape, to win some fresh soul to your view of the world? Of course, this depends on having a coherent worldview to begin with—some perspective on life and how it should be lived that is resistant to commercial seduction. Such a view includes a notion of limits and the rewards thereof; it values patience and celebrates special occasions; it recognizes and rewards accomplishment—and it cannot fail to notice the difference between an engaged child and one sedated by stuff. ✱

From Martha Fay, "Sedated by Stuff," *Civilization*, August–September 1999. Reprinted by permission.

Exercises

Do not refer to the selection for Exercises A and B unless your instructor directs you to do so.

A. DETERMINING THE MAIN IDEA AND PURPOSE

Choose the best answer.

_____ 1. The main idea of the selection is that
   a. today's parents are doing a poor job of raising their children.
   b. television advertising fosters the idea that happiness lies in buying things.
   c. the most important values in American society are money and the goods that money can buy.
   d. in buying too much stuff, American parents are teaching their children the wrong values.

_____ 2. With respect to the main idea, the writer's purpose is to
   a. criticize parents for engaging in a common practice.
   b. show the origins of a common practice.
   c. explain the effects of a common practice.
   d. denounce the media for fostering a common practice.

B. COMPREHENDING MAIN IDEAS

Choose the correct answer.

_____ **1.** The writer's main concern in this selection is

    a. commercial images of the good life.
    b. material greed.
    c. spiritual sedation.
    d. good parenting skills.

_____ **2.** When parents are asked why they buy so much for their children, they often reply

    a. "We can't help it."
    b. "Everyone else is doing it."
    c. "Stop us before we buy again."
    d. "We'll raise our child as we see fit."

_____ **3.** When the writer was growing up, she recalls that presents were

    a. either homemade or quite inexpensive.
    b. awarded only for good grades or good behavior.
    c. something special to mark a holiday or life passage.
    d. given as proof that her family loved her.

_____ **4.** The little boy who didn't want friends to come to his house because he didn't have Nintendo was learning a lesson early on, namely that

    a. children can be cruel.
    b. the impulse to buy starts at a young age.
    c. having material possessions means that one is accepted.
    d. games like Nintendo are a waste of time.

_____ **5.** Fay cites several reasons that parents spend money on their children so freely. Which *two* of these were *not* mentioned?

    a. They feel guilty about not spending enough time with their children.
    b. They see buying material possessions for their children as a way to improve their own social status.
    c. They enjoy spoiling their children.
    d. They think that spending money is fun.
    e. They have a harder time saying no than yes.
    f. They worry about cutting off their children from the culture of their peers.

_____ **6.** The writer maintains that parents need to give their children a different perspective, one that emphasizes the importance of

    a. being thrifty and doing without.
    b. establishing limits and being rewarded for accomplishments.
    c. delayed gratification.
    d. standing up for what one believes, not following what the crowd believes.

COMPREHENSION SCORE
Score your answers for Exercises A and B as follows:

A. No. right _____ × 2 = _____

B. No. right _____ × 1 = _____ (Note: For Exercise B5, count each answer as worth one-half point.)

Total points from A and B _____ × 10 = _____ percent

You may refer to the selection as you work through the remaining exercises.

C. DISTINGUISHING BETWEEN MAIN IDEAS AND SUPPORTING DETAILS
Label the following statements from paragraphs 2 and 3 as follows: MI if it represents a *main idea* and SD if it represents a *supporting detail*.

1. _____   It's unclear exactly when parents went from knowing what was good for kids to not knowing, but pretty much everybody agrees that things have taken a sharp turn for the worse in the greed department.

2. _____   Therapists tell horror stories about children drowning in plush and plastic tokens of affection.

3. _____   Parents tell tales on themselves.

4. _____   My friend Peter claims he cannot open the door to his tiny daughter's bedroom—it is stuffed to the four corners with Barbie dolls and Barbie equipment, with accessories and extras, with vacation houses, gyms, recreational vehicles, costumes, cosmetics.

5. _____   She is six; Barbie, as we all know, is a 40-year-old billionaire.

D. INTERPRETING MEANING
Write your answers to these questions in your own words.

1. In paragraph 1, Fay writes: "There are few subjects on which I feel as entitled to take a high moral tone as material greed." Explain why the author believes

this. _____

_____

2. _____   On whom does Fay place *most* of the blame for parents' persistence in overspending on their children? She primarily blames

    a. the parents themselves for being unable to say no.

    b. children, who know that whining will get what they want.

    c. television for beaming the message that happiness will come with acquiring things.

    d. our consumer society for making money the primary value.

3. The idea suggested in the title "Sedated by Stuff," is repeated in the last sentence when Fay mentions the difference between "an engaged child and one sedated by stuff." What does Fay mean by the word *engaged*? _____

_____

And what does she mean by the word *sedated*? _____

_____

E. ANALYZING STRUCTURE

Where appropriate, write your answers to these questions in your own words.

1. This essay has a clear introduction, body paragraphs supporting the main point, and conclusion. Identify the parts of the selection by writing the number or numbers of the paragraphs comprising each section in the spaces.

   Introduction: _____
   Body: _____
   Conclusion: _____

2. _____ Look again at paragraphs 12 and 13. Note that paragraph 12 asks why parents buy into the equation that having stuff means acceptance by peers. In relation to this paragraph, the purpose of paragraph 13 is to
   a. list several reasons.
   b. provide several examples.
   c. establish a contrast.
   d. define important terms.

3. _____ What is the purpose of paragraph 14 with respect to the whole article? It shows that some parents overspend for their children because they
   a. hope to compensate for a serious problem that can't be fixed.
   b. want to win their children's affection and gratitude.
   c. want to show their children that it isn't wrong to desire material things.
   d. hope to relieve their feelings of guilt about being poor parents.

F. UNDERSTANDING VOCABULARY

Look through the paragraphs listed below and find a word that matches each definition. Refer to the dictionary if necessary. An example has been done for you.

Ex. to scorn, hold in contempt [paragraph 1] _____disdain_____

1. something required for completion [1]: _____
2. excessive amount, oversupply [1]: _____
3. excessive amount, oversupply [4]: _____
4. words used as an excuse [6]: _____
5. one's equals [13]: _____
6. dropped suddenly and sharply [15]: _____

G. USING VOCABULARY

In parentheses before each sentence are some inflected forms of words from the selection. Study the context and the sentence. Then write the correct form in the space provided.

1. (*impulse, impulsive, impulsively*) The writer remembers that her family never bought items _____ when she was growing up.

2. (*persist, persistence, persistent, persistently*) Fay wonders why today's parents _____ in overspending for their children.

3. (*bombard, bombardment, bombarded*) Children from a very young age are _____ with advertising pitches on television telling them to buy or die lonely.

4. (*compensate, compensation, compensatory*) According to the writer, many parents buy excessive amounts of stuff for their children as _____ for their own failings as parents or to buy their love.

5. (*virtue, virtuous, virtuously*) Undoubtedly, Fay felt _____ when she adopted a "we-don't-need-it-and-don't-value-it" attitude.

H. PARAPHRASING AND SUMMARIZING EXERCISE

In the left column is a sentence from the selection, with a paraphrase of it on the right.

Original Passage

I was raised in perennial want of stuff, trained from infancy to pretend I didn't care—and to disdain those who did.

Paraphrase

I was brought up in a family that didn't have a lot of material things, and I was taught from a very young age to pretend that I didn't want things other children had or to feel contemptuous of children who did want such things.

First, study the paraphrase above. Then write a paraphrase of this sentence from paragraph 7:

Original Passage

Television is part of it, the agent of contagion certainly, if not the primary source—but you knew that. Children are bombarded from infancy with commercial images of how life is supposed to be lived, with products that scream, "Buy me or die lonely."

Paraphrase

_____

_____

_____

_____

_____

_____

I. TOPICS FOR WRITING OR DISCUSSION

1. Does Fay set herself up as a moral authority? Does she use any phrases that suggest she herself has not been immune to the impulse to spend?

2. What are some arguments against Fay's point of view? Are material goods really as harmful as Fay seems to suggest?

3. Write a short essay in which you explain how your parents taught you about the value of material possessions. Did your experiences echo those of children whom Fay writes about in her essay?

For Further Exploration

BOOK

Marie Winn's classic book, *The Plug-In Drug: Television, Computers and Family Life* (2002), was first published in 1977 and has recently been revised and updated. In this book, Winn examines the TV, computer, VCR, and video games and their damaging effects on those who indulge in them excessively.

MOVIES

• Apart from its futuristic theme—government agents fighting in a "Precrime" unit in the nation's capital—the 2002 film *Minority Report,* starring Tom Cruise and directed by Steven Spielberg, is a look ahead to the year 2054 and a culture that bombards its people with ads even more intrusively than occurs today. Product placement permeates this movie, with ads tailor-made for the character played by Cruise (Bulgari, Nike, and Guinness, for example) as he walks through public spaces.

• *The Truman Show* (1998), directed by Peter Weir and starring Jim Carrey and Laura Linney, offers an intriguing glimpse into the blurred lines between the fantasy we see on television and the emptiness of American culture. Carrey, an insurance salesman, is unaware that his entire life is an elaborate television show. His friends and relatives are actors; the town where he lives is a gigantic stage set. Even his wife, played by Linney, makes TV commercials in their kitchen while Truman looks on, not realizing what is really happening.

WEB SITES

The following two sites discuss the Barbie phenomenon and its impact on American culture:

• *www.otal.umd.edu/~vg/mssp96/ms07/cult.htm*
   ("Barbie's Effects on American Suburban Culture")

• *www.suite101.com/article.cfm/5671/38807*
   ("Barbie's Beginnings"—a history of Barbie in terms of American popular culture)

14

The Hunger for More

In the two previous selections, Paco Underhill and Martha Fay discussed two aspects of consumerism: the American love of shopping and the effects that the material goods we purchase have on our children's values. But why do Americans enjoy spending and acquiring so much? Why are we seemingly never satisfied with what we already have?

Lawrence Shames attempts to identify some reasons in his book The Hunger for More: Searching for Values in an Age of Greed, *published in 1989. In this excerpt from the first chapter, Shames examines the American frontier and its influence on our tradition of materialism. A former writer on ethical issues for* Esquire *magazine, Shames has also written for many national publications, among them the* New York Times, Vanity Fair, *and* Playboy.

Vocabulary Preview

WORD HISTORY

Optimists [paragraph 1]   Shames opens this selection with this sentence: "Americans have always been *optimists*." An *optimist* looks on the bright side of life and expects favorable outcomes. This word derives from the Latin root *optimus* ("best"). Its antonym or opposite is *pessimist,* which refers to a person who expects only unfavorable outcomes and views the future in a gloomy way. *Pessimist* derives from the Latin root *pessimus* ("worst"). You can remember these meanings well with this example: Let's say that you are stranded in the desert with a half-filled canteen of water. An *optimist* would view the canteen as being half full; a *pessimist* would view the canteen as half empty.

WORD PARTS

Re- [paragraphs 3 and 9]   The common prefix *re-* is attached to dozens of words in English to convey the idea of a repeated action. *Relocation* in paragraph 3 means the "process of locating again," while *recouped* in paragraph 9 means "recovered" as in a loss that is made up. However, not all words that begin with *re-* have this meaning: *Reconsider, recalculate, regenerate,* and *reimburse* do, but *register, regulate, residence,* and *rebuke* ("to scold") do not. Strip away the prefix and see if the root can stand alone. If it can, then the prefix likely has the meaning discussed.

What do these three words mean?

rehydrate   _____

rejuvenate   _____

revitalize   _____

213

WORD FAMILIES

Speculate, speculative, speculators [paragraphs 1 and 3]   Americans, Shames writes in the opening paragraph, "have always been optimists, and optimists have always liked to *speculate.*" This verb, and its relatives, *speculative* and *speculators,* all derive from the Latin word *specere* ("to watch," "to observe"). To *speculate,* in the sense that Shames uses the word, means to buy something risky with the idea that it may make a profit in the future. The root suggests here that one cannot "see" into the future, hence the risk. The connection with "watching" or "seeing" is more apparent in these words:

spectacle	a public performance, an object of interest (in other words, something worth looking at)
spectacular	describing an impressive or elaborate display (again, describing something worth looking at)
spectator	one who attends and sees a show or an event
spectacles	eyeglasses, enabling one to see clearly

LAWRENCE SHAMES

The Hunger for More

1   Americans have always been optimists, and optimists have always liked to speculate. In Texas in the 1880s, the speculative instrument of choice was towns, and there is no tale more American than this.

2   What people would do was buy up enormous tracts of parched and vacant land, lay out a Main Street, nail together some wooden sidewalks, and start slapping up buildings. One of these buildings would be called the Grand Hotel and would have a saloon complete with swinging doors. Another might be dubbed the New Academy or the Opera House. The developers would erect a flagpole and name a church, and once the workmen had packed up and moved on, the towns would be as empty as the sky.

3   But no matter. The speculators, next, would hire people to pass out handbills in the Eastern and Midwestern cities, tracts limning the advantages of relocation to "the Athens of the South" or "the new plains Jerusalem." When persuasion failed, the builders might resort to bribery, paying people's moving costs and giving them houses, in exchange for nothing but a pledge to stay until a certain census was taken or a certain inspection made. Once the nose-count was completed, people were free to move on, and there was in fact a contingent of folks who made their living by keeping a cabin on skids, and dragging it for pay from one town to another.

4   The speculators' idea, of course, was to lure the railroad. If one could create a convincing semblance of a town, the railroad might come through it, and a real town would develop, making the speculators staggeringly rich. By these devices a man named Sanborn once owned Amarillo.

5   But railroad tracks are narrow and the state of Texas is very, very wide. For every Wichita Falls or Lubbock there were a dozen College Mounds or Belchervilles, bleached, unpeopled burgs that receded quietly into the dust, taking with them large amounts of speculators' money.

6　　Still, the speculators kept right on bucking the odds and depositing empty towns in the middle of nowhere. Why did they do it? Two reasons—reasons that might be said to summarize the central fact of American economic history and that go a fair way toward explaining what is perhaps the central strand of the national character.

7　　The first reason was simply that the possible returns were so enormous as to partake of the surreal, to create a climate in which ordinary logic and prudence did not seem to apply. In a boom like that of real estate when the railroad barreled through, long shots that might pay 100,000 to one seemed worth a bet.

8　　The second reason, more pertinent here, is that there was a presumption that America would *keep on* booming—if not forever, then at least longer than it made sense to worry about. There would always be another gold rush, another Homestead Act, another oil strike. The next generation would always ferret out opportunities that would be still more lavish than any that had gone before. America *was* those opportunities. This was an article not just of faith, but of strategy. You banked on the next windfall, you staked your hopes and even your self-esteem on it; and this led to a national turn of mind that might usefully be thought of as the habit of more.

9　　A century, maybe two centuries, before anyone had heard the term *baby boomer,* much less *yuppie,* the habit of more had been installed as the operative truth among the economically ambitious. The habit of more seemed to suggest that there was no such thing as getting wiped out in America. A fortune lost in Texas might be recouped in Colorado. Funds frittered away on grazing land where nothing grew might flood back in as silver. There was always a second chance, or always seemed to be, in this land where growth was destiny and where expansion and purpose were the same.

10　　The key was the frontier, not just as a matter of acreage, but as idea. Vast, varied, rough as rocks, America was the place where one never quite came to the end. Ben Franklin explained it to Europe even before the Revolutionary War had finished: America offered new chances to those "who, in their own Countries, where all the Lands [were] fully occupied . . . could never [emerge] from the poor Condition wherein they were born."

11　　So central was this awareness of vacant space and its link to economic promise, that Frederick Jackson Turner, the historian who set the tone for much of the twentieth century's understanding of the American past, would write that it was "not the constitution, but free land . . . [that] made the democratic type of society in America." Good laws mattered; an accountable government mattered; ingenuity and hard work mattered. But those things were, so to speak, an overlay on the natural, geographic America that was simply *there,* and whose vast and beckoning possibilities seemed to generate the ambition and the sometimes reckless liberty that would fill it. First and foremost, it was open space that provided "the freedom of the individual to rise under conditions of social mobility."

12　　Open space generated not just ambition, but metaphor. As early as 1835, Tocqueville was extrapolating from the fact of America's emptiness to the observation that "no natural boundary seems to be set to the efforts of man." Nor was any limit placed on what he might accomplish, since, in that heyday of the Protestant ethic, a person's rewards were taken to be quite strictly proportionate to his labors.

13   Frontier; opportunity; more. This has been the American trinity from the very start. The frontier was the backdrop and also the raw material for the streak of economic booms. The booms became the goad and also the justification for the myriad gambles and for Americans' famous optimism. The optimism, in turn, shaped the schemes and visions that were sometimes noble, sometimes appalling, always bold. The frontier, as reality and as symbol, is what has shaped the American way of doing things and the American sense of what's worth doing.

14   But there has been one further corollary to the legacy of the frontier, with its promise of ever-expanding opportunities: given that the goal—a realistic goal for most of our history—was *more*, Americans have been somewhat backward in adopting values, hopes, ambitions that have to do with things *other than* more. In America, a sense of quality has lagged far behind a sense of scale. An ideal of contentment has yet to take root in soil traditionally more hospitable to an ideal of restless striving. The ethic of decency has been upstaged by the ethic of success. The concept of growth has been applied almost exclusively to things that can be measured, counted, weighed. And the hunger for those things that are unmeasurable but fine—the sorts of accomplishment that cannot be undone by circumstance or a shift in social fashion, the kind of serenity that cannot be shattered by tomorrow's headline—has gone largely unfulfilled, and even unacknowledged. ✳

From Lawrence Shames, *The Hunger for More: Searching for Values in an Age of Greed.* © 1989 by Lawrence Shames. Used by permission of Alfred A. Knopf, a division of Random House, Inc.

Exercises

Do not refer to the selection for Exercises A and B unless your instructor directs you to do so.

A. DETERMINING THE MAIN IDEA AND PURPOSE

Choose the best answer.

_____ **1.** The main idea of the selection is that

　　a. the American frontier, with its endless possibilities for opportunity and expansion, has shaped the country's national character.

　　b. Americans are by nature an optimistic people who are willing to gamble and take bold risks.

　　c. Americans believe in the Protestant ethic, the idea that one's rewards are proportionate to one's labors.

　　d. American values are being redefined as the nation experiences diminished opportunities and declining natural resources.

_____ **2.** With respect to the main idea concerning American cultural values and the American character, the writer's purpose is to

　　a. criticize, even condemn, them.

　　b. express regret for them.

　　c. examine the historical and geographic conditions that gave rise to them.

　　d. contrast them with older values and behavior patterns of earlier eras.

B. COMPREHENDING MAIN IDEAS

Choose the correct answer.

_____ **1.** Shames states that American optimism and speculation began in the 1880s with the

a. desire to escape the densely populated cities of the Midwest and the East.
b. promise of easy money during the Gold Rush era.
c. building of new towns in Texas.
d. coming of the railroad to the American frontier.

_____ **2.** Ultimately, land speculators hoped to attract

a. recent immigrants.
b. cattle ranchers.
c. railroads.
d. gold prospectors.

_____ **3.** Shames writes that when speculators lost money, they did not mind too much because they presumed that

a. the government would bail them out if they failed.
b. they could always keep on moving West.
c. the Homestead Act would be renewed every year.
d. America would continue to experience booms.

_____ **4.** The crucial concept to explain the American belief in opportunity and expansion was the

a. country's rich store of natural resources.
b. frontier, with its unlimited space.
c. American inclination for hard work.
d. country's strong democratic system.

_____ **5.** Shames writes that, from the beginning, the American "trinity" has been

a. ambition, wealth, and success.
b. booms, gambles, and high risk.
c. optimism, boldness, and social mobility.
d. frontier, opportunity, and more.

_____ **6.** The selection concludes with the idea that, in America, "the concept of growth" has been applied almost exclusively to

a. upward mobility.
b. things that can be measured.
c. the economy.
d. personal accomplishments and achievements.

COMPREHENSION SCORE

Score your answers for Exercises A and B as follows:

A. No. right _____ × 2 = _____

B. No. right _____ × 1 = _____

Total points from A and B _____ × 10 = _____ percent

You may refer to the selection as you work through the remaining exercises.

C. DISTINGUISHING BETWEEN MAIN IDEAS AND SUPPORTING DETAILS

Label the following statements from the selection as follows: MI if it represents a *main idea* and SD if it represents a *supporting detail.*

1. _____   The speculators' idea, of course, was to lure the railroad.

2. _____   If one could create a convincing semblance of a town, the railroad might come through it, and a real town would develop, making the speculators staggeringly rich.

3. _____   By these devices a man named Sanborn once owned Amarillo.

4. _____   But railroad tracks are narrow and the state of Texas is very, very wide.

5. _____   For every Wichita Falls or Lubbock there were a dozen College Mounds or Belchervilles.

6. _____   These were bleached, unpeopled burgs that receded quietly into the dust, taking with them large amounts of speculators' money.

D. INTERPRETING MEANING AND ANALYZING STRUCTURE

Where appropriate, write your answers to these questions in your own words.

1. In paragraph 2, Shames writes that the real-estate speculators would "start slapping up buildings" in Texas. What does this phrase suggest about the quality of these buildings? _____

2. _____   Look again at paragraphs 6–8. What kind of support does Shames use in this section?

    a. examples and illustrations
    b. steps in a process
    c. reasons
    d. definitions of unfamiliar terms

3. _____   Read paragraph 9 again. A good title for this paragraph would be

    a. "Nineteenth-Century Baby Boomers and Yuppies."
    b. "The Habit of More."
    c. "Second Chances."
    d. "Growth and Destiny."

4. In paragraph 12, Shames discusses the concept of the frontier as metaphor (an imaginative comparison to show an idea). What exactly does he mean?

_____

_____

5. _____ Which of the following sentences from the selection *best* states the main idea of the selection as a whole?

  a. "Americans have always been optimists, and optimists have always liked to speculate."
  b. "The next generation would always ferret out opportunities that would be still more lavish than any that had gone before."
  c. "Nor was any limit placed on what he might accomplish, since, in that heyday of the Protestant ethic, a person's rewards were taken to be quite strictly proportionate to his labors."
  d. "The frontier, as reality and as symbol, is what has shaped the American way of doing things and the American sense of what's worth doing."

E. UNDERSTANDING VOCABULARY

Look through the paragraphs listed below and find a word that matches each definition. Refer to the dictionary if necessary. An example has been done for you.

Ex. very dry, arid [paragraph 2]:   _____parched_____

 1. depicting, describing [3]:   _____
 2. representative group [3]:   _____
 3. outward appearance, barest trace [4]:   _____
 4. small towns [5]:   _____
 5. uncover or reveal by searching [8—two words]:   _____
 6. regained, made up for [9]:   _____
 7. squandered little by little, wasted [9]:   _____
 8. period of greatest popularity or success [12]:   _____
 9. stimulus, incentive [13]:   _____
10. causing consternation or dismay, terrible [13]   _____
11. a large indefinite number, innumerable [13]:   _____
12. natural consequence or effect [14]:   _____

F. USING VOCABULARY

Here are some words from the selection. Write an original sentence using each word that shows both that you know how to use the word and what it means.

1. *speculation* _____

2. *optimistic* _____

3. *prudent* _____

4. *presume* _____

5. *surreal* _____

G. PARAPHRASING EXERCISE

In the left column is a sentence from paragraph 14, with its paraphrase on the right:

Original Passage

In America, a sense of quality has lagged far behind a sense of scale. An ideal of contentment has yet to take root in soil traditionally more hospitable to an ideal of restless striving.

Paraphrase

Americans have always been more interested in quantity than quality. For this reason, we tend to value striving for a goal rather than being content when we have achieved something.

_____

Here are two sentences from paragraph 14. After you read them, write your own paraphrase in the space provided:

Original Passage

The concept of growth has been applied almost exclusively to things that can be measured, counted, weighed. And the hunger for those things that are unmeasurable but fine— the sorts of accomplishments that cannot be undone by circumstance or a shift in social fashion, the kind of serenity that cannot be shattered by tomorrow's headline—has gone largely unfulfilled, and even unacknowledged.

Paraphrase

_____

_____

_____

_____

_____

_____

_____

_____

H. LOCATING EVIDENCE

Go through the selection and locate any piece of information that supports the following idea:

As a society, the United States is paying the price for our "hunger for more."

Identify evidence by putting a star in the margin next to the sentence or by putting brackets around the words.

I.   TOPICS FOR WRITING OR DISCUSSION

1. Shames published the book from which this excerpt comes in 1989. How pertinent are his remarks in helping you understand the Internet and technology boom of the late 1990s and recent accounting scandals?

2. Shames strongly emphasizes the role of the frontier, with its symbolic and literal significance of unlimited land and unlimited opportunities. Based on your knowledge of American history and culture, what might be some other explanations that account for Americans' "hunger for more"?

3. Write a paragraph or two as a personal response to this sentence from the selection: "The ethic of decency has been upstaged by the ethic of success."

For Further Exploration

BOOK

In *Bad Land: An American Romance* (1996), Jonathan Raban examines a more recent but parallel phenomenon to the one Shames writes about here. At the turn of the century in the prairies of eastern Montana, settlers were promised 160 acres of free land. Pamphlets distributed by the railroad companies and the federal government touted the area's potential for wheat farming and promoted the now-discredited concept of "dry farming." Raban recounts the efforts of settlers to coax decent crops out of an environment that lacked sufficient rainfall. He brings us up-to-date on what life is like for residents of the little towns in this part of Montana.

MOVIE

A century after the Texas land speculators got rich selling worthless land to Midwesterners and Easterners, their twentieth-century counterparts have their own schemes, selling worthless stocks over the telephone to unsuspecting customers. The movie *Boiler Room* (2000), directed by Ben Younger and starring, among others, Ben Affleck, Vin Diesel, and Nia Long, exposes the inner workings of the sleazy "boiler room" operations associated with hucksters and hustlers.

WEB SITE

When I couldn't remember the name of the movie mentioned above, I searched the most comprehensive site for anything and everything about movies, The Internet Movie Database. You can search by title, actor/actress, director, theme, plot. The site also offers movie reviews by professional critics and ordinary movie buffs. The address is:

- *www.imdb.com.*

Making Inferences

Look carefully at this cartoon:

"I thought it was pretty good, for a book."

What can you conclude about the little boy from his remarks? The cartoonist does not tell us the boy's attitude toward books. He suggests or implies it, and from what he implies, we *infer* (draw a conclusion by reading into his remark) that the boy probably prefers to play video games or watch television than read books. You will practice making inferences like this in the readings in the next three parts of the text.

   Let's say that on a cloudy winter day you are driving north on a narrow mountain road. Suddenly, you notice that all of the cars coming toward you have their headlights on, and you wonder why. One possibility is that the cars are part of a funeral procession. Another is that they were just driving in an area in which headlights are required during the day (such as on narrow or windy roads) and that all the drivers forgot to turn off their lights at the end. A third is that they have just emerged from dense fog. Which of these conclusions is most likely? (Any one of them could be true, of course, but one is *probably* more likely than the other two.)

Usually the cars in a funeral procession have identifying stickers or signs on their windshields. And it would be unlikely that every single driver would forget to turn off the lights at the end of the narrow or windy section of road. So the most likely possibility is that a patch of dense fog lies ahead. Of course, if you reach the patch of dense fog as you proceed north, this inference will be confirmed by observation and experience.

As this example shows, we make inferences in the real world all the time. Here is another situation in which you'd be likely to make inferences: Suppose you live next door to a family named Sullivan. One morning you observe that the Sullivans' newspapers are piling up at their front door. From this fact, you might infer one of three things: (1) They are away on vacation; (2) they forgot to cancel their newspaper delivery; or (3) they forgot to ask someone to pick up the papers so as not to attract burglars.

These conclusions are *logical*; that is, they derive from the facts as you know them. However, they may not actually be *true*. The Sullivans may have been called away on a family emergency and simply were too distraught to realize that the newspapers would pile up. Or perhaps they were all stricken with the flu and have been unable to get out. A more far-fetched inference might be that they have all been murdered and that no one has detected the crime yet.

In the absence of any other information, however, the first set of inferences stated earlier are more likely to be accurate. This is the important point about inferences: They are statements more of *probability* than of fact.

When you make an inference, in reading or in life, you draw a logical conclusion, not from something you actually know, but rather from what you know to be true from experience. In reading, this process is called "reading between the lines," drawing a logical conclusion from what the writer suggests but does not state.

Many of my students find the inference questions in this text to be among the most challenging of the exercises. And the skill of drawing inferences is eminently worthwhile to develop if you are serious about becoming a more proficient reader. Making inferences means that you can move beyond literal or surface comprehension to gain a deeper understanding. Making good inferences also reinforces the thinking process, allows you to gain insights that lie beneath the surface, and extends your understanding of that subject.

In some of the inference sections in the remainder of the book, you will be asked to write a sentence or two in your own words stating an appropriate inference that you can draw from a particular passage. However, in most of the selections in Parts 3 and 5, you will be asked to label statements from the text using this key: Y (yes), N (no), or CT (can't tell). A "yes" answer means that the inference is *probably accurate.* It states something that the writer's words actually imply or suggest. A "no" answer means that the inference is *probably inaccurate,* either because it shows a misreading or a distortion of the writer's words. Or perhaps one part of the inference statement is accurate, but another part is not, making the whole statement inaccurate. A "can't tell" answer means that *you can't be sure one way or the other* whether the inference is logical or accurate. The writer does not mention anything that would allow you to draw such a conclusion, or the conclusion depends on something else you have read or have other knowledge of. In other words, you can't tell from *this* particular passage.

Before we look at some sample inference questions, let's examine the difference between a "no" and a "can't tell" answer in more detail. Think about this statement: Blue is a color, and north is a quality. Is this an accurate statement? The first part is fine, but the second part is not: north is a direction, not a quality. It's the same with inferences. In a complicated inference containing two ideas, if one idea is accurate and the other is not, mark it N. CT, on the other hand, means just that— you simply can't tell. To return to our earlier headlight example, if only one car coming toward you has its headlights on, you wouldn't have enough information to make an inference. (Some people prefer to drive with their lights on during the day, especially on narrow, windy roads, but this is not a generalization about all drivers that you can make from your driving experience.)

Let's begin with an excerpt from paragraph 2 of Selection 8, "Games Elephants Play," by Sheldon Campbell:

> In captivity, elephants best display their great intelligence in shows of various types, rapidly learning complex acts where it seems the trainer is constantly at risk and never harmed, or in the heavy, often difficult tasks they perform in India, Bangladesh, Sri Lanka, and Thailand.

Label these inferences Y, N, or CT.

1. _____ Most elephants are captured to perform in circuses.

2. _____ Elephants in India, Sri Lanka, Thailand, and Bangladesh are used as work animals.

3. _____ The author is an elephant trainer.

Now compare your answers with these:

  1. N   2. Y   3. CT

Here is an explanation of the answers: The answer to Inference 1 is N; it hinges almost solely on one little word—*or.* In this passage the writer is distinguishing between elephants captured to perform in "shows" and those captured for "heavy, often difficult tasks."

The answer to Inference 2 is Y, because the inference reflects the same distinction. The writer does not say what those tasks are, but he does say the tasks are difficult, so we can infer that they involve hard work of some sort, probably in the fields, though again Campbell does not say so. The key words, then, are *heavy, difficult,* and *tasks.*

Inference 3, however, is a good example of an inference that should be marked CT. There is no way to know whether or not Campbell is a trainer, at least not from this passage. One can write about elephants intelligently without training them!

When doing the inference exercises, don't make wild guesses. Always return to the selection, read the appropriate paragraph again, and think about the writer's words and what they suggest. To help you work through the exercises and to strengthen your understanding of what you read, consider these suggestions:

HOW TO MAKE ACCURATE INFERENCES
• Look up the meanings of any unfamiliar words, and consider all the definitions in context. • Think about the possibilities of interpretation based on the writer's words and phrases. • Look carefully at the way the statement is worded. Then return to the passage and locate the pertinent passage. Test the statement for accuracy. • When in doubt, ask your instructor for help or for further clarification.

In order to make reliable inferences, you need to pay close attention to the passage. First, look up the meanings of any unfamiliar words. You can't interpret a passage if you don't know what the author is saying. Next, consider the various meanings of the unfamiliar words in the passage. Words often have more than one meaning, so don't accept the first meaning you come upon in the dictionary. Make sure that the meaning you choose makes sense in context. Then, return to the exercise and look carefully at how the statement is worded. If the sentence has two parts, make sure you know whether both of them are logical inferences based on the text. Check the exercise against the text for accuracy. Finally, if you aren't sure about an answer, ask your instructor for help or for further clarification. But remember, good readers may disagree over the answers because inferences aren't always black or white. That's what makes them fun and challenging.

Let's look at some additional examples from three of the selections you have already read. This one is from Selection 9, "The Life and Death of a Western Gladiator," by Charles Finney:

[1] He could see things well enough within his limited range, but a five-inch-long snake can command no great field of vision. [2] He had an excellent sense of smell. [3] But, having no ears, he was stone deaf. [4] On the other hand, he had a pit, a deep pock mark between eye and nostril. [5] Unique, this organ was sensitive to animal heat. [6] In pitch blackness, Crotalus, by means of the heat messages recorded in his pit, could tell whether another animal was near and could also judge its size. [7] That was better than an ear.

Here are the questions:

1. _____ Rattlesnakes are nearly blind.

2. _____ The "pit," the rattlesnake's main sensing device, is used to detect the presence of potential victims and enemies.

3. _____ No other species of snake possesses a pit like the diamondback rattlesnake.

4. _____ Rattlesnakes locate their prey by smelling them, even from great distances.

5. _____ A rattlesnake is seriously handicapped by not being able to hear.

Inference 1 should be marked N. Notice these words in the first sentence: "can command no great field of vision." Although the snake can't see very far, he is certainly not "nearly blind." So this is an inaccurate reference. Inference 2 should be marked Y. It shows an accurate understanding of the pit and what it is used for—to locate the presence of other animals, whether they represent a potential threat or whether they be that night's dinner.

To answer Inference 3, you have to think carefully about what the word *unique* in sentence 5 means—"one of a kind." But it's not clear how Finney is using this word; it is ambiguous, capable of two possible interpretations. Does he mean that the rattlesnake's pit is unique to diamondback rattlesnakes or that the pit is unique compared to a snake's other sense organs? It's hard to tell, so CT is a safe answer in this case.

Inference 4 should be marked N. Look again at Finney's words in light of how the statement is worded: He writes in sentence 5 that the pit is "sensitive to animal heat," which doesn't involve smell. So Inference 4 is an example of misreading. Inference 5 is tricky, but it too should be marked N. Again, Finney's words suggest that the snake's being "stone deaf" is not a terrible handicap: You can figure out this answer by considering the contrasting phrase in sentence 4, "on the other hand," and also the last sentence, "That [the pit] was better than an ear."

Here is a slightly longer and more challenging practice passage from Geoffrey Crowley's article, "The Language Explosion," Selection 10:

[1] More fundamentally, they [little children] discover that words can have radically different meanings depending on how they're strung together. [2] Even before children start combining words on their own, most know the difference between "Big Bird is tickling Cookie Monster" and "Cookie Monster is tickling Big Bird." [3] That awareness marks the zenith of language development. [4] A chimp can learn to label things, and a high-powered computer can process more information in a minute than any person could handle in a lifetime. [5] But neither a chimp nor a mainframe [computer] is any match for a runny-nosed 3-year-old when it comes to reporting who did what to whom. [6] When a chimp with a signboard signals "Me banana you banana you," chances are he wants you to give him one, but the utterance could mean almost anything. [7] Three-year-olds don't talk that way. [8] The reason, most linguists agree, is that natural selection has outfitted the human brain with software for grammatical analysis. [9] As MIT linguist Noam Chomsky realized more than 30 years ago, the world's languages all build sentences from noun phrases ("The big dog") and verb phrases ("ate my homework"). [10] And toddlers who have never heard of grammar identify them effortlessly.

This time, write your answer in the space provided. Then below each answer, write a brief explanation of why you marked each one as you did or choose the phrase or sentence that led you to your answer. Be sure to refer back to the excerpt to study the exact wording.

1. _____   The human brain is inferior to the "brain" of a mainframe computer.

Explanation: _____

_____

_____

2. _____ The chimpanzee's words like "Me banana you banana you" are both incomprehensible and ungrammatical.

Explanation: _____

_____

_____

3. _____ The chimpanzee's words, like "Me banana you banana you," were simple for the chimpanzee to produce.

Explanation: _____

_____

4. _____ Chimpanzees' brains lack the software for grammatical analysis that is innate in humans.

Explanation: _____

_____

_____

_____

5. _____ The term *grammar* in this context means, simply, a way to connect one's thoughts meaningfully.

Explanation: _____

_____

6. _____ The sentence "Cookie Monster is tickling Big Bird" consists of a noun phrase and a verb phrase.

Explanation: _____

_____

_____

7. _____ One must study grammar in order to speak correctly, no matter what language environment he or she is raised in.

Explanation: _____

_____

_____

8. _____ The world's languages are more alike structurally than one might imagine.

Explanation: _____

_____

This process shows you the importance of rereading the relevant sentence or sentences carefully. In my experience, students make significant mistakes in their reading because they read inattentively or, more often, they go off wildly into their own interpretation based on their experience or based on an erroneous understanding of what the author has said.

Here is one final exercise for you to do on your own. It represents several inference questions from Selection 14 by Lawrence Shames, "The Hunger for More" on pages 214–216. The relevant paragraph numbers are indicated for you, so be sure to look back before you write your answer.

As before, write Y ("yes") if the inference is an accurate one, N ("no") if the inference is an inaccurate one, and CT ("can't tell") if the writer does not give you enough information to make an inference one way or the other. As before, explain your answer.

1. _____   The buildings that the land speculators built in Texas towns were well designed and carefully constructed. [paragraph 2]

Explanation: _____

2. _____   Developers named buildings the Grand Hotel and the New Academy and named towns "the Athens of the South" or "the new plains Jerusalem" to make them sound more impressive than they really were. [paragraph 3]

Explanation: _____

_____

3. _____   In the 1880s, the railroad companies would put a train through a Texas town only if the population was high enough to justify it. [paragraph 4]

Explanation: _____

4. _____   The majority of real-estate speculators made huge fortunes building towns in hopes of attracting the railroads. [paragraphs 6–7]

Explanation: _____

_____

5. _____   A prospector who lost a fortune in gold or silver or oil was almost always ruined financially. [paragraph 8]

Explanation: _____

_____

A final note: Ask your instructor for help if you are having difficulty with these inference questions.

PART THREE

Tackling More Challenging Prose

15

ERIC SCHLOSSER

Fast Food Nation: Behind the Counter

Eric Schlosser's best-selling book, Fast Food Nation: The Dark Side of the All-American Meal, *has become a contemporary classic. Schlosser, a correspondent for the* Atlantic Monthly *magazine, investigated McDonald's, Burger King, Taco Bell, Kentucky Fried Chicken, and other fast food chains in the tradition of an old-fashioned muckraker. (A muckraker is a journalist who thoroughly investigates and exposes misconduct, usually in a particular industry.) In looking at the "dark side" of the fast food industry, Schlosser shows how it has permanently changed potato production in Idaho and beef production in Iowa; meanwhile, the industry has contributed both to urban sprawl throughout the country and to a decline in Americans' health. In this selection, Schlosser uses the city of Colorado Springs as the backdrop for a behind-the-scenes look at how a typical McDonald's operates.*

Vocabulary Preview

WORD HISTORIES

Crucial [paragraph 11] A significant part of this selection examines the concept of "throughput"—a *crucial* measurement of the speed and volume of a factory's flow. Meaning "of supreme importance," *crucial* derives from *crux,* the Latin word for "cross." English has also adopted the Latin word *crux,* meaning "a crucial or critical point"; Christ died on a *crucifix;* and finally, the *cruciferous* class of vegetables (brussels sprouts, cauliflower, and cabbage) are so termed because the leaves and stems are cross-shaped. If you turn over a head of cabbage, you will see this cross-shaped structure clearly.

Altruism [paragraph 19] Because fast food restaurants need a constant supply of low-wage workers, Schlosser writes that these establishments often hire "the young, the poor, and the handicapped," though their motives are "hardly *altruistic.*" The English noun *altruism* means "unselfish concern for others' welfare" and derives from the French word *altruisme.* The *American Heritage Dictionary* credits the philosopher Auguste Comte with coining this word as an antonym to (a word that means the opposite of) *egoism.* It seems that Comte took the Italian root *altrui* ("other"), in turn from the Latin word *alter* (also meaning "other"), and added the suffix *-isme,* which is identical to the English suffix *-ism,* which you have already studied. Related words in English are *alter, alternate,* and *alternative.*

WORD PARTS

Automated [paragraph 4]   The word *automated* refers to "machinery or equipment that runs by itself, without human intervention or control." (Schlosser alludes to *automated* site selection software programs and robotic drink machines.) *Automatic* combines the Greek prefix *auto-* ("self") + *-matos* ("willing"). Many other words in English begin with *auto-*, among them *automobile* ("self-moving") and *autopsy* ("a medical examination of a corpse to determine the cause of death," from *auto-* + *opsis* ["sight"], or literally, "a seeing for oneself"). What do these words mean? Consult a dictionary if you are unsure.

automaton	_____
autocracy	_____
autonomy	_____
autograph	_____

WORD FAMILIES

Demographic [paragraph 4]   McDonald's Corporation employs commercial satellites to provide information about future *demographic* growth in order to locate new restaurants near areas with a growing population. The word *demographic* combines two Greek roots—*demos* ("people") + *graphos* ("writing")—though this etymology does not yield a helpful definition. *Demographic* actually refers to "characteristics of human population," from *demography*, "the study of human population size, growth, and related subjects." Other words that come from *demos* include *democracy* ("rule of the people") and *demagogue*, "a political leader who gains power by stirring up people's prejudices."

ERIC SCHLOSSER

Fast Food Nation: Behind the Counter

1   Despite all the talk in Colorado about aerospace, biotech, computer software, telecommunications, and other industries of the future, the largest private employer in the state today is the restaurant industry. In Colorado Springs, the restaurant industry has grown much faster than the population. Over the last three decades the number of restaurants has increased fivefold. The number of chain restaurants has increased tenfold. In 1967, Colorado Springs had a total of twenty chain restaurants. Now it has twenty-one McDonald's.

2   The fast food chains feed off the sprawl of Colorado Springs, accelerate it, and help set its visual tone. They build large signs to attract motorists and look at cars the way predators view herds of prey. The chains thrive on traffic, lots of it, and put new restaurants at intersections where traffic is likely to increase, where development is heading but real estate prices are still low. Fast food restaurants often serve as the shock troops of sprawl, landing early and pointing the way. Some chains prefer to play follow the leader: when a new McDonald's opens, other fast food restaurants soon open nearby on the assumption that it must be a good location.

3   Regardless of the billions spent on marketing and promotion, all the ads on radio and TV, all the efforts to create brand loyalty, the major chains must live

with the unsettling fact that more than 70 percent of fast food visits are "impulsive." The decision to stop for fast food is made on the spur of the moment, without much thought. The vast majority of customers do not set out to eat at a Burger King, a Wendy's, or a McDonald's. Often, they're not even planning to stop for food—until they see a sign, a familiar building, a set of golden arches. Fast food, like the tabloids at a supermarket checkout, is an impulse buy. In order to succeed, fast food restaurants must be seen.

4   The McDonald's Corporation has perfected the art of restaurant site selection. In the early days Ray Kroc flew in a Cessna to find schools, aiming to put new restaurants nearby. McDonald's later used helicopters to assess regional growth patterns, looking for cheap land along highways and roads that would lie at the heart of future suburbs. In the 1980s, the chain became one of the world's leading purchasers of commercial satellite photography, using it to predict sprawl from outer space. McDonald's later developed a computer software program called Quintillion that automated its site-selection process, combining satellite imagery with detailed maps, demographic information, CAD drawings, and sales information from existing stores. "Geographic information systems" like Quintillion are now routinely used as site-selection tools by fast food chains and other retailers. As one marketing publication observed, the software developed

by McDonald's permits businessmen to "spy on their customers with the same equipment once used to fight the cold war."

5   The McDonald's Corporation has used Colorado Springs as a test site for other types of restaurant technology, for software and machines designed to cut labor costs and serve fast food even faster. Steve Bigari, who owns five local McDonald's, showed me the new contraptions at his place on Constitution Avenue. It was a rounded, postmodern McDonald's on the eastern edge of the city. The drive-through lanes had automatic sensors buried in the asphalt to monitor the traffic. Robotic drink machines selected the proper cups, filled them with ice, and then filled them with soda. Dispensers powered by compressed carbon dioxide shot out uniform spurts of ketchup and mustard. An elaborate unit emptied frozen french fries from a white plastic bin into wire-mesh baskets for frying, lowered the baskets into hot oil, lifted them a few minutes later and gave them a brief shake, put them back into the oil until the fries were perfectly cooked, and then dumped the fries underneath heat lamps, crisp and ready to be served. Television monitors in the kitchen instantly displayed the customer's order. And advanced computer software essentially ran the kitchen, assigning tasks to various workers for maximum efficiency, predicting future orders on the basis of ongoing customer flow.

6   Bigari was cordial, good-natured, passionate about his work, proud of the new devices. He told me the new software brought the "just in time" production philosophy of Japanese automobile plants to the fast food business, a philosophy that McDonald's has renamed Made for You. As he demonstrated one contraption after another—including a wireless hand-held menu that uses radio waves to transmit orders—a group of construction workers across the street put the finishing touches on a new subdivision called Constitution Hills. The streets had patriotic names, and the cattle ranch down the road was for sale.

THROUGHPUT

7   Every Saturday Elisa Zamot gets up at 5:15 in the morning. It's a struggle, and her head feels groggy as she steps into the shower. Her little sisters, Cookie and Sabrina, are fast asleep in their beds. By 5:30, Elisa's showered, done her hair, and put on her McDonald's uniform. She's sixteen, bright-eyed and olive-skinned, pretty and petite, ready for another day of work. Elisa's mother usually drives her the half-mile or so to the restaurant, but sometimes Elisa walks, leaving home before the sun rises. Her family's modest townhouse sits beside a busy highway on the south side of Colorado Springs, in a largely poor and working-class neighborhood. Throughout the day, sounds of traffic fill the house, the steady whoosh of passing cars. But when Elisa heads for work, the streets are quiet, the sky's still dark, and the lights are out in the small houses and rental apartments along the road.

8   When Elisa arrives at McDonald's, the manager unlocks the door and lets her in. Sometimes the husband-and-wife cleaning crew are just finishing up. More often, it's just Elisa and the manager in the restaurant, surrounded by an empty parking lot. For the next hour or so, the two of them get everything ready. They turn on the ovens and grills. They go downstairs into the basement and get food and supplies for the morning shift. They get the paper cups, wrappers, card-

board containers, and packets of condiments. They step into the big freezer and get the frozen bacon, the frozen pancakes, and the frozen cinnamon rolls. They get the frozen hash browns, the frozen biscuits, the frozen McMuffins. They get the cartons of scrambled egg mix and orange juice mix. They bring the food upstairs and start preparing it before any customers appear, thawing some things in the microwave and cooking other things on the grill. They put the cooked food in special cabinets to keep it warm.

9   The restaurant opens for business at seven o'clock, and for the next hour or so, Elisa and the manager hold down the fort, handling all the orders. As the place starts to get busy, other employees arrive. Elisa works behind the counter. She takes orders and hands food to customers from breakfast through lunch. When she finally walks home, after seven hours of standing at a cash register, her feet hurt. She's wiped out. She comes through the front door, flops onto the living room couch, and turns on the TV. And the next morning she gets up at 5:15 again and starts the same routine.

10   Up and down Academy Boulevard, along South Nevada, Circle Drive, and Woodman Road, teenagers like Elisa run the fast food restaurants of Colorado Springs. Fast food kitchens often seem like a scene from *Bugsy Malone,* a film in which all the actors are children pretending to be adults. No other industry in the United States has a workforce so dominated by adolescents. About two-thirds of the nation's fast food workers are under the age of twenty. Teenagers open the fast food outlets in the morning, close them at night, and keep them going at all hours in between. Even the managers and assistant managers are sometimes in their late teens. Unlike Olympic gymnastics—an activity in which teenagers consistently perform at a higher level than adults—there's nothing about the work in a fast food kitchen that requires young employees. Instead of relying upon a small, stable, well-paid, and well-trained workforce, the fast food industry seeks out part-time, unskilled workers who are willing to accept low pay. Teenagers have been the perfect candidates for these jobs, not only because they are less expensive to hire than adults, but also because their youthful inexperience makes them easier to control.

11   The labor practices of the fast food industry have their origins in the assembly line systems adopted by American manufacturers in the early twentieth century. Business historian Alfred D. Chandler has argued that a high rate of "throughput" was the most important aspect of these mass production systems. A factory's throughput is the speed and volume of its flow—a much more crucial measurement, according to Chandler, than the number of workers it employs or the value of its machinery. With innovative technology and the proper organization, a small number of workers can produce an enormous amount of goods cheaply. Throughput is all about increasing the speed of assembly, about doing things faster in order to make more.

12   Although the McDonald brothers had never encountered the term "throughput" or studied "scientific management," they instinctively grasped the underlying principles and applied them in the Speedee Service System. The restaurant operating scheme they developed has been widely adopted and refined over the past half century. The ethos of the assembly line remains at its core. The fast food industry's obsession with throughput has altered the way millions of

Americans work, turned commercial kitchens into small factories, and changed familiar foods into commodities that are manufactured.

13   At Burger King restaurants, frozen hamburger patties are placed on a conveyor belt and emerge from a broiler ninety seconds later fully cooked. The ovens at Pizza Hut and at Domino's also use conveyor belts to ensure standardized cooking times. The ovens at McDonald's look like commercial laundry presses, with big steel hoods that swing down and grill hamburgers on both sides at once. The burgers, chicken, french fries, and buns are all frozen when they arrive at a McDonald's. The shakes and sodas begin as syrup. At Taco Bell restaurants the food is "assembled," not prepared. The guacamole isn't made by workers in the kitchen; it's made at a factory in Michoacán, Mexico, then frozen and shipped north. The chain's taco meat arrives frozen and precooked in vacuum-sealed plastic bags. The beans are dehydrated and look like brownish corn flakes. The cooking process is fairly simple. "Everything's add water," a Taco Bell employee told me. "Just add hot water."

14   Although Richard and Mac McDonald introduced the division of labor to the restaurant business, it was a McDonald's executive named Fred Turner who created a production system of unusual thoroughness and attention to detail. In 1958, Turner put together an operations and training manual for the company that was seventy-five pages long, specifying how almost everything should be done. Hamburgers were always to be placed on the grill in six neat rows; french fries had to be exactly 0.28 inches thick. The McDonald's operations manual today has ten times the number of pages and weighs about four pounds. Known within the company as "the Bible," it contains precise instructions on how various appliances should be used, how each item on the menu should look, and how employees should greet customers. Operators who disobey these rules can lose their franchises. Cooking instructions are not only printed in the manual, they are often designed into the machines. A McDonald's kitchen is full of buzzers and flashing lights that tell employees what to do.

15   At the front counter, computerized cash registers issue their own commands. Once an order has been placed, buttons light up and suggest other menu items that can be added. Workers at the counter are told to increase the size of an order by recommending special promotions, pushing dessert, pointing out the financial logic behind the purchase of a larger drink. While doing so, they are instructed to be upbeat and friendly. "Smile with a greeting and make a positive first impression," a Burger King training manual suggests. "Show them you are GLAD TO SEE THEM. Include eye contact with the cheerful greeting."

16   The strict regimentation at fast food restaurants creates standardized products. It increases the throughput. And it gives fast food companies an enormous amount of power over their employees. "When management determines exactly how every task is to be done . . . and can impose its own rules about pace, output, quality, and technique," the sociologist Robin Leidner has noted, "[it] makes workers increasingly interchangeable." The management no longer depends upon the talents or skills of its workers—those things are built into the operating system and machines. Jobs that have been "de-skilled" can be filled cheaply. The need to retain any individual worker is greatly reduced by the ease with which he or she can be replaced.

17   Teenagers have long provided the fast food industry with the bulk of its workforce. The industry's rapid growth coincided with the baby-boom expansion of that age group. Teenagers were in many ways the ideal candidates for these low-paying jobs. Since most teenagers still lived at home, they could afford to work for wages too low to support an adult, and until recently, their limited skills attracted few other employers. A job at a fast food restaurant became an American rite of passage, a first job soon left behind for better things. The flexible terms of employment in the fast food industry also attracted housewives who needed extra income. As the number of baby-boom teenagers declined, the fast food chains began to hire other marginalized workers: recent immigrants, the elderly, and the handicapped.

18   English is now the second language of at least one-sixth of the nation's restaurant workers, and about one-third of that group speaks no English at all. The proportion of fast food workers who cannot speak English is even higher. Many know only the names of the items on the menu; they speak "McDonald's English."

19   The fast food industry now employs some of the most disadvantaged members of American society. It often teaches basic job skills—such as getting to work on time—to people who can barely read, whose lives have been chaotic or shut off from the mainstream. Many individual franchisees are genuinely concerned about the well-being of their workers. But the stance of the fast food industry on issues involving employee training, the minimum wage, labor unions, and overtime pay strongly suggests that its motives in hiring the young, the poor, and the handicapped are hardly altruistic. *

From Eric Schlosser, *Fast Food Nation*. © 2001 by Eric Schlosser. Reprinted by permission of Houghton Mifflin Co. All rights reserved.

Exercises

Do not refer to the selection for Exercises A and B unless your instructor directs you to do so.

A. DETERMINING THE MAIN IDEA AND PURPOSE

Choose the best answer.

_____ **1.** The main idea of the selection is that

    a. the restaurant industry is the largest private employer in Colorado.

    b. McDonald's Corporation has perfected the process of selecting sites and standardizing every aspect of its restaurant operations.

    c. Colorado Springs is McDonald's test site for designing restaurant technology, for software, and for machines designed to cut labor costs.

    d. McDonald's is particularly successful because of its regimented approach to hiring and training workers and its standardized menu.

_____ 2. With respect to the main idea, the writer's purpose is to

    a. argue that the reader should not patronize McDonald's and other fast food restaurants.

    b. criticize fast food restaurants for putting independent restaurants out of business.

    c. examine some common business practices McDonald's employs that the average person might not be aware of.

    d. investigate the hiring, training, and salary practices McDonald's uses with its largely teenage workforce.

B. COMPREHENDING MAIN IDEAS

Choose the correct answer.

_____ 1. McDonald's and other fast food chains prefer to situate new restaurants

    a. in established neighborhoods with high population density.

    b. near areas of high traffic where land is still cheap and where future suburbs will develop.

    c. in inner-city neighborhoods where labor is cheap.

    d. along heavily traveled interstates and other major highways.

_____ 2. Despite all the money fast food companies spend on marketing, promotion, and advertising, most customers dine there because

    a. the food is cheap, filling, and good.

    b. fast food restaurants are everywhere and easy to patronize.

    c. they see a sign or a familiar building and stop in on impulse.

    d. they can eat a meal in a relatively short period of time.

_____ 3. To select new restaurant sites, McDonald's currently

    a. employs satellite photography and a computer software program.

    b. follows the lead of other fast food restaurants and locates stores near other existing establishments.

    c. takes customer surveys to find out where diners would like new restaurants to be built.

    d. chooses areas close to schools for a ready-made customer base.

_____ 4. The philosophy underlying the automated systems that make McDonald's restaurants run more productively originated in

    a. the Japanese automobile industry.

    b. the American automobile industry.

    c. Silicon Valley technology firms.

    d. McDonald's corporate headquarters.

_____ **5.** As used in the fast food industry, the term *throughput* refers to

   a. the number of customers who order their food at a fast food restaurant's drive-through window.

   b. increasing the speed of assembly and doing every step faster to produce more in a given time.

   c. shortening the amount of time customers eat inside the restaurant, thus ensuring faster customer turnover and higher profits.

   d. shortening the number of items on a restaurant's menu so that fewer employees are needed to assemble the food.

_____ **6.** Ultimately, Schlosser emphasizes two chief characteristics of fast food restaurants and their operations, namely

   a. efficiency and high quality.

   b. good career opportunities and fringe benefits.

   c. standardization and regimentation.

   d. genuine friendliness and a desire to serve.

COMPREHENSION SCORE

Score your answers for Exercises A and B as follows:

A. No. right _____ × 2 = _____

B. No. right _____ × 1 = _____

Total points from A and B _____ × 10 = _____ percent

You may refer to the selection as you work through the remaining exercises.

C. IDENTIFYING SUPPORTING DETAILS

Place an X in the space for each sentence from the selection that *directly* supports this main idea: "Teenagers have long provided the fast food industry with the bulk of its workforce."

1. _____ [Workers] are instructed to be upbeat and friendly.

2. _____ A McDonald's kitchen is full of buzzers and flashing lights that tell employees what to do.

3. _____ Instead of relying upon a small, stable, well-paid, and well-trained workforce, the fast food industry seeks out part-time, unskilled workers who are willing to accept low pay.

4. _____ Teenagers have been the perfect candidates for these jobs, not only because they are less expensive to hire than adults, but also because their youthful inexperience makes them easier to control.

5. _____ The industry's rapid growth coincided with the baby-boom expansion of that age group [teenagers].

6. _____ Since most teenagers still lived at home, they could afford to work for wages too low to support an adult, and until recently, their limited skills attracted few other employers.

7. _____ A job at a fast food restaurant became an American rite of passage, a first job soon left behind for better things.

8. _____ The flexible terms of employment in the fast food industry also attracted housewives who needed extra income.

9. _____ As the number of baby-boom teenagers declined, the fast food chains began to hire other marginalized workers: recent immigrants, the elderly, and the handicapped.

10. _____ English is now the second language of at least one-sixth of the nation's restaurant workers, and about one-third of that group speaks no English at all.

D. MAKING INFERENCES

For each of these statements write Y (yes) if the inference is an accurate one, N (no) if the inference is an inaccurate one, and CT (can't tell) if the writer does not give you enough information to make an inference one way or another.

1. _____ Since most customers stop at a fast food restaurant on impulse, it is important that its signs be conspicuous from the street. [paragraph 2]

2. _____ McDonald's is not the only fast food business to use geographic information systems; most of the other chains employ the same technology. [paragraph 2]

3. _____ Foreign countries welcome McDonald's outlets in their countries as symbols of American culture and progress. [essay as a whole]

4. _____ "Throughput" means that fast food outlets can save money by reducing labor costs. [paragraphs 11–12]

5. _____ Fast food chains prefer to hire teenagers to staff their restaurants because they are more energetic and more enthusiastic about work than are older workers. [paragraph 17]

E. INTERPRETING MEANING AND ANALYZING STRUCTURE

Where appropriate, write your answers to these questions in your own words.

1. Read paragraph 2 again. What purpose is served by Schlosser's use of these

   words: *predators, prey,* and *shock troops*? _____

   _____

   What do these phrases suggest about his point of view? _____

   _____

2. _____ Read paragraph 4 again. A good title for this paragraph would be
   a. "Restaurant Locations."
   b. "Uses for Commercial Satellite Photography."
   c. "How McDonald's Selects New Sites."
   d. "Site Selection Tools."

3. In your own words, state the main point of paragraph 5. _____

   _____

   Now list three important supporting details for that point. _____

   _____

   _____

4. In paragraphs 5 and 6 Schlosser refers to the equipment that he is shown at a McDonald's in Colorado Springs as *contraptions*. Why does he choose this word? What connotation or emotional feeling does it convey? _____

   _____

5. In paragraph 8 Schlosser uses the word *frozen* six times. Why? _____

   _____

6. In relation to the selection as a whole, how effective is the description of Elisa Zamot's typical workday at McDonald's? _____

   _____

7. Paragraph 13 consists only of several examples but no stated main idea. Based on the many details in the paragraph, what is Schlosser's point? _____

   _____

   _____

8. On balance, what is Schlosser's opinion of McDonald's hiring practices? _____

   _____

   _____

   _____

F. UNDERSTANDING VOCABULARY

Choose the best definition according to an analysis of word parts or the context.

_____ 1. to *assess* regional growth patterns [paragraph 4]:
   a. evaluate
   b. consider
   c. estimate
   d. research

_____ 2. *demographic* information [4]: the study of
   a. the relationship between advertising and profits
   b. natural resources
   c. political systems
   d. human population

_____ 3. her family's *modest* townhouse [7]:
   a. crowded, cramped
   b. plain, not showy
   c. well-lived in, comfortable
   d. untidy, messy

_____   **4.** a much more *crucial* measurement [11]:

      a. commonly accepted
      b. difficult to calculate
      c. accurate, precise
      d. critical, very important

_____   **5.** with *innovative* technology [11]:

      a. newly introduced
      b. sophisticated, complicated
      c. valuable, costly
      d. superior, outstanding

_____   **6.** the *ethos* of the assembly line [12]:

      a. unique design
      b. atmosphere, environment
      c. fundamental value, character
      d. purpose, function

_____   **7.** the strict *regimentation* [16]: characterized by

      a. haphazard order
      b. military power
      c. careful, thoughtful planning
      d. uniformity, rigid order

_____   **8.** its motives . . . are hardly *altruistic* [19]:

      a. beneficial
      b. unselfish
      c. questionable
      d. genuine

G. USING VOCABULARY

From the following list of vocabulary words, choose a word that fits in each blank according to both the grammatical structure of the sentence and the context. Use each word in the list only once. Do not change the form of the word. (Note that there are more words than sentences.)

accelerate	computerized	efficiency	marginalized
automated	cordial	flexible	obsession
coincided	declined	franchises	predators

1. One of Schlosser's primary complaints is that fast food companies like

McDonald's _____ urban sprawl because they regard cars and

their passengers the way _____ would look at prey.

2. Because every aspect of food "assembly" at a typical McDonald's is both

_____ and _____ , they operate at maximum

_____ .

3. Fast food chains like to hire teenagers because their hours fit into the outlets'

   _____ work hours, but they are increasingly hiring

   _____ workers like recent immigrants, the elderly, and the handicapped.

H. ANNOTATING EXERCISE

In the margin, annotate paragraphs 3 and 10.

I. TOPICS FOR WRITING OR DISCUSSION

1. Write a paragraph in which you summarize Schlosser's ideas about the effect fast food chain restaurants have on a community. Now write a second paragraph in which you examine the effects a particular fast food restaurant has had on your community. You might want to consider traffic patterns, eating habits, or employment matters.
2. Schlosser paints a rather grim picture of McDonald's and its fast food counterparts. What are some positive features that fast food restaurants have brought to American culture?
3. Do you eat at fast food restaurants regularly? If so, what are their attractions? If not, why not?

For Further Exploration

BOOK

In the same way that Schlosser exposes the underside of the fast food industry, Jessica Mitford, one of this country's best-known twentieth-century muckrakers, exposed the funeral industry in *The American Way of Death* (1963). This classic book, written in a bitingly humorous style, exposed the way funeral directors gouged their unsuspecting and vulnerable customers.

MOVIE

While not about fast food workers, *Clerks* (1994), directed by Kevin Smith, is a very funny look at the antics of a convenience store clerk and his buddy who works at the video store next door. The film was made in black and white for $27,000.

WEB SITES

Check out these fast food Web sites. Which site gives the most complete nutritional information about the food served at their establishments? Which site provides the easiest access to this information?

- *www.mcdonalds.com*
- *www.burgerking.com*
- *www.inandout.com*
- *www.jackinthebox.com*

16

VAL PLUMWOOD

Being Prey: Surviving a Crocodile Attack

Activist, academic, writer, and scholar, Val Plumwood is currently ARC Fellow at the Australian National University. She enjoys a worldwide reputation as a feminist theorist and a pioneer of environmental philosophy. The incident described in this excerpt occurred in February 1985 near the city of Darwin in Kakadu National Park located on the northern coast of Australia. The article was originally published in a different form in Travelers' Tales *(1999) and was reprinted in the* Utne Reader. *It was also selected for inclusion in* The Best Science and Nature Writing 2001.

Vocabulary Preview

WORD HISTORIES

Enticed [paragraph 1] The verb *entice* means "to attract by arousing hope or desire" or "to lure." Its modern meaning is more general than what the word originally meant in the Middle English root *enticen* and the French root *intitiare.* Both meant "to set afire."

Aboriginal and Indigenous [paragraphs 2, 5] *Aboriginal,* when capitalized, refers to the *indigenous* or original inhabitants of Australia. When written in lower case, *aboriginal* refers to the original inhabitants of any region, for example, the Ainu of Japan or the Indians of North and South America. Both words are of Latin origin: *Aboriginal* comes from the prefix *ab-* + *origine* ("beginning"), and *indigenous* derives from the Latin root *indigina,* "a native."

WORD PARTS

-ity (noun suffix) Four words in this selection illustrate this common noun suffix. (A *prefix,* you will remember, is a word part that comes at the beginning of a word that often indicates meaning. A *suffix* is a word part added to the end of a root, which makes the root into another part of speech. In other words, suffixes commonly indicate grammatical parts of speech rather than convey meaning.) The noun suffix *-ity* is added to adjectives to form abstract nouns that express a state or condition. In paragraph 10, then, *subjectivity* means "the condition of being subjective," and *timidity* in paragraph 3 means "the state of being timid." The selection also contains the words *integrity, eternity,* and *capacities* (the latter is the plural spelling).

WORD FAMILIES

Aquatic [paragraph 2] Plumwood writes that "the crocodile was a symbol of the power and integrity of this place and the incredible richness of its *aquatic* habitats." *Aqua* can refer both to the color blue-green (like the sea) and simply to water. Other examples of words in the family using this root are *aquaplane, aquarium, aqueous* (an adjective meaning "watery"), and *aqueduct* (a system for transporting water, *aqua + ducere* ["to lead"]).

VAL PLUMWOOD

Being Prey: Surviving a Crocodile Attack

1   In the early wet season, Kakadu's paperbark wetlands are especially stunning, as the water lilies weave white, pink, and blue patterns of dreamlike beauty over the shining thunderclouds reflected in their still waters. Yesterday, the water lilies and the wonderful bird life had enticed me into a joyous afternoon's idyll as I ventured onto the East Alligator Lagoon for the first time in a canoe lent by the park service. "You can play about on the backwaters," the ranger had said, "but don't go onto the main river channel. The current's too swift, and if you get into trouble, there are the crocodiles. Lots of them along the river!" I followed his advice and glutted myself on the magical beauty and bird life of the lily lagoons, untroubled by crocodiles.

2   Today, I wanted to repeat that experience despite the drizzle beginning to fall as I neared the canoe launch site. I set off on a day trip in search of an Aboriginal rock art site across the lagoon and up a side channel. The drizzle turned to a warm rain within a few hours, and the magic was lost. The birds were invisible, the water lilies were sparser, and the lagoon seemed even a little menacing. I noticed now how low the 14-foot canoe sat in the water, just a few inches of fiberglass between me and the great saurians,[1] close relatives of the ancient dinosaurs. Not long ago, saltwater crocodiles were considered endangered, as virtually all mature animals in Australia's north were shot by commercial hunters. But after a decade and more of protection, they are now the most plentiful of the large animals of Kakadu National Park. I was actively involved in preserving such places, and for me, the crocodile was a symbol of the power and integrity of this place and the incredible richness of its aquatic habitats.

3   After hours of searching the maze of shallow channels in the swamp, I had not found the clear channel leading to the rock art site, as shown on the ranger's sketch map. When I pulled my canoe over in driving rain to a rock outcrop for a hasty, sodden lunch, I experienced the unfamiliar sensation of being watched. Having never been one for timidity, in philosophy or in life, I decided, rather than return defeated to my sticky trailer, to explore a clear, deep channel closer to the river I had traveled along the previous day.

4   The rain and wind grew more severe, and several times I pulled over to tip water from the canoe. The channel soon developed steep mud banks and snags.

---

[1]*Saurians* refers to Sauria, the suborder of reptiles including lizards, crocodiles, and alligators. The Greek root is *sauros* or "lizard." (Ed.)

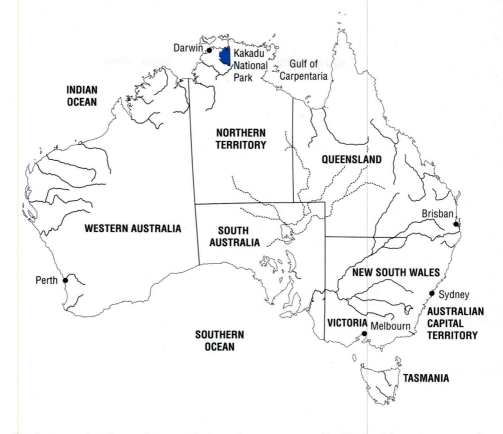

Farther on, the channel opened up and was eventually blocked by a large sandy bar. I pushed the canoe toward the bank, looking around carefully before getting out in the shallows and pulling the canoe up. I would be safe from crocodiles in the canoe—I had been told—but swimming and standing or wading at the water's edge were dangerous. Edges are one of the crocodile's favorite food-capturing places. I saw nothing, but the feeling of unease that had been with me all day intensified.

5   The rain eased temporarily, and I crossed a sandbar to see more of this puzzling place. As I crested a gentle dune, I was shocked to glimpse the muddy waters of the East Alligator River gliding silently only 100 yards away. The channel had led me back to the main river. Nothing stirred along the riverbank, but a great tumble of escarpment cliffs up on the other side caught my attention. One especially striking rock formation—a single large rock balanced precariously on a much smaller one—held my gaze. As I looked, my whispering sense of unease turned into a shout of danger. The strange formation put me sharply in mind of two things: of the indigenous Gagadgu owners of Kakadu, whose advice about coming here I had not sought, and of the precariousness of my own life, of human lives. As a solitary specimen of a major prey species of the saltwater crocodile, I was standing in one of the most dangerous places on earth.

6   I turned back with a feeling of relief. I had not found the rock paintings, I rationalized, but it was too late to look for them. The strange rock formation presented itself instead as a telos[2] of the day, and now I could go, home to trailer comfort.

7   As I pulled the canoe out into the main current, the rain and wind started up again. I had not gone more than five or ten minutes down the channel when, rounding a bend, I saw in midstream what looked like a floating stick—one I did not recall passing on my way up. As the current moved me toward it, the stick developed eyes. A crocodile! It did not look like a large one. I was close to it now but was not especially afraid; an encounter would add interest to the day.

8   Although I was paddling to miss the crocodile, our paths were strangely convergent. I knew it would be close, but I was totally unprepared for the great blow when it struck the canoe. Again it struck, again and again, now from behind, shuddering the flimsy craft. As I paddled furiously, the blows continued. The unheard of was happening; the canoe was under attack! For the first time, it came to me fully that I was prey. I realized I had to get out of the canoe or risk being capsized.

9   The bank now presented a high, steep face of slippery mud. The only obvious avenue of escape was a paperbark tree near the muddy bank wall. I made the split-second decision to leap into its lower branches and climb to safety. I steered to the tree and stood up to jump. At the same instant, the crocodile rushed up alongside the canoe, and its beautiful, flecked golden eyes looked straight into mine. Perhaps I could bluff it, drive it away, as I had read of British tiger hunters doing. I waved my arms and shouted, "Go away!" (We're British here.) The golden eyes glinted with interest. I tensed for the jump and leapt. Before my foot even tripped the first branch, I had a blurred, incredulous vision of great toothed jaws bursting from the water. Then I was seized between the legs in a red-hot pincer grip and whirled into the suffocating wet darkness.

10   Our final thoughts during near-death experiences can tell us much about our frameworks of subjectivity. A framework capable of sustaining action and purpose must, I think, view the world "from the inside," structured to sustain the concept of a continuing, narrative self; we remake the world in that way as our own, investing it with meaning, reconceiving it as sane, survivable, amenable to hope and resolution. The lack of fit between this subject-centered version and reality comes into play in extreme moments. In its final, frantic attempts to protect itself from the knowledge that threatens the narrative framework, the mind can instantaneously fabricate terminal doubt of extravagant proportions: *This is not really happening. This is a nightmare from which I will soon awake.* This desperate delusion split apart as I hit the water. In that flash, I glimpsed the world for the first time "from the outside," as a world no longer my own, an unrecognizable bleak landscape composed of raw necessity, indifferent to my life or death.

11   Few of those who have experienced the crocodile's death roll have lived to describe it. It is, essentially, an experience beyond words of total terror. The croc-

---

[2]*Telos* is a word of Greek origin meaning "the end result of a goal-oriented process." The word also appears on page 252.

odile's breathing and heart metabolism are not suited to prolonged struggle, so the roll is an intense burst of power designed to overcome the victim's resistance quickly. The crocodile then holds the feebly struggling prey underwater until it drowns. The roll was a centrifuge of boiling blackness that lasted for an eternity, beyond endurance, but when I seemed all but finished, the rolling suddenly stopped. My feet touched bottom, my head broke the surface, and coughing, I sucked at air, amazed to be alive. The crocodile still had me in its pincer grip between the legs. I had just begun to weep for the prospects of my mangled body when the crocodile pitched me suddenly into a second death roll.

12   When the whirling terror stopped again I surfaced again, still in the crocodile's grip next to a stout branch of a large sandpaper fig growing in the water. I grabbed the branch, vowing to let the crocodile tear me apart rather than throw me again into that spinning, suffocating hell. For the first time I realized that the crocodile was growling, as if angry. I braced myself for another roll, but then its jaws simply relaxed; I was free. I gripped the branch and pulled away, dodging around the back of the fig tree to avoid the forbidding mud bank, and tried once more to climb into the paperbark tree.

13   As in the repetition of a nightmare, the horror of my first escape attempt was repeated. As I leapt into the same branch, the crocodile seized me again, this time around the upper left thigh, and pulled me under. Like the others, the third death roll stopped, and we came up next to the sandpaper fig branch again. I was growing weaker, but I could see the crocodile taking a long time to kill me this way. I prayed for a quick finish and decided to provoke it by attacking it with my hands. Feeling back behind me along the head, I encountered two lumps. Thinking I had the eye sockets, I jabbed my thumbs into them with all my might. They slid into warm, unresisting holes (which may have been the ears, or perhaps the nostrils), and the crocodile did not so much as flinch. In despair, I grabbed the branch again. And once again, after a time, I felt the crocodile jaws relax, and I pulled free.

14   I knew I had to break the pattern; up the slippery mud bank was the only way. I scrabbled for a grip, then slid back toward the waiting jaws. The second time I almost made it before again sliding back, braking my slide by grabbing a tuft of grass. I hung there, exhausted. *I can't make it,* I thought. *It'll just have to come and get me.* The grass tuft began to give away. Flailing to keep from sliding farther, I jammed my fingers into the mud. This was the clue I needed to survive. I used this method and the last of my strength to climb up the bank and reach the top. I was alive!

15   Escaping the crocodile was not the end of my struggle to survive. I was alone, severely injured, and many miles from help. During the attack, the pain from the injuries had not fully registered. As I took my first urgent steps, I knew something was wrong with my leg. I did not wait to inspect the damage but took off away from the crocodile toward the ranger station.

16   After putting more distance between me and the crocodile, I stopped and realized for the first time how serious my wounds were. I did not remove my clothing to see the damage to the groin area inflicted by the first hold. What I could see was bad enough. The left thigh hung open, with bits of fat, tendon, and muscle showing, and a sick, numb feeling suffused my entire body. I tore up some clothing to bind the wounds and made a tourniquet for my bleeding thigh,

then staggered on, still elated from my escape. I went some distance before realizing with a sinking heart that I had crossed the swamp above the ranger station in the canoe and could not get back without it.

17   I would have to hope for a search party, but I could maximize my chances by moving downstream toward the swamp edge, almost two miles away. I struggled on, through driving rain, shouting for mercy from the sky, apologizing to the angry crocodile, repenting to this place for my intrusion. I came to a flooded tributary and made a long upstream detour looking for a safe place to cross.

18   My considerable bush[3] experience served me well, keeping me on course (navigating was second nature). After several hours, I began to black out and had to crawl the final distance to the swamp's edge. I lay there in the gathering dusk to await what would come. I did not expect a search party until the following day, and I doubted I could last the night.

19   The rain and wind stopped with the onset of darkness, and it grew perfectly still. Dingoes[4] howled, and clouds of mosquitoes whined around my body. I hoped to pass out soon, but consciousness persisted. There were loud swirling noises in the water, and I knew I was easy meat for another crocodile. After what seemed like a long time, I heard the distant sound of a motor and saw a light moving on the swamp's far side. Thinking it was a boat, I rose up on my elbow and called for help. I thought I heard a faint reply, but then the motor grew fainter and the lights went away. I was as devastated as any castaway who signals desperately to a passing ship and is not seen.

20   The lights had not come from a boat. Passing my trailer, the ranger noticed there was no light inside it. He had driven to the canoe launch site on a motorized trike and realized I had not returned. He had heard my faint call for help, and after some time, a rescue craft appeared. As I began my 13-hour journey to Darwin Hospital, my rescuers discussed going upriver the next day to shoot a crocodile. I spoke strongly against this plan: I was the intruder, and no good purpose could be served by random revenge. The water around the spot where I had been lying was full of crocodiles. That spot was under six feet of water the next morning, flooded by the rains signaling the start of the wet season.

21   In the end I was found in time and survived against many odds. A similar combination of good fortune and human care enabled me to overcome a leg infection that threatened amputation or worse. I probably have Paddy Pallin's incredibly tough walking shorts to thank for the fact that the groin injuries were not as severe as the leg injuries. I am very lucky that I can still walk well and have lost few of my previous capacities. The wonder of being alive after being held—quite literally—in the jaws of death has never entirely left me. For the first year, the experience of existence as an unexpected blessing cast a golden glow over my life, despite the injuries and the pain. The glow has slowly faded, but some of that new gratitude for life endures, even if I remain unsure whom I should thank. The gift of gratitude came from the searing flash of near-death knowledge, a glimpse "from the outside" of the alien, incomprehensible world in which the narrative of self has ended.

---

[3]"Bush" here refers to the Australian bush, the vast area of the country that is not settled. (Ed.)
[4]Dingoes are wild dogs native to Australia. (Ed.)

22 . . . [T]he story of the crocodile encounter now has, for me, a significance quite the opposite of that conveyed in the master/monster narrative. It is a humbling and cautionary tale about our relationship with the earth, about the need to acknowledge our own animality and ecological vulnerability. I learned many lessons from the event, one of which is to know better when to turn back and to be more open to the sorts of warnings I had ignored that day. As on the day itself, so even more to me now, the telos of these events lies in the strange rock formation, which symbolized so well the lessons about the vulnerability of humankind I had to learn, lessons largely lost to the technological culture that now dominates the earth. In my work as a philosopher, I see more and more reason to stress our failure to perceive this vulnerability, to realize how misguided we are to view ourselves as masters of a tamed and malleable nature. . . . ✳

From Val Plumwood, *Traveler's Tales.* © 1999 by Val Plumwood. Reprinted by permission of the author.

Exercises

Do not refer to the selection for Exercises A and B unless your instructor directs you to do so.

A. DETERMINING THE MAIN IDEA AND PURPOSE

Choose the best answer.

_____ 1. The main idea of the selection is that

    a. surviving a near-death crocodile attack gave the writer a glimpse into an incomprehensible part of nature and of human life.

    b. crocodiles are fiercely dangerous creatures who prey on humans if they venture into their waters.

    c. the writer's experience in the Australian bush was useful when she encountered a crocodile.

    d. in confronting her crocodile attacker, the writer learned that human endurance and the will to triumph can conquer every peril in nature.

_____ 2. With respect to the main idea, the writer's purpose is to

    a. describe an exotic location in a faraway place.

    b. tell a frightening story that gave her a new perspective on life.

    c. present an account of the writer's experience as a naturalist.

    d. observe and describe a powerful creature in its own environment.

B. COMPREHENDING MAIN IDEAS

Choose the correct answer.

_____ 1. Before she set off in a canoe to explore, the park ranger at Kakadu National Park told the writer not to

    a. venture into the main river channel.
    b. stay out in the water too long.
    c. climb onto the channel's muddy banks.
    d. be afraid of the park's crocodiles.

_____ 2. While the writer crossed the sandbar to see the place from a closer view, she initially felt both

    a. wonder and delight.
    b. unease and fear of danger.
    c. anxiety and panic.
    d. curiosity and a desire to see more.

_____ 3. When the writer first encountered the crocodile, she says that it resembled a

    a. partially submerged log.
    b. strange rock formation.
    c. dark shadow in the water.
    d. floating stick.

_____ 4. Plumwood writes that, when faced with danger, it is human nature to

    a. alter reality by doubting that the danger is real.
    b. feel terrified by the reality of the situation.
    c. feel intimately connected to the reality of the situation.
    d. adopt a purely objective point of view.

_____ 5. After the crocodile attacked the first two times, the writer was able to escape the crocodile's grasp by

    a. scrambling back into her canoe and paddling furiously.
    b. climbing to safety on the muddy bank away from the water.
    c. leaping into the branches of a nearby tree growing in the water.
    d. hitting the crocodile on the head with her canoe paddle.

_____ 6. As a result of her near-death experience, Plumwood

    a. decided to investigate potential dangers before setting off on such an adventure again.
    b. promised to seek the advice of experts before starting off on a dangerous journey.
    c. sustained crippling injuries to her leg.
    d. felt gratitude for the gift of life.

COMPREHENSION SCORE

Score your answers for Exercises A and B as follows:

A. No. right _____ × 2 = _____

B. No. right _____ × 1 = _____

Total points from A and B _____ × 10 = _____ percent

You may refer to the selection as you work through the remaining exercises.

C. IDENTIFYING SUPPORTING DETAILS

Place an X in the space for each sentence from the selection that *directly* supports this main idea: "Few of those who have experienced the crocodile's death roll have lived to describe it."

1. _____   It is, essentially, an experience beyond words of total terror.

2. _____   The crocodile's breathing and heart metabolism aren't suited to prolonged struggle.

3. _____   The roll is an intense burst of power designed to overcome the victim's resistance quickly.

4. _____   The crocodile then holds the feebly struggling prey underwater until it drowns.

5. _____   I prayed for a quick finish and decided to provoke it by attacking it with my hands.

6._____   After putting more distance between me and the crocodile, I stopped and realized for the first time how serious my wounds were.

D. MAKING INFERENCES

For each of these statements write Y (yes) if the inference is an accurate one, N (no) if the inference is an inaccurate one, and CT (can't tell) if the writer does not give you enough information to make an inference one way or another.

1. _____   Plumwood was an experienced canoeist. [article as a whole]

2. _____   The writer got into trouble and encountered crocodiles because the ranger's sketch of the waterways was wrong. [paragraph 3]

3. _____   If Plumwood had asked the Aboriginal Gagadgu owners of Kakadu Park for advice, they would undoubtedly have told her not to venture into the waterways in a canoe. [paragraph 5]

E. INTERPRETING MEANING AND ANALYZING STRUCTURE

Choose the best answer or write your answers to these questions in your own words.

1. _____ Which of the following sentences from the selection *best* represents the main idea?

   a. "As a solitary specimen of a major prey species of the saltwater crocodile, I was standing in one of the most dangerous places on earth."
   b. "Our final thoughts during near-death experiences can tell us much about our frameworks of subjectivity."
   c. "I struggled on, through driving rain, shouting for mercy from the sky, apologizing to the angry crocodile, repenting to this place for my intrusion."
   d. "The gift of gratitude came from the searing flash of near-death knowledge, a glimpse 'from the outside' of the alien, incomprehensible world in which the narrative of self has ended."

2. The first part of the essay establishes a mood that strongly contrasts with the mood after the attack. What contrasts in emotion are suggested?

   _____ and _____

3. Paragraph 10 is quite difficult. Study it carefully and also read the last sentence of paragraph 21, which repeats the same idea. To help you, first figure out what the words *inside* and *outside* refer to in the phrases "from the inside" and "from the outside." _____

   _____

   _____

   Then write a sentence summarizing Plumwood's main point in the paragraph. _____

   _____

   _____

4. _____ A good title for paragraph 11 would be

   a. "Experiencing Total Terror."
   b. "Why Crocodiles Kill."
   c. "An Unbelievable Experience."
   d. "Crocodile Behavior."

5. Look through paragraphs 11 and 12 again. List three phrases that convey the intense violence of the crocodile's attack. _____

   _____

   _____

6. What action probably saved Plumwood from dying?_____

_____

7. _____ Read paragraph 20 again. In it the writer strongly suggests that

    a. the park rangers eventually shot the crocodile that attacked her.

    b. she later regretted not requesting that the crocodile be killed.

    c. identifying the particular crocodile that had attacked her would be difficult.

    d. revenge is not a good motive for taking action.

F. UNDERSTANDING VOCABULARY

Look through the paragraphs listed below and find a word that matches each definition. Refer to the dictionary if necessary. An example has been done for you.

Ex. threatening, frightening [paragraph 2]   _____ menacing _____

1. the state of being whole and unimpaired [2]: _____

2. natural environments, surroundings [2]: _____

3. an intricate network, a labyrinth [3]: _____

4. soggy, full of water [3]: _____

5. referring to native inhabitants [5]: _____

6. not inclined to believe [9]: _____

7. agreeable, open to [10]: _____

8. make up, invent [10]: _____

9. gloomy, offering little hope [10]: _____

10. overwhelmed, nearly destroyed [19]: _____

G. USING VOCABULARY

Here are some words from the selection. Write an original sentence using each word that shows both that you know how to use the word and what it means.

1. *precariously*_____

_____

_____

2. *rationalize* _____

_____

_____

3. *delusion* _____

_____

_____

4. *repentance* _____

_____

_____

H. PARAPHRASING EXERCISE

Write a paraphrase of the last four sentences of paragraph 21, starting at "The wonder of being alive. . . ." _____

_____

_____

_____

_____

_____

_____

_____

_____

I.   TOPICS FOR WRITING OR DISCUSSION

1. Write a short narrative in which you describe an experience where you felt, as Plumwood did, "total terror." It does not have to be an incident as harrowing as a crocodile attack, but everyone has felt intense fear at one time or another.

2. Go to a good unabridged dictionary, in the library if necessary, and look up the meaning of the Greek word *hubris*. To what extent do Plumwood's actions reflect this emotion?

3. What are some devices that the writer uses to maintain interest and to create suspense and terror in the reader?

For Further Exploration

BOOKS

- Bill Bryson, *In a Sundrenched Country* (2000). This master travel writer journeyed through Australia and, in his characteristic humorous and self-effacing style, shows us the wonders of Australia from the remote and sparsely populated Outback to the cosmopolitan cities of Sydney and Melbourne.
- Jon Krakauer, *Into the Wild* (1996). Chris McCandless, newly graduated from Emory University in Atlanta, decided to fulfill a long-standing dream and live on his own in the Alaska wilderness. He traveled around the country working at odd jobs and saving money to finance his dream. Krakauer

writes a readable account of McCandless's attempt to survive in this modern saga of inexperience and hubris.

MOVIE

A Cry in the Dark (1988), directed by Fred Schepisi and starring Meryl Streep and Sam Neill, depicts the true story of Lindy Chamberlain, an Australian woman who was accused of killing her baby during a family vacation to Ayers Rock (a sacred Aboriginal site now called Uluru). Despite her protests of innocence— that the baby was carried off by a dingo—she had to stand trial. This is a dark film, portraying a couple whose actions earned them universal scorn from the Australian public.

WEB SITES

End the confusion over the difference between crocodiles and alligators by visiting this site:

- *www.lib.duke.edu/bes/reptiles/crockgator.htm*

Photographs of Kakadu National Park, along with other famous Australian sites, are available at these two addresses:

- *goaustralia.about.com/library/weekly/aa111799.htm*
- *www.galen-frysinger.org/kakadu.htm*

Photographs of Ayers Rock (uluru) and other Australian sites are available at:

- *www.australianexplorer.com.au/photographs/nt_landscape_ayers_rock.htm*

17

ELLIOTT WEST
Wagon Train Children

Elliott West is a Distinguished Professor of History at the University of Arkansas where he has twice been selected as the university's teacher of the year. His specialty is the social and environmental history of the American West. He has published five books, among them Growing Up with the Country: Childhood on the Far Western Frontier *(1989) and* The Contested Plains: Indians, Goldseekers and the Rush to Colorado. *Most of us have read of the hardships the nineteenth-century pioneers endured as they traveled west to California and Oregon. But for the children traveling overland, the experience must have been both exciting and unsettling. In this article, first published in* American Heritage, *the writer recounts the experiences of several children, drawn chiefly from diaries and memoirs they kept as they traveled on the Oregon Trail.*

Vocabulary Preview

WORD HISTORIES

Cannibalism [paragraph 27]   One of the memoirs quoted was written by a young girl who was a survivor of the Donner Party, an ill-fated group of emigrants on their way to Oregon. When their guide foolishly decided to take a different route, supposedly a shortcut through the mountains, the group became completely lost. Stranded in the Sierra Nevada mountains in northern California during an unusually harsh winter, several in the group died. Those who survived resorted to *cannibalism* to stay alive until they could be rescued.

   The word *cannibalism* is a corruption of *Caribales,* the name of a group of people living in Cuba and Haiti whom Christopher Columbus encountered when he landed in the New World. These tribes were fierce, and some were reported to be cannibals. European explorers used either word, *Canibales* and *Caribales,* to refer to the people of the West Indies. Somehow the incorrect name for the people became associated with their reputation for eating people.

WORD PARTS

Emigrants [paragraph 2]   People often wrongly think that *emigrants* and *immigrants* mean the same thing. Although both words come from the same Latin root *migrare* ("to move"), the prefixes make their meanings different. The prefix in *emigrate* comes from *ex-* ("away"), whereas the prefix in *immigrate* comes from *in-* ("in"). Thus, an *emigrant* is one who leaves ("moves from") one country or region, and an *immigrant* is one who enters ("moves into") a new country or region.

You will be able to remember the difference more clearly if you think of the phrases *emigrate from* and *immigrate to*.

WORD FAMILIES

Domains [paragraph 7]   One of the children wrote in her diary that the trip west "was like traveling over the great *domains* of a lost world." This word means "territory" or "realm." It derives from the French *domaine* ("property"), which in turn comes from the Latin word *dominus* ("lord"). This root, along with the related Latin word *domus* ("house"), is the source of a large family of English words, among which are the following:

dome	the hemispherical roof of a church or building, from *domus Dei* ("house of the Lord"), the most important feature of which was the domed roof
domestic	pertaining to the family or household
domesticate	to tame, to train to live with people in a household, said of animals
domicile	one's legal residence or home
dominion	territory or influence or control

ELLIOTT WEST

Wagon Train Children

1   The historian Francis Parkman, strolling around Independence, Mo., in 1846, remarked upon the "multitude of healthy children's faces . . . peeping out from under the covers of the wagons." Two decades later, a traveler wrote of husbands packing up "sunburned women and wild-looking children," along with shovels and flour barrels, in preparation for the journey West. In the gold fields of California in the 1850s, a chronicler met four sisters and sisters-in-law who had just crossed the Great Plains with 36 of their children. "They could," she wrote, "form quite a respectable village."

2   In the great overland migration that lasted from 1841 until the start of the Civil War, more than a quarter of a million people pushed their way from the Missouri valley to the Pacific coast. Probably at least 35,000 of them were young girls and boys; except during the Gold Rush, at least every fifth person on the trails was a child. Yet in all we read today, these thousands of young emigrants are infrequently seen and almost never heard.

3   The voices of many of them do survive, though. Some kept diaries along the way that have been preserved; many others wrote down their memories later. These records permit glimpses of a life that children of today might easily dream about—a child's life of adventure and purpose, of uncertainty and danger, albeit sometimes of sheer boredom. Once they reached their destinations and became settled, these children might well begin long years of isolation and monotony, but getting there was bound to be unpredictable and a challenge.

4   From Independence and St. Joseph and Council Bluffs their families packed into wagons usually no more than 5 feet by 10 feet and set out when the spring

grass was up. For the next six months they would roll and lurch westward for more than 2000 miles—across plains and deserts, along the Platte, Sweetwater, Humboldt, Carson, Malheur, Snake and Columbia rivers, and through the Rockies, Blue Mountains and Sierra Nevada.

5   Children had little idea what to expect. For most of them the trip at first seemed a lark. "Every day was like a picnic," a young girl remembered of her earliest weeks on the trail. A 7-year-old had finished nearly half the trip when a question suddenly dawned on him. "I was looking far away in the direction we were traveling, across a dreary sage plain . . . and I got to wondering where we were trying to get to." "To Oregon," someone answered.

6   One boy had heard the fantastic names upon the land and waited eagerly for the show: "I was looking for the Black Hills. Hills I saw, but they were not black. Blue River had faded out, Chimney Rock was only a sharp pointed rock on the top of a hill, not a chimney at all. The 'Devil's Backbone' was only a narrow ridge."

7   Much of the passing scene measured up easily. Children gawked at giant whirlwinds, boiling springs, chasms hundreds of feet deep, wide rivers and dried desert streams. Some passed for hours at a stretch through land black with bison. There were antelope that bounded from sight before the dust was raised behind them, dogs that sang, squirrels that yipped like dogs. The human inhabitants of the land were just as marvelous. Boys and girls who overcame their first fears traded jackknives and coffee for beadwork and moccasins, and in the bargain they got a taste of the exotic. "They amused us by eating grasshoppers," a girl of 12 told her diary. As another young girl put it, "It was like traveling over the great domains of a lost world."

8   Children whose recollections survive rarely complained about the closeness of life in a wagon—they seem to have welcomed it in a time of uprooting—but food was another matter. While they generally enjoyed antelope, bison and other new dishes of the Plains, there was much to rail at—like campside baking (bread "plentifully seasoned with mouse pills") and foul water ("drank red mud for coffee"). More than anything, they longed for fresh vegetables and fruit. Dried apples were brought along to ward off scurvy, but most youngsters found them a cruel mockery. An 11-year-old recommended them for their economy. "You need but one meal a day," he explained. "You can eat dried apples for breakfast, drink water for dinner and swell for supper."

9   Between the moments of excitement fell inevitable hours of boredom. Parents packed small libraries and organized school lessons to fill these hours; the children made up games. Many of the games would be instantly recognizable to both earlier and later generations—London Bridge, Run-Sheep-Run, Leapfrog, Button-Button. Girls and younger boys made wreaths and necklaces from wildflowers, a favorite pastime before the present century, and chanted handed-down rhymes and rounds.

10   By and large, they seemed to have preferred highly competitive games that stressed strategy. And they invented games of their own. One group of young boys found that when they dived onto a dead ox, its sun-bloated stomach would fling them back. This became a contest, with each competitor jumping harder and bouncing back farther. Finally a lanky boy sprinted, leaped head first—and

plunged deep into the rotting carcass. Only with difficulty did his friends pull him out.

11   The same group of boys were expected to find fuel for the company's evening fires, and this, too, turned into a competition. At the end of the day they organized teams and divided the area around the night's camp into districts. Each group scoured its section and tried to amass the largest pile of buffalo chips, driving away all chip-rustlers and claim-jumpers with barrages of dried dung.

12   Most of the work was not so light. Children herded, cooked, hunted, gathered water, cared for babies and did other important tasks. And circumstances often left a boy or girl with graver responsibilities. When his fatherless family was abandoned by a hired hand, 11-year-old Elisha Brooks drove the animals, stood guard at night and generally took charge.

13   At 14, Octavius Pringle was sent on a lifesaving ride of 125 miles to fetch food for his group. Children of 10 and under sometimes drove ox teams, cared for herds and took part in difficult family decisions, and ones only a little older served on guard duty and chose camping sites. When the challenge of the road left her parents floundering, a daughter barely in her teens virtually took over her family of 12. "They all depend on her," wrote a fellow traveler. "The children go to her in their troubles and perplexities, her father and mother can rely on her, and she is always ready to do what she can."

14   Young girls in particular had chances to fill new roles—and to taste the complications that came with them. Mary Ellen Todd, 11, learned to drive the oxen pulling her family to Oregon. Later she recalled: "How my heart bounded . . . when I chanced to hear father say to mother, 'Do you know that Mary Ellen is beginning to crack the whip?' Then how it fell again, when mother replied, 'I am afraid it isn't a very ladylike thing for a girl to do.' After this, while I felt a secret joy in being able to have power that sets things going, there was also some sense of shame. . . ."

15   Being lost or stolen could suddenly seem a real possibility on the trail. One 7-year-old sent to fetch a horse became disoriented and wandered for hours until he was found that night, miles from his party. Another, age 3, was found whimpering under some sagebrush a day after he walked away from camp.

16   "A dreadful fear of Indians was born and grown into me," remembered a girl who crossed the Plains at age 5 and had nightmares for years. Fed on stories of babies kidnapped by savages, children typically went into panic at their first sight of a Pawnee or Osage. An older boy recalled that the sight of scalps strung around a warrior's waist had "made me homesick"; many younger children, especially, never mastered their dread. Emma Shepherd wrote that every night on the trail was "full of terror" as she imagined that each breeze-blown bush was a skulking native.

17   But Indians were usually far more a help than a hindrance. Along the Sweetwater in 1852, a party of Crows took pity on a fatherless family and traveled with them for more than a week. It was quite a sight: Braves in panther robes rode before their favorite wives, tattooed and draped in mantles of bird skins, while behind them came the older women, dogs and finally an ox team with an exhausted white mother and her tattered brood of six. One of the boys remembered: "We were a wild West show."

18   Inevitably there were those who suffered terribly. An emigrant approaching the Sierra in 1850 would have passed children sitting on wagon ruts sucking on pork rinds and eating rawhide. A widow of the trail recalled that near the end of her trip, her nine famished children "all would go out in the woods and smoke the wood mice out of the logs and roast and eat them."

19   Accidents were most common when a restless boy or girl, clambering around a rolling and pitching wagon, fell beneath its wheels. A woman told of such a tumble by her rambunctious grandson: "It did not quite kill him, but it made the little rascal holler awfully."

20   Although fewer than one in 20 emigrants died on the way West, most youngsters seem to have confronted death in some way. They wrote often of Indian burial platforms, with their decaying corpses and bleaching bones, and they hardly could have missed the hundreds of travelers' graves beside the trail.

21   In 1852 a boy and his mother methodically counted 32 in a stretch of 14 miles. One young girl told of seeing a baby's skeleton picked clean and lying beside the road. Another sat down only to discover the foot of an Indian's corpse poking from the sand next to her, and yet another glimpsed a woman's head, a comb still in its hair, pulled from a shallow grave by scavengers.

22   Sights like these could feed a child's basic fears. Mary Ackley had already lost her mother to cholera when her father disappeared for several hours. She wrote: "I never felt so miserable in my life. I sat on the ground with my face buried in my hands, speechless. . . . What would become of us children?"

23   A gold-seeker wrote in his diary of 1852: "I was one day traveling alone and in advance of our teams when I overtook a little girl who had lingered far behind her company. She was crying, and as I took her into my arms I discovered that her little feet were bleeding by coming into contact with the sharp flint stones upon the road. I says why do you cry? Does your feet hurt you? See how they bleed. No (says she) nothing hurts me now. They buried my father and mother yesterday, and I don't want to live any longer. They took me away from my sweet mother and put her in the ground. . . ."

24   There is no indication that children died any oftener than adults on the road West, but parents probably buried more than 2000 of their young along the way. Only a tiny number were victims of Indians or wild beasts; most fell to diseases, especially cholera, which ravaged the travelers from 1849 to 1852. A far smaller number died from mishaps such as drownings, injuries by wagons and accidental poisonings or gunshots.

25   For a grim reminder of their vulnerability, children—those who could read—had only to look at the grave markers beside the road:

Our only child, Little Mary
Two children Killed by a Stampede, June 23, 1863
Jno. Hoover, died June 18. 49. Aged 12 yrs. Rest in peace, sweet boy, for thy
    travels are over

26   In October 1849, J. Goldsborough Bruff, a chronicler of the trail, rested just past the crest of the Sierra and watched the procession. Among the "rough-looking, hairy, dirty, ragged, jaded" emigrants were exhausted children of 10 carrying babies on their backs, and others leading cadaverous mules weighted

with men and women wracked with scurvy and ague. But he shared his camp-fire with a pair of boys who cheerfully encouraged their weeping, despondent parents, and he met a cocky 6-year-old who bragged of his bravery and en-durance: "I'm a great hand for walking." Along the soft, green sward of the Feather River, boys and girls laughed and played and napped.

27   As Bruff's observations suggest, children responded to the journey in count-less ways. But a thread can be found: Most of these youngest pioneers seem to have come through with resilience and optimism, and many learned early of their own strengths. Nothing illustrates this better than a letter written from Cal-ifornia in 1847 by Virginia Reed, at 13 a survivor of the tragic Donner party, whose terrible hardships in the snow of the Sierra Nevada had led them to can-nibalism. "O Mary, I have not wrote you half of the truble [we have had] but I hav wrote you anuf to let you know what truble is," she told her cousin. She fin-ished not with grief or self-pity but with a piece of offhand advice. "Don't let this letter dishaten anybody," she wrote. "Never take no cutof's* and hury along as fast as you can." ✳

*cutofs—Virginia Reed is referring to the cutoff the leader of the Donner Party took, supposedly a faster way through the Sierra Nevada mountains, which caused them to lose their way and become stranded for the winter.

From Elliott West, "The Youngest Pioneers," *American Heritage*, December 1985. Reprinted by permis-sion of American Heritage, a division of Forbes, Inc.

Exercises

Do not refer to the selection for Exercises A and B unless your instructor directs you to do so.

A. DETERMINING THE MAIN IDEA AND PURPOSE

Choose the best answer.

_____ 1. The main idea of the selection is that
   a. the diaries of the emigrant children showed that their lives were filled with adventure, uncertainty, challenge, danger, and fre-quently boredom.
   b. the experiences of emigrant children have largely been neglected.
   c. for the children who migrated with their families, the trip west was only the beginning of a life of boredom and isolation, which would continue long after they reached their destination.
   d. from 1841 until 1865 more than 250,000 people pushed their way west to the Pacific Ocean in a great overland migration.

_____ 2. With respect to the main idea, the writer's purpose is to
   a. persuade the reader to accept his opinion on a controversial issue.
   b. relate a series of stories.
   c. describe the scenery of the western Plains states.
   d. inform the reader about a part of American history.

B. COMPREHENDING MAIN IDEAS

Choose the correct answer.

_____ 1. Of the 250,000 emigrants who came west, the children probably numbered about
   a. 10,000.
   b. 35,000.
   c. 50,000.
   d. 100,000.

_____ 2. For the children, the greatest difficulty during the trip west was undoubtedly
   a. the lack of companionship of other children.
   b. the absence of a traditional schoolroom.
   c. the uncertainty about what they would find when they reached their destination.
   d. the close quarters they had to share with their families in the wagons.

_____ 3. The children complained most about
   a. the poor quality of the food.
   b. the lack of privacy in the wagons.
   c. the impossibility of making permanent friends.
   d. having to collect dried buffalo dung for fuel.

_____ 4. According to the author, the Indians that the emigrants encountered along the way were
   a. generally savage and hostile.
   b. terrified of the white travelers.
   c. usually more of a help than a hindrance.
   d. suspicious and distant in manner.

_____ 5. The most common danger for children along the route was
   a. being kidnapped by Indians.
   b. dying of starvation.
   c. getting scurvy.
   d. falling under the wagon wheels.

_____ 6. The disease that caused the most deaths among the emigrants from 1849 to 1852 was
   a. tuberculosis.
   b. scarlet fever.
   c. influenza.
   d. cholera.

COMPREHENSION SCORE

Score your answers for Exercises A and B as follows:

A. No. right _____ × 2 = _____

B. No. right _____ × 1 = _____

Total points from A and B _____ × 10 = _____ percent

You may refer to the selection as you work through the remaining exercises.

C. RECOGNIZING SUPPORTING DETAILS

Place an X in the space for each sentence from the selection that *directly* supports this main idea: "Most of the work was not so light. . . . And circumstances often left a boy or girl with graver responsibilities."

1. _____ Boys who were expected to find fuel for the evening fires turned the work into a competition.

2. _____ Children herded, cooked, hunted, gathered water, and cared for babies.

3. _____ One 11-year-old boy took charge of his family after his fatherless family was abandoned by a hired hand.

4. _____ At 14 another boy was sent on a lifesaving ride of 125 miles to fetch food for his group.

5. _____ When Mary Ellen Todd learned to crack a whip at the age of 11, her mother complained that it wasn't a very ladylike thing for a girl to do.

6. _____ In 1852 a party of Crow Indians took pity on a fatherless family and traveled with them for more than a week.

7. _____ Some children suffered terribly from hunger and malnutrition.

8. _____ In one way or another, most youngsters learned to confront death on the way west.

D. MAKING INFERENCES

For each of these statements write Y (yes) if the inference is an accurate one, N (no) if the inference is an inaccurate one, and CT (can't tell) if the writer does not give you enough information to make an inference one way or another.

1. _____ The kind of life that the emigrant children experienced as they moved west would be nearly impossible for American children today to duplicate. [paragraph 3]

2. _____ Diaries kept by children during the journey would probably represent a more accurate account of their experiences than would memoirs written as adults. [paragraph 3]

3. _____ Even if the children were uncertain about what they would find when they reached their destination, their parents knew. [paragraph 5 and essay as a whole]

4. _____ The names of some of the places the emigrants saw, like Devil's Backbone or the Black Hills, were an exaggeration. [paragraph 6]

5. _____ By the time of the great migration west, the great herds of bison had nearly disappeared because of overhunting. [paragraphs 7 and 8]

6. _____ The stories of savages kidnapping babies or killing children were simply not true and had no basis in fact. [paragraphs 16–17]

E. ANALYZING STRUCTURE AND SEEING RELATIONSHIPS

Where appropriate, write your answers for these questions in your own words.

1. This essay has a clear introduction, body, and a conclusion. Write the number of the paragraph(s) for each section of the essay.

   Introduction: _____
   Body   _____
   Conclusion: _____

2. _____ To support the main ideas in the article, the writer relies mainly on
   a. personal opinion.
   b. examples and illustrations taken from firsthand accounts.
   c. historical textbooks.
   d. stories that have been handed down from generation to generation.

3. Read the first sentence of paragraph 8, which suggests a contrast between

   two things. What is the writer contrasting? _____

   _____

4. _____ The writer intends the descriptive details in paragraph 21 to be
   a. gruesome.
   b. amusing.
   c. unbelievable.
   d. shocking.

5. Write the sentence from the article that represents West's overall characterization of these young pioneers. Also indicate the number of the paragraph in

   which it occurs. _____

   _____

6. _____ The writer's attitude toward the emigrant children is
   a. not evident from the essay.
   b. neutral, impartial.
   c. amazed, astonished.
   d. admiring, sympathetic.

F. UNDERSTANDING VOCABULARY

Choose the best definition according to an analysis of word parts or the context.

_____ 1. a child's life of uncertainty and danger, *albeit* sometimes of sheer boredom [paragraph 3—pronounced ŏl-bē´-ĭ t]:

a. although
b. including
c. in addition
d. finally

_____ 2. Children *gawked* at giant whirlwinds [7]:

a. were frightened of
b. marveled at
c. ran away from
d. stared at

_____ 3. *chasms* hundreds of feet deep [7]:

a. valleys
b. craters
c. narrow cracks
d. rivers

_____ 4. they got a taste of the *exotic* [7]: referring to something that is

a. weird, bizarre
b. foreign, unfamiliar
c. usual, ordinary
d. surprising, unexpected

_____ 5. there was much to *rail* at [8]:

a. criticize harshly
b. be grateful for
c. long or wish for
d. remember fondly

_____ 6. to *ward off* scurvy [8]:

a. cure
b. diagnose
c. prevent
d. cause

_____ 7. left her parents *floundering* [13]:

a. acting in confusion
b. wondering about the future
c. feeling ill
d. incapable of acting

_____ **8.** a grim reminder of their *vulnerability* [25]:

    a. imminent death

    b. ability to survive natural disasters

    c. lack of sensitivity

    d. defenselessness against injury or disease

_____ **9.** their weeping, *despondent* parents [26]:

    a. despised

    b. downhearted

    c. desperate

    d. devoted

_____ **10.** come through with *resilience* [27]: the ability to

    a. look at the positive side of life

    b. keep a sense of humor

    c. learn from one's mistakes

    d. recover from misfortune quickly

G. USING VOCABULARY

From the following list of vocabulary words, choose a word that fits in each blank according to both the grammatical structure of the sentence and the context. Use each word in the list only once. Do not change the form of the word. (Note that there are more words than sentences.)

barrage	domain	hindrance	scouring
destination	dread	inevitable	skulking
disoriented	exotic	monotony	strategy

1. It was _____ that life for children on the Oregon Trail would be characterized by _____ , but at the same time the Indians and the new scenery provided them with a taste of the _____ .

2. Some children never overcame their _____ of Indians, whom they imagined might be _____ around every bush or tree; in fact, however, the Indians the travelers encountered were generally more of a help than a _____ .

3. Emigrant children devised games that required some _____ ; even the task of _____ the countryside for buffalo chips was turned into a competition.

H. PARAPHRASING EXERCISE

Here is a sentence from paragraph 2 and a paraphrase of it.

Original Sentence

In the great overland migration that lasted from 1841 until the start of the Civil War, more than a quarter of a million people pushed their way from the Missouri valley to the Pacific Coast.

Paraphrase

More than 250,000 people made the great migration across the Plains from Missouri to the Pacific Coast between 1841 and the beginning of the Civil War.

After you study this paraphrase, write your own paraphrases of these sentences:

These records permit glimpses of a life that children of today might easily dream about—a child's life of adventure and purpose, of uncertainty and danger, albeit sometimes of sheer boredom. [paragraph 3]

Children whose recollections survive rarely complained about the closeness of life in a wagon—they seemed to have welcomed it in a time of uprooting—but food was another matter. [paragraph 8]

For a grim reminder of their vulnerability, children—those who could read—had only to look at the grave markers beside the road. [paragraph 25]

I.   TOPICS FOR WRITING OR DISCUSSION

1. Using both traditional print sources and the Internet, investigate what life was like for the emigrants after they arrived in the Gold Rush towns of California or Oregon and write a short paper summarizing your findings.

2. On balance, what is the central impression West conveys about emigrant children? If you grew up watching, say, *Little House on the Prairie,* which glorified life on the American frontier, how does West's selection change your perception of nineteenth-century frontier life in America?

For Further Exploration

BOOKS

- Francis Parkman's classic book *The Oregon Trail* remains the definitive work about his expedition to study the American Indians in the Great Plains and mountain states. The first edition was published in 1849. Parkman, a young 22-year-old graduate of Harvard College, along with his cousin, Quincy Adams Shaw, embarked on their transcontinental journey from New York to Oregon in 1846. Parkman's account of American Indians, their culture and customs, remains the most popular and widely read portrayal of that era.
- *Ordeal by Hunger: The Story of the Donner Party* (1992) by George Rippey Stewart relates the tragic story of the Donner Party (see footnote on page 266), which was stranded in the Sierra Nevada during one of the worst winters on record. To stay alive, the survivors resorted to cannibalism. Despite the grisly subject, Stewart recounts the story with compassion and objectivity.

MOVIES

- *The Emigrants* (1971), directed by Swedish director Jan Troell and starring Max von Sydow and Liv Ullmann, depicts the lives of Swedish immigrants who settled in Minnesota during the latter part of the nineteenth century.
- *The New Land* (1972) is a sequel to *The Emigrants.* It follows the same characters after their arrival in the New World.

WEB SITES

The following sites offer a wealth of information about the Oregon Trail:

- "All About the Oregon Trail"—*www.isu.edu/~trinmich/Allabout.html*
- "In Search of the Oregon Trail"—*www.pbs.org/opb/oregontrail/*
- "Oregon Trail: The Trail West"—*www.ku.edu/kansas/seneca/oregon/mainpage.html*

18 NELSON MANDELA
Long Walk to Freedom

Nelson Mandela, former president of South Africa, was imprisoned for twenty-six years for his outspoken stand on apartheid—the policy of "separateness" established early in the 20th century by South Africa's white-minority government. After his release in 1990, he continued to speak out against apartheid from his position as leader of the African National Congress (ANC). In 1994 South Africa held its first all-races election, and Mandela was elected president, ending white-minority rule in that long-troubled country. Long Walk to Freedom (1994) is Nelson Mandela's autobiography. In this selection, he explains the Xhosa tradition of circumcision, the ceremony whereby Xhosa boys become men.

Vocabulary Preview

WORD HISTORIES

Stoicism [paragraph 6]   Mandela writes, "Circumcision is a trial of bravery and *stoicism*; no anesthetic is used; a man must suffer in silence." The Stoics, from the word *stoicism*, were members of a Greek school of philosophy that flourished in the third century B.C.E. Zeno, who developed the Stoic philosophy, taught that "people should be free from passion, unmoved by joy or grief, and submit without complaint to unavoidable necessity." *Stoicism*, then, is the philosophy of enduring life's painful experiences without feeling.

Meander [paragraph 19]   After the circumcision ceremony, Mandela writes, "I walked back to the river and watched it *meander* on its way to where, many miles distant, it emptied into the Indian Ocean." The verb *meander* (pronounced mē-ăn´-dər) means to "wander aimlessly without direction." This word, of Greek origin, comes from the name of a river in Greece called *Maender*. Since Greece is a mountainous country, most rivers there flow down rapidly to the sea, but the river Maender was known for its unusual number of twists and turns. Thus, the English word *meander* describes anything that wanders from a straight course.

WORD PARTS

Bene- [paragraph 17]   A *benefactor* is a person who gives help or aid to another. The Latin prefix *bene-* means "well," and it begins many so-called loan words from Latin, among them *benefit, beneficial, benevolence* ("wishing well"), *benediction* ("good saying"), and *benign*.

What is a *beneficiary* of a life insurance policy? _____

_____

**WORD
FAMILIES**

Initiates [paragraph 12]   After the circumcision ceremony, Mandela writes that they became *abakhwetha*, "*initiates* into the world of manhood." As a verb, *initiate* comes from the Latin word *initiare*, meaning "to begin." As a noun, *initiate* refers to a new member who has been introduced into a group, either by means of a ceremony or of a test. Two other relatives in this word family are *initiation* (the ceremony, ritual, or test by which a person is admitted to a group) and *initial* (the first letter of a name or something that occurs at the beginning, like an *initial* step).

What does the word *initiative* mean?_____

NELSON MANDELA

Long Walk to Freedom

1   When I was sixteen, the regent[1] decided that it was time that I became a man. In Xhosa tradition, this is achieved through one means only: circumcision. In my tradition, an uncircumcised male cannot be heir to his father's wealth, cannot marry or officiate in tribal rituals. An uncircumcised Xhosa man is a contradiction in terms, for he is not considered a man at all, but a boy. For the Xhosa people, circumcision represents the formal incorporation of males into society. It is not just a surgical procedure, but a lengthy and elaborate ritual in preparation for manhood. As a Xhosa, I count my years as a man from the date of my circumcision.

2   The traditional ceremony of the circumcision school was arranged principally for Justice—the rest of us, twenty-six in all—were there mainly to keep him company. Early in the new year, we journeyed to two grass huts in a secluded valley on the banks of the Mbashe River, known as Tyhalarha, the traditional place of circumcision for Thembu kings. The huts were seclusion lodges, where we were to live isolated from society. It was a sacred time; I felt happy and fulfilled taking part in my people's customs and ready to make the transition from boyhood to manhood.

3   We had moved to Tyhalarha by the river a few days before the actual circumcision ceremony. These last few days of boyhood were spent with the other initiates, and I found the camaraderie enjoyable. The lodge was near the home of Banabakhe Blayi, the wealthiest and most popular boy at the circumcision school. He was an engaging fellow, a champion stickfighter and a glamour boy, whose many girlfriends kept us all supplied with delicacies. Although he could neither read nor write, he was one of the most intelligent among us. He regaled us with stories of his trips to Johannesburg, a place none of us had ever been before. He so thrilled us with tales of the mines that he almost persuaded me that to be a miner was more alluring than to be a monarch. Miners had a mystique; to be a miner meant to be strong and daring, the ideal of manhood. Much later, I realized that it was the exaggerated tales of boys like Banabakhe that caused so

[1]A ruler or governor. (Ed.)

many young men to run away to work in the mines of Johannesburg, where
they often lost their health and their lives. In those days, working in the mines
was almost as much of a rite of passage as circumcision school, a myth that
helped the mine-owners more than it helped my people.

4   A custom of circumcision school is that one must perform a daring exploit before the ceremony. In days of old, this might have involved a cattle raid or even a
battle, but in our time the deeds were more mischievous than martial. Two nights
before we moved to Tyhalarha, we decided to steal a pig. In Mqhekezweni there
was a tribesman with an ornery old pig. To avoid making noise and alarming
him, we arranged for the pig to do our work for us. We took handfuls of sediment from homemade African beer, which has a strong scent much favored by
pigs, and placed it upwind of the pig. The pig was so aroused by the scent that
he came out of the kraal,[2] following a trail we had laid, gradually made his way

---

[2]A South African word denoting either a rural village or an enclosure for livestock. Mandela probably
uses the word in the second sense. (Ed.)

to us, wheezing and snorting and eating the sediment. When he got near us, we captured the poor pig, slaughtered it, and then built a fire and ate roast pork underneath the stars. No piece of pork has ever tasted as good before or since.

5   The night before the circumcision, there was a ceremony near our huts with singing and dancing. Women came from the nearby villages, and we danced to their singing and clapping. As the music became faster and louder, our dance turned more frenzied and we forgot for a moment what lay ahead.

6   At dawn, when the stars were still in the sky, we began our preparations. We were escorted to the river to bathe in its cold waters, a ritual that signified our purification before the ceremony. The ceremony was at midday, and we were commanded to stand in a row in a clearing some distance from the river where a crowd of parents and relatives, including the regent, as well as a handful of chiefs and counselors, had gathered. We were clad only in our blankets, and as the ceremony began, with drums pounding, we were ordered to sit on a blanket on the ground with our legs spread out in front of us. I was tense and anxious, uncertain of how I would react when the critical moment came. Flinching or crying out was a sign of weakness and stigmatized one's manhood. I was determined not to disgrace myself, the group, or my guardian. Circumcision is a trial of bravery and stoicism; no anesthetic is used; a man must suffer in silence.

7   To the right, out of the corner of my eye, I could see a thin, elderly man emerge from a tent and kneel in front of the first boy. There was excitement in the crowd, and I shuddered slightly knowing that the ritual was about to begin. The old man was a famous *ingcibi*, a circumcision expert, from Gcalekaland, who would use his assegai[3] to change us from boys to men with a single blow.

8   Suddenly, I heard the first boy cry out, *"Ndiyindoda!"* (I am a man!), which we were trained to say in the moment of circumcision. Seconds later, I heard Justice's strangled voice pronounce the same phrase. There were now two boys before the *ingcibi* reached me, and my mind must have gone blank because before I knew it, the old man was kneeling in front of me. I looked directly into his eyes. He was pale, and though the day was cold, his face was shining with perspiration. His hands moved so fast they seemed to be controlled by an otherworldly force. Without a word, he took my foreskin, pulled it forward, and then, in a single motion, brought down his assegai. I felt as if fire was shooting through my veins; the pain was so intense that I buried my chin into my chest. Many seconds seemed to pass before I remembered the cry, and then I recovered and called out, *"Ndiyindoda!"*

9   I looked down and saw a perfect cut, clean and round like a ring. But I felt ashamed because the other boys seemed much stronger and braver than I had been; they had called out more promptly than I had. I was distressed that I had been disabled, however briefly, by the pain, and I did my best to hide my agony. A boy may cry; a man conceals his pain.

10   I had now taken the essential step in the life of every Xhosa man. Now, I might marry, set up my own home, and plow my own field. I could now be admitted to the councils of the community; my words would be taken seriously. At the ceremony, I was given my circumcision name, Dalibunga, meaning "Founder

[3]A spear or lance used by South African tribesmen. (Ed.)

of the Bungha," the traditional ruling body of the Transkei.[4] To Xhosa tradition-alists, this name is more acceptable than either of my two previous given names, Rolihlahla or Nelson, and I was proud to hear my new name pronounced: Dali-bunga.

11   Immediately after the blow had been delivered, an assistant who follows the circumcision master takes the foreskin that is on the ground and ties it to a corner of your blanket. Our wounds were then dressed with a healing plant, the leaves of which were thorny on the outside but smooth on the inside, which absorbed the blood and other secretions.

12   At the conclusion of the ceremony, we returned to our huts, where a fire was burning with wet wood that cast off clouds of smoke, which was thought to promote healing. We were ordered to lie on our backs in the smoky huts, with one leg flat, and one leg bent. We were now *abakhwetha,* initiates into the world of manhood. We were looked after by an *amakhankatha,* or guardian, who explained the rules we must follow if we were to enter manhood properly. The first chore of the *amakhankatha* was to paint our naked and shaved bodies from head to foot in white ocher, turning us into ghosts. The white chalk symbolized our purity, and I still recall how stiff the dried clay felt on my body.

13   That first night, at midnight, an attendant, or *ikhankatha,* crept around the hut, gently waking each of us. We were then instructed to leave the hut and go tramping through the night to bury our foreskins. The traditional reason for this practice was so that our foreskins would be hidden before wizards could use them for evil purposes, but, symbolically, we were also burying our youth. I did not want to leave the warm hut and wander through the bush in the darkness, but I walked into the trees and after a few minutes, untied my foreskin and buried it in the earth. I felt as though I had now discarded the last remnant of my childhood.

14   We lived in our two huts—thirteen in each—while our wounds healed. When outside the huts, we were covered in blankets, for we were not allowed to be seen by women. It was a period of quietude, a kind of spiritual preparation for the trials of manhood that lay ahead. On the day of our reemergence, we went down to the river early in the morning to wash away the white ocher in the waters of the Mbashe. Once we were clean and dry, we were coated in red ocher. The tradition was that one should sleep with a woman, who later may become one's wife, and she rubs off the pigment with her body. In my case, however, the ocher was removed with a mixture of fat and lard.

15   At the end of our seclusion, the lodges and all their contents were burned, destroying our last links to childhood, and a great ceremony was held to welcome us as men to society. Our families, friends, and local chiefs gathered for speeches, songs, and gift-giving. I was given two heifers and four sheep, and felt far richer than I ever had before. I who had never owned anything suddenly possessed property. It was a heady feeling, even though my gifts were paltry next to those of Justice, who inherited an entire herd. I was not jealous of

---

[4]Now a semi-independent area in southeast South Africa on the Indian Ocean, at the time Mandela was writing, it was a Black African Homeland. It received nominal independence in 1976. (Ed.)

Justice's gifts. He was the son of a king; I was merely destined to be a counselor to a king. I felt strong and proud that day. I remember walking differently on that day, straighter, taller, firmer. I was hopeful, and thinking that I might some-day have wealth, property, and status.

16   The main speaker of the day was Chief Meligqili, the son of Dalindyebo, and after listening to him, my gaily colored dreams suddenly darkened. He began conventionally, remarking on how fine it was that we were continuing a tradi-tion that had been going on for as long as anyone could remember. Then he turned to us and his tone suddenly changed. "There sit our sons," he said, "young, healthy, and handsome, the flower of the Xhosa tribe, the pride of our nation. We have just circumcised them in a ritual that promises them manhood, but I am here to tell you that it is an empty, illusory promise, a promise that can never be fulfilled. For we Xhosas, and all black South Africans, are a conquered people. We are slaves in our own country. We are tenants on our own soil. We have no strength, no power, no control over our own destiny in the land of our birth. They will go to cities where they will live in shacks and drink cheap alco-hol all because we have no land to give them where they could prosper and multiply. They will cough their lungs out deep in the bowels of the white man's mines, destroying their health, never seeing the sun, so that the white man can live a life of unequaled prosperity. Among these young men are chiefs who will never rule because we have no power to govern ourselves; soldiers who will never fight for we have no weapons to fight with; scholars who will never teach because we have no place for them to study. The abilities, the intelligence, the promise of these young men will be squandered in their attempt to eke out a liv-ing doing the simplest, most mindless chores for the white man. These gifts to-day are naught, for we cannot give them the greatest gift of all, which is freedom and independence. I well know that Qamata is all-seeing and never sleeps, but I have a suspicion that Qamata may in fact be dozing. If this is the case, the sooner I die the better because then I can meet him and shake him awake and tell him that the children of Ngubengcuka, the flower of the Xhosa nation, are dying."

17   The audience had become more and more quiet as Chief Meligqili spoke and, I think, more and more angry. No one wanted to hear the words that he spoke that day. I know that I myself did not want to hear them. I was cross rather than aroused by the chief's remarks, dismissing his words as the abusive comments of an ignorant man who was unable to appreciate the value of the education and benefits that the white man had brought to our country. At the time, I looked on the white man not as an oppressor but as a benefactor, and I thought the chief was enormously ungrateful. This upstart chief was ruining my day, spoiling the proud feeling with wrongheaded remarks.

18   But without exactly understanding why, his words soon began to work in me. He had planted a seed, and though I let that seed lie dormant for a long season, it eventually began to grow. Later, I realized that the ignorant man that day was not the chief but myself.

19   After the ceremony, I walked back to the river and watched it meander on its way to where, many miles distant, it emptied into the Indian Ocean. I had never crossed that river, and I knew little or nothing of the world beyond it, a world

that beckoned me that day. It was almost sunset and I hurried on to where our seclusion lodges had been. Though it was forbidden to look back while the lodges were burning, I could not resist. When I reached the area, all that remained were two pyramids of ashes by a large mimosa tree. In these ash heaps lay a lost and delightful world, the world of my childhood, the world of sweet and irresponsible days at Qunu and Mqhekezweni. Now I was a man, and I would never again play *thinti*, or steal maize, or drink milk from a cow's udder. I was already in mourning for my own youth. Looking back, I know that I was not a man that day and would not truly become one for many years. ✳

From Nelson Mandela, *Long Walk to Freedom*. © 1994, 1995 by Nelson Rolihlahla Mandela. By permission of Little, Brown and Company.

Exercises

Do not refer to the selection for Exercises A and B unless your instructor directs you to do so.

A. DETERMINING THE MAIN IDEA AND PURPOSE

Choose the best answer.

_____ **1.** The main idea of the selection is that
  a. all cultures conduct rituals to initiate boys into manhood.
  b. the circumcision ceremony is performed on teenaged Xhosa boys, the only way to become a man in that culture.
  c. uncircumcised Xhosa males are not eligible to become leaders.
  d. a boy must perform a daring exploit before the circumcision ritual.

_____ **2.** With respect to the main idea, the writer's purpose is to
  a. describe the circumcision procedure in medical terms.
  b. describe his emotional state before, during, and after the ceremony.
  c. honor the role this initiation ceremony plays in his culture.
  d. explain the tradition associated with the circumcision ceremony and his experience undergoing it.

B. COMPREHENDING MAIN IDEAS

Choose the correct answer.

_____ **1.** In the Xhosa tradition, an uncircumcised male
  a. is allowed to remain intact only in certain extreme cases, for reasons of health.
  b. has no rights to inherit, to marry, or to take part in tribal rituals.
  c. is an object of ridicule and jokes among the tribespeople.
  d. is allowed to remain intact if his family rejects the tradition.

_____ 2. The daring exploit that Mandela and his comrades performed before the ceremony was

    a. climbing the tallest tree in the vicinity.
    b. killing a leopard.
    c. stealing a pig.
    d. drinking homemade beer.

_____ 3. Bathing in the cold river waters before the ceremony was intended to

    a. test their endurance.
    b. purify them.
    c. baptize them.
    d. symbolically wash away their boyhood.

_____ 4. Flinching or crying out during the circumcision ceremony was considered disgraceful behavior because it

    a. ruined the ceremony for the other participants.
    b. showed disrespect for the elders and the circumcision expert.
    c. made the participants' relatives anxious and tense.
    d. stigmatized one's manhood.

_____ 5. To symbolize the destruction of the young men's last links to childhood, the final step in the ritual was to

    a. burn the seclusion lodges and everything in them.
    b. bathe again in the river.
    c. paint their bodies with white chalk.
    d. chant traditional tribal songs.

_____ 6. Chief Meligqili, the main speaker of the day, warned the initiates that the promise of manhood was an illusory one that could never be fulfilled because black South Africans were

    a. not well enough educated to get good jobs.
    b. a conquered people with no control over their own destiny.
    c. too content to work for low wages and not fight for a higher standard of living.
    d. too timid to fight their oppressors.

COMPREHENSION SCORE

Score your answers for Exercises A and B as follows:

A. No. right _____ × 2 = _____

B. No. right _____ × 1 = _____

Total points from A and B _____ × 10 = _____ percent

You may refer to the selection as you work through the remaining exercises.

C. IDENTIFYING SUPPORTING DETAILS

For each main idea stated here, find and write down two supporting details.

1. In Xhosa culture, the circumcision ceremony marks a significant step in a young boy's life. [paragraph 1]

   a. _____

   b. _____

   _____

   _____

2. Initially, Mandela was irritated by Chief Meligqili's remarks after the ceremony. [paragraph 17]

   a. _____

   _____

   b. _____

D. MAKING INFERENCES

For each of these statements write Y (yes) if the inference is an accurate one, N (no) if the inference is an inaccurate one, or CT (can't tell) if the writer does not give you enough information to make an inference one way or another.

1. _____ Not all males in Xhosa culture become circumcised. [paragraph 1]

2. _____ The circumcision ceremony that Mandela describes has more symbolic than actual practical value in terms of a man's worth to the community. [paragraph 1]

3. _____ The circumcision ceremony was arranged principally for Justice because he was the son of a king. [paragraphs 2 and 15]

4. _____ The young black South Africans who ran away to work in the mines were well informed about the working conditions before they began their jobs. [paragraph 3]

5. _____ Some of the boys who were circumcised with Mandela went on to become great chiefs and advisers to kings. [essay as a whole]

6. _____ Although only 16 at the time he was initiated, Mandela was well educated and well informed about South Africa's political situation, and he understood clearly the white role in black oppression. [paragraph 18]

E. INTERPRETING MEANING AND ANALYZING STRUCTURE

Where appropriate, write your answers to these questions in your own words.

1. _____   Which of the following sentences from the selection *best* states the thesis?

   a. "When I was sixteen, the regent decided that it was time that I became a man."
   b. "For the Xhosa people, circumcision represents the formal incorporation of males into society."
   c. "As a Xhosa, I count my years as a man from the date of my circumcision."
   d. "At the end of our seclusion, the lodges and all their contents were burned, destroying our last links to childhood, and a great ceremony was held to welcome us as men to society."

2. Explain the fundamental irony that underlies paragraphs 3 and 16, concerning black South Africans working in the mines. _____

   _____

3. Write the sentence that represents the main idea of paragraph 9. _____

   _____

4. _____   Look again at paragraph 12. A good title for this paragraph is

   a. "Concluding the Ceremony."
   b. "Becoming *Abakhwetha.*"
   c. "Symbols of Purity."
   d. "How We Were Initiated."

5. Paragraph 18 contains a metaphor, an imaginative comparison. Locate it and explain its meaning. _____

   _____

6. In your own words, explain the main idea of paragraph 19. _____

   _____

   _____

7. How would you describe Mandela as his character emerges from this autobiographical account? _____

   _____

F. UNDERSTANDING VOCABULARY

Choose the best definition according to an analysis of word parts or the context.

_____ **1.** the *camaraderie* was enjoyable [paragraph 3]:
- **a.** isolation from adults
- **b.** good fellowship among friends
- **c.** conversation, lighthearted talk
- **d.** anticipation of the future

_____ **2.** more mischievous than *martial* [4]:
- **a.** ridiculous, absurd
- **b.** far-fetched, incredible
- **c.** harmless, mild
- **d.** military, warlike

_____ **3.** *clad* only in blankets [6]:
- **a.** wrapped tightly
- **b.** clothed
- **c.** hidden
- **d.** identified

_____ **4.** *Flinching* or crying out [6]:
- **a.** screaming in terror
- **b.** becoming visibly nervous
- **c.** letting tears flow
- **d.** shrinking back in fear

_____ **5.** a trial of bravery and *stoicism* [6]:
- **a.** indifference to pain
- **b.** physical strength and endurance
- **c.** manliness
- **d.** heroism

_____ **6.** the last *remnant* [13]:
- **a.** scrap, small piece
- **b.** vestige, remainder
- **c.** example, illustration
- **d.** memory, reminiscence

_____ **7.** a *heady* feeling [15]:
- **a.** relieved
- **b.** anxious
- **c.** desirable
- **d.** exhilarating

_____ **8.** my gifts were *paltry* [15]:
- **a.** meager
- **b.** unwanted
- **c.** cherished
- **d.** generous

_____ 9. These gifts today are *naught* [16]:

     a. treasured
     b. undeserved
     c. nothing, of no value
     d. taken for granted

_____ **10.** I let that seed lie *dormant* [18]:

     a. inactive, but capable of coming alive
     b. undisturbed by any negative thoughts
     c. inflexible, unmoving
     d. unquestioned, unchallenged

G. USING VOCABULARY

In parentheses before each sentence are some inflected forms of words from the selection. Study the context and the sentence. Then write the correct form in the space provided.

1. (*allure, alluring*) The stories that Banabakhe told about working in the mines

by one of the initiates held great _____ for the other boys.

2. (*purify, purified, purification, pure*) Mandela and the other boys were

_____ by bathing in the cold waters of the river.

3. (*stoic, stoicism, stoically*) Above all, the boys had to withstand the pain of the

circumcision ceremony, _____ refusing to flinch or cry.

4. (*illusion, illusory, illusionary*) The main speaker warned the initiates that the

promise of manhood was at best an _____ that would never be
fulfilled.

5. (*prosperity, prosper, prospered, prosperous*) White South Africans were

_____ because black South Africans worked hard to maintain their
levels of wealth.

6. (*abuse, abused, abusiveness, abusive, abusively*) At the time, Mandela believed

that the chief spoke wrongly about the way whites supposedly _____
black workers.

H. LOCATING EVIDENCE

Go through the selection and locate any piece of information that supports this idea.

    The circumcision ceremony is an important ritual in Xhosa society.

To identify it, put a star in the margin next to the sentence or bracket the words.

I. TOPICS FOR WRITING OR DISCUSSION

1. How are young American boys initiated into rites of manhood? Write a short paper in which you contrast the Xhosa circumcision ceremony Mandela describes with American traditions.
2. What are the advantages of a formalized ritual such as the Xhosa have devised to initiate young boys to take part in the larger community?
3. If you have read Selection 7 by Andre Dubus, "Digging," on pages 112–118, write a short paper in which you contrast the cultures of North America and the Xhosa in South Africa, specifically in the ways boys are initiated into manhood.

For Further Exploration

BOOKS

- Alan Paton, *Cry, the Beloved Country* (1948). The most important novel to come out of South Africa, Paton's novel alerted the outside world to the system of apartheid.
- J. M. Coetzee, a South African writer, has published two memoirs about growing up in Capetown: *Boyhood: Scenes from Provincial Life* (1998) and *Youth: Scenes from Provincial Life II* (2002).
- Paul Theroux's most recent travel book, *Dark Star Safari* (2003), has two chapters on South Africa today. The Xhosa tradition of circumcising young men is still practiced.

MOVIE

Mandela (1996) is a documentary chronicling Nelson Mandela's life from his childhood, to his work with the African National Conference (ANC), his imprisonment, and finally his election as South Africa's first black president.

WEB SITES

Photos of South Africa are available at this site:

- *www.africaguide.com/country/safrica/photolib.htm*

Here are two sites devoted to Xhosa culture:

- *www.questconnect.org/africa_xhosa.htm*
- *www.speirstours.co.za/xhosa_culture.htm*

A good introduction to the life and times of Nelson Mandela is available at the Mandela Page:

- *www.anc.org.za/people/mandela/*

Finally, a way to keep up with current African affairs:

- *www.usafricaonline.com*

19 ANWAR F. ACCAWI
The Telephone

Anwar Accawi was born in 1943 and grew up in the small village of Magdaluna in southern Lebanon. There, because the town was isolated from the outside world, natural disasters served as a kind of calendar, whereby momentous events were remembered and passed down to younger generations. When a village resident proposed that the town get a telephone, the modern world intruded on the centuries-old traditions, and the lives of the residents of Magdaluna were never the same. This selection originally appeared in Accawi's memoir The Boy from the Tower of the Moon *(1999) and was also included in* Best American Essays *(2001). Accawi now teaches at the University of Tennessee's English Language Institute.*

Vocabulary Preview

WORD HISTORIES

Itinerant [paragraph 20]   Small villages like the one Accawi lived in often depend on tradespeople and traveling salesmen for news of the outside world. Such people are called *itinerant,* like the Catholic priest who visited Magdaluna. Similar to the word *itinerary,* meaning "a plan or proposed route for a trip," the related word *itinerant* describes a person who travels from place to place to perform a job. Both words come from the Latin noun *itiner,* meaning "journey."

Lucrative [paragraph 23]   The telephone brought many changes to Accawi's village, among them a loss of *"lucrative* business" he had enjoyed running errands for adults. Meaning "producing wealth or profit," *lucrative* follows the path that so many English words do: from Middle English *lucratif,* from Old French, and originally from Latin *lucrari* ("to profit" or "to gain") and from *lucrum* ("gain").

WORD PARTS

Telephone [title]   The common Greek prefix *tele-* means "at a distance," so that *telephone* literally combines *tele-* ("distance") and *phonos* ("sound"). *Tele-* precedes many new, usually technical words, in English. Here are a few besides the obvious *television* and *telescope:*

telegram	communication transmitted by wire; from *tele-* + *graphos* ("writing")
telepathy	communication through means other than the senses; from *tele-* + *pathy* ("feeling")
teleconference	a conference held among people in different locations

WORDS FROM FOREIGN LANGUAGES

Accawi also uses some unusual words from other languages. Among them are these:

myopic [paragraph 3]   nearsighted; from Greek *muopia*, originally from *muein* ("to close") + *ops* ("eye")

gendarme [13]   a police officer; from French *gens d'armes* ("mounted soldiers")

concierge [18]   a staff member at a hotel who assists guests; from French, but originally from the Latin word for "fellow slave" (*conservus*)

oasis [21]   a fertile green spot in the middle of a desert; also a place of refuge from unpleasantness; from Coptic, an Egyptian language (*ouahe*)

ANWAR F. ACCAWI

The Telephone

1   When I was growing up in Magdaluna, a small Lebanese village in the terraced, rocky mountains east of Sidon, time didn't mean much to anybody, except maybe to those who were dying, or those waiting to appear in court because they had tampered with the boundary markers on their land. In those days, there was no real need for a calendar or a watch to keep track of the hours, days, months, and years. We knew what to do and when to do it, just as the Iraqi geese knew when to fly north, driven by the hot wind that blew in from the desert, and the ewes knew when to give birth to wet lambs that stood on long, shaky legs in the chilly March wind and baaed hesitantly, because they were small and cold and did not know where they were or what to do now that they were here. The only timepiece we had need of then was the sun. It rose and set, and the seasons rolled by, and we sowed seed and harvested and ate and played and married our cousins and had babies who got whooping cough and chicken-pox—and those children who survived grew up and married *their* cousins and had babies who got whooping cough and chickenpox. We lived and loved and toiled and died without ever needing to know what year it was, or even the time of day.

2   It wasn't that we had no system for keeping track of time and of the important events in our lives. But ours was a natural—or, rather, a divine—calendar, because it was framed by acts of God. Allah himself set down the milestones with earthquakes and droughts and floods and locusts and pestilences. Simple as our calendar was, it worked just fine for us.

3   Take, for example, the birth date of Teta Im Khalil, the oldest woman in Magdaluna and all the surrounding villages. When I first met her, we had just returned home from Syria at the end of the Big War and were living with Grandma Mariam. Im Khalil came by to welcome my father home and to take a long, myopic look at his foreign-born wife, my mother. Im Khalil was so old that the skin of her cheeks looked like my father's grimy tobacco pouch, and when I kissed her (because Grandma insisted that I show her old friend affection), it was like kissing a soft suede glove that had been soaked with sweat and then

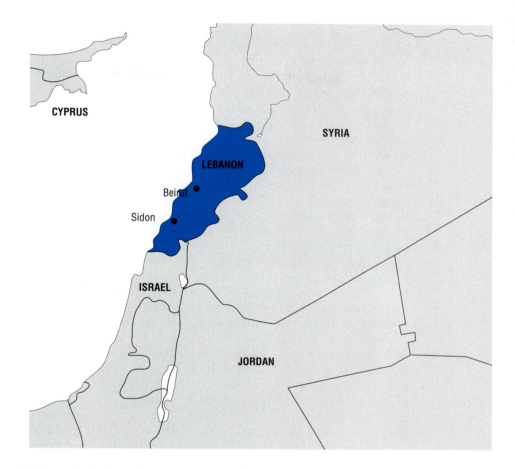

left in a dark closet for a season. Im Khalil's face got me to wondering how old one had to be to look and taste the way she did. So, as soon as she had hobbled off on her cane, I asked Grandma, "How old is Teta Im Khalil?"

4   Grandma had to think for a moment; then she said, "I've been told that Teta was born shortly after the big snow that caused the roof on the mayor's house to cave in."

5   "And when was that?" I asked.

6   "Oh, about the time we had the big earthquake that cracked the wall in the east room."

7   Well, that was enough for me. You couldn't be more accurate than that, now, could you? Satisfied with her answer, I went back to playing with a ball made from an old sock stuffed with other, much older socks.

8   And that's the way it was in our little village for as far back as anybody could remember: people were born so many years before or after an earthquake or a flood; they got married or died so many years before or after a long drought or a big snow or some other disaster. One of the most unusual of these dates was when Antoinette the seamstress and Saeed the barber (and tooth puller) got married. That was the year of the whirlwind during which fish and oranges fell

from the sky. Incredible as it may sound, the story of the fish and oranges was true, because men—respectable men, like Abu George the blacksmith and Abu Asaad the mule skinner, men who would not lie even to save their own souls—told and retold that story until it was incorporated into Magdaluna's calendar, just like the year of the black moon and the year of the locusts before it. My father, too, confirmed the story for me. He told me that he had been a small boy himself when it had rained fish and oranges from heaven. He'd gotten up one morning after a stormy night and walked out into the yard to find fish as long as his forearm still flopping here and there among the wet navel oranges.

9   The year of the fish-bearing twister, however, was not the last remarkable year. Many others followed in which strange and wonderful things happened: milestones added by the hand of Allah to Magdaluna's calendar. There was, for instance, the year of the drought, when the heavens were shut for months and the spring from which the entire village got its drinking water slowed to a trickle. The spring was about a mile from the village, in a ravine that opened at one end into a small, flat clearing covered with fine gray dust and hard, marble-sized goat droppings, because every afternoon the goatherds brought their flocks there to water them. In the year of the drought, that little clearing was always packed full of noisy kids with big brown eyes and sticky hands, and their mothers—sinewy, overworked young women with protruding collarbones and cracked, callused brown heels. The children ran around playing tag or hide-and-seek while the women talked, shooed flies, and awaited their turns to fill up their jars with drinking water to bring home to their napping men and wet babies. There were days when we had to wait from sunup until late afternoon just to fill a small clay jar with precious, cool water.

10   Sometimes, amid the long wait and the heat and the flies and the smell of goat dung, tempers flared, and the younger women, anxious about their babies, argued over whose turn it was to fill up her jar. And sometimes the arguments escalated into full-blown, knockdown-dragout fights; the women would grab each other by the hair and curse and scream and spit and call each other names that made my ears tingle. We little brown boys who went with our mothers to fetch water loved these fights, because we got to see the women's legs and their colored panties as they grappled and rolled around in the dust. Once in a while, we got lucky and saw much more, because some of the women wore nothing at all under their long dresses. God, how I used to look forward to those fights. I remember the rush, the excitement, the sun dancing on the dust clouds as a dress ripped and a young white breast was revealed, then quickly hidden. In my calendar, that year of drought will always be one of the best years of my childhood, because it was then, in a dusty clearing by a trickling mountain spring, I got my first glimpse of the wonders, the mysteries, and the promises hidden beneath the folds of a woman's dress. Fish and oranges from heaven . . . you can get over that.

11   But, in another way, the year of the drought was also one of the worst of my life, because that was the year that Abu Raja, the retired cook who used to entertain us kids by cracking walnuts on his forehead, decided it was time Magdaluna got its own telephone. Every civilized village needed a telephone, he said, and Magdaluna was not going to get anywhere until it had one. A telephone would link us with the outside world. At the time, I was too young to un-

derstand the debate, but a few men—like Shukri, the retired Turkish-army drill sergeant, and Abu Hanna the vineyard keeper—did all they could to talk Abu Raja out of having a telephone brought to the village. But they were outshouted and ignored and finally shunned by the other villagers for resisting progress and trying to keep a good thing from coming to Magdaluna.

12   One warm day in early fall, many of the villagers were out in their fields repairing walls or gathering wood for the winter when the shout went out that the telephone-company truck had arrived at Abu Raja's *dikkan,* or country store. There were no roads in those days, only footpaths and dry streambeds, so it took the telephone-company truck almost a day to work its way up the rocky terrain from Sidon—about the same time it took to walk. When the truck came into view, Abu George, who had a huge voice and, before the telephone, was Magdaluna's only long-distance communication system, bellowed the news from his front porch. Everybody dropped what they were doing and ran to Abu Raja's house to see what was happening. Some of the more dignified villagers, however, like Abu Habeeb and Abu Nazim, who had been to big cities like Beirut and Damascus and had seen things like telephones and telegraphs, did not run the way the rest did; they walked with their canes hanging from the crooks of their arms, as if on a Sunday afternoon stroll.

13   It did not take long for the whole village to assemble at Abu Raja's *dikkan.* Some of the rich villagers, like the widow Farha and the gendarme Abu Nadeem, walked right into the store and stood at the elbows of the two important-looking men from the telephone company, who proceeded with utmost gravity, like priests at Communion, to wire up the telephone. The poorer villagers stood outside and listened carefully to the details relayed to them by the not-so-poor people who stood in the doorway and could see inside.

14   "The bald man is cutting the blue wire," someone said.

15   "He is sticking the wire into the hole in the bottom of the black box," someone else added.

16   "The telephone man with the mustache is connecting two pieces of wire. Now he is twisting the ends together," a third voice chimed in.

17   Because I was small and unaware that I should have stood outside with the other poor folk to give the rich people inside more room (they seemed to need more of it than poor people did), I wriggled my way through the dense forest of legs to get a firsthand look at the action. I felt like the barefoot Moses, sandals in hand, staring at the burning bush on Mount Sinai. Breathless, I watched as the men in blue, their shirt pockets adorned with fancy lettering in a foreign language, put together a black machine that supposedly would make it possible to talk with uncles, aunts, and cousins who lived more than two days' ride away.

18   It was shortly after sunset when the man with the mustache announced that the telephone was ready to use. He explained that all Abu Raja had to do was lift the receiver, turn the crank on the black box a few times, and wait for an operator to take his call. Abu Raja, who had once lived and worked in Sidon, was impatient with the telephone man for assuming that he was ignorant. He grabbed the receiver and turned the crank forcefully, as if trying to start a Model T Ford. Everybody was impressed that he knew what to do. He even called the operator by her first name: "Centralist." Within moments, Abu Raja was talking

with his brother, a concierge in Beirut. He didn't even have to raise his voice or shout to be heard.

19   If I hadn't seen it with my own two eyes and heard it with my own two ears, I would not have believed it—and my friend Kameel didn't. He was away that day watching his father's goats, and when he came back to the village that evening, his cousin Habeeb and I told him about the telephone and how Abu Raja had used it to speak with his brother in Beirut. After he heard our report, Kameel made the sign of the cross, kissed his thumbnail, and warned us that lying was a bad sin and would surely land us in purgatory. Kameel believed in Jesus and Mary, and wanted to be a priest when he grew up. He always crossed himself when Habeeb, who was irreverent, and I, who was Presbyterian, were around, even when we were not bearing bad news.

20   And the telephone, as it turned out, was bad news. With its coming, the face of the village began to change. One of the first effects was the shifting of the village's center. Before the telephone's arrival, the men of the village used to gather regularly at the house of Im Kaleem, a short, middle-aged widow with jet-black hair and a raspy voice that could be heard all over the village, even when she was only whispering. She was a devout Catholic and also the village *shlikki*—whore. The men met at her house to argue about politics and drink coffee and play cards or backgammon. Im Kaleem was not a true prostitute, however, because she did not charge for her services—not even for the coffee and tea (and, occasionally, the strong liquor called arrack) that she served the men. She did not need the money; her son, who was overseas in Africa, sent her money regularly. (I knew this because my father used to read her son's letters to her and take down her replies, as Im Kaleem could not read and write.) Im Kaleem was no slut either—unlike some women in the village—because she loved all the men she entertained, and they loved her, every one of them. In a way, she was married to all the men in the village. Everybody knew it—the wives knew it; the itinerant Catholic priest knew it; the Presbyterian minister knew it—but nobody objected. Actually, I suspect the women (my mother included) did not mind their husbands' visits to Im Kaleem. Oh, they wrung their hands and complained to one another about their men's unfaithfulness, but secretly they were relieved, because Im Kaleem took some of the pressure off them and kept the men out of their hair while they attended to their endless chores. Im Kaleem was also a kind of confessor and troubleshooter, talking sense to those men who were having family problems, especially the younger ones.

21   Before the telephone came to Magdaluna, Im Kaleem's house was bustling at just about any time of day, especially at night, when its windows were brightly lit with three large oil lamps, and the loud voices of the men talking, laughing, and arguing could be heard in the street below—a reassuring, homey sound. Her house was an island of comfort, an oasis for the weary village men, exhausted from having so little to do.

22   But it wasn't long before many of those men—the younger ones especially—started spending more of their days and evenings at Abu Raja's *dikkan*. There, they would eat and drink and talk and play checkers and backgammon, and then lean their chairs back against the wall—the signal that they were ready to toss back and forth, like a ball, the latest rumors going around the village. And

they were always looking up from their games and drinks and talk to glance at the phone in the corner, as if expecting it to ring any minute and bring news that would change their lives and deliver them from their aimless existence. In the meantime, they smoked cheap, hand-rolled cigarettes, dug dirt out from under their fingernails with big pocketknives, and drank lukewarm sodas they called Kacula, Seffen-Ub, and Bebsi. Sometimes, especially when it was hot, the days dragged on so slowly that the men turned on Abu Saeed, a confirmed bachelor who practically lived in Abu Raja's *dikkan,* and teased him for going around barefoot and unshaven since the Virgin had appeared to him behind the olive press.

23   The telephone was also bad news for me personally. It took away my lucrative business—a source of much-needed income. Before the telephone came to Magdaluna, I used to hang around Im Kaleem's courtyard and play marbles with the other kids, waiting for some man to call down from a window and ask me to run to the store for cigarettes or arrack, or to deliver a message to his wife, such as what he wanted for supper. There was always something in it for me: a ten- or even a twenty-five-piaster piece. On a good day, I ran nine or ten of those errands, which assured a steady supply of marbles that I usually lost to Sami or his cousin Hani, the basket weaver's boy. But as the days went by, fewer and fewer men came to Im Kaleem's, and more and more congregated at Abu Raja's to wait by the telephone. In the evenings, no light fell from her window onto the street below, and the laughter and noise of the men trailed off and finally stopped. Only Shukri, the retired Turkish-army drill sergeant, remained faithful to Im Kaleem after all the other men had deserted her; he was still seen going into or leaving her house from time to time. Early that winter, Im Kaleem's hair suddenly turned gray, and she got sick and old. Her legs started giving her trouble, making it hard for her to walk. By spring she hardly left her house anymore.

24   At Abu Raja's *dikkan,* the calls did eventually come, as expected, and men and women started leaving the village the way a hailstorm begins: first one, then two, then bunches. The army took them. Jobs in the cities lured them. And ships and airplanes carried them to such faraway places as Australia and Brazil and New Zealand. My friend Kameel, his cousin Habeeb, and their cousins and my cousins all went away to become ditch diggers and mechanics and butcher-shop boys and deli owners who wore dirty aprons sixteen hours a day, all looking for a better life than the one they had left behind. Within a year, only the sick, the old, and the maimed were left in the village. Magdaluna became a skeleton of its former self, desolate and forsaken, like the tombs, a place to get away from.

25   Finally, the telephone took my family away, too. My father got a call from an old army buddy who told him that an oil company in southern Lebanon was hiring interpreters and instructors. My father applied for a job and got it, and we moved to Sidon, where I went to a Presbyterian missionary school and graduated in 1962. Three years later, having won a scholarship, I left Lebanon for the United States. Like the others who left Magdaluna before me, I am still looking for that better life. ✳

From Anwar Accawi, *The Boy from the Tower of the Moon.* © 1999 by Anwar Accawi. Reprinted by permission of Beacon Press, Boston.

Exercises

Do not refer to the selection for Exercises A and B unless your instructor directs you to do so.

A. DETERMINING THE MAIN IDEA AND PURPOSE

Choose the best answer.

_____ 1. The main idea of the selection is that

    a. life in the small village of Magdaluna was slow, simple, and un-eventful.

    b. the telephone brought many profound changes to Magdaluna, and, in turn, resulted in the town's downfall.

    c. the telephone made it possible for Magdaluna to connect to the outside world.

    d. the telephone brought many positive changes to Magdaluna.

_____ 2. With respect to the main idea, the writer's purpose is to

    a. contrast life in his village before and after the telephone's arrival.

    b. show what life was like in a small rural Lebanese village.

    c. praise new technology for its role in modernizing his homeland.

    d. persuade residents of isolated villages that they should remain that way if they hope to preserve their way of life.

B. COMPREHENDING MAIN IDEAS

Choose the correct answer.

_____ 1. The residents of Magdaluna kept track of time and key events in their lives by means of a particular kind of calendar, specifically

    a. news of the outside world brought by itinerant visitors.

    b. a Muslim calendar.

    c. natural disasters sent by Allah.

    d. ancient time-keeping devices like sundials and stone columns.

_____ 2. One especially memorable event occurred on the day Antoinette the seamstress married Saeed the barber, when the sky rained

    a. goat droppings and coins.

    b. locusts and other insects.

    c. fish and oranges.

    d. candy and little toys.

_____ 3. Accawi and his friends especially enjoyed the year of drought when tempers flared and women fought with each other, allowing the boys to

    a. have a day off from school to search for water.

    b. peek at what was under the women's clothing.

    c. be entertained by the spectacle of women rolling around in the dust.

    d. make bets on who the victor would be.

_____ **4.** Abu Raja, the owner of the *dikkan* or country store, proposed that Magdaluna get its own telephone and offered several reasons. Which one of these was *not* mentioned?

   a. A telephone was necessary in case of an emergency.
   b. A telephone would bring much-needed extra income for the villagers.
   c. The town would never be much of a town without one.
   d. A telephone would link the town to the outside world.

_____ 5. After the telephone arrived, the village center shifted to Abu Raja's store, whereas before the telephone arrived, the men of the town had spent the evenings

   a. at the home of Im Kaleem, who offered the men a place to relax and amuse themselves.
   b. at the local bar and restaurant drinking, eating, and talking politics.
   c. at home with their families.
   d. in the town's mosques.

_____ **6.** The most serious and long-reaching effect of the telephone on village life in Magdaluna was that its residents

   a. became more interested in the outside world and neglected local events and customs.
   b. realized that they had the best possible life right where they were.
   c. became dissatisfied and left to search for a better life.
   d. began to demand more sophisticated kinds of technology to improve their lives.

COMPREHENSION SCORE

Score your answers for Exercises A and B as follows:

A. No. right _____ × 2 = _____

B. No. right _____ × 1 = _____

Total points from A and B _____ × 10 = _____ percent

You may refer to the selection as you work through the remaining exercises.

C. MAKING INFERENCES

Write your answers to these questions in your own words.

1. Look again at the details in paragraph 1. What point is Accawi suggesting about life in Magdaluna? _____

_____

2. Again, in paragraph 1, why does Accawi say that the people of Magdaluna didn't need to know what year or what time of day it was? _____

_____

3. Accawi recounts the story some older men and his father told him about the heavens raining fish and oranges. Based on the evidence in the selection, do you think that story was true or not? _____ What evidence leads to your conclusion? _____

_____

4. Look at the last sentence of paragraph 10. Concerning Accawi and his friends, what does he mean to imply in the last sentence: "Fish and oranges from heaven . . . you can get over that"? _____

_____

_____

5. Accawi's friend Kameel didn't believe Accawi's account of the new telephone (see paragraph 19). What does this suggest about the telephone's significance to the larger community? _____

_____

6. What does Accawi imply about his earlier life in Magdaluna from the last sentence of the essay when he writes, "I am still looking for that better life"?

_____

D. INTERPRETING MEANING AND ANALYZING STRUCTURE

Where appropriate, write your answers to these questions in your own words.

1. What is the purpose of the illustration in paragraphs 3–7 when Accawi's grandmother tells him how old Teta Im Khalil was? What point does her answer reinforce? _____

_____

2. _____ Read paragraph 9 again. A good title for this paragraph is
   a. "The Year of the Drought."
   b. "A Fish-Bearing Twister."
   c. "How a Village Survived Without Water."
   d. "Allah's Milestones."

3. An *allusion* is a reference to something outside the text, and it is used to shed light on an idea by relating it to something that has gone before. Allusions can be from literature, mythology, history, or from a religious text like the Bible, among other sources. Paragraph 17 contains an allusion. First locate it and write it in the first space. _____

_____

Then explain why Accawi uses this allusion. _____

4. Consider carefully the changes that Accawi attributes (paragraphs 20 and 22) to the men who spent their evenings at Abu Raja's store. How did their conversations change?_____

_____

5. Ultimately, what effect did the telephone have on these men and on their lives?

_____

_____

6. *Irony* is a discrepancy between what we might expect to happen and what actually does happen. Do you see any irony in what Accawi writes in paragraph 24? _____

_____

E. UNDERSTANDING VOCABULARY

Choose the best definition according to an analysis of word parts or the context.

_____ **1.** We lived and loved and *toiled* [paragraph 1]:

  a. became ill
  b. worked hard
  c. produced children
  d. endured hardships

_____ **2.** floods and locusts and *pestilences* [2]:

  a. epidemic diseases
  b. long dry periods
  c. invasions by foreign armies
  d. punishments sent by divine beings

_____ **3.** women with *protruding* collarbones [9]: collarbones that appeared to be

  a. sunken
  b. broken
  c. sticking out
  d. conspicuous

_____ **4.** *amid* the long wait [10]:

  a. after
  b. during
  c. because of
  d. in the middle of

_____ **5.** they were finally *shunned* [11]:

  a. criticized harshly
  b. rejected, avoided
  c. banished permanently
  d. ridiculed, jeered at

_____ **6.** the *itinerant* Catholic priest [20]:
  a. widely respected
  b. scholarly, well educated
  c. entertaining, amusing
  d. traveling from place to place

_____ **7.** my *lucrative* business [23]:
  a. well established
  b. thriving, successful
  c. profitable, producing money
  d. important, useful

_____ **8.** only the old and the *maimed* [24]:
  a. sick
  b. unambitious
  c. stubborn
  d. disfigured

F. USING VOCABULARY

From the following list of vocabulary words, choose a word that fits in each blank according to both the grammatical structure of the sentence and the context. Use each word in the list only once. Do not change the form of the word. (Note that there are more words than sentences.)

desolate	gravity	lured	tampered
drought	ignorant	milestones	terrain
gendarme	incorporated	oasis	
grappled	irreverent	purgatory	

1. For the villagers of Magdaluna, time wasn't particularly important, unless

   someone had to go to court because he had _____ with the boundary markers; otherwise, the townspeople remained pretty much

   _____ of the more usual ways of marking time.

2. The story of the fish and oranges that rained down from heaven was an

   example of one of Allah's _____ . That story was so

   famous that eventually it became _____ into the village's calendar.

3. On the day that the telephone arrived in the village, everyone came to watch,

   _____ by the excitement; the _____ of the representatives showed how important they were and how important their errand was.

4. Eventually, however, Im Kaleem's house stopped being an _____ from the endless chores residents were required to perform, and as one family after another moved away, Magdaluna became almost

   _____ .

G. TOPICS FOR WRITING OR DISCUSSION

1. The telephone forever changed the lives of Magdaluna's townspeople. Write a paragraph summarizing the changes as Accawi describes them.
2. Does Accawi's account of the desolation that befell Magdaluna after the arrival of the telephone seem believable? Can you detect any other forces that might have contributed to the town's becoming "desolate and forsaken"?
3. Can you think of a technological device or invention that has caused similar disruption in a community, one that has produced far-reaching and mostly negative changes?

For Further Exploration

BOOK

Silicon Snake Oil (1996) by computer expert Clifford Stoll examines the computer revolution with a skeptical eye. Stoll discusses the overblown promises of technology and expresses his fears that the virtual reality offered by computers and video games will damage our ability to think and to experience real life first-hand.

MOVIE

For a humorous and dark look at the evils of technology, *Chicken Run* (2000), directed by Nick Park and Peter Lord, is a wonderful animated movie that undoubtedly appeals more to adults than to children. Made by the same animators who do the clever and inventive Wallace and Gromit cartoons, this offering is a spoof of what happens when a new piece of technology is invented—in this case, an amazing contraption for turning a live chicken into a chicken pot pie.

WEB SITES

The amount of information on the Web concerning technology and technological advancements and trends can be overwhelming. Here are four good sites to get you started:

- *www.cnet.com*
- *www.zdnet.com*
- *www.pcworld.com*
- *www.macworld.com*

20

ELLEN ALDERMAN AND CAROLINE KENNEDY

New Jersey v. T.L.O.: The School Search Cases

The right to privacy, which most Americans assume is guaranteed under the Constitution, has been eroding gradually over the past century. In fact, the Constitution does not guarantee this right, yet it has remained an American principle since the end of the nineteenth century. In 1890, Samuel D. Warren and Louis D. Brandeis (who later became a U.S. Supreme Court justice) wrote an article entitled "the Right to Privacy," which they defined as "the right to be let alone." They also argued for its counterpart—the right to sue for "invasion of privacy." The judicial system has upheld this principle ever since.

In The Right to Privacy *(1995), Ellen Alderman and Caroline Kennedy explore the changes that this fundamental tenet has undergone, and they examine the threat to our right to privacy as media and technology have become more sophisticated and intrusive. Alderman and Kennedy are attorneys who met when they were students at the Columbia University School of Law.*

This particular excerpt from their book describes a case involving two high school girls who were caught smoking in the school bathroom. The parents of one of the girls (here called "T.L.O." to protect her privacy) sued the district, and the case went all the way to the Supreme Court. In this selection, Alderman and Kennedy explain how this incident became a test case for the Fourth Amendment, particularly as it applies to searching students accused of misconduct.

Vocabulary Preview

WORD HISTORIES **Subtle [paragraph 17]** The word *subtle* is pronounced with a silent *b*; it means "so slight as to be difficult to detect or analyze." For example, a color may be subtle because it is so light; a remark may be subtle because it is indirect, rather than pointed. According to the *Dictionary of Word Origins* by Joseph T. Shipley, "this word survives in the figurative sense only; it is drawn from weaving. . . . Meaning of fine or delicate texture, it was applied to ideas the interweaving of which could not be discerned." The fibers in the woven cloth, in other words, were so expertly woven together that one couldn't see them individually. The Latin root *subtilis* ("of fine or delicate texture") comes from *sub* ("under") + *texere* ("to weave").

WORD PARTS

Contra- [paragraph 6]   One of the duties of Theodore Choplick, vice principal of the New Jersey high school where T.L.O. was a student, was to punish students caught with *contraband. Contraband* typically refers to goods that the law prohibits from being imported or exported (drugs, for example). The word, however, has a slightly broader meaning in this context, referring to any item forbidden on the premises, such as cigarettes, alcohol, or weapons. Meaning "opposite," the prefix *contra-* can be seen in these words:

contradiction	speaking against [*contra-* + *dicere* ("to speak")]
contraception	a means of preventing pregnancy
contravene	to act counter, to violate an order [*contra-* + *venire* ("to come between")]

What is a *contrarian?* _____

WORD FAMILIES

Suspension and Suspended [paragraph 7 and elsewhere; paragraph 11 and elsewhere]   The verb form *suspend,* in the context of *suspending* a student from school, as it is used in this essay, means "to bar for a period from a privilege, position, or office." One's driver's license, for example, can be *suspended* for various infractions. More literally, the word can also mean "to hang," from the Latin word that combines *sub-* ("under") + *pendere* ("to hang"). Other words in this family are *suspenders* (devices to hold up one's pants), *suspense* (literally, to leave one hanging), and *pendant,* a piece of jewelry that hangs from a necklace.

ELLEN ALDERMAN AND CAROLINE KENNEDY

New Jersey v. T.L.O.: The School Search Cases

The right of the people to be secure in their persons, houses, papers, and effects, against unreasonable searches and seizures, shall not be violated, and no Warrants shall issue, but upon probable cause, supported by Oath or affirmation, and particularly describing the place to be searched, and the persons or things to be seized.

The Fourth Amendment to the United States Constitution

1   Some of the chaos from the streets has spilled over into the nation's schools as well. In some areas, "schoolteacher" is now considered a high-risk job. Schools everywhere, not just in urban centers, have been trying to cope with increased disciplinary problems, rising drug use, and the potential for violence. To enter their schools, some children walk through metal detectors like those set up at airports to foil terrorist attacks. Many more students customarily have their lockers or desks searched by school officials. And some administrators have considered routine drug testing of all of their students.

2   Yet as widespread as these measures are, it is not clear that they are always constitutional. In general, the use of metal detectors and drug tests is considered

a search under the Fourth Amendment. But as late as the mid-1980s, the United States Supreme Court had not even ruled on whether the Fourth Amendment applied to public school officials, much less on the specific standards to be followed in a school setting. Ironically, the case that finally got the Court's attention in 1985 did not involve violence or weapons or any high-tech searches. Instead, the incident that sparked the landmark lawsuit was so old and familiar that in the light of today's problems, it almost seems quaint.

3   A New Jersey high school teacher opened the door to the girls' lavatory between class periods and walked into a cloud of smoke. Through the acrid haze, she saw two freshman girls lounging on the sinks and windowsill, smoking cigarettes. At this particular high school, smoking was allowed, but only in designated areas—which most definitely did not include the rest rooms. The teacher promptly led the two girls to the principal's office.

4   At the office, the students were confronted by Theodore Choplick, vice principal. At a public school, the vice principal is the disciplinarian, responsible for ferreting out wrongdoing and meting out punishment. Choplick has been in education for more than twenty years, mostly as a vice principal. He views his role as something approaching that of a surrogate parent. "We are responsible for them," he says of the students. "I treat them like they are my children. It's as simple as that." But times have changed and Choplick's job has changed with them.

5   In a measure of how dire the situation has become in some schools, Choplick says that his own suburban school, with a student population of twenty-six hundred, is "not totally out of control"—by which he means: "I have never feared for my life." Instead, Choplick says his New Jersey high school has "typical" problems, ranging from fistfights and truancy to teen pregnancy, alcohol, and more recently, drugs. Choplick says his students are involved mostly with marijuana and, less frequently, cocaine and LSD. Though he sees himself as a stand-in for parents, when the vice principal describes his job, he sounds more like a cop walking his beat.

6   "You have an idea who is dealing and you always keep your eye out," he says. "You position yourself in certain places in the hallway where you can get a vantage point. Or you suddenly walk in a different direction so you can sneak up on something." If Choplick finds students with contraband, he walks them down to his office. He says that one of the rules he learned early is never to discipline a student in front of others. "But," he continues, "when you walk the students, you always make sure they stay in front of you. You never lead the way because they will drop things off. If they're in front of you, you're able to see if they drop things along the way."

7   However, none of this was on Choplick's mind when the two freshman girls were brought to the office for smoking in the lavatory. Neither of the students was known to be a troublemaker or a drug user. "They were not ones I was watching," the vice principal says. "The ones we watched, we caught." Standing at a counter in the waiting area, he simply asked the girls if they had been smoking in the rest room. One of them said yes right away, and Choplick gave her the punishment mandated by the Board of Education: three days' suspension. However, when he turned to the second student, fourteen-year-old "T.L.O.," she

denied that she had been smoking in the rest room. Indeed, she denied that she smoked at all.

8   Choplick did not want to confront T.L.O. in front of her friend, so he asked her to step into his office. There, he again asked her if she had been smoking, and T.L.O. again denied it. So Choplick asked to see the girl's purse. It was something he had done dozens, maybe even hundreds, of times. "I had asked boys or girls before to empty their purses or give me their wallets. If they had book bags, we looked in the book bags. We did all of that," he says. In other words, Choplick never would have guessed that his actions over the next two minutes would be scrutinized by four separate state courts and, ultimately, nine justices of the United States Supreme Court.

9   Choplick opened T.L.O.'s purse and saw a pack of Marlboro cigarettes "sitting right on top there." He held the cigarettes in front of T.L.O. and accused her of lying. But as he did so, Choplick looked down into the purse again and this time saw a package of E-Z Widers. He says, "If you're a school administrator, you know E-Z Widers are rolling papers used for marijuana."

10   At that point, Choplick began to empty T.L.O.'s pocketbook. He found a pipe, several empty plastic bags, and one bag containing a tobacco-like substance. "You take the plastic bag and take a smell," Choplick says, "and you smell marijuana. And now you say, 'Whoa, whoa, whoa.'" He opened T.L.O.'s wallet, which contained $40 in singles. Then, opening a separate compartment, he found an index card with the heading "People Who Owe Me Money," followed by a list of names and amount of $1.00 or $1.50. Finally, Choplick found two letters apparently concerning marijuana sales.

11   He was surprised because T.L.O. had never been in trouble before. Nonetheless, he was certain, given what was now arrayed before him, that the fourteen-year-old was in the business of selling marijuana. Following board policy, Choplick notified T.L.O.'s parents first, then called the police. With her mother present, T.L.O. was given "Miranda" warnings and questioned by police officers. She first told them that the $40 was from her paper route. ("Give me a break" was Choplick's response.) Then the girl admitted that she had been selling marijuana in school and on that day had sold eighteen to twenty joints for $1.00 apiece. In accordance with board policy, T.L.O. was suspended from school for ten days—three days for smoking cigarettes in the girls' room and seven days for selling marijuana at school.

12   But the matter did not end there. The police turned the case over to the local prosecutor's office, which filed a complaint against T.L.O. in juvenile court. She was charged with delinquency based on possession of marijuana with intent to distribute.

13   T.L.O.'s parents hired an attorney and fought the charges on two fronts. They defended against the delinquency charge in juvenile court, and they went to civil court to contest T.L.O.'s suspension from school. In both courts, T.L.O.'s argument was the same: The vice principal's search of T.L.O.'s purse had violated her Fourth Amendment rights. Therefore, the evidence seized could not be used against her. Without the evidence of drug dealing, there would be no delinquency case against T.L.O., nor would there be any grounds for suspending her from school.

14   It all seemed perfectly straightforward. But it was nothing of the kind.

15   The United States Supreme Court had never ruled on whether the Fourth Amendment applied to school officials such as Vice Principal Choplick. Although the Court had long ago declared that students do not "shed their Constitutional rights . . . at the schoolhouse gate," there was an equally long tradition of deferring to school officials in recognition of their unique responsibilities. For Fourth Amendment purposes, the singular context of the public schools cuts both ways.

16   School officials are charged with the crucial task of educating our children. They are also charged with what today has become an equally awesome responsibility: that of keeping our children safe. Teachers and administrators need to be able to act swiftly and surely to maintain an environment where students can not just grow intellectually but also be assured of getting through the day in one piece.

17   There are also more subtle but equally important forces at work. One of the most essential lessons a public school teaches is that of citizenship. As early as 1943, the Supreme Court declared that that was reason enough "for scrupulous protection of Constitutional freedoms of the individual, if we are not to strangle the free mind at its source and teach youth to discount important principles of our government as mere platitudes." The lesson is taught not only in civics class but also by example. How school officials treat students suspected of wrongdoing—when and why they search—may be one of the most lasting lessons a child will learn.

18   Without a ruling from the Supreme Court, state and federal courts were, as one attorney put it, "all over the place." At one extreme, schoolteachers and administrators were considered to be *in loco parentis*—that is, "in place of a parent." Under this view, school officials were not bound by the Fourth Amendment and could search students and their belongings as freely as a parent could. At the other extreme, school officials were held to the strictest standards under the Fourth Amendment. Before they could search a student, they had to obtain a warrant based upon "probable cause" that a crime had been committed.

19   Taking a middle position, many courts held that public school officials were bound by the Fourth Amendment but that a less strict standard was appropriate. Under this compromise view, a search merely had to be "reasonable under all of the circumstances" to be considered constitutional.

20   Yet deciding that the Fourth Amendment does indeed apply to school officials raises still another question. If a search of a student is found to violate the Fourth Amendment, can the evidence seized in the search be turned over to the police, or must it be excluded from any criminal or even disciplinary proceedings? Does the so-called exclusionary rule apply in the school setting?

21   The exclusionary rule is one of the most controversial aspects of the Fourth Amendment. The rule is not specifically set out in the text of the amendment. Rather, in the criminal context the Supreme Court has decided that if a search violates the Fourth Amendment, then the evidence seized in that search cannot be used in court. Otherwise, the Court reasoned, there would be a right without a remedy. Law enforcement officials could not be counted on to follow the rules unless there was a penalty for violating them. Critics say that the exclusionary

rule allows an obviously guilty person to "get off on a technicality." Or, as Justice Benjamin Cardozo put it more colorfully, "The criminal is to go free because the constable has blundered."

22 Perhaps in the school setting, where courts often defer to school officials, the rule need not apply. On the other hand, it seems especially unfair to allow school officials to search students under a lesser standard than that which applies to suspected criminals, and also be able to use the evidence seized against students in disciplinary or even criminal proceedings. The Supreme Court had not ruled on these issues either.

23 Thus, T.L.O.'s "smoking in the girls' room" case began a roller-coaster ride through the courts. Three lower courts in New Jersey reached different conclusions regarding the legality of Choplick's search. Then it was the New Jersey Supreme Court's turn to scrutinize Vice Principal Choplick's actions. The court held that the Fourth Amendment applied to public schools, and that searches by school officials need only be "reasonable." But the New Jersey Supreme Court held that Choplick's search was *not* reasonable.

24 The court said that there had been no reasonable basis for opening T.L.O.'s purse in the first place. No one had furnished any information to Choplick indicating that the purse contained cigarettes. Furthermore, the mere presence of cigarettes in the bag did not prove that T.L.O. had been smoking them in the girls' room. And possessing cigarettes at school was not in itself an infraction, because smoking was allowed in certain areas. Even if opening the purse had been reasonable, the court continued, Choplick's "wholesale rummaging" was not. The court then declared that the exclusionary rule applied in the school setting. Therefore, the evidence found in T.L.O.'s purse should be suppressed.

25 Immediately, the state of New Jersey, represented by attorney Alan Nodes, asked the United States Supreme Court to review the case. However, Nodes did not ask the Court to reverse the state court's holding in its entirety. New Jersey was willing to accept that the Fourth Amendment applied to school officials with the lesser standard of "reasonableness." The state was even willing to accept the Court's decision that Choplick's search was not reasonable. But New Jersey did not want the exclusionary rule to be used for school searches. "We felt more comfortable asking for a modification of a judge-made rule, like the exclusionary rule, than asking for a modification of the Fourth Amendment," Nodes says.

26 When the Supreme Court agreed to hear the case, T.L.O.'s court-appointed attorney, Lois DeJulio, was not pleased. Noting recent cases in which the Supreme Court had cut back on Fourth Amendment protections, she says, "I was really kind of dreading what was going to happen next. . . . I was really very afraid that this would be the end of the Fourth Amendment for juveniles."

27 The person who was most unhappy about the case being reviewed by the High Court was the one who had started it all, T.L.O. "This was not a case where she set out to test constitutional rights," says DeJulio. Indeed, T.L.O.'s goal had simply been to get back in school. By the time the case reached the Supreme Court, T.L.O. not only had been readmitted to high school but had graduated and moved on with her life. Nonetheless, she was forever frozen in court papers as the fourteen-year-old caught smoking in the girls' room. Now that girl was going to become part of constitutional history.

28   In March of 1984, the Supreme Court heard oral arguments concerning whether the exclusionary rule should apply in the school setting. In June of 1984, the Court told the parties to back up and address a constitutional issue that they had not even raised. The Court wanted to use T.L.O.'s case to decide what role, if any, the Fourth Amendment should play in public schools.

29   In October of 1984, the parties were back before the Court, this time arguing about whether school officials were bound by the Fourth Amendment in the first place. On January 15, 1985, the Supreme Court finally issued its opinion.

30   The Court noted what anyone with a school-age child already knows. "In recent years, school disorder has often taken particularly ugly forms: drug use and violent crime in the schools have become major social problems." Nonetheless, the Court said that "the situation is not so dire that students in schools may claim no legitimate expectations of privacy." From this day forward, public school teachers and administrators would be bound by the Fourth Amendment.

31   However, the Court also held that because of the special circumstances relating to the school context, some "modification" of the usual Fourth Amendment rules would be necessary. Teachers would not be expected to obtain warrants before conducting a search in school. Nor would they be expected to train themselves in the "niceties" of the "probable cause" standard used by police officers. The search should simply be "reasonable under all of the circumstances." By this the Court meant two things. First, there must be reasonable grounds for suspecting that the search will turn up evidence that the student has violated either the law or school rules. Second, the search must not be excessively intrusive in light of the student's age and sex and the nature of the infraction.

32   Turning to T.L.O. and Mr. Choplick, the Court held that the search was "in no sense unreasonable." The Court agreed that the presence of cigarettes in T.L.O.'s purse did not prove conclusively that she had been smoking in the rest room. However, the Court held that conclusive proof was not necessary. It was enough that the cigarettes would corroborate the charge and undermine T.L.O.'s defense that she did not smoke at all. Addressing the New Jersey court's concern that no one had specifically told Choplick that there were cigarettes in T.L.O.'s purse, the Court stated, "If she did have cigarettes, her purse was the obvious place in which to find them." Once the purse was opened and Choplick saw the E-Z Wider cigarette papers in plain view, he was justified in looking further. From start to finish, the Court concluded, the vice principal's search was reasonable. Therefore, it was not necessary to resolve the question of whether the exclusionary rule should apply.

33   In dissent, Justices William Brennan and Thurgood Marshall declared: "Vice Principal Choplick's thorough excavation of T.L.O.'s purse was undoubtedly a serious intrusion on her privacy." The dissent decried the Court's creation of yet another exception to the clear command of the Fourth Amendment. According to the dissent, the new standard of "reasonable under all of the circumstances" not only watered down the privacy rights of students but also posed a practical problem for administrators. The dissent found the new standard to be ambiguous, stating that the only thing definite about it was that "it is *not* the same test as the 'probable cause' standard found in the text of the Fourth Amendment." The dissent predicted that after *T.L.O.*, school students' privacy rights would be

trampled and school administrators "would be hopelessly adrift as to when a search may be permissible." ✳

Exercises

Do not refer to the selection for Exercises A and B unless your instructor directs you to do so.

A. DETERMINING THE MAIN IDEA AND PURPOSE

Choose the best answer.

_____ 1. The main idea of the selection is that
- **a.** the social problems invading America's schools have required administrators to establish measures to protect students that may, in fact, be illegal.
- **b.** modifying the Fourth Amendment to allow students to be searched may result in their loss of privacy and cause disagreement over what constitutes a reasonable search.
- **c.** the Fourth Amendment to the Constitution protects citizens from illegal search and seizure.
- **d.** public school teachers have the same right as parents to search for harmful substances and for contraband.

_____ 2. With respect to the main idea, the writers' purpose is to
- **a.** explain the facts of the case against T.L.O. and interpret the rulings of various courts concerning it.
- **b.** explain the origins of the right to privacy provision.
- **c.** defend the Supreme Court's ruling in T.L.O.'s case.
- **d.** examine both arguments in the T.L.O. case and let the reader make up his or her own mind.

B. COMPREHENDING MAIN IDEAS

Choose the correct answer.

_____ 1. When Theodore Choplick asked T.L.O. if she had been smoking in the bathroom, she
- **a.** admitted that she had been.
- **b.** claimed the cigarettes belonged to a friend.
- **c.** denied smoking at all.
- **d.** refused to be questioned until she called an attorney.

_____ **2.** When Choplick searched T.L.O.'s purse, he found the following: $40, cigarettes, and

    a. a package of E-Z Widers and a bag of marijuana.
    b. a list of various drugs students had ordered from her.
    c. cocaine and speed.
    d. a gun.

_____ **3.** T.L.O.'s parents hired an attorney and sued the school district on the grounds that

    a. the parents allowed T.L.O. to smoke marijuana at home.
    b. she had never caused any trouble before, and this was a first offense.
    c. Choplick's search of her purse had violated her Fourth Amendment rights.
    d. she was a good student without a previous criminal record who deserved a second chance.

_____ **4.** In the view of many courts, public school officials were bound by a less strict interpretation of the Fourth Amendment, which was actually a compromise, holding that a search

    a. could be done only as a last resort to control known or suspected troublemakers.
    b. had to be reasonable under all circumstances.
    c. had to be conducted in front of the student's parents.
    d. could not take place without a judge's issuing a search warrant.

_____ **5.** The exclusionary rule states that

    a. evidence seized in violation of the Fourth Amendment can't be used in court.
    b. police have the right to search students without the school's or the parent's permission.
    c. a court must exclude all evidence obtained under false pretenses or without a warrant.
    d. people convicted of a crime must be excluded from testifying in a courtroom.

_____ **6.** In its decision, the U.S. Supreme Court ruled that Choplick's search of T.L.O.'s purse was

    a. "necessary to protect other students."
    b. "in no sense unreasonable."
    c. "unwarranted because of the relative harmlessness of the incident."
    d. "the result of inconclusive proof."

COMPREHENSION SCORE

Score your answers for Exercises A and B as follows:

A. No. right _____ × 2 = _____

B. No. right _____ × 1 = _____

Total points from A and B _____ × 10 = _____ percent

You may refer to the selection as you work through the remaining exercises.

C. LOCATING SUPPORTING DETAILS

For each main idea stated here, find and write down two details that support it.

1. [The New Jersey Supreme Court] said that there had been no reasonable basis for opening T.L.O.'s purse in the first place. [paragraph 24]

   a. _____

   _____

   b. _____

   _____

2. However, the [U.S. Supreme Court] also held that because of the special circumstances relating to the school context, some "modification" of the usual Fourth Amendment rules would be necessary. [paragraph 31]

   a. _____

   _____

   b. _____

   _____

D. MAKING INFERENCES

For each of these statements write Y (yes) if the inference is an accurate one, N (no) if the inference is an inaccurate one, and CT (can't tell) if the writer does not give you enough information to make an inference one way or another. The pertinent paragraph numbers are provided for you.

1. _____ The Supreme Court has ruled that metal detectors used in public schools are illegal. [paragraph 1]

2. _____ Theodore Choplick is a trusting man. [paragraphs 5 and 6]

3. _____ T.L.O. brought some of her subsequent legal problems on herself by lying when Choplick asked her if she been smoking. [paragraphs 7–11]

4. _____ The writers strongly imply that Choplick should either have not searched T.L.O.'s purse at all or not rummaged underneath the package of Marlboro cigarettes. [selection as a whole]

5. _____ T.L.O. had never sold marijuana before the day her purse was searched. [paragraph 11]

6. _____ Until T.L.O.'s case was heard, the Supreme Court had not ruled decisively on the Fourth Amendment as it applies to students. [paragraphs 15 and 18]

7. _____ Despite the four courts' interpretations in this case, all the judges agreed upon the meaning of the word *reasonable* as it applied to Vice Principal Choplick's search of T.L.O.'s purse. [paragraphs 23–25 and 31–32]

8. _____ In its ruling, the Supreme Court implied that although school officials are bound by the Fourth Amendment, students *are* in some ways different from ordinary citizens. [paragraphs 30–31]

E. INTERPRETING MEANING AND ANALYZING STRUCTURE

Where appropriate, write your answers to these questions in your own words.

1. Explain the irony in T.L.O.'s case reaching the Supreme Court, as the writers suggest at the end of paragraph 2. _____

   _____

   _____

2. How does Mr. Choplick characterize his role as vice principal? _____

   _____

   How do the writers characterize him? _____

   _____

   The two impressions are obviously quite different. What might be one reason that Choplick's image of himself and that of two outside observers are so different? _____

   _____

3. Read paragraph 17 again. Then explain the "lesson" that schools should teach students in civics classes and by their example in dealing with students suspected of wrongdoing. _____

   _____

   _____

4. Look at paragraph 21 again. Then write the sentence that represents the main idea. _____

   _____

5. In paragraph 23, Alderman and Kennedy write: "Thus, T.L.O.'s 'smoking in the girls' room' case began a roller-coaster ride through the courts." What does this metaphor mean?_____

_____

6. _____   Read paragraph 33, the conclusion, again. A good title for this paragraph would be

     a. "An Exception to the Fourth Amendment."
     b. "Trampling Students' Rights to Privacy."
     c. "Why Two Judges Dissented."
     d. "What Constitutes a Permissible Search."

F. UNDERSTANDING VOCABULARY

Look through the paragraphs listed below and find a word that matches each definition. Refer to the dictionary if necessary. An example has been done for you.

Ex. prevent, deter, thwart [paragraph 1]   foil

1. describing something of great significance, a turning point [2]   _____

2. odd, in an old-fashioned way [2]   _____

3. bitter, pungent, sharp-smelling [3]   _____

4. distributing, measuring out [4]   _____

5. serving as a substitute or replacement [4]   _____

6. dreadful, terrible, urgent [5 and 30]   _____

7. critical, most important, vital [16]   _____

8. meticulous, very careful, exacting [17]   _____

9. made a mistake, bungled, fouled up [21]   _____

10. violation, offense [31]   _____

11. prove, confirm, verify [32]   _____

12. disagreement, refusal to go along with the majority opinion [33]   _____

G. USING VOCABULARY

Here are some words from the selection. Write an original sentence using each word that shows both that you know how to use the word and what it means.

1. *ironically* _____

_____

2. *confront* _____

_____

3. *subtle* _____

_____

4. *exclude* _____

_____

5. *legality* _____

_____

6. *intrusive* _____

_____

7. *scrutinize* _____

_____

8. *ambiguous* _____

_____

H. PARAPHRASING EXERCISE

In the left column are three sentences from paragraph 30, with a paraphrase of them on the right.

Original Passage

The Court noted what anyone with a school-age child already knows. "In recent years, school disorder has often taken particularly ugly forms: drug use and violent crime in the schools have become major social problems." Nonetheless, the Court said that "the situation is not so dire that students in schools may claim no legitimate expectations of privacy. . . ."

Paraphrase

The Court observed what all parents know: Schools have recently experienced serious turmoil, especially from drugs and violence. But the Court also observed that these problems aren't so serious that students should be robbed of all aspects of their privacy.

_____

_____

_____

_____

Here is the last sentence of the article, which explains the dissenting opinion by Justices Brennan and Marshall. Study it carefully and then write a paraphrase of it.

Original Passage

The dissent predicted that after *T.L.O.,* school students' privacy rights would be trampled and school administrators "would be hopelessly adrift as to when a search may be permissible. . . ."

Paraphrase

_____

_____

_____

_____

_____

I.   TOPICS FOR WRITING OR DISCUSSION

1. Regardless of the law and various legal interpretations over whether the search of T.L.O.'s purse was reasonable or not, should principals or other school administrators have the right to search students' backpacks, purses, lockers, and so forth, if they suspect illegal activity?
2. In paragraph 15, the Supreme Court declared that students do not "shed their Constitutional rights . . . at the schoolhouse gate." The reference is to a case involving students who wore black armbands: *Tinker v. Des Moines Independent Community School District*, 393 U.S. 503 (1969). The case can be accessed at this Web site: *http://supct.law.cornell.edu/supct.* Type in "Tinker Des Moines" in the search box and scroll down to read the case.

For Further Exploration

BOOK

Caroline Kennedy's most recent book is *Profiles in Courage for Our Time* (2002). In it, she assembles a list of well-known writers who tell the stories of twenty-five people who won the Kennedy Profile in Courage award.

MOVIE

Midnight Express (1978), directed by Alan Parker and written by Oliver Stone, concerns the true story of a young American, Billy Hayes. Hayes foolishly tried to smuggle hashish out of Turkey on his return trip to the United States and was searched by the police as he tried to board the plane. He was imprisoned and suffered unnecessarily harsh treatment. The film is both brutal and cautionary, showing what happens when there are no restraints on a legal system.

WEB SITES

Read the entire 1985 Supreme Court ruling on the T.L.O. case at this site:

- Go to *http://supct.law.cornell.edu/supct/.* Then type "T.L.O." in the search box.

In addition, here is another site pertaining to Fourth Amendment cases:

- Opinions from legal experts and other writers on *New Jersey v. T.L.O.* can be found at *http://www.softcom.net/users/kareed/opinions.html.*

Maryland v. Wilson is an interesting search and seizure case, this one involving a passenger who was caught possessing cocaine after the driver was stopped. All of the documents pertaining to the case are available at:

- *http://supct.law.cornell.edu/supct/*

21

DAVID FERRELL

Badwater: The Ultra-Marathon

David Ferrell is a journalism graduate of California State University, Fullerton. He has written for the Los Angeles Times *since 1983. In 1997, the* Times *published Ferrell's series of feature articles on extreme sports, which was nominated for a Pulitzer Prize in feature writing in 1998. Other articles in the series described the extreme sports of ice climbing, monster truck races, Ultimate Fighting, extreme kayaking, and BASE jumping, an illegal and extremely dangerous form of parachuting that jumpers do from land-based objects. (BASE is an acronym for buildings, antennas, spans [bridges], and earth [cliffs].) This article describes an ultra-race called Badwater—a punishing 135-mile race from Badwater in California's Death Valley to Mt. Whitney, run in heat that can reach 118 degrees.*

Vocabulary Preview

WORD HISTORIES

Zealots [paragraph 7] According to Ferrell, the runners who attempt the Badwater marathon are *"zealots* who live to train, who measure themselves by their mental toughness." Coming from the noun *zeal* (from the Greek word *zelos*), *zealous* means "enthusiastically devoted to a cause, an ideal, or a goal," However, it also suggests that one is tirelessly diligent in pursuing the goal to the point of fanaticism. *Zealots* (written with a capital letter) refer to an extreme Jewish sect in Judea that flourished in the first century C.E. that advocated overthrowing Roman rule.

Alchemy [paragraph 28] In the Middle Ages, *alchemists* tried to transform base metals into gold. Ferrell describes the race's toll on the human body, writing "The body is already under enormous assault; the success of the hours ahead will hinge largely on the fickle *alchemy* of supplying it proper nutrition." In this context, *alchemy* refers to a process of transmuting or changing something from one form to another, in other words, changing the runners' food into sufficient energy to help them finish the race.

WORD PARTS

Eu- [paragraph 22] Many long-distance runners commonly experience *euphoria*, a feeling of intense well-being and pleasure. As Ferrell writes, "For superbly fit athletes, who train by doing 10 or 20 miles a day, the early stages of a long race often produce the *euphoric* sensation that they could go on forever." The Greek prefix *eu-* always means "well." (Be careful, however, not to confuse *eu-* with *eur-*, a prefix that generally denotes Europe.) Other words beginning with *eu-* are *euphony* (agreeable sound); *euphemism* (the substitution of an inoffensive term for one considered offensive or too explicit); and *eulogy* (a speech in praise of a person, usually of someone who has recently died). Consult your dictionary, if necessary, and define these words:

eugenics _____

euthanasia _____

Why did a popular new wave rock band of the 1980s call themselves the Eurhythmics? _____

WORD FAMILIES

Ignominious [paragraph 63]   In the Badwater race, "A runner who stops ceases to be a runner. It is a death of that identity, marked by an *ignominious* epitaph: 'Did not finish.'" The difficult word *ignominious* has its origin in the Latin root *nomen* ("name"), derived, in turn, from the Greek *onoma*. Meaning "dishonorable" or "disgraceful," *ignominius* has a strongly negative connotation. As Ferrell points out in the same paragraph, a runner considers the abbreviation "DNF" to be "foul with shame."

The noun form—ignominy—can be broken down like this: [*ig-* ("not") + *nomen* ("name" or "reputation")]. Other words containing the root *nomen* are *anonymity* (having no name); *nominal* (existing in name only); and oddly, the word *noun* itself, literally, the name of something.

DAVID FERRELL

Badwater: The Ultra-Marathon

1   Badwater is a madman's march, a footrace through the summer heat of the hottest spot in America. It extends 135 miles from a stinking water hole on the floor of Death Valley to a piney oasis 8,300 feet up the side of Mt. Whitney. The course is nothing but asphalt and road gravel. Feet and knees and shins ache like they are being whacked with tire irons. Faces turn into shrink-wrap.

2   Lisa Smith is 102 miles into it. She has been running, and now walking, for almost 27 hours, through yesterday's 118-degree heat, up 6,000 feet of mountain passes into a 40 mph head wind. The night brought her 40 minutes of sleep, if that—two catnaps.

3   Her feet are blistered and taped up, and she is wearing shoes with the toes cut out to relieve the pressure. Her right ankle, sprained twice since February, is so swollen she can no longer wear the air cast that was supporting it. She is also cramping with diarrhea.

4   "It's bad," she says, gasping. "My stomach is killing me."

5   Grimacing, spitting, bending over at times to fight the nausea, she trudges on, pushing down the undulating highway toward Keeler, a ramshackle mining outpost. Visible ahead is the serrated peak of Whitney, as distant as Oz. If she can

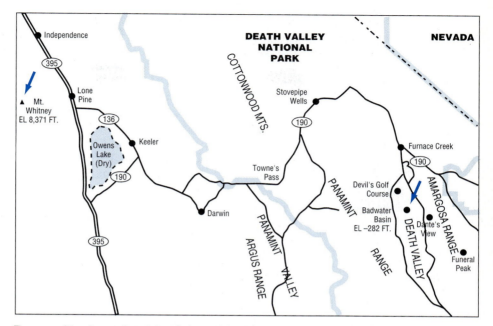

The course of the ultra-marathon starts at Badwater (right arrow) and ends at Mt. Whitney (left arrow).

hang on, it will take most of the day—and a 4,000 foot ascent over the final 13 miles—to get there.

6   Every year, two or three dozen elite ultra-marathoners come to Badwater, and every year Badwater beats them down. About a third fail to finish; after 50 miles or 70 miles or 110 miles, the torture exceeds their desire to go on, and they end up rolling away in their cars and minivans, faces covered with wet towels, their bodies stretched out like corpses.

7   For a thin slice of society—zealots who live to train, who measure themselves by their mental toughness—the ultra-marathon is the consummate test of human character. No other event in sport, except possibly a prizefight, is as punishing, as demanding of the mind and body. No other athlete is more revered than the distance runner. Indefatigable, heroic, celebrated in poetry and myth, the Greek soldier, Pheidippides, ran 26 miles from Marathon to Athens to herald victory over the Persians in 490 B.C., then collapsed and died. It was the first marathon. To fill the unforgiving minute, to persevere, is one of the highest ideals of man—who, after all, was born to hardship, cast from Eden.

8   The explosion of extreme sports in recent years has produced an unprecedented number of ultra-endurance races. Several thousand men and women travel the country—and abroad—competing in events from 30 miles to more than 300 miles. There are weeklong "adventure races" by foot, bike and kayak across Patagonia, South Africa, and Australia.

9   In Morocco, there is the Marathon des Sables—"the Marathon of the Sands"—a six-day trek, in stages, across 150 miles of the Sahara. Colorado has the Hardrock 100, snaking 100 miles through the 11,000-foot peaks of the San Juan

Mountains. In Alaska it's the Coldfoot, a 100-miler in October with the wind roaring and the temperatures plunging to 40 below.

10   Death Valley has Badwater: "probably the most physically taxing competitive event in the world," according to the runners' handbook, which warns that you could die out here—though no one yet has. "Heat illness or heat stroke . . . can cause death, kidney failure and brain damage. It is important that runners and crews be aware of the symptoms . . . vomiting, headache, dizziness, faintness, irritability, lassitude, weakness and rapid heart rate. . . . Heat stroke may progress from minimal symptoms to complete collapse in a very short period of time."

11   Twenty-seven runners have entered this year's 10th anniversary race, a field drawn from North America and Europe. Lisa, 36, is the only woman, a fitness trainer from Bernardsville, N.J., who has run 60 marathons—her fastest in 2 hours and 48 minutes—and four ultras. Bjarte Furnes, 23, a molecular biology student from Norway, is out to become the youngest ever to finish. Beacham Toler, 69, a retired boilermaker from Amarillo, Texas, is already the oldest; he aims to better a personal best by breaking 50 hours.

12   The course record, set five years ago, is 26 hours and 18 minutes, but few concern themselves with that or the first place prize money—$500. The main goal is to go the distance, because Badwater, like every extreme race, is less a competition among runners—whose training and talents vary widely—than it is a struggle between each runner and the miles. To conquer the course, you must get through it in less than 60 hours. Those who make it in under 48—two days and two nights—are awarded a special memento, a belt buckle, a modest hunk of bronze featuring a bas relief of the desert.

13   "If I don't make it, I'll be back every year until I do," vows U.S. Marine Corps Major W. C. Maples, 33, a second-time entrant from Camp Pendleton who stands now at the starting line, shortly before dawn. Three years back, during Utah's Wasatch 100, he got off the floor of an aid station despite hypothermia and winced through the last 50 miles with a stress fracture in his right leg.

14   But Badwater got him a year ago. The Major, as other runners call him, quit after vomiting up a bunch of pink, fleshy tissue that turned out to be part of his stomach lining. It was the only endurance race he failed to complete.

15   "I have fumed over that," he says. "One way I define a challenge is something that does not have a guaranteed outcome. I know that on my worst day I can strap on a pair of shoes and run 26 miles. But here, no matter what kind of shape you're in, there's no guarantee you're going to finish. I can relate to that. I train for combat. Combat does not have a guaranteed outcome."

THE BODY IS UNDER ENORMOUS ASSAULT

16   The race begins in the dawn glow of a clear, breezy morning, below a craggy cliff of the Amargosa Mountains on the valley's east rim. From a casino-hotel on the Nevada-California border, where the runners spent the night, it has taken more than 40 minutes to reach Badwater, so named for an acrid, amoeba-shaped pool of salt and brimstone just off the road. Its brittle white edges look like crusts of ice, but that is a desert illusion because the temperature at 5:30 A.M. is 92 degrees.

17   A weather-chipped placard notes that the earth here sinks to the lowest point in the Western Hemisphere: 282 feet below sea level. Minivans and cars fill a narrow parking lot. The support crews tend to number one to four people—wives, coaches, in-laws, friends, gurus, anyone willing to dispense water, food and exhortations. The vans are packed high with provisions—gallons of water, sandwiches, fruit, candy bars, protein bars, Gatorade, pretzels, crackers, salt tablets, sea salt, socks, shorts, blister pads, tape, towels, ankle braces, sunglasses, sunscreen, five or six pairs of shoes, and a bathroom scale.

18   Sahara hats are popular—white, Lawrence of Arabia headgear that shades the neck and cheeks. A few runners, like the Norwegian, wear them tailored to hold clumps of crushed ice, a cold skullcap. Dr. Dale Sutton, 57, a San Diego dentist, carries ice atop his head and in hanging pouches near his cheeks as well as in the pockets of his running togs: pinstriped blue pajamas sliced with ventilation holes. He is known as the Pajama Man.

19   Runners stretch, mingle and pose for pictures—all in eerie quiet, because it is so early, or because they are about to wage combat, or because the open desert sky swallows up most of the sound. At 6 A.M., they assemble on the road. No speeches, no fanfare. They are told to go. They take off to the whoops and claps of the support crews.

20   In all the miles to follow, these will be the only spectators; no one else will appreciate their toil, except perhaps the whizzing motorists and the occasional bystanders who have stopped for a Coke or radiator coolant in towns hardly larger than a gas station.

21   At first the road climbs gradually north along the valley floor, away from hills and escarpments named Funeral Peak, Coffin Canyon and Dante's View. The ruddy desert loam tilts toward ridges to the east and falls to the yellow-white valley bowl to the west. For long stretches there is almost no vegetation, just rocky fields divided by the winding asphalt.

22   They move at a fast, easy gait. For superbly fit athletes, who train by doing 10 or 20 miles a day, the early stages of a long race often produce the euphoric sensation that they could go forever. Runners like to savor it, aware of their own breathing, the length and balance of their strides.

23   "I focus on what I'm doing, how I'm feeling," says the man who takes the early lead, Eric Clifton, one of America's great ultra-marathoners. "I'm constantly monitoring myself, keeping my legs relaxed, running smoothly, keeping my arm relaxed. Is my face tensed up? I'm trying to be as efficient as possible."

24   The 39-year old movie buff, a theater projectionist from Crownsville, Md., has won more than half of the 68 ultra-marathons he has completed; he set an unofficial record last year by running a 100-miler in 13 hours and 16 minutes. Like most who venture into such extreme races, Eric began more modestly, running the two-mile in high school, later dabbling in 5- and 10-kilometer road races. Once he realized his own exceptional stamina, he advanced to marathons and triathlons, then ultra-marathon cycling races.

25   With his long, pendular strides and short, pink socks, Eric moves well in front, followed by a pack that includes Lisa and the Major, steady at 9 minutes per mile.

26   At 7 A.M., the sun emerges above the Amargosas; it is 105 degrees—in the shade. At 7:15, it is 108. At 7:25, it is 110. A hot, dry wind pushes the competitors

along. Dragonflies blow around in it. Tinder-dry weeds quiver in the canyon washes. At Furnace Creek, 17 miles out, the runners veer northwest on California 190, passing a borax museum and descending again into the yawning desolation of a dry lake bed where the thermometer reads 114. The asphalt is at least 20 degrees hotter.

27   Faces and shirts are sweat-soaked. Support vans play leapfrog with the runners, moving ahead a mile or so at a time. Runners stop briefly to drink, many alternating water and electrolyte supplements. How much they drink, eat, weigh, how hot they are, how fast they are going—every detail is logged by crew members, who take on the mien of anxious scientists, recording the vitals of subjects in some grotesque lab experiment.

28   The body is already under enormous assault; the success of the hours ahead will hinge largely on the fickle alchemy of supplying it proper nutrition. Sweat loss alone in this heat can exceed a gallon an hour. Dehydration is a constant danger. Usually, it is accompanied by the depletion of blood sugar and electrolytes—sodium, potassium and other ions that are vital to cells and muscles.

29   Cells die; muscles cramp. In extreme cases, the heart may go into fibrillation, which can be fatal. More often, the body channels extra blood to the heart and brain, robbing it from other places—the skin, kidneys and bowels. A runner gets the chills. Kidneys clog with protein from damaged muscles, damming up toxins in the blood. The walls of the empty bladder sometimes rub at the pubic bone, causing internal bleeding and producing an intense urge to urinate. Pieces of the bowel or stomach wall may slough off in diarrhea.

30   Rarely, the body temperature climbs high enough, 104 degrees, to affect the brain; the runner may slip into convulsions or a coma.

31   Drinking is a safeguard, but huge amounts of water may overwhelm the gastrointestinal tract, causing cramps, bloating, nausea. Even sports drinks may not contain enough electrolytes—or the body may not absorb them well enough—to prevent problems. It is often a matter of luck, experience or genetics that enables one runner to endure while the man behind him folds up like a scarecrow.

DISTANCE RUNNER'S RITE OF PASSAGE

32   Badwater delivers its earliest savagery to those from cooler climes. A Swiss runner with stomach cramps is the first to drop out. Bjarte, the Norwegian, vomits after 18 miles—the beginnings of an agonizing downward spiral that would end with his surrender, 10 hours later, at Mile 53, by which point he had thrown up, in the estimation of one crew member, at least 40 more times.

33   A 33-year-old Canadian, Paul Braden, once ran a Colorado 100-miler in which his blisters got so bad he had to cut off his shoes with scissors, drain the wounds and go the last 15 miles with sandals taped to his feet. But that was not as agonizing as the cramps and nausea he now suffers as he nears Devil's Cornfield, a grove of clumpy arrow weed bushes 36 miles out.

34   With the wind raking across the road, with the temperature reaching 118 degrees, Paul drops a red flag—a legal means of temporarily leaving the course—and accepts a car ride to Stovepipe Wells, a burg at 41 miles consisting of a motel, a saloon and a convenience store. There, officials from Hi-Tec, the

athletic gear company that sponsors the race, help him into the back of a refrigerated bottled-water truck. His legs keep cramping and he is screaming so loud that a few tourists wander over, trying to see what is going on.

35   A white-haired race official administers a carbonated electrolyte beverage whose effect is immediate: Paul vomits all over the truck bed. The theory is that his balky digestion—gummed up by too much fruit—will now return to normal. Looking queasy, Paul is driven back to his flag. He resumes, suffers more cramps, ends up resting, falling asleep and finally dragging himself back onto the road in the evening, when the worst of the heat is over.

36   Finishing the race is the rite of passage of the distance runner. The sport culls out the weak and rewards the dogged. The runner learns that pain is temporary, but the gulf between those who drop out and those who finish is vast and enduring. With every step, an investment is made. It is either lost on the roadside or it becomes a jackpot that you reap at the end.

37   Having completed Badwater three times, Barbara Warren, a San Diego sports psychologist, has found that "the deep satisfaction in life comes from this enormous achievement. You feel like a giant."

38   Often, athletes spend months training and planning for Badwater, which raises the emotional stake in how it turns out. Paul tried to prepare himself for Death Valley by traveling to Amarillo, Texas, a month beforehand, running 10 to 15 miles a day in 100-degree heat.

39   The Major began training for Badwater in January, expanding his regimen to include twice-monthly workouts in the desert near Borrego Springs. Every trip he ran 25 to 30 miles, alone, bored, baking in the sun. "By the end of June, I had put in almost 1,600 miles just for this one race," he says. There are other forces: All the Marines at Camp Pendleton who know he is representing the Corps— what will they think if he quits? The lessons he learned from his mother, who has spent 27 years battling a degenerative stomach disorder, and his grandfather, who survived the same malady until he was 87, still mowing his lawn at 86.

40   If you get through a thing like Badwater, a lot of life's other problems seem far more manageable, the Major says. But the moment you let yourself quit, you step onto a slippery slope. One day you quit at 90 miles and the next you quit at 60. Before long you are getting by with the minimum, rationalizing mediocrity.

41   "Quitting is a disease," he says. "I can't bear the idea of looking in a mirror and seeing a quitter."

42   The Major is now bearing down on the 50-mile mark, nine miles beyond Stovepipe. It is well into afternoon. The road climbs; it will reach 6,000 feet at the end of the 18-mile stretch to Towne's Pass in the Panamint Mountains. The wind is coming downhill, and it is directly in the runners' faces—a steady blast that seems to come from some humongous hair dryer. No one runs; they walk tilting into the wind at comical angles, like a bunch of Charlie Chaplins.

43   The Marine Corps flag snaps wildly from the rear of the Major's support van. His face, faintly freckled, is rigid, his eyes fixed on the road. All of his elaborate philosophy has been bludgeoned down into a tight-lipped, 10-word mantra: "Mind over matter: If you don't mind, it doesn't matter."

44   Much of the first half of the field is scattered along the 18-mile climb. Eric is still well in front—he's already through the pass—trailed by a runner from

Tennessee and then Lisa, in third place, but well back and struggling. Her 10- and 12-minute miles have disintegrated to this: a mile logged at a woeful 25 minutes.

45   Nauseated, weakened by diarrhea that began the night before the race—a result of nerves, her crew thinks—she is limping too, with an air cast supporting her bad right ankle. It is still hot—107 at 4:30 P.M.—and she has at least 24 hours to go.

46   She tries not to think about the punishment ahead. Long-haired and purposeful, a former springboard diver at the University of Wisconsin, she is a staunch believer in mental strength, spiritualism, holistic healing. Like the Major, she is inspired by the courage of others: her younger sister, Julie, a member of her support crew, who overcame life-threatening surgery to repair three small holes in her heart; her cousin Joe, who was Lisa's age when he died last year of AIDS.

47   "He got a tattoo in New Orleans," she says. "Seven guys all used the same needle. All seven of them are dead."

48   Music from a movie they enjoyed together, "The Last of the Mohicans," plays on her headphones.

49   All the runners are adrift out here, sorting through their thoughts, weighing the reasons to push on. A few miles behind Lisa is the 69-year-old Texan, Beacham, who slumps into a folding chair to gulp water from a plastic bottle.

50   "This right here is pretty agonizing," he says, but nothing of the ordeal shows on his face, thin as a hawk's. Beacham looks as if everything soft in him has boiled away on the hard roads—and maybe it has. He runs 3,000 miles a year, seven or eight ultra-marathons.

51   Despite a poor spell at 38 miles, where he had to lie down and take some chicken noodle soup, he is keeping up at a formidable pace. The drive seems to come from a fear of growing old, says crew member Jim Davis, who is 58. Ultras are especially important to Beacham because without them, without all the training, he would figure to start withering away.

52   "I think he wants to get in as many of them as he can," Jim says, "before he gets to where he can't."

HALLUCINATIONS NOT UNCOMMON

53   Evening is falling. The corrugated mountains near Towne's Pass glow warm orange and black, painted by slanting sunlight and shadows. Bruised clouds blow over the ridges. At 7:30, the sun sinks into the clouds rimming 6,585-foot Panamint Butte, gone until morning, and a soft violet haze settles over Death Valley. The plum-colored Amargosas, where the day began, are a ruffled curtain across the other side of the world.

54   The heat subsides—it is 86 degrees at 8:10, when the first automobile headlights fill the shadows. Eric, the race leader, descends into the Panamint Valley, where indolent followers of Charles Manson are still said to inhabit the brushy foothills near the Barker Ranch.

55   Eric is now feeling it. Downhills are murder on the thighs; after the intense early pace, his are aching like "somebody was beating them with baseball bats." At Mile 68, near a motel stop called Panamint Springs, he is passed by a 45-year-

old investor named David Jones, who has yet to take a rest. Even when he had to vomit, up at the pass, he turned his head, retched and pressed on.

56   David opens a substantial lead. With the light fading in a landscape of rolling hills and ridges, Eric and Lisa contend for second place. A quick glance up to a stream of purple-orange clouds and Lisa sees a face—her cousin Joe's face, a vision that lasts an instant and is gone. It inspires her, but also saddens her. She cries. She tells her crew about it. Soon, the sky deepens, and even those tangled clouds disappear, leaving her there on the road toiling.

57   The darkness takes over. She sees a shooting star and is heartened by whatever hope it might portend, but before long she is crying again.

58   Night is hard. Night is for demons. Night is when rationality shrinks away, slipping down a rabbit hole, and nothing remains but the black asphalt and black sky and the questions that flicker through shorting mental circuits, like: Where is the horizon, what creatures are out here, why does it matter, really, to keep on going?

59   Hallucinations are not uncommon. Two years ago, when she got through Badwater in less than 42 hours, her first ultra-marathon, Lisa had a conversation with her dead grandmother. She heard babies crying, Indians chanting. "I saw things flying through the air," she remembers. "All the trees on Whitney, I thought they were people climbing."

60   Others have seen dogs, herds of cows, miniature people pushing tiny sleds, women showering, cactuses magically transformed into rocket launchers, highway skid marks shooting away like harpoons, flying off to infinity. One runner remembers an elaborate bridge under construction, spanning the highway, with an office building next door. Only the next day, when he was driving back over the course and looking for it, did he learn from his crew that all of it was pixie dust.

61   The runners are illuminated for periods of time by headlights, until the support vans pull ahead, leaving them to catch up again. At the west rim of Panamint Valley is another climb, through a 4,000-foot pass called Father Crowley's. It is cool enough there for long sleeves and sweatpants; the runners change during the stops. Here and there, they nap—half an hour, an hour, rarely longer.

62   Two more drop out, one because of a long, purple thigh bruise, the result of a pinched nerve and tendinitis. Eric goes lame on the downside of Crowley's; he dawdles through 10 miles in six hours and quits at dawn at Mile 94. Having won so many times, he places no stigma on stepping away, regrouping, aiming for another race. That is not the case for the less accomplished. For most who quit, the failure is a trauma almost equal to the pounding of the miles.

63   A runner who stops ceases to be a runner. It is a death of that identity, marked by an ignominious epitaph: "Did not finish." The phrase is abbreviated on the printouts that list the winners, and the slang verb, "DNF-ing," has an obscene sound, foul with shame. The runner who succumbs often goes to extraordinary lengths for resurrection, training for months and traveling back to the same race, the same course, a year or two later, to try again.

64   Twenty-four hours have gone by. Fatigue seeps like ice water into bones and joints. Walking is the rule now. Rest stops lengthen. Closing their eyes, they get

leg massages. They take time to patch blisters, tape their feet, change shoes. They go up half a size when the swelling is bad. They drink hot soup and get up with the painful slowness of old men.

65   Gossip travels up and down the course in irregular pulses, moving from race officials to support crews, then to the runners. They crave information about the whereabouts of others, how they are doing. Eric's withdrawal is surprising news. It is rare now that one runner sees another, except on arduous grades or during long stops when someone is passed.

66   Lisa slips into third place. Beacham drops back into 10th, an hour ahead of the Major. Only twice during the night has Beacham slept, once for 15 minutes, another time for 20. He maintains a steady pace through Crowley's despite a blister on the ball of each foot, wounds that have been growing for almost 60 miles.

67   "It was pretty painful until I got them lanced," he says, his breath as sharp as piston stokes. "They hurt now, but I can stand it."

68   Beyond the pass, the road levels out near 4,000 feet, angling northwest along the Saline Valley and the dry Owens Lake bed: contoured terrain that grows nothing but rust-colored scrub. A wall of white mountains fills the far horizon. This is another of Badwater's psychological slams. One of those distant, chiseled peaks is Whitney.

69   "You can see the finish," says a runner, "but it's 51 miles away."

70   The sun climbs into the blue vastness of space and they pass one by one down the long, rippled road, a line of asphalt that runs forever.

71   "The sun's coming up, and pretty soon the sun will go down, and that's what you have to think about," says Dale, the Pajama Man, who at 7 A.M. is distracting himself, playing mental word games, his gangly limbs swinging as if they are loose in their sockets. "You have to disassociate your body from the pain."

72   At a drink stop, he sips slowly, to avoid spitting it up, and tries to gauge his progress.

73   "I have, what? Thirty-five miles to go?"

74   "No," a crew member tells him. "Forty-seven."

"IT'S BEYOND EXHILARATION"

75   In spite of the distance remaining, race officials are able to make a reasonably accurate projection of the finishers. They can see who is going well, the ones who will probably hang on.

76   David Jones, victorious only once in 57 prior marathons and ultra-marathons, is far ahead in first, already nearing Lone Pine, the tree-lined town at the base of Whitney. He is on his way to clocking 29 hours and 10 minutes, more than five hours ahead of the man in second.

77   Most of the top 10 runners will earn a buckle. Beacham's blisters will continue to plague him, but he is on his way to finishing in 43 hours and 53 minutes, well under his goal of 50 hours. The Major limps on a swollen right knee and is chafing so badly in the crotch that a streak of blood runs to the knee of his white sweatpants. His crew has dubbed him "Mad Mood Maples"; he is headed for a time of 45:15.

78   At least 18 others are also on the way to finishing. Seven have quit. That number might reach eight. Lisa is the one in doubt—the only remaining runner in serious trouble who has not yet withdrawn.

79   At 102 miles, she clings to third, reeling from her bad ankle and diarrhea and sleep loss. To go the next six miles to Keeler takes her four hours. Lone Pine is 16 miles beyond Keeler. Morning turns to afternoon. The sun beats down; temperatures soar into the 90s. The highway veers right into Long Pine, past an airport, motels, diners, then left at a traffic light onto the two-lane road up Whitney.

80   This final stretch, a 4,000 foot ascent over 13 winding miles, is by far the most daunting. It begins gradually—the road flanked by sagebrush and boulders and tall rock formations that look like brown crispy cereal all glued together. Soon it rises to impossible steepness.

81   Lisa is still on the lower slopes at 3 o'clock, taking ice treatments on her ankles. They are both so badly swollen they barely move. Coming out of the motor home, she is staggering. Turning uphill, her mirrored glasses catching the hot sun, she looks ready to cry. Two crew members walk alongside, ready in case she should collapse.

82   "Never, Never Quit," says a spray-painted slogan across the back of the motor home, but sometimes such lofty ideals must give way to reason. Her crew huddles in the road, discussing whether to make her stop. Her mother, Dot, squints up the mountain.

83   "It's scary," she says. "She doesn't want to give up. I think we're trying to make the decision for her. My theory is, live to race another day."

84   Arguing for surrender is that in two weeks she is scheduled to compete in a 300-mile adventure race, a team event for which she and her friends have paid hefty entrance fees. It is unthinkable to miss it, but the recovery from an ultra-marathon can take weeks. Most runners are fortunate to begin training again in six or seven days; stamina may not return for a month or two.

85   Lisa, though, doesn't always make the rational decision. Crew member Tony Di Zinno remembers an earlier adventure race, when she suffered a sprained ankle and a hairline fracture of her right leg on the second day out. She strapped on an air cast and kept going, six more days, 250 more miles.

86   Her hope had been to break the women's record for Badwater—36 hours and 19 minutes, set during a race that began at night. That goal is now out of reach. With eight miles to go, Lisa disappears into the motor home. Sister Julie stands outside, helpless, wondering if this is where Lisa will yield.

87   "She says she's never felt this bad," Julie says. "She can't bend her ankles, they're so swollen. There's no blood in her urine yet, but she thinks she lost her stomach lining."

88   For almost half an hour, there is only this still-life picture: the motor home under a cloudless sky, the rugged mountainside rising above it. Now and then a breeze stirs, but all the air seems to move at once, muffling sounds, preserving a strange hush. Insects clicking softly in the sagebrush. Inside, Lisa lies on her ravaged stomach. She will explain later that it is unwise at this point to sleep: The body begins to shut down. Instead, she meditates. In her mind she makes a list

of all those reasons she should quit, the complaints of 127 horrific miles, every negative thought. When the list is as long as she can make it, she lights a tiny imaginary fire—and she burns it.

89   The door opens. She is helped down to the pavement, and she turns to confront the mountain.

90   "I'm going to get to the top."

91   Upward, then, with the road growing steeper. Her ankles cannot handle the slope, and so she turns around, walking backward, tiny three-inch steps. Up, up, up, staring into the sky, Whitney rising behind her. At 5:45, she is well up the mountain, the road at last curving into the afternoon shadows.

92   Pine trees begin to appear. Her legs look puffed up, rubbery, but they keep moving. Where the road levels out she turns around, walking forward until it rises again. At 6 o'clock, she has less than four miles to go. Every step is precarious, but her mood soars—"it's beyond exhilarating"—and she talks in strained breaths about a book, "The Power Within," by Chuck Norris, and how its lessons helped her through the hard moments.

93   Less than a mile to go and the road rounds a steep turn. Lisa goes through it backward, her arms out, as if dizzy. Immediately, four Marines—the advance guard from the Major's group—jump out of a van and join her, like jet fighters forming an escort, but they drop away after the final curve, letting Lisa take the last hill alone.

94   Whitney Portals, where the race ends, is tucked within a nook of chalky granite: a clear pool fed by a plunging waterfall, hillsides thick with tall evergreens. A yellow tape is stretched across the road and Lisa hits it, finishing in 37 hours and 1 minute. It is not the record she wanted, but it is the fastest a woman has gone from a daytime start, when the racers cross the floor of Death Valley in the heat.

95   Officials, crew members and five or six bystanders surround her, applauding. She is weeping, relieved, overjoyed, falling into the embrace of her sister, her mom, her friends. She looks up at the sky and says thank you. A huge bouquet of red roses is placed in her arms, spilling over them in a glorious scene of triumph—a portrait somehow perfect, but also fleeting, because Lisa quickly hands the roses away.

96   "Can't hold them," she whispers. "They're too heavy."

From David Ferrell, "Far Beyond a Mere Marathon," *Los Angeles Times*, August 23, 1997. © 1997 Los Angeles Times. Reprinted by permission of *Los Angeles Times* Syndication.

POSTSCRIPT

In July 2002, Pam Reed of Tucson, Arizona, became the first woman ever to win the Badwater Marathon, running the course in 27 hours and 56 minutes. She also shattered the women's record. The 2002 race was especially grueling because the temperatures at one point reached 123 degrees. Lisa Smith also ran in the 2002 race. Twenty-four runners of the seventy-nine who entered had "DNF" next to their names on the leader board.

Exercises

Do not refer to the selection for Exercises A and B unless your instructor directs you to do so.

A. DETERMINING THE MAIN IDEA AND PURPOSE

Choose the best answer.

_____ 1. The main idea of the selection is that

    a. ultra-races like Badwater should be abolished or at least regulated by the government.

    b. ultra-marathoners like those who enter the Badwater race are the elite of the running world.

    c. for running zealots, an ultra-marathon like Badwater is the supreme test of human character and the ability to endure.

    d. every year two or three dozen runners enter the Badwater race, and every year Badwater beats them down.

_____ 2. With respect to the main idea, the writer's purpose is to

    a. convince the reader that reform of ultra-races like Badwater is necessary.

    b. explain how the Badwater ultra-race works and why runners enter such races.

    c. discuss the physiological changes and long-term physical damage caused by participating in ultra-marathon races.

    d. trace the history of ultra-marathon races.

B. COMPREHENDING MAIN IDEAS

Choose the correct answer.

_____ 1. Every year around a third of the runners who attempt the Badwater race fail to finish because

    a. their physicians and trainers make them stop to avoid permanent damage.

    b. the torture they experience is greater than their desire to go on.

    c. they realize that their training was not sufficient to complete the race.

    d. they collapse, unable to continue.

_____ 2. The *primary* physical danger to runners in the Badwater race is

    a. hypothermia.

    b. kidney failure.

    c. loss of memory.

    d. heat stroke.

_____ 3. The beginning point of the race is at Badwater, known specifically as the Western Hemisphere's
   a. highest point.
   b. hottest point.
   c. lowest point.
   d. only salt-and-brimstone pool.

_____ 4. For runners who participate in the Badwater race, the most serious offense, one that assumes enormous significance for everyone concerned, is
   a. not having a reliable crew along the course.
   b. attempting the race without preparing for it adequately.
   c. quitting before reaching the end.
   d. letting down their sponsors.

_____ 5. Ferrell writes that those runners who do not finish the course (those who have "DNF" written next to their names on the list of entrants) generally
   a. decide to give up running permanently.
   b. suffer such physical damage that they can no longer compete in ultra-races.
   c. are scorned and ridiculed by their fellow runners.
   d. train even harder for the race the next year.

_____ 6. Lisa Smith, the only woman to enter this particular year's race (in 1997), eventually made it to the finish line on Mt. Whitney by
   a. crawling on her hands and knees.
   b. walking backwards.
   c. experiencing a last-minute burst of energy.
   d. becoming revitalized by her family's support.

COMPREHENSION SCORE

Score your answers for Exercises A and B as follows:

A. No. right _____ × 2 = _____

B. No. right _____ × 1 = _____

Total points from A and B _____ × 10 = _____ percent

You may refer to the selection as you work through the remaining exercises.

C. DISTINGUISHING BETWEEN FACT AND OPINION

For each of the following statements from the selection, write F if the statement represents a factual statement that can be verified or O if the statement represents the writer's or someone else's subjective interpretation. The first two are done for you.

1. _____ Every year, two or three dozen elite ultra-marathoners come to Badwater, and every year Badwater beats them down.

2. _____ For a thin slice of society—zealots who live to train, who measure themselves by their mental toughness—the ultra-marathon is the consummate test of human character.

3. _____ About a third fail to finish; after 50 miles or 70 miles or 110 miles, the torture exceeds their desire to go on, and they end up rolling away in their cars or minivans, faces covered with wet towels, their bodies stretched out like corpses.

4. _____ No other event in sport, except possibly a prizefight, is as punishing, as demanding of the mind and body.

5. _____ No other athlete is more revered than the distance runner.

6. _____ To fill the unforgiving minute, to persevere, is one of the highest ideals of man—who, after all, was born to hardship, cast from Eden.

7. _____ The explosion of extreme sports in recent years has produced an unprecedented number of ultra-endurance races.

8. _____ Several thousand men and women travel the country—and abroad—competing in events from 30 miles to more than 300 miles.

D. MAKING INFERENCES

For each of these statements write Y (yes) if the inference is an accurate one, N (no) if the inference is an inaccurate one, or CT (can't tell) if the writer does not give you enough information to make an inference one way or another.

1. _____ Badwater is an unusual kind of ultra-marathon because the outcome is not guaranteed. [paragraph 15]

2. _____ For the runners who enter the Death Valley race, competition among them is keen, and their desire to place first is their main motivation to finish. [paragraph 12]

3. _____ During the race, participants must run at all times; walking is not permitted. [selection as a whole]

4. _____ If Lisa Smith had started the Badwater race at night, rather than during the day, her finish time would probably have been better. [selection as a whole]

5. _____ Runners from cool climates, for example, Switzerland or Norway, are at a disadvantage because they do not train in the hot-weather conditions that they will encounter in the real race. [paragraph 32]

6. _____ Ferrell is a marathon runner. [selection as a whole]

E. INTERPRETING MEANING AND ANALYZING STRUCTURE

Where appropriate, write your answers to these questions in your own words.

1. _____   Which sentence *best* represents the thesis of the article as a whole?
   a. "Badwater is a madman's march, a footrace through the summer heat of the hottest spot in America."
   b. "Every year, two or three dozen elite ultra-marathoners come to Badwater, and every year Badwater beats them down."
   c. "For a thin slice of society—zealots who live to train, who measure themselves by their mental toughness—the ultra-marathon is the consummate test of human character."
   d. "The explosion of extreme sports in recent years has produced an unprecedented number of ultra-endurance races."

Explain the reason for your answer. _____

_____

2. What are some characteristics of long-distance runners who enter ultra-marathons like the one Ferrell describes? List two or three qualities that the writer emphasizes. _____

_____

3. Identify three metaphors or similes—imaginative comparisons—in paragraph 1. _____

_____

4. An *allusion* is a reference to something outside a particular piece of writing. Allusions can refer to literature, religion, historical events, and so forth. In paragraph 5, Ferrell writes that the peak of Mt. Whitney is as distant as Oz, and at the end of paragraph 7, he writes, "To fill the unforgiving minute, to persevere, is one of the highest ideals of man—who, after all, was born to hardship, cast from Eden." Consult a dictionary if necessary, and explain these two allusions in your own words.

   Oz   _____

   _____

   Eden   _____

   _____

5. Look again at paragraphs 95 and 96, and then explain the irony in Lisa Smith's handing the bouquet of red roses away. _____

_____

F. UNDERSTANDING VOCABULARY

Choose the best definition according to an analysis of word parts or the context.

_____ **1.** the *undulating* highway [paragraph 5]:
   a. having a wavy appearance
   b. tortuous, twisting and turning
   c. poorly maintained
   d. radiating heat

_____ **2.** the *consummate* test [7]:
   a. well-publicized
   b. requiring energy
   c. impossible to complete
   d. supreme, perfect

_____ **3.** *indefatigable,* heroic [7]:
   a. athletic in appearance
   b. difficult to comprehend
   c. tireless
   d. handsome, attractive

_____ **4.** an *unprecedented* number [8]:
   a. infinite, uncountable
   b. having no previous example
   c. small, tiny
   d. having no equal, unsurpassed

_____ **5.** willing to dispense *exhortations* [17]:
   a. words of encouragement
   b. words to discourage
   c. complaints
   d. good fortunes

_____ **6.** the *mien* of anxious scientists [27]:
   a. interest, curiosity
   b. appearance, manner
   c. field of specialization
   d. politeness, courtesy

_____ **7.** The sport *culls* out the weak [36]:
   a. removes
   b. determines
   c. strengthens
   d. makes allowances for

_____ **8.** the same *malady* [39]:
   a. tension
   b. heredity
   c. illness
   d. adventure

_____ **9.** a *staunch* believer [46]:

    a. firm
    b. without much conviction
    c. enthusiastic
    d. unwilling

_____ **10.** The heat *subsides* [54]:

    a. grows worse
    b. remains the same
    c. lessens in intensity
    d. disappears

_____ **11.** the most *daunting* [80]:

    a. visible
    b. discouraging
    c. easy to accomplish
    d. irritating

_____ **12.** Every step is *precarious* [92]:

    a. easy to complete
    b. close to the goal
    c. uncertain, unstable
    d. exhausting, fatiguing

G. USING VOCABULARY

In parentheses before each sentence are some inflected forms of words from the selection. Study the context and the sentence. Then write the correct form in the space provided.

1. (*zeal, zealot, zealotry, zealous, zealously*) Ferrell describes the Badwater

marathon runners as _____ athletes who push themselves often beyond what is physically safe.

2. (*eeriness, eerie, eerily*) The morning that the race begins is _____ quiet.

3. (*euphoria, euphoric, euphorically*) Superbly fit athletes often feel a sense of

_____ , feeling as if they could run forever.

4. (*indolence, indolent, indolently*) One cannot say that ultra-marathon runners

view life _____ .

5. (*portent, portend, portentous, portentously*) A runner might look upon a

shooting star as a _____ of what is to come the next day.

6. (*ignominy, ignominious, ignominiously*) Quitting before the end is considered

an _____ defeat, marked by the insulting acronym "DNF."

H. SUMMARIZING EXERCISE

Read paragraph 36 again (left column). On the right is a summary of the information in it.

Original Passage

Finishing the race is the rite of passage of the distance runner. The sport culls out the weak and rewards the dogged. The runner learns that pain is temporary, but the gulf between those who drop out and those who finish is vast and enduring. With every step, an investment is made. It is either lost on the roadside or it becomes a jackpot that you reap at the end.

Summary

The runner who completes the race is rewarded for endurance and the ability to withstand pain, but the runner who drops out suffers emotional pain far worse than the physical discomfort during the race, and it lasts forever.

Study this summary. Then write a summary of paragraph 63.

Original Passage

A runner who stops ceases to be a runner. It is a death of that identity, marked by an ignominious epitaph: "Did not finish." The phrase is abbreviated on the printouts that list the winners, and the slang verb, "DNF-ing," has an obscene sound, foul with shame. The runner who succumbs often goes to extraordinary lengths for resurrection, training for months and traveling back to the same race, the same course, a year or two later, to try again.

Summary

I.   TOPICS FOR WRITING OR DISCUSSION

1. In what ways are the runners who subject themselves to the punishing demands of the Badwater marathon different from athletes who participate in regular athletic competition (non-extreme sports contests)?

2. What might be some reasons to account for the "explosion of extreme sports in recent years" that Ferrell notes in the article?
3. Write a paragraph in which you analyze some of the devices that Ferrell uses to make these runners' experiences so vivid and striking.

For Further Exploration

BOOK

Jon Krakauer, *Into Thin Air* (1997). A writer for *Outdoor* magazine, Krakauer took part in an ill-fated 1996 expedition to Mt. Everest that resulted in the deaths of eight climbers, including Rob Hall, one of Everest's most experienced and respected guides. Krakauer explores the factors leading up to the disaster and the reasons that Mt. Everest remains perhaps the ultimate challenge for extreme-sports enthusiasts.

MOVIE

Chariots of Fire (1981), a British film directed by Hugh Hudson, is the true story of two young men who trained for and participated in the 1924 Olympics. It received the Oscar for Best Picture.

WEB SITES

- David Ferrell's other stories in the *Times* extreme-sports series can be read at *www.latimes.com*. Go to the archives, enter the author's name, and scroll down to 1997. (There is a small fee for downloading.)
- Information and photographs about Death Valley are available here: *www.americansouthwest.net/california/death_valley/national_park.html*

Persuasive Writing and Evaluating Evidence

In this introductory section, these are the topics for discussion:

- The principles of persuasive writing
- How to read persuasive writing
- Types of claims
- The structure of an argument
- Kinds of evidence
- The refutation
- Bias

The Principles of Persuasive Writing

As you recall from the introduction to Part 1, to *persuade* is one of the primary purposes in writing. The art of persuasion is a worthwhile skill to develop. Consider its usefulness in practical terms. Let's say that you have been working at your current part-time job for a year; you think you have done a good job, you take on new responsibilities willingly and without complaint, you come on time, and you don't fool around on the job. But you haven't had a raise. How would you approach your boss to ask for a higher salary? What reasons would you give in support of your request? You might point to your fine qualities listed above. You would certainly wait to make sure that he or she was in a good mood and not stressed out about meeting deadlines or dealing with grumpy customers. You would point out your loyalty, your dedication to the job, and other equally stellar traits. And if you were lucky, you might succeed in getting that raise. This real-life example shows that understanding the tactics of persuasion can yield tangible rewards.

Learning to read persuasive prose with understanding and a critical eye also yields rewards. It is the basis on which our democratic society is built. A significant part of being a good citizen is finding out the issues of the day, weighing the arguments for and against proposed policies, and coming to a decision on your own, not one imposed on you by someone else. The right to make informed decisions on one's own is one of many rewards of living in a democratic country with a free press and the unhindered freedom to express oneself without fear of punishment, retaliation, or censorship, as occurs in repressive societies. More broadly, learning to see issues from a variety of perspectives, not merely from one person's (or our own) narrow point of view is an important part of becoming an educated citizen.

The six reading selections in Part 4 represent various styles of persuasive writing. Reading them and working through the exercises—which differ markedly from those in the rest of the text—will help you learn to read prose expressing an opinion.

The Aims of Persuasive Writing

Persuasive writing essentially aims to convince you in various ways of something. A person may try to convince you to accept his or her point of view. Politicians do this all the time, when they try to persuade us that they are the best candidate for public office. Someone may try to convince you to change your thoughts or behavior, as when a missionary exhorts you to embrace religion. Someone may try to persuade you to take action—quit smoking, protest against war, volunteer in a soup kitchen—or simply to consider that another point of view has merit. All of these are common aims of persuasion and of persuasive writing as well.

AIMS OF PERSUASIVE WRITING
• To convince you to accept a particular point of view
• To convince you to change your thinking
• To convince you to take action
• To convince you to at least consider that another point of view has merit

The six pieces representing persuasive writing come from many sources. Three are editorials originally published in the *Wall Street Journal,* the *Los Angeles Times,* and the *Boston Globe.* The *Washington Post* article is a feature piece by a science writer who presents the ethical problems associated with the very controversial issue of human cloning. The other two are opinion pieces taken from the *Utne Reader,* a magazine devoted to reprinting unusual material from the alternative press. The subjects are equally varied: one writer's theory about the cause of violence in adolescent males, the damage caused by excessive competition in sports, global warming, a reevaluation of the concept of heroism following the September 11 terrorist attacks, the problems of homeless and mentally ill people on the streets of Los Angeles, and human cloning.

How to Read Persuasive Writing

When you read the opinion pieces in Part 4 and in other sources like your daily newspaper, you should first ask yourself what the writer's purpose is and what is the aim of the essay or article. By definition, persuasive writing presents a controversial issue that is open to discussion. Also by definition, a persuasive piece will present the writer's subjective opinions. But there is wide latitude in what a persuasive writer can do: Some writers present two or even three points of view and leave you to make up your own mind about where you stand. Other writers make more obvious attempts to change your mind or to persuade you to adopt their position by resorting to bias, slanted language, emotional appeals, and other manipulative devices.

Whichever techniques the opinion writer uses, the most important step—and your starting point—is to determine his or her central *argument* (also called the *claim*), the proposition or idea to be backed and defended, which lies at the heart of the piece. Like the thesis statement in an *informative* (or *expository*) essay, the claim or argument in a persuasive piece may be either *stated* directly or *implied*. Those who study argumentation classify claims into three types: *claims of fact*, *claims of value*, and *claims of policy*.

Types of Claims

CLAIMS OF FACT

Claims of fact can be verified, measured, tested, and proved by citing factual evidence, the results of scientific research, or in the case of predictions, by the passage of time. Examples of claims of fact include:

- Smoking causes numerous health problems for long-term smokers.
- Genetically modified crops will help feed Third World nations.
- The Los Angeles Lakers will win another NBA title next year.

CLAIMS OF VALUE

Claims of value are harder to prove than are claims of fact, because claims of value involve matters of taste, morality, opinion, and ideas about right and wrong. Examples of such claims include:

- Community colleges offer students a good education at relatively little cost.
- Broccoli tastes better than spinach.
- *Minority Report* was an intriguing, engaging movie about a serious subject—the degree to which civil liberties can be abrogated to fight crime.

Support for claims of value would be in the form of reasons, examples, and personal experience.

CLAIMS OF POLICY

Claims of policy argue for a course of action, propose a change, or identify a problem that needs a solution. Note that these types of claims may include words like *should, must,* or *ought to*. Examples of claims of policy include:

- Because of overcrowded classes, Centerville Community College should raise its tuition so that more teachers can be hired.
- Elementary schools must do their part to discourage obesity in the nation's children and remove candy and soft drink machines from campuses.
- We ought to boycott movies that glamorize smoking and illegal drug use.

Claims of policy are typically supported by good reasons, facts and statistics, examples, or the testimony of authorities or experts.

The Structure of an Argument

An argumentative piece must be clearly organized if the writer is to get the point across effectively and to convince the audience to adopt the particular claim. Not every argument you read will look exactly like this. Many writers, for example, prefer to save the claim for the end of the piece, after assembling sufficient evidence. All good opinion pieces should include an introduction in which the author provides background, introduces the subject, perhaps engages the reader with an anecdote, and *may* contain the argument or claim, the body, which contains evidence to support or prove the claim, the refutation, a section, usually quite short, in which the writer considers *opposing views* and offers a counterargument against them (many editorials and persuasive pieces do not contain refutations), and a conclusion, which may contain the claim, recommend future action, give a warning about what will happen if the claim is not accepted, or state the seriousness of the problem.

The first step in reading opinion pieces is to locate the *claim* and then identify the *supporting evidence*. You may have to separate the two, because some writers mix the claim and the evidence in the same sentence. For example, consider this sentence:

> Because obesity has become such a serious health risk for our nation's children (the government estimates that 11 percent of American children are obese), our public schools should encourage children to walk or ride their bikes to school and should eliminate candy and snack food machines from school grounds.

Which part of the sentence represents the claim and which part represents the evidence? Write the claim in the first space.

Claim: _____

_____

Evidence: _____

_____

Kinds of Evidence

After you have located the writer's argument or claim, then you can identify and evaluate the *evidence* used to support it. Writers of opinion pieces may use a single kind of evidence, or they may combine various kinds. The most common kinds of evidence include facts and statistics, such as may appear in scientific studies, research reports, government-sponsored investigations, census reports, clinical tests, and so forth; examples and observations drawn from the writer's own experience or from his or her reading; or rational, plausible explanations that justify the writer's point of view and answer the question "why."

Let's look at a relatively short editorial to see if we can identify its structure. This piece is an unsigned editorial from the *Washington Post National Weekly Edition.* (An unsigned editorial means that it was written by a member of the newspaper staff without a byline identifying the particular writer.) I have annotated the piece for you, paragraph by paragraph, pointing out the significant elements.

1-2 Intro: Situation and reason for controversy: Planned Parenthood challenged right to patient records—privacy vs. law enforcement needs.

1   In May, a dead newborn baby was discovered in a recycling center in Storm Lake, Iowa. Police apparently had no leads and thought that finding the child's mother would be the best way to discover what had happened. So prosecutors subpoenaed records from area hospitals concerning women who had received positive pregnancy tests in the preceding nine months.

2   Others seem to have quietly complied, but a Planned Parenthood clinic balked—citing the medical records privacy of the women whom it serves—and went to court. A district court ordered that it turn over the records by Aug. 17. But the Iowa Supreme Court stayed that order, so the case could end up being a major legal showdown between medical privacy rights and law enforcement.

3–4 Body: Reason 1—investigation too broad, not focused on one person. 2—unlikely culprit would be found from PP's records. 3—PP's patients promised confidentiality.

3   It is routine enough for law enforcement to seek private medical information about a particular suspect in a case, so if authorities were investigating an individual, there would likely be no controversy. But the subpoena in Iowa is disturbing because it is so wildly broad. There is no particular reason to think that the baby's mother used this clinic, so the likelihood of a payoff to investigators is quite small.

4   But lots of innocent women did use the clinic and were promised confidentiality when they did so, and the cost to their privacy could be substantial. Some of these women likely had abortions—though the clinic in question does not perform them—and their families may not have known about their pregnancies. Some may have miscarried and wish to keep that secret. This is not the sort of pond in which fishing expeditions are appropriate.

5 Refutation: No one wants baby's killer to go free, but value of investigation must be weighed against damage. Conclu: Request must be narrower.

Claim: Should respect privacy of PP's patients.

5   Nobody wants to see a baby-killer go unpunished. But eventually, the likely efficacy of any investigative step must be measured against the damage it may do. It is certainly wrong to permit sweeping law enforcement access to this sort of sensitive information without a reasonable balancing of important privacy interests and an insistence that any request be as narrow as possible. That has not happened here. The medical privacy of Planned Parenthood's patients deserve more respect.

—"A Question of Medical Privacy," *The Washington Post,* August 11, 2002. © *The Washington Post.* Reprinted with permission.

First, read the annotations column and be sure that you know the meanings of any unfamiliar words in the editorial. Then in your own words, state the primary *claim* in this editorial. Next identify the type of claim—fact, value, or policy. (Note that there may be both a primary and a secondary type of claim.) Be sure not to include any supporting evidence in this section.

Claim: _____

_____

_____

_____

Now list four pieces of supporting evidence. Use the annotations to help you. After you write each one, identify the type of evidence according to this list: facts and statistics; examples and observations; good reasons; or quotation or testimony.

Evidence: _____

_____

_____

_____

_____

_____

_____

_____

Conclusion: _____

The Refutation

The final step in reading persuasive pieces is to look for a *refutation,* wherein the writer deals with the opposing side. Note that many editorial writers do not include a refutation, but when there is one, the writer usually *concedes* that there is some merit to the opposing side (after all, every question has two sides, and often more) and then takes one or two of the opposition's major arguments and *refutes* them, offering counterarguments against them. In the *Washington Post* editorial you just read, for example, the writer provides the briefest of refutations, when he or she says, "Nobody wants to see a baby-killer go unpunished. But eventually, the likely efficacy of any investigative step must be measured against the damage it may do."

Let's examine these two sentences in more detail. The first sentence represents a *concession;* the writer does not want to be thought heartless or lenient toward those who commit a vicious crime. The second sentence begins the *refutation,* starting with the word *but.* In effect, the writer is saying that although murderers should be punished, the way the state is going about identifying the murderer is wrong.

A real-life example will help you understand this process better. Let's say that you live near a dangerous intersection where several major accidents have occurred involving injuries to pedestrians who were trying to cross the street. You and your neighbors request a meeting of the municipal transportation and safety board at which you explain the problem, give evidence that the problem is serious, and offer a solution: The intersection is so dangerous that it needs a stoplight.

The safety director counters your proposal by saying that the city's budget is tight, that a new light will cost $100,000, and that the community has more pressing needs to meet. For example, the city has just committed the same amount of money to an after-school program for disadvantaged boys and girls. Hard to argue against that!

Still, you and your neighbors are convinced that your position is right. You prepare your refutation and come up with the following counterarguments:

1. An after-school program for disadvantaged youth is surely a worthy cause (your concession), but the board needs to reexamine its priorities. Saving the lives of pedestrians is more important. Also, a stoplight is the city's responsibility—an after-school club is not. It would be more appropriate to seek funding for a club from private grants and charitable foundations. (This is your first counterargument.)
2. Your second counterargument appeals to the board's conscience: If a stoplight isn't installed, more injuries will occur, and someone might die. Although $100,000 might seem like a lot of money for a simple stoplight, it will be money well spent. A human life is more precious than the $100,000 saved by not installing one. How many people must die or be seriously injured before the board decides that a light is necessary?
3. Your third counterargument appeals to the emotions: It's unconscionable that the board is willfully ignoring traffic hazards.
4. Finally, you offer some hard evidence refuting the board's contention that the town doesn't have enough money in its budget for the project: Recently, the local newspaper ran a series of articles criticizing some frivolous expenditures at City Hall. For example, the mayor redecorated her office at taxpayer expense, buying leather couches, matching chairs, an expensive Persian rug, and installing a bar; she also requisitioned a new limousine. Surely pedestrians' lives are more important than an elegant mayor's office and a fancy car.

Your refutation might work, or it might not, but at least you have dealt with your opponent's primary objections to spending this money.

These various counterarguments demonstrate the forms that a refutation can take. The writer may agree that there is some merit to the opposition but that the issue is more serious or complicated than the opponent realizes. The writer may argue that the opposing argument is somehow flawed. Finally, and probably most effective, the writer may admonish the opponent by warning of the consequences of not acting. Or the reverse might be appropriate. For example, when George W. Bush and many Republican supporters argued for going to war to remove the Iraqi leader Saddam Hussein, many writers, scholars, and government officials argued for *not* acting because attacking Iraq would have severe political and economic consequences.

When you read persuasive pieces, look for a refutation. The best opinion writers anticipate their opponents' objections and offer a rebuttal.

Bias

Last, when you read opinion pieces, look for evidence of *bias*—prejudice or unfair, preconceived ideas. Obviously, complete objectivity is humanly impossible, since we are all the products of our environment, ethnic and religious heritage, social class, and the like. Yet a writer should not come across as having an axe to grind—a particular point of view that he or she bludgeons the reader with. You can ask yourself if the writer treats the issue fairly, whether there is sufficient evidence to support the argument, and whether the writer appeals to your sense of reason or to your emotions (or perhaps to both). There is nothing wrong with a writer's appealing to the emotions, as long as you are aware that it is going on.

One other suggestion: You are not being wishy-washy if you read an editorial and are unable to come to a conclusion about which side you favor. Complex issues require complex analysis. And complex issues produce plenty of argument but few workable solutions. Good readers do not necessarily become immediate converts to one side or the other. Before taking a decisive stance that agrees with your general outlook and perspective, you can read more material expressing other points of view. Reading the op-ed pages of the daily newspaper and looking up information on the World Wide Web and in Internet newsgroups are important ways of getting more information about the serious issues of the day.

In sum, if you know what to look for when you tackle persuasive prose, your reading will be at once more critical and more intelligent; and this awareness will serve you well for the rest of your life.

PART FOUR

Reading about Issues

22

BILL McKIBBEN

The Environmental Issue from Hell

In this opinion piece, Bill McKibben writes about global warming, a problem he characterizes as "the great moral crisis of our time." McKibben is the author of The End of Nature *and* Enough: Staying Human in an Engineering Age. *This piece was originally published in the progressive newsmagazine* In These Times *and reprinted in the* Utne Reader.

Vocabulary Preview

WORD HISTORIES

Boycott [paragraph 12]   A *boycott* refers to the action of people banding together and refusing to buy or deal with a particular business, used as a tactic to force change. An *eponymous* word is a word derived from a person's name. *Boycott* comes from Charles G. Boycott, a nineteenth-century land agent for the English in Ireland. Boycott's story was a complicated one,[1] but in essence, he was run out of town after he refused to lower the rent of a couple of his tenants whose crops had failed. His name is now forever attached to the practice of boycotting, not just in English, but in other languages as well.

WORD PARTS

Equivalent [paragraph 3]   McKibben writes that driving a big SUV for one year is "the *equivalent* of opening your refrigerator door and then forgetting to close it for six years," in terms of the amount of carbon dioxide produced. The prefix *equi-* indicates "equality." *Equivalent* therefore means "equal in value or measure." Here are some other words with this prefix:

equilibrium	state of balance due to the equal action of opposing forces [*equi-* + *libra* ("balance")]
equinox	the two times of the year when the length of the day and the length of the night are approximately equal [*equi-* + *nox* or *noct-* ("night")]
equidistant	equally distant from one another

What does this word mean? Check a dictionary if you are unsure.

equivocal _____

---

[1]A fascinating account of Boycott and his troubles can be found in a little book written by his great great-niece: Rosie Boycott, *Batty, Bloomers, and Boycott: A Little Etymology of Eponymous Words* (1983). New York: Peter Bedrick Books, pp. 25–26.

**WORD
FAMILIES**

Magnitude [paragraph 2]   A microscope *magnifies* things or provides *magnification.* *Magnitude* means "great size or amount." All three words come from the root *magnus,* meaning "large" or "great." You can also see the same root in these two words:

magnificent   great in splendor, lavish
magnanimous   generous in giving or in forgiving an insult [*magnus* + *animus* ("spirit")]

If a student graduates from college *magna cum laude,* what does that mean? _____

_____

What is a real estate *magnate*? _____

BILL McKIBBEN

The Environmental Issue from Hell

1   When global warming first emerged as a potential crisis in the late 1980s, one academic analyst called it "the public policy problem from hell." The years since have only proven him more astute: Fifteen years into our understanding of climate change, we have yet to figure out how we're going to tackle it. And environmentalists are just as clueless as anyone else: Do we need to work on lifestyle or on lobbying, on photovoltaics or on politics? And is there a difference? How well we handle global warming will determine what kind of century we inhabit—and indeed what kind of planet we leave behind. The issue cuts close to home and also floats off easily into the abstract. So far it has been the ultimate "can't get there from here" problem, but the time has come to draw a road map—one that may help us deal with the handful of other issues on the list of real, world-shattering problems.

2   Typically, when you're mounting a campaign, you look for self-interest, you scare people by saying what will happen to us if we don't do something: All the birds will die, the canyon will disappear beneath a reservoir, we will choke to death on smog. But in the case of global warming, that doesn't exactly do the trick, at least in the time frame we're discussing. In temperate latitudes, climate change will creep up on us. Severe storms already have grown more frequent and more damaging. The progression of seasons is less steady. Some agriculture is less reliable. But face it: Our economy is so enormous that it takes those changes in stride. Economists who work on this stuff talk about how it will shave a percentage or two off the GNP over the next few decades. And most of us live lives so divorced from the natural world that we hardly notice the changes anyway. Hotter? Turn up the air-conditioning. Stormier? Well, an enormous percentage of Americans commute from remote-controlled garage to office parking garage—it may have been some time since they got good and wet in a rainstorm. By the time the magnitude of the change is truly in our faces, it will be too late to do much about it: There's such a lag time to increased levels of

carbon dioxide in the atmosphere that we need to be making the switch to solar and wind and hydrogen power right now to prevent disaster decades away. Yesterday, in fact.

3   So maybe we should think of global warming in a different way—as the great moral crisis of our time, the equivalent of the civil rights movement of the 1960s.

4   Why a moral question? In the first place, no one's ever figured out a more effective way to screw the marginalized and poor of this planet than climate change. Having taken their dignity, their resources, and their freedom under a variety of other schemes, we now are taking the very physical stability on which their already difficult lives depend.

5   Our economy can absorb these changes for a while, but consider Bangladesh for a moment. In 1998 the sea level in the Bay of Bengal was higher than normal, just the sort of thing we can expect to become more frequent and severe. The waters sweeping down the Ganges and the Brahmaputra rivers from the Himalayas could not drain easily into the ocean—they backed up across the country, forcing most of its inhabitants to spend three months in thigh-deep water. The fall rice crop didn't get planted. We've seen this same kind of disaster over the past few years in Mozambique and Honduras and Venezuela and other places.

6   And global warming is a moral crisis, too, if you place any value on the rest of creation. Coral reef researchers indicate that these spectacularly intricate ecosystems are also spectacularly vulnerable. Rising water temperatures are likely to bleach them to extinction by mid-century. In the Arctic, polar bears are 20 percent scrawnier than they were a decade ago: As pack ice melts, so does the opportunity for hunting seals. All in all, the 21st century seems poised to see extinctions at a rate not observed since the last big asteroid slammed into the planet. But this time the asteroid is us.

7   It's a moral question, finally, if you think we owe any debt to the future. No one ever has figured out a more thoroughgoing way to strip-mine the present and degrade what comes after—all the people who will ever be related to you. Ever. No generation yet to come will ever forget us—we are the ones present at the moment when the temperature starts to spike, and so far we have not reacted. If it had been done to us, we would loathe the generation that did it, precisely as we will one day be loathed.

8   But trying to launch a moral campaign is no easy task. In most moral crises, there is a villain—some person or class or institution that must be overcome. Once the villain is identified, the battle can commence. But you can't really get angry at carbon dioxide, and the people responsible for its production are, well, us. So perhaps we need some symbols to get us started, some places to sharpen the debate and rally ourselves to action. There are plenty to choose from: our taste for ever bigger houses and the heating and cooling bills that come with them, our penchant for jumping on airplanes at the drop of a hat. But if you wanted one glaring example of our lack of balance, you could do worse than point the finger at sport utility vehicles.

9   SUVs are more than mere symbols. They are a major part of the problem— we emit so much more carbon dioxide now than we did a decade ago in part

because our fleet of cars and trucks actually has gotten steadily less fuel efficient for the past 10 years. If you switched today from the average American car to a big SUV, and drove it for just one year, the difference in carbon dioxide that you produced would be the equivalent of opening your refrigerator door and then forgetting to close it for six years. SUVs essentially are machines for burning fossil fuel that just happen to also move you and your stuff around.

10   But what makes them such a perfect symbol is the brute fact that they are simply unnecessary. Go to the parking lot of the nearest suburban supermarket and look around: The only conclusion you can draw is that to reach the grocery, people must drive through three or four raging rivers and up the side of a canyon. These are semi-military machines, armored trucks on a slight diet. While they do not keep their occupants appreciably safer, they do wreck whatever they plow into, making them the perfect metaphor for a heedless, supersized society.

11   That's why we need a much broader politics than the Washington lobbying that's occupied the big environmental groups for the past decade. We need to take all the brilliant and energetic strategies of local grassroots groups fighting dumps and cleaning up rivers and apply those tactics in the national and international arenas. That's why some pastors are starting to talk with their congregations about what cars to buy, and why some college seniors are passing around petitions pledging to stay away from the Ford Explorers and Excursions, and why some auto dealers have begun to notice informational picketers outside their showrooms on Saturday mornings urging customers to think about gas mileage when they look at cars.

12   The point is not that such actions by themselves—any individual actions—will make any real dent in the levels of carbon dioxide pouring into our atmosphere. Even if you got 10 percent of Americans really committed to changing their energy use, their solar homes wouldn't make much of a difference in our national totals. But 10 percent would be enough to change the politics around the issue, enough to pressure politicians to pass laws that would cause us all to shift our habits. And so we need to begin to take an issue that is now the province of technicians and turn it into a political issue, just as bus boycotts began to make public the issue of race, forcing the system to respond. That response is likely to be ugly—there are huge companies with a lot to lose, and many people so tied in to their current ways of life that advocating change smacks of subversion. But this has to become a political issue—and fast. The only way that may happen, short of a hideous drought or monster flood, is if it becomes a personal issue first. ✷

From Bill McKibben, "The Environmental Issue from Hell," In *These Times*, April 30, 2001. Reprinted by permission.

Exercises

You may refer to the selection as you complete these exercises. Write your answers to these questions in the spaces provided.

A. IDENTIFYING THE CLAIM

1. Using your own words as much as possible, write down McKibben's central claim or proposition. Also indicate the number of the paragraph in which this claim is made. _____

_____

_____

2. Then decide if the claim is a claim of fact, a claim of value, or a claim of policy. Remember that an argument may include a secondary type of claim as well. _____

B. LOCATING EVIDENCE AND REFUTATION

1. One piece of evidence is listed for you. List two other major pieces of evidence that the writer uses to support the claim. Also characterize each piece of evidence according to whether it represents facts and statistics, examples and observations, good reasons, or quotation or testimony.

   a. Although we may not see the damage done because the changes in the atmosphere occur so slowly, there

   is already evidence of climate and seasonal changes. [observations]

   _____

   b. _____

   _____

   _____

   c. _____

   _____

   _____

2. Finally, if there is a refutation, list that as well. _____

_____

_____

C. IDENTIFYING SOLUTIONS

1. Does McKibben provide a solution to the problem he discusses? If so, write it in the space provided. Be sure to use your own words. _____

_____

_____

_____

2. What is your proposal to help solve this problem? _____

_____

_____

_____

D. USING VOCABULARY

Here are some words from the selection. Write an original sentence using each word that shows both that you know how to use the word and what it means. The number of the paragraph in which the word occurs in the selection is provided for you.

1. *astute* [paragraph 1] _____

_____

2. *penchant* [8] _____

_____

3. *heedless* [10] _____

_____

4. *advocating* [12] _____

_____

5. *subversion* [12] _____

_____

E. LOCATING EVIDENCE

Go through the editorial and locate the evidence that supports this idea:

Consumers who care about solving the problem of global warming should not buy SUVs.

To identify it, put a star in the margin next to the sentence or paragraph, or bracket the words.

F. TOPICS FOR WRITING OR DISCUSSION

1. Imagine that a good friend has decided to buy an SUV. Write a letter in which you try to convince the person to change his or her mind.
2. Write a refutation of your own to McKibben's opinion piece. Can you come up with two or three reasons in favor of buying an SUV?

For Further Exploration

WEB SITES

The first Web site gives an overview of the problem of global warming. It includes the next three sites as links, each one of which provides a wealth of information on the subject.

- *http://ingrid.ldeo.columbia.edu/dochelp/QA/Basic/globalwarming.html*
- *http://lwf.ncdc.noaa.gov/oa/climate/globalwarming.html*
- *http://www.ngdc.noaa.gov/paleo/globalwarming/home.html*
- *http://yosemite.epa.gov/oar/globalwarming.nsf/content/index.html*

Finally, this Web site was started to satirize and to "expose the ridiculous SUV trend."

- *http://poseur.4x4.org*

23

JAY WEINER

Sports Centered

Jay Weiner is a sportswriter for the Minneapolis newspaper the Star Tribune *and the author of a book on sports,* Stadium Games: Fifty Years of Big League Greed and Bush League Boondoggles. *This piece was reprinted in the* Utne Reader.

Vocabulary Preview

WORD HISTORIES

Renegade [paragraph 12] Weiner uses the word *renegade* to describe Curt Flood, who refused to be traded from his team, the St. Louis Cardinals. The word *renegade* refers to a person who rejects something, whether it is a religion, an authority, or allegiance to a particular group. Its meaning is clear from its etymology: The word came into English from the Spanish word *renegado,* from Latin, *renegare,* "to deny."

Behemoth [paragraph 14] Another word with an unusual history is *behemoth,* which Weiner uses to describe the sports "corporate entertainment behemoth." Pronounced bĭ-hē´-məth, this word describes something huge in both size and power. It derives from *behemoth,* a word from the Bible used to describe a huge animal or beast, possibly a hippopotamus. It comes from the Hebrew word for beast, pronounced bə-hē-môt.

WORD PARTS

Anti- [paragraphs 2 and 10] The prefix *anti-* appears three times in this selection: *anti-Semitism* in paragraph 2 and *antihero* and *anti-icon* in paragraph 10. This Greek prefix is typically attached to English words to denote "against" or "in opposition to," as in the common words *antiwar, anti-American,* and *antislavery. Anti-Semitism* refers to prejudice against Jews or the Jewish faith; an *antihero* is a modern hero, who lacks the qualities of a traditional hero; and *anti-icon* is a word that you won't find in the dictionary. Weiner made it up to explain the idea that many athletes act in ways that are in deliberate opposition to athletes' usual status as icons or representative symbols of their sport. As you can see, *anti-* is a most useful prefix.

Phobia [paragraph 19] *Homophobia* is fear of homosexuality, from the Greek word part *phobia* ("fear") + *homo-* ("same"). *Phobia* is attached to many English words, usually of Greek origin, to describe a persistent or abnormal fear. What do these common "phobia" words mean? Check a dictionary if you are unsure.

claustrophobia   _____
hydrophobia   _____
agoraphobia   _____
xenophobia   _____

WORD FAMILIES   **Autographs [paragraph 7]**   In previous selections, you were introduced to the elements that make up the word *autograph: auto-* meaning "self," *graphos* meaning "writing," and *graphein,* "to write." (The earlier words in which these word parts appeared were *automated* and *demographic.*) *Graph* is a common Greek word element that has two related meanings: "something that writes or records" and "something drawn or written." Here are some other words in this family:

phonograph   a device to play back music [*phono* ("sound") + *graph*]
telegraph   a device to transmit messages over long distances [*tele-* ("distance") + *graph*]
graphology   the study of handwriting [*graph* + *ology* ("study of")]
biography   a book about someone's life [*bio* ("life") + *graph*]

What is an *autobiography*?   _____

Allusions

Allusions are references to an idea outside the scope of the text, and writers often employ them to shed light on a subject in a new way. Allusions can be made to works of literature, history, the world of art, the Bible or other religious works, mythology, and so forth. In his conclusion, Weiner writes: "The tension of the competition is legitimate. The drama is high. And therein lies the essence of modern American sport. It's a good show, albeit *bread and circuses.*" *Albeit* means "although," and the phrase *bread and circuses* is an allusion to the Roman empire, when emperors provided food and circuses for the amusement of the population—in other words, everything to keep the population content. The *American Heritage Dictionary* lists this definition of *bread and circuses:* "Offerings, such as benefits or entertainments, intended to placate discontent or distract attention from a policy or situation."

JAY WEINER

Sports Centered

1   How far back must we go to remember that sports matter? How deeply into our personal and national pasts must we travel to recall that we once cared?

2   Do we have to return to 1936? Adolf Hitler tried to make the Olympics into a propaganda machine for anti-Semitism and racism. In that case, American track star Jesse Owens, demonstrating that the master race could be mastered at racing, stole Hitler's ideological show. Were not sports a vehicle of significant political substance then?

3   Or should we return to 1947 and Jackie Robinson? A baseball player integrated our "national pastime" a year before the U.S. Army considered African Americans equal. Robinson's barrier-break may have been largely based on ticket-selling economics for the Brooklyn Dodgers' owners, but didn't sports do something good?

4   Their fists raised, their dignity palpable, track stars Tommie Smith and John Carlos spread the American black power and student protest movements to the world when they stood on the victory stand at the 1968 Olympics in Mexico City. Politics and sports mixed beautifully then.

5   Remember when tennis feminist Billie Jean King took on an old fart named Bobby Riggs in 1973, boldly bringing the women's movement to the playing fields? That moment of sports theater stirred up sexual politics as much as any Betty Friedan essay or Miss America bra burning could ever do.

6   Sports had meaning. And sports were accessible.

7   Remember when your grandfather or your uncle—maybe your mother—took you to a game when you were a little kid? The hot dog was the best. The crowd was mesmerizing. The colors were bright. The crack of the bat under the summer sun, or the autumn chill wrapped around that touchdown run, was unforgettable. Back then, some nobody became your favorite player, somebody named Johnny Callison or Hal Greer or Clarence Peaks or Vic Hadfield, someone who sold cars in the off-season and once signed autographs for your father's men's club for a $50 appearance fee. Those "heroes" were working-class stiffs, just like us.

8   Now you read the sports pages—or, more exactly, the business and crime pages—and you realize you've disconnected from the institution and it from you. Sports is distant. It reeks of greed. Its politics glorify not the majestic drama of pure competition, but a drunken, gambling masculinity epitomized by sports-talk radio, a venue for obnoxious boys on car phones.

9   How can we reconcile our detachment from corporatized pro sports, professionalized college sports—even out-of-control kids' sports—with our appreciation for athleticism, with our memories? And how, after we sort it all out, can we take sports back?

10   Part of the problem is that we want sports to be mythological when, in our hearts, we know they aren't. So reclaiming sports requires that we come to grips with our own role in the myth-making. Owens, Robinson, Smith, Carlos, and King played to our highest ideals and so have been enshrined in our sports pantheon. But we've also made heroes of some whose legacies are much less clear-cut. Take Joe Namath, the 1960s quarterback who represented sexual freedom, or Bill Walton, the 1970s basketball hippie who symbolized the alienated white suburban Grateful Dead sports antihero. Neither deserves the reverence accorded Owens or Robinson or even King, but both captured the essence of their era. Or how about relief pitcher Steve Howe, who symbolized the evils of drug addiction in the '80s, or Mike Tyson, who currently plays the archetypal angry black male? No less than Tommie Smith and John Carlos, these anti-icons were emblematic of their age.

11   It may be discomfiting, but it's true: The power of sports and sports heroes to mirror our own aspirations have also contributed to the sorry state of the institution today. The women's sports movement Billie Jean King helped create proved a great

leap forward for female athletes, but it also created a generation of fitness *consumers,* whose appetite for Nikes and Reeboks created a new generation of Asian sweatshops.

12   Fans applauded the courage of renegade Curt Flood, the St. Louis Cardinals outfielder who in 1969 refused to be traded, arguing that baseball players should be free to play where they want to play. We cheered—all the way to the Supreme Court—his challenge to the cigar-smoking owners' hold on their pinstripe-knickered chattel. Now players can sell their services to the highest bidder, but their astronomical salaries—deserved or not—alienate us from the games as much as the owners' greed.

13   The greed isn't new, of course. The corporate betrayal of the fan is as traditional as the seventh-inning stretch. The Boston Braves moved to Milwaukee in 1953, and the Dodgers and New York Giants fled to California in 1958, for money, subsidized facilities, and better TV contracts. But what has always been a regrettable by-product of sports has suddenly become its dominant ethos. Our worship of sports and our worship of the buck have now become one and the same. So it shouldn't surprise us that we get the heroes we expect—and maybe deserve.

14   So how do we as a society reclaim sports from the corporate entertainment behemoth that now controls it? Some modest proposals:

15   • **Deprofessionalize college and high school sports.**

Let's ban college athletic scholarships in favor of financial aid based on need, as for any other student. And let's keep high school athletics in perspective. Why should local news coverage of high school sports exceed coverage given to the band, debating society, or science fair? Sports stars are introduced to the culture of athletic privilege at a very young age.

16   • **Allow some form of public ownership of professional sports teams.**

Leagues and owners ask us to pay for the depreciating asset of a stadium but give us no share of the appreciating asset of a franchise. Lease agreements between teams and publicly financed stadiums should also include enforceable community-involvement clauses.

17   • **Make sports affordable again.**

Sports owners call their games "family entertainment." For whose family? Bill Gates'? Owners whose teams get corporate subsidies should set aside 20 percent of their tickets at prices no higher than a movie admission. And, like any other business feeding at the public trough, they should be required to pay livable wages even to the average schmoes who sell hot dogs.

18   • **Be conscious of the messages sport is sending.**

Alcohol-related advertising should be banned from sports broadcasting. Any male athlete convicted of assaulting a woman should be banned from college and pro sports. Fighting in a sports event should be at least a misdemeanor and maybe a felony, rather than a five-minute stay in the penalty box.

19   Let's take the sports establishment by its lapels and shake it back toward us. Because even with all the maddening messages of male dominance, black servil-

ity, homophobia, corporate power, commercialism, and brawn over brains, sports still play an important role in many lives. When we watch a game, we are surrounded by friends and family. There are snacks and beverages. We sit in awe of the players' remarkable skills. We can't do what they do. They extend our youth. The tension of the competition is legitimate. The drama is high.

20   And therein lies the essence of modern American sport. It's a good show, albeit bread and circuses. And we just can't give it up. So why not take it back for ourselves as best we can, looking for ways to humanize an institution that mirrors our culture, understanding that those who own sport won't give it up without a fight, knowing that we like it too much to ever just walk away. *

From Jay Weiner, "Sports Centered," *Utne Reader,* January–February 2000. © 2000 by Jay Weiner. Reprinted by permission of the author.

Exercises

You may refer to the selection as you complete these exercises. Write your answers to these questions in the spaces provided.

A. IDENTIFYING THE CLAIM

1. Using your own words as much as possible, write the writer's central claim or proposition. Also indicate the number of the paragraph in which it is

    located. _____

    _____

    _____

2. Then decide if the claim is a claim of fact, a claim of value, or a claim of policy.

    Remember that an argument may have a secondary claim as well. _____

    _____

B. LOCATING EVIDENCE AND REFUTATION

1. One piece of evidence is listed for you. List three other major pieces of evidence that the writer uses to support the claim. Also characterize each piece of evidence according to whether it represents facts and statistics, examples and observations, good reasons, or quotation or testimony.

    a. Sports reeks of greed. [good reason]_____

    b. _____

        _____

        _____

    c. _____

        _____

d. _____

_____

2. Write the refutation, if there is one, in the space provided. _____

_____

_____

C. IDENTIFYING SOLUTIONS

1. Summarize in your own words the solutions Weiner proposes to return

sports to our memories of what sports used to be or should be. _____

_____

_____

_____

_____

_____

2. What is your proposal to help solve this problem? _____

_____

_____

D. USING VOCABULARY

Here are some words from the selection. Write an original sentence using each word that shows both that you know how to use the word and what it means. The number of the paragraph in which the word occurs in the selection is provided for you.

1. *palpable* [paragraph 4] _____

_____

2. *mesmerizing* [7] _____

_____

3. *epitomized* [8] _____

_____

4. *reconcile* [9]_____

_____

5. *archetypal* [10] _____

_____

6. *subsidized* [13] _____

_____

E. PARAPHRASING EXERCISE

Paraphrase paragraph 11.

Original Passage	Paraphrase
It may be discomfiting, but it's true: The power of sports and sports heroes to mirror our own aspirations have also contributed to the sorry state of the institution today. The women's sports movement Billie Jean King helped create proved a great leap forward for female athletes, but it also created a generation of fitness *consumers,* whose appetite for Nikes and Reeboks created a new generation of Asian sweatshops.	_____ _____ _____ _____ _____ _____ _____ _____ _____

F. TOPICS FOR WRITING OR DISCUSSION

1. Write a paragraph in which you reminisce about a sporting event that you attended. What made it special? Perhaps contrast that experience with a more recent one. Does your experience mirror Weiner's disaffection from sports?
2. Write a refutation of your own of Weiner's article, in particular justifying the high salaries commanded by professional athletes.

For Further Exploration

WEB SITES

Here is a list of "Best of the Web" devoted to sports, as published in the *San Francisco Chronicle* (March 13, 2001):

- *www.sports.yahoo.com*
- *www.espn.com*
- *www.sportsline.com*
- *www.sportsjones.com*
- *www.sportstalk.com*

An excerpt by Christopher Doob called "Competition in Sports," from his textbook *Sociology: An Introduction* (Wadsworth, 6th edition) is available at:

- *www.wadsworth.com/sociology_d/special_features/action/essays/sports.html*

24

MAGGIE GALLAGHER

Fatherless Boys Grow Up into Dangerous Men

This opinion piece was first published on the editorial page of the Wall Street Journal. *In it, Maggie Gallagher challenges the idea that poverty is the cause of increasing violence among American male youths. Gallagher is an affiliate scholar with the Institute for American Values, a conservative think-tank.*

Vocabulary Preview

WORD HISTORIES

Spree [paragraph 2]   *Spree* is an unusual word because it can have both a positive and a negative connotation, or emotional association, depending on the context. If one goes on a spending or a shopping *spree,* the result is fairly harmless, except for having to pay the bill. But a shooting *spree,* as mentioned in the introduction to this piece, is a different matter. The word means "a sudden indulgence in or an outburst of activity." It comes from the Scottish word for a cattle raid, *spreath.* Since cattle were regarded as standards of wealth, their theft—executed with "an outburst of activity"—constituted a crime, just as a crime or a shooting spree does today.

WORD PARTS

Co- [paragraphs 3 and 4]   Gallagher uses the word *coincidence* in paragraph 3 and *correlations* in paragraph 4. The prefix *co-* means "together." A *coincidence* refers to two events that occur at the same time, "together." A *correlation* is a correspondence or connection between two things. Other words that begin with *co-* are *coauthor, cooperate, coworker, co-conspirator.*

What does the word *coeducation* mean? _____

_____

WORD FAMILIES

Gynecology [paragraph 5]   Gallagher cites a research study done by Cynthia Harper, who, among other things, is a demographer in the department of obstetrics and *gynecology* at the University of California, San Francisco, medical school. Obstetrics is the branch of medicine that deals with prenatal care and childbirth; *gynecology* is the branch dealing with women's reproductive organs, from the Greek word element *gyno* or "woman." (A physician called an ob-gyn, therefore, both delivers babies and diagnoses problems with women's reproductive organs.) What do these two other words in this family mean?

polygyny   _____

            _____

            _____

misogyny   _____

Maggie Gallagher

Fatherless Boys Grow Up into Dangerous Men

1   George Moody, a 60-year-old man from Hinesville, Ga., had just checked into John's resort in Haines City, Fla., for a family reunion in April. He opened his hotel door, and three teens in ski masks opened fire. When police arrived they found five members of Mr. Moody's family, including a 10-year-old girl, wounded. "It was a random shooting," Sheriff Lawrence Crow told the Miami Herald. "It doesn't make any sense."

2   This was the final act of a four-day shooting spree undertaken by three boys, all under 18. Just another crime in America, not shocking enough to make the national news. But according to a new report, "Kids and Violence," by Florida's Family First organization, all three gunmen had one thing in common: they came from homes broken by divorce or unwed parenting.

3   Coincidence? Between 1980 and 1990 the homicide arrest rate for juveniles jumped 87%. Following rapid changes in family formation in the 1970s, youth violence rose sharply in the 1980s and '90s, even while it declined for adults over age 25.

4   Such correlations are merely hints that fatherlessness causes crime. Until recently, scientific evidence has been hard to come by. Researchers had long suspected a link between father absence and crime, but few had access to the kind of large nationally representative database needed to rule out alternative theories. Since boys raised by single parents disproportionately come from disadvantaged backgrounds, maybe it was not fatherlessness but poverty or discrimination that put them at risk of crime. Nor could most of these earlier studies distinguish between different sorts of disrupted families: Was it just children of unwed mothers who were at risk, or did divorce have similarly negative effects? Is a stepfather as good as a biological dad? How much does remarriage, which dramatically raises family income, do to restore to children the protection of a two-parent home?

5   To answer questions like these, Cynthia Harper, a demographer at the department of obstetrics and gynecology at the University of California, San Francisco, along with Princeton's Sara McLanahan, one of the nation's top family scholars, undertook what few researchers had in the past: a longitudinal look at how fam-

ily structure affects serious crime, using a large national database, the National Longitudinal Survey of Youth. Their study offers a unique opportunity to calculate the true costs of family breakdown and to compare different theories about the "root causes" of crime.

6   Ms. Harper and Ms. McLanahan followed 6,403 boys who were between the ages of 14 and 22 in 1979, up through their early 30s. They controlled for family background variables such as mother's educational level, race, family income and number of siblings, as well as neighborhood variables like the proportion of female-headed families in the neighborhood, unemployment rates, median income and even cognitive ability.

7   Here is what they found: Boys raised outside of intact marriages are, on average, more than twice as likely as other boys to end up jailed, even after controlling for other demographic factors. Each year spent without a dad in the home increases the odds of future incarceration by about 5%.

8   Boys raised by unmarried mothers are at greater risk, but mostly, it appears, because they spend more time without a dad. A child born to an unwed mother is about 2½ times as likely to end up imprisoned, while a boy whose parents split during his teenage years was about 1½ times as likely to be imprisoned.

9   Child support made no difference one way or another in the likelihood a boy will grow up to be a criminal. And sadly remarriage made things worse: Boys living in stepparent families were almost three times as likely to face incarceration as boys from intact families. In fact, note Ms. Harper and Ms. McLanahan, "the odds for youths from stepparent families are similar to those for youths who do not live with any parents, although these children, in addition to not having any parents care for them, are selected for more difficult family circumstances." Apparently stepfathers and children frequently compete for the time, attention and resources of the biological mother. Ms. Harper cautions, however, that "there may be lots and lots of households that benefit enormously from a stepfather. These are large national averages."

10   Poverty did make it more likely that a boy will be incarcerated as an adult. But "family structure was more important than income," reports Ms. Harper, though she'd like to see that finding replicated using other, more reliable income data. Though Ms. Harper and Ms. McLanahan's data don't prove this, I think their evidence suggests that, while the structural advantages of marriage (more time, more supervision and more money) help, the attachment between father and son may be the key. Fathers teach their sons lessons, directly and indirectly, about what it means to be a man. When boys identify with fathers who are loving and available, the likelihood lessens that they will define their masculinity in terms of rebellion and antisocial aggression.

11   Ms. Harper and Ms. McLanahan, for example, found that the very small number of teenage boys living with just their single fathers were no more likely to commit crimes than boys in intact families. But boys living with remarried dads faced rates of future incarceration as high as or higher than boys living with remarried mothers. Why? Perhaps because men who don't marry but care for their children single-handedly are unusually devoted fathers.

12   "Adolescents face a lot higher risks today than they used to," says Ms. Harper. "Fathers may be even more important now than in the past." Yet as the importance of fathers has grown, the likelihood that they're around has fallen:

By their teenage years, almost 40% of boys in Ms. Harper and Ms. McLanahan's study were not living with both their parents.

13   Since 1970, the divorce rate has doubled and the out-of-wedlock birth rate has tripled. Today, according to the latest Census Bureau statistics, one-third of all births and 44% of first births, are to unmarried mothers. The first heart-breaking victims of this revolution in social behavior may be the children of single parents themselves. But as George Moody found out, they are not the only victims.

From Maggie Gallagher, "Fatherless Boys Grow Up into Dangerous Men," *Wall Street Journal*, December 1, 1998. Reproduced by permission. www.copyright.com.

Exercises

You may refer to the selection as you complete these exercises. Write your answers to these questions in the spaces provided.

A. IDENTIFYING THE CLAIM

1. Using your own words as much as possible, write the writer's central claim or proposition. Also indicate the number of the paragraph in which it is

   located. _____

   _____

2. Then decide if the claim is a claim of fact, a claim of value, or a claim of policy. Remember that an argument may have a secondary claim as well. _____

   _____

B. LOCATING EVIDENCE AND THE REFUTATION

1. One piece of evidence is listed for you. List three other major pieces of evidence that the writer uses to support the claim. Also characterize each piece of evidence according to whether it represents facts and statistics, examples and observations, good reasons, or quotation or testimony.

   a. A carefully structured study conducted by two researchers turned up a g eat deal of evidence about the effects of family breakdown on young males. [testimony]

   b. _____

   _____

   _____

   c. _____

   _____

d. _____

_____

_____

2. Write the refutation, if there is one, in the space provided. _____

_____

_____

C. IDENTIFYING SOLUTIONS

1. Does Gallagher provide a solution to the problem she discusses? If so, write it in the space provided. Be sure to use your own words. _____

_____

_____

2. What is your proposal to help solve this problem? _____

_____

_____

_____

D. USING VOCABULARY

Here are some words from the selection. Write an original sentence using each word that shows both that you know how to use the word and what it means. The number of the paragraph where the word occurs in the selection is provided for you.

1. _random_ [paragraph 1] _____

_____

2. _coincidence_ [3] _____

_____

3. _discrimination_ [4] _____

_____

4. _cognitive_ [6] _____

_____

5. _intact_ [7] _____

_____

6. _replicated_ [10] _____

_____

E. SUMMARIZING INFORMATION

Write a summary of the information in paragraph 9.

Original Passage

Child support made no difference one way or another in the likelihood a boy will grow up to be a criminal. And sadly remarriage made things worse: Boys living in stepparent families were almost three times as likely to face incarceration as boys from intact families. In fact, note Ms. Harper and Ms. McLanahan, "the odds for youths from stepparent families are similar to those for youths who do not live with any parents, although these children, in addition to not having any parents care for them, are selected for more difficult family circumstances." Apparently stepfathers and children frequently compete for the time, attention and resources of the biological mother. Ms. Harper cautions, however, that "there may be lots and lots of households that benefit enormously from a stepfather. These are large national averages."

Summary

F. TOPICS FOR WRITING OR DISCUSSION

1. Do you see any flaws in the study conducted by Cynthia Harper and Sara McLanahan? Would it have strengthened the editorial if the authors of the study or Gallagher had spelled out exactly what kinds of crimes these young men were incarcerated for? Does Gallagher present the evidence in such a way that it is convincing?
2. What are some other reasons that adolescent boys can become violent? What might be som e other factors to account for the increase in boys' involvement with serious crimes since the 1970s?

For Further Exploration

WEB SITES

The following sites draw on the study done by Cynthia Harper and Sara McLanahan:

- "Kids and Violence," published by Family First: *www.familyfirst. net/violentstreets.htm*
- A second report titled "Effects of Divorce on America," sponsored by the Christian organization Peacemaker Ministries, also incorporates information from Harper's and McLanahan's study: *www.peacemakerministries. org/html/artic27.htm.*

These three sites offer help for fathers who want to be stronger influences in their children's lives:

- *www.fatherhoodproject.org*
- *www.fatherhood.org*
- *www.dadsempowered.org*

25

ALEX RAKSIN AND BOB SIPCHEN

Lost, Then Found: Helping People Off the Streets

Alex Raksin and Bob Sipchen are editorial writers for the Los Angeles Times. *In 2002, they won the Pulitzer Prize for editorial writing for a series of opinion pieces they published on the plight of mentally ill homeless people. This piece was part of the series.*

Vocabulary Preview

WORD HISTORIES

Graffiti [paragraph 2]   Most words in English that originated in Latin, the mother tongue of the Romance languages, entered by way of French. The word *graffiti* is unusual because it comes from Italian, another Romance language. Termed by critics "a scourge" and by advocates "public art," *graffiti* literally means "writing on the wall." It is a diminutive form of the Italian word *graffio,* "scratching" or "scribbling," from the Latin verb *graphein,* "to write." Although technically one should use the singular form *graffito* when describing a particular example of this type of writing, Americans generally use the plural form to indicate all such markings.

Skid Row [paragraph 13]   Every major city has a *skid row,* a place where the down-and-out, vagrants, and the homeless congregate and live. This slang expression developed as a variant form of *Skid Road,* a road consisting of logs or planks used for moving objects. Somehow *skid row,* originally associated with the place where loggers congregated, came to have a less savory meaning. Today, two related slang phrases derive from this concept: "to be on the skids" or "to hit the skids," referring to being on a downward path to ruin.

WORD PARTS

Para- [paragraph 1]   The Greek prefix *para-* has several meanings. Here are the two most common ones: (1) describing something "beyond," as in *paranormal* or *parapsychology,* and (2) referring to someone who is an "assistant" or a "subsidiary." *Paramedics,* then, mentioned in paragraph 1, assist other medical personnel. We see this meaning in the prefix of words like *paralegal* (someone who assists an attorney) and *paraprofessional* (someone who assists a professional person).

WORD FAMILIES

Civil and Civilian [paragraphs 3 and 6]   *Civil* and *civilian* both derive from the Latin root *civis,* "citizen." *Civic* describes things that relate to being a citizen, as in the phrases *civil liberties* or *civil rights.* The word *civilian* refers to an ordinary citizen, specifically someone who is not a member of the armed forces. Other words in this family using the root *civis* include *civilization, civilize, civic,* and *civility.*

Many high school students take *civics*. What does this course refer to? _____

_____

ALEX RAKSIN AND BOB SIPCHEN

Lost, Then Found: Helping People Off the Streets

1   On a corner in downtown Los Angeles, a man sprawls unconscious, genitals exposed, one shoe on the sidewalk beside a foot covered with oozing sores. Blood and spit gurgle in his open mouth. A man in a fruit company uniform walks by, unmoved. Speaking in Spanish and gesturing, he makes it clear that he sees no point in calling paramedics: There are too many of these people—drunk or on drugs or crazy. *"Perdido,"* he says. Lost.

2   As it happens, just around the corner, in the middle of San Julian Street, paramedics from Los Angeles City Fire Station No. 9 are already pounding another overdosed man's bare chest. A few feet away, a hot dog cart blares music and at least 85 people, many with wild, unfocused eyes, mill about watching, yakking, even dancing. A man slumped with several others against a graffiti-splattered wall lets out a slurred shout: "Let him go to heaven."

3   As late as the 1960s, people with mental illness and addictions were tossed into institutions with little concern for their civil liberties. Today many such people wander the streets. This is no more humane. It's time to help those who cannot act in their own best interests to move from the urban and suburban sidewalks and parks and into treatment for their ailments. It is for the sake of the sick, and also because the costs to taxpayers and civic pride are simply not acceptable. The firefighters and paramedics at Station No. 9 alone respond to about 70 calls a day, sometimes juggling as many as five simultaneous cases of drug or alcohol overdose amid the city's skid row sidewalk encampments. One way to slowly stop this senseless and relentless rescue operation is to put more teams of specialist public servants on the streets to ease people with mental illnesses and addictions off.

4   Craig McClelland and his partner, Suzanne Newberry, have been trained to do just that and to coax and cajole people from under bridges and out of the shrubbery caves they inhabit from East L.A. to the Westside.

5   Newberry is a nurse supplied by the county Department of Mental Health. McClelland is a deputy sheriff. The partners are one of the mental evaluation teams put together by the Los Angeles County Board of Supervisors in what Newberry calls "the joining of totally foreign agencies—public health and law enforcement." The Sheriff's Department and the Los Angeles Police Department have between them a total of about 30 such teams.

6   Dressed in civilian clothing, McClelland and Newberry drive their unmarked Crown Victoria through some of the county's least desirable real estate. McClel-

land summarizes the team's mission: "We try to find real solutions, long-term solutions, not just a quick fix."

7   To see how this works, walk with the partners into a ragged enclave of weather-beaten blue tarps, tents and cardboard boxes in an industrial area just east of the Civic Center. As some inhabitants stare glumly from a cluster of old mattresses that reek of body odor and urine, a middle-aged man in a black gaucho-style hat steps out to greet them.

8   The team's approach is to lift up tent flaps and tuck in gallons of water that Mc-Clelland talks the Sparkletts company into donating and hand out canned goods contributed by his church in Huntington Beach. They talk to those who will listen, suggesting shelters, offering to make contact with drug treatment programs.

9   Then they move on to the next spot where people hang their clothes on razor-wire-topped chain link or sleep beside dumpsters overflowing with rotting trash.

10   Slowly, people get to know them. One afternoon "Black Hat" approached. "Can you help me?" he said. "There's something wrong in my head."

11   Newberry is a short, red-haired woman who spent 20 years working in psychiatric emergency rooms. McClelland is a veteran of 13 years with the Sheriff's Department and an expert on substance abuse. When "Black Hat" bridled at the mention of going to a hospital, they knew how to quickly wrangle a psychiatrist and get him to the encampment to prescribe antipsychotic medication on the spot.

12   This middle-aged man still lives on that sidewalk, but a fog has lifted from his mind. Earlier this month McClelland and Newberry persuaded him to go with them to tour a facility that could provide housing and long-term treatment. They're hopeful he'll soon join the 5,000 people statewide whom such teams have moved off the street and into some sort of treatment and housing. It certainly beats jail, where locking up a mentally ill person can cost up to $600 a night—about the price of a suite at the Four Seasons.

13   What Newberry and McClelland do takes compassion, toughness and persistence. More such teams are needed. The alternative can be seen in the emergency medical madness that unfolds 24 hours a day in Los Angeles, where the paramedics at Station No. 9 alone go through five cases of latex gloves a month as they pump the chests and patch the wounds of people who will live and die on skid row streets. ✳

From Alex Raskin and Bob Sipchen, "Lost, Then Found: Helping People Off the Streets," *Los Angeles Times*, November 19, 2001. Reprinted by permission of the *Los Angeles Times* Syndication.

Exercises

You may refer to the selection as you complete these exercises. Write your answers to these questions in the spaces provided.

A. IDENTIFYING THE CLAIM

1. Using your own words as much as possible, write Raskin and Sipchen's central claim or proposition. Also indicate the number of the paragraph in which it is located. _____

_____

2. Then decide if the claim is a claim of fact, a claim of value, or a claim of policy. Remember that an argument may have a secondary claim as well. ____

_____

B. LOCATING EVIDENCE AND REFUTATION

1. One piece of evidence is listed for you. List three other major pieces of evidence that the writers use to support the claim. Also characterize each piece of evidence according to whether it represents facts and statistics, examples and observations, good reasons, or quotation or testimony.

a. The "lost" people mentioned in paragraphs 1 and 2 need help. [observations]

b. _____

_____

c. _____

_____

_____

d. _____

_____

_____

2. Write the refutation, if there is one, in the space provided. _____

_____

C. IDENTIFYING SOLUTIONS

1. Do Raksin and Sipchen provide a solution to the problem they discuss? If so, write it in the space provided. Be sure to use your own words. _____

_____

_____

2. What is your proposal to help solve this problem? _____

_____

D. USING VOCABULARY

Here are some words from the selection. Write an original sentence using each word that shows both that you know how to use the word and what it means. The number of the paragraph where the word occurs in the selection is provided for you.

1. *simultaneous* [paragraph 3] _____

_____

2. *relentless* [3] _____

_____

3. *cajole* [4] _____

_____

4. *glumly* [7] _____

_____

5. *wrangle* [11] _____

_____

6. *persistence* [13] _____

_____

E. LOCATING EVIDENCE

Go through the article and locate any piece of information that supports this idea:

> We need to find long-term solutions to the problem of mentally ill homeless people, not quick fixes.

To identify it, put a star in the margin next to the sentence or paragraph, or bracket the words.

F. TOPICS FOR WRITING OR DISCUSSION

1. Does your community have a policy for dealing with the homeless? Do some investigation, and write a short paper explaining how it works and, more important, whether it works.

2. Homeless advocates sometimes maintain that forcing people who live on the streets to move to treatment centers or to sleep in shelters violates their civil liberties. Comment on their objection.

For Further Exploration

WEB SITE

A more liberal view of the homeless issue in America can be found here:

• *http://usliberals.about.com/cs/welfarepoverty/*

26

NICHOLAS THOMPSON

Hero Inflation

In the aftermath of the terrorist attacks of September 11, 2001, journalists, thinkers, and media pundits representing every segment of the political spectrum sought to interpret this terrible event and its repercussions. In this opinion piece, first published on the editorial page of the Boston Globe, *Thompson questions the application of the word* hero *to the World Trade Center victims and rescuers. He prefaces his piece with this question: "When we put every victim of tragedy on a pedestal, what are we looking up to?" Thompson is a Markle Fellow at the New American Foundation (an independent, nonprofit public policy institute) and a correspondent for the* Boston Globe.

WORD HISTORIES

Pantheon [paragraph 11] Referring to the 350 firefighters who died in the World Trade Center, Thompson writes that they "now stand atop our national *pantheon*." Written with a small letter, *pantheon* refers to the gods of a people considered together as a group. When capitalized, *Pantheon* refers to the temple dedicated to the gods that still stands in Rome, Italy. Its etymology is from the Greek word *Pantheion*, "shrine of all the gods," and originally is from *pantheios*, "of all the gods." The word can be broken down into its component parts like this: *pan-* ("all") + *theos* (god). Here, the writer intends the first definition.

WORD PARTS

Syn- or Sym- [paragraph 3] Thompson states that "The victims of the terrorist attacks deserve tremendous *sympathy*." *Sympathy* means a mutual or shared feeling between one person and another. It comes from the Greek prefix *syn-*, also spelled *sym-*, meaning "together" or "with." The root *pathy* derives from the Greek root *pathos*, or "feeling," hence "feeling with another." Other words in English beginning with this prefix include the following:

symphony	an extended piece of music or the orchestra that plays it [*sym-* + *phone* ("sound")]
synagogue	a meeting place or building for worship and religious instruction in the Jewish faith [*syn-* + *agein* ("to lead")]
symbol	a representation of an idea, a sign [*sym-* + *ballein* ("to throw")]
symmetry	equal correspondence of structure on either side of a dividing line [*sym-* + *metron* ("measure")]

What does the word *symbiosis* mean? Look in the dictionary if you are unsure. _____

WORD FAMILIES

Immortalized [paragraph 5]   If a person is *immortalized,* then he or she has been made immortal (not literally, of course, but symbolically made to live forever). The word can be broken down like this: *im-* ("not") + *mortal* ("subject to death") + *-ize* ("to make"). *Mort* is a Latin root that came into French and then into English. Other words in this family include these:

mortal	subject to death
mortuary	a funeral home
mortgage	literally a "death pledge"
postmortem	a medical examination after death [*post-* ("after") + *mort*]

NICHOLAS THOMPSON

Hero Inflation

1   Since Sept. 11, America has become a nation of heroes. Stevie Wonder, Willie Nelson, and Bruce Springsteen played a "tribute to heroes" that raised $150 million for victims of the attacks. Firefighters and rescue workers have earned acclaim for heroism, but so has nearly everyone who directly suffered on that horrible morning.

2   "The fatalities of that day are all heroes and deserve to be honored as such," said Thomas Davis, a Republican congressman from Virginia, while successfully working to obtain a full burial plot in Arlington National Cemetery for the former National Guardsman who piloted the plane that crashed into the Pentagon.

3   The victims of the terrorist attacks deserve tremendous sympathy. They died tragically and often horrifically. But not all died in a way that people have previously described as heroic. And even the heroism attributed to the rescue workers stems as much from the country's needs in responding to the disaster as from what actually happened in the collapsing buildings.

4   It is long overdue that Americans appreciate their public servants. It is also necessary to honor those who died simply for being in America. But changing the definition of hero to accommodate tragic victims may actually weaken us by diminishing the idea of role models who perform truly extraordinary acts.

5   To the ancient Greeks, "heroes," such as Hercules or Odysseus, performed great deeds, frequently challenged the gods, and were immortalized after death. Heroes lived in times and realms halfway between gods and men and often were deemed to have brought prosperity to the people who praised them.

6   That definition gradually evolved in this country as Americans adapted it to the people most respected here. Heroes won that standing by courageously transforming the world—Martin Luther King Jr. or Mother Teresa for example. Or heroes could earn that title simply for incredible acts of bravery several steps above the call of duty—Oskar Schindler, a young girl who plunges into a dangerous icy river and saves a stranger's life, or maybe someone from battle such as Henry Johnson who fought off 20 Germans with a knife and a couple of hand grenades in World War I.

7   Roughly speaking, American heroes first needed bravery. But bravery is not sufficient because evil people can be brave, too. So, the second trait in American historical lore is nobility. Heroes must work toward goals that we approve of. Heroes must show ingenuity. Lastly, they should be successful. Rosa Parks wouldn't have been nearly as much of a hero if she hadn't sparked a boycott that then sparked a movement. Charles Lindbergh wouldn't have been nearly as heroized if the Spirit of St. Louis had crashed into the Atlantic, or if scores of other people had made the flight before.

8   Recently though, a fourth trait—victimhood—seems to have become as important as anything else in determining heroic status. Today heroes don't have to do anything; they just need to be noble victims.

9   For example, if J. Joseph Moakley was known at all nationally, it was as a hard-working Massachusetts congressman who almost always followed the Democratic Party line. But when he was stricken with leukemia, he became a national hero, earning praise from the president and seemingly everyone else in Washington. He was cited from the balcony, traditionally the spot reserved for heroes, by President Bush during the State of the Union message. (This paper even wrote about a letter received at his house addressed simply to "Joe Moakley, Hero.") His death earned almost as much newspaper coverage as the death this year of the 98-year-old Mike Mansfield, a giant of the U.S. Senate who served as majority leader longer than anyone in history and initiated the Senate Watergate Committee.

10   But that shouldn't surprise us. Books about overcoming adversity clog the bestseller lists, and perseverance during illness—any illness—is grist for the heroic mill. If John F. Kennedy wanted to run for president today, he might constantly mention his struggle against Addison's disease as opposed to emphasizing his exploits on his PT boat in the Pacific.

11   Of course, victimhood hasn't completely eclipsed action in our national selection of heroes. The biggest heroes have many of the virtues of traditional heroes but also are victims—for example, the 350 firefighters who died in the World Trade Center and who now stand atop our national pantheon. These men have been honored everywhere from the current cover of *Sports Illustrated* to a recent best-selling comic book that makes them into superheroes. They even inspired thousands of Halloween costumes.

12   But although the firemen who died in the Trade Center bravely fought the flames and led the evacuation, they did so as workers doing the best they could in their jobs—people trained by the city to rush into buildings and save others. Firefighters chose a very worthy line of work, but to die while doing it isn't completely different from, say, the computer programmers who stayed in the Trade Center and perished while desperately trying to preserve the data backing people's financial portfolios. Just after Christmas, a New Bedford policeman carried a woman out of a burning building. "I'm not a hero," he said upon emerging outside. "I'm just a worker."

13   There were no doubt some unconditional individual heroes on Sept. 11, including some of the people on United Flight 93 who fought the hijackers and individual firefighters and police who went well beyond the requirements of the job, but most of the other people who died in the attacks were simply victims,

much like the tens of thousands of innocent people killed in home fires, or on highways, every year.

14   They deserve our grief and their families and communities merit great sympathy. But it's time for a little more perspective when Congress almost unanimously passes a bill called the "True American Heroes Act" awarding Congressional Gold Medals—the highest honor that body can give—to every government official who died in the attacks, including Port Authority employees who were killed in their World Trade Center offices.

15   Of course, some of the hero-making is born of necessity. In the aftermath of the attacks, we needed to turn the narrative away from the horror of the images on television and our clear vulnerability. As soon as the buildings came down, we needed to build the victims up. It also helped to reclassify everyone on the opposing side as incorrigibly demonic and everyone on our side as paragons of virtue. After the 11th, the first part was easy and the second part took a little bit of work.

16   That wasn't of course a wholly bad thing. The inflation of the heroism of Sept. 11 surely helped the nation recover and pull together. Moreover, America probably didn't have enough heroes. An August *U.S. News and World Report* poll revealed that more than half of all Americans didn't consider a single public figure heroic. Right before the attacks, Anheuser Busch planned an ad campaign titled "Real American Heroes" that, among other things, saluted the inventor of the foot-long hot dog.

17   But just because the sometimes false focus on heroism helped the nation salve its wounds doesn't make such attitudes wholly good either. Heroes often end up as role models, a task not well suited for victims. Moreover, by lowering the bar for heroism, we cheapen the word and, in some ways, the exploits of people who have earned the right to be called that in the past.

18   Finally, when people earn classification as heroes, those acting in their names often try to take it a step too far. Last month, for example, the federal government announced plans to disburse about as much money this year to families of attack victims as the entire international aid community has slated to give to Afghanistan over the next decade—and that money will come in addition to incredible amounts of charitable aid also already raised. Nevertheless, a spokesman for a victims' lobby group immediately dissented, demanding more. "We are exploring our legal options and lining up attorneys," he said. Almost no criticism could be found in response.

19   Emerson once wrote that "every hero becomes a bore at last." Well, at least their lawyers and lobbyists do. ✳

From Nicholas Thompson, "Hero Inflation," *Boston Globe*, January 13, 2002. Used with permission. www.copyright.com.

Exercises

You may refer to the selection as you complete these exercises. Write your answers to these questions in the spaces provided.

A. IDENTIFYING THE CLAIM

1. Using your own words as much as possible, write Thompson's central claim or proposition. Also indicate the number of the paragraph in which it is

located. _____

_____

_____

2. Then decide if the claim is a claim of fact, a claim of value, or a claim of

policy. Remember that an argument may have a secondary claim as well.____

_____

B. LOCATING EVIDENCE AND REFUTATION

1. One piece of evidence is listed for you. List three other major pieces of evidence that the writer uses to support the claim. Also characterize each piece of evidence according to whether it represents facts and statistics, examples and observations, good reasons, or quotation or testimony.

   a. Applying the word *hero* to victims changes the definitions that have served us well since ancient Greece and throughout American history. A true hero in American culture has traditionally been someone who acted bravely to successfully change the world, who acted with nobility, and who showed ingenuity in his or her actions. Today we apply the word *heroes* to noble victims. [examples and observations]

   b. _____

_____

_____

   c. _____

_____

_____

   d. _____

_____

_____

2. Thompson intersperses refutations all through this selection. Try to find three examples and write them in the space provided.

a. _____

_____

_____

b. _____

_____

_____

c. _____

_____

_____

C. IDENTIFYING SOLUTIONS

1. Does Thompson provide a solution to the problem he discusses? If so, write it in the space provided. Be sure to use your own words. _____

_____

_____

2. What is your proposal to help solve this problem? _____

_____

_____

_____

D. ANNOTATING EXERCISE

In the margin, annotate paragraphs 15 and 16.

E. USING VOCABULARY

Here are some words from the selection. Write an original sentence using each word that shows both that you know how to use the word and what it means. The number of the paragraph where the word occurs in the selection is provided for you.

1. *acclaim* [paragraph 1]_____

_____

2. *deemed* [5]_____

_____

3. *initiated* [9] _____

_____

4. *adversity* [10] _____

_____

5. *perseverance* [10] _____

_____

6. *dissented* [18] _____

_____

F. TOPICS FOR WRITING OR DISCUSSION

1. Write a paragraph contrasting the Greek concept of a hero with the traditional American concept.
2. Write a refutation of this editorial in which you argue that victims of disasters such as the World Trade Center attack can and should be considered heroes.

For Further Exploration

WEB SITE

David Kennedy, professor of history at Stanford University, wrote an article titled "American Innocence Walks a Perilous Path," in which he discusses the issue of terrorism and the lessons of the terrorist attacks:

- *www.bayarea.com/mld/mercurynews/news/editorial/4029777.htm*

27 **RICK WEISS**

A Uniquely Human Debate

This opinion piece first appeared in the Washington Post National Weekly Edition. *Rick Weiss, formerly a writer for* Health *magazine, has been a science and medical reporter for the* Washington Post *since 1996, covering genetics, molecular biology, bioethics, and other topics in the life sciences. In this article, Weiss presents the arguments of a small group of people who have stated their cases for the freedom to be cloned or to clone another person and the concerns of bioethicists and legal scholars.*

WORD HISTORIES

Narcissism [paragraph 13]   In Greek mythology, Narcissus was a beautiful young man who was unable to love and who rejected everyone who developed romantic feelings for him. In one version of the myth, Nemesis, the goddess of revenge (see page 149), decreed that Narcissus would fall in love with himself. One day, he leaned over a pool of water, saw his own reflection, and immediately fell in love with his image. He lay next to the pool day after day, unable to take his gaze off his reflection. Eventually, he wasted away and died. The gods transformed his body into the flower we know today as *narcissus.* Ethicists are concerned that people who seek to clone themselves are only doing it out of "blatant *narcissism*"—excessive love of oneself.

Alchemy [paragraph 39]   Some people, Weiss writes, hope to clone themselves, to yield "better versions of themselves—through the *alchemy* of cloning." In the Middle Ages, *alchemists* were chemists who hoped to find a way to change base metals into gold. Today, we use the word *alchemy* to describe a process of changing or transmuting something from one form to another; in other words, scientists could use cloning *alchemy* to achieve an identical individual.

WORD PARTS

Bio- [selection as a whole]   Weiss alludes to *biologists* and *bioethicists.* The prefix *bio-* means "life." Thus a biologist studies life processes, from *bio-* + *ology* ("study of"), and a bioethicist studies ethical issues raised by new biological techniques like in vitro fertilization and cloning. Other words beginning with *bio-* are *biography*, the story of another person's life, and *biopsy*, an examination of an organism's tissue to determine disease.

What do these two words mean? Check a dictionary if you are unsure.

biodegradable   _____

biofeedback   _____

_____

WORD FAMILIES

Propel [paragraph 13]   The verb *propel* means "to move or to cause to move forward," and it can be broken down like this: *pro-* ("forward") + *pellere* ("to drive"). The related noun form is *propulsion*. English has several words from the roots *pellere* and *puls,* among them:

compel	to force or to drive someone to do something
compulsion	the noun form of *compel*
impel	to urge to action, to drive forward
impulse	the noun form of *impel*
repel	to drive back, to disgust
repulsion	the noun form of *repel*

FOREIGN PHRASES

Laissez-faire [paragraph 47]   This French phrase means "noninterference in other people's affairs." Its literal derivation from French is "let do," from *laissez* ("to let") + *faire* ("to do"). In this context, *laissez-faire* refers to the doctrine that the government should not regulate commerce, in this case, cloning.

RICK WEISS

A Uniquely Human Debate

1   Liz Catalan lives in a nice house in Miami. She does marketing for a cruise line. She's been married to a wonderful guy for five years. She is, in short, an ordinary woman of 41. Except that Catalan, who suffers from an untreatable form of infertility, has an extraordinary craving to be cloned. "I'm not crazy," says Catalan, whose ovaries went into premature failure years ago. "I just want to have a child of my own." Not a child made from a donor egg provided by someone she doesn't know. Not one adopted from halfway around the globe. She wants a baby genetically related to her. And if that means one who's genetically identical, then so be it.

2   Catalan is part of a small but serious cadre of would-be clonees, people who have studied the science, considered the issues and concluded that their pursuit of happiness might best be fulfilled by having themselves or a loved one cloned.

3   Their perspective is not countenanced on Capitol Hill, where Congress—although vigorously debating whether to allow the cloning of human embryos for research—is unified in its opposition to the creation of cloned babies. Nor is human cloning widely favored by the public. In a poll of Americans conducted last summer, almost 90 percent said scientists should not be allowed to use cloning to try to create children for infertile couples.

4   Yet many of those who wish to be cloned are not easily dismissed as kooks or cranks. And by bucking the majority view, they are pushing policymakers and the public to contemplate human futures unthinkable even a few years ago.

5   In fact, say ethicists and constitutional scholars, the cloning debate is important not because it will settle the question of whether cloning is "right" or "wrong"—it will not—but because it is forcing people to think more deeply about who we are

and what we want to become, as individuals and as a species. In our reflexive dismissal of human cloning, these experts say, there may be a missed opportunity to clarify what the issues really are and why they carry such emotional power.

6   Such soul-searching is one of the unanticipated but more immediate byproducts of a genetic revolution that is rewriting the rules of biology and society. It's an incremental revolution, without clear milestones that might make it easier to comprehend. And it is still largely confined to the laboratory. Yet it is being shaped not only by scientists but also by the basic longings that define the lives of ordinary people—people like Liz Catalan—who claim nothing less than a democratic right to be pioneers on the biomedical frontier.

7   "I'm willing and ready for whatever it takes," she says.

8   Human reproductive rights were far from Ian Wilmut's mind when he and his colleagues in Scotland took a skin cell from a 6-year-old ewe's udder, placed it in a laboratory dish, and—with a tiny bolt of electricity—fused it to an egg cell whose own genetic material had been removed. The result of that fusion was an embryo, which the Scottish team transferred to the womb of a surrogate mother sheep that, five months later, gave birth to a lamb named Dolly.[1]

9   Dolly offered the first living proof that mammals could be created from a single cell and without any contribution from a father. Centuries of scientific thinking collapsed in a heartbeat, and the social implications left people reeling. The day after Dolly's birth was announced, in February 1997, Washington University biologist Ursula Goodenough said pointedly that with human cloning, "there'd be no need for men."

10   President Bill Clinton responded immediately, ordering the National Bioethics Advisory Commission to study the topic and report back to him within 90 days. The commission's 120-page report, which remains the definitive critique of the technology, concluded that there was a lot to worry about.

11   Among the commission's concerns was that a clone might find it oppressive to know that his or her genetic life had already been lived, and feel robbed of the "open-ended future" that human rights advocates generally agree should be the birthright of every child. Moreover, a clone's "parent" might have onerous expectations as to how the clone should behave. Why else would someone be cloned, except to get a known quantity? "Cloning is a kind of Rorschach test for some of the worst excesses of parental hyper-expectations," says Thomas Murray, president of the Hastings Center, a bioethics think tank in Garrison, N.Y., who served on Clinton's bioethics commission.

12   The commission also warned that cloning could "undermine important social values by opening the door to a form of eugenics," genetic engineering. Republican Sen. Sam Brownback of Kansas, chief sponsor of a Senate bill to ban all cloning, echoes that thought. "Efforts to create human beings by cloning mark a new and decisive step toward turning human reproduction into a manufacturing process in which children are made in laboratories to preordained specifications," he said in February.

---

[1]In February 2003, Dolly was euthanized at the age of 6. She had developed a serious lung infection that could not be cured. (Ed.)

Dolly, the first cloned mammal.

13   But perhaps more than anything, what disturbs some ethicists is the literal self-promotionalism of it all. Cloning, after all, is about the ascendancy of the individual, the chance to propel one's genetic self into the future undiluted by another. Such "blatant narcissism," Murray says, can only undermine society.

14   Of course, some people want to clone others rather than themselves, most commonly a loved one, such as a child who met an untimely death. But ethicists foresee problems there, too. "This encourages all of us to view children as interchangeable commodities," says George Annas, a professor of health law at Boston University. "The death of a child thus need no longer be a singular human tragedy, but rather an opportunity to try to duplicate the no longer priceless deceased child."

15   Despite these and other concerns, Clinton's commission was not convinced that cloning posed unique or insurmountable social harms. It did recommend that Congress impose a moratorium on human cloning, but not on ethical or moral grounds. Rather, the commission was concerned about safety. And recognizing that research would likely overcome the miscarriages and deformities of early attempts, the commission recommended that any congressional ban automatically expire in five years.

16   Now five years have elapsed and, although the House has passed a ban, a divided Senate is only now considering similar bills. In the meantime, animal cloners have become increasingly adept. And a small number of doctors are compiling waiting lists of people who want to be cloned. Liz Catalan is on one of them.

17   She was a legal secretary for 15 years, during which she became well informed about a lot in medicine. She has thought about the possible problems, including the idea that clones might feel that their lives were already being lived, or had been lived, by another.

18   "I really, honestly think that clones could feel unique, depending on how you bring them up," Catalan says. "It happens all the time with identical twins."

19   Catalan's observation reflects a truth often overlooked in the age of the genome. With discoveries of genetic links to disease and personality announced every week, one could easily misbelieve that identity is written in the language of DNA. It is not. Our physical, cultural and social environments all influence what we become. Even Wilmut, who strongly opposes human cloning, has said he can easily tell his cloned sheep apart by their individual quirks, though all are genetic replicas.

20   "Having the same genome as another individual is no threat to the fact of human uniqueness or individuality," Brown University philosopher Dan Brock wrote in the April 12 issue of *Science*, "because the full identity, individuality or self of a person is determined by much more than the person's genome."

21   In fact, some have noted, clones might be expected to have less difficulty defining their own identities than twins typically have. Twins generally have to share both their genes and their environment. By contrast, a clone would likely be a generation younger than his or her parental twin.

22   As for the safety issues, Catalan and other cloning advocates cite the precedent of in-vitro fertilization, or IVF. Study after study has confirmed that babies conceived through IVF have significantly heightened odds of being born with medical and developmental problems (mostly due to IVF's higher prevalence of twins and triplets), yet no one demanded those data before the practice became widespread. And parents today are given the freedom to assess those risks and take them if they choose.

23   Similarly, some Jewish couples have 25 percent odds of giving birth to a baby with Tay-Sachs disease, a genetic condition that typically kills its victims by age 5. The federal government has not tried to stop them from having children. Why, advocates ask, is human cloning different?

24   Using safety concerns to set legal criteria for reproduction could have unintended consequences, says University of Alabama philosopher Gregory Pence. "If cloning one day becomes safer than sexual reproduction, will cloning then be the only [legal] way to have children—based on the good of future children?" Pence asked at a House subcommittee hearing last year. "To me, the essential moral question is whether human cloning is intrinsically wrong. But how can a new way of creating a family be intrinsically wrong?"

25   A family is all Liz Catalan wants. "I know it's not right for everyone," she says. "But I do personally believe that it should be up to each person. And if the only way a person can have a child of their own is to do this, and if they are willing to take a chance, then they should be able to."

26   At least a few doctors and scientists agree, and Catalan has been communicating with one of them: Kentucky fertility researcher Panos Zavos, who announced a year ago his intention to collaborate in an offshore human cloning effort. Catalan is one of more than 2,200 adults Zavos says are on his waiting list.

27   Zavos, who was invited to testify before a House subcommittee, isn't the only one claiming to have begun a cloning effort. Italian fertility doctor Severino Antinori has said he intends to produce a human clone as soon as he can. Last month he claimed to have three pregnancies underway, but others in the field are skeptical.

28   Meanwhile, leaders of the obscure Raelian religion, who believe that cloning can bring people closer to enlightenment and who say they've heard from 3,000 volunteers, announced in London earlier this year that they had begun a project to clone a terminally ill man. According to the Raelians, the unidentified man plans to stop taking his medications if the effort succeeds and die peacefully in the knowledge that he—or a reasonable facsimile of himself—may enjoy a second chance at life.

29   The Raelians don't stop with the dying, either; they are willing to clone the dead. Unlike Zavos and Antinori, who have said they will offer cloning only to infertile couples, the Raelians are offering their services to grieving relatives who want to see their loved ones again.

30   That offer could appeal to an especially motivated, distraught and vulnerable subset of potential clients, people like Kathy Gordon, whose tireless efforts to have her dead daughter cloned testify to the lengths to which some will go to heal a broken heart.

31   Gordon's eldest daughter, Emily, was 16 years old in 1997, when the news about Dolly the sheep came out. At the time, Gordon says, Emily spoke enthusiastically about the prospect of human cloning. Six months later she was killed by a drunk driver.

32   Devastated by the sudden loss, Kathy Gordon became obsessed with the idea of cloning a girl from some of Emily's cells. She spoke to the coroner soon after the accident and tried to have some tissues frozen in liquid nitrogen, but to no avail. She contacted many of the top scientists in the world of cloning, but those who replied, she says, simply "offered condolences." The few tubes of Emily's blood that remain today have been stored in refrigerators not cold enough to ensure proper preservation of her cells for cloning. But Gordon still harbors some hope that the technology will improve, allowing their use someday.

33   "I don't understand people who want to clone themselves," says Gordon, 42, a lab technician who lives in central Montana and has a doctorate in ethics. But cloning one's dead daughter is different, she says. "I'd trade everything I have today just to have Emily back."

34   Gordon rejects the idea that she would try to mold her new child into some preconceived persona. Don't all parents struggle with the dueling urges to shape a child and let that child become its own person? It's a struggle, Gordon says, that she'd be having with Emily if not for the accident that took her away.

35   And besides, she asks, since when does the government engage in the business of distinguishing between good and bad reasons for having a child? Surely, Gordon says, her freedom to reproduce is at least as compelling as a clone's right to be unique.

36   She has some case law on her side. The Supreme Court has recognized that "procreation" and the right to "have offspring" are fundamental rights, which means the government cannot restrict them without overwhelmingly good reason. "If the right of privacy means anything," the court said 30 years ago in *Eisenstadt v. Baird*, "it is the right of the individual . . . to be free from unwarranted governmental intrusion into matters so fundamentally affecting a person as the decision whether to bear or beget a child." Other cases offer similar language.

37   Of course, even cloning won't bring Gordon's daughter back, but Gordon knows that. She knows that cloning replicates nature, not nurture. But that's part of her inspiration.

38   Emily grew up in difficult circumstances during Gordon's previous marriage, Gordon says, declining to go into details. "But in the end, she turned out wonderfully," Gordon says. "If I could have a child with her predisposition to life, her humor, but have her grow up in this new life I've created for myself, which is much better now. I'm married to an attorney. I have all kinds of things now. . . ." Her voice trails off.

39   Any parent would want something better for his or her child. But what about people who want to better themselves—or make better versions of themselves— through the alchemy of cloning?

40   What about Jonathan Colvin?

41   Colvin, who is 34 and holds degrees in physics and philosophy, was a science fiction buff as a kid and remembers reading tales about human cloning long before it became scientifically plausible. Now he's a technical writer for a computer company in Vancouver.

42   He was born with cystic fibrosis, an inherited lung disease that could easily kill him within the next decade. There is no cure, but by adding a healthy version of the gene that's defective in CF, scientists have been able to "cure" individual cells taken from patients with the disease. Now Colvin wants scientists to do just that, and a little bit more: Take one of the trillions of cells in his body, fix the tiny molecular mutation that causes the disease, and then clone that single repaired cell to grow a new and literally improved copy of himself—a newborn Jonathan Colvin who would be free of the disease.

43   "In some respect, it would give me a second chance at life without CF," Colvin says. "It wouldn't be me, but it would be very similar to me."

44   To opponents, of course, Colvin's vision just feeds their worst fears that cloning will lead to a new eugenics. "Human nature itself lies on the operating table, ready for alteration," the University of Chicago's Leon Kass warned in the *New Republic* last spring. "We can see all too clearly where the train is headed, and we do not like the destination," wrote Kass, who is now chief of President Bush's Bioethics Council.

45   But Colvin does not see his situation in that light. He's not interested in building a superior human.

46   He doesn't want a kid with Michael Jordan's jumping genes or Georgia O'Keefe's artistic vision. He just wants to make a normal, healthy boy.

47   Colvin is not the only one who sees the specter of eugenics as an argument for, rather than against, laissez-faire human cloning. Think about the Nazi era,

when the state "knew" what was best, says Nick Bostrom, a philosopher at Yale University. Think about Scandinavia through the 1970s, when mentally handicapped people were "encouraged" to be sterilized.

48   In Bostrom's view, eugenics movements of decades past were problematic precisely because governments got involved in decisions about reproduction. "The best way to avoid these scenarios," he says, "is for people to make their own reproductive choices."

49   Recently Colvin has been getting some legal advice as to whether he might have a good case under the Canadian constitution favoring his right to clone a healthy version of himself. "Most of the objections I've heard so far are for religious reasons, which I believe should not be imposed on me, or because people are just plain scared," Colvin says. "They're afraid of science fiction, like 'The Attack of the Clones.'"

50   What Colvin fears is the possibility that his offspring would suffer as he has. Does the government really feel compelled to stop him from having a child with healthy, pink lungs? A child who need not think about every breath? "If anything," he says, "it would be socially irresponsible for me to clone myself and not knock out the CF." ✳

From Rick Weiss, "A Uniquely Human Debate," *The Washington Post* Weekly Edition, June 3–9, 2002. © 2002 *The Washington Post*. Reprinted with permission.

Exercises

You may refer to the selection as you complete these exercises. Write your answers to these questions in the spaces provided.

A. IDENTIFYING THE CLAIM

1. Using your own words as much as possible, write the writer's central claim or proposition. Also indicate the number of the paragraph in which it is

   located._____

   _____

   _____

   _____

2. Then decide if the claim is a claim of fact, a claim of value, or a claim of policy. Remember that an argument may have a secondary claim as well. _____

   _____

B. LOCATING EVIDENCE

1. Since Weiss presents both sides of the cloning debate, this exercise is divided into two parts. First, locate evidence in the article that presents arguments *against* cloning of human beings and those who are proponents of the tech-

nology. One piece of evidence offered by *opponents* of cloning is listed here. List three other major pieces of evidence that Weiss includes. Also characterize each piece of evidence according to whether it represents facts and statistics; examples and observations; good reasons; or quotation or testimony.

a. Cloning could open the door to eugenics, the practice of genetically engineering babies by selecting only those who possess certain desired traits, which occurred in Nazi Germany. [good reason]

b. _____

_____

c. _____

_____

d. _____

_____

2. Now do the same for those who favor cloning. One piece of evidence offered by *proponents* of cloning is listed here. List three other major pieces of evidence that Weiss lists as arguments for the practice. Also characterize each piece of evidence according to whether it represents facts and statistics; examples and observations; good reasons; or quotation or testimony.

a. Liz Catalan is infertile and wants to have a child genetically related to her, making her reject other methods of conception like using a donated egg. [example]

b. _____

_____

_____

_____

c. _____

_____

d. _____

_____

C. USING VOCABULARY

Here are some words from the selection. Write an original sentence using each word that shows both that you know how to use the word and what it means. The number of the paragraph where the word occurs in the selection is provided for you.

1. *surrogate* [paragraph 8]_____

_____

2. *implications* [9] _____

_____

3. *critique* [10] _____

_____

4. *oppressive* [11] _____

_____

5. *undermine* [12] _____

_____

6. *blatant* [13] _____

_____

7. *replica* [19] _____

_____

8. *precedent* [22] _____

_____

9. *criteria* [singular is *criterion*—24] _____

_____

10. *skeptical* [27] _____

_____

D. SUMMARIZING EXERCISE

Summarize the information in paragraph 11.

Original Passage

Among the commission's concerns was that a clone might find it oppressive to know that his or her genetic life had already been lived, and feel robbed of the "open-ended future" that human rights advocates generally agree should be the birthright of every child. Moreover, a clone's "parent" might have onerous expectations as to how the clone should behave. Why else would someone be cloned, except to get a known quantity? "Cloning is a

Summary

_____

_____

_____

_____

_____

_____

_____

_____

_____

kind of Rorschach test for some of the worst

excesses of parental hyper-expectations," says

Thomas Murray, president of the Hastings

Center, a bioethics think tank in Garrison,

N.Y., who served on Clinton's bioethics

commission.

_____

_____

_____

_____

_____

_____

E. TOPICS FOR WRITING OR DISCUSSION

1. Of the three proposals for cloning—Liz Catalan's, Kathy Gordon's, and John Colvin's—whose do you find most compelling, if any?
2. Weiss opens the article by noting that 90 percent of Americans oppose cloning as a way "to create children for infertile couples." Do you agree with the majority on this question? What about the other cases Weiss presents? Should a parent have the right to clone a dead child? Should someone who suffers from an incurable genetic disease be allowed to have the defective gene "repaired" and then a new, improved model cloned?
3. Write a paragraph or two in which you set forth your own reactions to this article, whether for or against the concept of cloning.

For Further Exploration

WEB SITES

The following sites provide a broad spectrum of information about cloning, its moral implications, and the scientific principles underlying this technique. The first is sponsored by PBS's *NewsHour* with Jim Lehrer:

- *http://www.pbs.org/newshour/health/cloning.html*

This site, sponsored by BBC news, includes coverage of the ethical problems associated with cloning, current research, definitions of key terms, and recent legislation:

- *http://news.bbc.co.uk/1/hi/uk/1130633.stm*

Patterns of Development and Transitions

In this final section, we will take up two important skills that are necessary for good comprehension of nonfiction prose: a recognition of various patterns of development. These include a list of facts or details, examples, reasons (cause and effect), process (sequential steps), and contrast (showing differences) as well as transitional elements.

Patterns of Development

Let's say that you are wrestling with a big decision that you must make about your future. You know that you are interested in helping people, and you come up with a list of careers in which such an interest would be required for someone to succeed and be happy. On a sheet of paper you note the following career choices: nurse, doctor, teacher, charity worker, mental health worker, social worker. What you have done is provide *examples,* specific instances of careers in which you could help others.

Now you have another decision facing you: Should you apply to the four-year state university fifty miles away or study for the first two years at your local community college and then transfer? Again, you write down the good and bad aspects of both institutions and analyze their differences. Now you're *contrasting.* And when your counselor asks you why you want to become, say, a social worker, you come up with some *reasons* why the field of social work appeals to you.

These logical processes, which we do all the time in our daily lives, are also present in writing. Called *patterns of development,* they refer to the internal logic of a passage, the way the writer gets his or her ideas across. The choice of the appropriate pattern of development hinges on the subject. But your starting point is to recognize that these patterns of development can pertain to our thought processes as well as to the pattern a writer imposes on his or her material. We will examine each pattern briefly; they are illustrated with some short passages. Studying these patterns will help you keep on track as you read and follow the writer's thinking process.

LISTING FACTS OR DETAILS

The pattern of *listing facts* or *details* is perhaps the simplest one to recognize. Following the main idea, each supporting sentence presents factual evidence to support the main assertion. Consider this passage from a *New Yorker* article on the grueling Tour de France cycling race held every summer. The American cyclist

Lance Armstrong has won this race four times, despite his bout with cancer. In this excerpt, Michael Specter supports the main idea—identified in the margin—with a listing of details that prove his point:

Physical demands on competitive cyclists are immense.

The physical demands on competitive cyclists are immense. One day, they will have to ride two hundred kilometres through the mountains; the next day there might be a long, flat sprint lasting seven hours. Because cyclists have such a low percentage of body fat, they are more susceptible to infections than other people. (At the beginning of the Tour, Armstrong's body is around four or five per cent; this season Shaquille O'Neal, the most powerful player in the N.B.A., boasted that his body-fat level was sixteen per cent.)

The Tour de France has been described as the equivalent of running twenty marathons in twenty days. During the nineteen-eighties and nineties, Wim H. M. Saris, a professor of nutrition at the University of Maastricht, conducted a study of human endurance by following participants in the Tour. . . .

Looking at a wide range of physical activities, Saris and his colleagues measured the metabolic demands made on people engaged in each of them. "On average, cyclists expend sixty-five hundred calories a day for three weeks, with peak days of ten thousand calories," he said. "If you are sedentary, you are burning perhaps twenty-five hundred calories a day. Active people might burn as many as thirty-five hundred. . . ."

—Michael Specter, "The Long Ride," *The New Yorker*

EXAMPLES

An *example* is a specific instance of something more general. As you saw earlier, nursing and social work are examples of fields involving helping people. Consider this paragraph about the Ohlone Indians who inhabited parts of Northern California hundreds of years ago. Malcolm Margolin begins with the statement that, in comparison to Europeans, Ohlones seemed lazy. (You can tell that the writer is challenging this observation because he puts the word *laziness* in quotation marks.) The examples have been briefly annotated for you in the margin. Note that the first example is preceded with the helpful transitional phrase, "for example," and the next three little examples follow logically from that connector.

Main idea: Episodic harvesting explains "laziness"

Examples: deer hunting—arduous

Acorn, seed, & salmon harvests—hard work but for short periods

No crops to cultivate, animals to tend, ditches to dig

The episodic character of the harvesting also helps explain another much noted Ohlone characteristic: their so-called "laziness." For them hard work came only in spurts. Deer hunting, for example, was an arduous pursuit that demanded fasting, abstinence, great physical strength, and single-mindedness of purpose. The acorn harvest, the seed harvest, and the salmon harvest also involved considerable work for short periods of time. But when the work was over, there was little else to do. Unlike agricultural people, the Ohlones had no fields to plow, seeds to plant, crops to cultivate, weeds to pull, domestic animals to care for, or irrigation ditches to dig or maintain. So at the end of a harvest they often gave themselves over to "entire indolence," as one visitor described it—a habit that infuriated the Europeans who assumed that laziness was sinful and that hard work was not just a virtue for a God-given condition of human life.

—Malcolm Margolin, *The Ohlone Way*

REASONS—CAUSE AND EFFECT

In Part 4, you saw that writers of persuasive prose may use good reasons to support their opinion. But *reasons,* answers to question "why," are often present in regular expository (explanatory) prose as well. Reasons comprise one-half of the cause–effect relationship, meaning that every effect (every situation, every problem) has a cause or a reason—or perhaps multiple reasons—to explain it. If you write, for example, "Vinh passed his English class because he studied hard every day and got help from a tutor," the *effect* is that Vinh passed his class, and the *reasons* or the *causes* are that he studied hard and had a tutor.

In this excerpt from Selection 9, "The Life and Death of a Western Gladiator," Charles Finney discusses the situation faced by a new-born diamondback rattlesnake:

> The direct rays of the sun could, in a short time, kill him. If the temperature dropped too low he would freeze. Without food, he would starve. Without moisture he would die of dehydration. If a man or a horse stepped on him he would be crushed.

Here is the passage printed again, with the cause–effect relationships marked for you. The causes are set in colored blocks and the effects are underlined. The arrows show the relationship between the two.

> The direct rays of the sun could, in a short time, kill him. If the temperature dropped too low he would freeze. Without food, he would starve. Without moisture he would die of dehydration. If a man or horse stepped on him he would be crushed.

Here is another example of a paragraph using the cause and effect pattern; however, unlike the one about the causes of death for a baby rattlesnake, this one begins with a single *cause* or *reason,* followed by a series of *effects.* Follow the annotations as you read.

Cause: Civil rights movement

Effects: gave us Dr. King; each other; material things; knowledge; pride; gave men a purpose; broke black servitude; heroes & leaders; hope; gave us history; a call to life

What good was the civil rights movement? If it had just given this country Dr. King, a leader of conscience for once in our lifetime, it would have been enough. . . . If the civil rights movement is "dead," and if it gave us nothing else, it gave us each other forever. It gave some of us bread, some of us shelter, some of us knowledge and pride, all of us comfort. It gave us our children, our husbands, our brothers, our fathers, as men reborn and with a purpose for living. It broke the pattern of black servitude in this country. . . . It gave us history and men far greater than Presidents. It gave us heroes, selfless men of courage and strength, for our little boys to follow. It gave us hope for tomorrow. It called us to life.

Because we live, it can never die.

—Alice Walker, "The Civil Rights Movement: What Good Was It?" *American Scholar*

PROCESS

If you want to make an omelet for your Sunday morning breakfast, you could follow a cookbook recipe or you could follow your instincts. Either way, you would go through a *process,* a series of steps that, if followed in order, would produce something edible. First you would crack three eggs into a bowl and beat them. Then you would heat a little butter in your pan. Next, you would grate some cheese and chop some onions, add the eggs to the pan, and so forth. Writers use the process pattern for two primary purposes: (1) to show how to do something, for example, how to make an omelet, how to change a flat tire, or how to burn CDs; or (2) to show how something occurred, for example, how glaciers formed during the Ice Age or how a surfer tackles a big wave.

In this illustrative paragraph, Sophie Petit-Zerman discusses the phenomenon of laughter and answers this question: "Is it true that laughing can make us healthier?" Each step in the process is numbered to help you follow the discussion:

> [Laughter is] undoubtedly the best medicine. For one thing it's exercise. [1] It activates the cardiovascular system, so heart rate and blood pressure increase, [2] then the arteries dilate, causing blood pressure to fall again. [3] Repeated short, strong contractions of the chest muscles, diaphragm, and abdomen increase blood flow into our internal organs, and forced respiration—the *ha! ha!*—makes sure that this blood is well oxygenated. [4] Muscle tension decreases, and indeed [5] we may temporarily lose control of our limbs, as in the expression "weak with laughter."
>
> —Sophie Petit-Zerman, "No Laughing Matter," *Discover*

CONTRAST

How does a Honda differ from a Toyota? How are high school English classes different from college English courses? What are the major differences between the two sports Web sites espn.com and sportsline.com? When a writer sets two subjects side by side and examines their differences, he or she is using the *contrast* pattern. In this example, Bruno Bettelheim explores the main idea stated in the first sentence by contrasting fairy tales and dreams. Again, study the annotations:

Differences between fairy tales & dreams

Open vs. disguised wish fulfillment

Relief of pressure and happy ending vs. lack of solution for inner pressures

> There are, of course, very significant differences between fairy tales and dreams. For example, in dreams more often than not the wish fulfillment is disguised, while in fairy tales much of it is openly expressed. To a considerable degree, dreams are the result of inner pressures which have found no relief, of problems which beset a person to which he knows no solution and to which the dream finds none. The fairy tale does the opposite: it projects the relief of all pressures and not only offers ways to solve problems but promises that a "happy" solution will be found.
>
> —Bruno Bettelheim, *The Uses of Enchantment: The Meaning and Importance of Fairy Tales*

<table>
<tr><td colspan="5" align="center">**PATTERNS OF DEVELOPMENT**</td></tr>
</table>

List of Facts or Details	Examples	Reason—Cause and Effect	Description of a Process	Contrast
Includes factual details to support the main idea.	Uses specific instances of something more general to support the main idea.	Offers reasons (show causes and effects) that explain why to support the main idea.	Explains the steps one needs to follow to support the main idea.	Sets two subjects side by side and examines their differences to support the main idea.

Transitional Elements

Sometimes called *markers, transitional elements* make the logical relationships between ideas clear. They "mark" the place where a writer shifts ideas or indicates a particular logical connection. In this way, they serve as a bridge between ideas, helping us follow the writer's thinking, keeping us on track, and showing us where a shift—sometimes a very subtle shift—in thought begins. As you will see, transitions can be either single words or phrases. And sometimes an entire paragraph may be used as a transition, pointing back to the preceding paragraph and, at the same time, pointing ahead to the next idea in the chain of ideas.

Some writers use lots of transitions; others use none at all. But when they are present, they are useful. Contrary to what some students may have been taught, transitions do not necessarily come at the beginning of sentences. They can appear in the middle of sentences or even at the end. By studying a number of examples, you will quickly become proficient at locating transitions. The most common types of transitional elements follow.

TRANSITIONS THAT INDICATE ADDITIONAL INFORMATION IS COMING

These transitions are most commonly used in the first two patterns: listing facts and details and offering examples. Here are some examples:

and
next
besides
in the same way
in addition
further
furthermore
moreover
next
also
first
second

Examples from the Reading Selections

At 18, I had grown tired. . . . I had seen too many dead across the pavement. . . . In addition, I had fallen through the cracks of two languages, unable to communicate well in any.

—Luis J. Rodriguez, "La Vida Loca: Two Generations of Gang Members"

Markman has shown that instead of testing endless hypotheses about each word's meaning, kids start from three basic assumptions. First, they figure that labels refer to whole objects, not parts or qualities. Second, they expect labels to denote classes of things . . . rather than individual items. Third, they assume that anything with a name can have only one.

—Geoffrey Cowley, "The Language Explosion"

TRANSITIONS THAT INTRODUCE EXAMPLES OR ILLUSTRATIONS

These transitions signal that a writer is going to give an example or illustration to reinforce a more general idea. Here are some examples:

for example
for instance
to illustrate
as a case in point
consider the following
namely

Examples from the Reading Selections

A 1993 U.S. Department of Education Report on illiteracy says 21–23 percent of U.S. adults—about 40 million—read minimally, enough to decipher an uncomplicated meeting announcement. Another 25–38 percent read and write only slightly better. For instance, they can fill out a simple form.

—Richard Wolkomir, "Making Up for Lost Time: The Rewards of Reading at Last"

It wasn't that we had no system for keeping track of time and of the important events in our lives. But ours was a natural—or, rather, a divine—calendar because it was framed by acts of God. . . . Simple as our calendar was, it worked just fine for us. Take, for example, the birth date of Teta Im Khalil, the oldest woman in Magdaluna and all the surrounding villages.

—Anwar F. Accawi, "The Telephone"

TRANSITIONS THAT SHOW CAUSE–EFFECT CONNECTIONS

Although not as common, there are a few transitional elements that signal a cause–effect relationship. Interestingly, there are no true transitional words that indicate *cause*. The writer can show cause only by using conjunctions like *because* or *for* (meaning "because") or by writing a phrase like *one reason for*, or other similar expressions. However, there are a few transitions that indicate *effect* or *result*. Here are six:

as a result
consequently
therefore
thus
then
hence

Examples from the Reading Selections

The vice principal's research of T.L.O.'s purse had violated her Fourth Amendment right. Therefore, the evidence seized could not be used against her. [shows result]

—Ellen Alderman and Caroline Kennedy, *"New Jersey v. T.L.O.: The School Search Cases"*

[Chief Megliquili is speaking]: "There sit our sons . . . young, healthy, and handsome, the flower of the Xhosa tribe, the pride of our nation. We have just circumcised them in a ritual that promises them manhood, but I am here to tell you that it is an empty, illusory promise, a promise that can never be fulfilled. For we Xhosas, and all black South Africans, are a conquered people. We are slaves in our own country." [means "because" and shows cause]

—Nelson Mandela, "Long Walk to Freedom"

TRANSITIONS THAT SHOW CHRONOLOGICAL ORDER OR TIME PROGRESSION

This group of transitions is particularly evident in the process pattern or in narratives. Writers use them to ensure a logical progression of steps or a logical sequence of events. Here are some examples:

then
meanwhile
later
after
eventually
soon
after a few days
next
in 2001

Examples from the Reading Selections

One kind-hearted lady who was trying to feed an elephant at the San Diego Zoo made the mistake of holding her purse and the peanut in the hand she stretched out across the moat. . . . Instead of taking the peanut the elephant grabbed the purse, which in the process fell open. The elephant then turned the purse upside down and emptied its contents on the ground. For the next several moments, while the formerly kindhearted lady watched helplessly, the elephant picked up all the objects one by one. . . . Eventually, the purse and its contents were rescued.

—Sheldon Campbell, "Games Elephants Play"

In March of 1984, the Supreme Court heard oral arguments concerning whether the exclusionary rule should apply in the school setting. In June of 1984, the Court told the parties to back up and address a constitutional issue they had not even raised.

In October of 1984, the parties were back before the Court, this time arguing about whether school officials were bound by the Fourth Amendment in the first place. On January 15, 1985, the Supreme Court finally issued its opinion.

—Ellen Alderman and Caroline Kennedy, "*New Jersey v. T.L.O.:* The School Search Cases"

TRANSITIONS THAT SHOW CONTRAST

This last group of transitions helps keep the reader on track when the writer is moving back and forth and between two subjects showing the differences. Consider these examples:

but
yet
still
however
nevertheless
nonetheless
on the other hand
in contrast
instead
whereas
while

Examples from the Reading Selections

Then he takes her home, and she lies on her bed, a conflicted, tortured soul, and weeps until dawn, whereas when Roger gets back to his place, he opens a bag of Doritos.

—Dave Barry, "Tips for Women: How to Have a Relationship with a Guy"

I was not happy to be part of the agricultural work force. I would have preferred working in a dress shop or baby-sitting, like my friends. But I had a dream that would cost a lot of money—college.

—Rose Del Castillo Guilbault, "The Conveyor-Belt Ladies"

While female elephants, even those that play games, are generally friendly and affable and in the Asian species fairly easy to train, male elephants are a different story.

—Sheldon Campbell, "Games Elephants Play"

TRANSITIONS	
Type of Transition	**Examples**
Additional Information	and, next, besides, in the same way, in addition, further, furthermore, moreover, next, also, first, second
Examples or Illustrations	for example, for instance, to illustrate, as a case in point, consider the following, namely
Cause–Effect Connections	*cause:* because, for *result:* as a result, consequently, therefore, thus, then, hence
Chronology	then, meanwhile, later, after, eventually, soon, after a few days, next, in 2001
Contrasts	but, yet, still, however, nevertheless, nonetheless, on the other hand, in contrast, instead, whereas, while

Some Final Considerations

As mentioned earlier, a writer is under no obligation to use transitional elements to make the reader's job easier. In the absence of transitions, how can you maintain focus, keep on track, and follow along with the writer's words. As stated frequently in this text, reading with a pencil in your hand—actively annotating—can help. Also actively thinking about the connections between ideas can help.

To illustrate, consider this short paragraph by Elliott West from "Wagon Train Children":

> Most of the work was not so light. Children herded, cooked, hunted, gathered water, cared for babies and did other important tasks. And circumstances often left a boy or girl with graver responsibilities. When his fatherless family was abandoned by a hired hand, 11-year-old Elisha Brooks drove the animals, stood guard at night and generally took charge.

What is the relationship between the first sentences and those that follow? What would be the best way for West to support the idea that for the children, the work along the trail "was not so light"? The only pattern of development that works here is *example,* and that's exactly what he does: West provides several short examples and one illustration of a fatherless family's son to prove his point. When transitional elements are absent, the reader must supply his or her own connections.

Finally, pay attention to repeated words and phrases. For example, read this opening paragraph from "Long Walk to Freedom" by Nelson Mandela and study the highlighted words and phrases:

> When I was sixteen, the regent decided that it was time that I became a man.
>
> In Xhosa tradition, this is achieved through one means only: circumcision. In
>
> my tradition, an uncircumcised male cannot be heir to his father's wealth,
>
> cannot marry or officiate in tribal rituals. An uncircumcised Xhosa man is a

contradiction in terms, for he is not considered a man at all, but a boy. For the Xhosa people, circumcision represents the formal incorporation of males into society. It is not just a surgical procedure, but a lengthy and elaborate ritual in preparation for manhood. As a Xhosa, I count my years as a man from the date of my circumcision.

The highlighted words and phrases are not there by accident. Mandela is a careful writer, and the repetition of the key words *Xhosa, circumcision, tradition,* and the synonyms *man* and *male* is deliberate. Paying attention to these repetitions makes this paragraph quite readable, even if the concepts are foreign.

PART FIVE

Mastering Difficult Prose

28

SCOTT ANDERSON

In Country

On September 11, 2001, terrorists hijacked airplanes and used them as missiles, flying them into the twin towers of New York's World Trade Center. Another plane crashed into the Pentagon in Washington, DC, but passengers on the fourth plane—supposedly headed either for the U.S. Capitol or the White House—somehow wrested control from the hijackers. That plane crashed into a field in Pennsylvania. In this article, first published in the November 2001 issue of Esquire, *war correspondent Scott Anderson describes the scene in New York after the World Trade Center buildings collapsed and concludes that, after reporting from a dozen wars in his career, the warfront was suddenly in his own country.*

The article's title, "In Country," reflects a recent American idiom referring to Vietnam. If an American soldier says that he was "in country," it means that he fought in Vietnam during the conflict that lasted from the mid-1960s to 1975, when Saigon fell to the North Vietnamese.

Vocabulary Preview

WORD HISTORIES

Charisma [paragraph 8]   *Charisma* means "a rare quality, applied to certain leaders who inspire devotion among their followers." It is most typically applied to political or religious leaders. For example, Adolf Hitler, John F. Kennedy, and Martin Luther King Jr. were often described as *charismatic*. This word comes into the English language from the Greek word *kharisma*, meaning "favor" or "divine gift."

Bizarre (Pejoration) [paragraph 34]   Anderson writes that the area where the World Trade Center's twin towers had once stood was "a *bizarre* scene." *Bizarre* means "strikingly odd," "farfetched," or "grotesque." The word has completely changed its meaning from the original. In French (*bizarre*), Spanish and Portuguese (*bizarro*), and Italian (*bizzarro*), the word originally meant "handsome" or "brave." According to the *Oxford Dictionary of English Etymology,* all these Romance languages (languages that were derived from Latin) got the word from the Basque word *bizarra*, which meant "beard," and wearing a beard was the mark of a swashbuckler, a dashing adventurer. Over time, the word changed meaning from something positive—"dashing" or "brave"—to something negative—"strange." This type of transformation is an example of *pejoration*, a process whereby a word shifts meaning over a long period of time from a positive meaning to a negative one.

WORD PARTS

-cracy [paragraph 8]   The word *meritocracy* is composed of two word elements: *merit* + *-cracy*, meaning "rule." The Greek suffix *kratia*, from *kratos*, originally meant "strength" or "power." Therefore, a meritocracy is a society in which the power lies in those who have achieved, in other words, those who merited it. A *democracy* describes rule by the people, from *demos* ("people") + *-cracy*. The suffix indicating a person is *-crat*, as in *democrat*.

Here are some other words ending with this useful suffix:

plutocracy	government by the wealthy [*ploutos* ("wealth") + *-cracy*]
aristocracy	government by the ruling class [*aristos* ("best") + *-cracy*]
bureaucracy	administration of a government or other organization by bureaus or departments

What is an *autocracy*? Check a dictionary if you are unsure. _____

_____

WORD FAMILIES

Rehydrate [paragraph 25]   The Greek element *hydra* or *hydro* means "water." In Greek mythology, Hydra was a many-headed monster that Hercules slayed, and it was also the name of a water serpent. *Rehydrate* means "to replenish fluids in the body," from *re-* ("again") + *hydra* + *-ate* (a common verb ending). The element *hydra* or *hydro* is the basis for a large family of words, among them:

hydroelectric	making electricity by converting water into energy
hydraulic	describing something moved by water under pressure
hydrometer	an instrument used to measure a fluid's specific gravity
hydrology	scientific study of water, its properties and distribution in soils
hydrothermal	relating to hot water
hydrophobia	fear of water

SCOTT ANDERSON

In Country

1   It is an odd thing, probably not what one would predict or remember afterward, but when a person encounters true horror, the body's first response almost always occurs in the hands. With women, the hands tend to immediately come up to cover the mouth or press the cheeks. Among men, they tend to form a steeple over the nose and mouth or to clutch tightly onto the sides of the head. It is as if, in this moment of utter incomprehension and helplessness, the hands are trying to give comfort.

2   I'm not sure where I first noticed this. It might have been in Belfast in 1989, when a large car bomb went off downtown and the people around me didn't know which way to run as glass rained down around us. Or it might have been before that, in Beirut in 1983 or in Sri Lanka in 1987, but it does seem to be a uni-

What remained of the World Trade Towers after their collapse September 11, 2001.

versal reflex, this thing with the hands. I saw it again at 9:59 on the morning of September 11 in New York City.

3   At that moment, I was standing on the roof of an apartment building in the East Village, watching the billows of white smoke pouring off the upper floors of the World Trade Center towers, perhaps two miles away. On the surrounding rooftops were scores, maybe hundreds, of other onlookers. At 9:59, there appeared to be a sudden bulging outward around the midpoint of Tower Two, a quick glittering of either fire or the morning sun reflecting off dislodged windows, and then Tower Two started straight down with a speed that seemed to defy gravity. On the rooftops all around me, men gripped their heads, women their faces. Just down from me, a man in his late thirties with a long ponytail and tattooed forearms began screaming, "No, no!" then dropped to his knees and wrapped his arms tightly over his chest. I remember looking at him with a mix of pity and envy—pity for his pain but envy because he was the first among us to find his voice, the first to move from shock to despair, and this seemed the healthiest reaction to have. I was still just standing there, mute, numb, clutching my head.

4   Over the past eighteen years, I've been to a dozen-odd war zones around the world. Usually, I went as a journalist, with all the detachment and comparative immunity that implies. Of course, there were times when both detachment and immunity fell away, when I witnessed things that affected me deeply, or I found myself in harm's way, but in all these places, I was, first and foremost, an outsider; what was happening fundamentally did not involve me, it was not my war. Nor could I ever reasonably claim to be shocked by what I saw; after all, I had gone there for the very purpose of seeing it. All that ended, as it did for

millions of other New Yorkers, on the morning of September 11. For the first time, I had not gone to war, but war had come to me—and with as little warning as it comes to most—and if a lot of it felt very familiar, a lot of it didn't at all.

5   After Tower One collapsed at 10:28, I left the apartment rooftop. Like everyone else in the city, I didn't know what to do, I just knew that I needed to do something, and maybe if I began to walk I would discover it. I started south, toward the plume of white smoke and dust in the sky.

6   The four lanes of First Avenue were virtually empty save for an occasional racing ambulance or police car, but along the sidewalks came a flood of people heading north. There was a hush to them, hardly anyone speaking, and here and there in the crowd was someone caked in fine beige powder. I don't think any of them knew where they were going, either, just away from the ugly cloud, further into the warmth and sunlight of this beautiful late-summer morning.

7   Walking against the current, I spotted a middle-aged businessman approaching at a brisk pace, weaving and overtaking "traffic" the way New Yorkers do on sidewalks. He was dressed in an expensive suit and clutched a fine leather briefcase, but it was as if he'd been dipped in buckwheat flour from head to toe, and the briskness of his walk was causing little spumes of dust to fly off him with each step. As we passed, he gave me a quick, slightly annoyed glance, as if to say, "What the hell are you looking at?" He obviously had been close when the towers came down, had undoubtedly sprinted for his life, and had done so in such blind terror that it never occurred to him to drop the briefcase. Now, a half hour and two miles away, he was still pumped up, still moving on the adrenaline that might give out on the next block or might carry him all the way to wherever he imagined he was headed.

8   In war, the fabric of society—the rules and laws and customs that are lived by—frays in direct proportion to one's nearness to the battlefield. In most wars, this fraying occurs over a distance of provinces or valleys or mountain ranges, but in New York on September 11 it was happening over the space of a few city blocks. By 11:00, the authorities were trying to establish a security perimeter at Canal Street, a demarcation line between civilization and madness that civilians would not be allowed past. The problem was, the police detailed to this task were just as lost and stunned as the rest of us; their authority had deserted them. A policeman stopped me, ordered me back. I nodded at him and continued on, and he simply turned to try his luck with someone else. Once past this line, authority had little to do with rank or uniforms; in the peculiar kind of meritocracy that takes over in a place of chaos, leadership now fell to anyone with the surety or charisma to seize it.

9   I first saw this at a forward triage unit being set up in the lobby of the Department of Health building near City Hall, where a black woman in her mid-thirties in a white coat was in command of people twice her age. Perhaps she was a doctor, perhaps a nurse, but her authority stemmed from her calm, her ability to focus on each person who came before her and to give them orders. It didn't matter if the commands she gave were impossible to fulfill, it was the certainty with which she gave them that made the rest of us trust her; in our collective impotence, we were all just looking for someone to tell us what to do.

10   I helped unload boxes of medical supplies coming off trucks, stacked them along the walls of the lobby. It felt good to do this, like I was being useful, and I

was spurred on by a man somewhere in the crowd who repeatedly shouted, "Come on, people, we have to get organized. They're going to be coming in any minute now." Except they didn't come in. No one came in. No one was coming out anymore from the awful cloud a few blocks away, and we were all just there—doctors, nurses, grunts like me—stacking boxes, erecting eyewash kits, making neat little arrays of gauze bandages and syringes and antiseptic wash, because it was only by staying busy that our minds could detach from the enormity of what had happened, could let us believe we were doing something to help.

11   After a time, I wandered outside. Another set of wooden barricades had been set out on the far side of the street, and as I walked toward them, a policewoman called out to me: "Sir, you're not allowed past there."

12   "Okay," I called back, and continued on. She was not a cop anymore; she knew it and I knew it, and if I'd had the presence of the woman in the Health Department lobby, I could have told the cop to go across the street and start counting paper cups and she would have done it.

13   I walked a little ways down a deserted side street, and, finally, out of the gloom came two women caked in dust. One was middle-aged and white, the other elderly and black with tightly braided hair, limping. I couldn't tell if they were friends or coworkers or simply found each other on the way out, but they were very protective of each other, the white woman hovering close as the other settled into a chair on the sidewalk. I asked if there was anything I could do for them; they thanked me and said they were fine.

14   "I was at my desk on the ninety-first floor," the white woman said. "I think the plane must have hit right above us, maybe on ninety-three or ninety-four. They told us to leave."

15   She told of her long descent down the stairwell of Tower One, how after a few flights she felt a second shudder, softer than the first, and figured this must have been from the other plane hitting Tower Two. She related all this in a flat, matter-of-fact voice, but her face was trembling, her knees unsteady.

16   "When I got outside, I saw people jumping. I didn't know they were people at first. I thought maybe it was just different things falling, you know? Maybe bits of the building or chairs or lamps. I really didn't know. Even now, I'm not sure that's what I saw, that maybe it wasn't people. Have you heard anything about people jumping?"

17   Her eyes were desperate and terribly sad, and they searched my face for a clue. I'd seen that look many times before—after car bombings or artillery attacks, on the faces of mothers looking for lost sons—and it seemed that her mind was trying to erase what her eyes had seen, that with the right words at this fragile moment, the memory might be erased altogether.

18   "No," I told her. "I haven't heard anything about that. There's a lot of wild rumors flying around, but I haven't heard that one."

19   This seemed to calm her, and I asked if she'd like me to find her a chair.

20   "No, thank you," she said, wiping at her cheek with shaking fingers. "I just want to stand for a while, wait for the others."

21   I stayed with them, and we all gazed down the side street from which they had emerged, from which any other survivors coming this way would probably

emerge. After a time, a lone figure appeared. She was a very pretty Hispanic woman in her mid-twenties, and she seemed oblivious to the fact that she had lost her shoes and was leaving behind drops of blood with each step. Just about the only way to reach someone in severe shock is to look directly into their eyes and talk softly, but this woman only stared straight ahead, so as she passed, I leaned close and whispered that she was bleeding, that there was a medical unit just ahead. She continued on without any indication she'd heard me.

22   We waited awhile longer, the two ladies and I, but no one else came down the street, and, finally, the white woman turned to her friend. "Well," she said, with that exaggerated exhalation that usually suggests impatience or that it's time to get motivated, "are you ready?"

23   The black woman nodded and got to her feet, and the two went off together down the sidewalk. I was sorry to see them go, because even just standing beside them in their vigil, I felt I was doing something. With them gone, I had no purpose again.

24   I came upon a large crowd gathered in Foley Square, in front of the New York Supreme Court building. Groups were being organized and corralled into little pens delineated with yellow police tape. It appeared most people were there to donate blood, their blood type marked in big black letters on their arms or T-shirts, and one young man moved about shouting in a hoarse voice, "O-negatives, we urgently need O-negatives." Except there was no one around to actually take blood, no vehicles to take anyone to a place where it might be done. It was organization for organization's sake, a plan of action being devised in the absence of either plan or action. But if it was absurd, it was also inspiring; what I was seeing was the very first steps toward rebuilding an ordered society in a corner of Manhattan where it had suddenly vanished, and it was being done with black Magic Markers and yellow police tape by the natural leaders among us.

25   At one corner of the park, search-and-rescue volunteers were being divided into various groups, and I joined the one consisting of current and former members of the military. I chose the group both because I figured it would be among the first to go in and because I was drawn to its self-appointed leader: an athletic, bespectacled man in his late thirties with a crew cut and a bullhorn. Through the hot afternoon, he put us through our paces, ordering us to "form up" in columns or "fall out," to "rehydrate" ourselves, to "listen up, and listen good" to whatever new bits of information he had gleaned from somewhere. "Stay loose, men, and stay focused," our "commander" exhorted us. "There's a lot of desperate people in there, and they're counting on us."

26   "We kept running over body parts," the fireman whispered. He was staring into my eyes with a pleading look, as if seeking forgiveness. "I mean, the ash was so thick, you'd see things in the street, but you couldn't tell what they were until you ran over them. I mean, what the fuck were we supposed to do?"

27   I nodded, patted him on the shoulder, and when I did, he let out a single sharp sob, almost like a hiccup. I looked past him at the 150 or so other firemen resting in a tunnel nearby.

28   At about four o'clock, I and the rest of the "military team" had been bused over to the West Side of Manhattan, just above the ruins. We had assumed we

were about to go in, but instead we'd been told that another high-rise building was about to collapse and were ordered back toward the West Side Highway. In our retreat, we'd come upon the firemen in the tunnel.

29   I'd heard many rumors over the course of that day—that the Capitol had been hit, that another hijacked plane was shot down over the Hudson River— but a recurrent one held that a huge number of New York City firefighters were dead or missing; as I passed the firemen, I studied their faces for some clue as to its validity. I couldn't detect a pattern. At some tables they were talking, even laughing at some shared story, while at the next table over they were sleeping or simply staring into space.

30   One day in Chechnya, I'd come upon a group of Russian soldiers stranded on a remote firebase. The night before, they'd been attacked by the rebels, had taken a number of casualties, but now, in the false calm of day, they were scattered over the ground, some sound asleep, others crying, others contentedly playing cards or listening to music. It occurred to me then how in moments of emotional collapse, we simply mimic those around us—if you sit next to a laugher, you laugh, next to a crier, you cry, that if you get enough shell-shocked people together in one place, you won't discern any pattern at all.

31   On the West Side Highway, we linked up with some of the other search-and-rescue teams waiting to go in and huddled around to wait some more. The sun set over the river and for a while, maybe a half hour, there was a stunning gold tinge to the sky and the buildings around us. Up the highway stretched a line of emergency vehicles and knots of waiting firemen and medics and police as far as the eye could see, and, as hard as it was for us to accept—and it was very, very hard—I think it began to dawn on all of us volunteers that if they were not going into the ruins and flames, neither were we.

32   At about midnight, I finally gave up hope and began the long walk north toward the perimeter line and the "normal" city that lay beyond. I remember that I passed a man walking his dog. For a fleeting instant, I felt an absolute rage at the sight, but the very next instant, I felt my eyes well up for reasons I wouldn't have been able to explain. I decided to keep to the quieter, less-peopled streets as I made my way home.

33   The following evening, I reached the edge of the disaster site, not as a "deputized" search-and-rescue volunteer but as a mere onlooker. A measure of official authority had been established by then, but only a measure; by cutting through the backstreets below the Brooklyn Bridge, I charted a path past the police barricades and emerged onto Broadway at the corner of Ann Street. Across the street, the graves of St. Paul's were covered in ash and scattered papers, and along the wall next to me was an enormous pile of crudely made wood stretchers. Yesterday, one of the construction teams had gone off to make stretchers, and here they sat, unused, never to be used, gathering ash from the fires that still burned.

34   Walking south on Broadway, I came to the corner of Liberty Street, just a block from where the World Trade towers had once stood. It was, of course, a bizarre scene, made more so by the ghostly glow of stage lights that illuminated the workers scrambling over the ruins. Enormous sections of the Tower Two facade jutted up at odd angles, and as shovels dug at the pile, little bursts of flame

appeared beneath. I stood on the corner and watched for a time, but what I eventually began to notice were all the shoes scattered in the street before me. There were ladies' pumps, men's dress shoes, high heels, but they all looked much the same, twisted and mangled by either their owner's flight or the wheels of emergency vehicles, all half sunken in the ash-mud that coated everything here.

35   I can recall only one other time that I've ever written about shoes. It was in a book I wrote with my brother, an oral history of five wars taking place around the world. In the epilogue I had tried to sum up what war now meant to me, and the image that came to me was of a young man, a lotus-blossom seller I had met in Sri Lanka, sitting in his hut and holding up a pair of small green shoes. Two years earlier, guerrillas had suddenly appeared at the Buddhist shrine where he sold his flowers and started shooting anyone not quick enough to get out of their way—and that included the man's five-year-old son. The boy had lost four inches of his left leg, and that was now compensated for by a four-inch heel on his left shoe.

36   "And I suppose for me that is war," were the last words I'd written in the book, "that for a variety of reasons, all of which sound good, men shoot the children of lotus-blossom sellers and leave behind them little green shoes."

37   And now here I was again, not in Sri Lanka or Chechnya, but on the corner of Broadway and Liberty Street in downtown Manhattan, looking at the shoes that war leaves behind, and all at once, in this place I had tried so hard to reach, I didn't want to stay any longer, I didn't ever want to see it again. ✳

From Scott Anderson, "In Country," *Esquire,* November 2001. © 2001 by Scott Anderson. Used by permission of ICM as agent for Scott Anderson.

Exercises

Do not refer to the selection for Exercises A and B unless your instructor directs you to do so.

A. DETERMINING THE MAIN IDEA AND PURPOSE

Choose the best answer.

_____ **1.** The main idea of the selection is that

   a. New Yorkers responded with an outpouring of energy and generosity after the World Trade Center buildings collapsed.

   b. the scene following the buildings' collapse was one of chaos and confusion.

   c. maintaining one's objectivity is difficult if not impossible when a journalist covers a war scene.

   d. the attacks turned New York into a war zone and New Yorkers into the dazed victims that are the mark of any war scene.

_____ **2.** With respect to the main idea, the writer's purpose is to

    a. relate his experiences, observations, and impressions of New York immediately after the attacks.

    b. assess the preparedness of New York to respond to the attacks.

    c. explain how New York City officials organized the first cleanup efforts.

    d. describe various war zones he has covered in the past.

B. COMPREHENDING MAIN IDEAS

Choose the correct answer.

_____ **1.** Anderson writes that when witnessing true horror, people the world over express their feelings by expressively using their

    a. eyes.

    b. entire bodies.

    c. heads.

    d. hands.

_____ **2.** As a war correspondent with eighteen years of experience, Anderson says that until that September day he had been able to

    a. develop a sense of humor and a keen eye for observing details.

    b. maintain detachment and immunity from the events around him.

    c. identify emotionally with war victims.

    d. demonstrate an inquisitive, curious nature and a tendency to be in the right place at the right time.

_____ **3.** In contrast to other war zones he has covered as a journalist, the New York scene was different because

    a. the nation was not at war.

    b. the battleground was limited to a few city blocks.

    c. the city had been unprepared for the attack and so complete chaos reigned.

    d. there were fewer deaths and injuries.

_____ **4.** Initially, authority had little to do with one's rank and uniform; instead, authority rested in

    a. ordinary citizens who showed leadership ability or charisma.

    b. Mayor Giuliani and other elected city officials.

    c. nurses, doctors, and other medical personnel.

    d. police officers, firefighters, and other assorted rescue workers.

_____ **5.** Throughout the selection, Anderson writes that he felt the need to

    a. go home to his family and escape the horror.

    b. take photographs of the scene.

    c. interview survivors to find out what they were thinking and how they were coping.

    d. find something useful to do.

_____ **6.** As Anderson stood near the site of the buildings' ruins the day after the attacks, he was struck in particular by the sight of

    a. dozens of pairs of mangled shoes.

    b. the amount of ash covering everything and everybody.

    c. the unused stretchers that no one needed now.

    d. the normal functioning of the city so close to the collapsed buildings.

COMPREHENSION SCORE

Score your answers for Exercises A and B as follows:

A. No. right _____ × 2 = _____

B. No. right _____ × 1 = _____

Total points from A and B _____ × 10 = _____ percent

You may refer to the selection as you work through the remaining exercises.

C. DISTINGUISHING BETWEEN MAIN IDEAS AND SUPPORTING DETAILS

Label the following statements from the selection as follows: MI if it represents a *main idea* and SD if it represents a *supporting detail.*

1. _____ It is an odd thing, probably not what one would predict or remember afterward, but when a person encounters true horror, the body's first response almost always occurs in the hands.

2. _____ With women, the hands tend to immediately come up to cover the mouth or press the cheeks.

3. _____ Among men, they tend to form a steeple over the nose and mouth or to clutch tightly onto the sides of the head.

4. _____ It is as if, in this moment of utter incomprehension and helplessness, the hands are trying to give comfort.

D. MAKING INFERENCES

For each of these statements write Y (yes) if the inference is an accurate one, N (no) if the inference is an inaccurate one, and CT (can't tell) if the writer does not give you enough information to make an inference one way or another.

1. _____ Scott Anderson has served in the military as well as working as a war correspondent.

2. _____ Detachment, immunity, and the inability to be shocked are most likely important qualities for a journalist sent on assignment to cover war zones.

3. _____ When covering a war in a foreign country, a war correspondent may feel like an outsider who is not personally involved in the activities he observes.

4. _____ We can infer from paragraph 8 that the New Yorkers who lived or worked closest to the World Trade Center area were more seriously affected by the terrorist attacks than those living in other parts of the city.

5. _____ Anderson had been asked by his employer to help in any way he could, by unloading boxes of medical supplies.

6. _____ Police officers were unable to do their jobs effectively because they too were in shock.

7. _____ Anderson refused to obey the policewoman's command (paragraphs 11 and 12) because he thought that the rules didn't apply to him as a journalist.

8. _____ In paragraphs 16–18, when Anderson tells the woman that he had not heard the rumor about people jumping from the building before it collapsed, he was telling the truth.

E. INTERPRETING MEANING AND ANALYZING STRUCTURE

Where appropriate, write your answers to these questions in your own words.

1. Why does Anderson begin with a description of people's hands as they witness horrible events? _____

_____

_____

2. What unites Anderson's description of the people he observes walking after the buildings collapsed? What do they seem to have in common?_____

_____

3. Read paragraph 17 again. Then explain what Anderson is saying. _____

_____

_____

4. _____ Which of the following is the best title for paragraph 24?
   a. "A Crowd in Foley Square"
   b. "The First Step in Rebuilding Order"
   c. "The Need for Blood"
   d. "Important Uses for Magic Markers and Police Tape"

5. _____ Consider again paragraphs 29 and 30. In them, Anderson is primarily
   a. giving examples.
   b. listing facts.
   c. comparing, finding similarities.
   d. contrasting, finding differences.
   e. expressing a personal opinion.

6. Read paragraphs 35 and 36 again, and then explain why Anderson includes the example of the lotus-blossom seller and the pair of small green shoes. ___

_____

7. _____ In the article as a whole, how does Anderson organize the ideas?

   a. in order of importance, from the least important to the most important
   b. in random order, so that the impressions have no particular order
   c. in chronological or time order

8. _____ Anderson's emotional attitude toward the events he describes, and especially in the last paragraph, can best be described as one of

   a. disbelief.
   b. a mixture of anger and horror.
   c. detachment.
   d. a mixture of sadness and regret.

F. UNDERSTANDING VOCABULARY

Choose the best definition according to an analysis of word parts or the context.

_____ **1.** just standing there, *mute,* numb [paragraph 3]:

   a. silent
   b. unmoving
   c. feeling no pain
   d. horrified

_____ **2.** detachment and comparative *immunity* [4]: a state of being

   a. unaffected by a situation
   b. emotionally involved in a situation
   c. protected by one's high position
   d. able to record events precisely

_____ **3.** the fabric of society . . . *frays* [8]:

   a. becomes unified, cemented
   b. becomes clearer
   c. unravels, comes apart
   d. is filled with danger

_____ **4.** a *demarcation* line [8]:

   a. point of no return
   b. line around the outside or perimeter
   c. a line forming a barrier
   d. a line indicating a separation

_____ **5.** standing beside them in their *vigil* [23]:

   a. moment of crisis
   b. moment of need
   c. period of observing or watching
   d. shock and dismay

_____ **6.** our "commander" _exhorted_ us [25]:

    a. urged

    b. threatened

    c. comforted

    d. organized

_____ **7.** you don't _discern_ any pattern [30]:

    a. form, make

    b. perceive, distinguish

    c. describe, show

    d. discuss, talk about

_____ **8.** sections of the Two Tower _facade_ [34]:

    a. interior offices

    b. foundation

    c. windows

    d. exterior walls

G. USING VOCABULARY

In parentheses before each sentence are some inflected forms of words from the selection. Study the context and the sentence. Then write the correct form in the space provided.

1. (_incomprehension, incomprehensible, incomprehensibly_) Anderson describes the gestures of onlookers as they stared _____ at the collapsing buildings.

2. (_charisma, charismatic, charismatically_) In the aftermath of the attacks, ordinary citizens often became leaders and organized people to start helping because they had _____ personalities that others responded to.

3. (_impotence, impotent, impotently_) Many onlookers felt _____ and unable to react because of their shock.

4. (_obliviousness, oblivious, obliviously_) One young Hispanic woman walked down the street, _____ to the fact that she was barefoot and trailing blood.

5. (_defy, defying, defiance, defiant, defiantly_) The second tower collapsed so quickly that the motion seemed to be _____ gravity.

H. PARAPHRASING EXERCISE

Paraphrase the following two excerpts:

Original Passage

Usually, I went as a journalist, with all the detachment and comparative immunity that implies. Of course, there were times when both detachment and immunity fell away, when I witnessed things that affected me deeply, or I found myself in harm's way, but in all these places, I was, first and foremost, an outsider; what was happening fundamentally did not involve me, it was not my war. [paragraph 4]

Paraphrase

_____

_____

_____

_____

_____

_____

_____

_____

Original Passage

In war, the fabric of society—the rules and laws and customs that are lived by—frays in direct proportion to one's nearness to the battlefield. In most wars, this fraying occurs over a distance of provinces or valleys or mountain ranges, but in New York on September 11 it was happening over the space of a few city blocks. By 11:00, the authorities were trying to establish a security perimeter at Canal Street, a demarcation line between civilization and madness that civilians would not be allowed past. [paragraph 8]

Paraphrase

_____

_____

_____

_____

_____

_____

_____

_____

_____

_____

_____

I. TOPICS FOR WRITING OR DISCUSSION

1. Write a short paper in which you describe what you were doing when you first heard about the terrorist attacks of September 11. Explain your initial reactions on that first day; then explain your emotional feelings after the shock wore off.
2. How did the terrorist attacks change the country? How did they change you? Your family? The way you view the world?

For Further Exploration

BOOKS

- William Langewiesche, *Unbuilding the World Trade Center* (2002). Veteran journalist Langewiesche had unprecedented access to Ground Zero in the weeks following the attacks. In this book, first excerpted in the *Atlantic Monthly,* he tells the behind-the-scenes story of the cleanup efforts.
- Tim O'Brien, *The Things They Carried* (1990). O'Brien's book presents a series of overlapping semi-autobiographical stories relating his experiences in Vietnam as a U.S. marine.

MOVIE

Apocalypse Now (1979), directed by Francis Ford Coppola and starring Marlon Brando and Martin Sheen, adapted Joseph Conrad's novel *Heart of Darkness* to depict the horrors of the Vietnam War.

WEB SITES

Photographs of Ground Zero, both after the attacks and during the cleanup effort, are available at these two sites:

- *http://library.thinkquest.org/CR0212088/grzero.htm*
- *www.digitaljournalist.org/issue0111/aris_intro.htm*

The design that won the international competition to build a memorial at the World Trade Center site was done by Daniel Libeskind, a Berlin architect. A description of his plan can be viewed at:

- *1010wins.com/topstories/winsnews_story_057183025.html*

29

JON KATZ
What Hath Goth Wrought?

The Columbine shootings in April 1999 shocked the nation and intensified discussion on a long-standing social problem in American high schools: the treatment of students who, for whatever reason, are perceived as different. The two perpetrators in the Columbine incident played violent video games and considered themselves Goths, dressing in long black dusters. They were preoccupied with bombs and other weapons. In this selection, first published in Brill's Content *and reprinted in the* Utne Reader, *Jon Katz examines the backlash against Goths, geeks, and other perceived misfits in American schools and the media's role in fostering misperceptions.*

Vocabulary Preview

WORD HISTORIES

Talismans [paragraph 1]   The word *talisman* means "an object with magical powers or offering protection" (like a rabbit's foot or a lucky penny). *Talisman* appears in several other languages: French (*talisman*), Spanish (*talismán*), Italian (*talismano*). All come from the Arabic word *tilasm,* and originally from Greek, *telesma,* meaning "consecration" or "ceremony."

Geeks [paragraphs 2 and elsewhere]   The word *geek* today refers to a person who is a whiz at technology, but it also suggests that the person—almost always male—is socially inept. The *American Heritage Dictionary* cites this unusual etymology:

> Our word *geek* is now chiefly associated with student and computer slang; one probably thinks first of a *computer geek.* In origin, however, it is one of the words American English borrowed from the vocabulary of the circus, which was a much more significant source of entertainment in the United States in the 19th and early 20th century than it is now. Large numbers of traveling circuses left a cultural legacy in various and sometimes unexpected ways. For example, Superman and other comic book superheroes owe much of their look to circus acrobats, who were similarly costumed in capes and tights. The circus sideshow is the source of the word *geek,* "a performer who engaged in bizarre acts, such as biting the head off a live chicken."

The dictionary goes on to list the original language with a question mark, saying that it is perhaps an alteration of the German word for fool—*gek.*

Hysteria [paragraphs 3 and 7]   The noun *hysteria* and the related adjective *hysterical* are of Greek origin. The noun actually refers to a kind of neurosis, but it can also mean "excessive fear or any other strong emotion," which is how Katz uses the word in these contexts to describe the media's reaction to the Columbine killings. To modern readers the word's origin will likely seem sexist: The Greek word for *uterus* was *hustera,* and the Greek word *hysterikos* ("suffering in the womb") reflects the ancient belief that the disease was caused by disturbances in the uterus and that more women than men suffered from it.

WORD PARTS

Penta-, semi-, deca-, unif- (and other numerical prefixes)   English contains a large number of Latin and Greek prefixes referring to numbers. Do not worry about remembering which language they come from, because many of the same prefixes are found in both languages. A *pentagram,* mentioned in paragraph 1, is a five-sided star thought to have mystical significance. In Greek, *penta-* means "five." *Semi-,* as in the word *semifinalist* (also in paragraph 1) means literally a "half" finalist. *Decade,* mentioned in paragraph 13, refers to a period of ten years, from *deca-* (in Greek, *deka*), the prefix for "ten." And finally, *unifying* in paragraph 15 combines *uni-* ("one") with *ficare* ("to make"). Here are some other words beginning with numerical prefixes:

hemisphere	*hemi-* (half)
monotheism, monopoly, monotone	*mono-* (one)
biannual, bimonthly, bisexual	*bi-* (two)
duet	*duo-* (two)
trimester, tricycle, triplets	*tri-* (three)
centipede, century, bicentennial	*cent-* (one hundred)
millennium, millipede, millimeter	*mille-* (one thousand)

WORD FAMILIES

Subsequent [paragraph 10]   Katz wrote "two *subsequent* columns" after his first one was posted on the Web site Slashdot. This word means "following in time or in order." It derives from the Latin root *sequi-,* meaning "to follow." This same root is at the heart of a large number of word "relatives," among them:

sequence	the following of one thing after another
consequence	something that results (or follows) from an action or condition
consecutive	following successively and without interruption, as in "a consecutive order of events"
sequel	something that follows or continues; used to describe a second movie or book that follows the first, as in *Star Wars* or *Men in Black*

JON KATZ

What Hath Goth Wrought?

1   An e-mail that begins this way stands out: "I'm a Goth/Wiccan in Alabama, and for the crime of wearing black lipstick, a trench coat, and a pentagram, I've been a social outcast for four years. In some ways I've had it better than many of your re-

spondents: I'm graduating at the top of my class as a National Merit Scholar with a 1,600 SAT, a finalist for the Alabama All-State Academic Team, and a semi-finalist for the Presidential Scholars, among other things. I'll matriculate at Yale University. I hold these things up as talismans to protect me; all my awards are thin paper shields to keep me safe from the hatred that surrounds me and my friends."

2   The message came from Jennifer Andress, a senior at Bob Jones High School in Madison, Alabama. A self-described Wiccan (the pagan religion commonly associated with witchcraft) and Goth (the broody subculture marked by industrial music, black clothing, white makeup, and a preoccupation with death), she is a member of an obsessive, brainy community of oddballs, misfits, geeks, and nerds who know what it's like to be outcasts.

3   The massacre near Littleton, Colorado, in April hit their world like a bomb. Like so many other kids who don't fit into conventional notions of "normal," Jennifer found the massacre and resulting media-fueled hysteria appalling.

4   "It hurts," she wrote. "Why do people assume that a kid in a black trench coat must be a psychotic murderer instead of a National Merit Scholar? Or a kid who plays Doom? Or wears white makeup? Or listens to Marilyn Manson or industrial music? Or spends as much time on the Net as his or her classmates do on the football or soccer field?"

5   Although many geeks are happy, well-adjusted, popular, and athletic, many are not. They grasp the reality of the alienated, the anger of those who inhabit a world that isn't made for them, doesn't work for them or reflect their values, and sometimes systematically excludes and humiliates them—a brutal fact of life in middle school and high school. And if life was painful before Littleton, it got worse afterward. The media coverage was grotesque, even outrageous. Even serious journalists accepted and transmitted the idea that two students turned to mass murder because they played nasty computer games associated with the gloomy (but nonviolent) Goths, or had access to Internet bomb-making sites.

6   Dumb and demonstrably false as it is (an estimated 20 million Americans, mostly kids, are into video and computer games; hardly any commit mass murder), this idea was so prevalent that most of the country actually came to believe it. The week after the massacre, a Gallup poll suggested that more than 80 percent of Americans agreed that the Internet was at least partly responsible for the Colorado killings.

7   And who could blame them? CBS's *60 Minutes* devoted a segment to this question: "Are Video Games Turning Kids into Killers?" *Time* magazine ran grainy pictures of the two killers under this cover line: "The Monsters Next Door." Hundreds of newspapers and TV stations ran stories linking computer games, Goths, Web sites, and other "aberrant," "abnormal," and "weird" behavior to mass murder. These messages were almost guaranteed to panic parents and students and to stampede educators into overreaction. Instead of being a force for truth, clarity, and calm, the media transmitted hysteria. The cost of being different—already high—went way up.

8   Overnight, geeks, misfits, and oddballs became instant suspects in a kind of "geek profiling," a national hunt for the strange.

9   Three days after the massacre, I wrote a column called "Why Kids Kill" on Slashdot, a Web site with a large geek following. It was reprinted on the

Freedom Forum's Web site, Free! I suggested in the column that ties between violence and popular culture are fuzzy at best, and that what caused these mass killings remains unclear.

10   In two subsequent columns I reprinted some of the messages I got in response. Describing the cruel reality these kids face just because they're different, the messages were wrenching and irrefutable. They couldn't be subjected to journalism's noxious and eternal culture of debate, because these were kids reflecting on their own experience. More e-mails poured in, reporting that students had been sent home for dressing strangely and that schools had installed hot lines to report odd peers. Kids who expressed sympathy or understanding for the Littleton killers were called into counseling or banned from class. Ditto for kids who admitted in newspaper articles and class discussions that they had sometimes felt enraged to the point of committing violence. Even kids who played computer games were offered psychiatric help.

11   "Help me, please," e-mailed JDT from a high school in Illinois. "My social studies teacher asked if we wanted to talk about Littleton. I said I had some sense of how those two kids might have been driven crazy by cruel students, since it happens to me. I said I had thought of taking my father's gun to school when I was in the ninth grade and was so angry. I was sent home. When I got there, three detectives were going through my room."

12   School life, reported Jane D., had become insane. "We were all called into an assembly and asked to turn in our friends who were moody, emotional, angry at the way they were treated in school. That's everybody I know!" Another student wrote that he felt much safer with the people blasting him on the video game Quake than he did in his high school hallways.

13   The Net sent these voices into homes, schools, offices, and newsrooms around the country to a degree I'd never seen in nearly a decade of writing online. Geek kids had taken to their computers to launch a media revolution. While journalists, educators, and therapists were telling the world about the state of American kids, the kids were using the Net to speak for themselves. My columns quoting the Slashdot kids were read on National Public Radio, discussed at MIT, entered into the *Congressional Record,* reprinted and referred to in magazines and newspapers like the *Economist,* the *New York Times,* the *Los Angeles Times,* and several others.

14   Reaching far beyond their computers into the heart of mainstream media, these kids made big news. They used technology to fight back and speak out, and many journalists heard them. They changed the way the media work. Kids who were voiceless suddenly had a voice.

15   "You speak for us," Jennifer said at the end of her message to me. "Take our stories and let them know what is happening here." Her message was an especially haunting and, in an odd way, unifying one, transcending the killings and their aftermath. It was a reminder of what it really means to be a journalist, new or old. ✳

From Jon Katz, "What Hath Goth Wrought?" *Utne Reader,* November–December 1999. Reprinted by permission of the author.

Exercises

Do not refer to the selection for Exercises A and B unless your instructor directs you to do so.

A. DETERMINING THE MAIN IDEA AND PURPOSE

Choose the best answer.

_____ 1. The main idea of the selection is that as a result of the Columbine killings,

   a. geeks in American high schools face social isolation, alienation, and now intense attention from the media.
   b. people who are different are often treated unfairly by the crowd.
   c. parents and school educators are fearful about the harmful influence of Goth, video games, industrial music, and strange clothing.
   d. though stereotyping of geeks is inevitable, it is also unfair.

_____ 2. With respect to the main idea, the writer's purpose is to

   a. trace the history of the Goth movement among America's disaffected teenagers.
   b. warn the public about the dangers that geeks and other misfits represent.
   c. explain the media's role in fostering hysteria about geeks and other alienated teenagers who are perceived as different.
   d. recommend that the media change the way it covers massacres and other similar events.

B. COMPREHENDING MAIN IDEAS

Choose the correct answer.

_____ 1. Katz writes of Jennifer Andress, from Madison, Alabama, who describes herself as both a Goth and a "Wiccan." The word *Wiccan* refers to someone who

   a. believes in the mystical powers of the pentagram.
   b. practices a pagan religion associated with witchcraft.
   c. dresses in black, wears white makeup, and is preoccupied with death.
   d. has a superior command of computer technology and video games.

_____ 2. The primary source of the hysteria that followed the Columbine massacre primarily came from the

   a. nation's high school administrators.
   b. parents of those who had been victimized and persecuted for being different.
   c. students who consider themselves "normal."
   d. national media, including newspapers and television.

_____ **3.** Katz writes that a brutal fact of high school is the practice of

  a. excluding those who aren't interested in athletics or other socially accepted activities.
  b. making everyone conform to a single high standard.
  c. excluding and humiliating those who are considered different.
  d. introducing guns and violence from the streets into schools.

_____ **4.** A week after the Columbine massacre, a Gallup poll was released showing that 80 percent of Americans believed that the responsibility for the killings lay with

  a. the Internet.
  b. the media, especially network television.
  c. the Goth culture.
  d. the killers' parents.

_____ **5.** Katz states that the connection between violence and popular culture

  a. needs further research by social scientists and teachers.
  b. is unclear.
  c. is impossible to ignore.
  d. is only part of the picture, since other factors may be connected, too.

_____ **6.** The kids who wrote to various Internet sites launched a media revolution, Katz says, and in the process

  a. made the American public understand that those who aren't perceived as "normal" should not be persecuted.
  b. explained why they dress and act as they do.
  c. gained more converts to Goth and geek culture.
  d. changed the way the media works.

COMPREHENSION SCORE

Score your answers for Exercises A and B as follows:

A. No. right _____ × 2 = _____

B. No. right _____ × 1 = _____

Total points from A and B _____ × 10 = _____ percent

You may refer to the selection as you work through the remaining exercises.

C. DISTINGUISHING BETWEEN FACT AND OPINION

For each of the following statements from the selection, write F if the statement represents a factual statement that can be verified or O if the statement represents the writer's or someone else's subjective interpretation.

1. _____ Like so many other kids who don't fit into conventional notions of "normal," Jennifer found the [Columbine] massacre and resulting media-fueled hysteria appalling.

2. _____ Although many geeks are happy, well-adjusted, popular, and athletic, many are not.

3. _____ They grasp the reality of the alienated, the anger of those who inhabit a world that isn't made for them . . . and sometimes systematically excludes and humiliates them—a brutal fact of life in middle school and high school.

4. _____ And if life was painful before Littleton, it got worse afterward. The media coverage was grotesque, even outrageous.

5. _____ The week after the massacre, a Gallup poll suggested that more than 80 percent of Americans agreed that the Internet was at least partly responsible for the Colorado killings.

D. MAKING INFERENCES

For each of these statements write Y (yes) if the inference is an accurate one, N (no) if the inference is an inaccurate one, and CT (can't tell) if the writer does not give you enough information to make an inference one way or another.

1. _____ The word *normal* with regard to high school students' behavior is both obvious and easy to define.

2. _____ Katz is concerned about the way geeks and other supposed "misfits" are treated because he was a misfit himself in high school.

3. _____ Kids who play Doom, dress in black, or listen to Marilyn Manson's music are probably not very good students or interested in school.

4. _____ The journalists who blamed the Columbine killings on violent video and computer games lacked hard evidence to show the connection between such entertainment and violence.

5. _____ Katz was impressed with the way the geek kids responded to media attacks by launching their own campaign to speak of their experiences.

6. _____ Katz has a high opinion of the mass media.

E. INTERPRETING MEANING

Where appropriate, write your answers to these questions in your own words.

1. Consider the article title, "What Hath Goth Wrought?" which is a play on a quotation, "What Hath God Wrought." This latter quotation is from the Bible (see Numbers 23:23) but was more recently used by Samuel F. B. Morse in the first telegraphic message he sent to his partner on May 24, 1844.[1] What does

   this phrase mean? Look up *wrought* before you answer._____

   _____

   _____

[1]Cited in Bartlett's *Familiar Quotations,* 14th edition.

2. _____   Which of the following is the best title for paragraph 7?

    a. "The Mass Media and Columbine"
    b. "Goth Culture and the Media"
    c. "The Media's Role in Creating Hysteria"
    d. "Why the American Media Should Be Regulated"

3. In paragraph 9, what evidence does Katz offer to support the idea that "ties

between violence and popular culture are fuzzy at best." _____

_____

F. UNDERSTANDING VOCABULARY

From the following list of vocabulary words, choose a word that fits in each blank according to both the grammatical structure of the sentence and the context. Use each word in the list only once. Do not change the form of the word. (Note that there are more words than sentences.)

aberrant	humiliated	massacre	transcend
conventional	hysteria	media	transmitted
excluded	irrefutable	peers	wrenching

1. Katz believes that the members of the _____ are primarily

responsible for creating _____ in the public after the Columbine

_____ .

2. Students who were perceived as acting different from _____ kids

told _____ stories about the way their _____ treated them.

3. Students wrote about being systematically _____ and

_____ if they indulged in so-called _____

behavior or played violent video games.

G. USING VOCABULARY

Here are some words from the selection. Write an original sentence using each word that shows both that you know how to use the word and what it means.

1. *appalling* [paragraph 3] _____

_____

2. *grotesque* [5] _____

_____

3. *transmit* or *transmitted* [5] _____

_____

4. *subsequent* [10]_____

_____

5. *irrefutable* [10] _____

_____

6. *transcending* [15] _____

_____

H. PARAPHRASING EXERCISE

Here is paragraph 8 and a paraphrase of it:

Original Passage

Overnight, geeks, misfits, and oddballs became instant suspects in a kind of "geek profiling," a national hunt for the strange.

Paraphrase

_____

_____

_____

_____

Study this paraphrase. Now paraphrase these two sentences from paragraph 10:

Original Passage

Describing the cruel reality these kids face just because they're different, the messages were wrenching and irrefutable. They couldn't be subjected to journalism's noxious and eternal culture of debate, because these were kids reflecting on their own experience.

Paraphrase

_____

_____

_____

_____

_____

_____

I.   TOPICS FOR WRITING OR DISCUSSION

1. Does Katz provide sufficient support for his contention in paragraph 5 that following the Columbine shootings "the media coverage was grotesque, even outrageous"? Explain.
2. Couldn't one argue that high school students who dress like Goths or who purposely act "different" *want* to be treated differently and that therefore they shouldn't complain when they're persecuted?
3. Write a paragraph or two in which you describe the situation in your high school regarding people who were considered bizarre or different. How were they treated? Was there peer pressure to make unconventional students conform? How did the conventional and unconventional groups get along? Based on your experience, is Katz exaggerating the "brutal fact of life" in America's high schools today, or is he telling it the way it really is?

For Further Exploration

BOOK

Jon Katz's article was the basis of a book he later published, *Geeks: How Two Lost Boys Rode the Internet Out of Idaho* (2001), which examines in much greater detail the pervasive custom of stereotyping those who are perceived to be different in American high schools.

MOVIE

Welcome to the Dollhouse (1996), directed by Todd Solondz and starring Heather Matarazzo, parodies the problem of peer pressure and its effect on a seventh-grade girl, who must learn to deal with her nasty classmates and her unsympathetic, self-absorbed family.

WEB SITE

Investigate the Web site that Katz cites as instrumental in changing the media's perception of geeks and see if your findings are consistent with Katz's:

- *www.slashdot.com*

30

ARTHUR ZICH

Japanese Americans: Home at Last

The internment of Japanese American citizens in 1942, under Executive Order 9066 signed by President Franklin D. Roosevelt, was a black mark in the nation's history. This article examines the treatment of the Issei, the first generation of Japanese immigrants, when they arrived in this country and their internment during World War II. Originally published in the National Geographic *magazine, this article was included in* From the Field, *an anthology of the best writing over the magazine's 110-year history.*

A former editor at Newsweek *and foreign correspondent for Time-Life, Arthur Zich is a frequent contributor to* National Geographic *and other magazines. After graduating from Dartmouth College, he studied at Yale's Institute of Far East Languages, becoming fluent in Mandarin Chinese. A resident of Half Moon Bay, California, he travels frequently to China and Asia on assignment. He is currently working on a memoir of his forty years covering stories in Asia.*

Vocabulary Preview

WORD HISTORIES

Sabotage and saboteur [paragraphs 3 and 32] A *saboteur* commits *sabotage*, or treacherous activity within his or her own nation, especially in wartime; in other words, *sabotage* is deliberate subversion. (The French suffix *-eur* is comparable to *-er* or *-or* in English.) The etymology of these words is unusual. The root comes from the French word *sabot*, or "old shoe." Here is Joseph Shipley's explanation:

> [The word *sabotage*] does not mean to throw a shoe, instead of a monkey wrench into the machinery. It is the old peasant type of shoe, which became a slang word meaning an inferior tool or workman; hence [French] *saboter*, to work badly. With the rise of trade union activity, it took on the sense of deliberately bad work. It is suggested, however, that the current use springs from peasants' trampling their landlords' crops.[1]

[1]*Dictionary of Word Origins*, p. 308.

Shroud [paragraph 71]   The word *shroud* can be either a noun or a verb. Zich writes, "For a long time, Japanese Americans *shrouded* the wartime experience from the world, from themselves, and from their own children behind 40 years of silence." The use here is more metaphorical than literal, meaning "to shut off from the light" or "to screen." Literally, however, a *shroud* refers to a winding sheet, the linen or cotton cloth traditionally used to wrap a body for burial. But its derivation suggests that this modern meaning is a recent one: The word originally referred simply to any garment—an example of the linguistic process called *specialization*.

WORD PARTS

Dis- [paragraph 3]   The prefix *dis-* has several meanings, but we will look at only one in this section. In the word *disloyalty* (the crime most Japanese American residents were accused of), the prefix *dis-* indicates simply "not." Other words beginning with this prefix are *distrust, dissimilar, disorder, discomfort,* and *disapprove*.

WORD FAMILIES

Credo [paragraph 19]   *Credo* in Latin means literally "I believe" (from the Latin *credere*) and refers to a belief or creed. To refresh your memory, here are the other words in this family: *credibility, incredible, incredulous,* and *credit*.

ARTHUR ZICH

Japanese Americans: Home at Last

1   On the day in May 1942 when American soldiers took her and her family to the concentration camp, the very last thing Mary Tsukamoto did was sweep the house. "I had to leave it clean," she explains. "We didn't know how long we'd be gone."

2   Mrs. Tsukamoto was one of nearly 120,000 American citizens and alien residents of Japanese ancestry who, after the Japanese attack on Pearl Harbor, were uprooted from West Coast homes, farms, and businesses and herded, most of them, into assembly centers in racetracks and fairgrounds. Later they were transported to ten desolate concentration camps—the term used by President Franklin D. Roosevelt himself, whose Executive Order 9066, signed February 19, 1942, put them there.

3   Categorized by this presidential action as potential spies and saboteurs, they remained behind barbed wire for an average term of two and a half years. The ordeal devastated the life's work of Issei (first generation Japanese in the United States), costing them millions in lost property and income. It deprived their Nisei (second generation) offspring, born in the U.S., of liberty and the rights of citizenship. It fractured families along political and generational lines. Above all, in branding them as disloyal without charge or trial, it inflicted on Japanese Americans a gnawing sense of shame—for some to the third and fourth generations.

4   In the years since the war Japanese Americans have surmounted most of the social obstacles erected against them. They have risen so high and so fast, in fact, that they have been called a model minority—an epithet they deplore as simplis-

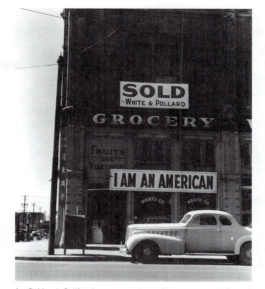

An Oakland, California, grocery store whose owner was forced to close it because of the evacuation order. Source: © The Dorothea Lange Collection, The Oakland Museum of California. Gift of Paul S. Taylor.

tic, condescending, and forgetful of their traumatic history in the United States. Dr. Ford H. Kuramoto, director of Hollywood Mental Health Service, calls the stigma of internment "a psychic skeleton in the closet."

5   Mary Tsukamoto, retired now after 26 years of teaching in Florin, California, still loves to talk to children of Japanese ancestry about old country culture. "They look up at me with their big eyes," she relates, "and ask, again and again, 'Was Great-grandpa really guilty when they put him in the concentration camp?' "

6   Windblown and seasick, 18-year-old Yuki Torigoe stood at the rail as the salt-caked steamer *Siberia Maru* slipped through the Golden Gate into San Francisco Bay. Like a score of other "picture brides" descending the ship's gangplank, she looked from her husband's photograph to the faces of the men in the dockside throng. It was May 1914. Less than a month before, at her home in Kurashiki, she had knelt before a Shinto altar in her finest kimono and married, by proxy, a man she had never met—a man who was then 5,500 miles away, running a small shop in Watsonville, California.

7   "Somehow we all just found each other," Mrs. Torigoe, now 90 and widowed, remembers. "Some of the other brides were crying: Their husbands turned out to be 20 years older than their photos. But we all went off in cars for a mass American wedding at the hotel."

8   Of the 214,000 Japanese immigrants who arrived in the United States in the first two decades of the 20th century, fewer than 30,000 were women. Perhaps half were picture brides; most were a decade or more younger than their

husbands. Many immigrants were impoverished farmers from southern prefectures like Hiroshima. But they carried in their hearts a fierce pride in Japan's rising power, a profound commitment to its stern, traditional values—*on* (duty to family and country); *giri* (a moral indebtedness, as to a parent, that cannot be repaid); *gaman* (stoic endurance)—and a burning determination to work hard in America, make good, and return to their beloved homeland.

9   "They had no intention of staying," Yuji Ichioka, researcher at the Asian American Studies Center of the University of California, Los Angeles, explains. "They were sojourners—birds of passage."

10   America did not invite them to stay. As Asians they were barred from U.S. citizenship—"the single most important factor affecting the Issei in this country," Ichioka avers. "It kept them out of the American political process and left them defenseless against discriminatory legislation."

11   From 1907 through 1948 anti-Japanese bills were introduced in every session of the California legislature. In 1907 a gentlemen's agreement between the United States and Japan halted immigration of male laborers. In 1913 a California law banned purchase of land by aliens "ineligible to citizenship." Seven years later a similar law prevented them from leasing land. Then, in 1924, a new U.S. Immigration Act slammed the door on Japanese immigration completely.

12   The Japanese settled for whatever wages they could get—often half what whites were paid for similar labor. Most turned to farming, laboring under Japanese bosses in picking, packing, and pruning gangs that began work by lantern light well before dawn and finished long past dark.

13   Michiko Tanaka, who left Hiroshima for California in 1923 and bore 13 American children, recalls the life. "Until the internment camp, I worked in the fields right up to the day each baby was born," she says. "We would finish the work, wrap our children in blankets—and move on. Papa loved to gamble and drink. All the Issei men did. Me, he never talked to. The children, Papa harangued: 'Learn your culture! Learn Japanese! As long as you look Japanese, you are going to *be* Japanese.'"

14   "Papa knew the struggle was futile—that as long as we lived here Americanization was going to gobble us up," says the Tanakas' daughter Akemi Kikumura, a cultural anthropologist. "But he fought it as long as he lived. That was my father's way."

15   Nonetheless, the Issei sought places to put down roots. Some managed to buy or lease farms before alien land measures passed into law. Some put titles in the names of their American-born children or of trusted American friends. In all, the Japanese never owned or leased more than 4 percent of California's improved cropland. But by 1920, sales of Issei farm produce accounted for more than 10 percent of the total value of all commercial truck crops in California.

16   "Japanese neighbors grew up as sanctuaries against outside hostility," Dr. Kikumura goes on. "They became, in effect, extended families." The Japanese community in San Mateo, south of San Francisco, was typical. By 1924 the town had both a Buddhist and a Christian church. A chapter of the Japanese Association of America was resolving commercial disputes and staging annual picnics. There were six billiard parlors and an apartment house complete with backyard

tea garden and redwood *o-furo* (hot tub bath), where Issei men gathered on Saturday nights to soak away cares, sip sake, and strum the samisen (three-stringed banjo). Tanomoshi, an informal savings and loan system, helped provide capital for local businesses serving local needs. "Default meant disgrace to the borrower and his family," Dr. Kikumura explains. "No one would have dreamed of it."

17   For boys, most communities had a Scout troop, a baseball team, and a kendo (Japanese fencing) and sumo (wrestling) club. Girls joined the Camp Fire Girls and odori (Japanese dance) groups. Nisei males, growing up in this mixed world of old Japan and new America, were separated from their fathers by an average age difference of 38 years. Three-fourths of the parents were Buddhist; most knew little English. The majority of the children were Christian; all spoke English, and few spoke Japanese.

18   Parental word was law. There was virtually no juvenile delinquency. Teachers ranked second only to parents. "Honor or shame to the family name would be brought according to the success or failure of the child in school," wrote Seattle sociologist S. Frank Miyamoto. After-school Japanese-language classes only created more cultural conflict. Retired U.S. Army Maj. Tom Kawaguchi, 64, director of Go For Broke, Inc., a Japanese-American veterans' organization based in San Francisco, tells how one Nisei saw it: "I hated every minute of it. Hell, I wanted to be an *American!*"

19   This sentiment was shared by many members of the influential Japanese American Citizens League (JACL), founded in 1929. Issei, denied U.S. citizenship, still looked on Japan as their motherland, still felt its emotional tug. But their Nisei sons and daughters adopted the JACL credo: "I am proud that I am an American citizen of Japanese ancestry," and they pledged to defend the United States "against all enemies." Seattle Issei Yoshisada Kawai articulated the Issei's dilemma: "I felt a turmoil deep in my mind," he told an interviewer at 81. "I did not want my sons to take arms against my mother country. But I owed this country a lot. I was crushed between human affection and giri."

20   Kamechiyo Takahashi, 94, of San Mateo, recalls her own family circumstance: "We'd saved a goodly amount over the years to build a home of our own. Then, when it looked as if war was imminent, Mr. Takahashi said he thought we should take the money and go back to Japan. But our two sons said, 'Wait! We're Americans! Our world is here.' So we built our house and moved into it in the fall of 1941."

21   Just a few weeks later Mrs. Takahashi, busy in the kitchen, heard a radio blaring in the living room. "I couldn't understand the English," she recalls. "All I could hear was the announcer shouting." It was Sunday, December 7.

22   "Just visualize that day! The Pacific Fleet, our first line of defense, was all but sunk! Our second line was the West Coast, where the heaviest concentration of Japanese and people of Japanese descent resided. And we were getting it straight from the horse's mouth—from intercepted cable traffic out of Tokyo, which we code-named MAGIC—that the Japanese were setting up an espionage-sabotage network on the coast. There was only one thing to do, and that was move those people out of there!"

23   The speaker is New York lawyer John J. McCloy, 91, Assistant Secretary of War under President Franklin D. Roosevelt.

24   "Earl Warren, the attorney general out there in California [afterward Chief Justice of the United States], had been pleading with the White House: 'For God's sake! Move the Japanese!'

25   "The President called Francis Biddle, the Attorney General, into his office.

26   "'Francis,' the President said, 'are you in favor of this move?'

27   "'Oh yes, Mr. President,' said Biddle. 'But I want to see it carried out *humanely.*'

28   "'That's exactly what I want to do,' the President said. 'You help draw the order'—and right then and there, Biddle did. The President went on: 'And I want the Army to carry it out!'

29   "When he heard of the plan, Chief of Staff General George Marshall pleaded: 'Please, Mr. President, we've got our hands full.'

30   "'No,' said the President. 'No civilian agency can do this. I want the Army to take it on.'

31   "We were faced with what Mr. Churchill called the 'bloody dilemmas.' I said, 'We're going to have litigation about this, but we better go ahead and do it. We don't know where their next attack is coming from.' I didn't give a damn whether they were citizens or not."

32   Scholars have questioned the necessity of President Roosevelt's action, pointing out that the Office of Naval Intelligence, the Federal Bureau of Investigation, and President Roosevelt's own special investigator all assured Washington that there was no evidence of espionage or sabotage by Japanese Americans. Dr. Peter Irons, associate professor of political science at the University of California, San Diego, who conducted an exhaustive study of 2,000-plus MAGIC messages, concludes: "The MAGIC cables do not implicate Japanese Americans in any sabotage or espionage activity. They provide no substantiation for concern on the President's part about the loyalty of Japanese Americans on the West Coast."

33   "We're charged with wanting to get rid of the Japs for selfish reasons," said the secretary of California's Grower-Shipper Vegetable Association in the *Saturday Evening Post* in May 1942. "We do."

34   Declared U.S. Congressman John Rankin of Mississippi: "This is a race war." But whatever else is said, ultimate responsibility was the President's. As McCloy states: "Franklin Roosevelt was the only man in the world who could sign that order relocating those people. And he signed it." Reflected Attorney General Biddle in his memoirs: "The Constitution has never greatly bothered any wartime President."

35   On the West Coast, FBI agents and local police rounded up more than 2,000 suspected security risks: Japanese-language and martial-arts teachers, Buddhist priests, community leaders. Among the targets were picture bride Yuki Torigoe and her husband, who ran a small watch-repair and gun shop in Watsonville, California: "That very morning they took Mr. Torigoe away. I didn't see him again for nearly a year."

36   The President's order had little effect on Hawaii. Fewer than 2,000 Japanese were taken into custody. Hawaii's 158,000 Japanese represented 37 percent of the population and an even higher percentage of the skilled labor force. "Without them," says Franklin Odo, director of ethnic studies at the University of Hawaii at Manoa, "Hawaii simply couldn't have functioned."

This famous photo, by Dorothea Lange, is titled, "Manzanar Relocation Center—July 3, 1942." It depicts the guardhouse and living quarters. Source: National Archives.

37   A civilian War Relocation Authority (WRA) was established to assist in the evacuation. Its first director, Milton S. Eisenhower, brother of the general, envisioned the agency overseeing a humane resettlement program that would put the uprooted Japanese back to work in public and private jobs throughout the inland states. But the reception Eisenhower received at a meeting with the governors and attorneys general of ten western states on April 7, 1942, convinced him that such a scheme had no hope of realization. Wyoming Governor Nels Smith warned that if Eisenhower's plan were attempted "there would be Japs hanging from every pine tree." Explained Idaho Attorney General Bert Miller: "We want to keep this a white man's country." Eisenhower resigned.

38   "So," says Yuji Ichioka, "the great fire sale got under way." Evacuation notices, posted on telephone poles, gave some Japanese just two days to dispose of the possessions of a lifetime. A few, like Mary Tsukamoto and her husband, were able to leave homes and property in the care of trusted friends. Most had to deal with bargain hunters and profiteers.

39   Mary Oda's family, who farmed 30 acres in the San Fernando Valley, had just two weeks to dispose of a new $1,200 tractor, three cars, three trucks, and all their crops. "In all," recalls Dr. Oda, now a physician practicing near the former family homesite, "we got $1,300. We couldn't argue. We had to leave."

40   When evacuation day arrived, Norman Mineta,[2] who was then ten and later became a U. S. congressman from San Jose, put on his Cub Scout uniform. At the 1942 commencement exercises of the University of California at Berkeley, the top scholar was absent. Harvey Itano, who recorded four years of straight A's, was in the Sacramento assembly center. Explained university president Robert G. Sproul: "His country has called him elsewhere."

41   Hoping thereby to prove their patriotism, the majority of Japanese Americans went off to the internment camps without a whisper. Exhorted JACL president Saburo Kido: "Let us leave with a smiling face and courageous mien. Let us look upon ourselves as the pioneers of a new era looking forward to the greatest adventure of our times."

[2]George W. Bush appointed Norm Mineta to be Secretary of Transportation. (Ed.)

42   "Like a lot of couples then, we got married just before the evacuation so we wouldn't be separated," remembers Dr. Kazuyuki Takahashi, retired now after 23 years in internal medicine at Oakland's Kaiser Hospital. Adds his wife, Soyo, "We honeymooned at Santa Anita assembly center."

43   The racetrack, near Pasadena, was converted into a holding area for Japanese Americans, pending construction of permanent concentration camps. At Santa Anita the Takahashis shared a single, manure-speckled horse stall, and one roll of toilet paper a week, with another newlywed couple. "Manure dust kept drifting down from the walls and ceilings," Doctor Takahashi relates. Soyo adds: "We had four wood-frame cots, with straw-filled mattresses, jammed in crosswise with a blanket hanging down the middle for privacy. After a couple of weeks, mushrooms began growing up through the floor."

44   Kaz tacked up wrapping paper to block the manure dust; Soyo hung a Stanford pennant. "Something great and something American may come out of all this," young Kaz wrote in June 1942. "In the meantime we live on from day to day, not unhappily but in a fog of uncertainty about the future."

45   By September, ten camps had been constructed in the wilds of Arkansas, Arizona, California, Colorado, Idaho, Utah, and Wyoming. Rohwer, Arkansas, was surrounded by mosquito- and snake-infested swamps and became a quagmire when the rains came. Poston, Arizona, got so hot that people jokingly renamed the camp Roastin', poured water on their canvas cots, and slept outdoors trying to keep cool—until dust storms drove them back inside.

46   California's Manzanar—where the Takahashis were moved in the fall of 1942—was typical: wood-frame, tar-paper barracks, armed guards in sentry towers, barbed wire. An American flag fluttered over the gates. Each barracks consisted of four 20-by-20 foot rooms furnished with an oil stove and a bare hanging bulb. There were no closets, Takahashi wrote, "no shelves, no table or chair, not even a nail to hang one's hat." Open showers and latrines offered no privacy.

47   Five doctors cared for the camp's 10,000 people. Mary Oda lost her father, older brother, and a sister in the scant space of seven months. Tom Watanabe, now of Chicago, lost his wife and twin girls in childbirth. "What haunted me," Watanabe says, "was that for years I didn't know what they did with the bodies."

48   To ease the wartime labor shortage, the WRA allowed some internees to work outside the camps. The plan, for the most part, was successful—but not always. Nancy Araki and her parents left Amache, Colorado, to start a farm at American Fork, Utah. "I slept on a sofa under the living-room window," she recalls. "I was just falling asleep one night when someone threw a brick through the glass. My father moved us back into a camp."

49   The camps weren't trouble free either. "The air has been tense and explosive for the past several months," Takahashi wrote as the winter of 1942 set in. Small, pro-Japanese gangs were trying to have their way by a reign of terror, he explained. Some, though not all of the Kibei—that is, American-born citizens educated in Japan—were openly pro-Japanese. The "thoroughly American" internees were keeping quiet because "we all realize that Americanism has somehow skipped the Japanese Americans. . . ."

50   Two days before Pearl Harbor's first anniversary, one of the pro-American JACL leaders at Manzanar, Fred Tayama, was severely beaten. Three Kibei were arrested for the assault. Next day a riot erupted—the worst violence of the evacuation. Two internees were killed by military police, ten others were wounded. "We stayed in our quarters. We were frightened," Dr. Takahashi relates now.

51   To separate loyal from disloyal individuals and to identify those who might be called up for military service, the government in February 1943 required internees over 16 to fill out a loyalty questionnaire. Question 27 asked Nisei males: "Are you willing to serve in the armed forces of the United States on combat duty, wherever ordered?" Question 28 asked: "Will you swear unqualified allegiance to the United States . . . and forswear any form of allegiance or obedience to the Japanese emperor . . . ?"

52   Some 9,000 answered the questions "no-no," qualified their answers, or refused to respond at all. All persons giving so-called no-no answers were summarily branded disloyal. Most were eventually removed from their camps and segregated for the duration at Tule Lake, California. But more than 65,000, about 85 percent of the internees who responded, answered "yes-yes," affirming their loyalty. "It was *my* country and I wanted to defend it," says Tom Kawaguchi. "It was that simple." Explains Hawaii's Senator Daniel K. Inouye, who lost an arm in combat and earned the Distinguished Service Cross, America's second highest decoration for bravery: "We were fighting two wars—one against the Axis overseas and another against racism at home."

53   The 23,000 Nisei who fought for the country of their birth averaged five feet four inches in height and 125 pounds in weight, with M1 rifle and grenades. They wore shirts with 13 1/2-inch necks, pants with 26-inch waists, and size three boots. They won more than 18,000 decorations for bravery, including a Medal of Honor, 52 Distinguished Service Crosses, 560 Silver Stars, 28 with oak-leaf clusters, and no fewer than 9,486 Purple Hearts.

54   Nisei were barred from enlisting in the Navy and Marines, but 6,000 served as Army military intelligence specialists in the Pacific. They were attached to about 130 units from eight different countries and the armies of China. According to Gen. Charles Willoughby, intelligence chief for Gen. Douglas MacArthur, they shortened the war against Japan by two years.

55   Their single most valuable exploit, says Shig Kihara, one of the founders of the Army's Japanese-language school at the Presidio in San Francisco, was cracking Operation Z., Japan's strategic plan for the defense of the Philippines and the Marianas. The result of that effort was the U.S. naval victory in the Battle of Leyte Gulf and the final destruction of the Japanese fleet.

56   In Europe, the mainland Nisei's 442nd Regimental Combat Team, combined overseas with the Hawaiian 100th Battalion, took for its motto "Go For Broke." Fighting in Italy and southern France, the 100/442nd emerged for its size and length of service as the most decorated unit in American history—earning eight Presidential Unit Citations and taking 300 percent casualties.

57   Its most celebrated mission was the October 1944 rescue of the "Lost Battalion"—a unit of the Texas 36th Infantry Division, which had been cut off and was being chewed to pieces in the Vosges Mountains of France. In furious fighting

over six days, the 100/442nd suffered more than 800 casualties to rescue 211 members of the Lost Battalion.

58   Fifth Army Commanding Gen. Mark Clark told them: "The whole United States is proud of you."

59   Not quite. Having survived three major campaigns, T/Sgt. Shig Doi hitch-hiked back to Auburn, California. With his duffel bag on his shoulder and a Bronze Star on his chest, the diminutive hero topped the crest of a hill and looked down onto his hometown. Doi still shuts his eyes at the bitter recollection: "Every store on Main Street had a 'No Japs Wanted' sign out front."

60   Tule Lake, the last of the concentration camps, closed for good in March 1946. At least a third of all Japanese-American truck farmers on the West Coast found their lands ruined or lost to foreclosure. Japanese neighborhoods everywhere were gone, their rented homes and shops taken over by war workers who had flooded into the region.

61   Soyo Takahashi found her parents' home in Palo Alto filled with migrants sleeping ten to a room. After three wartime years as a cook in an Idaho labor camp, John Saito's mother, Sakuyo, had saved enough money for a down payment on a modest house in southwest Los Angeles; the day she tried to move in, she was handed an injunction. "Restrictive covenant," Saito explains. "A thousand-dollar fine and/or a year in jail if we move in. We sold—for a song."

62   It has been estimated that Japanese-American losses totaled 400 million dollars—in 1942 dollars. In 1948 Congress appropriated 38 million dollars to settle claims, but the processing was so snarled that the internees settled for an average of a dime on the dollar. Mary Oda's mother, a former teacher who turned to field labor to support herself, carried the ashes of her dead husband, son, and daughter around in an urn for six years, unable to afford a proper funeral. She finally settled for $1,800 just to see them buried.

63   Some injustices were redressed. In 1952 JACL helped win repeal of California's alien land laws, and Congress granted the Issei's right to citizenship at last. Among those who applied is Michiko Tanaka, now 81. "I have 11 children living and 22 grandchildren, all citizens," she said. "I'm entitled."

64   Social barriers fell too. Nisei men and women found that traditional Japanese values had become marketable commodities in America. "The Japanese work ethic—personal discipline, deference to authority, high productivity, and emphasis on quality—corresponds to the old Protestant ethic," explains UCLA sociologist Harry Kitano. "Once these qualities were ridiculed, despised. Now they dovetail with the needs of the American marketplace."

65   Twenty-five years after the camps were closed, the average personal income of Japanese Americans was 11 percent above the national average; average family income was 32 percent higher. A higher proportion of Japanese Americans were engaged in professional occupations than were whites. By 1981, an astonishing 88 percent of Sansei (third generation) children were attending college, and of these, 92 percent planned professional careers. In California, where more than a third of the nation's 720,000 Japanese Americans reside (88 percent of them U.S. born), family income remains 15 percent above the statewide average.

Wrote sociologist William Petersen: "Even in a country whose patron saint is Horatio Alger, there is no parallel to this success story."

66 And it's a story told over and over again. Paul Terasaki, 56, grew up on the poor side of Los Angeles, where his father had the ill fortune to open a bakery in 1941. The family spent the war years in the desert camp at Gila River, Arizona. Terasaki worked his way through UCLA, earning a doctorate in immunology-embryology, and studied with Nobel laureate Sir Peter Medawar at University College in London. Today Dr. Terasaki heads UCLA's Terasaki Laboratory, recognized as a pioneer in the crucial area of tissue-matching for organ transplants.

67 The late Minoru Yamasaki and his bride, Teruko, shared a one-bedroom New York apartment with his parents and younger brother during the war years. Before the war, Yamasaki spent his days boxing imported china; nights, he struggled toward a master's degree in architecture at New York University. The crowning achievement of his career: Manhattan's twin-tower, 110-story World Trade Center.

68 The first Japanese-American astronaut, Lt. Col. Ellison Onizuka of the U.S. Air Force, who died with six other crew members when the space shuttle *Challenger* exploded last January 28,[3] had dreamed of spaceflight since boyhood. At 13 he had stood on the black lava shores of the Big Island of Hawaii and looked up at the night sky, filled with wonder at the flight of Alan B. Shepard, Jr., America's first man in space. This is how Elli Onizuka described his own first flight in 1985:

69 "I looked down as we passed over Hawaii and thought about all the sacrifices of all the people who helped me along the way. My grandparents, who were contract laborers; my parents, who did without to send me to college; my schoolteachers, coaches, and ministers—all the past generations who pulled together to create the present. Different people, different races, different religions—all working toward a common goal, all one family."

70 Postwar Japanese-American success gave rise to the media catchphrase "model minority." The term makes virtually every Japanese American wince. Some resent being held up for other races to emulate. "It's the whites who are the model. We're still the minority," says one San Francisco attorney. "The term measures us against them, on *their* terms." Others object that the label obscures the many human problems—from neglected elders and broken marriages to kids strung out on drugs—that Japanese Americans share with other Americans.

71 Many Sansei grew up torn between their parents' unspoken shame and a fierce new American pride in ethnic identity. For a long time, Japanese Americans shrouded the wartime experience from the world, from themselves, and from their own children behind 40 years of silence, a resigned shrug, and the phrase *shikata-ga-nai* (nothing can be done). "Anger, shame, humiliation—all are part of it," says Dr. Edward Himeno, a psychiatrist who has worked extensively with Nisei camp victims.

72 "The Sansei absorbed the emotions their parents bottled up," says Dr. Himeno. "They grew up feeling 'there's something wrong with me, and I don't know what it is.'" Congressman Robert Matsui, interned as a one-year-old, offers an illustration: "I remember about age 14 sitting on the back porch with a friend. He said, 'Gee, I wish I weren't Japanese.' I said, 'Yeah, me too.'"

[3]This article was published in 1986 seven years before the terrorist attacks against the World Trade Center mentioned in paragraph 67, and a short time after the *Challenger* explosion. (Ed.)

73   Some Sansei turned their anger inward. "I did heroin, every drug I could find," relates Vietnam combat veteran Mike Watanabe, now executive director of Los Angeles' Asian American Drug Abuse Program (AADAP). "I wasn't proud of my heritage as an Asian American and wanted to assert my own identity—even if it was a destructive one." Eventually, Watanabe says, he understood that he was proud of being Japanese American. He got off drugs, earned a master's degree, and dedicated himself to social work at AADAP, a storefront community clinic in Los Angeles' multiracial, working-class Crenshaw district. Says Watanabe: "In the ten years I've been here, we've treated thousands of Japanese Americans for drug abuse."

74   Other Sansei moved to set their ethnic record right. In 1980 five Sansei attorneys crafted a brief laying out the constitutional violations surrounding the camp experience. In 1983 these attorneys and a team of more than 100 volunteer lawyers and law students forced reopening of the three convictions the Supreme Court upheld in 1943 and 1944. In the first of the cases—that of Fred Korematsu, who was tried for resisting internment—a U.S. district court judge in San Francisco cleared the conviction, declaring that our institutions must "protect all citizens from the petty fears and prejudices that are so easily aroused."

75   The most momentous of the legal actions was finally getting Congress to establish a commission in 1980 to investigate the facts and circumstances surrounding FDR's Executive Order 9066. For the first time Japanese Americans came forward and publicly recounted their experiences in the camps. Men and women wept as they testified, "After 40 years," says Dr. Kuramoto, "the emotional boil was lanced, and the healing process was begun."

76   After hearing testimony from some 750 witnesses, the commission concluded that Executive Order 9066 was not justified by military necessity, that "a grave injustice" had been done to those interned, and that the broad historical causes behind the order were "race prejudice, war hysteria, and a failure of political leadership." The commission recommended the appropriation of 1.5 billion dollars as compensation to the victims. "It was a redemption," says Warren Furutani of UCLA's Asian American Studies Center. "The victims weren't guilty—and the Sansei finally found out what their parents had been through."

77   Their problem now was to find out who they were themselves. Sansei Philip Gotanda, 35, of San Francisco, perhaps the most prolific of young Japanese-American playwrights, went to live in rural Japan to try to answer the question, "How Japanese am I?" "I had the language down pretty well," he relates. "I was wearing the clothes, getting around fine, feeling comfortable. And one day, walking down the street, I had a profound experience: I suddenly realized that all the faces I'd been seeing in the movies and on television, all the faces of the people on the street, were Japanese. Everyone looked like me. For the first time in my life, I was anonymous."

78   Gotanda pauses, as if to let the experience sink in anew. "I think it gave me the vantage point to accept the fact that I am not Japanese," he says. "For better or for worse I am an American."

79   And what did Gotanda do then?

80   "I came home," he says with a smile. ✳

From Arthur Zich, "Japanese Americans: Home at Last," *National Geographic*, April 1986. Reprinted by permission of the author.

Exercises

Do not refer to the selection for Exercises A and B unless your instructor directs you to do so.

A. DETERMINING THE MAIN IDEA AND PURPOSE

Choose the best answer.

_____ 1. The main idea of the selection is that
   a. President Roosevelt's Executive Order 9066 changed Americans' perception of Japanese Americans in the United States.
   b. Japanese Americans accused of spying and sabotage were sent to internment camps.
   c. the internment of Japanese Americans during World War II had profound psychological and economic consequences for those interned and for their descendants.
   d. the internment represented a stigma and a "psychic skeleton in the closet" for Japanese Americans.

_____ 2. With respect to the main idea, the author's purpose is to
   a. trace the history of Japanese Americans in the United States, from their immigration to the period after the war ended.
   b. argue that Japanese Americans interned during the war receive fair compensation.
   c. question the motives of those who supported Japanese internment camps.
   d. recite the accomplishments of Japanese Americans and their role as a "model minority."

B. COMPREHENDING MAIN IDEAS

Choose the correct answer.

_____ 1. The wartime internment of Japanese Americans had many tragic results, the most important of which, according to Zich, was
   a. their being branded as disloyal to their country.
   b. the feeling of suspicion they provoked in Americans.
   c. the loss of their property and livelihoods.
   d. their inability to serve in the U.S. armed forces.

_____ 2. Japanese Americans resent the label "model minority," believing that the term
   a. detracts from other minority groups' struggles to win civil rights.
   b. is inaccurate and unfair.
   c. is condescending and simplistic.
   d. embarrasses them by singling them out for special praise.

_____ 3. The JACL (Japanese American Citizens League) adopted a credo by which its Nisei members, representing the second generation, pledged that they were proud to be "American citizens of Japanese ancestry"

    a. but that they would not take up arms against America.

    b. and that they would stay neutral in the war.

    c. but that they would return to Japan as soon as the war ended.

    d. and that they would defend America against its enemies.

_____ 4. With regard to accusations that Japanese had been engaging in espionage and sabotage, Zich makes it clear that

    a. there was sufficient evidence to warrant internment.

    b. there was no evidence to warrant internment.

    c. there was questionable evidence, and the government decided it was better to be safe than sorry.

    d. scholars disagree about the strength of the evidence.

_____ 5. During the winter of 1942, the atmosphere, in one camp at least, was

    a. festive and cheerful.

    b. sullen and subdued.

    c. quiet and peaceful.

    d. tense and explosive.

_____ 6. Regarding their parents' experience in the camps, many of the Sansei felt

    a. anger and shame.

    b. confusion and ambivalence.

    c. pride and self-respect.

    d. understanding and compassion.

COMPREHENSION SCORE

Score your answers for Exercises A and B as follows:

A. No. right _____ × 2 = _____

B. No. right _____ × 1 = _____

Total points from A and B _____ × 10 = _____ percent

You may refer to the selection as you work through the remaining exercises.

C. MAKING INFERENCES

Write your answers to these questions in your own words.

1. What might be one reason that the government chose desolate locations for concentration camps? _____

_____

2. In paragraph 2, Zich writes, "It [the ordeal of internment] fractured families along political and generational lines." What do you think was the cause of this "fracturing"? _____

_____

3. What was the motivation for the Japanese to begin coming to this country? (See paragraph 8.) _____

_____

4. From what the author writes in paragraphs 10–12, how would you characterize the American government's treatment of Japanese residents? _____

_____

5. From paragraph 19, why did the Issei, the first generation of Japanese in the United States, continue to regard Japan as their motherland? _____

_____

6. Throughout the article, but particularly in paragraphs 39–41, the author suggests one reason that the Japanese were so acquiescent about their relocation. As he writes, they went to the camps "without a whisper." What is it? _____

_____

_____

7. If there was never any evidence that Japanese Americans had been disloyal, engaging in sabotage or espionage activity, why, then, were they interned? Write down the two reasons implied in paragraphs 33 and 46._____

_____

_____

8. Pearl Harbor, site of the famous 1941 Japanese attack, is in Hawaii. Yet Japanese in Hawaii were not sent to internment camps. Why not, according to what the writer suggests in paragraph 36? _____

_____

D. INTERPRETING MEANING AND ANALYZING STRUCTURE

Where appropriate, write your answers to these questions in your own words.

1. The introduction to many essays and articles sometimes uses what is called a "funnel pattern," in which the writer introduces the topic in a general way with background or by using anecdotes (as this article does), after which comes the thesis statement or main idea. How do the opening three paragraphs of this article represent this funnel pattern? Where is the thesis located?

    _____

    _____

2. Look at paragraph 6. What is the meaning of the phrase "picture bride"? _____

    _____

    _____

3. What evidence is provided in paragraph 15 to support this implied idea:

    Japanese farms were highly productive? _____

    _____

4. _____   Which of the following is the best title for paragraph 16?
    a. "Japanese Communities"
    b. "Japanese Neighborhoods: A Refuge from the Outside World"
    c. "Religious and Social Activities in Japanese Communities"
    d. "Issei Forms of Entertainment"

5. With respect to the article as a whole, explain the function of paragraphs

    53–59: _____

    And paragraphs 66–80: _____

    _____

6. At the end of paragraph 65, Zich quotes sociologist William Petersen as saying, "Even in a country whose patron saint is Horatio Alger, there is no parallel to this success story." Explain this sentence. If necessary, look up the

    allusion to Horatio Alger. _____

    _____

    _____

    _____

    _____

E. UNDERSTANDING VOCABULARY

Look through the paragraphs listed below and find a word that matches each definition. Refer to the dictionary if necessary. An example has been done for you.

Ex. strongly disapprove of, condemn [paragraph 4] _____deplore_____

1. overcome, defeated [4] _____

2. descriptive term [4] _____

3. useless, in vain [14] _____

4. however, nevertheless [15] _____

5. belief, doctrine [19] _____

6. feeling of extreme confusion [19] _____

7. about to occur [20] _____

8. treachery, deliberate subversion [32] _____

9. manner, appearance, expression [41] _____

10. boggy area filled with muck and mud [45] _____

11. remedied, corrected [63] _____

12. courteous respect for [64] _____

13. cringe in pain [70] _____

14. imitate, follow the example of [70] _____

F. USING VOCABULARY

In parentheses before each sentence are some inflected forms of words from the selection. Study the context and the sentence. Then write the correct form in the space provided.

1. (*desolation, desolate, desolately*) It is certain that the internees felt complete

   _____ when they first arrived at the camps.

2. (*condescension, condescend, condescending, condescendingly*) Japanese Americans resent being termed a model minority because they think it is both simplistic

   and _____ .

3. (*futility, futile, futilely*) The Issei (or first generation) tried _____ to keep their children from becoming Americanized.

4. (*strategy, strategize, strategic, strategically*) Japan's _____ in implementing Operation Z was to defend the Philippines and Mariana Islands.

5. (*obscurity, obscured, obscurely*) The rapid rise of Japanese Americans after the

   war _____ the fact that many suffered from anger, alienation, and other psychological problems.

6. (*redemption, redeem, redeeming*) The American government attempted to

_____ itself by appropriating $1.5 billion to compensate those victims who had been forcibly relocated to internment camps.

G. SUMMARIZING EXERCISE

On a separate sheet of paper, write a summary in which you contrast (show the differences between) the attitudes of interned Japanese American adults and those of their children.

H. TOPICS FOR WRITING AND DISCUSSION

1. Go to the library or search the World Wide Web for information about the role of William Randolph Hearst's newspaper chain, the Hearst Corporation, in the campaign to relocate Japanese Americans to internment camps.
2. Has the government sufficiently compensated the former internees? Again, do some research on the push to compensate former Japanese American internees.

For Further Exploration

BOOKS

- Jeanne Wakatsuki Houston, *Farewell to Manzanar* (1973). The author was 7 years old when her family was ordered to go to Manzanar in California's Owens Valley along with over 10,000 other Japanese Americans, mostly from Los Angeles. The years of forced detention were hard, and Houston's retelling of her family's experience is poignant but restrained.
- David Guterson, *Snow Falling on Cedars* (1994). This novel is set in the 1950s, after the end of World War II, but lingering mistrust remains for the Japanese American fishermen and berry farmers who live on one of Puget Sound's islands. When a man is found murdered, a Japanese American fisherman is the first suspect.
- Dorothea Lange, *Executive Order 9066* (1972). This famous collection of photographs captures the many moods of Japanese Americans, recording their lives before and during their internment.

MOVIES

- PBS documentary, *Children of the Camps*
- PBS documentary, *Conscience and the Constitution*

WEB SITES

"Women Come to the Front," sponsored by the Library of Congress, features photographs by Dorothea Lange:

- *www.loc.gov/exhibits/wcf/wcf0001.html*

These sites from the Museum of the City of San Francisco give an overview of Lange's work, photographs, editorials from the period, historical information, and many links on the subject of the Japanese internment:

- *www.sfmuseum.org/hist/lange.html*
- *www.sfmuseum.org/war/evactxt.html*

Remembering Manzanar, a site devoted to a relocation camp mentioned in the article, is available here:

- *www.qnet.com/~earthsun/remember.htm*

31

JARED DIAMOND
Easter's End

"Easter's End," first published in Discover *(a magazine devoted to the world of science), is a thought-provoking look at the civilization that flourished on Easter Island in Polynesia. In it, Jared Diamond describes what the civilization was like when it reached its peak between 1200 and 1500, marked in particular by the hundreds of mysterious and huge stone statues, called* moai, *along the coast. But the civilization—including both human and plant life—eventually declined. Diamond offers some hypotheses to explain why, and in telling Easter Island's story, Diamond finds a grim parallel for modern human civilization.*

Jared Diamond is currently a professor of physiology at the UCLA School of Medicine and a contributing editor of Discover. *He has led many expeditions to New Guinea and the Solomon Islands. Some of his* Discover *columns were collected in* The Third Chimpanzee: The Evolution and Future of the Human Animal. *His most recent book,* Guns, Germs, and Steel: The Fates of Human Societies *(1997), investigates the role of geography on human societies and their evolution. It was awarded the Pulitzer Prize in 1998 in the category of general nonfiction.*

Vocabulary Preview

WORD HISTORIES

Mogul [paragraph 31]   Diamond only half-humorously compares the enormous statues carved and erected by Easter Islanders to the huge, ostentatious houses that media *moguls* like Aaron Spelling and Marvin Davis have built in Los Angeles in a game of "let's see who can top this." The word *mogul* derives from the Persian and Arabic word *mugul*, originally from a similar Mongolian word. A *mogul* was originally a member of the force that conquered India in 1526. In English, however, the word more typically denotes a rich and powerful person.

Chaos [paragraph 34]   Diamond describes the *chaos* that replaced the centralized government on Easter Island, as its food surpluses diminished. Our word *chaos* refers to total disorder and confusion. It derives from a Greek word that originally referred to the great void, the primal emptiness out of which order (the Greek *cosmos*) was made.

WORD PARTS

Extra- [paragraph 13]   In English, many compound words are formed with the prefix *extra-*, meaning "outside" or "beyond." *Extraterrestrial* describes an inhabitant of another world, combining the prefix with *terra*, the Latin root for "earth." Other words beginning with this prefix are *extraordinary, extramarital, extracurricular,* and *extrasensory.*

WORD FAMILIES

Revived [paragraph 4]   Diamond writes that his interest in Easter Island was *revived* because of new research and analysis conducted by paleontologists and other researchers studying the animals and plants that once lived there. *Revive* means "to bring back to life." The Latin verb *vivere* ("to live") and the noun *vita* ("life") have given rise to other words in this linguistic family, among them: *vital* (essential for life), *vitamin* (an essential food element), *revitalize* (to give new life to), *vivid* (lifelike), and *vivacious* (full of life, animation, and spirit). What is the meaning of this word?

vivisection   _____

JARED DIAMOND

Easter's End

1   Among the most riveting mysteries of human history are those posed by vanished civilizations. Everyone who has seen the abandoned buildings of the Khmer, the Maya, or the Anasazi is immediately moved to ask the same question: Why did the societies that erected those structures disappear?

2   Their vanishing touches us as the disappearance of other animals, even the dinosaurs, never can. No matter how exotic those lost civilizations seem, their framers were humans like us. Who is to say we won't succumb to the same fate? Perhaps someday New York's skyscrapers will stand derelict and overgrown with vegetation, like the temples at Angkor Wat and Tikal.

Mysterious statues, called *moai*, on Easter Island.

3   Among all such vanished civilizations, that of the former Polynesian society on Easter Island remains unsurpassed in mystery and isolation. The mystery stems especially from the island's gigantic stone statues and its impoverished landscape, but it is enhanced by our associations with the specific people involved: Polynesians represent for us the ultimate in exotic romance, the background for many a child's and an adult's vision of paradise. My own interest in Easter was kindled over 30 years ago when I read Thor Heyerdahl's fabulous accounts of his *Kon-Tiki* voyage.

4   But my interest has been revived recently by a much more exciting account, one not of heroic voyages but of painstaking research and analysis. My friend David Steadman, a paleontologist, has been working with a number of other researchers who are carrying out the first systematic excavations on Easter intended to identify the animals and plants that once lived there. Their work is contributing to a new interpretation of the island's history that makes it a tale not only of wonder but of warning as well.

5   Easter Island, with an area of only 64 square miles, is the world's most isolated scrap of habitable land. It lies in the Pacific Ocean more than 2,000 miles west of the nearest continent (South America), 1,400 miles from even the nearest habitable island (Pitcairn). Its subtropical location and latitude—at 27 degrees south, it is approximately as far below the equator as Houston is north of it—help give it a rather mild climate, while its volcanic origins make its soil fertile. In theory, this combination of blessings should have made Easter a miniature paradise, remote from problems that beset the rest of the world.

6   The island derives its name from its "discovery" by the Dutch explorer Jacob Roggeveen, on Easter (April 5) in 1722. Roggeveen's first impression was not of a paradise but of a wasteland: "We originally, from a further distance, have considered the said Easter Island as sandy; the reason for that is this, that we counted as sand the withered grass, hay, or other scorched and burnt vegetation, because its wasted appearance could give no other impression than of a singular poverty and barrenness."

7   The island Roggeveen saw was a grassland without a single tree or bush over ten feet high. Modern botanists have identified only 47 species of higher plants native to Easter, most of them grasses, sedges, and ferns. The list includes just two species of small trees and two of woody shrubs. With such flora,[1] the islanders Roggeveen encountered had no source of real firewood to warm themselves during Easter's cool, wet, windy winters. Their native animals included nothing larger than insects, not even a single species of native bat, land bird, land snail, or lizard. For domestic animals, they had only chickens.

8   European visitors throughout the eighteenth and early nineteenth centuries estimated Easter's human population at about 2,000, a modest number considering the island's fertility. As Captain James Cook recognized during his brief visit in 1774, the islanders were Polynesians (a Tahitian man accompanying Cook was able to converse with them). Yet despite the Polynesians' well-deserved fame as a great seafaring people, the Easter Islanders who came out to Roggeveen's and Cook's ships did so by swimming or paddling canoes that Roggeveen described

---

[1]Plants as a group; often used with *fauna*, or animals as a group. (Ed.)

as "bad and frail." Their craft, he wrote, were "put together with manifold small planks and light inner timbers, which they cleverly stitched together with very fine twisted threads. . . . But as they lack the knowledge and particularly the materials for caulking and making tight the great number of seams of the canoes, these are accordingly very leaky, for which reason they are compelled to spend half the time in bailing." The canoes, only ten feet long, held at most two people, and only three or four canoes were observed on the entire island.

9   With such flimsy craft, Polynesians could never have colonized Easter from even the nearest island, nor could they have traveled far offshore to fish. The islanders Roggeveen met were totally isolated, unaware that other people existed. Investigators in all the years since his visit have discovered no trace of the islanders' having any outside contacts: not a single Easter Island rock or product has turned up elsewhere, nor has anything been found on the island that could have been brought by anyone other than the original settlers or the Europeans. Yet the people living on Easter claimed memories of visiting the uninhabited Sala y Gomez reef 260 miles away, far beyond the range of the leaky canoes seen by Roggeveen. How did the islanders' ancestors reach that reef from Easter, or reach Easter from anywhere else?

10   Easter Island's most famous feature is its huge stone statues, more than 200 of which once stood on massive stone platforms lining the coast. At least 700 more, in all stages of completion, were abandoned in quarries or on ancient roads between the quarries and the coast, as if the carvers and moving crews had thrown down their tools and walked off the job. Most of the erected statues were carved in a single quarry and then somehow transported as far as six miles—despite heights as great as 33 feet and weights up to 82 tons. The abandoned statues, meanwhile, were as much as 65 feet tall and weighed up to 270 tons. The stone platforms were equally gigantic: up to 500 feet long and 10 feet high, with facing slabs weighing up to 10 tons.

11   Roggeveen himself quickly recognized the problem the statues posed: "The stone images at first caused us to be struck with astonishment," he wrote, "because we could not comprehend how it was possible that these people, who are devoid of heavy thick timber for making any machines, as well as strong ropes, nevertheless had been able to erect such images." Roggeveen might have added that the islanders had no wheels, no draft animals, and no source of power except their own muscles. How did they transport the giant statues for miles, even before erecting them? To deepen the mystery, the statues were still standing in 1770, but by 1864 all of them had been pulled down, by the islanders themselves. Why then did they carve them in the first place? And why did they stop?

12   The statues imply a society very different from the one Roggeveen saw in 1722. Their sheer number and size suggest a population much larger than 2,000 people. What became of everyone? Furthermore, that society must have been highly organized. Easter's resources were scattered across the island: the best stone for the statues was quarried at Rano Raraku near Easter's northeast end; red stone, used for large crowns adorning some of the statues, was quarried at Puna Pau, inland in the southwest; stone carving tools came mostly from Aroi in the northwest. Meanwhile, the best farmland lay in the south and east, and the best fishing grounds on the north and west coasts. Extracting and redistributing

all those goods required complex political organization. What happened to that organization, and how could it ever have arisen in such a barren landscape?

13   Easter Island's mysteries have spawned volumes of speculation for more than two and a half centuries. Many Europeans were incredulous that Polynesians—commonly characterized as "mere savages"—could have created the statues or the beautifully constructed stone platforms. In the 1950s, Heyerdahl argued that Polynesia must have been settled by advanced societies of American Indians, who in turn must have received civilization across the Atlantic from more advanced societies of the Old World. Heyerdahl's raft voyages aimed to prove the feasibility of such prehistoric transoceanic contacts. In the 1960s the Swiss writer Erich von Däniken, an ardent believer in Earth visits by extraterrestrial astronauts, went further, claiming that Easter's statues were the work of intelligent beings who owned ultramodern tools, became stranded on Easter, and were finally rescued.

14   Heyerdahl and Von Däniken both brushed aside overwhelming evidence that the Easter Islanders were typical Polynesians derived from Asia rather than from the Americas and that their culture (including their statues) grew out of Polynesian culture. Their language was Polynesian, as Cook had already concluded. Specifically, they spoke an eastern Polynesian dialect related to Hawaiian and Marquesan, a dialect isolated since about A.D. 400, as estimated from slight differences in vocabulary. Their fishhooks and stone adzes resembled early Marquesan models. Last year DNA extracted from 12 Easter Island skeletons was also shown to be Polynesian. The islanders grew bananas, taro, sweet potatoes, sugarcane, and paper mulberry—typical Polynesian crops, mostly of Southeast Asian origin. Their sole domestic animal, the chicken, was also typically Polynesian and ultimately Asian, as were the rats that arrived as stowaways in the canoes of the first settlers.

15   What happened to those settlers? The fanciful theories of the past must give way to evidence gathered by hardworking practitioners in three fields: archeology, pollen analysis, and paleontology.

16   Modern archeological excavations on Easter have continued since Heyerdahl's 1955 expedition. The earliest radiocarbon dates associated with human activities are around A.D. 400 to 700, in reasonable agreement with the approximate settlement date of 400 estimated by linguists. The period of statue construction peaked around 1200 to 1500, with few if any statues erected thereafter. Densities of archeological sites suggest a large population; an estimate of 7,000 people is widely quoted by archeologists, but other estimates range up to 20,000, which does not seem implausible for an island of Easter's area and fertility.

17   Archeologists have also enlisted surviving islanders in experiments aimed at figuring out how the statues might have been carved and erected. Twenty people, using only stone chisels, could have carved even the largest completed statue within a year. Given enough timber and fiber for making ropes, teams of at most a few hundred people could have loaded the statues onto wooden sleds, dragged them over lubricated wooden tracks or rollers, and used logs as levers to maneuver them into a standing position. Rope could have been made from the fiber of a small native tree, related to the linden, called the hauhau.

However, that tree is now extremely scarce on Easter, and hauling one statue would have required hundreds of yards of rope. Did Easter's now barren landscape once support the necessary trees?

18   That question can be answered by the technique of pollen analysis, which involves boring out a column of sediment from a swamp or pond, with the most recent deposits at the top and relatively more ancient deposits at the bottom. The absolute age of each layer can be dated by radiocarbon methods. Then begins the hard work: examining tens of thousands of pollen grains under a microscope, counting them, and identifying the plant species that produced each one by comparing the grains with modern pollen from known plant species. For Easter Island, the bleary-eyed scientists who performed that task were John Flenley, now at Massey University in New Zealand, and Sarah King of the University of Hull in England.

19   Flenley and King's heroic efforts were rewarded by the striking new picture that emerged of Easter's prehistoric landscape. For at least 30,000 years before human arrival and during the early years of Polynesian settlement, Easter was not a wasteland at all. Instead, a subtropical forest of trees and woody bushes towered over a ground layer of shrubs, herbs, ferns, and grasses. In the forest grew tree daisies, the rope-yielding hauhau tree, and the toromiro tree, which furnishes a dense, mesquite-like firewood. The most common tree in the forest was a species of palm now absent on Easter but formerly so abundant that the bottom strata of the sediment column were packed with its pollen. The Easter Island palm was closely related to the still-surviving Chilean wine palm, which grows up to 82 feet tall and 6 feet in diameter. The tall, unbranched trunks of the Easter Island palm would have been ideal for transporting and erecting statues and constructing large canoes. The palm would also have been a valuable food source, since its Chilean relative yields edible nuts as well as sap from which Chileans make sugar, syrup, honey, and wine.

20   What did the first settlers of Easter Island eat when they were not glutting themselves on the local equivalent of maple syrup? Recent excavations by David Steadman, of the New York State Museum at Albany, have yielded a picture of Easter's original animal world as surprising as Flenley and King's picture of its plant world. Steadman's expectations for Easter were conditioned by his experiences elsewhere in Polynesia, where fish are overwhelmingly the main food at archeological sites, typically accounting for more than 90 percent of the bones in ancient Polynesian garbage heaps. Easter, though, is too cool for the coral reefs beloved by fish, and its cliff-girded coastline permits shallow-water fishing in only a few places. Less than a quarter of the bones in its early garbage heaps (from the period 900 to 1300) belonged to fish; instead, nearly one-third of all bones came from porpoises.

21   Nowhere else in Polynesia do porpoises account for even 1 percent of discarded food bones. But most other Polynesian islands offered animal food in the form of birds and mammals, such as New Zealand's now extinct giant moas and Hawaii's now extinct flightless geese. Most other islanders also had domestic pigs and dogs. On Easter, porpoises would have been the largest animal available—other than humans. The porpoise species identified at Easter, the common dolphin, weighs up to 165 pounds. It generally lives out at sea, so it could not

have been hunted by line fishing or spearfishing from shore. Instead, it must have been harpooned far offshore, in big seaworthy canoes built from the extinct palm tree.

22   In addition to porpoise meat, Steadman found, the early Polynesian settlers were feasting on seabirds. For those birds, Easter's remoteness and lack of predators made it an ideal haven as a breeding site, at least until humans arrived. Among the prodigious numbers of seabirds that bred on Easter were albatross, boobies, frigate birds, fulmars, petrels, prions, shearwaters, storm petrels, terns, and tropic birds. With at least 25 nesting species, Easter was the richest seabird breeding site in Polynesia and probably in the whole Pacific.

23   Land birds as well went into early Easter Island cooking pots. Steadman identified bones of at least six species, including barn owls, herons, parrots, and rail. Bird stew would have been seasoned with meat from large numbers of rats, which the Polynesian colonists inadvertently brought with them; Easter Island is the sole known Polynesian island where rat bones outnumber fish bones at archeological sites. (In case you're squeamish and consider rats inedible, I still recall recipes for creamed laboratory rat that my British biologist friends used to supplement their diet during their years of wartime food rationing.)

24   Porpoises, seabirds, land birds, and rats did not complete the list of meat sources formerly available on Easter. A few bones hint at the possibility of breeding seal colonies as well. All these delicacies were cooked in ovens fired by wood from the island's forests.

25   Such evidence lets us imagine the island onto which Easter's first Polynesian colonists stepped ashore some 1,600 years ago, after a long canoe voyage from eastern Polynesia. They found themselves in a pristine paradise. What then happened to it? The pollen grains and the bones yield a grim answer.

26   Pollen records show that destruction of Easter's forests was well under way by the year 800, just a few centuries after the start of human settlement. Then charcoal from wood fires came to fill the sediment cores, while pollen of palms and other trees and woody shrubs decreased or disappeared, and pollen of the grasses that replaced the forest became more abundant. Not long after 1400 the palm finally became extinct, not only as a result of being chopped down but also because the now ubiquitous rats prevented its regeneration: of the dozens of preserved palm nuts discovered in caves on Easter, all had been chewed by rats and could no longer germinate. While the hauhau tree did not become extinct in Polynesian times, its numbers declined drastically until there weren't enough left to make ropes from. By the time Heyerdahl visited Easter, only a single, nearly dead toromiro tree remained on the island, and even that lone survivor has now disappeared. (Fortunately, the toromiro still grows in botanical gardens elsewhere.)

27   The fifteenth century marked the end not only for Easter's palm but for the forest itself. Its doom had been approaching as people cleared land to plant gardens; as they felled trees to build canoes, to transport and erect statues, and to burn; as rats devoured seeds; and probably as the native birds died out that had pollinated the trees' flowers and dispersed their fruit. The overall picture is among the most extreme examples of forest destruction anywhere in the world: the whole forest gone, and most of its tree species extinct.

28   The destruction of the island's animals was as extreme as that of the forest: without exception, every species of native land bird became extinct. Even shell-fish were overexploited, until people had to settle for small sea snails instead of larger cowries. Porpoise bones disappeared abruptly from garbage heaps around 1500; no one could harpoon porpoises anymore, since the trees used for constructing the big seagoing canoes no longer existed. The colonies of more than half of the seabird species breeding on Easter or on its offshore islets were wiped out.

29   In place of these meat supplies, the Easter Islanders intensified their production of chickens, which had been only an occasional food item. They also turned to the largest remaining meat source available: humans, whose bones became common in late Easter Island garbage heaps. Oral traditions of the islanders are rife with cannibalism; the most inflammatory taunt that could be snarled at an enemy was "The flesh of your mother sticks between my teeth." With no wood available to cook these new goodies, the islanders resorted to sugarcane scraps, grass, and sedges to fuel their fires.

30   All these strands of evidence can be wound into a coherent narrative of a society's decline and fall. The first Polynesian colonists found themselves on an island with fertile soil, abundant food, bountiful building materials, ample lebensraum,[2] and all the prerequisites for comfortable living. They prospered and multiplied.

31   After a few centuries, they began erecting stone statues on platforms, like the ones their Polynesian forebears had carved. With passing years, the statues and platforms became larger and larger, and the statues began sporting ten-ton red crowns—probably in an escalating spiral of one-upmanship, as rival clans tried to surpass each other with shows of wealth and power. (In the same way, successive Egyptian pharaohs built ever-larger pyramids. Today Hollywood movie moguls near my home in Los Angeles are displaying their wealth and power by building ever more ostentatious mansions. Tycoon Marvin Davis topped previous moguls with plans for a 50,000-square-foot house, so now Aaron Spelling has topped Davis with a 56,000-square-foot house. All that those buildings lack to make the message explicit are ten-ton red crowns.) On Easter, as in modern America, society was held together by a complex political system to redistribute locally available resources and to integrate the economies of different areas.

32   Eventually Easter's growing population was cutting the forest more rapidly than the forest was regenerating. The people used the land for gardens and the wood for fuel, canoes, and houses—and, of course, for lugging statues. As forest disappeared, the islanders ran out of timber and rope to transport and erect their statues. Life became more uncomfortable—springs and streams dried up, and wood was no longer available for fires.

33   People also found it harder to fill their stomachs, as land birds, large sea snails, and many seabirds disappeared. Because timber for building seagoing canoes vanished, fish catches declined and porpoises disappeared from the table. Crop yields also declined, since deforestation allowed the soil to be eroded by rain and wind, dried by the sun, and its nutrients to be leeched from it. Intensified chicken production and cannibalism replaced only part of all those lost

[2]German word meaning "living space." (Ed.)

foods. Preserved statuettes with sunken cheeks and visible ribs suggest that people were starving.

34   With the disappearance of food surpluses, Easter Island could no longer feed the chiefs, bureaucrats, and priests who had kept a complex society running. Surviving islanders described to early European visitors how local chaos replaced centralized government and a warrior class took over from the hereditary chiefs. The stone points of spears and daggers, made by the warriors during their heyday in the 1600s and 1700s, still litter the ground of Easter today. By around 1700, the population began to crash toward between one-quarter and one-tenth of its former number. People took to living in caves for protection against their enemies. Around 1770 rival clans started to topple each other's statues, breaking the heads off. By 1864 the last statue had been thrown down and desecrated.

35   As we try to imagine the decline of Easter's civilization, we ask ourselves, "Why didn't they look around, realize what they were doing, and stop before it was too late? What were they thinking when they cut down the last palm tree?"

36   I suspect, though, that the disaster happened not with a bang but with a whimper. After all, there are those hundreds of abandoned statues to consider. The forest the islanders depended on for rollers and rope didn't simply disappear one day—it vanished slowly, over decades. Perhaps war interrupted the moving teams; perhaps by the time the carvers had finished their work, the last rope snapped. In the meantime, any islander who tried to warn about the dangers of progressive deforestation would have been overridden by vested interests of carvers, bureaucrats, and chiefs, whose jobs depended on continued deforestation. Our Pacific Northwest loggers are only the latest in a long line of loggers to cry, "Jobs over trees!" The changes in forest cover from year to year would have been hard to detect: yes, this year we cleared those woods over there, but trees are starting to grow back again on this abandoned garden site here. Only older people, recollecting their childhoods decades earlier, could have recognized a difference. Their children could no more have comprehended their parents' tales than my eight-year-old sons today can comprehend my wife's and my tales of what Los Angeles was like 30 years ago.

37   Gradually trees became fewer, smaller, and less important. By the time the last fruit-bearing adult palm tree was cut, palms had long since ceased to be of economic significance. That left only smaller and smaller palm saplings to clear each year, along with other bushes and treelets. No one would have noticed the felling of the last small palm.

38   By now the meaning of Easter Island for us should be chillingly obvious. Easter Island is Earth writ small. Today, again, a rising population confronts shrinking resources. We too have no emigration valve, because all human societies are linked by international transport, and we can no more escape into space than the Easter Islanders could flee into the ocean. If we continue to follow our present course, we shall have exhausted the world's major fisheries, tropical rain forests, fossil fuels, and much of our soil by the time my sons reach my current age.

39   Every day newspapers report details of famished countries—Afghanistan, Liberia, Rwanda, Sierra Leone, Somalia, the former Yugoslavia, Zaire—where soldiers have appropriated the wealth or where central government is yielding

to local gangs of thugs. With the risk of nuclear war receding, the threat of our ending with a bang no longer has a chance of galvanizing us to halt our course. Our risk now is of winding down, slowly, in a whimper. Corrective action is blocked by vested interests, by well-intentioned political and business leaders, and by their electorates, all of whom are perfectly correct in not noticing big changes from year to year. Instead, each year there are just somewhat more people, and somewhat fewer resources, on Earth.

40   It would be easy to close our eyes or to give up in despair. If mere thousands of Easter Islanders with only stone tools and their own muscle power sufficed to destroy their society, how can billions of people with metal tools and machine power fail to do worse? But there is one crucial difference. The Easter Islanders had no books and no histories of other doomed societies. Unlike the Easter Islanders, we have histories of the past—information that can save us. My main hope for my sons' generation is that we may now choose to learn from the fates of societies like Easter's. ✷

From Jared Diamond, "Easter's End," *Discover*, August 1995. © 1995 Jared Diamond. Reprinted with permission of the author.

Exercises

Do not refer to the selection for Exercises A and B unless your instructor directs you to do so.

A. DETERMINING THE MAIN IDEA AND PURPOSE

Choose the best answer.

_____   1.   The main idea of the selection is that, among all vanished civilizations, the former Polynesian society on Easter Island remains unsurpassed in mystery and isolation *and*

    a. sparks our imagination and interest in other remote and vanished civilizations.

    b. paleontologists have been conducting research to identify the plants and animals that once flourished there.

    c. is the world's most isolated scrap of habitable land.

    d. the scientific research being done there offers us a new interpretation of the island's history, presenting a parallel to the dangers confronting modern civilization.

_____   2.   With respect to the main idea, the author's purpose is to

    a. warn us that the disaster and chaos that befell Easter Island could also happen to us.

    b. trace the history of human civilization on Easter Island.

    c. describe the statues on Easter Island and explain how they were built and erected.

    d. show the painstaking work and important scientific contribution that paleontologists add to the world's store of knowledge.

B. COMPREHENDING MAIN IDEAS

Choose the correct answer.

_____ 1. Which geographical characteristics of Easter Island's should have made it a "miniature paradise, remote from problems that beset the rest of the world"?

    a. Its fertile soil and ample water supply.
    b. Its remoteness, fertile soil, and mild climate.
    c. Its industrious population and position as a regional trading center.
    d. Its bountiful food supply and convenient location for nearby islands.

_____ 2. When the Dutch explorer Jacob Roggeveen arrived on Easter Island in 1722, he found

    a. a paradise.
    b. densely forested land.
    c. well-tended, productive farm plots.
    d. a wasteland.

_____ 3. Until recently, the biggest mystery surrounding the huge stone statues lining Easter Island's coast was

    a. why islanders had carved them in the first place.
    b. where islanders had found the stone to carve them from.
    c. how the islanders had been able to transport them and erect them, given their huge size and the island's lack of wood, draft animals, and power.
    d. why the islanders pulled them down.

_____ 4. Researchers in archeology, pollen analysis, and paleontology excavating Easter Island have found that it had, in fact,

    a. been barren for years, thus deepening the mystery.
    b. at one time been extensively forested with various kinds of trees.
    c. been colonized by advanced societies of American Indians.
    d. contained plants and animals never identified or associated with any other Polynesian island.

_____ 5. The Easter Islanders that explorers encountered in the 1700s paddled frail, rickety canoes rather than large, sturdy seagoing canoes other Polynesian islanders constructed. These canoes were of poor quality because

    a. all the island's palm trees had been cut down and had become extinct.
    b. the island's self-sufficiency made it unnecessary for strong canoes to travel elsewhere.
    c. the older generations who knew how to build strong canoes had failed to pass their skills down to succeeding generations.
    d. the islanders became apathetic and lazy and didn't care about shoddy handiwork.

_____ **6.** Diamond speculates that Easter's civilization declined

    a. so slowly that the residents didn't realize from generation to generation what was really happening.

    b. very quickly, wiped out by a combination of unfortunate and cataclysmic events.

    c. despite the residents' best efforts to regenerate it.

    d. in the same fashion and for the same reasons that all the other civilizations in Polynesia declined.

COMPREHENSION SCORE

Score your answers for Exercises A and B as follows:

A. No. right _____ × 2 = _____

B. No. right _____ × 1 = _____

Total points from A and B _____ × 10 = _____ percent

You may refer to the selection as you work through the remaining exercises.

C. DISTINGUISHING BETWEEN MAIN IDEAS AND SUPPORTING DETAILS

The following sentences come from paragraphs 27 and 28. Label them as follows: MI if the sentence represents a *main idea* and SD if the sentence represents a *supporting detail*.

1. _____ The fifteenth century marked the end not only for Easter's palm but for the forest itself.

2. _____ Its doom had been approaching as people cleared land to plant gardens; as they felled trees to build canoes, to transport and erect statues, and to burn; as rats devoured seeds; and probably as the native birds died out that had pollinated the trees' flowers and dispersed their fruit.

3. _____ The overall picture is among the most extreme examples of forest destruction anywhere in the world: the whole forest gone, and most of its tree species extinct.

4. _____ The destruction of the island's animals was as extreme as that of the forest: without exception, every species of native land bird became extinct.

5. _____ Even shellfish were overexploited, until people had to settle for small sea snails instead of larger cowries.

6. _____ Porpoise bones disappeared abruptly from garbage heaps around 1500; no one could harpoon porpoises anymore, since the trees used for constructing the big seagoing canoes no longer existed.

D. DRAWING CONCLUSIONS

Mark an X before any of these statements that represent reasonable conclusions you can draw from this selection.

1. _____   The most serious threat to our survival lies in overpopulation.

2. _____   Reconstructing the civilization on Easter Island and the reasons for its decline would not have been possible without the research done by paleontologists and biologists.

3. _____   Those Easter Islanders who tried to warn the younger generation about their harmful practices were dismissed as eccentrics or doomsayers.

4. _____   The people who inhabit Easter Island today are making every attempt to recapture its past glory.

5. _____   It is not within our power to change the course of civilization; cultures are born, flourish, and die, just as all life on earth does, and human intervention in a society's evolution is futile.

6. _____   Written records—the mark of literate societies—are a better way of preserving descriptions of an area's landscape than are oral tales handed down from generation to generation.

7. _____   Despite the technological advancements that our civilization has produced, it is likely that earth in the future—with its billions of people and dwindling resources—could succumb to the same fate as befell the Easter Islanders.

E. INTERPRETING MEANING AND ANALYZING STRUCTURE

Where appropriate, write your answers to these questions in your own words.

1. _____   Which of the following would be a good title for paragraph 3?
   a. "An Adult's Vision of Paradise"
   b. "Easter Island: An Exotic Romance"
   c. "Easter Island: A Vanished Civilization of Mystery and Isolation"
   d. "Polynesian Paradise"

2. Describe the kinds of evidence that Diamond uses to reinforce his theory that Easter Island, at one time, was a fertile, productive island, capable of sustaining life. Review the introduction to Part 4, if necessary. _____

_____

3. Look through paragraphs 31–36 and find two parallels Diamond makes between the Easter Islanders and issues and/or behavior in our civilization today.

_____

4. In paragraph 36, what words and phrases show us that Diamond's ideas are hypothetical and not factual?_____

_____

5. Find the quotation and identify the number of the paragraph that represents the *single* most important reason Diamond cites to explain Easter Island's demise._____

6. Look again at almost any of the paragraphs throughout the body of the article and determine what they have in common structurally. _____

_____

7. In the last two paragraphs, what is the fundamental irony that Diamond implies? _____

_____

_____

8. _____   Which of the following best describes Diamond's *tone,* or emotional attitude, in this piece?
   a. neutral, informative, and objective
   b. somber, concerned, and admonishing
   c. philosophical, reflective, and pensive
   d. provocative, shrill, and inflammatory

F. UNDERSTANDING VOCABULARY

Choose the best definition according to an analysis of word parts or the context.

_____ 1. a *paleontologist* has been working [paragraph 4]: one who studies
   a. islands
   b. rocks
   c. animals and birds
   d. plant and animal fossils

_____ 2. a scrap of *habitable* land [5]:
   a. arable, able to be cultivated
   b. able to be reached, navigable
   c. suitable for living
   d. usable, available

_____ 3. *devoid* of heavy thick timber [11]:
   a. completely lacking
   b. favored, blessed
   c. unaccustomed to using
   d. existing in large quantities

_____ **4.** Europeans were *incredulous* [13]:

    a. filled with wonder, astonished
    b. skeptical, disbelieving
    c. easily fooled, gullible
    d. fascinated, intrigued

_____ **5.** the *feasibility* of such contacts [13]: the ability to be

    a. observed
    b. instructed
    c. imitated
    d. brought about

_____ **6.** *ardent* believer [13]:

    a. passionate, enthusiastic
    b. staunchly rigid
    c. recently converted
    d. peculiar, eccentric

_____ **7.** Among the *prodigious* numbers [22]:

    a. huge
    b. small
    c. indeterminate
    d. stretching to infinity

_____ **8.** a *pristine* paradise [25]:

    a. populous
    b. neglected
    c. unspoiled
    d. breathtaking

_____ **9.** the most inflammatory *taunt* [29]:

    a. slang expression
    b. practice
    c. insult
    d. popular saying

_____ **10.** *ostentatious* mansions [31]:

    a. offensive, repugnant
    b. costly, expensive
    c. esthetically designed
    d. pretentiously showy

G. USING VOCABULARY

Here are some words from the selection. Write an original sentence using each word that shows both that you know how to use the word and what it means.

  1. *succumb* [paragraph 2] _____

_____

2. *barrenness* [6]: _____

_____

3. *manifold* [8]: _____

_____

4. *implausible* [16]: _____

_____

5. *strata* [19]: _____

_____

6. *haven* [22]: _____

_____

7. *squeamish* [23]: _____

_____

8. *ubiquitous* [26]: _____

_____

9. *moguls* [31]: _____

_____

10. *suffice* [40]: _____

_____

H. PARAPHRASING AND SUMMARIZING EXERCISE

1. Paraphrase these sentences from paragraph 38:

Original Passage

By now the meaning of Easter Island for us
should be chillingly obvious. Easter Island is
Earth writ small. Today, again, a rising population confronts shrinking resources.

Paraphrase

_____

_____

_____

_____

2. Paragraph 36 is one of the most moving passages in the article. Summarize it
   in twenty-five to thirty words._____

_____

_____

I. TOPICS FOR WRITING OR DISCUSSION

1. Search in the library or on the World Wide Web for information that offers a different theory to explain the decline of Easter Island's civilization. Write a short report summarizing your findings.

2. What evidence in the article makes Diamond's hypothesis irrefutable?

3. Do some research and report on what life is like on Easter Island now.

For Further Exploration

BOOKS

- Paul Theroux, *The Happy Isles of Oceania* (1992). Theroux is a seasoned traveler and travel writer whose grumpy attitude has given him the reputation of being somewhat of a curmudgeon. Still, this is a readable and engaging account of his journey around the islands of Oceania to Polynesia.
- Thor Heyerdahl, *Kon-Tiki: Across the Pacific by Raft* (1950). This classic story is about six men who undertook a raft trip across the Pacific.

MOVIE

On the Beach (1959) directed by Stanley Kramer and starring Gregory Peck, Ava Gardner, and Anthony Perkins, shows a nightmarish vision of nuclear warfare. With the exception of Australia, the world has been destroyed, and the movie shows the characters' lives as they wait for the fallout to come their way.

WEB SITES

Information about Easter Island is available at these three sites. The first is Easter Island's home page, which includes several links:

- *www.netaxs.com/~trance/rapanvi.html*

"Easter Island in Three Dimensions" features photographs of the island in both two and three dimensions:

- *www.3dphoto.net/stereo/world/latin_america/chile/easter/easter.html*

Finally, this site, "Images of Sites in Easter Island," shows rock art, petroglyphs, and the moai by a British photographer and archeologist:

- *www.le.ac.uk/archaeology/rug/image_collection/hier/pn/r1.html*

32

BARBARA EHRENREICH

Nickel and Dimed: On (Not) Getting By in America

Barbara Ehrenreich is a contributing editor of Harper's *magazine and the author of several books, including* Fear of Falling *and* Blood Rites. *In January 1999,* Harper's *published a long essay, a portion of which is reprinted here. That piece later led to a full-length book of the same title. Ehrenreich's mission was to find out how people manage to live on minimum wage, but instead of engaging in a more traditional research study, she decided to join the low-wage workforce. She found low-paying jobs in several different regions of the country, for example, working as a WalMart clerk in Michigan; as a cleaning woman for Merry Maids in Portland, Maine; and as a waitress in Key West, Florida, the subject of this particular excerpt.*

Vocabulary Preview

WORD HISTORIES

Atavistic [paragraph 8]   The word *atavistic* came into English from French (*atavique*), and the French word comes from the Latin word *atavus,* meaning "ancestor." The word combines the Latin elements *atta* ("father") + *avus* ("grandfather"). When Ehrenreich states that she found housekeeping appealing, "for reasons both *atavistic* and practical," she is referring to the fact that her mother had cleaned houses before she was born. The word, then, describes the process of a trait or a characteristic returning after a period of absence.

Agape [paragraph 17]   When Ehrenreich and the other waitresses put extra croutons on a diner's salad or pick up the tab for pie and milk from someone who is down on his luck, she writes that "maybe the same levels of *agape* can be found throughout the 'hospitality industry.'" *Agape* (pronounced ă-găp-́ā) is a Greek word meaning "love," but it describes a love that is spiritual in nature, rather than sexual.

Proletarian [paragraph 19]   The words *proletarian* and *proletariat* both refer to the working classes. (In his classic antitotalitarian novel *1984,* George Orwell used the short form, *prole.*) Derived from Latin, the word *proletariat* referred to the group of people who were the lowest class of citizens in the Roman Empire. The word may have a positive or negative context, depending on the way it is used. Ehrenreich uses it positively, suggesting in the phrase "in some dreamy *proletarian* idyll" that some writers romanticize the lives of common workers. However, her experiment proved this romanticism to be naive.

WORD PARTS

Il- [paragraph 17]   The word *illicit* combines the negative prefix *il-* and the Latin root *licitus* ("lawful"). If something is illicit, it is unlawful or not sanctioned by either custom or law. The prefix *il-* precedes words that begin with *l*, making them easier to pronounce. In this way, it is related to the other negative prefixes, *in-, im-,* and *ir-*. Other words beginning with this prefix include *illiterate, illegible,* and *illegal.* Do not confuse it with the prefix *ill-*, which means "badly," as in *ill-fated* or *ill-mannered.*

-logy [paragraphs 3 and 4]   The study of human societies is called *anthropology,* which combines the Greek elements *anthropo-* ("human") and *logy* ("study of" or "science"). Here are some other words ending in this useful suffix:

archeology	the study of antiquity, of man's past culture
biology	the study of animal and plant life
etymology	the study of word origins
pathology	the scientific study of the nature of disease
theology	the study of God and of divine truths

WORD FAMILIES

Anthropo- [paragraphs 3 and 4]   As you saw in the above segment, the Greek root *anthropo-* means "human." Therefore, an anthropologist studies the social and cultural development and behavior of various peoples. Two other words in this linguistic family are *anthropocentric,* the belief that man is the central part of the final aim of the universe, and *anthropomorphism,* the practice of attributing human motivations or characteristics to nonhuman things. What do these two words mean? Consult a dictionary if you are unsure.

anthropophagus	_____
misanthrope	_____

BARBARA EHRENREICH

Nickel and Dimed: On (Not) Getting By in America

1   At the beginning of June 1998 I leave behind everything that normally soothes the ego and sustains the body—home, career, companion, reputation, ATM card—for a plunge into the low-wage workforce. There, I become another, occupationally much diminished "Barbara Ehrenreich"—depicted on job-application

forms as a divorced homemaker whose sole work experience consists of house-keeping in a few private homes. I am terrified, at the beginning, of being un-masked for what I am: a middle-class journalist setting out to explore the world that welfare mothers are entering, at the rate of approximately 50,000 a month, as welfare reform kicks in. Happily, though, my fears turn out to be entirely un-warranted: during a month of poverty and toil, my name goes unnoticed and for the most part unuttered. In this parallel universe where my father never got out of the mines and I never got through college, I am "baby," "honey," "blondie," and, most commonly, "girl."

2   My first task is to find a place to live. I figure that if I can earn $7 an hour—which, from the want ads, seems doable—I can afford to spend $500 on rent, or maybe, with severe economies, $600. In the Key West area, where I live, this pretty much confines me to flophouses and trailer homes—like the one, a pleasing fif-teen-minute drive from town, that has no air-conditioning, no screens, no fans, no television, and, by way of diversion, only the challenge of evading the landlord's Doberman pinscher. The big problem with this place, though, is the rent, which at $675 a month is well beyond my reach. All right, Key West is expensive. But so is New York City, or the Bay Area, or Jackson Hole, or Telluride, or Boston, or any other place where tourists and the wealthy compete for living space with the peo-ple who clean their toilets and fry their hash browns.[1] Still, it is a shock to realize that "trailer trash" has become, for me, a demographic category to aspire to.

3   So I decide to make the common trade-off between affordability and conve-nience, and go for a $500-a-month efficiency thirty miles up a two-lane highway from the employment opportunities of Key West, meaning forty-five minutes if there's no road construction and I don't get caught behind some sun-dazed Canadian tourists. I hate the drive, along a roadside studded with white crosses commemorating the more effective head-on collisions, but it's a sweet little place—a cabin, more or less, set in the swampy back yard of the converted mo-bile home where my landlord, an affable TV repairman, lives with his bartender girlfriend. Anthropologically speaking, a bustling trailer park would be prefer-able, but here I have a gleaming white floor and a firm mattress, and the few resident bugs are easily vanquished.

4   Besides, I am not doing this for the anthropology. My aim is nothing so mist-ily subjective as to "experience poverty" or find out how it "really feels" to be a long-term low-wage worker. I've had enough unchosen encounters with poverty and the world of low-wage work to know it's not a place you want to visit for touristic purposes; it just smells too much like fear. And with all my real-life as-sets—bank account, IRA, health insurance, multiroom home—waiting indul-gently in the background, I am, of course, thoroughly insulated from the terrors that afflict the genuinely poor.

---

[1]According to the Department of Housing and Urban Development, the "fair-market rent" for an effi-ciency is $551 here in Monroe County, Florida. A comparable rent in the five boroughs of New York City is $704; in San Francisco, $713; and in the heart of Silicon Valley, $808. The fair-market rent for an area is defined as the amount that would be needed to pay rent plus utilities for "privately owned, de-cent, safe, and sanitary rental housing of a modest (non-luxury) nature with suitable amenities." [Ehrenreich's note. The "fair market rent" would be higher today—much higher in New York City or San Francisco. (Editor)]

5   No, this is a purely objective, scientific sort of mission. The humanitarian rationale for welfare reform—as opposed to the more punitive and stingy impulses that may actually have motivated it—is that work will lift poor women out of poverty while simultaneously inflating their self-esteem and hence their future value in the labor market. Thus, whatever the hassles involved in finding child care, transportation, etc., the transition from welfare to work will end happily, in greater prosperity for all. Now there are many problems with this comforting prediction, such as the fact that the economy will inevitably undergo a downturn, eliminating many jobs. Even without a downturn, the influx of a million former welfare recipients into the low-wage labor market could depress wages by as much as 11.9 percent, according to the Economic Policy Institute (EPI) in Washington, D.C.

6   But is it really possible to make a living on the kinds of jobs currently available to unskilled people? Mathematically, the answer is no, as can be shown by taking $6 to $7 an hour, perhaps subtracting a dollar or two an hour for child care, multiplying by 160 hours a month, and comparing the result to the prevailing rents. According to the National Coalition for the Homeless, for example, in 1998 it took, on average nationwide, an hourly wage of $8.89 to afford a one-bedroom apartment, and the Preamble Center for Public Policy estimates that the odds against a typical welfare recipient's landing a job at such a "living wage" are about 97 to 1. If these numbers are right, low-wage work is not a solution to poverty and possibly not even to homelessness.

7   It may seem excessive to put this proposition to an experimental test. As certain family members keep unhelpfully reminding me, the viability of low-wage work could be tested, after a fashion, without ever leaving my study. I could just pay myself $7 an hour for eight hours a day, charge myself for room and board, and total up the numbers after a month. Why leave the people and work that I love? But I am an experimental scientist by training. In that business, you don't just sit at a desk and theorize; you plunge into the everyday chaos of nature, where surprises lurk in the most mundane measurements. Maybe, when I got into it, I would discover some hidden economies in the world of the low-wage worker. After all, if 30 percent of the workforce toils for less than $8 an hour, according to the EPI, they may have found some tricks as yet unknown to me. Maybe—who knows?—I would even be able to detect in myself the bracing psychological effects of getting out of the house, as promised by the welfare wonks at places like the Heritage Foundation. Or, on the other hand, maybe there would be unexpected costs—physical, mental, or financial—to throw off all my calculations. Ideally, I should do this with two small children in tow, that being the welfare average, but mine are grown and no one is willing to lend me theirs for a month-long vacation in penury. So this is not the perfect experiment, just a test of the best possible case: an unencumbered woman, smart and even strong, attempting to live more or less off the land.

8   On the morning of my first full day of job searching, I take a red pen to the want ads, which are auspiciously numerous. Everyone in Key West's booming "hospitality industry" seems to be looking for someone like me—trainable, flexible, and with suitably humble expectations as to pay. I know I possess certain traits that

might be advantageous—I'm white and, I like to think, well-spoken and poised—but I decide on two rules: One, I cannot use any skills derived from my education or usual work—not that there are a lot of want ads for satirical essayists anyway. Two, I have to take the best-paid job that is offered me and of course do my best to hold it; no Marxist rants or sneaking off to read novels in the ladies' room. In addition, I rule out various occupations for one reason or another: Hotel front-desk clerk, for example, which to my surprise is regarded as unskilled and pays around $7 an hour, gets eliminated because it involves standing in one spot for eight hours a day. Waitressing is similarly something I'd like to avoid, because I remember it leaving me bone tired when I was eighteen, and I'm decades of varicosities and back pain beyond that now. Telemarketing, one of the first refuges of the suddenly indigent, can be dismissed on grounds of personality. This leaves certain supermarket jobs, such as deli clerk, or housekeeping in Key West's thousands of hotel and guest rooms. Housekeeping is especially appealing, for reasons both atavistic and practical: it's what my mother did before I came along, and it can't be too different from what I've been doing part-time, in my own home, all my life.

9   So I put on what I take to be a respectful-looking outfit of ironed Bermuda shorts and scooped-neck T-shirt and set out for a tour of the local hotels and supermarkets. Best Western, Econo Lodge, and HoJo's all let me fill out application forms, and these are, to my relief, interested in little more than whether I am a legal resident of the United States and have committed any felonies. My next stop is Winn-Dixie, the supermarket, which turns out to have a particularly onerous application process, featuring a fifteen-minute "interview" by computer since, apparently, no human on the premises is deemed capable of representing the corporate point of view. I am

conducted to a large room decorated with posters illustrating how to look "professional" (it helps to be white and, if female, permed) and warning of the slick promises that union organizers might try to tempt me with. The interview is multiple choice: Do I have anything, such as child-care problems, that might make it hard for me to get to work on time? Do I think safety on the job is the responsibility of management? Then, popping up cunningly out of the blue: How many dollars' worth of stolen goods have I purchased in the last year? Would I turn in a fellow employee if I caught him stealing? Finally, "Are you an honest person?"

10   Apparently, I ace the interview, because I am told that all I have to do now is show up in some doctor's office tomorrow for a urine test. This seems to be a fairly general rule: if you want to stack Cheerio boxes or vacuum hotel rooms in chemically fascist America, you have to be willing to squat down and pee in front of some health worker (who has no doubt had to do the same thing herself). The wages Winn-Dixie is offering—$6 and a couple of dimes to start with—are not enough, I decide, to compensate for this indignity.[2]

11   I lunch at Wendy's, where $4.99 gets you unlimited refills at the Mexican part of the Superbar, a comforting surfeit of refried beans and "cheese sauce." A teenage employee, seeing me studying the want ads, kindly offers me an application form, which I fill out, though here, too, the pay is just $6 and change an hour. Then it's off for a round of the locally owned inns and guesthouses. At "The Palms," let's call it, a bouncy manager actually takes me around to see the rooms and meet the existing housekeepers, who, I note with satisfaction, look pretty much like me—faded ex-hippie types in shorts with long hair pulled back in braids. Mostly, though, no one speaks to me or even looks at me except to proffer an application form. At my last stop, a palatial B&B, I wait twenty minutes to meet "Max," only to be told that there are no jobs now but there should be one soon, since "nobody lasts more than a couple weeks." (Because none of the people I talked to knew I was a reporter, I have changed their names to protect their privacy and, in some cases perhaps, their jobs.)

12   Three days go by like this, and, to my chagrin, no one out of the approximately twenty places I've applied calls me for an interview. I had been vain enough to worry about coming across as too educated for the jobs I sought, but no one even seems interested in finding out how overqualified I am. Only later will I realize that the want ads are not a reliable measure of the actual jobs available at any particular time. They are, as I should have guessed from Max's comment, the employers' insurance policy against the relentless turnover of the low-wage workforce. Most of the big hotels run ads almost continually, just to build a supply of applicants to replace the current workers as they drift away or are fired, so finding a job is just a matter of being at the right place at the right time

[2]According to the *Monthly Labor Review* (November 1996), 28 percent of work sites surveyed in the service industry conduct drug tests (corporate workplaces have much higher rates), and the incidence of testing has risen markedly since the eighties. The rate of testing is highest in the South (56 percent of work sites polled), with the Midwest in second place (50 percent). The drug most likely to be detected—marijuana, which can be detected in urine for weeks—is also the most innocuous, while heroin and cocaine are generally undetectable three days after use. Prospective employees sometimes try to cheat the tests by consuming excessive amounts of liquids and taking diuretics and even masking substances available through the Internet. [Editor's note]

and flexible enough to take whatever is being offered that day. This finally happens to me at one of the big discount hotel chains, where I go, as usual, for housekeeping and am sent, instead, to try out as a waitress at the attached "family restaurant," a dismal spot with a counter and about thirty tables that looks out on a parking garage and features such tempting fare as "Pollish [sic] sausage and BBQ sauce" on 95-degree days. Phillip, the dapper young West Indian who introduces himself as the manager, interviews me with about as much enthusiasm as if he were a clerk processing me for Medicare, the principal questions being what shifts can I work and when can I start. I mutter something about being woefully out of practice as a waitress, but he's already on to the uniform: I'm to show up tomorrow wearing black slacks and black shoes; he'll provide the rust-colored polo shirt with HEARTHSIDE embroidered on it, though I might want to wear my own shirt to get to work, ha ha. At the word "tomorrow," something between fear and indignation rises in my chest. I want to say, "Thank you for your time, sir, but this is just an experiment, you know, not my actual life."

13   So begins my career at the Hearthside, I shall call it, one small profit center within a global discount hotel chain, where for two weeks I work from 2:00 till 10:00 P.M. for $2.43 an hour plus tips.[3] In some futile bid for gentility, the management has barred employees from using the front door, so my first day I enter through the kitchen, where a red-faced man with shoulder-length blond hair is throwing frozen steaks against the wall and yelling, "Fuck this shit!" "That's just Jack," explains Gail, the wiry middle-aged waitress who is assigned to train me. "He's on the rag again"—a condition occasioned, in this instance, by the fact that the cook on the morning shift had forgotten to thaw out the steaks. For the next eight hours, I run after the agile Gail, absorbing bits of instruction along with fragments of personal tragedy. All food must be trayed, and the reason she's so tired today is that she woke up in a cold sweat thinking of her boyfriend, who killed himself recently in an upstate prison. No refills on lemonade. And the reason he was in prison is that a few DUIs caught up with him, that's all, could have happened to anyone. Carry the creamers to the table in a monkey bowl, never in your hand. And after he was gone she spent several months living in her truck, peeing in a plastic pee bottle and reading by candlelight at night, but you can't live in a truck in the summer, since you need to have the windows down, which means anything can get in, from mosquitoes on up.

14   At least Gail puts to rest any fears I had of appearing overqualified. From the first day on, I find that of all the things I have left behind, such as home and identity, what I miss the most is competence. Not that I have ever felt utterly competent in the writing business, in which one day's success augurs nothing at all for the next. But in my writing life, I at least have some notion of procedure: do the research, make the outline, rough out a draft, etc. As a server, though, I am beset by requests like bees: more iced tea here, ketchup over there, a to-go

---

[3]According to the Fair Labor Standards Act, employers are not required to pay "tipped employees," such as restaurant servers, more than $2.13 an hour in direct wages. However, if the sum of tips plus $2.13 an hour falls below the minimum wage, or $5.15 an hour, the employer is required to make up the difference. This fact was not mentioned by managers or otherwise publicized at either of the restaurants where I worked. [Ehrenreich's note]

box for table fourteen, and where are the high chairs, anyway? Of the twenty-seven tables, up to six are usually mine at any time, though on slow afternoons or if Gail is off, I sometimes have the whole place to myself. There is the touch-screen computer-ordering system to master, which is, I suppose, meant to minimize server-cook contact, but in practice requires constant verbal fine-tuning: "That's gravy on the mashed, okay? None on the meatloaf," and so forth—while the cook scowls as if I were inventing these refinements just to torment him. Plus, something I had forgotten in the years since I was eighteen: about a third of a server's job is "side work" that's invisible to customers—sweeping, scrubbing, slicing, refilling, and restocking. If it isn't all done, every little bit of it, you're going to face the 6:00 P.M. dinner rush defenseless and probably go down in flames. I screw up dozens of times at the beginning, sustained in my shame entirely by Gail's support—"It's okay, baby, everyone does that sometime"—because, to my total surprise and despite the scientific detachment I am doing my best to maintain, I care.

15   The whole thing would be a lot easier if I could just skate through it as Lily Tomlin in one of her waitress skits, but I was raised by the absurd Booker T. Washingtonian precept that says: If you're going to do something, do it well. In fact, "well" isn't good enough by half. Do it better than anyone has ever done it before. Or so said my father, who must have known what he was talking about because he managed to pull himself, and us with him, up from the mile-deep copper mines of Butte to the leafy suburbs of the Northeast, ascending from boilermakers to martinis before booze beat out ambition. As in most endeavors I have encountered in my life, doing it "better than anyone" is not a reasonable goal. Still, when I wake up at 4:00 A.M. in my own cold sweat, I am not thinking about the writing deadlines I'm neglecting; I'm thinking about the table whose order I screwed up so that one of the boys didn't get his kiddie meal until the rest of the family had moved on to their Key Lime pies. That's the other powerful motivation I hadn't expected—the customers, or "patients," as I can't help thinking of them on account of the mysterious vulnerability that seems to have left them temporarily unable to feed themselves. After a few days at the Hearthside, I feel the service ethic kick in like a shot of oxytocin, the nurturance hormone. The plurality of my customers are hard-working locals—truck drivers, construction workers, even housekeepers from the attached hotel—and I want them to have the closest to a "fine dining" experience that the grubby circumstances will allow. No "you guys" for me; everyone over twelve is "sir" or "ma'am." I ply them with iced tea and coffee refills; I return, mid-meal, to inquire how everything is; I doll up their salads with chopped raw mushrooms, summer squash slices, or whatever bits of produce I can find that have survived their sojourn in the cold-storage room mold-free.

16   There is Benny, for example, a short, tight-muscled sewer repairman, who cannot even think of eating until he has absorbed a half hour of air-conditioning and ice water. We chat about hyperthermia and electrolytes until he is ready to order some finicky combination like soup of the day, garden salad, and a side of grits. There are the German tourists who are so touched by my pidgin "Willkommen" and "Ist alles gut?" that they actually tip. (Europeans, spoiled by their trade-union-ridden, high-wage welfare states, generally do not know that

they are supposed to tip. Some restaurants, the Hearthside included, allow servers to "grat" their foreign customers, or add a tip to the bill. Since this amount is added before the customers have a chance to tip or not tip, the practice amounts to an automatic penalty for imperfect English.) There are the two dirt-smudged lesbians, just off their construction shift, who are impressed enough by my suave handling of the fly in the piña colada that they take the time to praise me to Stu, the assistant manager. There's Sam, the kindly retired cop, who has to plug up his tracheotomy hole with one finger in order to force the cigarette smoke into his lungs.

17   Sometimes I play with the fantasy that I am a princess who, in penance for some tiny transgression, has undertaken to feed each of her subjects by hand. But the non-princesses working with me are just as indulgent, even when this means flouting management rules—concerning, for example, the number of croutons that can go on a salad (six). "Put on all you want," Gail whispers, "as long as Stu isn't looking." She dips into her own tip money to buy biscuits and gravy for an out-of-work mechanic who's used up all his money on dental surgery, inspiring me to pick up the tab for his milk and pie. Maybe the same high levels of agape can be found throughout the "hospitality industry." I remember the poster decorating one of the apartments I looked at, which said "If you seek happiness for yourself you will never find it. Only when you seek happiness for others will it come to you," or words to that effect—an odd sentiment, it seemed to me at the time, to find in the dank one-room basement apartment of a bellhop at the Best Western. At the Hearthside, we utilize whatever bits of autonomy we have to ply our customers with the illicit calories that signal our love. It is our job as servers to assemble the salads and desserts, pouring the dressings and squirting the whipped cream. We also control the number of butter patties our customers get and the amount of sour cream on their baked potatoes. So if you wonder why Americans are so obese, consider the fact that waitresses both express their humanity and earn their tips through the covert distribution of fats.

18   Ten days into it, this is beginning to look like a livable lifestyle. I like Gail, who is "looking at fifty" but moves so fast she can alight in one place and then another without apparently being anywhere between them. I clown around with Lionel, the teenage Haitian busboy, and catch a few fragments of conversation with Joan, the svelte fortyish hostess and militant feminist who is the only one of us who dares to tell Jack to shut the fuck up. I even warm up to Jack when, on a slow night and to make up for a particularly unwarranted attack on my abilities, or so I imagine, he tells me about his glory days as a young man at "coronary school"—or do you say "culinary"?—in Brooklyn, where he dated a knockout Puerto Rican chick and learned everything there is to know about food. I finish up at 10:00 or 10:30, depending on how much side work I've been able to get done during the shift, and cruise home to the tapes I snatched up at random when I left my real home—Marianne Faithfull, Tracy Chapman, Enigma, King Sunny Ade, the Violent Femmes—just drained enough for the music to set my cranium resonating but hardly dead. Midnight snack is Wheat Thins and Monterey Jack, accompanied by cheap white wine on ice and whatever AMC has to offer. To bed by 1:30 or 2:00, up at 9:00 or 10:00, read for an hour while my

uniform whirls around in the landlord's washing machine, and then it's another eight hours spent following Mao's central instruction, as laid out in the Little Red Book, which was: Serve the people.

19   I could drift along like this, in some dreamy proletarian idyll, except for two things. One is management. If I have kept this subject on the margins thus far it is because I still flinch to think that I spent all those weeks under the surveillance of men (and later women) whose job it was to monitor my behavior for signs of sloth, theft, drug abuse, or worse. Not that managers and especially "assistant managers" in low-wage settings like this are exactly the class enemy. In the restaurant business, they are mostly former cooks or servers, still capable of pinch-hitting in the kitchen or on the floor, just as in hotels they are likely to be former clerks, and paid a salary of only about $400 a week. But everyone knows they have crossed over to the other side, which is, crudely put, corporate as opposed to human. Cooks want to prepare tasty meals; servers want to serve them graciously; but managers are there for only one reason—to make sure that money is made for some theoretical entity that exists far away in Chicago or New York, if a corporation can be said to have a physical existence at all. Reflecting on her career, Gail tells me ruefully that she had sworn, years ago, never to work for a corporation again. "They don't cut you no slack. You give and you give, and they take."

20   Managers can sit—for hours at a time if they want—but it's their job to see that no one else ever does, even when there's nothing to do, and this is why, for servers, slow times can be as exhausting as rushes. You start dragging out each little chore, because if the manager on duty catches you in an idle moment, he will give you something far nastier to do. So I wipe, I clean, I consolidate ketchup bottles and recheck the cheesecake supply, even tour the tables to make sure the customer evaluation forms are all standing perkily in their places—wondering all the time how many calories I burn in these strictly theatrical exercises. When, on a particular dead afternoon, Stu finds me glancing at a *USA Today* a customer has left behind, he assigns me to vacuum the entire floor with the broken vacuum cleaner that has a handle only two feet long, and the only way to do that without incurring orthopedic damage is to proceed from spot to spot on your knees.

21   On my first Friday at the Hearthside there is a "mandatory meeting for all restaurant employees," which I attend, eager for insight into our overall marketing strategy and the niche (your basic Ohio cuisine with a tropical twist?) we aim to inhabit. But there is no "we" at this meeting. Phillip, our top manager except for an occasional "consultant" sent out by corporate headquarters, opens it with a sneer: "The break room—it's disgusting. Butts in the ashtrays, newspapers lying around, crumbs." This windowless little room, which also houses the time clock for the entire hotel, is where we stash our bags and civilian clothes and take our half-hour meal breaks. But a break room is not a right, he tells us. It can be taken away. We should also know that the lockers in the break room and whatever is in them can be searched at any time. Then comes gossip; there has been gossip; gossip (which seems to mean employees talking among themselves) must stop. Off-duty employees are henceforth barred from eating at the

restaurant, because "other servers gather around them and gossip." When Phillip has exhausted his agenda of rebukes, Joan complains about the condition of the ladies' room and I throw in my two bits about the vacuum cleaner. But I don't see any backup coming from my fellow servers, each of whom has subsided into her own personal funk; Gail, my role model, stares sorrowfully at a point six inches from her nose. The meeting ends when Andy, one of the cooks, gets up, muttering about breaking up his day off for this almighty bullshit.

22   Just four days later we are suddenly summoned into the kitchen at 3:30 P.M. even though there are live tables on the floor. We all—about ten of us—stand around Phillip, who announces grimly that there has been a report of some "drug activity" on the night shift and that, as a result, we are now to be a "drug-free" workplace, meaning that all new hires will be tested, as will possibly current employees on a random basis. I am glad that this part of the kitchen is so dark, because I find myself blushing as hard as if I had been caught toking up in the ladies' room myself: I haven't been treated this way—lined up in the corridor, threatened with locker searches, peppered with carelessly aimed accusations—since junior high school. Back on the floor, Joan cracks, "Next they'll be telling us we can't have sex on the job." When I ask Stu what happened to inspire the crackdown, he just mutters about "management decisions" and takes the opportunity to upbraid Gail and me for being too generous with the rolls. From now on there's to be only one per customer, and it goes out with the dinner, not with the salad. He's also been riding the cooks, prompting Andy to come out of the kitchen and observe—with the serenity of a man whose customary implement is a butcher knife—that "Stu has a death wish today."

23   Later in the evening, the gossip crystallizes around the theory that Stu is himself the drug culprit, that he uses the restaurant phone to order up marijuana and sends one of the late servers out to fetch it for him. The server was caught, and she may have ratted Stu out or at least said enough to cast some suspicion on him, thus accounting for his pissy behavior. Who knows? Lionel, the busboy, entertains us for the rest of the shift by standing just behind Stu's back and sucking deliriously on an imaginary joint.

24   The other problem, in addition to the less-than-nurturing management style, is that this job shows no sign of being financially viable. You might imagine, from a comfortable distance, that people who live, year in and year out, on $6 to $10 an hour have discovered some survival stratagems unknown to the middle class. But no. It's not hard to get my co-workers to talk about their living situations, because housing, in almost every case, is the principal source of disruption in their lives, the first thing they fill you in on when they arrive for their shifts. After a week, I have compiled the following survey:

- Gail is sharing a room in a well-known downtown flophouse for which she and a roommate pay about $250 a week. Her roommate, a male friend, has been hitting on her, driving her nuts, but the rent would be impossible alone.
- Claude, the Haitian cook, is desperate to get out of the two-room apartment he shares with his girlfriend and two other, unrelated, people. As far as I can determine, the other Haitian men (most of whom only speak Creole) live in similarly crowded situations.

- Annette, a twenty-year-old server who is six months pregnant and has been abandoned by her boyfriend, lives with her mother, a postal clerk.
- Marianne and her boyfriend are paying $170 a week for a one-person trailer.
- Jack, who is, at $10 an hour, the wealthiest of us, lives in the trailer he owns, paying only the $400-a-month lot fee.
- The other white cook, Andy, lives on his dry-docked boat, which, as far as I can tell from his loving descriptions, can't be more than twenty feet long. He offers to take me out on it, once it's repaired, but the offer comes with inquiries as to my marital status, so I do not follow up on it.
- Tina and her husband are paying $60 a night for a double room in a Days Inn. This is because they have no car and the Days Inn is within walking distance of the Hearthside. When Marianne, one of the breakfast servers, is tossed out of her trailer for subletting (which is against the trailer-park rules), she leaves her boyfriend and moves in with Tina and her husband.
- Joan, who had fooled me with her numerous and tasteful outfits (hostesses wear their own clothes), lives in a van she parks behind a shopping center at night and showers in Tina's motel room. The clothes are from thrift shops.[4]

25   It strikes me, in my middle-class solipsism, that there is gross improvidence in some of these arrangements. When Gail and I are wrapping silverware in napkins—the only task for which we are permitted to sit—she tells me she is thinking of escaping from her roommate by moving into the Days Inn herself. I am astounded: How can she even think of paying between $40 and $60 a day? But if I was afraid of sounding like a social worker, I come out just sounding like a fool. She squints at me in disbelief, "And where am I supposed to get a month's rent and a month's deposit for an apartment?" I'd been feeling pretty smug about my $500 efficiency, but of course it was made possible only by the $1,300 I had allotted myself for start-up costs when I began my low-wage life: $1,000 for the first month's rent and deposit, $100 for initial groceries and cash in my pocket, $200 stuffed away for emergencies. In poverty, as in certain propositions in physics, starting conditions are everything.

26   There are no secret economies that nourish the poor; on the contrary, there are a host of special costs. If you can't put up the two months' rent you need to secure an apartment, you end up paying through the nose for a room by the week. If you have only a room, with a hot plate at best, you can't save by cooking up huge lentil stews that can be frozen for the week ahead. You eat fast food, or the hot dogs and styrofoam cups of soup that can be microwaved in a convenience store. If you have no money for health insurance—and the Hearthside's niggardly plan kicks in only after three months—you go without routine care or prescription drugs and end up paying the price. Gail, for example, was fine until she ran out of money for estrogen pills. She is supposed to be on the company plan by now, but they claim to have lost her application form and need to begin the paperwork all over again. So she spends $9 per migraine pill to control the

---

[4]I could find no statistics on the number of employed people living in cars or vans, but according to the National Coalition for the Homeless's 1997 report "Myths and Facts About Homelessness," nearly one in five homeless people (in twenty-nine cities across the nation) is employed in a full- or part-time job. [Ehrenreich's note]

headaches she wouldn't have, she insists, if her estrogen supplements were covered. Similarly, Marianne's boyfriend lost his job as a roofer because he missed so much time after getting a cut on his foot for which he couldn't afford the prescribed antibiotic.

27   My own situation, when I sit down to assess it after two weeks of work, would not be much better if this were my actual life. The seductive thing about waitressing is that you don't have to wait for payday to feel a few bills in your pocket, and my tips usually cover meals and gas, plus something left over to stuff into the kitchen drawer I use as a bank. But as the tourist business slows in the summer heat, I sometimes leave work with only $20 in tips (the gross is higher, but servers share about 15 percent of their tips with the busboys and bartenders). With wages included, this amounts to about the minimum wage of $5.15 an hour. Although the sum in the drawer is piling up, at the present rate of accumulation it will be more than a hundred dollars short of my rent when the end of the month comes around. Nor can I see any expenses to cut. True, I haven't gone the lentil-stew route yet, but that's because I don't have a large cooking pot, pot holders, or a ladle to stir with (which cost about $30 at Kmart, less at thrift stores), not to mention onions, carrots, and the indispensable bay leaf. I do make my lunch almost every day—usually some slow-burning, high-protein combo like frozen chicken patties with melted cheese on top and canned pinto beans on the side. Dinner is at the Hearthside, which offers its employees a choice of BLT, fish sandwich, or hamburger for only $2. The burger lasts longest, especially if it's heaped with gut-puckering jalapeños, but by midnight my stomach is growling again.

28   So unless I want to start using my car as a residence, I have to find a second, or alternative, job. I call all the hotels where I filled out housekeeping applications weeks ago—the Hyatt, Holiday Inn, Econo Lodge, HoJo's, Best Western, plus a half dozen or so locally run guesthouses. Nothing. Then I start making the rounds again, wasting whole mornings waiting for some assistant manager to show up, even dipping into places so creepy that the front-desk clerk greets you from behind bulletproof glass and sells pints of liquor over the counter. But either someone has exposed my real-life housekeeping habits—which are, shall we say, mellow—or I am at the wrong end of some infallible ethnic equation: most, but by no means all, of the working housekeepers I see on my job searches are African Americans, Spanish-speaking, or immigrants from the Central European post-Communist world, whereas servers are almost invariably white and monolingually English-speaking. When I finally get a positive response, I have been identified once again as server material. Jerry's, which is part of a well-known national family restaurant chain and physically attached here to another budget hotel chain, is ready to use me at once. The prospect is both exciting and terrifying, because, with about the same number of tables and counter seats, Jerry's attracts three or four times the volume of customers as the gloomy old Hearthside. ✳

From Barbara Ehrenreich, "Nickel and Dimed: On (Not) Getting By in America," *Harper's,* January 1999. © 1999 by Barbara Ehrenreich. Reprinted by permission.

Postscript

Ehrenreich took a waitress job at Jerry's, working the morning and lunch shift at the Hearthside and then working the 2–10 P.M. shift at Jerry's. When she arrived at Jerry's on her second day, one of her fellow waitresses greeted her with surprise, saying, "Well, it's good to see you again. Hardly anyone comes back after the first day."

Exercises

Do not refer to the selection for Exercises A and B unless your instructor directs you to do so.

A. DETERMINING THE MAIN IDEA AND PURPOSE
Choose the best answer.

_____ 1. The main idea of the selection is that low-wage earners in America
    a. benefit both economically and socially from the reforms in the welfare system.
    b. find it possible to survive on minimum wage, but it takes luck, sacrifice, and generosity from their family and friends.
    c. suffer the most in a recession because they tend to be unskilled and undereducated.
    d. find it nearly impossible to survive on minimum wage because their wages cannot cover rent or other necessities of life.

_____ 2. With respect to the main idea, the author's purpose is to
    a. demonstrate through personal experience the truth of her claim.
    b. convince the reader of the need for further welfare reform.
    c. complain how hard the life of a waitress is.
    d. examine some common workplace practices that alienate low-wage workers.

B. COMPREHENDING MAIN IDEAS
Choose the correct answer.

_____ 1. When Ehrenreich first conceived of her plan, she was terrified initially that she
    a. wouldn't have enough experience to do the jobs she applied for.
    b. would be recognized and exposed as a journalist.
    c. would not earn enough money to live on.
    d. would abandon the project early if she became too discouraged.

_____ 2. Ehrenreich believes that reform of the welfare system

    a. was long overdue and that its much-needed policy will lift women out of poverty and give them self-esteem.

    b. was simply a political ploy to win over conservative voters.

    c. offered too rosy a view of its benefits and may contribute to a worsening economy and depressed wages.

    d. did not go far enough because there aren't enough job-training programs to help low-skilled workers get jobs.

_____ 3. According to the National Coalition for the Homeless, in 1998, in order to afford a one-bedroom apartment, a worker must earn an hourly wage of

    a. $5.25.

    b. $6.35.

    c. $7.50.

    d. $8.89.

_____ 4. After searching newspaper ads for housekeeping jobs at various motels and hotels, Ehrenreich concluded that

    a. she was overqualified for these jobs.

    b. no one would hire her because she is white.

    c. the continual ads are merely employers' insurance to maintain a steady supply of workers to replace those who quit.

    d. the poor economy had caused a downturn in tourism, which affected the hospitality industry's low-wage employees.

_____ 5. At low-wage establishments, Ehrenreich complains that managers

    a. are more concerned with squeezing every nickel out for the corporation than with serving customers well or treating employees fairly.

    b. deliberately flout employment laws because they know that their employees need the work and won't complain.

    c. conduct mandatory drug tests because they want to run a clean operation.

    d. violate labor laws and pay less than minimum wage.

_____ 6. As Ehrenreich got to know her coworkers, she discovered that, for almost all of them, the one source of disruption in their lives was

    a. problems with personal relationships.

    b. the inability to get ahead because of their lack of skills and education.

    c. their problems with housing.

    d. substance abuse problems.

COMPREHENSION SCORE

Score your answers for Exercises A and B as follows:

A. No. right _____ × 2 = _____

B. No. right _____ × 1 = _____

Total points from A and B _____ × 10 = _____ percent

You may refer to the selection as you work through the remaining exercises.

C. IDENTIFYING SUPPORTING DETAILS

Place an X in the space for each sentence from the selection that *directly* supports this main idea: "There are no secret economies that nourish the poor; on the contrary, there are a host of special costs."

1. _____   I'd been feeling pretty smug about my $500 efficiency, but of course it was made possible only by the $1,300 I had allotted myself for start-up costs when I began my low-wage life.

2. _____   If you can't put up the two months' rent you need to secure an apartment, you end up paying through the nose for a room by the week.

3. _____   If you have only a room, with a hot plate at best, you can't save by cooking up huge lentil stews that can be frozen for the week ahead.

4. _____   You eat fast food, or the hot dogs and styrofoam cups of soup that can be microwaved in a convenience store.

5. _____   The seductive thing about waitressing is that you don't have to wait for payday to feel a few bills in your pocket, and my tips usually cover meals and gas, plus something left over to stuff into the kitchen drawer I use as a bank.

D. MAKING INFERENCES

Write your answers to these questions in your own words.

1. What can you infer might be the "humanitarian rationale for welfare" that Ehrenreich alludes to in paragraph 5? _____

_____

2. Read the end of paragraph 9 again. What can you infer about Winn-Dixie from the computer interview questions the writer must answer? What seem to be the company's main concerns about its employees? _____

_____

_____

3. From the end of paragraph 12, what can you infer was the reason that Phillip hired Ehrenreich so quickly for a waitress job? _____

4. Read paragraphs 15–17 again. How does the writer treat her dining patrons?

_____

_____

5. What is the general impression of managers in terms of the way they treat their employees, as Ehrenreich describes them? _____

_____

_____

6. In paragraph 27, Ehrenreich writes that she has not yet bought a large cooking pot, pot holders, or a ladle so that she could make an inexpensive dish like lentil stew. Why not? _____

_____

E. INTERPRETING MEANING AND ANALYZING STRUCTURE

Where appropriate, write your answers to these questions in your own words.

1. In paragraph 3, what does Ehrenreich mean when she writes, "anthropologically speaking, a bustling trailer park would be preferable"? _____

_____

2. _____ Which of the following is the best title for paragraph 5?
   a. "A Scientific Mission"
   b. "A Defense of Welfare Reform"
   c. "Welfare Reform: Rosy Theory and Hard Facts"
   d. "The Humanitarian Rationale for Welfare Reform"

3. Explain why Ehrenreich decided to live in the world of the low-wage worker instead of just pretending that she was working and adding up the figures?

Read paragraph 7 again before answering the question. _____

_____

_____

4. Where in the essay does Ehrenreich anticipate objections to her plan or suspicion that since she is a middle-class white woman who has never known poverty, the experiment may be unrepresentative of the problems faced by

workers who are stuck in dead-end jobs? _____

_____

_____

5. Read paragraph 9 again. Explain Ehrenreich's reaction to Winn-Dixie's interview process. _____

6. In paragraph 10, what does Ehrenreich think about low-wage employees having to submit to a urine test to detect the presence of drugs? _____

   _____

   What phrase reveals her attitude?_____

7. What does Ehrenreich mean at the end of paragraph 17 when she talks about how waitresses measure out pats of butter and sour cream?_____

   _____

   _____

8. In paragraph 28, Ehrenreich describes her own house keeping habits as "mellow." What does she mean?_____

F. UNDERSTANDING VOCABULARY

Look through the paragraphs listed below and find a word that matches each definition. Refer to the dictionary if necessary. An example has been done for you.

Ex. needless, having no justification, groundless
    [paragraph 1]   _____unwarranted_____

1. avoiding, escaping [2]   _____

2. defeated, conquered [3]   _____

3. intending to inflict punishment [5]   _____

4. a flowing in, mass arrival [5]   _____

5. ordinary, commonplace [7]   _____

6. extreme poverty, destitution [7]   _____

7. suggesting favorable circumstances [8]   _____

8. poor, impoverished [8]   _____

9. troublesome, oppressive [9]   _____

10. steady, persistent, unremitting [12]   _____

11. nimble, moving lightly and quickly [13]   _____

12. violation of the law, breaking a rule [17]   _____

13. secret, not practiced openly [17]   _____

14. criticisms, harsh reprimands [21]   _____

15. incapable of being wrong [28]   _____

G. USING VOCABULARY

Write the correct inflected form of the base word (in parentheses) in each of the following sentences. Be sure to add the appropriate ending to fit the grammatical requirements of the sentence. Refer to your dictionary if necessary.

1. (*indulgence, indulge, indulgent, indulgently*) Ehrenreich states that, unlike actual low-earning workers, in her real life she can _____ herself with bank accounts and other trappings of a comfortable life.

2. (*prosperity, prosper, prosperous, prosperously*) Optimists argue that welfare reform will result in greater _____ for former recipients.

3. (*viability, viable, viably*) Ehrenreich defends the _____ of her research project, claiming that it is both _____ and scientific.

4. (*futility, futile, futilely*) The Hearthside does not allow employees to enter through the front door, as Ehrenreich says, in a _____ attempt to convey an atmosphere of gentility.

5. (*improvidence, improvident, improvidently*) Some of her coworkers at first appear to spend money _____ , for example, by taking a room at a Days Inn rather than renting a small room or apartment.

H. SUMMARIZING EXERCISE

Summarize paragraph 5. _____

_____

_____

_____

I. TOPICS FOR WRITING OR DISCUSSION

1. What is your emotional reaction to Ehrenreich's experiment? Does her method seem like the best way to assess the problems low-wage earners face every day of their lives, or not? Did her approach impress you, or do you have objections?

2. In paragraph 6, Ehrenreich presents statistics to show the problems unskilled workers face: Minimum-wage jobs don't pay a living wage. She ends the paragraph by writing, "If these numbers are right, low-wage work is not a solution to poverty and possibly not even to homelessness." Write a short essay in which you respond to this statement. If she is right, then what *is* the solution?

For Further Exploration

BOOK

Iain Levison, *A Working Stiff's Manifesto: A Memoir* (2002). This slim book offers a similar view of low-paying jobs and the toll they take on people. Working as a deli clerk, meat cutter, and salmon slimer (a salmon slimer removes the scales from freshly caught salmon), Levison describes the underside of these worlds with a wicked sense of humor.

MOVIE

The Devil and Miss Jones (1941), directed by Sam Wood and starring Jean Arthur and Charles Coburn, tells the story of a tycoon (Coburn) who takes a job in one of his own stores to thwart an effort among employees (including Arthur) to unionize. After being humiliated himself, he becomes a leader in the effort to unionize.

WEB SITE

Ehrenreich's book received a large amount of coverage in the press, with mixed reviews of her methods and findings. Go to your favorite search engine (Google, Netscape, Yahoo, or another), do a search by typing in the title of the book, and see what the critics had to say about this work.

Credits

Photo Credits

Page 50, © Bill Ross/Corbis; p. 130, © Terry Whittaker/Frank Lane Picture Agency/Corbis; page 137, © Jeff Vanuga/Corbis; page 175, © Sue Owrutsky; page 237, © Susan Van Etten/PhotoEdit; page 389, © Reuters NewMedia, Inc./Corbis; page 413, © AFP/Corbis; page 439, Courtesy The Dorothea Lange Collection, The Oakland Museum of California, City of Oakland. Gift of Paul S. Taylor; page 439, Courtesy The Dorothea Lange Collection, The Oakland Museum of California; page 458, © Wolfgang Kaehler/Corbis; page 479, © Jason Fulford.

Text Credits

Source and copyright information for the readings appear at the end of each reading. Other text credits include: Pages 17, 18, 19, and 20, From *American Heritage Dictionary of the English Language,* 4th Ed. Reprinted by permission of Houghton Mifflin & Co. Page 20 (top) From *Merriam-Webster's Online Dictionary 2003.* Reprinted by permission of Merriam-Webster Incorporated, www.Merriam-Webster.com.

Index of Authors and Readings

Index of Vocabulary Preview Words